Invasive Species

With clima   , the risks
presented   griculture and
economies   me. Governments
world-wide a   ing   reate by   engthening quarantine
and biosecurity. This book   comprel   eview of risk-based techniques that help policy makers and regulators to protect national interests from
invasive pests and pathogens before, at and inside national borders. Selected from
the research corpus of Australia and New Zealand's Centre of Excellence for
Biosecurity Risk Analysis, this book provides solutions that reflect scientific rigour
coupled with practical, hands-on applications. Focussing on surveillance, stochastic modelling, intelligence gathering, decision making and risk communication, the
contents combine the strengths of risk analysts, mathematicians, economists, biolo-
gists and statisticians. The book presents tested scientific solutions to the greatest
challenges faced by quarantine and biosecurity policy makers and regulators today.

Andrew P. Robinson is Reader and Associate Professor in Applied Statistics, and
Director of the Centre of Excellence for Biosecurity Risk Analysis (CEBRA), at
the University of Melbourne. He works on biosecurity at national borders, inspection surveillance systems and performance metrics for regulatory inspectorates.

Terry Walshe is Decision Scientist at the Australian Institute of Marine Science. His
research deals with the intersection of technical and social dimensions of marine
science and marine management.

Mark A. Burgman is Professor of Risk Analysis and Environmental Policy at the
Centre for Environmental Policy, Imperial College, London, United Kingdom. He
works on ecological modelling, conservation biology and risk assessment.

Mike Nunn is Research Program Manager at the Australian Centre for International
Agricultural Research (ACIAR). He has particular interests in epidemiology, risk
analysis, emerging diseases, zoonoses, nutrition-sensitive agriculture and strategic
foresight.

Invasive Species

Risk Assessment and Management

Edited by

ANDREW P. ROBINSON

School of Mathematics and Statistics, University of Melbourne, Victoria, Australia

TERRY WALSHE

Australian Institute of Marine Science, Queensland, Australia

MARK A. BURGMAN

Centre for Environmental Policy, Imperial College, London, United Kingdom.

MIKE NUNN

Australian Centre for International Agricultural Research, Australian Capital Territory, Australia

CAMBRIDGE
UNIVERSITY PRESS

CAMBRIDGE
UNIVERSITY PRESS

University Printing House, Cambridge CB2 8BS, United Kingdom

One Liberty Plaza, 20th Floor, New York, NY 10006, USA

477 Williamstown Road, Port Melbourne, VIC 3207, Australia

4843/24, 2nd Floor, Ansari Road, Daryaganj, Delhi – 110002, India

79 Anson Road, #06-04/06, Singapore 079906

Cambridge University Press is part of the University of Cambridge.

It furthers the University's mission by disseminating knowledge in the pursuit of
education, learning, and research at the highest international levels of excellence.

www.cambridge.org
Information on this title: www.cambridge.org/9780521146746
DOI: 10.1017/9781139019606

© Cambridge University Press 2017

First published 2017

Printed in the United Kingdom by TJ International Ltd, Padstow Cornwall

A catalogue record for this publication is available from the British Library.

Library of Congress Cataloging-in-Publication Data
Names: Robinson, Andrew (Andrew P.) | Walshe, Terry. |
Burgman, Mark A. | Nunn, Mike (Michael)
Title: Invasive species: risk assessment and management / edited by Andrew Robinson,
School of Mathematics and Statistics, University of Melbourne, Victoria Australia,
Terry Walshe, Australian Institute of Marine Science, Australia, Mark Burgman, Centre for
Environmental Policy, Imperial College, London, United Kingdom,
Mike Nunn, Australian Centre for International Agricultural Research, ACT Australia.
Description: Cambridge: Cambridge University Press, 2017. |
Includes bibliographical references and index.
Identifiers: LCCN 2016052790 | ISBN 9780521765961 (hardback) | ISBN 9780521146746 (pbk.)
Subjects: LCSH: Introduced organisms – Control. | Pests – Control |
Invasive plants – Control. | Alien plants – Control. | Biosecurity.
Classification: LCC QH353.I58285 2017 | DDC 363.7/8–dc23
LC record available at https://lccn.loc.gov/2016052790

ISBN 978-0-521-76596-1 Hardback
ISBN 978-0-521-14674-6 Paperback

Contents

Contributors

Ruth Beilin
School of Ecosystem and Forest Sciences, University of Melbourne, Parkville, Victoria, Australia

Yakov Ben-Haim
Faculty of Mechanical Engineering, Technion, Haifa, Israel

Mark A. Burgman
Centre for Environmental Policy, Imperial College, London, United Kingdom

Rob Cannon
Australian Government Department of Agriculture and Water Resources (Retired), Canberra, Australian Capital Territory, Australia

Tuong Nhu Che
Crawford School of Public Policy, Australian National University, Canberra, Australian Capital Territory, Australia

Hoang Long Chu
Crawford School of Public Policy, Australian National University, Canberra, Australian Capital Territory, Australia

John W. Coulston
USDA Forest Service, Southern Research Station, Knoxville, Tennessee, USA

Brendan D. Cowled
Ausvet Animal Health Services, East Toowoomba, Queensland, Australia

Jane Elith
School of BioSciences, University of Melbourne, Parkville, Victoria, Australia

David R. Fox
Environmetrics Australia Pty. Ltd., Beaumaris, Victoria, Australia

M. Graeme Garner
Australian Government Department of Agriculture and Water Resources, Canberra, Australian Capital Territory, Australia

Jane Gilmour
Research Associate, Centre of Excellence for Biosecurity Risk Analysis (CEBRA), School of Biosciences, University of Melbourne Parkville, Victoria, Australia

Geoff Grossel
Australian Government Department of Agriculture and Water Resources, Canberra, Australian Capital Territory, Australia

Pham Van Ha
Crawford School of Public Policy, Australian National University, Canberra, Australian Capital Territory, Australia

Cindy E. Hauser
School of BioSciences, University of Melbourne, Parkville, Victoria, Australia

Marta Hernández-Jover
School of Animal & Veterinary Science, Charles Sturt University, Wagga Wagga, New South Wales, Australia

Susan M. Hester
Centre of Excellence for Biosecurity Risk Analysis (CEBRA), University of New England, Armidale, New South Wales, Australia

Owen Jones
School of Mathematics and Statistics, University of Melbourne, Parkville, Victoria, Australia

John M. Kean
AgResearch Limited, Ruakura Research Centre, Hamilton, New Zealand

Frank H. Koch
Department of Forestry and Environmental Resources, North Carolina State University and USDA Forest Service, Eastern Forest Environmental Threat Assessment Center, Asheville, North Carolina, USA

Tom Kompas
Centre of Excellence for Biosecurity Risk Analysis (CEBRA), University of Melbourne, Parkville, Victoria, Australia

Kevin B. Korb

School of Information Technology Monash University, Clayton, Victoria, Australia

Aidan Lyon

Department of Philosophy, University of Maryland, College Park, Maryland, USA

Tony Martin

Formerly Department of Agriculture and Food, Bunbury, Western Australia

Ann E. Nicholson

School of Information Technology, Monash University, Clayton, Victoria, Australia

Mike Nunn

Australian Centre for International Agricultural Research, Canberra, Australian Capital Territory, Australia

Joanne M. Potts

The Analytical Edge Pty. Ltd., Blackmans Bay, Tasmania, Australia

David M. Richardson

Centre for Invasion Biology, Department of Botany and Zoology, Stellenbosch University, Stellenbosch, South Africa

Andrew P. Robinson

Centre of Excellence for Biosecurity Risk Analysis (CEBRA), University of Melbourne, Parkville, Victoria, Australia

John Rolfe

School of Business and Law, Central Queensland University, North Rockhampton, Queensland, Australia

Tracy M. Rout

Environmental Decisions Group, University of Queensland, Brisbne, Queensland, Australia

Michael C. Runge

USGS Patuxent Wildlife Research Center, Laurel, MD

Martin Shield

Connected Analytics, Melbourne, Victoria, Australia

Jessica Sibley
Australian Government Department of Agriculture and Water Resources, Canberra, Australian Capital Territory, Australia

William D. Smith
Formerly USDA Forest Service, Southern Research Station, Asheville, North Carolina, USA

Daniel A. Spring
Centre of Environmental and Economic Research, The University of Melbourne, Victoria, Australia.

Tamara Sysak
School of Social Sciences, University of the Sunshine Coast, Sunshine Coast, Queensland, Australia

Colin J. Thompson
School of Mathematics and Statistics, University of Melbourne, Victoria, Australia

Terry Walshe
Australian Institute of Marine Science, Townsville, Queensland, Australia

Michael P. Ward
Faculty of Veterinary Science, University of Sydney, Camden, New South Wales, Australia

Jill Windle
School of Business and Law, Central Queensland University, North Rockhampton, Queensland, Australia

Denys Yemshanov
Natural Resources Canada, Canadian Forest Service, Great Lakes Forestry Centre, Sault Ste. Marie, Ontario, Canada

Foreword
Towards Evidence-Based and Risk-Weighted Strategies for Biosecurity

Globalisation has radically increased the magnitude and scale of the human-mediated movement of species. Species' ranges are no longer defined by natural dispersal mechanisms and biogeographical barriers. International travel and commerce have developed new trade routes, markets and products, and rapid climate change and associated factors continue to shape existing pathways and open new ones (Essl et al., 2015). The overall extent and magnitude of impacts is increasing rapidly, as is the diversity of types of impact and problems associated with the framing of issues and implicit assumptions regarding impacts of biological invasions (Essl et al., 2016).

The interest in understanding and managing the phenomenon of biological invasions has exploded in recent decades. Charles Elton's 1958 book *The Ecology of Invasions by Animals and Plants* is widely acknowledged as the starting point for focussed scientific attention on biological invasions (Richardson & Pyšek, 2007). In the 1980s, a major international programme under the auspices of the Scientific Committee on Problems of the Environment (SCOPE) was the impetus for a major upsurge in interest in invasions. Substantial progress has been made in understanding the 'nuts and bolts' of biological invasions (Richardson, 2011b). Despite many advances in invasion science, however, the magnitude and complexity of problems associated with biological invasions continue to escalate in all parts of the world (Richardson, 2011a).

The applied side of invasion science has morphed into the domain of *biosecurity* in which biogeography and ecology are important but where economic and socio-political issues increasingly dominate agendas (Figure 1). Biosecurity is a relatively new term, entering the scientific lexicon only in the late 1980s and the *Oxford English Dictionary* in 2005 (Hulme, 2012a). Various definitions exist, but in its broadest sense biosecurity covers 'all activities aimed at managing the introduction of new species to a particular region and mitigating their impacts should they become established…, [including] the regulation of intentional (including illegal) and unintentional introductions and the management of weeds and animal pests by central and local government, industry and other stakeholders' (Hulme, 2012a, p. 304). Emerging biosecurity strategies typically include international treaties and standards, cooperative efforts, inspections in host countries and at ports of entry, quarantine, intelligence and treatment of shipments (Elferink & van der Weijden, 2011).

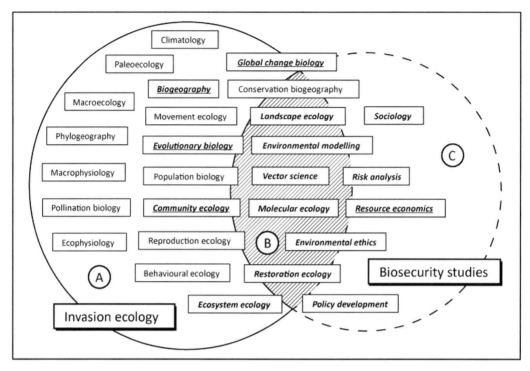

Figure 1.   Fields of research on issues relating to biological invasions (the main fields are underlined). Research in fields at the left of the diagram (zone A) are largely those that produce systems knowledge; those closer to and within zone B produce target knowledge; and those within zone B and into zone C largely comprise transformation knowledge. Boundary management occurs towards the right of the diagram (see text for details). Zones A, B and C together define the domain of invasion science.
[Reproduced, with permission, from Richardson (2011b).]

Most countries have legislation and policies aimed at biosecurity, but the magnitude of the problem is so large and the challenges of dealing with all the many interacting drivers of biological invasions are so daunting that only a few wealthy countries are devoting anything near the resources required to systematically reduce the rate and impacts of biological invasions. How much should a country spend to reduce problems associated with invasive species? The economics of preventing invasions is receiving much attention. Results of several studies suggest that expensive interventions are justified (e.g. Leung et al., 2002; Keller et al., 2007; Williams et al., 2010), but other authors question whether currently applied risk assessment methods are accurate enough to achieve their aim (e.g. Hulme, 2012b). A key aspect of the complexity relates to pathways of introduction and dissemination of non-native species. In most cases, we simply know too little about introduction pathways to apply effective management (Essl et al., 2015). Even where we do know the most important pathways, implementing effective interventions is becoming increasingly complicated. For example, the World Trade Organization requires that any trade restrictions invoked for biosecurity purposes must be science based, and should be 'least trade restrictive' (Shine et al., 2000). The science on which to base decisions on achieving a balance between 'least trade restrictive' and what is most effective to protect people and the environment is still under development. Countries are free to set their own levels of acceptable risk. Substantial work has been done recently to apply the latest advances in risk assessment methods in the biosecurity arena, but major advances in this sphere are in many cases being thwarted by the inherent complexity of the many interacting processes that mediate progress along the introduction–naturalisation–invasion continuum (Blackburn et al., 2011). The lack of objective criteria for assessing the risk of different categories of impacts has also hindered the formulation of robust policies and protocols (Blackburn et al., 2014). A promising approach in this regard is the Environmental Impact Classification for Alien Taxa (EICAT) framework which proposes using a scheme for evaluation impacts of invasive species that is similar to that applied by the International Union for Conservation of Nature (IUCN) to evaluate the threat of extinction of native species in *The IUCN Red List of Threatened Species* (www.iucnredlist.org/; Hawkins et al., 2015). Widespread adoption of this scheme could pave the way for a standardised approach for reporting impacts, thereby alleviating some of the current problems in the implementation of standards.

This book presents a timely and authoritative review of the fundamental challenges that face us in implementing effective and sustainable biosecurity measures, drawing largely on the particular challenges facing Australia. Contributions deal with state-of-the-art methods that are available to inform objective decision making. These include fundamental assessments to evaluate the quality and value of information, options for predicting distributions of non-native species, models for understanding the dynamics of diseases, cost benefit analyses for biosecurity decisions, and key requirements for surveillance and monitoring. Of huge importance, and well covered in the book, is the key challenge of ensuring that risks and potential options for biosecurity are accurately communicated to all stakeholders.

I greatly enjoyed reading the chapters in this volume. I have no doubt that the contributions will result in improved management of one of the most challenging problems of our time.

DAVID M. RICHARDSON

References

Blackburn, T. M., Essl, F., Evans, T., et al. (2014). Towards a unified classification of alien species based on the magnitude of their environmental impacts. *PLoS Biology*, 12(5), e1001850.

Blackburn, T. M., Pyšek, P., Bacher, S., et al. (2011). A proposed unified framework for biological invasions. *Trends in Ecology & Evolution*, 26(7), 333–339.

Elferink, E., & van der Weijden, W. (2011). Ecoterrorism and biosecurity. In D. Simberloff and M. Rejmánek (eds.), *Encyclopedia of biological invasions* (pp. 183–187). Berkeley: University of California Press.

Essl, F., Bacher, S., Blackburn, T. M., et al. (2015). Crossing frontiers in tackling pathways of biological invasions. *BioScience*, 65, 769–782.

Essl, F., Hulme, P. E., Jeschke, J. M., et al. (2016). Scientific and normative foundations for the valuation of alien species impacts: Thirteen core principles. *BioScience* (in press).

Hawkins, C. L., Bacher, S., Essl, F., et al. (2015). Framework and guidelines for implementing the proposed IUCN Environmental Impact Classification for Alien Taxa (EICAT). *Diversity and Distributions*, 21(11), 1360–1363.

Hulme, P. E. (2012a). Biosecurity: the changing face of invasion biology. In D. M. Richardson (ed.), *Fifty years of invasion ecology*, (pp. 301–314). Hoboken, NJ: Wiley-Blackwell..

Hulme, P. E. (2012b). Weed risk assessment: A way forward or a waste of time? *Journal of Applied Ecology*, 49(1), 10–19.

Keller, R. P., Lodge, D. M., & Finnoff, D. C. (2007). Risk assessment for invasive species produces net bioeconomic benefits. *Proceedings of the National Academy of Sciences of the United States of America*, 104(1), 203–207.

Leung, B., Lodge, D. M., Finnoff, D., et al. (2002). An ounce of prevention or a pound of cure: Bioeconomic risk analysis of invasive species. *Proceedings of the Royal Society of London Series B: Biological Sciences*, 269(1508), 2407–2413.

Richardson, D. M. (ed.). (2011a). *Fifty years of invasion ecology: The legacy of Charles Elton*. Oxford: Wiley-Blackwell.

Richardson, D. M. (2011b). Invasion science: The roads travelled and the roads ahead. In D. M. Richardson (ed.), *Fifty years of invasion ecology: The legacy of Charles Elton* (pp. 397–407). Oxford: Wiley-Blackwell.

Richardson, D. M., & Pyšek, P. (2007). Classics in physical geography revisited: Elton, C.S. 1958: The *ecology of invasions by animals and plants. Progress in Physical Geography*, 31, 659–666.

Shine, C., Williams, N., & Gündling, L. (2000). *A guide to designing legal and institutional frameworks on alien invasive species*. Gland, Switzerland: International Union for Conservation of Nature (IUCN).

Williams, F., Eschen, R., Harris, A., et al. (2010). *The economic cost of invasive non-native species on Great Britain*. Wallingford: Center for Agriculture and Biosciences International (CABI).

1 The Allocation of Inspection Resources

Owen Jones, Andrew P. Robinson, Martin Shield and Jessica Sibley

1.1 Introduction

Inspection is carried out by biosecurity protection authorities to detect and exclude biosecurity contaminations, by customs services to intercept illegal weapons and drugs, by taxation organisations to verify taxation returns and by environmental protection authorities to determine the levels of pollutants in public goods. In this chapter, we focus on inspections performed by regulators to ensure that a process complies with regulations. Our specific interest is border inspections for biosecurity contaminations.

We define inspection as the examination of a unit to determine whether or not it is compliant with relevant regulations. In the present context, an inspection will determine whether the unit contains biosecurity risk material. A typical unit could be an international passenger, a sea container or a pallet of goods. Inspection usually involves examining the unit and any accompanying packaging, and depending on the nature of the unit, inspection may also involve the examination of a sample taken from the unit. For example, the inspection of a consignment of oranges might focus on a random sample of 600 oranges, and the inspection of a consignment of coffee beans might focus on one or more samples of coffee beans extracted from the container by means of a probe.

We will assume that units arrive sequentially and that there is no logical demarcation in the flow of arrivals that could be used to define a collection of units to serve as a basis for structuring an inspection system. Therefore, although traditional methods may be used to determine the procedure for sampling from a unit such as a container, they are not appropriate for deciding how many or which units to inspect. Rather, as each unit arrives, a decision must be made on whether or not to inspect it. We will suppose that our inspection criteria are updated after every N-th arrival, for some fixed N. In particular, after every N-th arrival, we update our estimate of the non-compliance rate and adjust the frequency of our inspections accordingly.

The frequency of inspections is determined by three requirements: to intercept non-compliant units, to estimate the contamination level and to deter maleficent agents. We will assume that the only data that we have on the non-compliance rate of arriving units are the results of previous inspections. Moreover, we do not wish to use data from more than N past arrivals because we want our estimates to be current. Thus the frequency of inspections directly affects the quality of our estimates. When contaminated units are identified, they are destroyed, treated or re-exported so that they do not present a biosecurity threat. The specific action taken will not affect our analysis here. Finally, although it is clear that when inspections are well publicised and the penalties for infraction are sufficient, the knowledge of inspection may influence the behaviour of importers; we make no attempt to model this feedback here.

The frequency of inspections will generally increase with the estimated rate of contamination, although see Cannon (2009) and Press (2009). The frequency of inspections will therefore be low when the estimated rate is negligible but should not be allowed to decrease so much that it becomes impossible to detect an important increase in the contamination frequency within a reasonable time frame. When the sampling rate is low, detecting a contaminated unit can cause a spike in the estimate of the contamination rate that may misleadingly portend a change in the baseline rate. A further consideration is that, assuming we update our estimated contamination rate after every N-th arrival, our inspection regime should allow for a rapid increase in the inspection frequency if there is an important increase in the number of non-compliant units detected. A brief review of inspection resource allocation strategies can be found in Robinson et al. (2011); see also Cannon (2009).

Robinson et al. (2008, 2011) developed the import risk inspection sampling (IRIS) algorithm with the goal of determining an inspection level that reflects the joint needs to intercept non-compliant units and maintaining adequate estimates of contamination levels. The IRIS algorithm allows the manager to choose the length N of the review period, but does not allow changing the inspection frequency between the review periods if there is evidence of an increase in the contamination frequency. In this chapter, we show how to combine the IRIS algorithm with the different sampling or alert modes used by Dodge (1943) and Dodge and Torrey (1951) in the continuous sampling plan (CSP) and its variants. The combined algorithm retains the convenience of regular review periods while including mechanisms to trigger periods of high-frequency inspections.

This chapter is structured as follows. We develop a conceptual framework for the inspection process in Section 1.2. We review and extend the IRIS algorithm in Section 1.3. We introduce the CSP in Section 1.4 and discuss how to combine it with IRIS and why this might be useful. In Sections 1.2, 1.3 and 1.4, we assume that we are acting on a single homogeneous pathway of units. In Section 1.5 we consider the problem of pathways that are too small to get adequate estimates of the contamination level, and suggest a way of combining pathways using our IRIS–CSP hybrid algorithm. We then test our approach using a simulation experiment based on inspection data.

1.2   Conceptual Framework

In this section we present a conceptual framework for the inspection process that we will use to describe our inspection algorithms. Here, we use the vocabulary and context most suited to biosecurity inspection, but the principles are quite general.

We define an inspection *unit* as the entity upon which inspection is performed. Diverse kinds of units are of interest, and the method for inspection of each depends on the characteristics of the unit. Examples of units include people, consignments of imported goods and containers of commodities. Inspection units are analogous to sampling units in sampling theory.

We define a *pathway* as a sequence of units that are deemed to be similar by the inspectorate and over which the inspectorate has some regulatory authority. Defining a pathway as a collection of like units is subjective because there are numerous hierarchical levels of collections of units. For example, a pathway could comprise all air passengers, all passengers who arrive from a certain departure point or all passengers who have been out of the country for more than six weeks. Similarly, in the case of imported coffee beans, a pathway could comprise all consignments of coffee beans, all consignments from a certain supplier, all consignments from a specific country, all consignments to a particular importer or any combination of these. Pathways are analogous to infinite populations in sampling theory.

We assume that inspection of a unit yields a binary result: the unit is deemed to be contaminated (non-compliant) or not contaminated (compliant). We also suppose that the *effectiveness*, w, of inspections is known and constant for any given pathway. This means that a non-compliant unit that is inspected will be detected with a known probability w. In general, this probability will not be known and must be estimated using a procedure called an *endpoint survey*.

Consider the k-th unit that arrives at the inspection point from a given pathway. We define the *approach rate*, p_k, as the probability that the unit is non-compliant. The p_k is indexed by k because, in general, we allow it to change over time, although in practice we expect any change to be gradual, perhaps with occasional jumps. We define the *sampling rate*, s_k, as the probability that the k-th unit is inspected, and we define the *leakage rate*, r_k, as the probability that the unit is non-compliant and allowed past the inspection point. Thus, $r_k = (1 - w s_k) p_k$. Broadly speaking, our goal is to choose a value of s_k that is as small as possible while keeping r_k at an acceptable level. An important feature of the IRIS algorithm is that when determining s_k, it specifically makes allowance for uncertainty in our estimate of r_k. It is also important to know how quickly the sampling rate increases when there is an increase in p_k, to which end we incorporate the CSP methodology.

Our definition of the leakage rate gives the probability that a unit arriving at the inspection point is non-compliant but still gets through. We could also consider the probability that a unit that leaves the inspection point is non-compliant (the post-inspection leakage rate). These probabilities will be the same in the case of rectifying inspections, in which detected non-compliant units are made compliant and then released. In the case of non-rectifying inspections, the post-inspection leakage rate will always be higher than the leakage rate. However, when p_k is small, which is often the case, the two will be close because the proportion of units that are rejected will be small.

We collect units into groups of sizes $N_1, N_2,\ldots$, where the first N_2 units to arrive are considered to belong to group 1, the next N_2 to group 2, and so on. We assume that the group sizes are known in advance. The groups could be natural groupings, such as containers on a ship or passengers on an aeroplane, or they could be units that arrive during a given time period, say every three months. In the latter case, the group sizes can only be estimated ahead of time and will not be known for certain. The accuracy of these estimates is not of particular importance when we look at the performance of our inspection algorithms (see Section 1.5.1).

To measure performance we use the long-run average leakage rate, either theoretical or estimated. For a given approach rate p, the average outgoing quality, AOQ(p), is defined as the long-run average leakage rate when the approach rate $p_k = p$ is constant, under the assumption that units are independent and inspections are perfectly accurate ($w = 1$).[1] For a specific data sample, the estimated long-run average leakage rate is the sample outgoing quality (SOQ). Note that by long-run average leakage rate we mean the proportion of the given pathway that is non-compliant and undetected.

1.3　　The IRIS Algorithm

Throughout this section, we assume that the approach rate $p_k = p$ is constant. The IRIS algorithm is an ad hoc procedure designed to ensure that the leakage rate is kept below a set level with a given probability as long as the approach rate does not increase. Even when p is very small, we inspect frequently enough that our estimate of p remains acceptably accurate.

Suppose that in the first block of N_1 units there were n_1 inspections that found x_1 non-compliant units, giving us a point-estimate for p of $\hat{p}_1 = x_1 / (wn_1)$. Our aim is to choose n_2, the number of units to inspect from the next block of size N_2.

We start by adding a positive bias to $\hat{p}_1$ to allow for error and uncertainty in our estimate. Let $\hat{p}_* = \hat{p}_1 + \varepsilon$ be our biased estimate. Next, suppose that we sample n_2 units from the second block of N_2 units and find X_2 non-compliant units. Let $p_2 = X_2 / (wn_2)$ be the estimate of p obtained from these inspections, then $\mathrm{E}P_2 = p$ and $\mathrm{Var}P_2 = p(1 - wp)/(wn_2)$. Given these,[2] we adopt the following model for p using a beta distribution:

$$P \sim \mathrm{beta}(\hat{p}_* w' n_2 + 0.5, (1 - \hat{p}_*)w' n_2 + 0.5) \quad \text{where} \quad w' = \frac{(1 - \hat{p}_*)w}{1 - w\hat{p}_*}. \quad (1.1)$$

---

[1] The term average outgoing quality was first used by Dodge (1943), who also used the average outgoing quality limit, AOQL = $\max_p$AOQ(p), to give an overall measure of the effectiveness of an inspection policy. Lieberman (1953) went a step further and proposed the unrestricted average outgoing quality limit, UAOQL, which is an upper bound for the long-run average leakage rate for any sequence of p_k, not just constant sequences.

[2] We are treating the sample units as independent and identically distributed observations and not as a sample from a finite population of size N_2. This is because we are estimating the long-run approach rate, not just the approach rate for the second sampling period.

Under this model, conditional on $\hat{p}_*$, P has mean

$$\frac{\hat{p}_* + \delta}{1 + 2\delta} \quad \text{where} \quad \delta = \frac{1}{2w'n_2} \tag{1.2}$$

and variance.

$$\frac{(\hat{p}_* + \delta)(1 - \hat{p}_* + \delta)}{w'n_2(1 + 2\delta)^2(1 + 4\delta)} = \frac{\hat{p}_*(1 - \hat{p}_*)}{w'n_2} + \delta' = \frac{\hat{p}_*(1 - w\hat{p}_*)}{wn_2} + \delta' \quad \text{where} \quad \delta' = O(\delta). \tag{1.3}$$

The δ term is included so that, even if $\hat{p}_*$ is very small, P has a mean and variance bounded away from 0.

Given P, our estimate of the leakage rate, r, for the next block is $R = (1 - ws)P$, where $s = n_2 / N_2$ is the proportion of the next block to be sampled. We take as our (positively biased) point estimate of r the $100(1 - \alpha)\%$ point of R, where α is specified by the manager, for example 0.10. That is, if betainv is the inverse of the beta density,

$$\hat{r}_2 = (1 - ws) \quad \text{betainv}(1 - \alpha, \hat{p}_*w'n_2 + 0.5, (1 - \hat{p}_*)w'n_2 + 0.5). \tag{1.4}$$

This construction allows the manager to apply a level of surety to the estimate, providing a platform for risk-averse inspection strategies if the consequences of failure are large. Writing $s = n_2 / N_2$ we see that by putting $\hat{r}_2 = r$, where r is our target leakage rate, we get an equation for n_2. Equation 1.4 is easily solved numerically by using a root-finding algorithm.

When the IRIS algorithm was originally introduced by Robinson et al. (2008, 2011), they suggested that ε, the bias added to $\hat{p}_1$ to get $\hat{p}_*$, should be such that $\hat{p}_*$ corresponds to a percentage point from a beta distribution with mean approximately $\hat{p}_1$ and variance proportional to $1 / n_2$. However, if $\hat{p}_*$ depends on n_2, then Eq. 1.4 and $\hat{p}_*$ need to be solved iteratively. That is, we choose a $\hat{p}_*$ to start then solve Eq. 1.4 to get n_2, which gives us a new $\hat{p}_*$. Using this $\hat{p}_*$, we solve Eq. 1.4 again to get a new n_2 and thus a new $\hat{p}_*$. We continue until $\hat{p}_*$ and n_2 converge. We have included ε in our description because it is present in the original IRIS algorithm. However, the algorithm already includes a mechanism to deal with the uncertainty in our estimates, namely the α in Eq. 1.4. In practice, adding ε to $\hat{p}_1$ does not add a great deal to the robustness of the method and we now suggest that it can be omitted.

1.3.1 Bayes–IRIS

Although the IRIS algorithm produces reasonable sampling rates in operational settings (Robinson et al., 2011), the ad hoc nature of the algorithm makes it difficult to justify theoretically. In the remainder of this section we use a Bayesian approach to derive an analogous algorithm from first principles. We call the resulting algorithm Bayes–IRIS, and although it results in a rather different equation for n_2, it produces solutions similar to those of the IRIS algorithm in many operational settings.

We suppose that the first review period has just finished and we are planning for the second review period. In the first review period, we sampled n_1 out of N_1 units and found x_1 non-compliant units. Our goal is to choose n_2, the number of units to sample from the next N_2, so that the leakage rate is kept below a threshold r with probability $1 - \alpha$. We will suppose initially that inspections are error free, that is, $w = 1$.

As before, we start with an estimate of p. We use a Bayesian approach so that our estimate takes the form of a distribution. We deliberately choose not to use any information from before the first review period when estimating p. This is because we want our estimate to be current and capable of responding quickly to changes in the approach rate. Let P_0 be a distribution that represents our estimate at the start of the first review period based on no information. In Bayesian terminology, P_0 is called a non-informative prior. We use the usual choice of non-informative prior for a probability, the beta(0.5, 0.5) distribution.[3]

$$P_0 \sim \text{beta}(0.5, 0.5). \tag{1.5}$$

At the end of the first review period, we update our distribution for p based on the observed number of compliant and non-compliant units. We call this P_1 (the posterior distribution), and standard calculations give us

$$P_1 \sim \text{beta}(x_1 + 0.5, n_1 - x_1 + 0.5). \tag{1.6}$$

Now suppose that we take a sample of size n_2 from the N_2 units that arrive during the second review period. Let X_2 be the number of non-compliant units in that sample. If we knew p, then X_2 would have a binom(n_2, p) distribution. Instead, using our distribution P_1 for p, we obtain the distribution of X_2 by integrating the binomial distribution over the possible values of p. The resulting distribution is known as the beta-binomial. We write $X_2 \sim \text{beta-binom}(n_2, x_1 + 0.5, n_1 - x_1 + 0.5)$, and we have

$$P(X_2 = x_2) = \binom{n_2}{x_2} \frac{\beta(x_2 + x_1 + 0.5, n_2 - x_2 + n_1 - x_1 + 0.5)}{\beta(x_1 + 0.5, n_1 - x_1 + 0.5)}, \tag{1.7}$$

where $\beta(a, b)$ is the beta function evaluated at (a, b).

Given X_2, the leakage rate is $R_2 = (1 - n_2 / N_2) X_2 / n_2 = \left(\dfrac{1}{n_2} - \dfrac{1}{N_2} \right) X_2$, and requiring $P(R_2 > r) \leq \alpha$ is equivalent to requiring $P\left(X_2 > \dfrac{r n_2 N_2}{N_2 - n_2} \right) \leq \alpha$. Our sample size for the second sampling period is the smallest n_2 for which

---

[3] Note that some authors such as Tuyl et al. (2009) argue that beta(1, 1) is a better choice (the uniform prior). However, the beta (0.5, 0.5) prior, which is an example of a Jeffreys prior, is still the most commonly used. Practically, the difference is apparent only when we have a very small sample size, n_1, in which case the Jeffreys prior favours extreme probabilities (closer to 0 or 1) more than the uniform prior does.

$$\sum_{x_2=0}^{\lfloor rn_2 N_2/(N_2-n_2)\rfloor} \binom{n_2}{x_2} \frac{\beta(x_2 + x_1 + 0.5, n_2 - x_2 + n_1 - x_1 + 0.5)}{\beta(x_1 + 0.5, n_1 - x_1 + 0.5)} \geq 1 - \alpha, \qquad (1.8)$$

where the truncated brackets around the upper limit of the sum mean to round down to the next integer.

1.3.2 Bayes–IRIS with Imperfect Inspections

When dealing with imperfect inspections, the Bayesian analysis in Section 1.3.1 becomes more complicated. As before, we use $P_0 \sim \mathrm{beta}\,(0.5, 0.5)$ as a prior for p at the start of the first review period. In addition, we suppose that w, the probability of successfully identifying a non-compliant unit being inspected, has the following prior distribution that is independent of P_0

$$1 - W_0 \sim \mathrm{beta}\,(a_w, b_w). \qquad (1.9)$$

At the end of the first review period, having observed x_1 non-compliant units from n_1 inspected units, p and w have the following joint posterior density (Gaba & Winkler, 1992):

$$f_{P_1, W_1}(p, w | x_1, n_1) = \sum_{y=0}^{n_1 - x_1} c_y f_\beta(p; n_1 - y + 0.5, y + 0.5)$$
$$\times f_\beta(1 - w; n_1 - x_1 - y + a_w, x_1 + b_w), \qquad (1.10)$$

where $f_\beta(\cdot; a, b)$ is the beta(a, b) density, $c_y = a_y / \sum_{z=0}^{n_1 - x_1} a_z$, and

$$a_y = \binom{n_1 - x_1}{y} \beta(n_1 - y + 0.5, y + 0.5)\beta(n_1 - x_1 - y + a_w, x_1 + b_w). \qquad (1.11)$$

In the sum, we can interpret y as the true number of compliant units from the n_1 that were sampled.

In the case where p is small and w is known exactly, the posterior of p is approximately gamma distributed (Johnson & Gastwirth, 1991):

$$P_1 \approx \mathrm{gamma}\,(x_1 + 0.5, w(n_1 - x_1) - 0.5). \qquad (1.12)$$

Given a distribution for P_1, we can again obtain a distribution for X_2 by integrating the binomial distribution over the possible values of p. Again, by fixing w and supposing p to be small, we get

$$P(X_2 = x_2) \approx \binom{n_2}{x_2} \frac{(w(n_1 - x_1) - 0.5)^{x_1 + 0.5}}{(n_2 - x_2 + w(n_1 - x_1) - 0.5)^{x_1 + x_2 + 0.5}} \frac{\Gamma(x_1 + x_2 + 0.5)}{\Gamma(x_1 + 0.5)}, \quad (1.13)$$

where $\Gamma(a)$ is the gamma function evaluated at a. (Note that this is not a true distribution because summing the right-hand side over $x_2 = 0, \ldots, n_2$ does not give 1. The approximation is, nonetheless, reasonable for small x_2.) Putting

$R_2 = (1 - n_2 / N_2) X_2 / n_2$ and requiring $P(R_2 > r) \leq \alpha$, we can calculate n_2 as before. Our sample size for the second sampling period is the smallest n_2 for which

$$\sum_{x_2=0}^{\lfloor r n_2 N_2 / (N_2 - n_2) \rfloor} \binom{n_2}{x_2} \frac{(w(n_1 - x_1) - 0.5)^{x_1 + 0.5}}{(n_2 - x_2 + w(n_1 - x_1) - 0.5)^{x_1 + x_2 + 0.5}} \frac{\Gamma(x_1 + x_2 + 0.5)}{\Gamma(x_1 + 0.5)} \geq 1 - \alpha. \quad (1.14)$$

1.4   The CSP Algorithm

The IRIS algorithm allows for periodic updating of the sampling rate, and in particular makes sure that the sampling rate does not drop too low when few non-compliant units are detected, but it does not respond quickly to a sudden increase in the non-compliance rate. In contrast, the CSP is designed to increase the sampling rate quickly if a cluster of non-compliant units is detected, and then reduce it again if the non-compliance proves to be short lived. The CSP was introduced by Dodge (1943) and later extended by Dodge and Torrey (1951) and Govindaraju and Kandasamy (2000). We present a general description of the CSP that covers most schemes, including the multilevel plans of Lieberman and Solomon (1955).

We suppose that we have $K \geq 2$ states that represent how alert we are to non-compliant units, with state 1 the least alert and state K the most alert. For each state k, we have a sampling rate f_k, a window length g_k (also called a clearance number), and compliance numbers c_k^+ and c_k^- that are used to determine when to change to a different alert level. If a unit arrives while we are in state k, we will inspect it with probability f_k. If we are in state k and c_k^+ or more of the previous g_k items inspected in state k are non-compliant then we increase the alert level (by one or more levels). If c_k^- or fewer of the previous g_k items inspected in state k have been non-compliant then we decrease the alert level (by one or more levels). We can increase the alert level after only c_k^+ inspections, but we need at least g_k before we can decrease it. Lieberman and Solomon (1955) restrict themselves to the case where $c_k^- = 0$, and suppose that changes in state are by just one level at a time.

In Tables 1.1 to 1.3 we give details for some CSP algorithms. Here, the *Up destination* is the state you move to when increasing the alert level and the *Down destination* is the state you move to when decreasing the alert level. Values for the AOQ are taken from Stephens (1995) and give the theoretical long-run average leakage rate. Here, $q = 1 - p$.

When applying CSP-1, CSP-2 or CSP-3, we need to choose a sampling rate, f, and one or more window sizes. The usual approach is to start with an acceptable leakage rate, r, and a range of plausible approach rates, $[p^-, p^+]$. Using the AOQ, we can then get a set of potential parameters. For example, for CSP-3 we have

$$S = \{(f, g_c, g_a) : \text{AOQ}(p) \leq r \quad \text{for all} \quad p \in [p^-, p^+]\}.$$

We can then choose parameters from S according to some secondary consideration such as minimising f or g_c. Unfortunately, this approach is very much dependent

Table 1.1. CSP-1 algorithm

$$\mathrm{AOQ}(p) = \frac{p(1-f)q^g}{f(1-q^g)+q^g}$$

Alertness state	Sampling rate	Window size	Up threshold	Up destination	Down threshold	Down destination
2 (census)	1	g			0	1
1 (sampling)	f	1	1	2		

From Dodge (1943).

Table 1.2. CSP-2 algorithm

$$\mathrm{AOQ}(p) = \frac{p(1-f)q^{g_c}(2-q^{g_a})}{f(1-q^{g_c})(1-q^{g_a})+q^{g_c}(2-q^{g_a})}$$

Alertness state	Sampling rate	Window size	Up threshold	Up destination	Down threshold	Down destination
3 (census)	1	g_c			0	1
2 (alert)	f	g_a	1	3	0	1
1 (sampling)	f	1	1	2		

From Dodge and Torrey (1951).

Table 1.3. CSP-3 algorithm

$$AOQ(p) = \frac{p(1-f)q^{g_c}(1+q^4(1-q^{g_a}))}{f(1-q^{g_c})(1-q^{g_a+4})+q^{g_c}(1-q^4(1-q^{g_a}))+4fpq^{g_c}}$$

Alertness state	Sampling rate	Window size	Up threshold	Up destination	Down threshold	Down destination
4 (census)	1	g_c			0	1
3 (limbo)	1	4	1	4	0	2
2 (alert)	f	g_a	1	4	0	1
1 (sampling)	f	1	1	3		

From Dodge and Torrey (1951).

on the value of p^+ and can result in values of f that are too small if p^+ is small or values of f that are too large if p^+ is too large. If f is too small then the algorithm is too slow to respond to changes in p and we have no guarantee of the statistical value of the information gained from our inspections. If f is too large then we waste resources through unnecessary sampling.

1.4.1   Combining IRIS and CSP

Our response to the problem of parameter selection for the CSP algorithm is to combine it with the IRIS algorithm. At the end of each review period, we choose f using IRIS to achieve a given leakage rate, r, with a confidence of $100(1-\alpha)\%$. Given f, we then choose the window sizes g, or g_a and g_c according to secondary considerations, which may be operational.

As before, we suppose that units arrive in blocks or review periods of size N_1, N_2, and so forth. Suppose that during period 1 we used a CSP algorithm with base sampling rate f_1. (At any time k, the actual sampling rate, S_k, will be either f_1 or 1.) Given that we observed x_1 non-compliant units out of n_1 units inspected during period 1, we can estimate n_2 using IRIS as described in Section 1.3. The base sampling rate for period 2 is then $f_2 = n_2 / N_2$.

For example, suppose that we wish to combine CSP-1 and IRIS to determine an inspection algorithm for a given pathway. If in the previous batch of $N_1 = 1000$ units, $n_1 = 500$ were inspected and $x_1 = 1$ non-compliant units were found. The goal is to choose n_2, the number of units to inspect from the next batch of size $N_2 = 1000$. We assume that we want the prediction distribution of the leakage rate to be lower than 1% with probability 0.95 and that the inspection effectiveness, w, is known to be 0.9. Solving Eq. 1.4 for n_2 yields a sampling rate of $s = n_2 / N_2 = 0.479$, which we round to 0.5. To choose the window length g for the CSP-1 algorithm, in the absence of any other criteria, we can use the formula for the AOQ given in Table 1.1. [Graphs of this function can be found in Dodge (1943).] Using the point estimate $p = x_1 / n_1 = 1 / 500$ and $f = s = 0.5$ from the preceding, we can choose g to achieve the desired AOQ. For example, for an AOQ of less than 0.095%, the clearance number (window length) would be $g = 0.5$.

Alternatively, in some circumstances the clearance number can be interpreted directly as a burden on the importer, representing a period of intense scrutiny during which the importer needs to demonstrate proper compliance. Given this interpretation, the magnitude could be chosen to reflect expert opinion.

The IRIS algorithm is well suited to a slowly changing approach rate, with reviews at fixed points in time. It is not designed to continually monitor for a sudden increase in the approach rate, and it doesn't have an automatic reaction if this occurs. There is no need to monitor for a decrease in the approach rate under IRIS; we just wait until the next review point.

CSP algorithms provide an immediate measured response to any increase in the approach rate. CSP algorithms enable us to increase the sampling rate temporarily when there is a suspicion that the approach rate has increased, and then reduce it if there is not a problem. Where the CSP algorithms have problems, however, is in the choice of parameters f and g (or g_a and g_c). Using the IRIS algorithm to choose f means that we can choose g (or g_a and g_c) safe in the knowledge that we have already controlled the expected leakage rate and how large it could reasonably be. We also know that our overall sampling rate will be large enough to ensure that we will continue to have a good estimate of the approach rate. In the example given earlier, we chose f so that the leakage rate would be below 1% with 95% confidence. We then chose g so that the *expected* leakage rate would be 0.095%.

We note that IRIS may also be combined with other adaptive sampling technologies, such as the sampling plan A algorithm (Wald & Wolfowitz, 1945), or with the run-length based method of Bourke (2002). However, this approach would not work with algorithms that use multiple sampling rates, such as the multilevel plans of Lieberman and Solomon (1955), or algorithms that adjust the sampling rate dynamically, such as the credit methods of Baillie and Klaassen (2006) and Klaassen (2001). Covering the combination of IRIS and these tools is beyond the scope of this chapter.

1.5 Aggregation of Pathways

The IRIS algorithm supposes that arriving units are grouped into review periods of size N. If N is too small then the sampling rate required to give an accurate estimate will be very high. Because we want our estimates to depend only on recent data, the choice of N depends on how quickly units arrive on the pathway of interest. That is, a review period will typically be limited to a certain length of time, and N is then the (expected or estimated) number of units to arrive in that time.

For some pathways, the volumes are too small to enable the collection of statistically useful information. This is generally a result of trying to achieve homogeneous risk within each pathway. That is, to get groupings of similar units with a similar risk of contamination, we have to subdivide the set of all arriving units into pathways that are individually too small for meaningful analysis. Conversely, in many situations, such as customs and quarantine inspections, we have some control over the rate at which units arrive, by appropriately grouping units into pathways of similar types.

We form pathways by grouping similar units, and we assume that the arrival of contaminated units in one pathway is independent of the arrival of contaminated units in other pathways. Given this assumption, we still have a great deal of leeway over the level of aggregation that determines a pathway and hence the arrival rate. For example, a pathway may consist of all rice shipments, all rice shipments from a particular country or all rice shipments from a particular supplier. We need to choose pathways that are large enough that we get enough inspections in each review period so that we can estimate the approach rate well. But the pathways should not be so large that they include diverse types of units with very different risks of non-compliance. Our approach to this problem is to collect a number of sub-pathways into a single pathway that is large enough to give reasonable estimates using IRIS, as explained earlier, and then use a CSP algorithm to determine dynamic sampling rates separately for each sub-pathway.

Suppose that we have k sub-pathways, and in the previous review period there were $N_1(i)$ arrivals, $n_1(i)$ inspections and $x_1(i)$ contaminated units found in sub-pathway i. We will suppose that the effectiveness of inspections is w for all sub-pathways, although this can be easily generalised. If we let $n_1 = \sum_i n_1(i)$ and $x_1 = \sum_i x_1(i)$, then we put $\hat{p}_* = \hat{p}_1 = x_1/(wn_1)$, as in Section 1.3. We can now solve Eq. 1.4 to get n_2, the total number of desired inspections for the next review period across all sub-pathways. Let $N_2(i)$ be the number of arrivals in sub-pathway i during the next review period and put $N_2 = \sum_i N_2(i)$. Clearly, we need $N_2 \geq n_2$, which means either that the review period is long enough that the individual $N_2(i)$ are large enough, or that the number, k, of aggregated sub-pathways is large enough. Given n_2 and N_2, we get the sampling rate $s = n_2/N_2$ for the coming review period. Now, given S we apply a CSP algorithm *separately* to each sub-pathway but using the same base sampling rate $f = s$ in each case. The window sizes for sub-pathway i, namely $g(i)$ (or $g_a(i)$ and $g_c(i)$), can be different for different i.

The advantage of this methodology is that we can get enough data for a reasonable estimate of the approach rate averaged across the different sub-pathways. The disadvantage comes when the approach rate is very different across the different pathways, in which case we risk oversampling the more compliant pathways. Undersampling the less compliant pathways is less of a risk because the IRIS algorithm has error built in and because we are applying a CSP algorithm to each sub-pathway.

1.5.1   Simulation Experiment

In this section, we describe a simulation experiment to test the effect of aggregating sub-pathways. Each of the CSP-1, CSP-2 and CSP-3 algorithms were trialled, with a variety of clearance numbers, g or g_c and g_a. Rather than estimate f using the IRIS algorithm, we just used a range of suitable values to demonstrate the utility of combining sub-pathways whatever the value of f. The simulation experiment was performed using inspection data for a product imported by 20 or so different suppliers based in a single country. A complete inspection record was available for these data, and for the purposes of the experiment, we assumed that the inspections were error free.

Using three-month review periods, the rate at which units arrive from each supplier is too small to give a good estimate of the approach rate so we combine them for the purposes of estimating p. In practice, we would do this using the IRIS methodology described in Sections 1.3 and 1.4.1. For the purpose of this simulation, we consider a variety of values for f and g (or g_c and g_a) to give a more thorough assessment of the effect of aggregating pathways. Once we have our parameters, our goal is to compare the effect of applying a CSP algorithm separately to each sub-pathway, with the effect of applying the algorithm to the aggregated arrivals. That is, should we keep a separate inspection history and alert level for each sub-pathway, or should we just have a single inspection history and alert level that we apply to them all? The basis of the comparison was the SOQ, the estimated long-run leakage rate for the given sample of units.

For the data in question there is reason to believe that the approach rate varies across suppliers and it is intuitively reasonable to have a methodology that can sample one sub-pathway more than others. In our case, the mechanism that enables this is the alert level. The advantage of this strategy is that it focuses inspection resources onto areas in which there is the possibility of a higher approach rate. The disadvantage is that extra inspection effort may be undertaken in sub-pathways that are relatively clean because the base sampling rate, f, is inflated by the sub-pathways that have contamination.

The available inspection history comprised 1,516 inspections, 157 (10.4%) of which were non-compliant. The inspection dates ranged from 1 December 2005 to 2 April 2011, which is nearly five and a half years. Consignments (units) were imported from 20 unique suppliers, two of whom exported overwhelmingly larger volumes than the others. The experiment involved 100 replicates of all possible combinations of the following factors:

- Strata – none, supplier
- Inspection Rule – CSP-1, CSP-2 and CSP-3
- Sampling Fraction – $f = 0.10, 0.33$ and 0.50
- Clearance Number – $g = g_c = g_a = 5, 10$ and 20

Here, the strata label refers to the characteristic used to divide the consignments into sub-pathways. This design yielded 5,400 simulations.

The simulations involved sorting the inspection data by time and then unit by unit using the CSP algorithm to determine whether or not each unit would have been inspected. A unit is always inspected if the alert level of its sub-pathway is in census mode, but otherwise, a unit is inspected at random with probability f. Because of the use of random numbers to simulate the sampling process, the outcome of the inspection algorithm is random and the simulation was repeated 100 times for each candidate design. For the purposes of calculating the SOQ, only inspections from 2008 onwards were used, leaving out the two years of earlier inspections so that they act as a burn-in period for the algorithm.

1.5.2   Results

The results of the simulation experiment are presented in Figure 1.1, which gives the average leakage rate by scenario as a function of the number of consignments that were inspected. Each point represents the mean of 100 simulations. Each of the combinations of design and stratifying variable has nine points that represent different values of the sampling fraction, f, and clearance number, $g = g_c = g_a$. The straight diagonal line represents the expected trajectory if purely random sampling is performed.

The standard errors of the mean leakage rate ranged from 0.026% to 0.076%, and the standard errors of the mean inspection counts ranged from 1.2 to 5 consignments, which suggest that the locations of the points are reasonably precise.

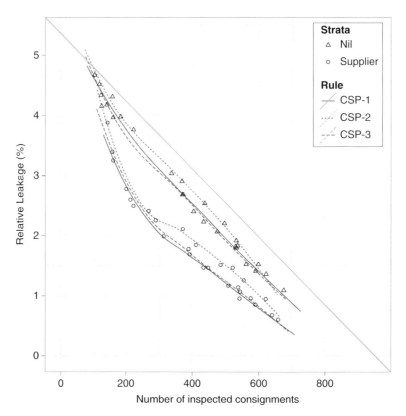

Figure 1.1. Simulation results. The x-axis reports the number of consignments inspected during the reporting period, the y-axis shows the SOQ, that is, the percentage of the pathway volume that is noncompliant and undetected.

We see that, regardless of which version of CSP is used and what inspection parameters are selected, stratifying the pathway by supplier improves the inspection performance considerably for this type of unit. This means that the approach rate varies between suppliers, which further suggests that keeping and using supplier-level inspection histories will increase the efficiency of the inspection process. The improvement seemed to be greatest at the mid-range of the inspection counts; with too few inspections the contaminated pathways were poorly detected, and with too many inspections the effort wasted on relatively clean pathways reduced the benefits of stratification. CSP-1 and CSP-3 performed approximately as well as each other, and both were slightly better than CSP-2.

In this example, each unit belonged to a unique sub-pathway. By using multiple variables to stratify the data, units may belong to more than one sub-pathway. For example, we may stratify by supplier and country of origin. In such a case we can maintain a separate alert level for each sub-pathway and then sample each unit according to its highest alert level.

A simulation experiment using historical data provides a useful way of deciding whether or not to include a particular stratification variable in the algorithm.

Theoretical AOQ values, such as those reported in Tables 1.1 to 1.3, are useful for the purposes of general comparison, but when reliable historical inspection data are available, the algorithms can be compared better using simulation.

1.6   Acknowledgements

The authors are grateful to Rob Cannon for useful conversations, Brendan Woolcott for assisting with the data and Dr Enrico Perotti and Louise van Meurs for advice and support.

References

Baillie, D. H. & Klaassen, C. A. J. (2006). Credit to and in acceptance sampling. *Statistica Neerlandica*, 60(3), 283–291.

Bourke, P. D. (2002). A continuous sampling plan using CUSUMs. *Journal of Applied Statistics*, 29(8), 1121–1133.

Cannon, R. M. (2009). Inspecting and monitoring on a restricted budget – where best to look? *Preventative Veterinary Medicine*, 92, 163–174.

Dodge, H. F. (1943). A sampling inspection plan for continuous production. *Annals of Mathematical Statistics*, 14(3), 264–279.

Dodge, H. F. & Torrey, M. N. (1951). Additional continuous sampling plans. *Industrial Quality Control*, 7(5), 7–12.

Gaba, A. & Winkler, R. L. (1992). Implications of errors in survey data: A Bayesian model. *Management Science*, 38(7), 913–925.

Govindaraju, K. & Kandasamy, C. (2000). Design of generalized CSP-C continuous sampling plan. *Journal of Applied Statistics*, 27(7), 829–841.

Johnson, W. O. & Gastwirth, J. L. (1991). Bayesian inference for medical screening tests: Approximations useful for the analysis of acquired immune deficiency syndrome. *Journal of the Royal Statistical Society. Series B (Methodological)*, 53(2), 427–439.

Klaassen, C. A. J. (2001). Credit in acceptance sampling on attributes. *Technometrics*, 43(2), 212–222.

Lieberman, G. J. (1953). A note on Dodge's continuous inspection plan. *Annals of Mathematical Statistics*, 24(3), 480–484.

Lieberman, G. J. & Solomon, H. (1955). Multi-level continuous sampling plans. *Annals of Mathematical Statistics*, 26(4), 686–704.

Press, W. H. (2009). Strong profiling is not mathematically optimal for discovering rare malfeasors. *Proceedings of the National Academy of Sciences of the USA*, 106(6), 1716–1719.

Robinson, A. P., Burgman, M. A., Atkinson, W., et al. (2008). *AQIS import clearance data framework.* Technical Report 0804. Melbourne, Australia: Australian Centre of Excellence for Risk Analysis, the University of Melbourne.

Robinson, A. P., Burgman, M. A. & Cannon, R. (2011). Allocating surveillance resources to reduce ecological invasions: Maximising detections and information about the threat. *Ecological Applications*, 21(4), 1410–1417.

Stephens, K. S. (1995). *How to perform continuous sampling*, 2nd ed. ASQC Basic References in Quality Control, Vol. 2: Statistical Techniques. Milwaukee, WI: American Society for Quality Control, Statistics Division.

Tuyl, F., Gerlach, R. & Mengersen, K. (2009). Posterior predictive arguments in favour of the Bayes-Laplace prior as the consensus prior for binomial and multinomial parameters. *Bayesian Analysis*, 4(1), 151–158.

Wald, A. & Wolfowitz, J. (1945). Sampling inspection plans for continuous production which insure a prescribed limit on the outgoing quality. *Annals of Mathematical Statistics*, 16(1), 30–49.

2 Tools for Designing and Evaluating Post-Border Surveillance Systems

Susan M. Hester, Cindy E. Hauser and John M. Kean

2.1 Introduction

Biosecurity surveillance is the collection, collation, analysis, interpretation and timely dissemination of information on the presence, distribution or prevalence of pests or diseases and the plants or animals that they affect (MAFBNZ, 2009b as cited in Acosta & White, 2011). When undertaken post-border, biosecurity surveillance activities are carried out for a variety of purposes: to achieve market access, to detect new pests and diseases sufficiently early to allow for cost-effective management, to establish the boundaries of a known pest or disease population and to monitor the progress of existing containment or eradication programmes. Integrated and efficient surveillance plans are essential for effective allocation of limited biosecurity resources, successful pest control and the maintenance of important export markets.

In this chapter, we provide a brief overview of many of the theoretical methods and models for designing and evaluating post-border surveillance, but our focus is on the readily applicable tools that have emerged from this theoretical work. These tools range in character from rules of thumb and simple formulae to simulation models with user-friendly interfaces. We discuss how each tool fits into the post-border surveillance framework, where to locate a particular tool and the contexts in which each tool has been applied. A more detailed explanation of key theoretical methods and models can be found in other chapters of this book; for example, predicting the spread of invasives is found in Chapters 5 and 6, optimising resource allocation is in Chapter 15, while the theory behind eradication, scenario trees and pathways analysis is given in Chapters 16 and 17.

Our discussion assumes that the reader has some knowledge of the many concepts and methods from economics and statistics that are relevant to post-border surveillance. Rather than include an explanation of these, we refer the reader to Chapter 10 for a discussion of economic concepts, and to Chapter 18 for a discussion on key statistical concepts and well-known sampling designs. We do, however, include a discussion on the likelihood of detecting a pest or disease that is central to the quantitative surveillance tools reviewed in this chapter.

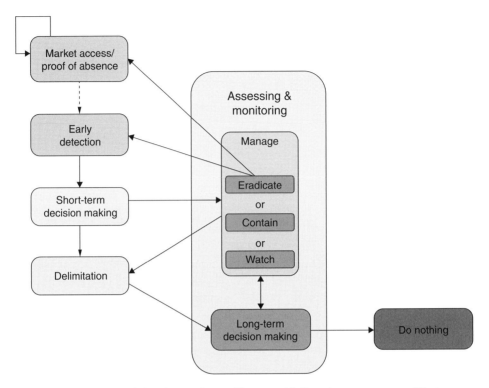

Figure 2.1.   Conceptual diagram of the phases of surveillance and infestation management (Hester et al., 2010a).

2.2   Tools for Surveillance of a Single Species

The process for prioritising multiple species and projects for surveillance was outlined in Chapter 1. In this section, we assume that a particular taxon has been identified as warranting surveillance. The type of surveillance needed will depend on the status of the taxon, whether it is present or absent and the goals for its management. As the presence, absence or distribution of a species changes over time, management goals may change and surveillance plans should also adapt.

The post-border surveillance framework illustrated in Figure 2.1 represents the way in which post-border surveillance activities relate to each other. Detections arising from surveys that are undertaken when a pest or disease is thought to be absent (for the purposes of market access or early detection) lead to short-term decision making to determine the appropriate initial response. Protocol may dictate that eradication be the automatic response; alternatively, delimitation may be required to estimate the full spatial extent of the incursion. Knowledge of the incursion's extent would allow for longer-term decision making, such as prediction of the damages that the incursion might cause and the resources required for candidate management strategies that aim to eradicate, contain, or simply watch the incursion with little interference (monitoring). Over time, further delimitation surveys may be required in the evaluation of the management programmes, and depending on the outcome, the aims of management may change. The management option to do nothing would be appropriate if further active management cannot be justified.

In Sections 2.2.1 to 2.2.4, we review surveillance approaches in the context of these various purposes – market access, early detection, delimitation and monitoring. We also explore methods and tools for understanding the interaction between surveillance and decision making, and for estimating the likelihood of detecting a pest or disease, the *detectability*, in the post-border surveillance context.

2.2.1 Surveillance for Market Access

Post-border surveillance for the purposes of securing or maintaining market access is undertaken to define the pest and disease status of a country or regions within a country. Based on international standards, trading partners may develop an agreement that specifies the surveillance standards required to establish and maintain area freedom status for specific pests and diseases. Countries that are members of the World Trade Organization have their international trade in plant and animal products governed by a series of rules, guidelines and standards; see Hester et al. (2010a) for a discussion of these. Essentially, countries or jurisdictions are required to use science-based evidence, confirmed by targeted surveys, to support their claims that a pest or disease is absent. Where possible, this targeted surveillance should be complemented by other sources of information such as scientific publications, research data, documented field observations and other non-survey data. Evidence may be provided either by structured surveys, which are often enhanced by passive surveillance, or by qualitative assessment of data from a variety of sources, usually by a panel of experts.

When claims of area freedom are based on structured surveys, the decisions on how and where to look for a target pest or disease depend on whether the aim of surveillance is detection or monitoring. Detection surveillance involves looking for pests and diseases that are not known to be present, while delimitation and monitoring surveillance are used to verify the characteristics of a known pest population and are undertaken under a limited number of agreements for which market access from areas of low pest prevalence is allowed (e.g. FAO, 2008).

Detection surveillance using structured surveys provides evidence that a pest or disease is absent. Where these surveys are undertaken and no pest is found, the results may be used to show that there is a particular level of confidence (e.g. 95%) that the pest would have been found even if it were present at a very low prevalence (e.g. 0.05%). When pest-specific or disease-specific guidelines for a structured population-based survey have not been given, appropriate statistical practices should be followed and documented. McMaugh (2005) gives a thorough account of the steps and relevant statistical concepts involved in detection surveillance for plant pests, and Cameron (1999) and OIE (2015) provide this information for animals. A readily available set of web-based tools (Epitools; Hester et al., 2015; Sergeant, 2009) can assist with survey designs for estimating disease prevalence or

Table 2.1. Surveillance tools for market access

Technique	Use of technique	Application and reference(s)	Available tools
Survey design	Providing evidence of area freedom when sensitivity and specificity ≠ 1, or sampling with replacement	Area surveys of animals (Cameron & Baldock, 1998a, b; Cannon, 2001; Cannon & Roe, 1982)	Formulae for sample size in reference FreeCalcV2: http://epitools.ausvet.com.au/content.php?page=FreeCalc2 Epi Tools Suite: http://epitools.ausvet.com.au/content.php?page=home
Survey design	Providing evidence of freedom from a disease	Various case studies presented (Cameron, 1999; McMaugh, 2005)	Formulae available in references
Bayesian belief networks	Providing evidence of area freedom in multiple-component systems	Foot and mouth disease, classical swine fever, Denmark (Hood et al., 2009)	Netica®: www.norsys.com/ GeNie and SMILE: www.bayesfusion.com/
Stochastic scenario tree models	Providing evidence of area freedom	Classical swine fever, Denmark (Martin et al., 2007a, b) Survey of an invertebrate, Barrow Island, Western Australia (Barrett et al., 2010) and a vertebrate (Jarrad et al., 2011)	Procedure and formulae available in reference PopTools: www.poptools.org AusVet Freedom software: http://freedom.ausvet.com.au/

for demonstrating freedom from diseases in animal herds, and is also applicable to plant-health surveillance surveys (see Table 2.1).

Alternatively, data from structured non-random surveillance may be used to support claims of area freedom. For animals, this may include information from 'general surveillance', which would include data from reporting or notification programmes, control programmes/health schemes, targeted testing/screening, antemortem and postmortem inspections, laboratory investigation records, biological specimen banks, sentinel units, field observations, farm production records or wildlife disease data (OIE, 2015). Martin et al. (2015) describe the structure of a stochastic spreadsheet-based model (General Surveillance Assessment Tool) that is used to estimate the sensitivity of general surveillance in the Australian livestock sector and to predict the median time to first detection of livestock diseases.

In some countries, results from sentinel site surveys are used to support claims of area freedom for a large range of pests and diseases of plants and animals. To maximise the chance of early detection, sentinel sites (trees, traps or animals) are selected at locations where there is thought to be a high likelihood of a pest or disease incursion, for example, at ports that receive international vessels. The sentinel sites are then surveyed regularly for evidence of a pest or disease incursion (Stevens, 2008).

When surveillance uncovers evidence of pest or disease presence, area freedom status may be revoked. Managers then generally focus resources on delimitation and eradication monitoring, as described in Sections 2.2.3 and 2.2.4. Meanwhile, an effort is usually made to identify the origin of the pest or disease and determine how it arrived, to manage the introduction pathway more effectively. If eradication is successful, reinstatement of area freedom status will depend on the terms of individual trading agreements, and is likely to depend on the life cycle of the pest. In some cases, trade with areas of low pest prevalence is allowed, and monitoring surveys are used to provide continued evidence of low pest prevalence (e.g. DAFF, 2004; FAO, 2008).

The main strength of structured surveys to demonstrate area freedom is that a quantifiable probability estimate for the presence of the pest or disease can be calculated based on well-established sampling theory and methods. The main disadvantage is that these surveys can be very expensive because large sample sizes are required to provide high statistical confidence that the prevalence of the disease is at, or near, zero (Ausvet Animal Health Services, n.d.). Survey costs may be an important constraint and will often determine the level of surveillance that may be undertaken. In this context, the optimal level of surveillance activity (e.g. number of blood tests or surveys, or level of enforcement) will be that which minimises the sum of the expected present value of all the costs associated with pest or disease incursion over an infinite time horizon. For example, Kompas and Che (2003) developed a model that can be used to determine the optimum surveillance level for a pest given the likely arrival time, biological characteristics, surveillance expenditure before detection and production losses before and after detection. When applied to ovine Johne's disease in Western Australia, the optimal quarantine programme should be of a severity that potentially allows entry of one infected sheep every eleven years (Kompas & Che, 2003). This approach was also used to estimate the optimal level of surveillance for foot-and-mouth disease in the United States (Kompas et al., 2006) and for wood borers and bark beetles in New Zealand (Epanchin-Niell et al., 2014).

Several recently developed techniques based on scenario tree models can use data from a range of different surveillance activities to calculate a quantitative estimate for the probability of detection, which can be used to support claims of freedom of disease or infection. Scenario trees are a way to represent a hierarchy of information about a system; these were developed for biosecurity by Martin et al. (2007a) and are explained more fully in Chapter 17. Where the analysis of very complex surveillance systems leads to the construction of large scenario trees, spreadsheets or other specialist computer software must be used (e.g. @Risk: Palisade Corporation, 2015; and Poptools: Hood, 2010). Hood et al. (2009) showed how some scenario trees can be simplified using matrix algebra or Bayesian belief networks. While it may be difficult for a biosecurity manager to use the matrix method to derive the more compact scenario trees, it is likely that biosecurity managers can use readily available Bayesian network software such as Netica® (Norsys Software Corporation, n.d.) and SMILE (Decision Systems Laboratory, n.d.) to represent scenario trees and use them to support claims of pest and disease freedom (Table 2.1).

Readily available tools that have evolved from the methods discussed in this section, and which can be used for market-access surveillance, are listed in Table 2.1.

2.2.2   Surveillance for Early Detection

As is the case with surveillance for market access, surveillance for early detection aims to find invasions of new pests and diseases early enough to enable effective and efficient management (including eradication or containment). In practice, the aims of early detection and proof of freedom often operate together. However, in the case of early detection, we assume that there is no trade imperative or proscriptive protocol for surveillance, and because of this, additional tools and methods are available.

Surveillance for early detection is particularly challenging because there is often little or no information available about where, when and how a new target species will arrive in a country or region (Kean et al., 2008), but the expectation is that a particular pest or disease will arrive eventually. There is a trade-off between using resources to find incursions early and using resources to manage the incursions once detected; the earlier an incursion is detected, the fewer the resources required for subsequent management compared with finding the incursion when it has spread further (Epanchin-Niell et al., 2012).

Identifying Where to Look

Pathways analysis (see Chapter 1) may be used to identify the entry and spread of an invasive species, where a pathway represents any means enabling the potential entry and spread of pests and diseases. Thomas et al. (2007) combined risk analysis with pathways analysis to enable ranking of the relative risk of weed-spread pathways in Victoria, Australia, so that resources for surveillance could be prioritised accordingly. The criteria developed for the risk assessment framework were weighted using an analytical hierarchical process, with weights determined using a software tool called Catchment Decision Assistant©. The tool helps users to structure the problem into a hierarchy of criteria, and then systematically rates and weights the relative importance of each criterion as it contributes to overall risk. The software also connects the decision-making framework to geographic information systems; Barrett et al. (2010) used the software to predict likely entry points for an invasive ant, and from that prediction, were able to determine where surveillance resources should be focused.

Simple mathematical models have also been used to identify where surveillance should be undertaken. Perry and Vice (2009) used a simple model to identify islands in the Pacific Ocean that were at high risk of brown tree snake entry and establishment as a result of transport and cargo movements from Guam, where this species is a serious problem. Information on the risk of establishment could be used to inform interdiction policies on Pacific islands where the threat of snake arrival is determined to have changed. Similarly, surveillance effort can be focused by combining spatially explicit information on the relative likelihoods of entry and establishment to generate relative risk maps (e.g. East et al., 2013; Magarey et al., 2011).

Identifying How to Look

Once the locations of early detection efforts have been determined, managers must decide how to undertake the surveillance. Often, a combination of active and passive surveillance is appropriate for early detection. *Active surveillance* is undertaken by pest-management agencies through targeted surveys, while *passive surveillance* involves public vigilance, where members of the community or an industry report possible new incursions (Hester and Cacho, 2017).

In principle, active surveillance techniques for early detection are the same as those discussed in the context of market access, but without any immediate trade imperative or prescribed survey protocol that insists on a particular testing intensity or density of traps. Nevertheless, to ensure that survey results are meaningful, it is important that statistically appropriate survey design and sampling techniques be used (see Chapter 18). MacKenzie and Royle (2005) provide a useful discussion on survey design and selection of sampling sites when attempting to describe the level of occupancy of a region or landscape. Berec et al. (2015) evaluate the effects of different spatial arrangements of traps or sampling points and show that it matters less and less as the sensitivity of the sampling method declines. The applicability of various sampling methods for simulated populations of an invasive plant is discussed in Rew et al. (2006). Barrett et al. (2010) derived formulae for calculating the number of surveillance system units that would be required to detect non-indigenous species, with a given statistical power and a specified number of independent individuals. The surveillance system can comprise structured surveys, trapping methods, incidental sightings by non-experts and any other detection method for which the sensitivity and footprint are known or can be reasonably estimated. The methodology of Barrett et al. (2010) was subsequently extended to a non-indigenous vertebrate pest: the black rat on an island (Jarrad et al., 2011).

Passive surveillance has often detected new incursions of invasive pests and diseases (Cacho et al., 2010; Hester & Cacho, 2012). Although not directly under the control of biosecurity managers, the efficacy of passive surveillance can be influenced through targeted education and in the way that reports are processed and followed up (Froud et al., 2008). Surveillance information can be gathered from the general public using telephone hotlines (Froud et al., 2008), but it may often be more effective to target the skills of farmers, private veterinarians and specialised pest-detection groups such as those of the National Plant Diagnostic Network in the United States, Weedspotters (Morton & Harris, 2008; Queensland Government, n.d.) and CropSafe (Agriculture Victoria, n.d) in Australia and the Garden Bird Health Initiative in the United Kingdom (UFAW, 2005). This type of surveillance information can be combined with other surveillance data using scenario trees (Martin et al., 2007a; see also Chapter 17) and can be incorporated into new designs or analysed after the fact using the methods advanced by Barrett et al. (2010).

Identifying How Hard to Look

A range of methods and tools can be used to help determine surveillance effort, based on effective survey frequency, survey intensity, time spent at a site or the optimal search effort that should be expended in the detection process.

Harris et al. (2001) and Brown et al. (2004) tackled the issue of search frequency when the ability to detect a species improves over time due to its increased spread. Recommendations for weed surveillance intervals are given for a range of weeds in a range of habitat types, and these depend on the rate of weed growth, the ability to detect a weed and the cost of controlling the weed. The model was made available as a spreadsheet (see Table 2.2).

Survey *intensity*, the number of survey units (e.g. traps, nets or sample points) required for a given area, is related to the population size and detectability of the pest or disease and has been investigated for a range of pests and diseases (see Section 2.3). For the special case when a survey unit is sure to detect a pest when present, Green and Young (1993) showed that the number of survey units required for 95% confidence in detection is simply three divided by the target population density. Barrett et al. (2010) extended this method to select the appropriate survey intensity when the probability of detection in a sample unit is less than one. They showed how disparate sampling methods could be combined to quantify the overall power of a survey. Similar principles underpin stochastic scenario tree models (Martin et al., 2007a, 2007b; see also Chapter 17).

The optimal search effort that should be applied to detecting a pest or disease has been investigated with a range of models. In the simulation model of Cacho et al. (2006, 2007) and Hester et al. (2010b), search theory concepts are incorporated into a population model and the costs of search and control are calculated as functions of the amount of search effort, which is the decision variable. This approach is extended in Panetta et al. (2011) and Hester et al. (2013) to show the effectiveness of search and control efforts in changing the status of a weed infestation from active (weed is detectable above ground) to monitored (no recruits detected). A user-friendly spreadsheet model for exploring the effect of changing levels of search effort using the methods of Cacho et al. (2006) is freely available (Cacho & Pheloung, 2007; see Table 2.2).

Mehta et al. (2007), Hauser and McCarthy (2009) and Epanchin-Niell et al. (2012) provided other examples of models that can be used to explore optimal search effort. Hauser and McCarthy (2009) used an occupancy model, a detection model and an economic analysis to identify how surveillance effort should be allocated across a heterogeneous landscape using both benefit–cost analysis and cost–effectiveness analysis. The optimal surveillance effort can be implemented using a readily available spreadsheet tool (Hauser, 2009; see Table 2.2).

Table 2.2. Surveillance tools for early detection

Technique	Use of technique	Application and reference(s)	Available tools
Scenario trees	Designing multi-element surveillance systems to a specified statistical power	Survey of an invertebrate, Barrow Island, Western Australia (Barrett et al., 2010) and survey of a vertebrate (Jarrad et al., 2011); insect trapping (Kean, 2015)	Formulae available in references
Numerical simulation	Determining time between surveys	Five habitat types, two or three weed types in each habitat (Brown et al., 2004, Harris et al., 2001)	Excel® spreadsheet model; email request to simon@harrisconsulting.co.nz
Simulation model	Determining eradication feasibility for various search efforts	Four hypothetical weed scenarios (Cacho & Pheloung, 2007) and for the eradication of miconia in far-north Queensland (Hester et al., 2010b)	Weed search: www.une.edu.au/staff-profiles/business/ocacho
Spatial model of detection and treatment	Determining effort allocation across landscape; costs vs. benefits of early detection	Orange hawkweed, Victoria (Hauser, 2009; Hauser & McCarthy, 2009)	Spreadsheet model email request to: chauser@unimelb.edu.au
Qualitative analysis	Developing a model for community-based detection	Weed detection network in Australia (Morton & Harris, 2008)	Template available in reference
Analytical hierarchical process	Ranking the relative risk of weed-spread pathways	Weed spread in Victoria, Australia (Thomas et al., 2007)	Catchment Decision Assistant© software discussed in Itami and Cotter (1999)
Modified failure-time model	Measuring time to detection	Two invasive grass species, threatened native plant, Victoria (Garrard et al., 2008, 2009)	Computer code for simulating data and calling WinBUGS model in R contained in Garrard et al. (2008, 2009)

Garrard et al. (2009) developed models based on environmental and observer variables for designing optimal surveillance strategies for early detection of weeds. They also discussed a trait-based model of plant detection time that may be used to provide estimates of detectability where no species-specific detection model exists (Garrard et al., 2008, 2009, 2013). This information is useful in prioritising surveillance activities and the amount of resources to allocate to surveillance (see Section 2.4). Computer code for implementing the method in the Bayesian freeware WinBUGS is provided in Garrard et al. (2008; see Table 2.2).

The range of readily deployable tools that can assist in early detection surveillance is given in Table 2.2. Tools range from qualitative analysis techniques through to simulation models and scenario trees.

2.2.3   Surveillance for Delimitation

The aim of surveillance undertaken for delimitation is to establish the boundaries of a known incursion of a pest or disease. In theory, delimitation should be undertaken as quickly as possible because the invasive species continues to spread while searching is taking place. This increases the probability of escape, the extent of the invasion and the ultimate effort required to manage the invasion (Leung et al., 2010).

Where to Look

Initially, delimitation surveillance efforts focus on determining the likely means of introduction as well as the method, amount and direction of dispersal from both the known infestation and from the original site of incursion. The initial detection site should be used as a starting point for gathering the required information, although this site will not necessarily be the initial point of introduction.

Trace-back and trace-forward techniques, combined with pathways analysis, can be used to gather information on introduction and spread. Trace-back enquiries are used to locate the likely original site of introduction, and if this is successful, trace-forward activities will then help to locate areas, objects or animals that might be infested and will need to be surveyed. Australia's National Livestock Information System and New Zealand's National Animal Identification and Tracing scheme are examples of formal tracing schemes that could be used in the context of delimiting an incursion of a pest or disease of livestock (MAFBNZ, 2009a; MLA, n.d; NAIT, n.d.).

Pathways analysis (see Section 2.2.2) can give additional information about possible dispersal mechanisms and is often used in conjunction with trace-forward and trace-back techniques in delimitation surveillance. This was the case in the delimitation of Siam weed (*Chromolaena odorata*) in Australia (QNRM, 2006) where pathways identified as high risk became the basis of trace-forward investigations. Detailed behavioural simulation models have recently been developed to suggest the proximal source location of insects caught in surveillance traps (Guichard et al., 2012), but further advances in trapping technology, specifically time-stamping captures, are needed before these tools can be operationalised. When there has been time to establish the habitat preferences of an invasive species, dispersal and habitat suitability models can be used to identify areas prone to invasion. Hastings et al. (2005) reviewed and synthesised recent developments in the study of the spread of invasive species and gave examples of where models have been tested with data. Habitat suitability models are used to describe the habitat types that have been invaded, and can subsequently be used to identify similar areas that might also harbour the invader or are more likely to face the most immediate threat of being invaded. Elith and Leathwick (2009) provide a review of habitat models (including history, cross-disciplinary features and diverse uses) as well as their use as a tool for predicting the suitability of new environments for a given species. Václavík and Meentemeyer (2009), Smolik et al. (2010) and Chapter 6 also provide useful information on modelling the spread of invasive species. Habitat suitability models that could be applied in a delimitation context range from non-linear regression models (Shaffi et al., 2003) to dispersal models combined with habitat suitability to predict weed occurrence across a landscape (Fox et al., 2009; Williams et al., 2008). Fox et al. (2009) reported the development of a surveillance support tool that can be used to assist in the delimitation and management of weed incursions. The geographic information system-based tool simulates invasions of plants across differing landscapes and through a range of dispersal mechanisms, and was used to evaluate the effectiveness of Chilean needle grass surveillance and to develop rules-of-thumb for future weed management. Hauser et al. (2016a) adapted their previous early detection surveillance optimisation (Hauser & McCarthy, 2009; Table 2.2) to accommodate known infestations and prioritise delimitation survey effort to high-risk areas beyond the known invasion extent. Their method was tested on a hawkweed eradication program in Australia, with survey priority maps proving a useful guide for managers about where surveillance effort should be allocated on the ground. Panetta and Lawes (2005) suggest that when information on habitat preferences is sparse and models of dispersal for new incursions do not exist, the delimitation strategy should involve systematic, intensive surveys in the local vicinity of known occurrences in conjunction with surveys in other areas that are selected based on putative dispersal behaviour and potential pathways of spread. This approach was further developed by Leung et al. (2010; see Section 2.2.3). In some cases, Cartesian methods may be used to focus surveillance effort where delimitation is the focus. For example, Meats (1998) used the results from sentinel trapping grids to estimate the location of epicentres of fruit fly populations from those detected in the traps.

How to Look

As with early detection, delimitation may use data arising from active or passive surveillance activities. For delimitation, resources can be better targeted because the identity and some of the distribution of the target pest is known. For example, passive surveillance was a key component of the attempts to delimit Siam weed and red imported fire ants in Queensland, Australia, where the community and various stakeholder groups were targeted through paid television advertising, direct mail-outs, letterbox drops, public relations events and press and radio coverage (Cacho et al., 2012; QNRM, 2006).

Active surveillance for delimitation should exploit the principles for survey design outlined in McMaugh (2005), Section 2.2.1 and Chapter 18. Pests and weeds that are detected early will often exist in low-density clustered distributions, for which adaptive cluster sampling (Thompson, 1990) is well suited. Spatial clustering implies that when one pest is found, nearby locations are much more likely than random locations to also have the pest (Philippi, 2005). Smith et al. (2003) demonstrated adaptive cluster sampling for rare (but not invasive) mussel species, while Philippi (2005) used this technique to determine the abundance and spatial distribution of a rare plant.

Conventional surveys may be impractical for determining the extent of an incursion when large areas are involved or when terrain impedes location access due to the high costs of searching. Remote sensing (aerial photography, multispectral airborne sensors and satellite imagery) may be used as a surveillance tool for delimitation when the pest is easily distinguished from its surroundings. For example, remote sensing has been used to estimate the extent of prickly acacia across 29,000 km^2 of the Mitchell grasslands of northern Australia (Lawes & Wallace, 2008), to quantify and map invasive species on a floodplain in Nebraska (Narumalani et al., 2009) and for quick and economical detection of small disjunct areas of yellow hawkweed (*Hieracium pratense*) over large areas in northern Idaho (Carson et al., 1995) and alpine areas of eastern Australia (Hung & Sukkarieh, 2015).

How to Achieve Delimitation

Panetta and Lawes (2005) suggest two rules-of-thumb for evaluating progress towards achieving delimitation: (1) that the cumulative area of known infestation becomes stable over time; and (2) that there is a decrease in the detection ratio (the total area of newly discovered infestation divided by the annual total area searched) over time. However, theory on how to determine the invasion boundary is sparse. Leung et al. (2010) presented one of very few published methods for rapidly delimiting the invasion boundary of a spreading organism, but it has not yet been developed into a readily applicable tool. Leung et al. (2010) developed a delimitation algorithm for circumstances when the site of the initial detection is known but there is no knowledge about the initial invasion site or the direction and extent of dispersal. The approach is based on probability and sampling theory and uses data assembled from the search process to draw inferences about the extent of the invasion. Although this method provides a useful starting point, it requires a very large sample effort and is not effective for low-density populations. The approach of Hauser et al. (2016a) was a suitable alternative for delimiting a sparse population of king devil hawkweed (*Hieracium praealtum*) in Australia.

In some cases, particularly during the early stages of an incursion investigation, a full and accurate delimitation may not be required; instead investigators may need to know only whether the invasion is already too widespread for certain management actions (e.g. eradication) to be feasible. In these cases, adequate information

Table 2.3. Surveillance tools for delimitation

Technique	Use of technique	Application and reference(s)	Available tools
Simulation model	Simulating dispersal; to evaluate surveillance and management	Weeds: applied to Chilean needle grass (Fox et al., 2009)	Surveillance support model: www.uq.edu .au/lir/weedtoolbox
Trace-forward, pathways analysis	Informing delimitation surveys	Siam weed, Queensland, Australia (QNRM, 2006)	Practical example in reference
Targeted detection surveys	Partial delimitation to enable rapid decision making during incursion investigation	Pasture tunnel moth, eucalyptus leaf beetle (Kean et al., 2015)	Formulae in reference

for decision making may be provided by a relatively inexpensive detection survey. Kean et al. (2015) describe this approach in more detail, give simple formulae for designing an appropriate survey and demonstrate how this approach has been used in recent insect invasions.

Delimitation of most invasive pests and diseases is a challenging process and the range of methods available is limited. Table 2.3 presents the few tools available that can be used to undertake delimitation surveillance and assist in achieving the goal of delimitation.

2.2.4   Surveillance for Monitoring

The progress of ongoing infestation management requires regular assessment and monitoring. Active surveillance can be used for continued delimitation, identifying sites that require control effort and observing changes in population density at known sites of infestation. It is important that the survey design and the data collected serve the objectives of the programme. We classify the objective of a programme broadly as eradication, containment or watching without interference (see Figure 2.1). Identifying which objective is most suitable for any particular case is discussed in Section 2.4 on long-term decision making.

When the programme objective is containment, surveillance resources should usually be targeted at the invasion front or barrier zone. One notable project of this type is the Slow the Spread programme against gypsy moth in the United States. Sharov et al. (1998) found that the most cost-effective solution was to place the highest density of traps ahead of the population front at a distance determined by how far new colonies can arise from the established infestation. Bogich et al. (2008) extended this work with a spatially implicit model of the area infested by gypsy moth to determine trap densities that minimise the expected costs of a gypsy moth eradication programme (Figure 2.2), and Epanchin-Niell et al. (2012) used a similar approach for optimising gypsy moth trapping across heterogeneous landscapes.

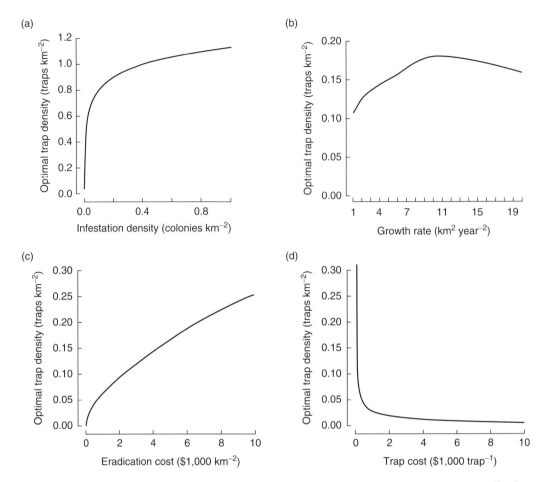

Figure 2.2. Optimal trap density as a function of **(a)** infestation density, **(b)** growth rate, **(c)** eradication cost and **(d)** trap cost for a five-year gypsy moth eradication programme.
[Reprinted with permission from Bogich, T. L., Liebhold, A. M. & Shea, K. (2008). To sample or eradicate? A cost minimization model for monitoring and managing an invasive species. Journal of Applied Ecology, 45(4), 1134–1142.]

In other cases, appropriate surveillance strategies will be influenced by the distribution of the infestation, which may be measured by remote sensing (see Section 2.2.3) and those targeted surveillance designs that are useful for early detection (see Section 2.2.2). Approaches that consider only pest presence or absence (e.g. Hauser & McCarthy, 2009) may not offer efficient designs when there is high variability in infestation size and the time required for treatment. The spatially explicit simulation model of Fox et al. (2009) offers an alternative for weed surveillance, with demographics and dispersal taken into account together with a range of surveillance strategies that can be explored and evaluated (Table 2.4).

Surveillance that is targeted for rapid control response is not well suited to observing changes in an infestation's density and distribution, and will often lead to biased

Table 2.4. Surveillance tools for monitoring

Technique	Use of technique	Application and reference(s)	Available tools
Simulation model	Simulating pest dispersal and growth, evaluate surveillance and management	Chilean needle grass in Queensland, Australia (Fox et al., 2009)	Surveillance support model: www.uq.edu.au/lir/weedtoolbox
Survey design	Gathering information on the extent and density of a pest or disease	Eight case studies (McMaugh, 2005)	Formulae in reference
Statistical methods	Inferring extinction time from sighting records	General (Rivadeneira et al., 2009)	Excel® spreadsheet: http://esapubs.org/archive/ecol/E090/084/suppl-1.htm
Optimisation, stochastic dynamic programming	Determining cost-effectiveness of further eradication monitoring when sample effort is known	Bitterweed in Queensland, Australia (Regan et al., 2006)	Rules-of-thumb in reference
Optimisation, stochastic dynamic programming	Determining cost-effectiveness of further eradication monitoring based on sighting records	Bitterweed in Queensland, Australia (Rout et al., 2009a)	Rules-of-thumb in reference
Robust optimisation, info-gap	Determining robustness of eradication monitoring	Rout et al. (2009b)	Rules-of-thumb in reference

estimates (McMaugh, 2005). In the latter case, statistical sampling designs – such as random, variable probability or stratified sampling – are preferable (see McMaugh, 2005; Royle et al., 2009; Samalens et al., 2007; Wikle & Royle, 1999; Table 2.4). Occupancy modelling can be used to detect changes in extent and guide future sampling (e.g. Field et al., 2005; Fitzpatrick et al., 2009).

As a programme approaches successful eradication, pest populations may be present at very low densities. Targeted surveillance plans, similar to those used for market access (Section 2.2.1) and early detection (Section 2.2.2), are most effective for finding those last individuals and evaluating eradication success. When sampling effort and detectability can be quantified (see Section 2.3), the probability of successful eradication can be derived from simple probability models together with environmental and survey data (e.g. Kean & Suckling, 2005). A range of sighting methods were reviewed and evaluated by Rivandeira et al. (2009), who concluded that most perform well when sampling effort is relatively homogeneous through time, even if absolute sampling intensity is unknown. These authors also supplied an Excel® spreadsheet for estimating extinction time from sighting records (Table 2.4). Bayesian methods have been used to quantify the success of vertebrate eradication programmes based on shooting or trapping methods (Ramsey et al., 2009; Solow et al., 2008; Anderson et al., 2013). Benefit–cost criteria can be overlaid onto these eradication probability models to identify when surveillance can be concluded and eradication can be declared successful (Regan et al., 2006; Rout et al., 2009a, 2009b; Table 2.4). This is discussed in detail in Chapter 16.

Planning the distribution, intensity and duration of surveillance resources in a monitoring programme requires careful consideration of the status of the infestation and the objectives of the programme. It is important to periodically assess and re-evaluate management, as infestation status and objectives change. In Section 2.4, we describe tools that can support this process for decision making.

2.3   Estimating Detection Probability

A common theme in all of the surveillance tools reviewed in Section 2.2 is the relationship between surveillance effort and the probability of detecting a population of the unwanted target organism. Confusingly, the term *detectability* has been used loosely in the literature to denote the probability of detecting an individual (e.g. Cacho et al., 2007), a population (e.g. Wintle et al., 2004) or a species (e.g. Mehta et al., 2007). If all individuals are similar, then the probability of detecting a target population, which we call *apparency* (*a*), depends on the *detectability* (*d*) of individuals (sometimes termed observability, trappability or sample efficacy) and the population size (*N*) within the searched area as $a = 1 - (1 - d)^N$.

Both detectability and apparency (collectively referred to as detection probabilities) are determined by the characteristics of the target species, the survey method and the sampling effort (e.g. mean search time) used, and may also depend on site, time or size. For many sampling methods, detectability also varies with distance from the sample point or transect. Because most sampling techniques were developed to measure the *relative* difference in population sizes over time or space, few have had their detection ability characterised. A special challenge for post-border surveillance is that an *absolute* estimate for detectability is required to interpret the zero results (apparent absences) that comprise much of the data collected.

2.3.1   Controlled Experiments for Measuring Detectability

Controlled experiments are one way to characterise the detectability of a particular target taxon with a specific sampling method. These generally involve calibration against another sampling method, release–recapture studies or techniques involving non-independent samples.

Calibration experiments simultaneously sample the same population using two or more techniques, where the detectability is known for one technique. The results then allow the detectability of the second technique to be estimated. For example,

Fleischer et al. (1985) calibrated various methods of sampling cotton pests against one another, and Byers et al. (1989) calculated the effective attraction radius of bark beetle pheromone traps by calibration against passive traps.

Alternatively, mark–release–recapture (MRR) methods allow the population size to be identified, enabling detectability to be estimated in various ways (Krebs & Boonstra, 1984). It is worth noting that MRR may be used with taxa that are not normally associated with these methods. For example, some studies have released a known population of plants (Hauser et al. 2015; Moore et al., 2011) or simulacra, such as plastic insects and plants or artificially induced disease symptoms (Bulman et al., 1999; Hauser et al., 2012, 2016b; Mangano et al., 2011), to estimate detectability in manual inspection surveys. Sterile insect releases for eradication or population suppression may also be used as MRR experiments to quantify detection probability (e.g. Kean & Suckling, 2005).

With an appropriate MRR design, it may be possible to quantify the influence of covariates, such as local environment, weather and searcher identity, on detectability (e.g. Chen et al., 2009; Christy et al., 2010; Yackel-Adams et al., 2011). MRR studies are also particularly useful for quantifying distance sampling (Buckland et al., 2001; Thomas et al., 2010) when detectability depends on the distance from a central sample point (e.g. insect trap) or transect line (as in visual surveys for plants). The relationship between detectability and distance may be used to derive an *effective sampling distance* that is equivalent to the area or volume beneath the curve in one dimension (e.g. Cacho et al., 2006), two dimensions (e.g. Kean, 2015; Turchin & Odendaal, 1996) or three dimensions (e.g. Byers, 2009), as appropriate for the sampling method (transect walks, insect population trapping and flying insect trapping respectively). This allows the overall efficacy of a surveillance system to be modelled as a function of the spatial deployment of samples (Kean, 2015), and thereby facilitates the design of optimal surveillance systems.

In cases in which neither calibration nor MRR techniques are feasible, it may still be possible to estimate detectability using non-independent samples. For example, if a population is repeatedly sampled without replacement, then an accumulation curve may be derived (e.g. McCallum, 2005) and detectability estimated from the slope and shape of the curve. For visual sampling, detectability can be estimated using double-observer methods, in which two observers simultaneously sample the same population (Nichols et al., 2000). Alternatively, it may be possible to infer the detectability of trappable insects by measuring the degree of trap interference at different spacings (e.g. Bacca et al., 2006; Suckling et al., 2015). Although the trap interference effect is well known (e.g. van der Kraan & Deventer, 1982; Wall & Perry, 1978), the methods necessary to estimate detectability from field results are not well developed.

2.3.2 Empirical Approaches to Estimating Detection Probabilities

A range of statistical techniques have been developed for simultaneously estimating apparency or detectability together with either local population size or probability

Table 2.5. Tools that can be used for estimating population apparency or detectability

Technique	Use of technique	Application and reference(s)	Available tools
Distance sampling	Quantifying detectability with distance	Thomas et al. (2010)	Specialised software: www .ruwpa.st-and.ac.uk/ distance/
	Estimating apparency from point survey data	Wintle et al. (2004)	Software PRESENCE: www.mbr-pwrc.usgs.gov/ software/doc/presence/ presence.html MARK: www.phidot.org/ software/mark/ CAPTURE: www.mbr-pwrc.usgs.gov/ software/captureshtml SURVIV: www.mbr-pwrc.usgs.gov/ software/surviv.shtml
	Estimating apparency and site occupancy	American toads, spring peepers (MacKenzie et al., 2002)	Software PRESENCE: www.mbr-pwrc.usgs.gov/ software/doc/presence/ presence.html
Zero-inflated binomial distribution	Estimating apparency and site occupancy	Woodland birds, forest-dwelling frogs, mound-spring invertebrates (Tyre et al., 2003)	R add-on to fit zero-inflated binomial distributions to biological survey data by maximum-likelihood estimation
Zero-inflated distributions	Estimating apparency and site occupancy	Mallard duck, Cherokee darter (Wenger & Freeman 2008)	R and WinBUGS code: http:// esapubs.org/archive/ecol/ E089/166/suppl-1.htm
	Optimal allocation of effort in detection and site occupancy studies	Amphibians in Yellowstone National Park, USA (Bailey et al., 2007)	Software GENPRES: www.mbr-pwrc.usgs.gov/ software
	Estimating apparency and site occupancy	Breeding birds (Rota et al., 2009)	R code: www3.interscience .wiley.com/journal/ 122681954/suppinfo

of occupancy (e.g. MacKenzie et al., 2002; Peterson & Bailey, 2004; Tyre et al., 2003; Table 2.5). Those based on empirically fitting zero-inflated distributions, which include many zero counts, seem to give the best estimates for population apparency (Wintle et al., 2004), prompting further advances in zero-inflated models (e.g. Joseph et al., 2009a; Wenger & Freeman, 2008). Meanwhile, sampling theory has been developed to determine the optimal strategy for data collection to parameterise the models. This may involve the choice of specific sampling methods (e.g. Cacho et al., 2007; Rew et al., 2006) or optimising the trade-off between temporal and spatial replication (e.g. Bailey et al., 2007; MacKenzie & Royle, 2005). For relatively immobile species, such as plants, the time spent searching at each site may be optimised, rather than the number of repeat visits (Garrard et al., 2008; Hauser et al., 2015).

A limitation of most empirical approaches is that they require a relatively large data set (but see MacKenzie et al., 2005), which constrains their use in biosecurity surveillance. In addition, they are inappropriate when there is significant change in local population size or habitat occupancy over time (Rota et al., 2009). This will be the case for many recent border incursions, and the models may give misleading results when the efficacy of different searchers is highly heterogeneous (Fitzpatrick et al., 2009). Empirical methods, which are not necessarily cheaper than experimental approaches, may be less likely to be useful for estimating detectability for biosecurity surveillance.

2.4   Decision Making

Justifiable and efficient surveillance is planned in the context of decision making. Surveys should be designed so that their data support and inform future decisions and management with a clear plan for how these data will be incorporated. Here, we discuss tools that aid decision making for pest incursion management, but take a broader view than just survey design. Some tools provide guidance on whether it is most prudent to eradicate, contain or not control an incursion, and other tools guide resource allocation among different activities, such as control, surveillance and research. Some models explicitly include the contribution of surveillance to overall management; others focus on other management activities and rely only implicitly on survey data.

2.4.1   Short-term Decision Making

Short-term decision making may be required immediately following the first detection of a species (Figure 2.1). In some cases, particularly when the species is a known economic threat, a protocol may have been agreed upon prior to detection, and management of the infestation can proceed immediately. In the absence of such a plan, a rapid assessment of the threat posed by the species is needed. Is establishment and spread likely under local conditions? What impact is the species anticipated to have on the local environment? A first assessment and any management strategies arising from it are typically surrounded by much uncertainty.

It is potentially more cost effective to eliminate an infestation at this early, uncertain stage than to embark on eradication later when the magnitude of the threat has been assessed in more detail and the species may have spread and caused damage. For example, Harris and Timmins (2009) analysed data from fifty-eight New

Zealand weed control projects and estimated that if a new infestation of a known weed is found, it should be controlled immediately if control (including follow-up surveillance) will cost less than NZ$47 000. Furthermore, a newly found plant of unknown weediness should be controlled immediately if control will cost less than NZ$7 000 (although this figure is likely to be an underestimate). In the first instance, feasibility of eradication can be assessed by comparing the time required to treat an infestation with the time interval during which individuals can be detected and accessed for treatment before they mature (Edwards & Leung, 2009; Table 2.6). Meta-analyses of eradication programmes (e.g. Tobin et al., 2014) have identified factors, including population size, that significantly affect the costs of eradication programmes and their likelihood of success. The Global Eradication and Response Database (GERDA; Kean et al., 2016; Table 2.6) provides an online tool for assessing the likely success and cost of an eradication programme based on past outcomes against similar species.

2.4.2   Long-term Decision Making

After the initial response, incursion management requires further periodic decision making. As an infestation is delimited, a more detailed threat assessment becomes possible and long-term management plans can be developed. Is the purpose of management to eradicate, contain or watch the species? What resources can, or should, be deployed for this purpose? Part III of this book addresses a range of decision-making issues in detail. We support structured decision-making approaches to develop sensible and defensible strategies. Much of the literature on decision making for incursion management focuses on benefit–cost analyses in particular (see Chapter 10). Risk return approaches are also consistent with benefit–cost and cost–effectiveness analyses.

Long-term decision making may be required even before a species of concern has arrived. Chapter 14 shows how structured decision making can be used to identify species of concern. It also shows how resources might be best allocated to quarantine activities that prevent species entry and to surveillance activities for effective detection if, or when, the species enters. Leung et al. (2002) also weighed the cost of preventing an invasion against the costs of treating an established infestation.

Many studies have taken a benefit–cost approach and applied optimisation methods to identify the intensity of control that will minimise the total expected time-discounted costs of control and the damage caused by the target species (see review by Epanchin-Niell & Hastings, 2010). These studies assume, however, that the distribution (and sometimes, density) of the pest population is known with certainty. The optimal control intensity derived by these studies may not explicitly relate to the objectives of eradication, containment or watching, and the anticipated long-term outcome of optimal control may implicitly shift (e.g. from eradication to containment) as the incursion and its management proceed. High-control intensity is justifiable when the threatened system is highly valued and highly threatened by the

Table 2.6. Summary of deployable tools and techniques for long-term decision making

Technique	Use of technique	Application and reference(s)	Available tools
Model comparison	Determining feasibility of eradication	*Ciona intestinalis*, a tunicate affecting blue mussels in Canada (Edwards & Leung, 2009)	Equations and rules-of-thumb in reference
Meta-analysis of past experiences	Determining feasibility and cost of eradication	Kean et al. (2016); Tobin et al. (2014)	GERDA: http://b3.net .nz/gerda
Optimisation by calculus	Determining optimal expenditure on control to minimise the costs of control and damage	Leung et al. (2005)	Rules-of-thumb in reference
Optimisation using a factored Markov decision process and algebraic decision diagrams	Prioritising infestation control among sites connected by dispersal	Chadès et al. (2011)	Rules-of-thumb; see also: www .youtube.com/ watch?v=wuOvbCu_ nJc;www .youtube.com/ watch?v=UMsKMd-X8QE; www .youtube.com/ watch?v=muLzZ-3hIvM
	Evaluating progress towards weed eradication. Corrects and extends Panetta and Lawes (2007)	Hester et al. (n.d.) using equations from Burgman et al. (2013)	MoniTool: www.acera .unimelb.edu.au/ materials/software .html
Optimisation using Symbolic Perseus algorithm for spatial partially observable Markov decision process	Prioritising infestation monitoring and control among sites connected by dispersal	Chadès et al. (2011)	Rules-of-thumb (see Section 2.4.2) and software
Optimisation by stochastic dynamic programming	Allocating resources between broad-scale searches, targeted searches and knowledge acquisition	Red imported fire ants (*Solenopsis invicta*) in south-east Queensland (Baxter & Possingham, 2011)	Rules-of-thumb (see Section 2.4.2)

pest, and when methods of control are sufficiently effective in mitigating damage (Leung et al., 2005; Table 2.6). Discount rates and reduced time horizons reduce the perceived benefits of control (Epanchin-Niell & Hastings, 2010 and citations therein; Chapter 10).

The feasibility and optimal duration of an eradication programme depend on the relationship between control costs and pest density (Epanchin-Niell & Hastings, 2010). If it becomes increasingly difficult to treat individuals as they become scarcer, then slow, delayed or no eradication may be preferred over a high-intensity rapid eradication programme. Nevertheless, populations may be eradicable if they have a tendency to decline further when at low density. As the probability of reinvasion increases, the value of eradication decreases, although it may still be warranted. The benefit–cost approach, and most guidelines arising from it, require that the value of the threatened system and control costs can be measured or estimated, when in reality, measuring the value of a system can be difficult if attributes of the system are not directly traded in the marketplace.

The relationship between control and the management purpose (eradicate, contain or no control) has been addressed explicitly in models of infestation spread from an introduction point (Cacho et al., 2008; Carrasco et al., 2009; Sharov & Liebhold, 1998). Assuming that damage caused is proportional to the area (but not density) of the infestation, it is optimal to target control at its perimeter. The outcome of control – eradication, containment, delay or no control – is expressed through the infestation's rate of spread (which can be positive or negative). The optimal control strategy depends on the infestation's uncontrolled rate of spread, its extent when first discovered and the duration of non-detectable life stages. The optimal control strategy may even switch over time as the infestation's extent changes.

Other control-focused studies have addressed how to most effectively target control resources among life history stages (Buhle et al., 2005; Hastings et al., 2006) or across space (Bogich & Shea, 2008; Chadès et al., 2011; Moody & Mack 1988; Taylor & Hastings, 2004). With the exception of Chadès et al. (2011), these studies assume that the distribution of the pest is known, presumably from surveillance data. Moody and Mack (1988) and Taylor and Hastings (2004) explored the utility of targeting outlier populations (comparable to Sharov and Liebhold's (1998) barrier zones in Section 2.2.4) versus the core infestation. Blackwood et al. (2010) and Chadès et al. (2011; Table 2.6) build spatially explicit networks of infestation based on their level of connectivity to identify where control efforts should be targeted. Chadès et al. (2011) explored a range of network motifs, finding that optimal control effort depends on the structure of the network and the stage of the infestations. Control effort should be prioritised to sources before sinks, shifting attention to neighbouring sites, and to least connected sites and clusters before addressing the most connected infestations. The extended network model of Chadès et al. (2011) accommodates imperfect survey information and includes software that can solve problems involving up to only six sites. To maximise the probability of eradication, optimal strategies generally apply control and survey effort repeatedly, especially to well-connected sites, even if the species is not observed.

Panetta and Lawes (2007; see Table 2.6) propose weed delimitation and extirpation criteria that require few inputs and account for imperfect detectability. These criteria can be plotted through time as an *eradograph* to assess progress towards eradication. When a programme is successful, the extirpation criterion will be larger than the seed longevity (non-detection time) of the species, while the delimitation criterion will approach zero. Figure 2.3a reproduces Panetta and Lawes's (2007) eradograph for branched broomrape, where the latter few years of data suggest a failure to delimit the infestation effectively. Eradograph trends that indicate that eradication measures are not currently successful also indicate which components of management would gain most benefit from more resources (see Figure 2.3b). Burgman et al. (2013) retain the original structure of Panetta and Lawes' (2007) eradograph but propose different metrics that improve biological interpretability. A user-friendly spreadsheet model (Monitool; Hester et al., n.d.) for exploring progress towards delimitation and extirpation using the methods of Burgman et al. (2013) is freely available (see Table 2.6).

There are more sophisticated ways of recognising the value of information supplied by surveillance. The rate of pest removal may provide information on total pest abundance, allowing for removal strategies that serve the dual purposes of population control and improved knowledge for future control (D'Evelyn et al., 2008). Alternatively, resources may need to be divided between separate surveillance and control activities (Ndeffo Mbah & Gilligan, 2010). In Chapter 15, the value of additional delimitation surveys is estimated before deciding whether or not to eradicate a newly discovered species.

Baxter and Possingham (2011; Table 2.6) investigated the optimal allocation of resources to broad-scale surveys (to assist delimitation), targeted surveys (to assist control) and research to improve species distribution models and hence the accuracy of future targeted surveys. They found that over the long term, there is a benefit to investing in research, at the expense of survey and control, in early time steps. However, this may also yield rapid population spread during that initial period. Other heuristic strategies may provide more acceptable results (see Figure 2.4), although the long-term probability of eradication is likely to be substantially lower (97% vs. 59%, in Baxter and Possingham's example).

For effective incursion management, surveillance must be understood and designed in the context of other management activities such as research and control. Tools that guide the allocation of resources between surveillance and other activities must acknowledge the quality of data obtained from surveillance, which will usually be imperfect. More common are studies that assume perfect and complete surveillance data (i.e. full knowledge of pest distribution), and which recommend optimal levels of pest control. Although these studies contribute important findings for cost-effective management, they may underestimate the cost and overestimate the feasibility of successful pest control if they are adopted without further consideration of the role surveillance plays.

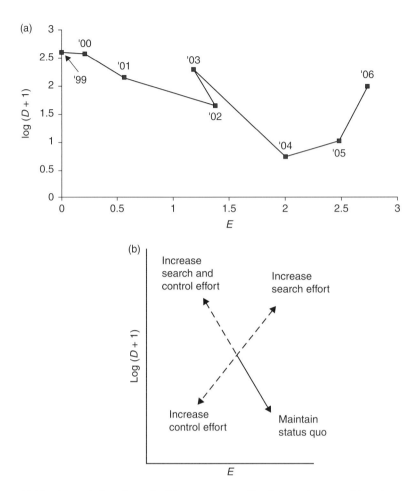

Figure 2.3.   **(a)** Eradograph for a branched broomrape eradication project, graphing the extirpation criterion E against the delimitation criterion $\log(D + 1)$. [Reprinted with permission from Burgman, M. A., McCarthy, M. A., Robinson, A. et al. (2013). Improving decisions for invasive species management: reformulation and extensions of the Panetta–Lawes eradication graph. Diversity and Distributions, 19(5–6), 603–607.] **(b)** Recommended resource deployment as a function of eradograph trend.
[Reprinted with permission from Panetta, F. D. & Lawes, R. (2007). Evaluation of the Australian branched broomrape (Orobanche ramosa) eradication program. Weed Science, 55(6), 644–651.]

2.5   Discussion

The outcome of successful biosecurity surveillance is a reduction in the risk that pests and diseases will become established or spread in a country or region, particularly those pests and diseases that have the potential to cause considerable harm to agricultural production, trade opportunities, human health or valued ecosystems.

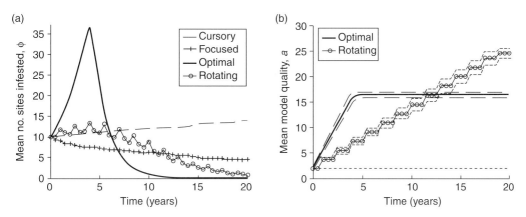

Figure 2.4.   Simulated performance of invasive species management over 20 years. **(a)** Comparison of four management strategies: cursory widespread searches; intensive focused searches; optimal state-dependent strategy recommended by stochastic dynamic programming; and continual rotating between cursory search, model-improvement and focused search. **(b)** Acquisition of knowledge when the optimal and rotational strategies are implemented. The two non-learning strategies (cursory and focused searching) remain at the initial level of $a = 2$ (dotted line).
[Reprinted with permission from Baxter, P. W. J. & Possingham, H. P. (2011). Optimizing search strategies for invasive pests: Learn before you leap. Journal of Applied Ecology, 48(1), 86–95.]

In this chapter, we have reviewed methods and tools for post-border surveillance with a view to assisting biosecurity managers to translate their observations and data on invasive species into management recommendations. Biosecurity managers are routinely faced with a range of surveillance problems and resource allocation decisions. Their decisions often need to be made rapidly, sometimes under close political scrutiny, so tools based on sound theory, which can be applied quickly and easily, are of great benefit. For this reason, we have highlighted tools that are freely available for use in each aspect of post-border surveillance and that require limited technical expertise to apply.

We have also covered the more technical methods and models that have been developed in the area of post-border surveillance, but not all of these have resulted in readily usable tools. There is a notable lack of tools that can be used to rapidly delimit an incursion. Tools to analyse absence-rich data, where sampling activities commonly result in the organism not being located, are also lacking. Biosecurity managers will, therefore, continue to benefit from the development of tools that use the more technical methods recently developed in this area.

Indeed, some techniques for analysing biosecurity surveillance data, such as stochastic scenario trees (Chapter 17), may involve complexities that preclude the development of simple and meaningful rules-of-thumb. Some additional training will be required if biosecurity managers are to become competent in using the software developed for creating scenario trees.

In such cases, it will be important for the scientists, statisticians and analysts working on behalf of biosecurity managers to involve managers and stakeholders in the process of obtaining results. Managers may also benefit when surveillance tools are presented in terms of economic tools with which they are familiar, such as benefit–cost analysis (Chapter 10) and control charts (Chapter 3).

Although the theories of zero-inflated distributions (Wenger & Freeman, 2008) and information contained in null data (e.g. Chapter 18) are developing rapidly, few authors have packaged their results in a form that is useful for managers. A key exception that is identified here is Epitools (Hester et al., 2015; Sergeant, 2009), a suite of tools that assist in surveillance design and proving area freedom.

The political nature of biosecurity means that decision makers must be well informed of the assumptions and uncertainties underlying the results from analyses of surveillance data. This may be especially challenging for authors providing simplified software black boxes or rule-of-thumb solutions.

Finally, it may not be easy for biosecurity managers to stay abreast of the new tools that could help them to make better decisions about surveillance systems. To realise fully the benefits of their work, scientists should carefully consider technology transfer. Reviews, such as this one, may go some way towards that goal, but there can be no substitute for biosecurity managers and scientists working together to realise their shared goal of better post-border surveillance systems.

2.6   Acknowledgements

This chapter arises from research funded by the Centre of Excellence for Biosecurity Risk Analysis. The authors acknowledge the financial and other support provided by the Department of Agriculture and Water Resources, the University of Melbourne, Australian Mathematical Sciences Institute and the Australian Research Centre for Urban Ecology. CEH was supported by the Australian Research Council's Linkage Projects funding scheme (project number LP100100441). JMK was partially funded by New Zealand's Better Border Biosecurity research programme (www.b3nz.org).

The authors are grateful to Mark Burgman for advice and support throughout the construction of the report and chapter, and to the following people for discussions and comments on past drafts: Andrew Robinson, Terry Walshe, Lois Ransom, Paul Pheloung, Mike Cole, Dane Panetta, Oscar Cacho, Bernie Dominiak, Greg Hood, Andrew Tomkins, Stephen Dibley, Joslin Moore, Aaron Dodd, Dean Paini, Nichole Hammond, Brendan Murphy, Tracy Rout, Mark Stanaway, Tony Pople, Peter Baxter, Iadine Chadès, Natalie Karavarsamis, Indriati Bisono, staff of the NT Department of Resources who spoke at a project meeting on 26 and 27 October 2009 and an anonymous reviewer. We thank Tiffany Bogich, Dane Panetta, Peter Baxter, Mark Burgman and their publishers for allowing us to reproduce their figures.

References

Acosta, H. & White, P. (2011). *Atlas of biosecurity surveillance*. Ministry of Agriculture and Forestry, Wellington, New Zealand. Available from www.mpi.govt.nz/mpi-surveillance-guide/atlas.pdf

Agriculture Victoria (n.d). *CropSafe program*. Available from http://agriculture.vic.gov.au/agriculture/grains-and-other-crops/grain-and-crop-health/cropsafe-program

Anderson, D. P., Ramsey, D. S. L., Nugent, G., et al. (2013). A novel approach to assess the probability of disease eradication from a wild-animal reservoir host. *Epidemiology and Infection*, 141(7), 1509–1521.

AusVet Animal Health Services. (n.d.). *Analysis of complex surveillance systems*. Available from http://freedom.ausvet.com.au/pmwiki/pmwiki.php?n=Freedom.FreedomTrail

Bacca, T., Lima, E. R., Picanço, M. C., Guedes, R. N. C. & Viana, J. H. M. (2006). Optimum spacing of pheromone traps for monitoring the coffee leaf miner *Leucoptera coffeella*. *Entomologia Experimentalis et Applicata*, 119(1), 39–45.

Bailey, L. L., Hines, J. E., Nichols, J. D. & MacKenzie, D. I. (2007). Sampling design trade-offs in occupancy studies with imperfect detection: Examples and software. *Ecological Applications*, 17(1), 281−290.

Barrett, S., Whittle, P., Mengersen, K. & Stoklosa, R. (2010). Biosecurity threats: The design of surveillance systems, based on power and risk. *Environmental and Ecological Statistics*, 17(4), 509–519.

Baxter, P. W. J. & Possingham, H. P. (2011). Optimising search strategies for invasive pests: Learn before you leap. *Journal of Applied Ecology*, 48(1), 86–95.

Berec, L., Kean, J. M., Epanchin-Niell, R., Liebhold, A. M. & Haight, R. G. (2015). Designing efficient surveys: Spatial arrangement of sample points for detection of invasive species. *Biological Invasions*, 17(1), 445–459.

Blackwood, J., Hastings, A. & Costello, C. (2010). Cost-effective management of invasive species using linear-quadratic control. *Ecological Economics*, 69(3), 519–527.

Bogich, T. L., Liebhold, A. M. & Shea, K. (2008). To sample or eradicate? A cost minimization model for monitoring and managing an invasive species. *Journal of Applied Ecology*, 45(4), 1134–1142.

Bogich, T. & Shea, K. (2008). A state-dependent model for the optimal management of an invasive metapopulation. *Ecological Applications*, 18(3), 748–761.

Brown, J. A., Harris, S. & Timmins, S. (2004). Estimating the maximum interval between repeat surveys. *Austral Ecology*, 29(6), 631−636.

Buckland, S. T., Anderson, D. R., Burnham, K. P., et al. (2001). *Introduction to distance sampling: Estimating abundance of biological populations*. Oxford: Oxford University Press.

Buhle, E. R., Margolis, M. & Ruesink, J. L. (2005). Bang for buck: Cost-effective control of invasive species with different life histories. *Ecological Economics*, 52(3), 355−366.

Bulman, L. S., Kimberley, M. O. & Gadgil, P. D. (1999). Estimation of the efficiency of pest detection surveys. *New Zealand Journal of Forestry Science*, 29(1), 102−115.

Burgman, M. A., McCarthy, M. A., Robinson, A., et al. (2013). Improving decisions for invasive species management: Reformulation and extensions of the Panetta-Lawes eradication graph. *Diversity and Distributions,* 19(5–6): 603–607.

Byers, J. A. (2009). Modeling distributions of flying insects: Effective attraction radius of pheromone in two and three dimensions. *Journal of Theoretical Biology*, 256(1), 81–89.

Byers, J. A., Anderbrant, O. & Löfqvist, J. (1989). Effective attraction radius: A method for comparing species attractants and determining densities of flying insects. *Journal of Chemical Ecology*, 15(2), 749−765.

Cacho, O. J., Hester, S. & Spring, D. (2007). Applying search theory to determine the feasibility of eradicating an invasive population in natural environments. *Australian Journal of Agricultural and Resource Economics*, 51(4), 425−443.

Cacho, O. J. & Pheloung, P. (2007). *Weed Search*. Available from www.une.edu.au/staff-profiles/business/ocacho

Cacho, O., Reeve, I., Tramell, J. & Hester, S. (2012). *Valuing community engagement in biosecurity surveillance.* Final Report, ACERA 1004 B 2d. Melbourne, Australia: University of Melbourne. Available from http://cebra.unimelb.edu.au/__data/assets/pdf_file/0006/1290516/1004B_OID7_Report.pdf

Cacho, O. J., Spring, D., Hester, S. & Mac Nally, R. (2010). Allocating surveillance effort in the management of invasive species: A spatially-explicit model. *Environmental Modelling and Software*, 25(4), 444–454.

Cacho, O. J., Spring, D., Pheloung, P. & Hester, S. (2006). Evaluating the feasibility of eradicating an invasion. *Biological Invasions*, 8(4), 903−917.

Cacho, O. J., Wise, R. M., Hester, S. M. & Sinden, J. A. (2008). Bioeconomic modeling for control of weeds in natural environments. *Ecological Economics*, 65(3), 559−568.

Cameron, A. R. (1999). *Survey toolbox for livestock diseases – A practical manual and software package for active surveillance in developing countries.* ACIAR Monograph 54. Canberra, Australia: Australian Centre for International Agricultural Research.

Cameron, A. R. & Baldock, F. C. (1998a). A new probability formula for surveys to substantiate freedom from disease. *Preventive Veterinary Medicine*, 34(1), 1–17.

Cameron, A. R. & Baldock, F. C. (1998b). Two-stage sampling in surveys to substantiate freedom from disease. *Preventive Veterinary Medicine*, 34(1), 19–30.

Cannon, R. M. (2001). Sense and sensitivity–designing surveys based on an imperfect test. *Preventive Veterinary Medicine*, 49(3–4), 141–163.

Cannon, R. M. & Roe, R. T. (1982). *Livestock disease surveys: A field manual for veterinarians.* Bureau of Resource Science, Department of Primary Industry. Canberra, Australia: Australian Government Publishing Service.

Carrasco, L. R., Baker, R., MacLeod, A., Knight, J. D. & Mumford, J. D. (2009). Optimal and robust control of invasive alien species spreading in homogeneous landscapes. *Journal of the Royal Society Interface*, 7(44), 529–540.

Carson, H. W., Lass, L. W. & Callihan, R. H. (1995). Detection of yellow hawkweed (*Hieracium pratense*) with high resolution multispectral digital imagery. *Weed Technology*, 9(3), 477–483.

Chadès, I., Martin, T. G., Nicol, S., et al. (2011). General rules for managing and surveying networks of pests, diseases and endangered species. *Proceedings of the National Academy of Sciences of the USA*, 108(20), 8323–8328.

Chen, G., Kéry, M., Zhang, J. & Ma, K. (2009). Factors affecting detection probability in plant distribution studies. *Journal of Ecology*, 97(6), 1383–1389.

Christy, M. T., Yackel Adams, A. A., Rodda, G. H., Savidge, J. A. & Tyrrell, C. L. (2010). Modelling detection probabilities to evaluate management and control tools for an invasive species. *Journal of Applied Ecology*, 47(1), 106–113.

DAFF (Department of Agriculture, Fisheries and Forestry). (2004). *Report for the importation of bananas from the Philippines. Revised draft import risk analysis.* Biosecurity Policy Memorandum 2004/19. Canberra, Australia: Department of Agriculture.

Decision Systems Laboratories. (n.d.). *About GeNIe and SMILE.* Available from www .bayesfusion.com/

D'Evelyn, S. T., Tarui, N., Burnett, K. & Roumasset, J. A. (2008). Learning-by-catching: Uncertain invasive-species populations and the value of information. *Journal of Environmental Management*, 89(4), 284–292.

East, I. J., Wicks, R. M., Martin, P. A. J., et al. (2013). Use of a multi-criteria analysis framework to inform the design of risk based general surveillance systems for animal disease in Australia. *Preventive Veterinary Medicine*, 112(3–4), 230–247.

Edwards, P. K. & Leung, B. (2009). Re-evaluating eradication of nuisance species: Invasion of the tunicate, *Ciona intestinalis. Frontiers in Ecology and the Environment*, 7(6), 326–332.

Elith, J. & Leathwick, J. R. (2009). Species distribution models: Ecological explanation and prediction across space and time. *Annual Review of Ecology Evolution and Systematics*, 40, 677–697.

Epanchin-Niell, R. S., Brockerhoff, E. G., Kean, J. M. & Turner, J. A. (2014). Designing cost-efficient surveillance for early detection and control of multiple biological invaders. *Ecological Applications*, 24(6), 1258–1274.

Epanchin-Niell, R. S., Haight, R. G., Berec, L., Kean, J. M. & Liebhold, A. M. (2012). Optimal surveillance and eradication of invasive species in heterogeneous landscapes. *Ecology Letters*, 15(8), 803–812.

Epanchin-Neill, R. S. & Hastings, A. (2010). Controlling established invaders: integrating economics and spread dynamics to determine optimal management. *Ecology Letters*, 13(4), 528–541.

FAO (Food and Agriculture Organization of the United Nations). (2008). *Establishment of areas of low pest prevalence for fruit flies (Tephritidae). International Standards for Phytosanitary Measures Publication* No. 30. Available from www.acfs.go.th/sps/downloads/ ISPM_30.pdf

Field, S. A., Tyre, A. J. & Possingham, H. P. (2005). Optimizing allocation of monitoring effort under economic and observational constraints. *Journal of Wildlife Management*, 69(2), 473–482.

Fitzpatrick, M. C., Preisser, E. L., Ellison, A. M. & Elkinton, J. S. (2009). Observer bias and the detection of low-density populations. *Ecological Applications*, 19(7), 1673–1679.

Fleischer, S. J., Gaylor, M. J. & Edelson, J. V. (1985). Estimating absolute density from relative sampling of *Lygus lineolaris* (Heteroptera: Miridae) and selected predators in early to mid-season cotton. *Environmental Entomology*, 14(6), 709–717.

Fox, J. C., Buckley, Y. M., Panetta, F. D., Bourgoin, J. & Pullar, D. (2009). Surveillance protocols for management of invasive plants: Modelling Chilean needle grass (*Nassella neesiana*) in Australia. *Diversity and Distributions*, 15(4), 577–589.

Froud, K. J., Oliver, T. M., Bingham, P. C., Flynn, A. R. & Rowswell, N. J. (2008). Passive surveillance of new exotic pests and diseases in New Zealand. In K. J. Froud, A. I. Popay & S. M. Zydenbos (eds.), *Surveillance for biosecurity: Pre-border to pest management* (pp. 97–110). Hastings, New Zealand: New Zealand Plant Protection Society.

Garrard, G. E., Bekessy, S. A., McCarthy, M. A. & Wintle, B. A. (2008). When have we looked hard enough? A novel method for setting survey effort protocols for flora surveys. *Austral Ecology*, 33(8), 986–998.

Garrard, G., Bekessy, S. & Wintle, B. (2009). *Determining necessary survey effort to detect invasive weeds in native vegetation communities.* Final Report, ACERA Project 0906. Melbourne, Australia: University of Melbourne.

Garrard, G. E., McCarthy, M. A., Williams, N. S. G., Bekessy, S. A. & Wintle, B. A. (2013). A general model of detectability using species traits. *Methods in Ecology and Evolution*, 4(1), 45–52.

Green, R. H. & Young, R. C. (1993). Sampling to detect rare species. *Ecological Applications*, 3(2), 351–356.

Guichard, S., Kriticos, D. J., Leriche, A., Kean, J. M. & Worner, S. P. (2012). Individual based modelling of moth dispersal to improve biosecurity incursion response. *Journal of Applied Ecology*, 49(1), 287–296.

Harris, S., Brown, J. & Timmons, S. (2001). *Weed surveillance – How often to search? Science for Conservation* 175. Wellington, New Zealand: Department of Conservation.

Harris, S. & Timmins, S. M. (2009). *Estimating the benefit of early control of all newly naturalised plants. Science for Conservation* 292. Wellington, New Zealand: Department of Conservation.

Hastings, A., Cuddington, K., Davie, K. F., et al. (2005). The spatial spread of invasions: New developments in theory and evidence. *Ecology Letters*, 8(1), 91–101.

Hastings, A., Hall, R. J. & Taylor, C. M. (2006). A simple approach to optimal control of invasive species. *Theoretical Population Biology*, 70(4), 431–435.

Hauser, C. E. (2009). Where and how much? A spreadsheet that allocates surveillance effort for a weed. *Plant Protection Quarterly*, 24(3), 94–97.

Hauser, C. E., Garrard, G. E. & Moore, J. L. (2015). Estimating detection rates. In F. Jarrad, S. Low Choy & K. Mengersen (eds.), *Biosecurity surveillance: Quantitative approaches* (pp. 151–166). Wallingford UK: CABI.

Hauser, C. E., Giljohann, K. M., Rigby, M., Herbert, K., Curran, I., Pascoe, C., Williams, N. S. G., Cousens, R. D. & Moore, J. L. (2016a). Practicable methods for delimiting a plant invasion. *Diversity and Distributions,* 22, 136–147.

Hauser, C. E. & McCarthy, M. A. (2009). Streamlining 'search and destroy': cost-effective surveillance for invasive species management. *Ecology Letters*, 12(7), 683–692.

Hauser C. E., Moore J. L., Giljohann K. M., Garrard G. E. & McCarthy M. A. (2012). Designing a detection experiment: Tricks and trade-offs. In V. Eldershaw (ed.), *Proceedings of the 18th Australasian Weeds Conference*, (pp. 267–272). Weed Society of Victoria, October 2012.

Hauser, C. E., Veltheim, I., Crase, B. & Guillera-Arroita, G. (2015). *Evaluation of a sniffer dog for detecting invasive hawkweeds (Hieracium spp) on the Bogong High Plains*. Report to Victorian Department of Economic Development, Jobs, Transport and Resources, Melbourne, Australia.

Hauser, C. E., Weiss, J., Guillera-Arroita, G., McCarthy, M. A., Giljohann, K. M. & Moore, J. L. (2016b). Designing detection experiments: three more case studies. In R. Randall, S. Lloyd, & C. Borger (eds.), *Proceedings of the 20th Australasian Weeds Conference*. Weeds Society of Western Australia, September 2016, pp. 171–178. http://caws.org.au/awc/2016/awc201611711.pdf

Hester, S. M., Brooks, S. J., Cacho, O. J. & Panetta, F. D. (2010b). Applying a simulation model to the management of an infestation of Miconia (*Miconia calvescens*) in the wet tropics of Australia. *Weed Research*, 50(3), 269–279.

Hester S. M. & Cacho, O. J. (2012). Optimising search strategies in managing biological invasions: A simulation approach. *Human and Ecological Risk Assessment*, 18(1), 181–199.

Hester, S. M. & Cacho, O. J. (2017). The contribution of passive surveillance to invasive species management. *Biological Invasions*, 19(3), 737–748.

Hester, S. M., Cacho, O. J., Panetta, F. D. & Hauser, C. E. (2013). Economic aspects of weed risk management. *Diversity and Distributions*, 19(5–6), 580–589.

Hester, S., Hauser, C., Kean, J., Walshe, T. & Robinson, A. (2010a). *Post-border surveillance techniques: Review, synthesis and deployment*. Milestone Report 1, ACERA 1004. Melbourne, Australia: University of Melbourne. Available from www.acera.unimelb.edu.au/materials/endorsed/1004_final-report.pdf

Hester, S., Herbert, K. & Cook, J. (n.d.). *MoniTool: A weed eradication and monitoring tool*, version 3. Available from http://cebra.unimelb.edu.au/publications/acera_reports/surveillance

Hester, S. M., Sergeant, E., Robinson, A. P. & Schultz, G. (2015). Animal, vegetable, or … ? A case study in using animal-health monitoring design tools to solve a plant-health surveillance problem. In F. Jarrad, S. Low-Choy & K. Mengersen (eds.), *Biosecurity surveillance: Quantitative approaches* (pp. 313–333). Wallingford, UK: CABI.

Hood, G. M. (2010). *PopTools*, version 3.2.5. Available from www.poptools.org

Hood, G. M., Barry, S. C. & Martin, P. A. J. (2009). Alternative methods for computing the sensitivity of complex surveillance systems. *Risk Analysis*, 29(2), 1686–1698.

Hung, C. & Sukkarieh, S. (2015). Using robotic aircraft and intelligent surveillance systems for orange hawkweed detection. *Plant Protection Quarterly*, 30(3), 100–102.

Itami, R. & Cotter, M. (1999). Application of Analytical Hierarchy Process to rank issues, projects and sites in integrated catchment management. In *Multiple objective decision support systems for managing watersheds and natural resources,* 2nd International Conference (*MODSS'99*), Brisbane.

Jarrad, F., Barrett, S., Murray, J., et al. (2011). Improved design method for biosecurity surveillance and early detection of nonindigenous rats. *New Zealand Journal of Ecology*, 35(2), 132–144.

Joseph, L. N., Elkin, C., Martin, T. G. & Possingham, H. P. (2009). Modeling abundance using N-mixture models: The importance of considering ecological mechanisms. *Ecological Applications*, 19(3), 631–642.

Kean, J. M. (2015). The effective sampling area of traps: estimation and application. In R. M. Beresford, K. J. Froud, J. M. Kean & S. P. Worner (eds.), *The plant protection data toolbox* (pp. 67–76)., Christchurch, New Zealand: New Zealand Plant Protection Society.

Kean, J. M., Burnip, G. M. & Pathan, A. (2015). Detection survey design for decision making during biosecurity incursions. In F. Jarrad, S. Low-Choy & K. Mengersen (eds.), *Biosecurity surveillance: Quantitative approaches* (pp. 238–250). Wallingford, UK: CABI.

Kean, J. M., Phillips, C. B. & McNeill, M. R. (2008). Surveillance for early detection: Lottery or investment? In K. J. Froud, A. I. Popay & S. M. Zydenbos (eds.), *Surveillance for biosecurity: Pre-border to pest management* (pp. 11–17)., Hastings, New Zealand: New Zealand Plant Protection Society.

Kean, J. M. & Suckling, D. M. (2005). Estimating the probability of eradication of painted apple moth from Auckland. *New Zealand Plant Protection*, 58, 7–11.

Kean, J. M., Suckling, D. M., Sullivan, N. J. et al. (2016). *Global eradication and response database*. Available from http://b3.net.nz/gerda

Kompas, T. & Che, N. (2003). *A practical optimal measure: Papaya fruit fly in Australia*. Draft Report to National Office of Animal and Plant Health, Australia (unpublished).

Kompas, T., Che, N., & Ha, P. V. (2006). An optimal surveillance measure against foot-and-mouth disease in the United States. Working Paper 06-11. Canberra, Australia: Crawford School of Economics and Government, Australian National University.

Krebs, C. J. & Boonstra, R. (1984). Trappability estimates for mark-recapture data. *Canadian Journal of Zoology*, 62(12), 2440–2444.

Lawes, R. A. & Wallace, J. F. (2008). Monitoring an invasive perennial at the landscape scale with remote sensing. *Ecological Management and Restoration*, 9(1), 53–59.

Leung, B., Cacho, O. & Spring, D. (2010). Searching for non-indigenous species: rapidly delimiting the invasion boundary. *Diversity and Distributions*, 16(3), 451–460.

Leung, B., Finnoff, D., Shogren, J. & Lodge, D. (2005). Managing invasive species: Rules of thumb for rapid assessment. *Ecological Economics*, 55(1), 24–36.

Leung, B., Lodge, D. M., Finnoff, D., et al. (2002). An ounce of prevention or a pound of cure: Bioeconomic risk analysis of invasive species. *Proceedings of the Royal Society of London B: Biological Sciences*, 269(1508), 2407–2413.

MacKenzie, D. I., Nichols, J. D., Lachman, G. B., et al. (2002). Estimating site occupancy rates when detection probabilities are less than one. *Ecology*, 83(8), 2248–2255.

MacKenzie, D. I., Nichols, J. D., Sutton, N., Kawanishi, K. & Bailey, L. L. (2005). Improving inferences in population studies of rare species that are detected imperfectly. *Ecology*, 86(5), 1101–1113.

MacKenzie, D. I. & Royle, J. A. (2005). Designing occupancy studies: General advice and allocating survey effort. *Journal of Applied Ecology*, 42(6), 1105–1114.

MAFBNZ (Ministry of Agriculture and Forestry Biosecurity New Zealand). (2009a). *Review of selected cattle identification and tracing systems worldwide: Lessons for the New Zealand National Animal Identification and Tracing (NAIT) Project*. MAF Biosecurity New Zealand Information Paper No 2009/03. Available from https://mpi.govt.nz/document-vault/6394

MAFBNZ (Ministry of Agriculture and Forestry Biosecurity New Zealand). (2009b). *Biosecurity surveillance strategy 2020*. Wellington, New Zealand: MAF Biosecurity New Zealand,

Magarey, R. D., Borchert, D. M., Engle, J. S., et al. (2011). Risk maps for targeting exotic plant pest detection programs in the United States. *EPPO Bulletin*, 41(1), 46–56.

Mangano, P., Hardie, D., Speijers, J., et al. (2011). The capacity of groups within the community to carry out plant pest surveillance detection. *The Open Entomology Journal*, 5(1), 15–23.

Martin, P. A. J., Cameron, A. R., Barford, K., Sergeant, E. S. G. & Greiner, M. (2007b). Demonstrating freedom from disease using multiple complex data sources 2: Case study – classical swine fever in Denmark. *Preventive Veterinary Medicine*, 79(2–4), 98–115.

Martin, P. A. J., Cameron, A. R. & Greiner, M. (2007a). Demonstrating freedom from disease using multiple complex data sources 1: A new methodology based on scenario trees. *Preventive Veterinary Medicine*, 79(2–4), 71–97.

Martin, P. A. J., Langstaff, I., Iglesias, R. M., East, I. J., Sergeant, E. S. G. & Garner, M. G. (2015). Assessing the efficacy of general surveillance for detection of incursions of livestock diseases in Australia. *Preventive Veterinary Medicine*, 121(3–4), 215–230.

McCallum, D. A. (2005). A conceptual guide to detection probability for point counts and other count-based survey methods. In *USDA Forest Service General Technical Report*, pp. 754–761.

McMaugh, T. (2005). *Guidelines for surveillance for plant pests in Asia and the Pacific*. ACIAR Monograph No. 119. Canberra, Australia: Australian Centre for International Agricultural Research.

Meats, A. (1998). Cartesian methods of locating spot infestations of the papaya fruit fly *Bactrocera papayae* Drew and Hancock within the trapping grid at Mareeba, Queensland, Australia. *General and Applied Entomology*, 28, 57–60.

Mehta, S. V., Haight, R. G., Homans, F. R., Polasky, S. & Venette, R. C. (2007). Optimal detection and control strategies for invasive species management. *Ecological Economics*, 61(2–3), 237–245.

MLA (Meat and Livestock Australia). (n.d.). *National Livestock Identification System*. Available from www.mla.com.au/Meat-safety-and-traceability/National-Livestock-Identification-System

Moody, M. E. & Mack, R. N. (1988). Controlling the spread of plant invasions: the importance of nascent foci. *Journal of Applied Ecology*, 25(3), 1009–1021.

Moore, J. L., Hauser, C. E., Bear, J. L., Williams, N. S. G. & McCarthy, M. A. (2011). Estimating detection-effort curves for plants using search experiments. *Ecological Applications*, 21(2), 601–607.

Morton, J. and Harris, W. (2008). *Weed Spotters guide: A guide for regional bodies to deliver a Weed Spotters network in their regions*. CRC for Australian Weed Management. Available from www.wsq.org.au/Publications/CRC%20WS%20regional%20guide_WEB.pdf

NAIT (National Animal Identification and Tracing) (n.d.). *Annual report 2013*. Available from www.nait.co.nz/assets/Annual-reports/Annual-Report-2013.pdf

Narumalani, S., Mishra, D. R., Wilson, R., Reece, R. & Kohler, A. (2009). Detecting and mapping four invasive species along the floodplain of North Platte River, Nebraska. *Weed Technology*, 23(1), 99–107.

Ndeffo Mbah, M. L. & Gilligan, C. A. (2010). Balancing detection and eradication for control of epidemics: Sudden oak death in mixed-species stands. *PLoS ONE*, 5(9), e12317.

Nichols, J. D., Hines, J. E., Sauer, J. R., et al. (2000). A double-observer approach for estimating detection probability and abundance from point counts. *The Auk*, 117(2), 393–408.

Norsys Software Corporation. (n.d.). *Netica^TM application*. Available from www.norsys.com/netica.html

OIE (World Organisation for Animal Health). (2015). *Terrestrial Animal Health Code – 2015*. Available from www.oie.int/eng/normes/Mcode/en_sommaire.htm

Palisade Corporation. (2015). *User's guide @RISK: Risk analysis and simulation add-in for Microsoft Excel*, version 7, August 2015. Available from www.palisade.com/downloads/documentation/7/EN/RISK7_EN.pdf

Panetta, F. D., Cacho, O. J., Hester, S. & Sims-Chilton, N. (2011). Estimating and influencing the duration of weed eradication programmes. *Journal of Applied Ecology*, 48(4), 980–988.

Panetta, F. D. & Lawes, R. (2005). Evaluation of weed eradication programs: the delimitation of extent. *Diversity and Distributions*, 11(5), 435–442.

Panetta, F. D. & Lawes, R. (2007). Evaluation of the Australian branched broomrape (*Orobanche ramose*) eradication program. *Weed Science*, 55(6), 644–651.

Perry, G. & Vice, D. (2009). Forecasting the risk of brown tree snake dispersal from Guam: A mixed transport-establishment model. *Conservation Biology*, 23(4), 992–1000.

Peterson, J. T. & Bayley, P. B. (2004). A Bayesian approach to estimating presence when a species is undetected. In W. L. Thompson (ed.), *Sampling rare or elusive species* (pp. 173–188). London: Island Press.

Philippi, T. (2005). Adaptive cluster sampling for estimation of abundances within local populations of low-abundance plants. *Ecology*, 86(5), 1091–1100.

QDPIF (Queensland Department of Primary Industries and Fisheries). (2008). *National fire ant eradication program progress report 2007–2008*. Oxley, Australia: Queensland Department of Primary Industries and Fisheries.

QNRM (Queensland Department of Natural Resources and Mines) (2006). *Siam weed national delimiting survey report*. Brisbane, Australia: Department of Natural Resources, Mines and Water.

Queensland Government (n.d.) *Weedspotters' network Queensland*. Available from www.qld .gov.au/environment/plants-animals/plants/herbarium/weed-spotters/

Ramsey, D. S. L., Parkes, J. & Morrison, S. A. (2009). Quantifying eradication success: The removal of feral pigs from Santa Cruz Island, California. *Conservation Biology*, 23(2), 449–459.

Regan, T. J., McCarthy, M. A., Baxter, P. W. J., Dane Panetta, F. & Possingham, H. P. (2006). Optimal eradication: When to stop looking for an invasive plant. *Ecology Letters*, 9(7), 759–766.

Rew, L. J., Maxwell, B. D., Dougher, F. L. & Aspinall, R. (2006). Searching for a needle in a haystack: Evaluating survey methods for non-indigenous plant species. *Biological Invasions*, 8(3), 523–539.

Rivadeneira, M. M., Hunt, G. & Roy, K. (2009). The use of sighting records to infer species extinctions: An evaluation of different methods. *Ecology*, 90(5), 1291–1300.

Rota, C. T., Fletcher Jr, R. J., Dorazio, R. M. & Betts, M. G. (2009). Occupancy estimation and the closure assumption. *Journal of Applied Ecology*, 46(6), 1173–1181.

Rout, T. M., Salomon, Y. & McCarthy, M. A. (2009a). Using sighting records to declare eradication of an invasive species. *Journal of Applied Ecology*, 46(1), 110–117.

Rout, T. M., Thompson, C. J. & McCarthy, M. A. (2009b). Robust decisions for declaring eradication of invasive species. *Journal of Applied Ecology*, 46(4), 782–786.

Royle, J. A., Nichols, J. D., Karanth, K. U. & Gopalaswamy, A. M. (2009). A hierarchical model for estimating density in camera-trap studies. *Journal of Applied Ecology*, 46(1), 118–127.

Samalens, J. C., Rossi, J. P., Guyon D., et al. (2007) Adaptive roadside sampling for bark beetle damage assessment. *Forest Ecology and Management*, 253(1–3), 177–187.

Sergeant, E. S. G. (2009). *Epitools epidemiological calculators*. AusVet Animal Health Services and Australian Biosecurity Cooperative Research Centre for Emerging Infectious Disease. Available from http://epitools.ausvet.com.au

Shafii, R., Price, W. J., Prather, T. S., Lass, L. W. & Thill, D. C. (2003). Predicting the likelihood of yellow starthistle (*Centaurea solstitialis*) occurrence using landscape characteristics. *Weed Science*, 51(5), 748–751.

Sharov, A. & Liebhold, A. M. (1998). Bioeconomics of managing the spread of exotic pest species with barrier zones. *Ecological Applications*, 8(3), 833–845.

Sharov, A. A., Liebhold, A. M. & Roberts, E. A. (1998). Optimizing the use of barrier zones to slow the spread of gypsy moth (Lepidoptera: Lymantriidae) in North America. *Journal of Economic Entomology*, 91(1), 165–174.

Sindel, B. S., van der Meulen, A., Coleman, M. & Reeve, I. (2008). *Pathway risk analysis for weed spread within Australia: Final report to Land and Water Australia (UNE61)*, Armidale, Australia: University of New England.

Smith, D. R., Villella, R. F. & LeMarié, D. P. (2003). Application of adaptive cluster sampling to low-density populations of freshwater mussels. *Environmental and Ecological Statistics*, 10(1), 7–15.

Smolik, M. G., Dullinger, S., Essl, F., et al. (2010). Integrating species distribution models and interacting particle systems to predict the spread of an invasive alien plant. *Journal of Biogeography*, 37(3), 411–422.

Solow, A., Seymour, A., Beet, A. & Harris, S. (2008). The untamed shrew: On the termination of an eradication programme for an introduced species. *Journal of Applied Ecology*, 45(2), 424–427.

Stevens P. M. (2008). High risk site surveillance (HRSS) – an example of best practice plant pest surveillance. In I. Popay, K. Froud & S. Zydenbos (eds.), *Surveillance for biosecurity: Pre-border to pest management* (pp. 127–134). Christchurch, New Zealand: New Zealand Plant Protection Society.

Suckling, D. M., Stringer, L. D., Kean, J. M., et al. (2015). Spatial analysis of mass trapping: How close is close enough? *Pest Management Science*, 71(10), 1452–1461.

Taylor, C. M. & Hastings, A. (2004). Finding optimal control strategies for invasive species: A density-structured model for *Spartina alterniflora*. *Journal of Applied Ecology*, 41(6), 1049–1057.

Thomas, L., Buckland, S. T., Rexstad. E. A., et al. (2010). Distance software: Design and analysis of distance sampling surveys for estimating population size. *Journal of Applied Ecology*, 47(1), 5–14.

Thomas, N., Steel, J., King, C., Hunt, T. & Weiss, J. (2007). *Tackling weeds on private land initiative: Weed spread pathway risk assessment – stage 2*. Melbourne, Australia: Department of Sustainability and Environment, Department of Primary Industries, Victoria.

Thompson, S. K. (1990). Adaptive cluster sampling. *Journal of the American Statistical Association*, 85(412), 1050–1059.

Tobin, P. C., Kean, J. M., Suckling, D. M., et al. (2014). Determinants of successful arthropod eradication programs. *Biological Invasions*, 16(2), 401–414.

Turchin, P. & Odendaal, F. J. (1996). Measuring the effective sampling area of a pheromone trap for monitoring population density of southern pine beetle (*Coleoptera: Scolytidae*). *Environmental Entomology*, 25(3), 582–588.

Tyre, A. J., Tenhumberg, B., Field, S. A., et al. (2003). Improving precision and reducing bias in biological surveys: Estimating false-negative error rates. *Ecological Applications*, 13(6), 1790–1801.

UFAW (Universities Federation for Animal Welfare). (2005). *Feeding garden birds: Best practice guidelines*. Available from www.ufaw.org.uk/shop/publications/product/feeding-garden-birds-best-practice-guidelines

Václavík, T. & Meentemeyer, R. K. (2009). Invasive species distribution modeling (iSDM): Are absence data and dispersal constraints needed to predict actual distributions? *Ecological Modelling*, 220(23), 3248–3258.

van der Kraan, C. & van Deventer, P. (1982). Range of action and interaction of pheromone traps for the summerfruit tortrix moth, *Adoxophyes orana* (F.v.R.). *Journal of Chemical Ecology*, 8(10), 1251–1262.

Wall, C. & Perry, J. N. (1978). Interactions between pheromone traps for the pea moth, *Cydia nigricana* (F.). *Entomologia Experimentalis et Applicata*, 24(2), 155–162.

Wenger, S. J. & Freeman, M. C. (2008). Estimating species occurrence, abundance, and detection probability using zero-inflated distributions. *Ecology*, 89(10), 2953–2959.

Wikle, C. K. & Royle, J. A. (1999). Space-time dynamic design of environmental monitoring networks. *Journal of Agricultural, Biological, and Environmental Statistics*, 4(4), 489–507.

Williams, N. S. G., Hahs, A. K. & Morgan, J. W. (2008). A dispersal-constrained habitat suitability model for predicting invasion of alpine vegetation. *Ecological Applications*, 18(2), 347–359.

Wintle, B. A., McCarthy, M. A., Parris, K. M. & Burgman, M. A. (2004). Precision and bias of methods for estimating point survey detection probabilities. *Ecological Applications*, 14(3), 703–712.

Yackel Adams, A. A., Stanford, J. W., Wiewel, A. S. & Rodda, G. H. (2011). Modelling detectability of kiore (*Rattus exulans*) on Aguiguan, Mariana Islands, to inform possible eradication and monitoring efforts. *New Zealand Journal of Ecology*, 35(2), 145–152.

3 Control Charts for Biosecurity Monitoring and Surveillance

David R. Fox

3.1 Introduction

The words *monitoring* and *surveillance* are sometimes confused and used interchangeably. Although both activities share common features of observation, data collection, analysis and assessment, there is a subtle distinction in terms of intent, which in turn has implications for the design and analysis of the monitoring or surveillance programme. The following clarifies the distinction between monitoring and surveillance:

> *Surveillance* is the structured collection and analysis of data for the purpose of detecting incursions of new or emerging disease or infection in an area, or for demonstrating freedom from a disease or infection. *Monitoring*, in contrast, is conducted for the purpose of assessing changes in the level or distribution of disease in an area. The main distinction is that surveillance is concerned with exotic disease, while monitoring is concerned with endemic disease.
>
> (National Aquatic Animal Health Technical Working Group, 2004, p. 2)

Surveillance activities are further classified according to two objectives: early detection of incursions of disease or demonstration of freedom from disease, which we shall denote as mode I and mode II surveillance respectively.

While statistics has always played a key role in monitoring and surveillance activities, more recent national and international protocols have attempted to balance statistical rigidity with operational flexibility. Thus we see, for example, the World Organisation for Animal Health requiring demonstration of freedom from disease to meet some level of statistical confidence (e.g. 95%) without being prescriptive about the statistical methods by which that objective is to be assessed. Indeed, the World Organisation for Animal Health acknowledges that there is 'considerable latitude available to Members to provide a well-reasoned argument to prove that absence of … infection is assured at an acceptable level of confidence' (World Organisation for Animal Health, 2010b, p. 5). This considerable latitude is both a blessing and a curse. The advantages are increased flexibility and adaptability, while the downside is a lack of comparability between different procedures and the increased risk of deliberate or unintentional misuse of statistical methods. Vague definitions such as 'acceptable level of confidence' do not help either.

The literature on monitoring and surveillance for invasive pests and plants also lacks specificity with respect to the identification of quantitative tools and methods for the detection of trends, anomalies or outbreaks. For example, Westbrooks' (2004) paper on new approaches for early detection of invasive plants in the United States provides no guidance as to how the early detection is to be achieved. Likewise, the United States Government's National Biological Information Infrastructure's Early Detection and Rapid Assessment programme is silent on the quantitative aspects of early detection (National Invasive Species Council, 2003).

This chapter provides an overview of a class of statistical tools and methods that are well suited to biosecurity monitoring and surveillance activities. Collectively, these methods fall under the umbrella of statistical process control (SPC). Specifically, we will be looking at the role of control charts for both monitoring and mode I (early detection) surveillance activities. Control charts are unlikely to prove useful for demonstrating freedom from a disease or pest (mode II surveillance) because the absence of disease or pest threats results in data streams that comprise only zeros. Demonstrating the absence of a disease or pest is an inferential problem and is better addressed using conventional tools of statistical inference such as hypothesis testing.

A common requirement of all statistical surveillance techniques is to – as quickly and as accurately as possible – detect important changes that occur in a stochastic process at an unknown time (Sonesson & Bock 2003). Many of the reported techniques use likelihood-based methods to detect step changes in a parameter of interest (e.g. process mean or variance). Although a number of papers have appeared on statistical surveillance in the context of epidemiology, public health and syndromic surveillance (Doherr & Audigé, 2001; Höhle & Paul, 2008; Marshall et al., 2004; Sonesson & Bock, 2003), relatively little has been published that illustrates applications to biosecurity monitoring.

This chapter examines the basics of control charts, starting with the Shewhart chart and various moving average charts, and then progressing to specialist charts for the time-between-events and the more contemporary Bayesian methods. More detailed information on specific SPC techniques can be found in any standard reference on the topic (e.g. Montgomery, 2012).

It is important to note that there are no universally accepted norms or conventions when using control charts for biosecurity. Indeed, the notion of advance or early warning systems for biosurveillance has been challenged on account of high rates of false alarms, inadequate lead times and a lack of evidence of success. Critics claim that despite more than 10 years of experience, there is no evidence that a single bioterrorism attack has been thwarted as a result of systematic surveillance. As noted by Mostashari and Hartman (2003), no surveillance system has provided early warning of bioterrorism, and no large-scale bioterrorist attack has occurred since existing systems were instituted. Demonstrating that a surveillance programme has reduced the likelihood of events that are yet to occur, or that may never occur, will always be difficult.

3.1.1   SPC

SPC can be broadly defined as the collection of mathematical and statistical tools used to monitor and manage quality. This definition reveals the original context of SPC – to control the quality of manufactured items in an industrial process or setting. These days, the word *control* is de-emphasised and is usually either dropped[1] or replaced by *improvement*. SPC methods rely largely on data visualisation techniques and as such are primarily descriptive in nature. While control limits and other triggering mechanisms use tools of statistical inference, the primary objective is not inferential. That is, we are not so concerned about testing hypotheses *per se* as we are about describing the state of the process.

The development of SPC techniques can be traced back to the First World War and shortly thereafter with the introduction of the Shewhart control chart by the American physicist Walter A. Shewhart in the 1920s. General acceptance and uptake of SPC tools in the West was relatively slow until it was realised that a major contributing factor to the high productivity and quality of Japanese manufactured goods was that country's enthusiastic embrace of a total quality philosophy espoused by leading American statistician and quality advocate W. Edwards Deming.

The 1980s saw a resurgence of interest in SPC under the banner of total quality management. The Six Sigma philosophy was conceived during this time in response to Motorola's desire to achieve a tenfold reduction in product failure levels within five years. The Six Sigma methodology (based on the steps define, measure, analyse, improve and control) underpins the objectives of process improvement, reduced costs and increased profits.

Despite some negative experiences in the manufacturing sector, total quality management made a substantial contribution to quality improvement. The use of SPC methods in environmental contexts has been a more recent development – particularly with respect to water quality monitoring (ANZECC & ARMCANZ, 2000; Burgman, 2005; MacNally & Hart, 1997; Morrison, 2008).

The challenge for SPC in biosecurity is not so much the fine-tuning of existing processes, but to identify radically new processes that alert us to impending threats with sufficient lead time to be useful. We next look at the adoption and uptake of SPC methods in biosecurity.

SPC and Biosecurity

Environmental applications of total quality management and SPC techniques have been identified only more recently despite the need for robust and reliable monitoring and surveillance systems. Fox (2001) attributed this to a lack of cross-talk between industrial statisticians and the environmental statisticians. Whatever the reasons, the slow uptake of SPC tools for environmental monitoring meant that

---

[1] The American Society for Quality Control changed its name to the American Society for Quality on 1 July 1997.

critical assessments of environmental conditions and important decisions about responses relied heavily on conventional tools of statistical inference. The ecologists' statistical toolkit was generally standard issue; t-tests, analysis of variance, analysis of similarities and multidimensional scaling were widely used, while the relatively simple techniques of Xbar-S charts, exponentially weighted moving average (EWMA) charts and capability analysis were virtually unheard of.

The use of control charts for mode I surveillance programmes has found particular application in syndromic surveillance of human populations. These applications were motivated by bioterrorism attacks in the United States when high-grade anthrax spores was sent via the United States Postal Service following the events of 11 September 2001. Exposure to anthrax initially produces flu-like symptoms in humans. Thus, the objective of syndromic surveillance is to provide an early warning mechanism by monitoring data on flu indicators (such as admissions to hospital emergency departments, sales of over-the-counter cold and flu medications and absenteeism levels) and an analysis of spatial clustering of outbreaks. Kulldorff (1997) developed a spatial scan statistic to help with the latter, while control charts were an obvious first candidate for the former.

Syndromic surveillance for counter-terrorism (e.g. www.bt.cdc.gov/surveillance/ears/) is a relatively recent development, while similar systems have been used for some time now to detect outbreaks, patterns and trends in diseases and epidemics (e.g. www.satscan.org/). Although these techniques do not appear to have had any appreciable uptake in Australia or elsewhere around the world in quarantine inspection and biosecurity, control charting has been suggested as an effective means of detecting trends for meat hygiene assessments (Commonwealth of Australia, 2002) and has also been recommended for detecting spatial and temporal clusters in veterinary monitoring (Carpenter, 2001). Hall and Golding (1998) discuss the use of control charts in testing waste streams from wastewater treatment plants, and Stark et al. (2006) examine risk-based veterinary surveillance approaches to protecting livestock and consumer health although control charting is not mentioned.

Although syndromic surveillance has not been widely used in the context of invasive species, the threat is no less tangible. Animal disease agents including those transmissible to humans have the potential to be used as biological weapons. They are particularly attractive because they have wide economic and social ranging impacts and are readily available (World Organisation for Animal Health, 2010a). As noted by Fricker (2011), some bioagents have symptoms in their prodromal stages that are similar to those of naturally occurring diseases. Syndromic surveillance may be useful in this setting, although, as we have already noted, a major barrier to uptake is the difficulty in proving that any of these systems has made a difference or even do what they're meant to do.

Control Charting Basics – The Shewhart Chart

At its simplest, a Shewhart chart is essentially a time series plot of some process measurement or attribute – the former being used for quantitative data (e.g. the time between outbreaks) and the latter for qualitative data (e.g. presence or absence

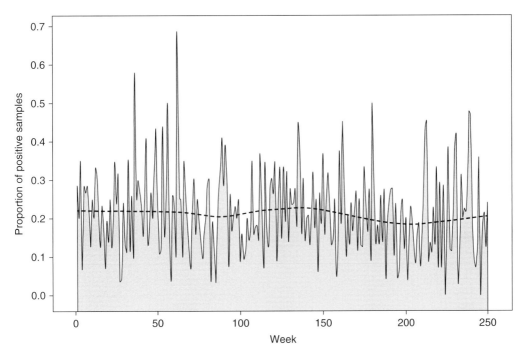

Figure 3.1. Times series plot of invasive species detection rate for a fictitious weekly monitoring programme. Dashed is a loess smooth.

of a disease or condition). For quantitative data we can choose to track individual readings or a statistic such as the mean or standard deviation of subgroups of observations. A Shewhart chart is differentiated from a simple time series plot by the incorporation of control limits that are determined from the statistical properties of the phenomenon being observed and are designed to provide an early warning mechanism for impending or out-of-control situations.

To motivate the discussion of control charting, we examine the time series plot of some artificial invasive pest monitoring data. Figure 3.1 shows the proportion of samples resulting in a detection of an invasive species for a weekly monitoring programme and is thus referred to as a P-chart. The dashed line in Figure 3.1 is the result of applying a loess local smoothing procedure (Cleveland, 1979) to the monitoring data. The idea behind loess smoothing (and other similar procedures) is that the high-frequency oscillations can be removed by taking a subset of the data and replacing individual data points by some statistic (such as the median of the data in the subset). In this way, the relatively noisy data are smoothed. The degree of smoothing can be varied to reveal different features in the time series data. In the case of Figure 3.1, the trend over time is flat with no particular anomalies indicated although the individual data are quite variable. One way of helping address the significance of the observed variations is through the use of control charts.

The simplest control chart is essentially Figure 3.1 with the addition of upper and lower control limits. The computation of control limits depends on the type of

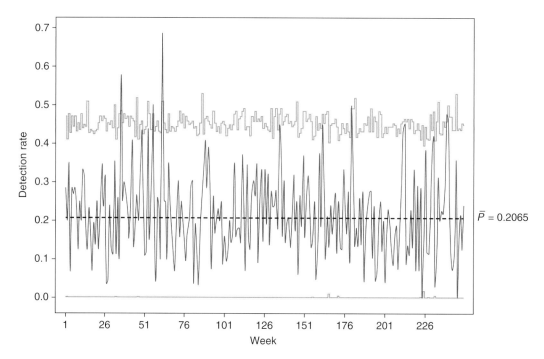

Figure 3.2.   P-chart for invasive species detection rate data with software-computed upper and lower two-sigma limits shown in grey.

control chart and distributional assumptions underlying the response-generating mechanism. As a rule-of-thumb, warning limits are placed at ± 2 standard deviations on either side of the mean response, while action limits are placed at ± 3 standard deviations on either side of the mean response. The computation of control limits for proportion data (such as the detection rates in Figure 3.1) requires care because the variance of the computed proportion is invariably a function of the magnitude of the proportion, and this in turn affects the width of the limits. Although these calculations could be done manually, it is easier to have computer software (such as the qcc package in R) do it (Figure 3.2).

Note that the upper and lower control limits in Figure 3.2 are not constant. This is because the number of samples inspected each week varied. The overall mean rate of detection is indicated by the dashed line in Figure 3.2, which suggests that approximately 21% of all samples resulted in a positive detection, with a small number of violations or excursions outside the control limits. By itself, this chart raises no particular concerns, other than the two or three occasions when the proportion was significantly high and a couple of occasions when it was significantly low. How to respond to excursions beyond the control limits is a matter for the investigator to decide and will depend on a number of factors including whether the limit is a warning or an action limit. Typically, the triggering of a warning limit results in increased surveillance, whereas the triggering of an action limit results in further

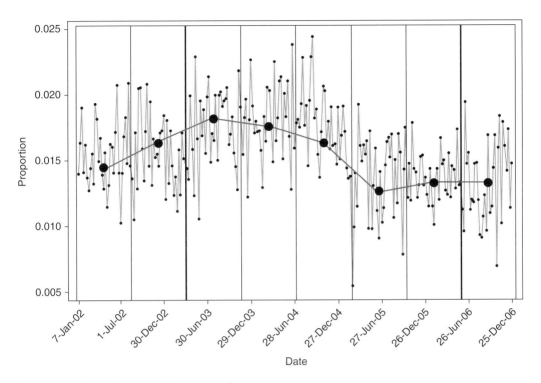

Figure 3.3.   Smoothing using block averaging.

investigations to identify causes or some form of physical intervention. Other more sophisticated response plans can be devised around more complex patterns of triggering such as the number of runs above and below a limit or alternating patterns of above and below limits.

For data that are collected over time, a number of time-based control charts are available. Some of the more common and useful ones are described next.

Process Smoothing

The simplest way of smoothing over time is by block averaging. Figure 3.3 shows time series data for a detection rate divided into a number of non-overlapping blocks of constant width. The average of the data in each block is computed and plotted at the centre of the block. These points can be connected by straight-line segments to reveal a smoother version of the series.

Block averaging is a relatively unsophisticated smoothing method and has some potential difficulties – not least of which is that the mean of each block is computed without reference to the rest of the series. In other words, there is no history built into the mean of an individual block and the smoothed series can still exhibit some erratic jumps. To overcome this, we can take the basic block or window width and step it across the series so that there is overlap. This is achieved by replacing

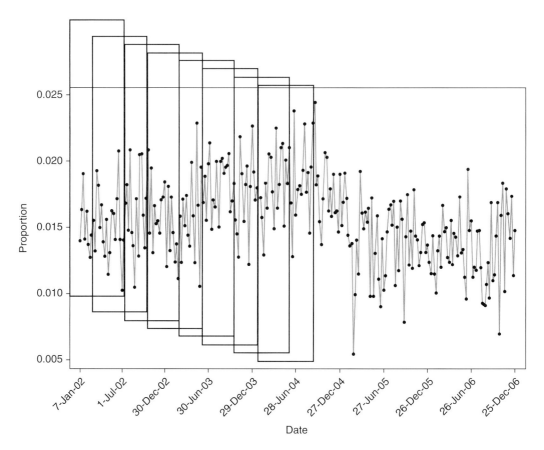

Figure 3.4. Moving average scheme. A block or 'window' is stepped incrementally over the series and the block mean computed and plotted.

the oldest k observations with the most recent k observations. The block averages result in a moving average of the original series (Figure 3.4). An example of a moving average plot for detection rate data is shown in Figure 3.5. The points plotted in Figure 3.5 are the averages of all observations in the window and not individual measurements. A horizontal line in Figure 3.5 is placed at the mean of all these averages (and is denoted as $\bar{\bar{X}}$).

By adjusting the parameters of the moving average plot, different levels of smoothing can be achieved. For example, Figure 3.6 shows a moving average plot for the proportion data using the averages of three-weekly subgroups. With this degree of smoothing, the underlying trend is more evident.

Time-weighted Charts

The block or moving average charts give equal importance (or weighting) to all data in the current window. Although this may be appropriate in some situations, it does not accord with the usual notion that the greater the time separation, the less relevant the data are. Time-weighted control charts such as the EWMA are more

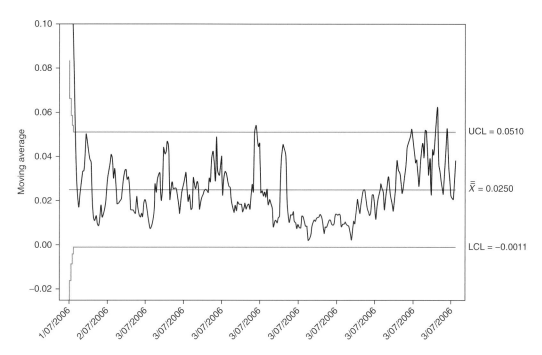

Figure 3.5. Illustrative example of moving average chart of weekday inspection data. Subgroup size = 1; MA length = 5.

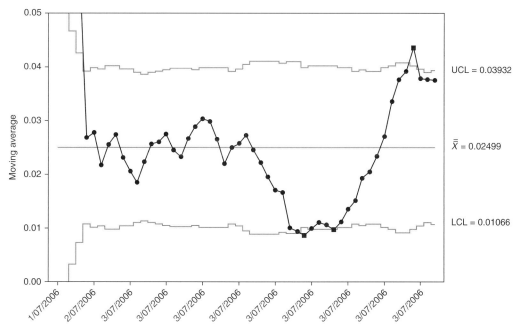

Figure 3.6. Moving average for weekday inspection failure rate. Subgroup size defined by week of year (usually 5); MA length = 4.

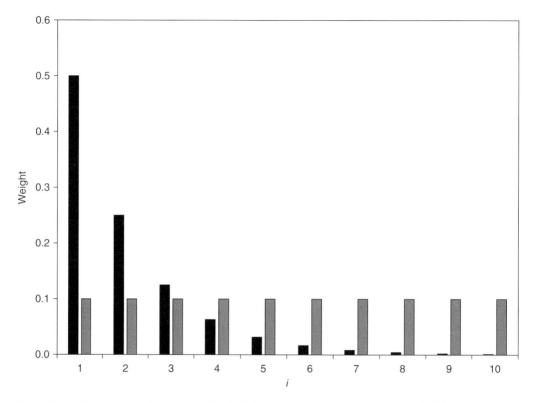

Figure 3.7.   Comparison of exponentially declining weights (black bars) compared with equal-weighting scheme (grey bars) for $k = 10$ subgroups.

flexible because the relative weightings given to recent and historical data can be specified.

By way of example, suppose we wish to form a weighted average of the current observation and the $(k - 1)$ most recent values. That is, we are interested in forming the weighted mean $\bar{X}_1 = \alpha X_1 + \alpha^2 X_2 + \cdots + \alpha^k X_k$, where the weighting factor is α. The requirement that $\bar{X}_1$ is an unbiased estimator of the true mean imposes the constraint $\sum_{i=1}^{k} \alpha^i = 1$, and for a given k, the solution to this is the root of the equation $\alpha^k - 2\alpha + 1 = 0$. For example, if $k = 10$, we find $\alpha = 0.5002$. A plot of these weights compared with the simple arithmetic mean is shown in Figure 3.7.

The recursive formula for computing values of the EWMA chart is $\text{EWMA}_t = \alpha X_t + (1 - \alpha)\text{EWMA}_{t-1}$ $0 < \alpha < 1$. In other words, the current EWMA is a weighted average of the current data value and the EWMA in the preceding period. The determination of α for the computation of the EWMA is largely a subjective decision that will reflect the investigator's desire to balance the degree of responsiveness (small α) and the degree of smoothing (larger α).

Figure 3.8 shows the EWMA chart for the weekday failure rate data with $\alpha = 0.2$.

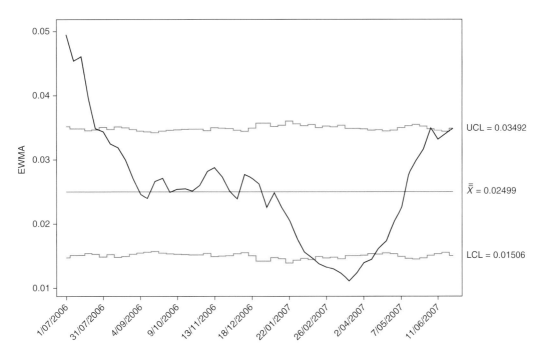

Figure 3.8. EWMA chart for data shown in Figure 3.5. Subgroup size defined by week of year (usually 5); EWMA weight = 0.2.

3.1.2   Time between Events

We have seen how control charts can be used to monitor variables (e.g. the number of invasions detected) or attributes (e.g. the proportion of samples having a biosecurity threat). When events (e.g. the arrival of an invasive species) occur randomly in time, an alternative approach is to monitor the inter-arrival time or the time between the occurrences of successive events. An advantage of this approach is that we do not have to wait until the end of some aggregation period (e.g. week, month or year) to obtain a measurement; it is available as soon as there has been a detection. However, some modifications to the standard charts are required to accommodate the fact that the distribution of inter-arrival times is usually (highly) non-normal. Details of the theoretical development can be found in Radaelli (1998). More recently, control charts for the number of cases between events (so-called g and h charts) have been developed and applied to monitoring hospital-acquired infections and other relatively rare adverse health-related events (Benneyan, 2001a, 2001b).

By way of example, consider Figure 3.9, which depicts the pattern of biosecurity detections over time. By measuring the white spaces (i.e. computing the differences $t_{i+1} - t_i$) in Figure 3.9, we obtain data on the inter-arrival times.

Our analysis of the inter-arrival data commences with an inspection of basic distributional properties (Figure 3.10).

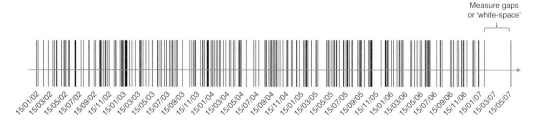

Figure 3.9. Pattern of inter-arrival times as measured by the 'white space' between biosecurity detections (black vertical lines).

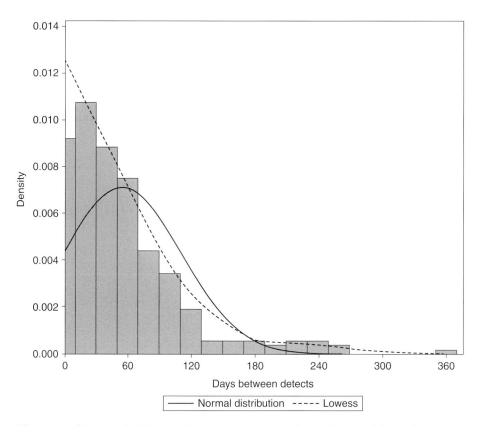

Figure 3.10. Histogram of inter-arrival times with smoothed version (dashed line) and theoretical normal distribution (black line) overlaid. The normal distribution provides a poor description of these data (evidenced by the both the shape and probability mass associated with negative values of days between detects).

It is clear from Figure 3.10 that these data are highly skewed and that the normal distribution is not an appropriate probability model.

The smoothed histogram in Figure 3.10 suggests that a J-shaped probability model is more appropriate. One such model is the negative exponential probability distribution. This choice is also supported by statistical theory that says that if events occur randomly in time according to a Poisson probability model with an average rate of arrival of λ per time, then the distribution of the inter-arrival time is a negative exponential with parameter λ. The probability density function for the negative exponential is given by Eq. 3.1 and the corresponding cumulative distribution function is given by Eq. 3.2.

$$f_X(x) = \lambda e^{-\lambda x}, \quad \lambda, x > 0 \tag{3.1}$$

$$F_X(x) = 1 - e^{-\lambda x}, \quad \lambda, x > 0. \tag{3.2}$$

For this distribution, the mean is $\frac{1}{\lambda}$ and the variance is $\frac{1}{\lambda^2}$. It is readily apparent from Eqs. 3.1 and 3.2 that the variance increases or decreases with an increasing or decreasing mean; this is a violation of a basic assumption of many conventional statistical techniques that assume constant variance. Thus, control limits computed under the (incorrect) assumption of constant variance will not perform as anticipated because they will result in triggering rates that differ from the nominal triggering rates.

One simple way of estimating the parameter λ is to equate the theoretical and sample means. In this case, we have $\frac{1}{\lambda} = 7.713$ and hence our estimate is $\hat{\lambda} = \frac{1}{7.713} = 0.130$. A plot of the histogram of the data with a negative exponential distribution having $\hat{\lambda} = 0.130$ overlaid is shown in Figure 3.11. The adequacy of this fit is readily seen by comparing the empirical and theoretical cumulative distribution functions (Figure 3.12).

The false triggering due to the non-normality of the data is evident in the I-chart[2] of Figure 3.13. There are two ways of overcoming this. The first is to modify the control chart to account for the non-normality. The second approach is to transform the data so that they are normally distributed (or approximately so) and then apply standard control charting techniques to the transformed data.

3.1.3 Control Chart for Time-between-Events

Rather than transform the data as described Section 3.1.2, alternative methods have been developed that modify existing control charts for use with untransformed (and non-normal) data. Radaelli (1998) describes procedures for setting control limits for both one- and two-sided control charts for inter-arrival times. Only the one-sided case is considered here because we are generally interested only in tracking significant deviations in one direction (e.g. a lower control limit to alert the investigator to a decreasing inter-arrival time between biosecurity events).

Let X_i be the ith inter-arrival time. An out-of-control situation is declared if $X_i < T_L$ in the case of decreasing inter-arrival times (i.e. increasing counts) or

---

[2] An I-chart is simply a control chart for individual observations (i.e. ungrouped data).

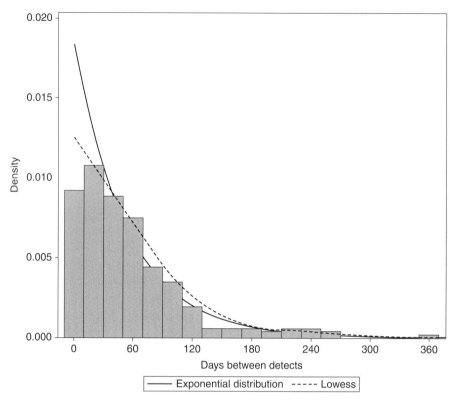

Figure 3.11.   Histogram of days between detects. Smoothed histogram indicated by dashed line; theoretical exponential distribution depicted by black curve.

$X_i > T_U$ in the case of increasing inter-arrival times (i.e. decreasing counts) where T_L and T_U are suitably[3] chosen positive constants. Suppose that an in-control situation corresponds to a mean inter-arrival time of λ_0^{-1}(where λ is the parameter in Eq. 3.1), then using Eq. 3.2, it can be determined that

$$P\left[X_i < T_L \,|\, \lambda = \lambda_0\right] = 1 - e^{-\lambda_0 T_L} \qquad (3.3)$$

$$P\left[X_i > T_U \,|\, \lambda = \lambda_0\right] = e^{-\lambda_0 T_U}. \qquad (3.4)$$

Equations 3.3 and 3.4 are analogous to the type I error in a hypothesis test: it is the probability of a false positive. As in statistical hypothesis testing, the type I error rate (α) is set to be some arbitrarily small value (e.g. $\alpha = 0.05$). The upper and lower control limits can be determined by setting Eqs. 3.3 and 3.4 equal to α and solving for either T_L or T_U. Thus we have

---

[3] Because the definition of suitable or appropriate control limits is context dependent, no generic definition can be provided. However, as a general guide, this will be determined largely by considerations of balancing the rate of false positives (i.e. exceeding a limit when the process is in control) and false negatives (i.e. the non-triggering of a limit when the process is out of control).

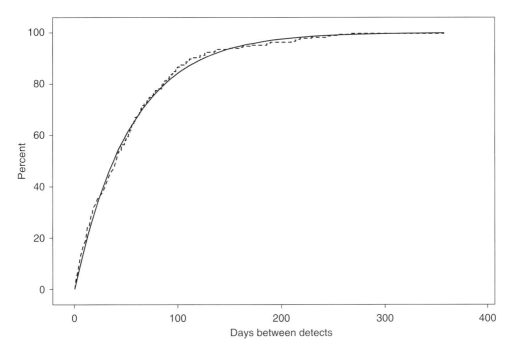

Figure 3.12. Empirical cumulative distribution function for days between detects (dotted line) and theoretical exponential cumulative distribution function (solid line).

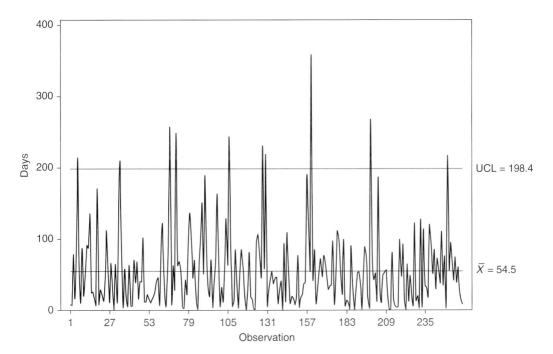

Figure 3.13. Chart of individual values of days between detects (I-chart) with three-sigma limit indicated (grey horizontal line).

$$T_L = -\lambda_0^{-1} \ln(1-\alpha) \tag{3.5}$$

$$T_U = -\lambda_0^{-1} \ln(\alpha). \tag{3.6}$$

In addition to having a low α, we also require our control chart to signal correctly an important deviation from in control conditions. Suppose we wish to detect a change from λ_0 to λ_1 with some high probability $(1-\beta)$, where $\lambda_1 = k\lambda_0$ and k is an arbitrary constant with $k > 1$ for a one-sided lower control chart and $k < 1$ for a one-sided upper control chart. That is,

$$P\left[X_i < T_L \mid \lambda = \lambda_1\right] = 1 \quad e^{-k\lambda_0 T_L} = (1-\beta) \qquad \text{(lower chart)} \tag{3.7}$$

$$P\left[X_i > T_U \mid \lambda = \lambda_1\right] = e^{-k\lambda_0 T_U} = (1-\beta). \qquad \text{(upper chart)} \tag{3.8}$$

Again, drawing a parallel with statistical hypothesis testing, we recognise β in Eqs. 3.7 and 3.8 as the probability of a type II error.

Substituting T_L and T_U in Eqs. 3.7 and 3.8, respectively, we obtain

$$(1-\beta) = 1 - e^{k\ln(1-\alpha)} \qquad \text{(lower chart)} \tag{3.9}$$

$$(1-\beta) = e^{k\ln(\alpha)}. \qquad \text{(upper chart)} \tag{3.10}$$

The performance characteristics for lower and upper one-sided charts are shown in Figures 3.14 and 3.15, respectively. Both of these figures show that the ability to detect even relatively large shifts (e.g. a doubling or halving) in the mean inter-arrival time is low (typically less than 0.2) for values of α less than 0.1. For example, using a 10% level of significance (i.e. $\alpha = 0.10$), the one-sided chart of Figure 3.14 suggests that there is a less than 20% chance of detecting a doubling (i.e. $k = 2$) of the mean arrival rate (or a halving of the inter-arrival time).

So far we have provided a review of basic statistical concepts as well as introducing some common control charting techniques that have been advocated elsewhere (Carpenter, 2001; Commonwealth of Australia, 2002) as being particularly suited to monitoring for temporal trends and aberrations in biosecurity-related applications. Control charts are particularly well suited to the visualisation and assessing of moderate to large volumes of time-based data. As such, control charts would be expected to have greater utility for container inspection regimes say, than for detecting the occurrence of an invasive species.

Control charts need to be viewed as just one method in a toolkit of available techniques that can potentially assist field officers and biosecurity risk assessors in identifying unusual or aberrant trends. For events having very low probabilities of occurrence (e.g. rare invasive species), the monitoring of time between outbreaks is a potentially more useful quantity to be charting, although as shown, the statistical power (ability to identify real shifts correctly in the mean time between events) using traditional charting techniques is relatively low. In Section 3.2 we look at a newer approach to control charting that has the potential to improve detection capabilities through the incorporation of extra information in the form of prior knowledge or expert opinion.

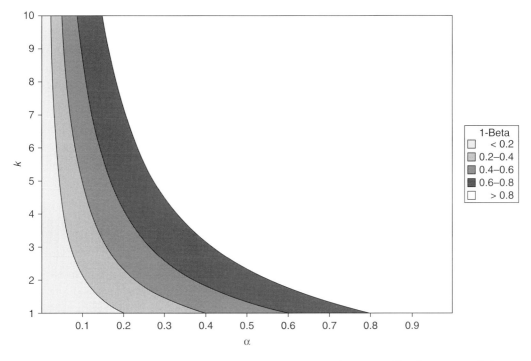

Figure 3.14. Performance characteristics (as measured by Eq. 3.9) for a one-sided, lower control chart.

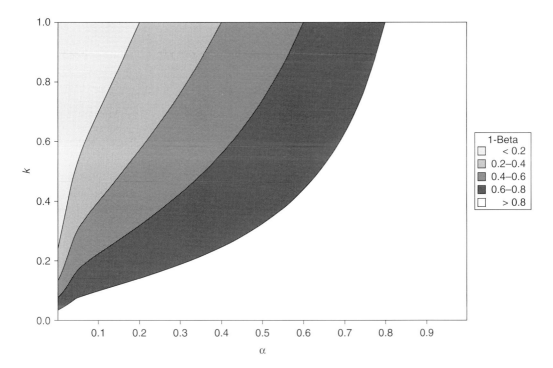

Figure 3.15. Performance characteristics (as measured by Eq. 3.10) for a one-sided, upper control chart.

Since the events of 11 September 2001, there has been a substantial research push in the area of syndromic surveillance with the accompanying development of new approaches and methods for detecting unusual patterns in a space–time continuum. Some of these techniques would appear to have direct applicability to monitoring for invasive species, although to date there has been little published on this application.

3.2   Bayesian Control Charting

Over the last decade, there has been considerable interest in the use of Bayesian statistical methods in the life sciences (e.g. McCarthy, 2007). Most of this interest has been focused on alternative approaches to conventional hypothesis testing frameworks and relatively little attention has been given to control charting methods.

In this section, we recast some of the previously discussed methods by explicitly incorporating prior belief about the state of the monitored system and adaptively updating the alerting mechanisms. The methodology is developed in the context of routine inspection of quarantine import inspections, but the potential applications extend to other areas of biosurveillance where data are being gathered over time and early warning triggers are required.

Many biosecurity surveillance and monitoring programmes lend themselves to a statistical approach because they invariably involve small sampling fractions and have an overarching requirement to balance the cost of sampling with the probability of failing to detect a threat. Here we focus on the temporal component of monitoring – that is, detecting important shifts or aberrations in monitored data in close to real time.

We have already seen that control charting methods have a number of attributes that make them particularly well suited to the task of identifying abnormal trends in biosecurity monitoring, such as an early-warning capability and easily communicated visual displays of historical results. Although some of these tools (such as the EWMA chart) have the ability to couple past and present observations, they are conventionally data-driven approaches that do not readily accommodate expert opinion or existing understanding about the underlying response-generating process. This is potentially an important consideration, particularly when monitoring a new disease or species for which historical data do not exist.

Another difficulty with standard control charting tools is that they are constructed using models that assume that process parameters are known exactly and observations are independently and identically distributed (Tsiamyrtzis & Hawkins, 2007). This is problematic in biosecurity applications because parameter values are rarely known and the assumption of independently and identically distributed data is frequently violated – particularly for time series data that often exhibit moderate to strong autocorrelation. More recently, Bayesian control charting methods have been developed to help overcome some of these limitations. Baron (2001) used the theory of optimal stopping of Markov sequences to develop efficient algorithms for the detection of a distributional change in sequentially collected data, and Hamada (2002) used Bayesian tolerance interval control limits in the context of attribute sampling.

In Section 3.3, we describe a Bayesian control charting approach that has been motivated by Menzefricke (2002), who used Bayesian predictive distributions to derive rejection regions for various monitoring applications.

Although it is beyond the scope of this book to provide a comprehensive review of Bayesian statistics, we shall digress momentarily to explain some of the underlying concepts. Readers requiring a more comprehensive treatment with applications to control charting may find the collection of papers in Colosimo and del Castillo (2007) a useful entry point.

3.2.1   Bayesian Statistics – Basic Concepts

The control charting methods discussed so far fall within the realm of frequentist statistics. This mode of statistical thinking is by far the most common and forms the core of nearly all undergraduate statistics courses. The frequentist view of the world is one in which the only admissible probabilities are those that can be expressed as the ratio of the number of outcomes that are favourable to the event under consideration to the total number of outcomes. Alternatively, probabilities can be thought of as the limiting value of the relative frequency of some phenomenon – hence the term frequentist statistics. A point of clear demarcation between frequentist and Bayesian statistics is the role of subjective probability. Subjective probability is eschewed in a frequentist framework; for Bayesians it is central.

The term Bayesian derives from the Rev. Thomas Bayes (b. 1702, London d. 1761). Bayes was not known as a mathematician and his only significant work, 'Essay towards solving a problem in the doctrine of chances', was published posthumously in the *Philosophical Transactions of the Royal Society of London* in 1763. Although a largely turgid piece of work, Bayes' essay identified a fundamental proposition in probability. This was a profound insight and provided a logical and consistent way of updating a prior belief or probability in the light of new evidence. The formula was named Bayes' rule after him. The updated probability is referred to as the posterior probability. Unlike frequentist statistical inference, which tests hypotheses or estimates (unknown) parameters on the basis of information contained in data alone, the Bayesian paradigm combines prior belief about unknown parameters with evidence from data using Bayes' rule. More formally, the aim of Bayesian inference is to make inferences about a parameter θ or future observation $\tilde{y}$ using probability statements that are conditional on the data y. Both parameters and future observations are treated as random variables in a Bayesian framework, and we talk of the posterior density of θ [denoted $p(\theta|y)$] and the posterior predictive density of y [denoted $p(\tilde{y}|y)$].

The simplest version of Bayes' rule for two events, A and B, says that the conditional probability that event A occurs given that event B has occurred is given by the formula $P(A|B) = \dfrac{P(A \cap B)}{P(B)}$, where the probability in the numerator is the joint probability (i.e. the probability that both A and B occur). Bayes' theorem applies equally to probability density functions. Thus if y denotes data and θ denotes some parameter or vector of parameters, then $P(y|\theta) = \dfrac{P(y \cap \theta)}{P(\theta)} = \dfrac{P(y, \theta)}{P(\theta)}$ and the numerator is the joint probability density function for y and θ. The roles of y and θ can be interchanged in this formula so that $P(\theta|y) = \dfrac{P(\theta \cap y)}{P(y)} = \dfrac{P(y, \theta)}{P(y)}$. A comparison of $P(y|\theta)$ and $P(\theta|y)$ reveals that $P(y, \theta) = P(\theta)P(y|\theta) = P(y)P(\theta|y)$. Finally, substituting this last expression for $P(y, \theta)$ into the expression for $P(\theta|y)$ gives Bayes' rule for probability functions:

$$P(\theta|y) = \frac{P(\theta)P(y|\theta)}{P(y)}.$$

(3.11)

This formula takes a prior probability density for θ [i.e. $P(\theta)$] and converts it into a posterior probability density $P(\theta|y)$ via the term $\dfrac{P(y|\theta)}{P(y)}$, which is called the Bayes factor. The denominator in the expression for the posterior density does not involve θ and only serves to normalise the probability density function (i.e. make it integrate to unity). Inference for θ based on the posterior is therefore unaffected by working with $P(\theta|y) \propto P(\theta)P(y|\theta)$ instead of the normalised posterior. Thus we see that the posterior distribution is proportional to the product of the prior and the likelihood of the data. In frequentist inference, only the likelihood is used; in Bayesian statistics, the likelihood is modified by our prior belief.

In Section 3.3, we describe a Bayesian control charting approach to biosurveillance. The motivation in the present context is that conventional (i.e. non-Bayesian or frequentist) approaches to control charting need to be primed with hard data in the absence of known parameter values. Although this might not be an issue in a manufacturing context, where production data are both plentiful and continuous, it is problematic for the monitoring of processes for which little background data are available. This problem becomes particularly acute for the development of a surveillance programme aimed at detecting a new threat for which there are no prior data. Similarly, in the case of monitoring a rare phenomenon, data paucity is axiomatic. In these cases, the monitoring data will comprise a string of zeros corresponding to no detect outcomes. Frequentist statistical methods will estimate the rate of occurrence as zero with a standard error of zero. The Bayesian paradigm, on the other hand, commences with the specification of a prior density for the parameter of interest (e.g. the true rate of occurrence) and continually updates this as new data become available.

3.3 A Bayesian Control Chart for Biosurveillance

The following development assumes attribute sampling, where at time t, n_t units are selected from a total volume of trade comprising N_t units and the result of inspection is a binary outcome: pass or fail. The time index t will generally represent daily increments. On each sampling occasion, two related control charting questions are considered: (1) Is the observed failure rate for the current sample within acceptable limits? (2) Is the cumulative failure rate for all samples inspected to date within acceptable limits? These objectives mirror the detection of pulse and press stresses in natural ecosystem management (Underwood, 1994). In answering questions (1) and (2), we wish to incorporate both historical monitoring data and prior information on the true failure rate, θ. We do this through the use of a conditional probability distribution for the data given θ and a prior probability model for θ. These two elements can be combined to obtain a predictive distribution for a new sample. The mathematical detail is provided in Section 3.3.1. Readers not interested in this can skip forward.

3.3.1 Mathematical Detail

The problem as formulated leads us to consider the random variable X_t, which is the number of failed units in the sample of n_t taken at time t. Assuming independent Bernoulli trials for each inspected unit, the conditional distribution of $X_t | \theta$ is binomial (we have dropped the time subscript to improve clarity where it is understood that all results pertain to the current sample unless otherwise indicated):

$$f_{X|\theta}(x|\theta) = \binom{n}{x} \theta^x (1-\theta)^{n-x} \; ; \; x = \{0,1,\dots n\}, 0 < \theta < 1. \qquad (3.12)$$

Uncertainty in the true failure rate, θ, is reflected in the prior distribution, $p(\theta)$. A suitable choice for $p(\theta)$ is the beta density:

$$p(\theta;a,b) = \frac{1}{\beta(a,b)} \theta^{a-1} (1-\theta)^{b-1}; \; 0 < \theta < 1, \; a > 0, \; b > 0. \qquad (3.13)$$

Initial values for the a and b parameters in Eq. 3.13 can be chosen according to various strategies depending on how much or how little we know about the true rate of risk for a particular commodity, country, test, and so forth. Robinson et al. (2009) discuss some of these strategies in the context of food imports and recommended the use of a Jeffrey's prior corresponding to $a = 0.5$ and $b = 0.5$. A plot of this Jeffrey's prior and two vague or non-informative prior densities are shown in Figure 3.16.

3.3.2 Updating the Prior

The underlying principle in the adaptive monitoring process is that our estimate of the true failure rate is constantly revised as new data are gathered. In the early

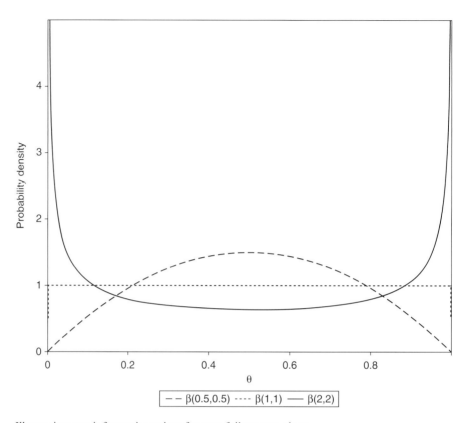

Figure 3.16. Illustrative non-informative priors for true failure rate, theta.

stages of monitoring, our probability model for the true failure rate will be driven by prior information.

At each time increment, the current prior probability for θ is updated using standard Bayesian methods to generate a posterior marginal probability density function. The procedure is described below.

At time t we have available the history of observed failures up to and including the current observation. We denote this as $\{x_1, x_2, \ldots, x_N\}$, where $N = \sum_{i=1}^{t} n_i$ is the total number of sampled units. We let Y denote the total number of failures at time t (i.e. $Y = \sum_{i=1}^{t} X_i$). For a stable process, the distribution of Y is also binomial with parameters (N, θ). However, N will rapidly become large (i.e. greater than ~30), and provided θ is not close to either 0 or 1, the binomial distribution is well approximated by a Poisson distribution with mean $N\theta$.

The marginal posterior distribution for Y as a function of the parameters a and b is

$$p(y|a,b) = \int_0^1 l(y|\theta) p(\theta|a,b) d\theta, \qquad (3.14)$$

where $l\left(y|\theta\right)$ is the likelihood of the data (y) given θ. Thus, Eq. 3.14 can be written as

$$p\left(y|a,b\right)=\int_{0}^{1}\left[\frac{e^{-N\theta}\left(N\theta\right)^{y}}{y!}\right]\frac{1}{B(a,b)}\theta^{a-1}\left(1-\theta\right)^{b-1}d\theta. \qquad (3.15)$$

Equation 3.15 can be evaluated using numerical integration or computed using Eq. 3.16 [a derivation of Eq. 3.14 is provided in Fox (2009)].

$$p\left(y|a,b\right)=\frac{N^{y}}{y!}\prod_{j=0}^{y-1}\left(\frac{j+a}{j+a+b}\right)\left\{1+\sum_{m=1}^{\infty}\left[\prod_{r=0}^{m-1}\frac{y+a+r}{y+a+b+r}\right]\frac{\left(-N\right)^{m}}{m!}\right\};$$
$$y=\{0,1,\ldots N\},\ a,b>0. \qquad (3.16)$$

At time t we have available the data $\{(N_{1},Y_{1}),(N_{2},Y_{2}),\ldots,(N_{t},Y_{t})\}$. The likelihood is thus

$$l(a,b;y)=\prod_{i=1}^{t}p(X_{i}=y_{i}-y_{i-1}|a,b); \quad y_{0}=0. \qquad (3.17)$$

The maximum likelihood estimates $\hat{a}$ and $\hat{b}$ at time t are found by simultaneously solving Eqs. 3.18a and 3.18b.

$$\hat{a}=\left\{a:\frac{\partial l(a,b;y)}{\partial a}\bigg|_{\hat{a}}=0\right\} \qquad (3.18a)$$

$$\hat{b}=\left\{b:\frac{\partial l(a,b;y)}{\partial b}\bigg|_{\hat{b}}=0\right\}. \qquad (3.18b)$$

The updated distribution for θ at time t is Eq. 3.13 with parameters $\hat{a}$ and $\hat{b}$. We use this posterior to obtain the predictive distributions for the number of failures (X_{t+1}) in the next sample of units to be inspected and the cumulative number of failures (Y_{t+1}).

3.3.3 Predictive Distributions for X_{t+1} and Y_{t+1}

The predictive distribution for X_{t+1} can be written as

$$p\left[X_{t+1}|y_{t}\right]=\int_{0}^{1}f\left(x_{t+1}|\theta\right)p\left(\theta|y\right)d\theta, \qquad (3.19)$$

where $p\left(\theta|y\right)=\dfrac{p(y|\theta)\,p(\theta)}{p(y)};p(y)=\int_{0}^{1}p(y|\theta)\,p(\theta)\,d\theta$ and $p(\theta)$ based on the most recent estimate using Eq. 3.13 with parameters $\{\hat{a},\hat{b}\}$.

Fox (2009) shows that $p\left[X_{t+1}\mid y_t\right]$ is given by Eq. 3.20.

$$p\left[X_{t+1}\mid y_t\right]=\binom{n_{t+1}}{x_{t+1}}\frac{\beta\left(x_{t+1}+y_t+a,n_{t+1}-x_{t+1}+b\right)}{\beta\left(y_t+a,b\right)}\frac{\left\{1+\sum\limits_{m=1}^{\infty}\left[\prod\limits_{r=0}^{m-1}\dfrac{x_{t+1}+y_t+a+r}{n_{t+1}+y_t+a+b+r}\right]\dfrac{\left(-N_t\right)^m}{m!}\right\}}{\left\{1+\sum\limits_{m=1}^{\infty}\left[\prod\limits_{r=0}^{m-1}\dfrac{y_t+a+r}{y_t+a+b+r}\right]\dfrac{\left(-N_t\right)^m}{m!}\right\}}.$$

$$(3.20)$$

We next consider the predictive distribution for Y_{t+1}. First, it can be seen that $p\left(Y_{t+1}=s\mid Y_t=y\right)=p\left(X_{t+1}=s-y\right)$. The unconditional distribution of X_{t+1}, $p\left(X_{t+1}\right)$ is obtained as follows:

$$p\left(X_{t+1}\right)=\int_0^1 p\left(X_{t+1}\mid\theta\right)p\left(\theta\right)d\theta,$$

$$(3.21)$$

where $p\left(X_{t+1}\mid\theta\right)\overset{d}{\sim}\mathrm{bin}(n_{t+1},\theta)$ and $p\left(\theta\right)\overset{d}{\sim}\mathrm{beta}(a,b)$. Thus, $p\left(X_{t+1}\right)$ is a beta-binomial distribution and the predictive distribution for Y_{t+1} is therefore

$$p\left(Y_{t+1}=s\mid Y_t=y\right)=\binom{n_{t+1}}{s-y}\frac{\beta\left(s-y+a,n_{t+1}-s+y+b\right)}{\beta\left(a,b\right)}.$$

$$(3.22)$$

We next discuss how the predictive distributions are used to set control limits for routine inspection programmes.

3.3.4   Adaptive Control Limits

The idea of a control limit is to provide an early warning that the underlying response-generating mechanism has departed from an assumed stable state. In the present context we wish to set two limits (designated RL_1 and RL_2) on the number of failures in the next batch of sampled units. RL_1 is set such that, when exceeded, it draws our attention to the fact that there are more failures in that particular sample of n units than would be expected. Exceeding RL_2 signifies an unusually high number of failures that would significantly increase the cumulative failure rate. Clearly, the two limits are related because triggering of RL_2 implies triggering of RL_1, although the converse is not necessarily true. Thus, the second limit will tend to be more liberal than the first.

$(1-\alpha)100\%$ response levels RL_1 and RL_2 are obtained by solving Eqs. 3.23 and 3.24 respectively.

$$RL_1\left(\alpha;n_{t+1},y\right)=\left\{r:\sum_{x=r}^{n_{t+1}}p\left(X_{t+1}=r\mid Y_t=y\right)\ge\alpha\ \wedge\ \sum_{x=r-1}^{n_{t+1}}p\left(X_{t+1}=r\mid Y_t=y\right)<\alpha\right\}$$

$$(3.23)$$

$$RL_2\left(\alpha;n_{t+1},y\right)=\left\{r:\sum_{x=r}^{n_{t+1}}p\left(Y_{t+1}=r\mid Y_t=y\right)\ge\alpha\ \wedge\ \sum_{x=r-1}^{n_{t+1}}p\left(Y_{t+1}=r\mid Y_t=y\right)<\alpha\right\}.$$

$$(3.24)$$

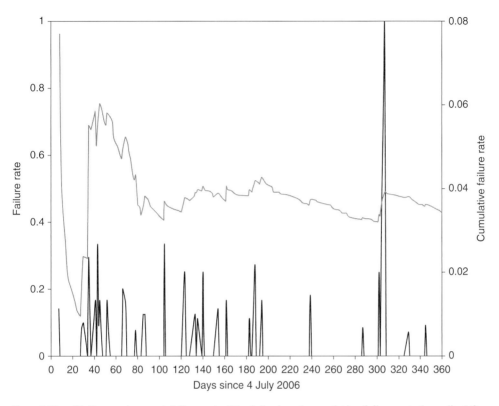

Figure 3.17. Daily consignment failure rate (black line) and cumulative failure rate (grey line) for invasive species detected in imported plant material.

3.4 Example – An Adaptive Control Chart for Shipping Container Inspections

The previous concepts are illustrated using fictitious data relating to the detection of an invasive species in plant material imported by shipping containers. A total of 1,718 inspections were made to give a pass or fail result for each consignment.

3.4.1 Updating the Prior

For the purpose of illustrating the proposed control charting methods, we have aggregated the results on a daily basis (as was done for the construction of the P-chart in Figure 3.2) and simply noted the number of failures x_t out of n_t consignments on day t. A plot of the observed daily failure rate and cumulative failure rate is shown in Figure 3.18. Initial estimates of the failure rate are highly variable although they ultimately converge to about 3%, as evidenced by the grey trace in Figure 3.17.

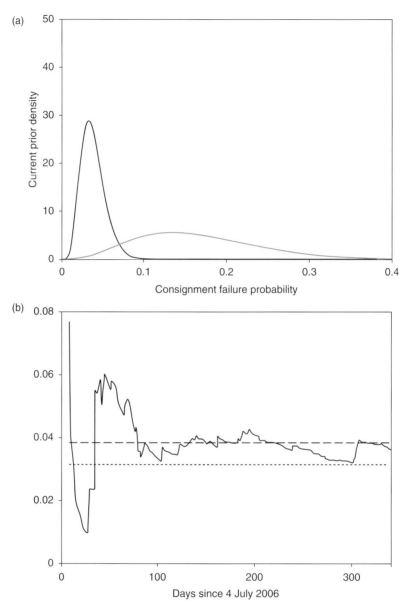

Figure 3.18.   Top: Original (subjective) prior density (grey curve) and posterior density (black curve) for true failure rate after one year. Bottom: Empirical cumulative failure rate (black line), overall mean failure rate (dotted line) and mean of posterior distribution after one year (dashed line).

We initially assumed a beta(4,20) distribution for the prior on θ, which has 99% of its probability mass between zero and 0.374, a mean of 0.167 and a modal value of 0.136. This choice reflects little or no prior knowledge about θ other than we expect it to be less than 0.4. Using the methods of the previous sections, we can update the prior at any point in time using all the information available at that time. This could be as frequently as every day or once a month. Figure 3.18 shows the situation at the end of a year of monitoring.

The top panel in Figure 3.18 shows the initial beta(4,20) prior (grey curve) and the posterior density at the end of the one-year period (black curve). The posterior is a beta(6.248,165.337) distribution that has a mean of 0.036, a median of 0.035 and a modal value of 0.031; 99% of the posterior distribution lies in the interval (0, 0.08). The lower panel of Figure 3.18 shows the cumulative failure rate as a function of time since monitoring

It is evident from Figure 3.18 and the related distributional summaries that the relatively vague prior has been considerably sharpened after a year of monitoring. The posterior density is compactly centred about the overall failure rate of 0.03, and a Bayesian 95% highest posterior density credibility interval for the true consignment failure rate is readily determined to be {0.011, 0.065}. The upper limit of a one-sided 95% credibility interval is 0.063, which suggests that a failure rate of more than the equivalent of 1 in 16 is evidence of a significant increase in import failure. A more refined instrument for alerting to changing failure status has been provided in the form of the two triggers, RL_1 and RL_2. We next illustrate how these operate in the present example.

3.4.2   Setting Adaptive Triggers

By way of example, suppose the current date is 7 August 2006 and we wish to place approximate 99% limits on the number of detects for the following day. There were a total of 128 consignments since the start of our monitoring period (we take this to be 4 July 2006) and three of these failed inspection, giving a current failure rate of 2.3%. Solving Eqs. 3.18a and 3.18b, we obtain the maximum likelihood estimates $\hat{a} = 3.805$ and $\hat{b} = 167.819$. There are 17 consignments on 8 August 2006. With $N = 128, y = 3$, $n = 17$ and $\alpha = 0.01$, we use Eq. 3.12 to determine $RL_1 = 2$ and Eq. 3.12 to determine $RL_2 = 2$. Because the outcome of the inspections is a discrete random variable, Eqs. 3.12 and 3.13 will generally not be able to be satisfied exactly. In this case, the actual value for α is 0.008 for RL_1 and 0.01 for RL_2 as distinct from the nominal $\alpha = 0.01$. An analysis of the data shows there were five failures on 8 August 2006 and this outcome would have tripped both triggers for further investigation.

In the early stages of monitoring, RL_1 and RL_2 will be quite close (in this case they are identical), reflecting the fact that not much data have been gathered and a significant increase in failure rate on any one occasion has a relatively large impact on the cumulative failure rate. As monitoring progresses, there will be greater separation between RL_1 and RL_2, although the difference will still be small given the relatively small sample sizes involved. By way of example, we advance to 28 June 2007. By this time, there have been 1,680 consignments resulting in 58 failures. The approximate $\alpha = 0.01$ triggers for the following day's 15 consignments are $RL_1 = 2$ and $RL_2 = 3$. The actual result was zero, which is clearly acceptable.

3.4.3   Discussion

The adoption of a Bayesian framework has allowed us to extend traditional control charting methods to accommodate expert option or prior belief about the monitored process. Furthermore, the Bayesian approach provides some other important enhancements. For example, ignorance about a new or previously undetected threat is readily accommodated and the intrinsic updating of prior information means that these methods are evolutionary, learning and adaptive. We believe that these are important prerequisites for successful biosecurity surveillance and monitoring systems.

It is important to distinguish between monitoring activities that aim to predict or forecast future events and those that aim to alert or flag the existence of an abnormal event. A comprehensive biosurveillance monitoring strategy will incorporate both proactive and reactive components. Control charting techniques are reactive, but depending on how they are constructed and implemented, they can provide a close to real-time monitoring capability. A difficulty with proactive systems, such as those used in syndromic surveillance, is that forecasting (particularly rare events) is exceedingly difficult, with success depending very much on model choice and parameterisation.

As noted by Burkhom et al. (2007), a critical issue for syndromic surveillance and forecasting systems is their sensitivity to expected and unexpected data outliers. Burkhom et al. (2007, p. 4216) go on to state further that 'for unexpected outliers, we have implemented automated outlier removal schemes to avoid baseline contamination for the adaptive regression, but such schemes can produce unexpected effects and need further study'. We regard this as a flawed strategy for two reasons: (1) An expected outlier is an oxymoron and (2) The automated removal of observations that are, in some sense, aberrant is to be strenuously avoided. It was precisely because of the automated removal of outliers that the hole in the ozone layer was initially undetected. It was only when the offending data were reinstated and the time series data reanalysed that the seriousness of the problem became apparent. Given that the utility of forward-looking systems is critically dependent on which data are included or excluded in the modelling process, it seems to us that data screening tools such as control charts have an important role to play in the development of forecasting tools.

Hitherto, Bayesian methods have not been widely used in biosecurity or biosurveillance applications, but a number of papers have appeared recently, which suggests that there is a growing awareness of the potential utility of this statistical paradigm. Wong et al. (2005) used Bayesian networks to extend the Population-wide Anomaly Detection and Assessment algorithm for syndromic surveillance, while Hogan et al. (2007) describe a Bayesian aerosol release detector that combines medical surveillance and meteorological data to provide an early warning capability for the release of *Bacillus anthracis*. More recently, Lu et al. (2011) proposed the use of Markov switching models to identify outbreak patterns in syndrome count time series data and gave an example using data relating to human health syndromes.

Future work could usefully focus on the elicitation of prior probability distributions as well as the incorporation of other covariates.

References

ANZECC and ARMCANZ. (2000). Australian and New Zealand guidelines for fresh and marine water quality. National Water Quality Management Strategy Paper No. 4. Canberra, Australia: Australian and New Zealand Environment and Conservation Council & Agriculture and Resource Management Council of Australia and New Zealand.

Baron, M. I. (2001). Bayes stopping rules in a change-point model with a random hazard rate. *Sequential Analysis*, 20(3), 147–163.

Benneyan, J. C. (2001a). Number-between g-type statistical quality control charts for monitoring adverse events. *Health Care Management Science*, 4(4), 305–318.

Benneyan, J. C. (2001b). Performance of number-between g-type statistical quality control charts for monitoring adverse events. *Health Care Management Science*, 4(4), 319–336.

Burgman, M. (2005). *Risks and decisions for conservation and environmental management.* Cambridge: Cambridge University Press.

Burkhom, H. S., Murphy, S. P. & Shmueli, G. (2007). Automated time series forecasting for biosurveillance. *Statistics in Medicine*, 26(22), 4202–4218.

Carpenter, T. E. (2001). Methods to investigate spatial and temporal clustering in veterinary epidemiology. *Preventative Veterinary Medicine*, 48(4), 303–320.

Cleveland, W. S. (1979). Robust locally weighted regression and smoothing scatterplots. *Journal of the American Statistical Association*, 74(368), 829–836.

Colosimo, B. M. & del Castillo, E., eds. (2007). *Bayesian process monitoring, control and optimization.* Boca Raton, FL: Chapman and Hall/CRC.

Commonwealth of Australia (2002). *Meat hygiene assessment: Objective methods for the monitoring of processes and products*, 2nd ed. Canberra, Australia: Commonwealth of Australia. Available from www.daff.gov.au/SiteCollectionDocuments/aqis/exporting/meat/elmer3/index/methods-microbiological-test-meat/meat_hygiene_assessment_2nd_ed.pdf

Doherr, M. G. & Audigé, L. (2001). Monitoring and surveillance for rare health-related events: A review from the veterinary perspective. *Philosophical Transactions of the Royal Society B: Biological Sciences*, 356(1411), 1097–1106.

Fox, D. R. (2001). Environmental power analysis – A new perspective. *Environmetrics*, 12(5), 437–449.

Fox, D. R. (2009). *Statistical methods for biosecurity monitoring and surveillance.* Report 06-05. Melbourne, Australia: Australian Centre of Excellence for Risk Analysis, the University of Melbourne.

Fricker, R. D., Jr. (2011). Biosurveillance: Detecting, tracking, and mitigating the effects of natural disease and bioterrorism. In J. J. Cochran, L. A. Cox, P. Keskinocak, J. P. Kharoufeh & J. C. Smith (eds.),. *Wiley encyclopedia of operations research and management science.* Hoboken, NJ: John Wiley and Sons.

Hall, J. A. & Golding, L. (1998). *Standard methods for whole effluent toxicity testing: Development and application.* NIWA Client Report MfE80205. Hamilton, New Zealand: National Institute of Water and Atmospheric Research.

Hamada, M. (2002). Bayesian tolerance interval control limits for attributes. *Quality and Reliability Engineering International,* 18(1), 45–52.

Hogan, W. R., Cooper, G. F., Wallstrom, G. L., Wagner, M. M. & Depinay, J. (2007). The Bayesian aerosol release detector: An algorithm for detecting and characterizing outbreaks caused by an atmospheric release of Bacillus anthracis. *Statistics in Medicine,* 26(29), 5225–5252.

Höhle, M. & Paul, M. (2008). Count data regression charts for the monitoring of surveillance time series. *Computational Statistics and Data Analysis,* 52(9), 4357–4368.

Kulldorff, M. (1997). A spatial scan statistic. *Communications in Statistics: Theory and Methods,* 26(6), 1481–1496.

Lu, H.-M., Zeng, D. & Chen, H. (2011). Markov switching models for outbreak detection. In M. Thurmond, D. Zeng, C. Castillo-Chavez, H. Chen & W. B. Lober (eds.), *Infectious disease informatics and biosurveillance (pp. 111–144).* New York: Springer Science+Business Media.

McCarthy, M. A. (2007). *Bayesian methods for ecology.* Cambridge: Cambridge University Press.

MacNally, R. & Hart, B. T. (1997). Use of CUSUM methods for water-quality monitoring in storages. *Environmental Science and Technology,* 31(7), 2114–2119.

Marshall, C., Best, N., Bottle, A. & Aylin, P. (2004). Statistical issues in the prospective monitoring of health outcomes across multiple units. *Journal of the Royal Statistical Society A: Statistics in Society,* 167(3), 541–559.

Menzefricke, U. (2002). On the evaluation of control chart limits based on predictive distributions. *Communication in Statistics – Theory and Methods,* 31(8), 1423–1440.

Montgomery, D. C. (2012). *Introduction to statistical quality control,* 7th ed. Hoboken, NJ: John Wiley & Sons.

Morrison, L. (2008). The use of control charts to interpret environmental monitoring data. *Natural Areas Journal,* 28(1), 66–73.

Mostashari, F. & Hartman, J. (2003). Syndromic surveillance: A local perspective. *Journal of Urban Health,* 80(Suppl 1), i1–i7.

National Aquatic Animal Health Technical Working Group (2004). *Principles for the design and conduct of surveys to show presence or absence of infectious disease in aquatic animals.* Available from www.daff.gov.au/SiteCollectionDocuments/animal-plant/aquatic/field-guide/4th-edition/amphibians/surveillance.pdf

National Invasive Species Council (2003*). General guidelines for the establishment and evaluation of invasive species early detection and rapid response systems,* version 1. Washington, DC: Department of the Interior. Available from www.invasivespecies.gov/global/EDRR/EDRR_documents/Guidelines%20for%20Early%20Detection%20&%20Rapid%20Response.pdf

Radaelli, G. (1998). Planning time-between-events Shewhart control charts. *Total Quality Management,* 9(1), 133–140.

Robinson, A., Burgman, M., Atkinson, W., et al. (2009). *Import clearance data framework.* ACERA Project 0804 Final Report. Melbourne, Australia: Australian Centre of Excellence for Risk Analysis, University of Melbourne.

Sonesson, C. & Bock, D. (2003). A Review and discussion of prospective statistical surveillance in public health. *Journal of the Royal Statistical Society. Series A (Statistics in Society),* 166(1), 5–21.

Stark, K. D. C., Regula, G., Hernandez, J., et al. (2006). Concepts for risk-based surveillance in the field of veterinary medicine and veterinary public health: Review of current approaches. *BMC Health Services Research*, 6, 20.

Tsiamyrtzis, P. & Hawkins D. M. (2007). *Bayesian process monitoring, control and optimization.* Boca Raton, FL: Chapman & Hall/CRC.

Underwood, A. J. (1994). On beyond BACI: Sampling designs that might reliably detect environmental disturbance. *Ecological Applications*, 4(1), 3–15.

Westbrooks, R. G. (2004). New approaches for early detection and rapid response to invasive plants in the United States. *Weed Technology*, 18(5), 1468–1471.

Wong, W. K., Cooper, G. F., Dash, D. H., et al. (2005). Population-wide anomaly detection. In *Proceedings of the International Workshop on Data Mining Methods for Anomaly Detection*, 21 August 2005, Chicago. Available from www.cs.uiuc.edu/class/fa05/cs591han/kdd05/docs/dmmad.pdf

World Organisation for Animal Health (2010a). *Bioterrorism fact sheet.* Available from www.oie.int/fileadmin/Home/eng/Current_Scientific_Issues/ docs/pdf/BIOTE_EN_FS%20.pdf

World Organisation for Animal Health (2010b). *Terrestrial animal health code 2010*, Article 10.4.27. Available from http://web.oie.int/eng/normes/mcode/en_chapitre_1.10.4.htm

4 Open-Source Intelligence Gathering and Open-Analysis Intelligence for Biosecurity

Geoff Grossel, Aidan Lyon and Mike Nunn

4.1 Introduction

Open-source intelligence is the analysis product of publicly available information that has been collected, sorted and archived. *Open-analysis intelligence* is the analysis of freely available information that is done out in the open by an engaged user community. A country's national security agency may mine Twitter for data and analyse this information to predict social uprisings. This would be an example of open-source intelligence but not an example of open-analysis intelligence because the analysis of the information is confidential. An example of open-analysis intelligence is the www.rdtn.org website that analysed crowdsourced measurements of radioactivity in Japan after the 2011 earthquake to map levels of radioactivity across the nation.

We have developed an online system called IBIS (International Biosecurity Intelligence System) that performs both open-source intelligence and open-analysis intelligence with the goal of tracking and forecasting terrestrial animal, aquatic animal and plant diseases. The result is a practical application that provides real-time and relevant information to decision makers with the ultimate goal of providing early warning, better planning and improving response times to animal and plant health issues and disease threats.

Public health intelligence gathering systems already exist on the Internet, for example, HealthMap and ProMED (Madoff, 2004). These websites have a *one health* perspective (One Health, 2011) that encompasses diseases of humans, animals and plants. Others, such as the World Animal Health Information Database operated by the World Organisation for Animal Health, focus on animal diseases and are emerging as vast and invaluable biosecurity intelligence resources.

These systems offer broadly similar services – albeit with subtle differences – around a central theme of aggregating both open-source and contributed content. They are heavily biased towards news aggregation, and with the exception of HealthMap's Flu Near You and Outbreaks Near Me apps, they are noticeably light on useful analysis output. None of the systems provides tools (other than discussion threads) that are freely available to the user community to conduct any collaborative or open-intelligence analysis of the information gathered.

There are no systems devoted solely to animal or plant diseases. The systems are slowly converging, and there is increasingly more collaboration – particularly between the two most prominent public health systems, ProMED and HealthMap. However, there will always be an opportunity for boutique or generic intelligence websites that are tailor made to fill analysis gaps and offer much needed services that take the next step beyond simply aggregating and organising information to offer an open-analysis intelligence application with some effective yet easy-to-use analysis tools.

Our approach in designing our first model website, AquaticHealth.net, was to integrate components from the existing systems that would have the most utility for aquatic animal biosecurity and add new tools where the demands required or where opportunities emerged during development. Our resulting IBIS website, which hosts aquatic, plant and animal intelligence systems, represents a departure from pre-filtered and owner-controlled systems. Rather than a broad approach to open-source intelligence gathering, we give the user community as much control as possible over the gathering and organisation of information, and then also provide the means to produce meaningful outputs with open-analysis intelligence tools. This allows for a collegiate community to concentrate directly on issues relevant to them. We call this approach *open-source intelligence gathering and open-analysis intelligence for biosecurity* with the aim of promoting crowdsourcing and active engagement in initiating and contributing to collaborative strategic intelligence analysis, and control over scanning, gathering and content. Not all analysis needs to be crowdsourced or conducted openly online. The open-source information can be used by discretion of decision makers for confidential analysis. This can be especially important when information is commercially sensitive, there are trade implications or when unfounded public perceptions and expectations need to be managed appropriately (e.g. in the national interest).

Governments need to be mindful that responsive and effective analysis of rapidly reported information that is already in the public domain, with or without official approval, is a more transparent mechanism for responsive decision making than private analysis of classified information – which is often criticised as resulting in avoidance of critical issues and delays in responsive action against disease risks. It is for this very reason that independently managed applications such as ProMED exist today. Governments are also beginning to understand that transparency and being held accountable for critical emergency decision making are directly the result of prompt and proactive disclosure of facts. This understanding stems from the realisation that the risks associated with complex problems are greater when you know something but do nothing (for whatever reason) than if you publicly disclose the facts as they are known at the time and immediately anticipate, plan or initiate an appropriate response. For example, a competent authority may, for managing public perceptions, sensitivities and for strategic trade reasons, not release information associated with an emerging disease problem, such as oyster herpesvirus, because the disease may not be nationally or internationally reportable, suitable diagnostics are lacking or because unfavourable public perception of the word *herpes* may seriously affect critical trade periods (e.g. the release of conditioned oysters during a short distribution window over the Christmas or summer holiday period). In the absence of prompt public disclosure the competent authority will not be held to account and thus may delay a critical and timely emergency response in favour of a short-term trade gain. Such a strategic delay is a false economy because disease spreads rapidly in the aquatic environment, and a delay all too often results in establishment and spread of the disease and serious consequences for the industry at the regional and potentially the national level. Sustained healthy trade and responsive action to an emerging disease threat can coexist when managed responsibly.

In situations involving nationally and internationally reportable diseases, most competent authorities are obliged to promptly report nationally and to the World Organisation for Animal Health respectively via their established reporting mechanisms. Notwithstanding such obligations, if we scan the data held in the World Organisation for Animal Health's disease notification recording system, the World Animal Health Information Database, it is clearly evident this is not always the case. The risk associated with the spread of diseases in globally traded aquatic animals and their products from non-reporting member countries alone justifies the need for effective open-source, open-intelligence applications to detect risk early so that appropriate responsive action can be taken.

4.2   Designing AquaticHealth.net

Our starting point was to develop a dedicated aquatic biosecurity intelligence information gathering system by examining existing web-based systems to identify features that may be particularly important for aquatic biosecurity. We examined a range of criteria including search strategies, language search and translation capabilities, mapping capabilities and the structure and logic of information filters (Lyon et al., 2012). The most significant ways in which the systems differ is their reliance on automated software rather than human beings for content gathering and analysis. Some such as BioCaster (biocaster.nii.ac.jp) are fully automated, whereas ProMED is at the other end of the information collection spectrum and is completely human based. We have opted for a balanced mixture of automated and human crowdsourcing – an open call to an undefined group, usually composed of people appropriate for a task, to contribute to an analysis or to solve a problem (Brabham, 2008). We believe that this is the best approach to take to generate human-mediated analysis.[1] For a comprehensive analysis of the functionality and technology behind AquaticHealth.net and the subsequent International Biosecurity Intelligence System application, see Lyon et al. (2013).

The technology for developing open-source, open-analysis intelligence applications is not new. What separates applications like AquaticHealth.net from, for example, HealthMap is not the ability to collect and organise open-source data

---

[1] See also Floridi (2009) for a more theoretical assessment of Web 2.0 and Web 3.0 technologies.

but the capacity to offer the user complete and unfiltered control of searching and then provide a set of easy to use vertically integrated applications to generate outputs in the form of intelligence reports from which health management decisions relating to disease risks can be based. An essential feature of an open-source intelligence application is the ability to keep abreast of the latest technology in the intelligence-reporting domain. To achieve this, the applications must resource and sustain a dynamic research community. Integrated analysis tools must continually be researched, constructed and uploaded as early as possible so that feedback from the user community can direct continual improvement of the systems or determine the usefulness, relevance and life span of the tools.

4.3   Wiki-based Open-Intelligence Analysis

Our research and development strategy is based around the adage *fail early and often*. We initially attempted to encourage user engagement by contributing to wiki pages as a simple form of open-analysis intelligence. A range of diseases were set up and seeded with rudimentary information around which narratives could be built, but they also included extensive reference to the site's reports. Topics were originally selected for placement into two categories: specific diseases and other topics. We seeded approximately 20 wiki entries as subjects using aquatic diseases of concern that were mostly diseases listed by the World Organisation for Animal Health. Each wiki entry also included a forecasting section, in which users could record educated guesses about where diseases are likely to spread next. The open-source nature of the wiki was intended to allow users to have fluid debates about the forecasts. All revisions of the wiki entries were recorded and made viewable by all users, and topics were limited only to the imagination of the system users.

By tracking the use of the wiki entries over time, it became apparent that the registered user community, now growing substantially in number, did not fully engage and contribute, and generally showed little interest. We concluded that the wiki entries were not working in the way we had anticipated. Nielsen (2011), an advocate of open science, proposes that open science wikis often fail because people, particularly those with careers in science, do not want to contribute to something of little or no benefit to the advancement of their careers. People would rather write articles, even substandard articles, for peer-reviewed journals because this kind of publication is far more beneficial to them individually. Nielsen proposes that this is not due to some kind of selfishness of the individuals, but rather the consequences of the wrong incentive structures being in place. A large component of hiring decisions, tenure reviews and promotions are the number of publications an individual has accumulated. Furthermore, open contribution may compromise contractual research obligations and intellectual property rights.

Nielsen's explanation for failed open science wikis may partly account for the failure of our wikis. However, the failure cannot so much be attributed to the wikis themselves, but to the original seed topics we chose. The failure of the wikis was not complete and some aspects were successful. By testing the various wiki topics, we found community engagement was successful if the topic, or the subject within a specific disease wiki, was consistent with what we were trying to accomplish – active and collaborative open-analysis intelligence of emerging disease issues, capturing emerging disease trends, forecasting and capturing other interesting hot issues and topics that can be tracked and analysed with the goal of improving early warning and responsive action to aquatic animal health issues, threats and disease outbreaks. Trying to engage registered users to update general disease information in the disease-focused topics was never the intention of an intelligence gathering and analysis website. Hence, the failure of wiki topics that were out of scope and the need to develop an alternative online application that is appealing, collaborative and yet simple. Nielsen (2011) argues that one of the challenges in making open science succeed is the creation of a more user-friendly online tool that encourages participation throughout the network, such as the open science website (www .openscience.org).

4.4   Blog-based Open-Intelligence Analysis

Like Nielsen, we believe our challenge is to find the most appropriate online format to create engagement in open-analysis intelligence. We have therefore moved to a new hybrid wiki-blog analysis platform called Emerging Issues. It has the same goal of promoting open-analysis intelligence, but does so by focusing on what the users of the site care about most: disease outbreaks or events that might be disease outbreaks, emerging issues, and forecasting disease outbreaks. Emerging Issues was born out of the failure of the original out-of-scope wiki topics with the exception of a wiki titled *Emerging Diseases for 2011* and from the forecasting sections of the disease-specific wikis. The simple and attractive core function of these wiki features was that they achieved our primary goal; they successfully captured events for further analysis and resulted in user engagement.

Entries in the Emerging Issues wiki blog feature a title and date, a window for all users to provide content, a forecasting section, links to related reports, share functions, comments and a map. The systems have now stabilised on a functional and meaningful model that provides an easy-to-use analysis tool for our registered user community to construct intelligence reports. The forecasting applications retained from some of the older wikis in AquaticHealth.net proved to be accurate and potentially very useful for improving biosecurity planning and health management in aquaculture and fisheries. These forecasts have been transferred to the most relevant Emerging Issues wiki blog.

For example, oyster herpes-related summer mortality in Pacific oyster culture was used as one of the original wiki topics. As emerging patterns in the global spread of the disease became apparent, the information was fed into the OsHV–1 wiki. The resulting prediction was that oyster herpes presents the greatest single disease risk to the Australian Pacific oyster industry. Eight months after this prediction was made, the Australian and New Zealand Pacific oyster industries both incurred outbreaks of oyster herpes-related summer mortality. In more examples, similar predictions were made prior to disease outbreaks in bivalve mollusc aquaculture in the United States and Vietnam.

To date, all four forecasts made during 2010–2012 have proven to be correct. The latest Emerging Issues wiki-blog forecast is that the marine fish disease known as viral nervous necrosis will cause significant problems in the emerging grouper aquaculture sector throughout the Southeast Asia region during 2012–2013. This forecast is scheduled to play out over the long term, but recent scientific reports from China indicate that this forecast was correct and has now run its course. Another forecast made in February 2012 was that amoebic gill disease will cause major problems on salmon farms in Scotland and eventually spread to Norway in the advent of favourable warm conditions sometime in the next three to five summer seasons (e.g. the summers of 2012–2014), amoebic gill disease had already re-emerged in southern regions of Norway in December 2012, and the forecast was therefore accurate but unexpectedly early. Emerging Issues currently arise at a rate of one or two issues every two months, and are all updated on a regular basis when new information becomes available. Our research focus for future analysis tools is to provide tools that are effective in producing meaningful outputs, are easy to use and promote collaboration within the user community. We are investigating forecasting tools, predictive modelling and cluster analysis, geospatial analysis, Delphi analysis and network analysis. The challenges we face with the tools are similar to the problems encountered with our original wiki: we need to transition the research into a user-friendly interface, load the tools to the website as early as possible and refine them according to feedback from users.

4.5 Content and Analysis Quality

An often-encountered concern about AquaticHealth.net, mostly by practising or publishing aquatic animal health scientists, is the quality of the information it collects. Scientists and aquatic animal health experts in government roles argue that to be of any value, disease outbreak information must be either an evidence-based peer-reviewed scientific publication or officially endorsed information released by government or an immediate disease notification from the World Organisation for Animal Health.

It is neither the intention nor function of our online intelligence gathering and analysis tools to be filters that are selective about the quality of information that enters the sites. The website's information collection capabilities function to collect all the available electronic information coming into the Internet, from Twitter, YouTube videos, scientific journal articles, World Organisation for

Animal Health immediate disease notifications, ProMed reports, and so forth. Our tools intelligently — with the help of humans — sort the information, add-value to it and archive it so that it can be retrieved later when an intelligence analyst is attempting to determine trends in the data, such as an emerging disease trend over a two-year period. For example, the information can be used in a similar way to a journalist investigating a story. An emerging disease trend may start by alerting the analyst to a disease outbreak problem of unknown aetiology, but the initial seed information may have a sketchy unverified source such as a YouTube video file and a tweet uploaded to the Internet by an interested bystander. Nevertheless, early seed information like this may be crucial in confirming the first event in a series of disease events leading to a new and concerning emerging disease problem.

To assist in later analysis, our online tools have the capability to crowdsource quality judgments through the four-star ranking system of reports and user comments attesting to the quality of the information. However, even if information is of poor quality, analysts can provide early disease trend information to aquatic health decision makers so that preparations for responsive action can be made. The intelligence analyst can interrogate the veracity of the information and verify the validity of the source during the course of investigating a disease trend or other issue and provide a comment or rank the information accordingly. More often than not, disease outbreaks in the aquatic environment will spread quickly to their natural limits with devastating impacts and consequences. Expensive emergency responses are then centred on containment, disposal and decontamination, rather than directing valuable and finite resources towards prevention. Aquatic health managers are keenly aware that consideration of timely information and early actions that are responsive and preventive are the primary and most effective considerations when managing biosecurity in the aquatic environment, and that waiting for high-quality reports to be published, such as scientific papers or official government reports, is an ineffective approach to responsive aquatic health management.

Another criticism we have encountered from aquatic animal health experts is the issue of peer review, especially of our forecasts and analysis featuring in the Emerging Issues section of the website. We do have peer review, but it isn't the standard scholarly peer review process that publishing scientists are familiar with (i.e. the traditional process of sending out articles to a narrowly defined field of, usually anonymous, expert reviewers). All our information is open source in the public domain and viewable by anyone on the Internet at any time. Registered users can, either anonymously or not, comment on or criticise anything without approval from a moderator in an open and transparent manner. Non-registered users can do the same, but someone within a trusted group in the network approves the comment first. All review comments are available for scrutiny, and any registered user can make alterations, discuss improvements and access previous versions of the analysis to track and debate changes. We are mindful of creating an environment that does not shut down the debate and actively encourages an open discussion about all content. The open peer review process we have adopted is also a post-publication review process, which is arguably more suitable for our purposes because we rely on open-intelligence analyses being collaborative, ongoing and updated as necessary, and directly targeted to the engaged demographic using our online tools.

There is potential for politically biased reporting to the site. Lobbyists for environmental groups have used the site to post information to all users via submission of disease news articles. However, the site's user community, although interested in browsing through all content in the context of reading the range of information available to them, is generally not the direct target for this kind of lobbying. As a result, the site has proven to be an ineffective information dissemination avenue that the lobbyists no longer pursue. There are further ways in which this lobbying pressure can be mitigated. Although the open and democratic nature of the site allows the possibility of pushing particular agenda, it also allows for effective crowdsourced agenda control. If a user starts promoting misleading information, other users can quickly comment on, or even edit, that information to explain to everyone else that the information is contentious. We have had some users who joined the site to publish all articles from their own website; fortunately, the community quickly corrected this and unpublished all of the irrelevant reports. The overall effect was that all relevant reports from that site were published and brought to people's attention and all irrelevant reports remained in the raw data scan and industry news feeds. The system isn't fool-proof, but no system is, and there is no reason to think that this system is especially prone to being gamed. We believe this is because the website is of little general interest outside the community of users. There is little opportunity to promote causes, increase sales or solicit money from the registered user community.

4.6   Conclusion

Our online intelligence gathering and analysis tools are an example of what can be achieved in today's technologically democratised world. Many of the key elements of our websites are outsourced. In their short history, our online applications have been used to capture emerging disease information, analyse and track disease trends, map diseases, organise data, perform basic predictive modelling, contribute to future health planning, provide biosecurity alerts, build biosecurity risk profiles and support responsive decision-making relating to imports and exports.

The power of raw data feeding into discussion and analysis in real-time is immense. Our sites offer the capacity to intelligently process raw information in real-time with the added function of unlimited application. Our mission is to create openness in animal and plant health. We will work to establish a system of transparency, public participation, collaboration and trust. Openness will strengthen animal and plant health and promote efficiency and effectiveness in biosecurity. We hope to establish an effective open-intelligence community over time to build critical mass for supporting the implementation of positive and responsive action (adapted from Obama, 2009).

References

Brabham, D. C. (2008). Crowdsourcing as a model for problem solving. *Convergence: International Journal of Research into New Media Technologies*, 14(1), 75–90.

Floridi, L. (2009). Web 2.0 vs. the semantic web: A philosophical assessment. *Episteme*, 6(1), 25–37.

Lyon, A., Nunn, M., Grossel, G. & Burgman, M. (2012). Comparison of web-based biosecurity intelligence systems: BioCaster, EpiSPIDER and HealthMap. *Transboundary and Emerging Diseases*, 59(3), 223–232.

Lyon, A., Nunn, M., Grossel, G. & Burgman, M. (2013). Using internet intelligence to manage biosecurity risks: A case study for aquatic animal health. *Diversity and Distributions*, 19(5–6), 640–650.

Madoff, L. C. (2004). ProMED-mail: An early warning system for emerging diseases. *Clinical Infectious Diseases*, 39(2), 227–232.

Nielsen, M. (2011). *Reinventing discovery: The new era of networked science*. Princeton, NJ: Princeton University Press.

Obama, B. (2009). *Subject: Transparency and open government, 23901*. Federal Register/Vol. 74, No. 97/Thursday, May 21, 2009/Notices Memorandum for the Heads of Executive Departments and Agencies. Available from www.whitehouse.gov/the_press_office/TransparencyandOpenGovernment/

One Health. (2011). *1st International One Health Congress*. Available from www.onehealth2011.com/

5 Predicting Distributions of Invasive Species

Jane Elith

5.1 Introduction

In a newly invaded region, invasive species can progress through the stages of introduction, establishment and dispersal to a full range. There is currently much worldwide interest in predicting distributions of invasive species, and many organisations will be faced with questions of whether and how to embark on such a task, or how to interpret predictions that others have provided. This chapter provides information on predicting the final stage, commonly referred to as the potential distribution, of the species in the invaded range. In contrast, Chapter 6 discusses methods for modelling the whole invasion process.

The names for these predictions of invasive species distributions can be confusing because the same terms can be used for distinctly different aims and models. So here, regardless of other uses of the words, mention of pest risk mapping, climate matching, niche mapping and predicting potential distributions will all mean the same thing: a model or process that aims to produce a map of areas that are likely to be suitable for the species. The advantages of these maps are obvious: species can be screened for those likely to become pests (i.e. likely to cause harm), monitoring programs can target areas most likely to be infested, arrangements can be established for cost sharing between jurisdictions over a large region and so on (Brunel et al., 2010; Cook et al., 2007; Richardson & Thuiller, 2007).

Many governments, agencies and organisations now invest in some form of pest risk mapping. As yet, there appears to be no complete system for mapping; most are examples, or case studies for particular species, or prototype systems. For instance, Pratique (https://secure.fera.defra.gov.uk/pratique/index.cfm) is a European Union initiative broadly targeting pest risk analysis, but with components focusing on mapping ranges. In the United States, the Animal and Plant Health Inspection Service conducts risk assessments using NAPPFAST (Magarey et al., 2007), while in Australia, the Department of Agriculture and Water Resources has frequently used a simple climate matching system (CLIMATE) to predict climate suitability for species of biosecurity concern (e.g. Bomford et al., 2010). Globally, there is interest in linking biodiversity databases with modelling tools to facilitate pest risk mapping anywhere in the world, but there is understandable uncertainty about the likely quality of the outputs.

This chapter begins with a brief discussion of approaches for modelling broad ecological units or climates (Section 5.2). The focus then shifts to single species models, covering the conceptual bases (Section 5.3), touching on mechanistic models (Section 5.4) and then focusing on methods using species distribution records and environmental data to predict distributions (Section 5.5). The chapter includes a mix of commentary based on my own research, review and advice, with the intention of providing interpretation of the current state of the science and commentary on useful ways forward.

5.2   Community or Climate-based Mapping

Some approaches to modelling potential ranges of invasive species focus on biological or environmental units aggregated above the species level. For instance, Richardson and Thuiller (2007) predicted the global distribution of seven South African biomes. They suggested that the results, which were essentially a biologically oriented climate matching, would be useful for screening species' introduction risks. Baker et al. (2000) reviewed applications of climate-based mapping that mapped climate without reference to species responses, giving examples both in environmental space (e.g. the early climographs of Cook, 1925) and geographic space (e.g. the Match Climates option in CLIMEX; see Box 5.2 and Sutherst, 2003). Brunel et al. (2010) proposed that Köppen–Geiger climate zones and world hardiness zones provide ecoclimatic information relevant to screening potential invasive plant species for the European and Mediterranean Plant Protection Organization. Thomas and Ohlemüller (2010) used rainfall and temperature information to map similar climates both locally (within 1000 km of a target cell) and globally. They then estimated likelihood of invasion (*invasibility*) by assuming that similar non-local climates represent potential source locations of invasive species. Their maps comparing risks under current and future climates suggested increases in invasibility with climate change (e.g. Figure 5.1).

These types of models or data summaries can be used to develop an understanding of general patterns of invasions. They can also give a broad overview of whether a region is even remotely likely to be suitable for a species of concern (or alternatively, whether the climates of two regions overlap and, therefore, whether one poses a potential risk for the other). In that sense, these models could be considered useful background information or a first step for assessing invasive potential.

5.3   The Conceptual Basis for Predicting Potential Distributions of Invasive Species

In many situations, predictions are needed for a particular species. Users require mapped estimates of where species could persist in a given region, and this is related to questions about the biotope – i.e. the geographic location of the species' niche.

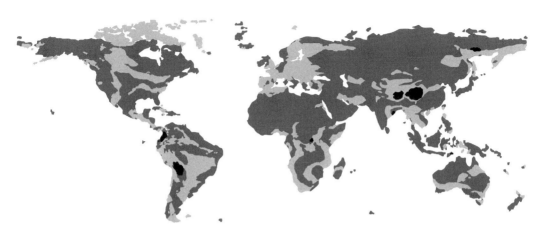

Figure 5.1. Change in invasibility index from 1931–1960 to 2041–2050, under the HadCM3 climate model, A2 emission scenario. Future long-distance invasion risk is increased in the dark grey areas and decreased in light grey areas. Black areas have no analogous climates in the future, so invasion risk is not calculable.
[Reproduced with permission from Thomas, C. D. & Ohlemüller, R. (2010). Climate change and species' distributions: An alien future? In C. Perrings, H. Mooney & M. Williamson (eds.), Bioinvasions and globalization: Ecology, economics, management and policy (pp. 19–29). Oxford: Oxford University Press. See source for full details.]

In the species modelling arena most niche definitions rely on Hutchinson's viewpoint (Hutchinson, 1957) – namely that the fundamental niche is a multidimensional hypervolume with 'permissive conditions and requisite resources as its axes' (Colwell & Rangel, 2009, p. 19651), in which every point corresponds to a state that would allow the species to exist indefinitely. The dimensions of this niche are limited to the subset of all possible conditions that directly affect the fitness of the organism (Kearney, 2006). In practice, modellers often focus on the species' response to climate, although this is neither essential nor most relevant for some species and spatial extents (Hulme, 2003). For a clear explanation of Hutchinson's niche ideas, the links between niche (environmental) and biotope (geographic) space and implications for species modelling, see Colwell and Rangel (2009).

The full fundamental niche need not be apparent at a given time. The concept of the *potential* niche was introduced by Jackson and Overpeck (2000) to describe those portions of the fundamental niche (those environments) that actually exist somewhere in geographic space at a specified time. The idea of modelling the potential distribution of an invasive species in a region is related to this definition. The *realised* niche (where the species actually occurs) is usually a smaller environmental volume (or geographic area) than the fundamental and potential niches. Hutchinson (1957) saw the realised niche as a subset of the fundamental niche, limited by biotic interactions – for instance, by the presence of competitors or predators, or the absence of mutualists. Others (e.g. Pulliam, 2000) refined the definition to allow for source-sink theory and dispersal limitations. Thus, sink populations can allow the realised niche to be larger than the fundamental niche, and constraints to dispersal and past disturbances can limit the realised niche beyond the effects of biotic interactions.

These differences between the realised and fundamental niches are relevant to invasive species, particularly when we consider the realised niche in native ranges versus the global potential or fundamental niche. Invasive species often persist in environments in their invaded ranges that either were not occupied by them (because of dispersal or biotic limitations) or were non-existent in their native range. That is, invasive species are able to expand into parts of their fundamental niche that are not available in their native range (Le Maitre et al., 2008). Methods best suited to modelling the potential distribution of an invasive species in any new region are therefore those that most directly estimate the fundamental niche. Although these will usually overestimate the final distribution of the invasive species in the invaded range, they will at least show what areas could be occupied if the species is able to spread everywhere and if biotic conditions are suitable.

A final complication in modelling invasive species is that their spread may not simply represent the expression of the fundamental niche as set by the gene pool in their native range. Instead, new conditions in the invaded range may provoke adaptive evolution (Colwell & Rangel, 2009; Huey et al., 2005). Although not a priority for this chapter, methods for exploring adaptive genetic change and predicting traits likely to be under selection pressure are relevant to invasive species and are an important topic for understanding the ecology and biogeography of invasive species (Ackerly, 2003; Alexander & Edwards, 2010).

5.4   Methods Aiming to Model and Map the Fundamental Niche: Mechanistic Models

Section 5.3 provides reasoning for preferring methods that model biological traits that are directly related to the fundamental niche of the species. I refer to these as *mechanistic models* because they focus on mechanisms or processes rather than patterns. Mechanistic models could – depending on the way the model is set up – include ecophysiological models, biophysical models, life-history models, phenological models, foraging energetic models and models based on functional traits (Buckley et al., 2010; Kearney & Porter, 2009; Morin & Lechowicz, 2008). For our purposes, the main criterion for considering a model to be mechanistic is that it attempts to capture the dominant processes contributing to survival and fecundity, and it links these processes to environmental data in a way that enables mapped predictions of the niche. These models are not fitted to species location data, and are, therefore, free from the problem that occurrence records are tied to the realised niche. Instead, they focus on the processes and physiological limits that constrain the distribution and abundance of a species.

Kearney and Porter (2009) review the potential to apply principles of biophysical ecology to modelling species distributions and include information on how to model key functional traits of a range of organisms (e.g. dry-skinned and wet-skinned ectotherms, endotherms, aquatic organisms and plants). Their software (NicheMapper; www.zoology.wisc.edu/faculty/por/por.html) is available, although it is quite complex to use and further development is underway to make it more broadly accessible (M. Kearney, personal communication, 2014). Examples of applications include Kearney and Porter (2004), Kearney et al. (2008, 2010) and Porter et al. (2002). These models require information on the morphology, physiology and behaviour of species (e.g. how endotherms balance metabolic rate and heat loss at various temperatures), and a means for translating the environment experienced by the animal to the landscape-scale geographic information system data usually available for mapping.

In related examples, Buckley et al. (2010) use three mechanistic models (a biophysical model, a life-history model and a foraging energetic model) to model a butterfly and a lizard; Morin and others (Chuine & Beaubien, 2001; Morin & Lechowicz, 2008; Morin & Thuiller, 2009) use a phenological model, Phenofit, to model trees. Phenofit focuses on the impacts of physiological stress on fitness, and on the synchronisation of developmental stages with seasonal variations in climate (Morin & Thuiller, 2009).

These authors and others (e.g. Hijmans & Graham, 2006) have compared mechanistic models with *correlative* models based on relationships between observed species locations and measured or estimated environmental conditions. These comparisons often show congruence of predictions in the regions in which the correlative model was trained, and a range of outcomes (from congruence to dissimilarity) for predictions for novel times or places (Kearney et al. 2010; Morin & Thuiller 2009). Kearney and Porter (2009) compare the likely strengths and weaknesses of mechanistic and correlative models, and Dormann et al. (2012) provide an interesting discussion of the apparent dichotomy between mechanistic and correlative models.

Mechanistic models are the subject of active research programmes, but are less frequently attempted than correlative models owing to the complexity of the models and the time it takes to gather appropriate data and fit models. It is conceptually appealing to focus on process and understand the constraints to distribution, because these will then be applicable to any geographic region or future time, providing the species does not evolve different tolerances in new environments. Despite the fact that mechanistic models are theoretically well suited to invasive species and several reviews recommend them (e.g. Buckley et al., 2010; Gallien et al., 2010; Kearney & Porter, 2009), few applications to invasive species exist (but see Elith et al. (2010) and Kearney et al. (2008) for a cane toad example). Of course, even though compatible with the modelling problem, mechanistic models will not be perfect. The most likely errors and uncertainties stem from the need to identify key processes (is there enough information to pinpoint these, and is the model sufficient to include and combine them appropriately?); parameterise the models appropriately (are relevant experimental data available? Buckley et al., 2010; Kearney & Porter, 2009); and match microclimate or laboratory measurements to the broad-scale climatic variables available for mapping. Given the time and expertise needed to fit mechanistic models, I expect them to be most useful for species of exceptional importance, or as a guide to likely distributions if generalised versions can be made available to serve as templates for sets of physiologically similar species.

5.5   Methods That Use Information on the Realised Niche

Most predictions of a species' invasion potential are based on models fitted to observed location data (Venette et al., 2010). Data from the native range (and perhaps additional records) are used to characterise and predict suitable conditions elsewhere. The commentary in this section is oriented towards key issues that arise in fitting, and predicting with, correlative models. In other words, it is more about the process of thinking about the data and the modelling problem than it is about one technique versus another. This reflects my viewpoint that the issues are critically important, and the modelling problem is one that requires careful thought.

Throughout, I will use the term *correlative models* (see Box 5.1 and Dormann et al., 2012) to refer to most of these models because they are pattern-based models that quantify the relationship between a species presence (or presence–absence or abundance) and a set of environmental covariates. That is, I use *correlation* in the broad sense of relationships between variables, in this case between a response (the species) and one or more predictors or covariates. A model that does not fall completely into this class is CLIMEX (Box 5.2), which relies on species records but has a more process-based orientation than correlative species distribution models (SDMs). The term *pest risk models* will include CLIMEX, but SDMs or correlative models will not. This is for convenience of discussion; obviously CLIMEX could also be termed an SDM. Box 5.1 provides background to the more general (and original) use of correlative models for modelling species other than invasive species and introduces the phrase *equilibrium SDM* for such applications, Box 5.2 describes CLIMEX, and Box 5.3 outlines the broad classes of correlative models. Table 5.1 summarises key references and examples of invasive species applications. If you are unfamiliar with correlative models, reading the boxes should give enough background for the following sections. Note that correlative models – sometimes with additional components to include processes of dispersal – have been used to fit and predict distributions entirely in the invaded range. These models are generally not considered here (but see Section 5.5.2) because they require specialised methods and are usually relevant only where a species has been in a country for a considerable time.

Box 5.1 The General Use of Correlative Models in Ecology

Correlative methods include a range of techniques variously referred to as species distribution models (SDMs), ecological niche models, bioclimatic envelopes, profile methods or climate matching techniques. None of these were originally designed to model invasive species. Instead, they were intended for modelling (and perhaps mapping) a species–environment relationship, but only using the current distribution of the species within the sampled geographic extent (Elith & Leathwick, 2009b). I will refer to this original use as *equilibrium SDM*, even though ecologists will recognise that use of the word *equilibrium* opens up many questions about time frame, dispersal barriers, effects of disturbance and so on (Franklin, 2010; Peterson et al., 2011). It is important to keep this history in mind when reading the SDM literature and when considering the range of methods available because the history provides context for interpreting what people have done and why they have done it. For instance, some equilibrium SDMs use geographic space rather than environmental space as the predictors of occurrence (e.g. convex hulls, kernel density estimators and kriging; Elith & Leathwick, 2009b). These might be useful where data are very sparse or where geographic space strongly determines distributions, but they are not useful for predicting the distribution of invasive species in new geographically remote areas. The more common use of environmental predictors is based on the belief that – at most scales and in most regions – environment is important in structuring distributions (Section 5.5.4).

The literature on SDMs has expanded rapidly since 2000, and tutorials, books and reviews are regularly emerging; see, for example, Austin (2002, 2007), Elith and Leathwick (2009b), Franklin (2010), Guisan and Thuiller (2005), Guisan and Zimmermann (2000); Pearson (2007), Peterson et al. (2011) and Schröder (2008). Equilibrium SDMs have been fitted for terrestrial, marine and freshwater species, and from macroecological (coarse grain, large extent) to local (fine grain, small extent) scales. Models using well-designed survey data and ecologically relevant predictor variables have produced useful insights and reliable predictions to new sites within the sampled regions (Bio et al., 2002; Leathwick & Austin, 2001; Ysebaert et al., 2002). Predictions have provided key inputs for conservation planning and resource management, identifying new sites for rare species surveys and global analyses of species distributions (Ferrier, 2002; Fleishman et al., 2001; Rangel et al., 2006; Zimmermann et al., 2007). Because equilibrium SDMs aim to predict within the range of the training data, users have tended to evaluate their performance at points within that range (e.g. using cross-validation) or by assessing whether the modelled relationships are ecologically sensible.

5.5.1 Issue 1: What Niche Can Be Characterised by These Models?

Section 5.3 discusses fundamental and realised niches, a critical issue for pest risk models. The dual concepts of environmental (niche) and geographic (biotope) space make it clear that to characterise the environmental niche well, records of species locations must be taken from regions in which the species has had opportunity to spread (geographically) to all suitable locations. Hence, it is logical to focus on places where the species is most likely to be at equilibrium (i.e. the native range).

Table 5.1. Example correlative methods for modelling species distributions

General class	Model (abbreviation)	Species data	Partial plots for effect on response	Comment	References for (a) explaining model and (b) invasive application
Expert model	Habitat suitability index (HSI)	Expert	Yes	Use expert knowledge for shape of species response	(a) Burgman et al. (2001) (b) Inglis et al. (2006)
Expert model	Expert	Expert / presence	No	Use expert knowledge to select variables and perhaps to inform about presence	(a, b) Rodda et al. (2009)
Climate envelope	BIOCLIM	Presence	No	Delimits climate envelope using only presence data, sometimes using percentiles; prediction from most extreme (limiting) variable	(a) Busby (1991) (b) Booth et al. (1988)
Machine learning	One-class support vector machines	Presence	No	Few uses, but being included in some ensembles	(a) Hastie et al. (2009) (b) Drake & Bossenbroek (2009); Guo et al. (2005)
Factor analysis	Ecological niche factor analysis (ENFA)	Presence-background	No	Also known as Biomapper	(a) Hirzel et al. (2002) (b) Steiner et al. (2008)
Machine learning	Genetic algorithm for ruleset production (GARP)	Presence-background	No	Widely used; final model is an average over best selected rules	(a, b) Peterson (2003)
Machine Learning	Maximum entropy (MaxEnt)	Presence-background	Yes	Widely used; complexity of model can be adjusted by choice of features and adjusting regularisation	(a) Elith et al. (2011); Phillips et al. (2006) (b) Rodda et al. (2011)
Regression	Generalised linear models (GLMs) or generalised additive models (GAMs)	Various	Yes	Statistical regression methods; generalised additive models allow smoothed data-driven functions	(a) Hastie et al. (2009) (b) Mellert et al. (2011)

Regression	Non-parametric multiplicative regression	Various	Yes	Implemented in Hyperniche; only found invasive examples use invaded range data	(a) McCune (2006); (b) Reusser & Lee (2008)
Machine Learning	Decision tree	Various	Yes	Also known as classification and regression trees; more often used for decision analysis (e.g. on whether species will become invasive or not)	(a) De'ath & Fabricius (2000); Hastie et al. (2009); (b) Václavík & Meentemeyer 2009 (only in invasive range)
Machine Learning	Ensembles of trees: boosted regression trees (BRT), or random forests (RF)	Various	Some	Most invasive species examples are within ensembles; automatically model interactions unless stumps used	(a) Hastie et al. (2009); (b) Broennimann et al. 2007
Machine Learning	Artificial neural nets	Various	Some	One of the earliest machine learning methods to be used in species modelling; regarded as a good general purpose algorithm	(a) Hastie et al. (2009); (b) Gevrey and Worner (2006)
Ensembles	Ensembles of any type of models	Not applicable	No	Several examples emerging, with varied approaches for selecting the component models	(a) Thuiller (2003); (b) Broennimann et al. (2007); Stohlgren et al. (2010)

It is not possible to make a definitive statement about exactly what niche is being modelled by equilibrium SDMs (Box 5.1), but it is most closely related to the realised niche (Austin, 2002; Austin et al., 1990; Colwell & Rangel, 2009; Jiménez-Valverde et al., 2008; Soberon & Nakamura, 2009). The species data, choice of predictor variables and modelling method all affect the outcome. For instance, imagine being fortunate enough to have a large, comprehensive and unbiased sample of the abundance of a species across its whole range. From these data, one might expect to model the realised niche successfully. However, if the available predictor variables fail to represent some important dimension of the niche (e.g. soil phosphorus for plants needing high levels of phosphorus) or the modelling method is incapable of fitting the shape of the true relationship, then the niche will be imperfectly modelled. The aim, therefore, in fitting an SDM for an invasive species is to do as much as possible to characterise the realised niche well (excluding sink populations), and beyond that, to move towards approximating the fundamental niche. An early application of this idea (Booth et al., 1988) expanded the native range climatic profile for 13 eucalypt species using forestry trial plot results from Africa, intending to characterise better the fundamental niche to inform successful tree introductions for plantations. Sections 5.5.2 to 5.5.7 include discussion on how species records, predictors, the model and the prediction extent all affect how accurately the realised niche is modelled, and resulting implications for prediction of invasive potential.

Similar issues apply to CLIMEX (Box 5.2) because the model is often primarily fitted using location data. The CLIMEX predicted distribution may be closer to the realised niche than the fundamental niche, depending on the extent to which the dispersal of the species has been limited and on the amount of additional physiological data (Lawson et al., 2010). Physiological data, if reliable and if successfully rescaled to be consistent with the predictor information, should allow the prediction to edge closer to the fundamental niche (Box 5.2).

For predicting potential distributions of invasive species, one drawback of being tied to observation records is that biotic interactions affect the outcome: the realised niche in the native range is usually affected by pathogens, pests, competitors and predators. In some instances, invasive species have shown evidence of release from inhibiting biotic factors, and models from the native ranges where biotic interactions were important but unquantified have not been good predictors of distributions in the invaded range (Le Maitre et al., 2008). This is an inherent weakness of models based on the realised niche. Biotic interactions are notoriously difficult to include as predictors because their effects are almost always confounded with the effects of other covariates (Leathwick & Austin, 2001). Researchers often assume that biotic interactions vary enough across the species range that a reasonably sized sample will smooth over local biotic effects. This will apply only sometimes, and the use of these models for predicting other than the realised niche is problematic. Solutions may not exist, but one way to counteract this problem is to collate available knowledge on the impact of biotic interactions on the native range of a species and use that as a guide to likely errors in predicted distributions. Further, recent progress in methods for modelling species co-occurrences (Ovaskainen et al., 2010; Pollock et al., 2014) can provide strong inference about likely interspecific effects. However, SDMs for species without significant pathogens, pests and competitors are likely to be the most accurate.

Box 5.2 CLIMEX

CLIMEX is a commercially available modelling method that was first published in the 1980s and has now been applied to many species and adopted worldwide in various agencies and governmental departments (Sutherst, 2003; Sutherst & Maywald, 1985). It was specifically developed for modelling invasive species. The primary output is a mapped prediction of the favourability of a set or grid of locations for a given species. The model also produces a suite of information to allow further understanding of species response to climate. CLIMEX requires location records of a species in its native range, and uses these with climate data and other optional relevant information (locations of persistent populations in invaded regions, relative abundance, seasonal phenology and laboratory data) to infer a species' climatic requirements. The model is based on population process concepts of how a species responds to environment, and attempts to characterise growth and stress responses to weekly climatic conditions. The version current at time of writing (version 3; Sutherst et al., 2007) of CLIMEX includes six growth indices (temperature, moisture, light, radiation, substrate and diapause/dormancy) over which a seventh index, biotic interactions, can be used as a multiplier. There are up to eight stress indices based on temperature and moisture (heat, cold, dry, wet and their interactions, e.g. hot and dry) plus two constraints to persistence that can be imposed over all others: length of growing season and obligate diapause/dormancy/vernalisation. The indices and constraints aim to cover the major mechanisms by which terrestrial species respond to their environments.

The model is conceptualised as providing two main seasons for the species: one for population growth and one for population survival. This is directly relevant to invasive species because new geographical regions can be determined as holding suitable environments for population persistence or population growth, the latter most related to pest status. In fitting the model, decisions are required about which indices or constraints are relevant to the species, and how to estimate their parameters. Growth indices relate to seasonal population growth and mostly require four parameters to be set (see inset graph in which parameters are T0 to T3). Stress indices are defined by a threshold value and an accumulation rate, and stress is assumed to accumulate exponentially with time. Parameters are often set by starting with template values and then iteratively altering them and assessing the effects of the changes on predicted distributions, usually by comparing with known locations in the native, and perhaps invaded, ranges (Section 5.5.2; Kriticos et al., 2011; Sutherst, 2003; Sutherst & Maywald, 1985).

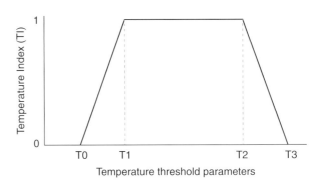

Example of a growth index based on temperature.

Experimental results or expert knowledge can be used to set parameters; these may require subjective adjustment so that they are directly relevant to the long-term averaged climate data (Section 5.5.4) used in the model. Underpinning the model with as many experimentally derived parameters as possible lowers the reliance on location data and should ultimately produce a more biologically relevant model, provided the experimental data are correct and relevant to field conditions.

Final mapped values include the annual average esoclimatic index (Eqs. 5.1 and 5.2) and annual average growth index (Eqs. 5.1 and 5.2). The model is estimated using weekly data so that seasonal variation in suitability can be inferred. This can be a major advantage over applications of correlative models that do not include seasonality predictors. Variation in climatic suitability across years can also be explored through the use of yearly rather than long-term averaged data and based on the assumption that these yearly variations are meaningful to the species. The components of the final indices are multiplicative (Eqs. 5.1 and 5.2), meaning that a low value for any will result in a low prediction. Each component index is scaled from 0 to 1, meaning that each included component contributes equally to the outcome.

The weekly growth index is

$$\boxed{GI_W = TI_W \times MI_W \times RI_W \times SV_W \times LI_W \times DI_W}$$ (5.1)

where the indices on the right side are weekly temperature, moisture, radiation, substrate, light and diapause indices, respectively.

The esoclimatic index is

$$\boxed{EI = GI_A \times SI \times SX}$$ (5.2)

where GI_A is the annual growth index (mean of GI_W), SI is the annual stress index (comprising multiplicative cold, dry, heat and wet stresses) and SX is the annual stress interaction index (comprising multiplicative cold–dry, cold–wet, hot–dry and hot–wet stresses).

Authors refer to this as a process-oriented or mechanistic model (e.g. Kriticos & Leriche, 2010) because (1) the model components consider environmental impacts on the species in a growth and stress framework, similar to process-based population models; and (2) growth and stress are calculated for weekly time steps across the year, mimicking population responses. However, the common use of species data to help fit CLIMEX models creates a clear distinction from the mechanistic models described in Section 5.4.

The strengths of CLIMEX for prediction of potential distributions are that it provides a coherent framework for including a range of information (expert knowledge, laboratory data, geographic locations and records of relative abundance) and simple tools for exploring the effect of competitors and mutualists on species distributions. Its authors have emphasised the importance of understanding both the ecology of the species and the frailty of the data, and they have invested time and effort into explaining the model and correcting poor applications. The component indices (e.g. figure above) are restricted to being relatively simple and are constructed so they must define physiological limits, meaning that they should predict sensibly outside their ranges. Nevertheless, if the model is used to predict to novel climates and if species locations are the only available data, the model will be uninformed about the species' response in the novel climates, as for other SDMs (Section 5.5.5).

The structure and assumptions of CLIMEX bring limitations for pest risk mapping, as do those of any model. As explained in Section 5.5, reliance on location data has consequences for the modelled niche (Section 5.5.1) and for sensitivity to sample size (Section 5.5.2). The model structure might be incorrect for some species; responses might be more complex or smoother than the programmed piecewise linear model and growth and stress might not comprise multiplicative responses to variables that are equally weighted. The model focuses mainly on climate, and inference will be limited (particularly for species with few presence records) if other abiotic variables, biotic interactions, dispersal limitations and disturbances also have an impact on presence records.

While CLIMEX has been widely applied, many modellers choose alternative methods of analysis. Their reasons may include (1) corporate ownership of CLIMEX influencing cost and willingness of public data modellers to use it; (2) limitation to one software implementation that restricts innovations by users, programmable links to other commonly used software (e.g. R) and use of batch files for sensitivity analyses; (3) a perception that the coarse gridded output provides less useful spatial detail than that attainable from SDMs applied to finer scale data (this may well be a false impression, depending on the quality of input data, and it is also a historic problem because finer grain data are now available; Kriticos et al., 2012); (4) temporal extent: the existing climate data packaged with the program spans from 1961 to 1990 and this may not be relevant to recent invasions; and (5) possibly an aversion to methods that appear to require more research and perhaps more subjective decisions.

Box 5.3 Overview of Modelling Methods for Correlative Species Distribution Models

A plethora of methods exist for modelling equilibrium species distributions, and a growing body of reviews and texts describes and compares them (Elith & Leathwick, 2009a, 2009b; Franklin, 2010; Guisan & Zimmermann 2000; Peterson et al., 2011; Renner et al. 2015; Thuiller et al., 2008; Zimmermann, 2000). Table 5.1 provides examples of several techniques with key references and invasive species mapping examples. Free versions for all of the tabled methods are available. Here, I will simply give an overview of the main categories of models and the important differences affecting their use for invasive species modelling.

One set of methods (the true presence-only methods) models environments at presence locations, making no comparison with the range of environments in the broader landscape or at absence sites. Envelope methods are one example. These define the hyper-rectangle that bounds species records in multidimensional environmental space, in some cases dealing with relative frequencies of records (e.g. by quantifying percentiles of the distribution). Variables can be weighted equally or unequally, or the response to the most limiting variable can be used for prediction (as in BIOCLIM; Nix, 1986). Related techniques (Franklin, 2010) use distance metrics, such as the Gower metric or Mahalanobis distance, to predict the environmental similarity between records of occurrence and all unvisited sites. A modern machine learning method, the one-class support vector machine, has also been applied to modelling invasive species (Drake & Bossenbroek, 2009; Guo et al., 2005). This focuses on finding boundaries that optimally separate occupied environments from all others.

Conceptually, the appeal of this group of methods is that it deals directly with the most common type of data available – presence-only records – and requires none of the additional decisions or assumptions about relevant regions, samples in place of absences and so forth that other techniques require. This group is dependent on a representative sample of presence locations (as are others), and is adversely affected by bias in the records (e.g. towards urban centres; Aikio et al., 2010) because there is generally no information on what has been sampled. Presence-only methods suffer from the problem that they cannot distinguish between landscape availability of environments and habitat suitability, because they include no analysis of available conditions. Presence-only methods are also subject to the usual problems of chance correlations with irrelevant predictors. Some techniques are somewhat biologically unrealistic (e.g. those that equally weight variables). Nevertheless, some are currently preferred in biosecurity because they are relatively simple to use and interpret.

All other methods require comparison of presence points with some other class. Some methods were developed especially for modelling equilibrium distributions based on presence-only data (e.g. ENFA, GARP and MaxEnt, Table 5.1).

Others are techniques were designed for modelling binomial (i.e. two-class) data (or in some cases counts or continuous responses) which can be adapted in various ways if used with presence-only species records. Examples include regression and classification methods such as generalised linear models and generalised additive models, decision trees, ensembles of trees including boosted regression trees and random forests. Artificial neural networks are also used. Details of how these methods work are varied and best left to dedicated publications (Table 5.1). All are fitted to species records and environmental data. Many rely on additive terms within the model (e.g. generalised linear models, generalised additive models, boosted regression trees and MaxEnt), which means that even if conditions are suboptimal according to one variable, another can compensate. In contrast, non-parametric multiplicative regression (Table 5.1) is based on multiplicative terms and is therefore more like CLIMEX (Box 5.2) in model structure. Many are capable of modelling interactions between variables (i.e. the response to one variable depends on the value of another). Common applications of several (e.g. generalised linear models and generalised additive models) tend to ignore this capacity, whereas others (e.g. boosted regression trees, random forests and MaxEnt) allow it by default.

Comparisons of methods show that for modelling species at equilibrium, the methods vary in their abilities to retrieve known responses and predict within the training range of the data (Elith & Graham, 2009; Elith et al., 2006; Heikennen et al., 2007; Moisen & Frescino, 2002). For instance, MaxEnt, tree ensembles and regression methods flexible enough to fit ecologically plausible relationships tend to perform well. Comparisons for invasive species modelling are more difficult because the truth about the potential distribution in the invaded range is unknown. There seems to be a general opinion emerging that smoother models (ones less tightly fitted to the known records) are more likely to predict well, because they do not focus on details of the sampled distribution that might result from survey biases, local responses to biota and so on. Smoother models can be fitted for methods capable of highly complex fits by limiting degrees of freedom and model complexity (e.g. Elith et al., 2010; Falk & Mellert, 2011; Merow et al., 2014). I do not think there is enough information yet to make strong conclusions about this idea, although the reasoning seems logical. Studies with artificial species would be useful but are rare.

More generally, in my opinion, a good approach for choosing a particular method is to consider information on its known performance, theoretical aspects of how it works and technical details, including whether its settings can be easily altered and explored and whether it will run well with the types and amounts of data likely to be used. Understanding how a method works, and the implications of default or selected settings, is particularly important for invasive species. Further comments on correlative models, particularly the challenges in using them for pest risk mapping, are included in the discussion of important issues (Sections 5.5.1 to 5.5.7).

5.5.2   Issue 2: How Species Records Affect the Predicted Distribution

All pest risk mapping methods benefit from accurate records across the full native range of the species. This will be universally true because the aim is to characterise all environments in which the species can persist. *Accurate* includes both locational accuracy and taxonomic accuracy. Locational accuracy refers to whether the co-ordinates properly represent the sample to a precision relevant to the grain of the environmental data, while taxonomic accuracy refers to whether the record is truly for the species of interest (Anderson, 2012; Elith & Leathwick, 2009a Elith et al., 2013; Funk & Richardson, 2002; Hortal et al., 2008; Reddy & Davalos, 2003; Robertson et al., 2010; Schulman et al., 2007). Record date is also important to accuracy because the record needs to be relevant to the temporal range covered by the available predictors.

Number of records, and their frequency in both environmental and geographic space, has varying importance depending on the modelling method. For instance, CLIMEX can be affected by the number of records, depending on the amount of physiological data available. Without physiological data, CLIMEX requires at least one record in each of the important combinations of environmental conditions (the axes of the environmental space defined by the predictors) inhabited by the species (Lawson et al., 2010). Geographic proximity of records is unimportant in CLIMEX, and having more than one record in a given environmental combination does not help model fitting, except to confirm that the conditions are suitable. Having few records most limits the number of parameters that can be meaningfully fitted in CLIMEX when the records are from locations with similar climates. In these cases, some indices have to remain undefined, or a range of values fitted and their effects on the outcome evaluated (van Klinken et al., 2009).

Similar limitations apply to correlative SDMs because response data (in this case, species records) are needed to fit model parameters, and having few records limits how many parameters can be fitted, that is, they limit the complexity of the model (in regression, this concept is called events per variable; Harrell Jr, 2006). Further, most correlative SDM methods use the relative frequency of records in different environments to determine relative suitability and sample bias will affect them. This problem is particularly severe for presence-only data (i.e. records of presence that are unaccompanied by records of absence) because there is no information on survey effort, including where the species was not found (Phillips et al., 2009). A model may reflect biases in survey effort more than the distribution of the species. There appears to be little research targeted at defining typical biases for invasive species records (e.g. if collectors tend to record presences in unexpected environments rather than randomly), although in the equilibrium SDM literature, research on quantifying biases and methods for dealing with them in models is gradually emerging (e.g. Dorazio, 2014; Fithian et al., 2014; Hortal et al., 2008; Phillips et al., 2009; Warton et al., 2013). There are some examples for invasive species (Wolmarans et al., 2010; Wu et al., 2005), but the topic needs ongoing attention. Even if the records are a random sample of the species distribution, distance between records should be checked. Correlative SDMs assume that each record is an independent sample, which is untrue for records in very close proximity (Legendre, 1993). Methods for examining spatial autocorrelation in model residuals are useful for diagnosing problems (Bio et al., 2002; Dormann et al., 2007; Rangel et al., 2006). All of these issues imply that data need to be carefully screened before use. This is particularly important when using data from online databases because errors and duplication of records are extremely common (Graham et al., 2004; Robertson et al., 2010).

The type of data (e.g. presence-only, presence–absence or abundance) is also important. Presence-only data are most often used in invasive species SDMs because they are the most common type available and efforts at digitising and correcting them are active and ongoing (Graham et al., 2004; and see sources for data in Herborg et al., 2009; Woodbury & Weinstein, 2008). Rapidly developing technologies offer intriguing possibilities for gathering and storing data (including citizen science projects and the use of mobile phones to capture images and upload data). However, there are many reasons for preferring presence–absence data for correlative modelling because they provide information on what has been surveyed (see Section 5.5.3). Abundance data would be even more useful for invasive species if they indicated the relative fitness of the species across a landscape (e.g. Hooten et al., 2007; Olfert et al., 2006; van Klinken et al., 2009), but only if such relationships were similar in invaded ranges. Several SDM methods can use, or at least be informed by, abundance data. These include CLIMEX and generalised regression methods that can model count data (e.g. Poisson regression; Fithian & Hastie, 2013; Potts & Elith, 2006). For invasive species, presence–absence and abundance data will only be reliable in regions that have been occupied long enough for the species to have had opportunity to persist (and reach stable population states in the case of abundance data) or to die out. Because the aim is to characterise suitable conditions as comprehensively as possible (Section 5.5.1), it is worth gathering all reliable records that are available (i.e. from multiple sources and surveys, but without creating duplicates). Combining data across different surveys does create some difficulties because differing survey efforts will result in differing densities of presence records, but methods are starting to emerge (Fithian & Hastie, 2013; Fithian et al., 2015; Hulme & Weser, 2011).

A final consideration is whether to restrict the model to one based on native range data or include records from the invaded range. The use of presence or abundance records from the invaded range is a two-edged sword. The advantage is that records from the invaded range are likely to expand the representation of environments and biota (Jiménez-Valverde et al., 2011) and can potentially edge the modelled niche towards the fundamental niche. This is the logic in using records from the invaded range in CLIMEX (e.g. van Klinken et al., 2009), and they can also be useful for strict presence-only (one-class) methods (e.g. Booth et al., 1988), although the lack of equilibrium in the invaded range brings difficulties for interpreting relative frequencies of occurrence in places with active invasion fronts. For two-class methods (Box 5.3), the use of records from the invaded range creates additional conceptual problems in relation to how to set the non-positive case (see Section 5.5.3) and how to make a composite dataset that reflects consistent survey effort. Several studies support the use of some invaded range data (e.g. Broennimann & Guisan, 2008). In the extreme (i.e. the majority of data from invaded ranges) the lack of equilibrium in that the invaded range is certain to cause problems for correlative models unless sophisticated models are used to adjust for variation in propagule pressure and the geographic (spatial) processes of spread (Cook et al., 2007; Elith et al., 2010; Rouget & Richardson, 2003; Williams et al., 2008). All of these problems relating to lack of equilibrium in the invaded range stem from violation of the basic assumption of SDMs (Franklin, 2010), that records are sufficiently well structured to give information on the environments suitable for the species. A species that is spreading will have records that mix environmental preferences with spatial dispersal limitations, and the effects are difficult to untangle.

5.5.3   Issue 3: The Different Views of Background Records, Pseudo-absences and Absences

As discussed in Box 5.3, many of the correlative SDM methods applied to presence-only data compare the presence records (the positive case) with another case (note: see Table 5.1 for method abbreviations used hereafter). This approach is used for equilibrium SDMs based on natural history collections (e.g. museums, herbaria, online data portals; Graham et al., 2004) and for quantifying resource use by animals within available areas (Manly, 2002). The meaning of the non-positive case varies in subtle but important ways. For some methods and interpretations, non-positive is taken to mean background, landscape or available locations – conditions that can be characterised independently of where the species is present. That interpretation applies to ENFA and MaxEnt and increasing evidence shows it to be the best approach for modelling presence-only data with logistic regression. Presence–background enables a coherent view of how to use regression models for such data (Fithian & Hastie, 2013; Keating & Cherry, 2004; Phillips et al., 2009; Phillips & Elith, 2011; Renner et al. 2015; Ward et al., 2009). So far, most uses of regression (e.g. generalised linear models, generalised additive models and boosted regression trees) with presence-only or background data use naïve models. These do not specifically deal with the problems of presence-only or background data (e.g. that the background points might have a presence at or near them) and do not attempt to model the actual probability of presence because prevalence is unknown (e.g. Elith et al., 2006). Although these appear to work reasonably well in some cases, they are not ideal, and current statistical research unifying ideas of density estimation, inhomogeneous Poisson point process models, logistic regression and MaxEnt (Renner et al. 2015) show how to best treat presence–background data in SDMs.

Other viewpoints treat the non-positive case as absence or pseudo-absence. The term *pseudo-absence* is used interchangeably in the literature to refer to either background or implied absence, but here it will mean implied absence. Methods that avoid presence records in sampling pseudo-absences implicitly accept this second view of the data. These include GARP and some uses of regression. For regression, pseudo-absences are placed either anywhere except where presences occur or outside a geographic or environmental buffer around presence records. For instance, Engler et al. (2004) used one model to discover areas with low predicted probability of presence and then sampled these to use as pseudo-absences in regression. The species modelling literature (for both equilibrium and invasive species) includes several suggestions about how to establish sensible locations for pseudo-absences or to define reliable absences in the absence of surveyed absences (Le Maitre et al., 2008; Lobo et al., 2010), and new papers with new suggestions keep emerging. However, the background viewpoint requires fewer ad hoc decisions about both position and number of background or pseudo-absence samples, and allows a more rigorous statistical framework (Renner et al. 2015).

Across both of these interpretations, correlative models require decisions about the extent (i.e. the landscape area) to be sampled for background or pseudo-absence points. Users of GARP and MaxEnt have not always understood the importance of this decision, failing to recognise that the model samples the background from any region with data in the gridded predictor variables supplied by the user. So, for instance, if global maps are used without masks for a species whose native range is within South America, the background will be sampled from the whole world. This implies that the species has had the opportunity to reach anywhere and occurs only in South America (Figure 5.2). Unlimited dispersal opportunity is uncommon. Instead, background extent should be restricted to a region that could reasonably be assumed to have been available to the species (Barve et al., 2011; Elith et al., 2011).

True absence data (through comprehensive survey) are relatively rare, but bring several advantages. For instance, absence data provide information on what has been surveyed, and overcome many problems in survey bias. For invasive species modelling, absence data are likely to be useful only in the native range, unless there is clear evidence in the invaded range that the species has had sufficient time and opportunity to spread to, and persist in, surveyed areas, or unless specialised models are used (e.g. Václavík & Meentemeyer, 2009). There has been some discussion of the disadvantages of absence data in the correlative distribution modelling literature, although to my mind, this is overstated. Biotic interactions, dispersal constraints and disturbances affect the distribution of absences (e.g., Jiménez-Valverde et al., 2008), but presence records will be affected similarly, so these impacts should not be used to argue against using absence data (Elith et al., 2011). Presence–absence records are valuable and worth collecting because they remove the need to assume random surveys or deal with survey bias. The important problem with survey-based absence records stems from imperfect detection (i.e. false-negative records; Hirzel & Le Lay, 2008; Jiménez-Valverde et al., 2008), but there are now a number of methods available for dealing with imperfect detection in correlative SDMs (e.g. Eraud et al., 2007; Hooten et al., 2007; Wintle et al., 2004). Data need to be used at a grain (spatial resolution) relevant to the species and application, and fine-scale absences may not be informative (e.g. Falk & Mellert, 2011). CLIMEX does not formally use absence data, although information on absence is required or assumed in fitting

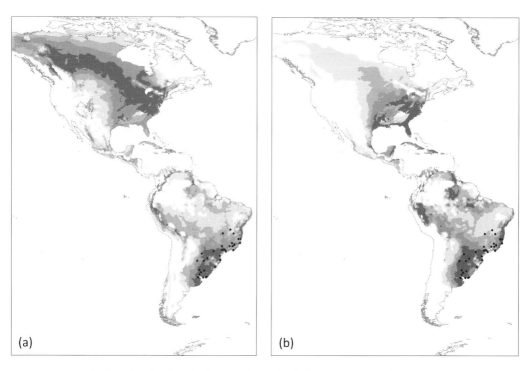

Figure 5.2. Predictions for the distribution of a hypothetical species located in South America (black dots) using **(a)** background of South America and **(b)** background of the whole world. Predictions were obtained from MaxEnt with linear and quadratic features and five candidate predictors (aridity, humidity, mean temperature of the wettest quarter, highest monthly temperature and minimum monthly precipitation). Shading show the logistic output predictions: darkest is high (1.0 to 0.8) and pale grey is low (0.2 to 0.05).

stress indices (which bound the geographic distribution). In the face of considerable uncertainty about absence, the effect of various assumptions could be explored in sensitivity analyses of the parameters limiting the stress indices.

What this all means for invasive species modelling is that users need to be aware of the assumptions of their method and the requirements for background or absence data. Concepts of the niche and accessible environments are important (Section 5.3). I expect it will take some time to come to a coherent view of the best way to treat these data in correlative methods, so users need to stay abreast of developments.

5.5.4   Issue 4: Choice of Predictor Variables

SDMs for invasive species usually focus on climatic variables. This is partly because climate dominates distributions at the global scale (see discussion of scale in Elith & Leathwick, 2009b) and partly because the only globally coherent terrestrial datasets to date have been climate based, usually long-term averaged data (for examples and sources see Franklin, 2010; Herborg et al., 2009; Woodbury & Weinstein, 2008). However, a broader range of data is becoming available. For terrestrial species, data for soils, topography and measures of climate variability and climate close to the ground are being prepared globally, some at fine resolution (B. McGill & R. Guralnick, personal communication, 2012; Kearney et al. 2014), and coarse resolution marine datasets are now available with a suite of useful predictors (e.g. Tyberghein et al., 2012). Methods are also developed for modelling river networks and summarising environmental conditions throughout the network while taking connectivity into account (Leathwick et al., 2008), although global rivers databases suitable for modelling are currently unavailable. Within the next 10 years, it is reasonable to expect substantial improvements in the quality and quantity of globally complete and biologically relevant predictors for both marine and terrestrial ecosystems. Additional predictors will provide more opportunity to select scales relevant to the modelling problem and use predictors most directly relevant to the species of interest. I expect that predictors that characterise climate extremes and variability and climate close to the ground will be particularly useful for modelling invasive species because they characterise processes and impacts important to species' persistence (e.g. Zimmermann et al., 2009).

This issue of selecting ecologically relevant predictors for correlative models is particularly important for modelling invasive species, and is also discussed in the equilibrium SDM literature. Two viewpoints are evident. The first is that intelligent prior selection of predictors, informed by existing knowledge and theory, will create the firmest foundation for a useful model (Austin & Van Niel, 2011; MacNally, 2000). Mellert et al. (2011) call this hypothesis-driven modelling. Austin (2002) argues strongly for the use of proximal predictors that are functionally relevant and best represent the resources and direct gradients that influence species. Distal predictors – such as elevation or ocean depth – rarely affect species distributions directly, but instead do so indirectly through their relationships with proximal predictors such as temperature. The problem with using distal predictors is that they are relevant to the species only through their correlations with proximal predictors, and these correlations tend to change across landscapes and continents. A model fit in one region cannot be guaranteed to predict reliably in another region that has different correlations between variables (Dormann et al., 2013; Elith et al., 2010; Jiménez-Valverde et al., 2011). The concept of choosing ecologically relevant predictors merges with the thinking behind mechanistic models, and some have discussed the possibility of using mechanistic models to provide physiologically informed predictors for correlative models (Elith et al., 2010; Kearney et al., 2010; Morin & Thuiller, 2009).

The alternative view, that a model should be given the full suite of available predictors so that it can discover the most relevant, is common in data mining and machine learning. Analyses using machine learning methods and hundreds or thousands of predictors have had impressive results in some fields of data analysis, but their success relies on large and unbiased samples of the measured response, and these are rarely available for invasive species.

There are many examples of careful selection of variables for invasive species modelling (e.g. Drake & Bossenbroek, 2009; Rodda et al., 2011; Thuiller et al., 2005). It is also not hard to find examples of the alternative approach – the most common being the use of all 19 temperature and rainfall variables from the Worldclim dataset (Hijmans et al., 2005). So far, there is limited critique in the literature of the effect of these choices, and very few studies include sensitivity analyses of the effect of these choices on model predictions. However, examples are emerging (Le Maitre et al., 2008; Peterson & Nakazawa, 2008; Rodda et al., 2011; Rödder & Lötters, 2010) that confirm the importance of informed selection of directly relevant variables. It is hard to test whether proximal variables can be reliably identified from an available set either by expert knowledge or by modelling, and this needs further exploration. Once a candidate set of variables is selected, iteration between model fitting and evaluation (Sections 5.5.6 and 5.5.7) might suggest the need for changes to the set of candidate variables (e.g. Falk & Mellert, 2011).

Issues of variable selection from extensive geographic information system datasets are not relevant to most CLIMEX analyses (Box 5.2) because the supplied data are limited to a selection of variables available at the time of development and deemed relevant by the authors. These are long-term averaged terrestrial climate data (temperature, rainfall and humidity) that are either site based (corresponding to approx. 3,000 meteorological stations worldwide) or gridded at 0.5 degree (approx. 50 km). Additional data can be added by users, and finer resolution gridded data are now available for use within CLIMEX (Kriticos & Leriche, 2010; Kriticos et al., 2012).

5.5.5   Issue 5: Novel Environments

In many cases, models fitted to native range data will be predicting into novel environments. This is true for all methods because it is related to the data used to fit the models. The general problem of using correlative models to predict to new geographic regions is often termed *transferability*; when this involves prediction to new environments, *extrapolation* is occurring. Here, the interplay between geographic and environmental space comes to the fore: new geographic regions need not, but often do, harbour new environments.

Protocols have been suggested for dealing with novel environments in CLIMEX. Where predictor values are very different in the invaded range from those for which data are available, it is recommended that parameters for the relevant indices are either not set or a range of likely options examined (van Klinken et al., 2009). Much of the early correlative SDM literature on transferability of models either failed to determine whether novel environments occur or used methods for identifying novelty (such as simple data summaries or principal component analyses) that – although useful – weren't spatially mapped (e.g. Randin et al., 2006). This makes the results of these studies difficult to interpret. Mapping novel environments (Elith et al., 2010; Mesgaran et al., 2014; Williams et al., 2007) helps interpretation of model output and guides users as to where predictions may be highly unreliable.

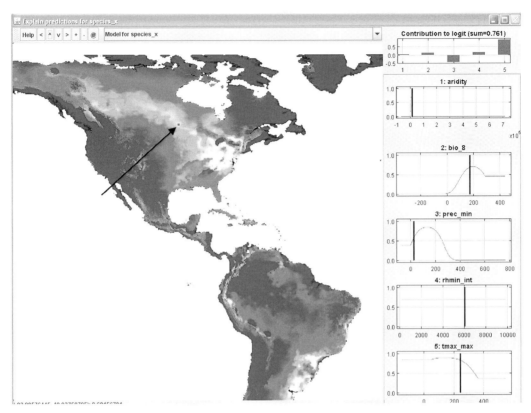

Figure 5.3.   Example of a tool for exploring components of predictions for the species modelled in Figure 5.2. The right pane shows components of the prediction (top panel) and partial plots for each predictor; vertical bold lines show the conditions at the location indicated by the arrow. This is from an interactive map produced by MaxEnt (Elith et al. 2010).

Novel environments can occur either because the climates in the invaded range are outside the ranges of the training data as assessed on a univariate basis, or they can occur because new combinations emerge, implying changed correlations between variables. If environments are outside the bounds of the data (whether in univariate or multivariate space), knowledge of how the model extrapolates is essential (see column on partial plots in Table 5.1). That is, outside the range of the training data, what trend does the fitted function follow? It is surprising that there has been so little attention to this in the SDM literature for invasive species, although perhaps that reflects the complexity of the topic. Models are usually fitted over multiple predictors, and the only simple way to assess extrapolation is to view partial response plots and the like (i.e. one variable at a time, where the response over the others is held at some constant value; e.g. Figure 5.3, right column). Although useful, this approach does not provide a complete picture. For models including interactions (e.g. models based on decision trees, or regression models with interaction terms), understanding how the model predicts in multidimensional environmental space is important (Zurell et al., 2012).

The main concern is that using a correlative model to extrapolate beyond the range of the training data is using it outside the realm of safe practice. The models have not been developed for this problem, and methods have not been developed for controlling the models appropriately. Research is only now starting to emerge in which models have been carefully controlled through choice of predictors, limiting degrees of freedom in transformations of predictors and controlling the edges of fitted functions (e.g. by weighting data; Mellert et al., 2011). I envisage future research on how to fit models that predict well in likely directions of change, how to identify novel environments (including substantially changed correlation structures) and how to control model behaviour to predict in ecologically realistic ways. Simulated data can be useful for exploring how models extrapolate (Fensterer, 2010). Modelling methods that have no facility for visualising fitted functions (Table 5.1) are failing to report vital information, and methods where fitted functions can be controlled (e.g. specialised splines in regression models) will be more easily extended for this application. CLIMEX (Box 5.2) and NAPPFAST (Magarey et al., 2007) were specifically developed for invasive species and have functions that are more likely to be appropriately controlled (depending on how well the model is developed). There is no reason why correlative models could not also be developed to use prior information from experts or experiments to control how the model extrapolates.

5.5.6   Issue 6: Evaluating Predictions

SDMs for species at equilibrium can be evaluated in various ways, for instance, by assessing variable importance and fitted functions and deciding whether the model is consistent with ecological knowledge about the species (Elith & Leathwick, 2009a, 2009b), by exploring the patterns in residuals and by testing predictive performance, ideally at independent sites not used in model training. Emphasis is usually on the last, and statistical summaries including area under the receiver operating characteristic curve, kappa and explained deviance are generally given precedence (Fielding & Bell, 1997; Franklin, 2010; Pearce & Ferrier, 2000).

Some of these methods (particularly the site-based statistical summaries) have been carried over from equilibrium SDM research into invasive species modelling, but they are often not particularly appropriate (Jiménez-Valverde et al., 2011). The aim of model evaluation should be to test whether the model is appropriate for its intended application (Rykiel, 1996). Because prediction in the native range is not the aim, the fact that a model can do this successfully is reassuring but not ultimately a strong test. The problem is clear: the potential distribution in the invaded range is unknown and test data are not available. The main question is whether the model fitted in the native range is relevant to the invaded range. Distributional data in the invaded range are unlikely to provide a reliable test of model performance because the species is likely to be invading; presences may not indicate persistence and absences will be unreliable. More attention should be given to the problem of evaluation, including how to simulate data that is useful for model testing (Austin et al., 2006; Fensterer, 2010). Models need to be assessed for their ecological relevance: by using expert knowledge, by sourcing additional data including physiological information or by comparison with completely independent models that do not use distributional records. Evaluation could also address questions about the sensitivity of the model to choices made in the modelling process (see Section 5.5.7). Methods for perturbing or resampling data that tested model behaviour in environments most common in the invaded range might also be useful. Because the problem of predicting potential invasive distribution is – from a modelling viewpoint – quite similar to the problem of predicting changes in distribution with climate change, progress on evaluation methods in that arena is likely to be transferable to invasive species (for an interesting example, see Falk & Mellert, 2011).

5.5.7   Issue 7: Dealing with Uncertainty

This section relies on a mix of information from equilibrium SDMs and invasive species applications (including models of spread in invaded ranges) because most pest risk mapping examples focus on only one component of uncertainty. Uncertainty in predictions emanates from multiple sources, including those discussed in Sections 5.5.2 to 5.5.4, and choice of modelling method and its settings (Box 5.3, Table 5.1). While there have been a number of theoretical treatments and reviews of sources of uncertainty in correlative equilibrium SDMs and related fields (Ascough et al., 2008; Barry & Elith, 2006; Elith et al., 2002; Kangas & Kangas, 2004; Leyk et al., 2005; Rocchini et al., 2011), relatively little has been done in practice to characterise the effect of likely uncertainties on modelled predictions (but see Dormann et al., 2008; Elith et al., 2013; Gutzwiller & Barrow, 2001; Johnson & Gillingham, 2008; Leung et al., 2012; van Niel & Austin, 2007). This is largely because it is difficult to quantify errors, and the problem seems overwhelming once possible errors are scoped. Uncertainty is only partly characterised by confidence intervals from models (Elith et al., 2002; Kuhn et al., 2006). Rocchini et al. (2011) emphasise the need for maps of ignorance to depict areas where the reliability of predictions is either known or unknown and suggest potential approaches for producing these.

   Most research has targeted important components of uncertainty, including bias in species records (e.g. Argaez et al., 2005; Hortal et al., 2008; Rodda et al., 2011), uncertainty in predictors (Kriticos & Leriche, 2010; van Niel & Austin, 2007), differences between modelling methods (Pearson et al., 2006) and different parameterisations of one model (Hartley et al., 2006). Ensembles of correlative methods are favoured by some modellers (e.g. Araujo et al., 2005; Caphina & Anastácio, 2010; Roura-Pascual et al., 2009, Stohlgren et al., 2010; Thuiller, 2003) as a means of dealing with the sometimes extreme variation in predictions across methods. Their aim is to emphasise agreement of predictions and to quantify model-based uncertainty. However, these are not problem free, particularly for invasive species. Ensemble SDM methods are usually based on standard application of the component modelling methods (e.g. generalised linear models, generalised additive models, Mahalanobis distance and boosted regression trees;

Table 5.1), with default settings chosen by the ensemble programmer and any weighting of the ensemble components based on predictive performance to some set of sites. Because point-based predictive performance is usually impossible to evaluate meaningfully for invasive species, the ensemble components are often simply averaged (Araújo & New, 2007). It is unclear whether variation between components of the ensemble (i.e. between individual methods) is largely due to unrealistic models that have not been thoroughly explored and evaluated rather than real uncertainty between predictions. In my opinion, use of ensembles is a good idea only if the component models have been rigorously evaluated (e.g. Falk & Mellert, 2011). There are several reasons for this. Available species data sets are rarely so large and error-free that a model can be left to sort out the mess. The shapes of modelled responses require evaluation. Default settings may not be appropriate; the model might be too complex (as is often the case with machine learning methods using standard settings) or too simple (linear fits in GLMs). The extent of extrapolation needs to be evaluated, especially as it interacts with the shape of the modelled response (Section 5.5.6).

A useful approach for exploring uncertainty in any model is to fit multiple parameterisations to test the many judgments made in fitting the model (Elith et al., 2013; Ray & Burgman, 2006; Taylor & Kumar, 2012; van Klinken et al., 2009). Another angle for exploring uncertainty is to ask what type and amount of uncertainty would lead to a changed decision based on the model, or whether a decision or action is robust to estimated uncertainty (e.g. Elith et al., 2013; Moilanen et al., 2006; Yemshanov et al., 2010; see Chapters 6, 12 and 13 in this volume). Alternatively, adaptive surveillance approaches can be used by starting with models based on existing information (even if inadequate) and then iteratively updating the models with new information resulting from actions aimed at achieving some mix of management and data collection (McCarthy & Parris, 2008; Rout et al., 2014).

Although it might be easier to believe that a model is accurate, it is important to face the range of likely uncertainties and to communicate them in a way that aids decision making and future data collection. Further research – focusing on how to make practically useful evaluations of uncertainty – will progress informed use of predictions (Venette et al., 2010).

5.6   Conclusions

Many practitioners will need to use models based on data from the realised niche, whether as a stop-gap measure before better methods are available or because these might remain one of the only options for many species. An obvious question is which method to adopt. In my opinion, because these models require understanding, a better question is what expertise to develop. A skilled analyst is important for understanding the issues; they can also learn more than one method and choose methods that suit their data and species. Methods such as CLIMEX have been specifically developed for invasive species and have some features that make them safer to use (e.g. the way their indices can be controlled to extrapolate beyond the realised niche). These methods will not suit all species and all situations, and it is useful to continue development of other methods and tools. Some researchers are optimistic that correlative models will predict with high precision (e.g. Peterson, 2003); although that may be true for some species at some scales of evaluation, I believe that the issues discussed in this chapter make substantial errors reasonably likely. I am hopeful that ongoing developments will produce models better suited to the task and tools to help practitioners to better understand predictions and their uncertainties.

5.7   Acknowledgements

Thanks to Terry Walshe, Yvonne Buckley, Matt Hill and Karl Mellert for thoughtful comments on drafts and Stuart Elith for help with artwork.

References

Ackerly, D. D. (2003). Community assembly, niche conservatism, and adaptive evolution in changing environments. *International Journal of Plant Sciences*, 164(3 Suppl), S165–S184.

Aikio, S., Duncan, R. P. & Hulme, P. E. (2010). Herbarium records identify the role of long-distance spread in the spatial distribution of alien plants in New Zealand. *Journal of Biogeography*, 37(9), 1740–1751.

Alexander, J. M. & Edwards, P. J. (2010). Limits to the niche and range margins of alien species. *Oikos*, 119(9), 1377–1386.

Anderson, R. P. (2012). Harnessing the world's biodiversity data: Promise and peril in ecological niche modeling of species distributions. *Annals of the New York Academy of Sciences*, 1260, 66–80.

Araújo, M. B. & New, M. (2007). Ensemble forecasting of species distributions. *Trends in Ecology & Evolution*, 22(1), 42–47.

Araújo, M. B., Whittaker, R. J., Ladle, R. J. & Erhard, M. (2005). Reducing uncertainty in projections of extinction risk from climate change. *Global Ecology & Biogeography*, 14(6), 529–538.

Argaez, J. A., Christen, J. A., Nakamura, M. & Soberon, J. (2005). Prediction of potential areas of species distributions based on presence-only data. *Environment and Ecological Statistics*, 12(1), 27–44.

Ascough, J. C. II, Maier, H. R., Ravalico, J. K. & Strudley, M. W. (2008). Future research challenges for incorporation of uncertainty in environmental and ecological decision-making. *Ecological Modelling*, 219(3–4), 383–399.

Austin, M. P. (2002). Spatial prediction of species distribution: An interface between ecological theory and statistical modelling. *Ecological Modelling*, 157(2–3), 101–118.

Austin, M. P. (2007). Species distribution models and ecological theory: A critical assessment and some possible new approaches. *Ecological Modelling*, 200(1–2), 1–19.

Austin, M. P., Belbin, L., Meyers, J. A., Doherty, M. D. & Luoto, M. (2006). Evaluation of statistical models used for predicting plant species distributions: Role of artificial data and theory. *Ecological Modelling*, 199(2), 197–216.

Austin, M. P., Nicholls, A. O. & Margules, C. R. (1990). Measurement of the realized qualitative niche: Environmental niches of five eucalyptus species. *Ecological Monographs*, 60(2), 161–177.

Austin, M. P. & van Niel, K. P. (2011). Improving species distribution models for climate change studies: Variable selection and scale. *Journal of Biogeography*, 38(1), 1–8.

Baker, R. H. A., Sansford, C. E., Jarvis, C. H., et al. (2000). The role of climatic mapping in predicting the potential geographical distribution of non-indigenous pests under current and future climates. *Agriculture, Ecosystems & Environment*, 82(1–3), 57–71.

Barry, S. C. & Elith, J. (2006). Error and uncertainty in habitat models. *Journal of Applied Ecology*, 43(3), 413–423.

Barve, N., Barve, V., Jiménez-Valverde, A., et al. (2011). The crucial role of the accessible area in ecological niche modeling and species distribution modeling. *Ecological Modelling*, 222(11), 1810–1819.

Bio, A. M. F., De Becker, P., De Bie, E., Huybrechts, W., & Wassen, M. (2002). Prediction of plant species distribution in lowland river valleys in Belgium: Modelling species response to site conditions. *Biodiversity and Conservation*, 11(12), 2189–2216.

Bomford, M., Barry, S. C. & Lawrence, E. (2010). Predicting establishment success for introduced freshwater fishes: A role for climate matching. *Biological Invasions*, 12(8), 2559–2571.

Booth, T. H., Nix, H. A., Hutchinson, M. F. & Jovanovic, T. (1988). Niche analysis and tree species introduction. *Forest Ecology and Management*, 23(1), 47–59.

Broennimann, O. & Guisan, A. (2008). Predicting current and future biological invasions: Both native and invaded ranges matter. *Biology Letters*, 4(5), 585–589.

Broennimann, O., Treier, U. A., Müller-Schärer, H., et al. (2007). Evidence of climatic niche shift during biological invasion. *Ecology Letters*, 10(8), 701–709.

Brunel, S., Branquart, E., Fried, G., et al. (2010). The EPPO prioritization process for invasive alien plants. *EPPO Bulletin*, 40(3), 407–422.

Buckley, L. B., Urban, M. C., Angilletta, M. J., et al. (2010). Can mechanism inform species' distribution models? *Ecology Letters*, 13(8), 1041–1054.

Burgman, M. A., Breininger, D. R., Duncan, B. W. & Ferson, S. (2001). Setting reliability bounds on habitat suitability indices. *Ecological Applications*, 11(1), 70–78.

Busby, J. R. (1991). BIOCLIM – A bioclimate analysis and prediction system. In C. R. Margules & M. P. Austin (eds.), *Nature conservation: Cost effective biological surveys and data analysis* (pp. 64–68). Canberra, Australia: CSIRO.

Capinha, C. & Anastácio, P. (2010). Assessing the environmental requirements of invaders using ensembles of distribution models. *Diversity and Distributions*, 17(1), 13–24.

Chuine, I. & Beaubien, E. G. (2001). Phenology is a major determinant of tree species range. *Ecology Letters*, 4(5), 500–510.

Colwell, R. K. & Rangel, T. F. (2009). Hutchinson's duality: The once and future niche. *Proceedings of the National Academy of Sciences of the USA*, 106(Suppl 2), 19651–19658.

Cook, D. C., Thomas, M. B., Cunningham, S. A., Anderson, D. L. & De Barro, P. J. (2007). Predicting the economic impact of an invasive species on an ecosystem service. *Ecological Applications*, 17(6), 1832–1840.

Cook, W. C. (1925). The distribution of the alfalfa weevil (*Phytonomus posticus* Gyll.). A study in physical ecology. *Journal of Agricultural Research*, 30(5), 479–491.

De'ath, G. & Fabricius, K. E. (2000). Classification and regression trees: A powerful yet simple technique for ecological data analysis. *Ecology*, 81(11), 3178–3192.

Dorazio, R. M. (2014). Accounting for imperfect detection and survey bias in statistical analysis of presence-only data. *Global Ecology and Biogeography*, 23(12), 1472–1484.

Dormann, C. F., Elith, J., Bacher, S., et al. (2013). Collinearity: A review of methods to deal with it and a simulation study evaluating their performance. *Ecography*, 36(1), 27–46.

Dormann, C. F., McPherson, J. M., Araújo, M. B., et al. (2007). Methods to account for spatial autocorrelation in the analysis of species distributional data: A review. *Ecography*, 30(5), 609–628.

Dormann, C. F., Purschke, O., García-Márquez, J., Lautenbach, S. & Schröder, B. (2008). Components of uncertainty in species distribution analysis: A case study of the Great Grey Shrike. *Ecology*, 89(12), 3371–3386.

Dormann, C. F., Schymanski, S. J., Cabral, J., et al. (2012). Correlation and process in species distribution models: Bridging a dichotomy. *Journal of Biogeography*, 39(12), 2119–2131.

Drake, J. M. & Bossenbroek, J. M. (2009). Profiling ecosystem vulnerability to invasion by zebra mussels with support vector machines, *Theoretical Ecology*, 2(4), 189–198.

Elith, J., Burgman, M. A. & Regan, H. M. (2002). Mapping epistemic uncertainties and vague concepts in predictions of species distribution. *Ecological Modelling*, 157(2–3), 313–329.

Elith, J. & Graham, C. (2009). Do they? How do they? WHY do they differ? On finding reasons for differing performances of species distribution models. *Ecography*, 32(1), 66–77.

Elith, J., Graham, C. H., Anderson, R. P., et al. (2006). Novel methods improve prediction of species' distributions from occurrence data. *Ecography*, 29(2), 129–151.

Elith, J., Kearney, M. & Phillips, S. J. (2010). The art of modelling range-shifting species. *Methods in Ecology and Evolution*, 1(4), 330–342.

Elith, J. & Leathwick, J. R. (2009a). The contribution of species distribution modelling to conservation prioritization. In A. Moilanen, K. A. Wilson & H. Possingham (eds.), *Spatial conservation prioritization: Quantitative methods & computational tools* (pp. 70–93). New York: Oxford University Press.

Elith, J. & Leathwick, J. R. (2009b). Species distribution models: Ecological explanation and prediction across space and time. *Annual Review of Ecology, Evolution and Systematics*, 40(1), 677–697.

Elith, J., Phillips, S. J., Hastie, T., et al. (2011). A statistical explanation of MaxEnt for ecologists. *Diversity and Distributions*, 17(1), 43–57.

Elith, J., Simpson, J., Hirsch, M. & Burgman, M.A. (2013) Taxonomic uncertainty and decision making for biosecurity: Spatial models for myrtle/guava rust. *Australasian Plant Pathology*, 42(1), 43–51.

Engler, R., Guisan, A. & Rechsteiner, L. (2004). An improved approach for predicting the distribution of rare and endangered species from occurrence and pseudo-absence data. *Journal of Applied Ecology*, 41(2), 263–274.

Eraud, C., Boutin, J.-M., Roux, D. & Faivre, B. (2007). Spatial dynamics of an invasive bird species assessed using robust design occupancy analysis: The case of the Eurasian collared dove (*Streptopelia decaocto*) in France. *Journal of Biogeography*, 34(6), 1077–1086.

Falk, W. & Mellert, K. H. (2011). Species distribution models as a tool for forest management planning under climate change: Risk evaluation of *Abies alba* in Bavaria. *Journal of Vegetation Science*, 22(4), 621–634.

Fensterer, V. (2010) *Statistical methods in niche modelling for the spatial prediction of forest tree species.* Diploma thesis, Ludwig-Maximilians-University Munich. www.osti.gov/eprints/topicpages/documents/record/277/2903664.html

Ferrier, S., Watson, G., Pearce, J. & Drielsma, M. (2002). Extended statistical approaches to modelling spatial pattern in biodiversity in northeast New South Wales. I. Species-level modelling. *Biodiversity and Conservation*, 11(12), 2275–2307.

Fielding, A. H. & Bell, J. F. (1997). A review of methods for the assessment of prediction errors in conservation presence/absence models. *Environmental Conservation*, 24(1), 38–49.

Fithian, W., Elith, J., Hastie, T. & Keith, D. (2015). Bias correction in species distribution models: Pooling survey and collection data for multiple species. *Methods in Ecology and Evolution*, 6(4), 424–438.

Fithian, W. & Hastie, T. (2013) Statistical models for presence-only data: Finite-sample equivalence and addressing observer bias. *Annals of Applied Statistics*, 7(4), 1917–1939.

Fleishman, E., Macnally, R., Fay, J. P. & Murphy, D. D. (2001). Modeling and predicting species occurrence using broad-scale environmental variables: An example with butterflies of the Great Basin. *Conservation Biology*, 15(6), 1674–1685.

Franklin, J. (2010). *Mapping species distributions: Spatial inference and prediction.* Cambridge: Cambridge University Press.

Funk, V. A. & Richardson, K. S. (2002). Systematic data in biodiversity studies: Use it or lose it. *Systematic Biology*, 51(2), 303–316.

Gallien, L., Münkemüller, T., Albert, C. H., Boulangeat, I. & Thuiller, W. (2010). Predicting potential distributions of invasive species: Where to go from here? *Diversity and Distributions*, 16(3), 331–342.

Gevrey, M. & Worner, S. P. (2006). Prediction of global distribution of insect pest species in relation to climate by using an ecological informatics method. *Journal of Economic Entomology*, 99(3), 979–986.

Graham, C. H., Ferrier, S., Huettman, F., Moritz, C. & Peterson, A. T. (2004). New developments in museum-based informatics and applications in biodiversity analysis. *Trends in Ecology and Evolution*, 19(9), 497–503.

Guisan, A. & Thuiller, W. (2005). Predicting species distribution: Offering more than simple habitat models. *Ecology Letters*, 8(9), 993–1009.

Guisan, A. & Zimmermann, N. E. (2000). Predictive habitat distribution models in ecology. *Ecological Modelling*, 135(2–3), 147–186.

Guo, Q., Kelly, M. & Graham, C. H. (2005). Support vector machines for predicting distribution of sudden oak death in California. *Ecological Modelling*, 182(1), 75–90.

Gutzwiller, K. J. & Barrow, W. C., Jr. (2001). Bird-landscape relations in the Chihuahuan Desert: Coping with uncertainties about predictive models. *Ecological Applications*, 11(5), 1517–1532.

Harrell, F. E., Jr. (2006). *Regression modeling strategies: With applications to linear models, logistic regression, and survival analysis,* 2nd ed. New York: Springer Science+Business Media.

Hartley, S., Harris, R. & Lester, P. J. (2006). Quantifying uncertainty in the potential distribution of an invasive species: Climate and the Argentine ant. *Ecology Letters*, 9(9), 1068–1079.

Hastie, T., Tibshirani, R. & Friedman, J. H. (2009). *The elements of statistical learning: Data mining, inference, and prediction,* 2nd ed. New York, NY: Springer Science + Business Media.

Heikkinen, R. K., Luoto, M., Kuussaari, M. & Toivonen, T. (2007). Modelling the spatial distribution of a threatened butterfly: Impacts of scale and statistical technique. *Landscape and Urban Planning*, 79(3–4), 347–357.

Herborg, L. M., Drake, J. M., Rothlisberger, J. D. & Bossenbroek, J. M. (2009). Identifying suitable habitat for invasive species using ecological niche models and the policy implications of range forecasts. In R. P. Keller, D. M. Lodge, M.A. Lewis & J.F. Shogren (eds.), *Bioeconomics of invasive species: Integrating ecology, economics, policy and management* (pp. 63–82). New York: Oxford University Press.

Hijmans, R. J., Cameron, S. E., Parra, J. L., Jones, P. G. & Jarvis, A. (2005). Very high resolution interpolated climate surfaces for global land areas. *International Journal of Climatology*, 25(15), 1965–1978.

Hijmans, R. J. & Graham, C. H. (2006). The ability of climate envelope models to predict the effect of climate change on species distributions. *Global Change Biology*, 12(12), 1–10.

Hirzel, A. H., Hausser, J., Chessel, D., & Perrin, N. (2002). Ecological-Niche factor analysis: how to compute habitat-suitability maps without absence data? *Ecology*, 83(7), 2027–2036.

Hirzel, A. H. & Le Lay, G. (2008). Habitat suitability modelling and niche theory. *Journal of Applied Ecology*, 45(5), 1372–1381.

Hooten, M. B., Wikle, C. K., Dorazio, R. M. & Royle, J. A. (2007). Hierarchical spatiotemporal matrix models for characterizing invasions. *Biometrics*, 63(2), 558–567.

Hortal, J., Jiménez-Valverde, A., Gómez, J. F., Lobo, J. M. & Baselga, A. (2008). Historical bias in biodiversity inventories affects the observed environmental niche of the species. *Oikos*, 117(6), 847–858.

Huey, R. B., Gilchrist, G. W. & Hendry, A. P. (2005). Using invasive species to study evolution: Case studies with *Drosophila* and salmon. In D. F. Sax, J. J. Stachowicz & S. D. Gaines (eds.), *Species invasions: Insights into ecology, evolution and biogeography* (pp. 139–164). Sunderland, MA: Sinauer Associates.

Hulme, P. E. (2003). Biological invasions: Winning the science battles but losing the conservation war? *Oryx*, 37(2), 178–193.

Hulme, P. E. & Weser, C. (2011). Mixed messages from multiple information sources on invasive species: A case of too much of a good thing? *Diversity and Distributions*, 17(6), 1152–1160.

Hutchinson, G. E. (1957). Concluding remarks. *Cold Spring Harbour Symposium on Quantitative Biology*, 22, 415–427.

Inglis, G. J., Hurren, H., Oldman, J. & Haskew, R. (2006). Using habitat suitability index and particle dispersion models for early detection of marine invaders. *Ecological Applications*, 16(4), 1377–1390.

Jackson, S. T. & Overpeck, J. T. (2000). Responses of plant populations and communities to environmental changes of the late quaternary. *Paleobiology*, 26(Sp 4), 194–200.

Jiménez-Valverde, A., Lobo, J. M. & Hortal, J. (2008). Not as good as they seem: The importance of concepts in species distribution modelling. *Diversity and Distributions*, 14(6), 885–890.

Jiménez-Valverde, A., Peterson, A., Soberón, J., et al. (2011). Use of niche models in invasive species risk assessments. *Biological Invasions*, 13(12), 2785–2797.

Johnson, C. J. & Gillingham, M. P. (2008). Sensitivity of species-distribution models to error, bias, and model design: An application to resource selection functions for woodland caribou. *Ecological Modelling*, 213(2), 143–155.

Kangas, A. S. & Kangas, J. (2004). Probability, possibility and evidence: Approaches to consider risk and uncertainty in forestry decision analysis. *Forest Policy and Economics*, 6(2), 169–188.

Kearney, M. (2006). Habitat, environment and niche: What are we modelling? *Oikos*, 115(1), 186–191.

Kearney, M. R., Isaac, A. P. & Porter, W. P. (2014). Microclim: Global estimates of hourly microclimate based on long-term monthly climate averages. *Scientific Data*, 1, 140006.

Kearney, M., Phillips, B. L., Tracy, C. R., et al. (2008). Modelling species distributions without using species distributions: The cane toad in Australia under current and future climates. *Ecography*, 31(4), 423–434.

Kearney, M. & Porter, W. P. (2004). Mapping the fundamental niche: Physiology, climate and the distribution of nocturnal lizards across Australia. *Ecology*, 85(11), 3119–3131.

Kearney, M. & Porter, W. (2009). Mechanistic niche modelling: Combining physiological and spatial data to predict species' ranges. *Ecology Letters*, 12(4), 334–350.

Kearney, M. R., Wintle, B. A. & Porter, W. P. (2010). Correlative and mechanistic models of species distribution provide congruent forecasts under climate change. *Conservation Letters*, 3(3), 203–213.

Keating, K. A. & Cherry, S. (2004). Use and interpretation of logistic regression in habitat selection studies. *Journal of Wildlife Management*, 68(4), 774–789.

Kriticos, D. J. & Leriche, A. (2010). The effects of spatial data precision on fitting and projecting species niche models. *Ecography*, 33(1), 115–127.

Kriticos, D. J., Watt, M. S., Potter, K. J. B., et al. (2011). Managing invasive weeds under climate change: Considering the current and potential future distribution of *Buddleja davidii*. *Weed Research*, 51(1), 85–96.

Kriticos, D. J., Webber, B. L., Leriche, A., et al. (2012) CliMond: Global high-resolution historical and future scenario climate surfaces for bioclimatic modelling. *Methods in Ecology and Evolution*, 3(1), 53–64.

Kühn, I., Bierman, S. M., Durka, W. & Klotz, S. (2006). Relating geographical variation in pollination types to environmental and spatial factors using novel statistical methods. *New Phytologist*, 172(1), 127–139.

Lawson, B. E., Day, M. D., Bowen, M., van Klinken, R. D. & Zalucki, M. P. (2010). The effect of data sources and quality on the predictive capacity of CLIMEX models: An assessment of *Teleonemia scrupulosa* and *Octotoma scabripennis* for the biocontrol of *Lantana camara* in Australia. *Biological Control*, 52(1), 68–76.

Le Maitre, D. C., Thuiller, W. & Schonegevel, L. (2008). Developing an approach to defining the potential distributions of invasive plant species: A case study of *Hakea* species in South Africa. *Global Ecology and Biogeography*, 17(5), 569–584.

Leathwick, J. R. & Austin, M. P. (2001). Competitive interactions between tree species in New Zealand's old-growth indigenous forests. *Ecology*, 82(9), 2560–2573.

Leathwick, J. R., Elith, J., Chadderton, L., Rowe, D. & Hastie, T. (2008). Dispersal, disturbance, and the contrasting biogeographies of New Zealand's diadromous and non-diadromous fish species. *Journal of Biogeography*, 35(8), 1481–1497.

Legendre, P. (1993). Spatial autocorrelation: Trouble or new paradigm? *Ecology*, 74(6), 1659–1673.

Leung, B., Roura-Pascual, N., Bacher, S., et al. (2012) TEASIng apart alien species risk assessments: A framework for best practices. *Ecology Letters*, 15(12), 1475–1493.

Leyk, S., Boesch, R. & Weibel, R. (2005). A conceptual framework for uncertainty investigation in map-based land cover change modelling. *Transactions in GIS*, 9(3), 291–322.

Lobo, J. M., Jiménez-Valverde, A. & Hortal, J. (2010). The uncertain nature of absences and their importance in species distribution modelling. *Ecography*, 33(1), 103–114.

MacNally, R. (2000). Regression and model-building in conservation biology, biogeography and ecology: The distinction between – and reconciliation of – 'predictive' and 'explanatory' models. *Biodiversity and Conservation*, 9(5), 665–671.

Magarey, R. D., Fowler, G. A., Borchert, D. M., et al. (2007). NAPPFAST: An internet system for the weather-based mapping of plant pathogens. *Plant Disease*, 91(4), 336–345.

Manly, B. F. J., McDonald, L. L., Thomas, D. L., McDonald, T. L. & Erickson, W. P. (2002). *Resource selection by animals: Statistical design and analysis for field studies*, 2nd ed. Dordrecht, the Netherlands: Kluwer Academic.

McCarthy, M. A. & Parris, K. M. (2008). Optimal marking of threatened species to balance benefits of information with impacts of marking. *Conservation Biology*, 22(6), 1506–1512.

McCune, B. (2006). Non-parametric models with automatic interactions. *Journal of Vegetation Science*, 17(6), 819–830.

Mellert, K. H., Fensterer, V., Küchenhoff, H., et al. (2011). Hypothesis-driven species distribution models for tree species in the Bavarian Alps. *Journal of Vegetation Science*, 22(4), 635–646.

Merow, C., Smith, M. J., Edwards, T. C., Jr., et al. (2014). What do we gain from simplicity versus complexity in species distribution models? *Ecography*, 37(12), 1267–1281.

Mesgaran, M. B., Cousens, R. D. & Webber, B. L. (2014). Here be dragons: A tool for quantifying novelty due to covariate range and correlation change when projecting species distribution models. *Diversity and Distributions*, 20(10), 1147–1159.

Moilanen, A., Wintle, B., Elith, J. & Burgman, M. (2006). Uncertainty analysis for regional-scale reserve selection. *Conservation Biology*, 20(6), 1688–1697.

Moisen, G. G., Freeman, E. A., Blackard, J. A., et al. (2006). Predicting tree species presence and basal area in Utah: A comparison of stochastic gradient boosting, generalized additive models, and tree-based methods. *Ecological Modelling*, 199(2), 176–187.

Moisen, G. G., & Frescino, T. S. (2002). Comparing five modeling techniques for predicting forest characteristics. *Ecological Modelling*, 157(2–3), 209–25.

Morin, X. & Lechowicz, M. J. (2008). Contemporary perspectives on the niche that can improve models of species range shifts under climate change. *Biology Letters*, 4(5), 573–576.

Morin, X. & Thuiller, W. (2009). Comparing niche- and process-based models to reduce prediction uncertainty in species range shifts under climate change. *Ecology*, 90(5), 1301–1313.

Nix, H. A. (1986). A biogeographic analysis of Australian elapid snakes. In N. Longmore (ed.), *Atlas of elapid snakes of Australia* (pp. 4–15). Canberra, Australia: Australian Government Publishing Service.

Olfert, O., Hallett, R., Weiss, R. M., Soroka, J. & Goodfellow, S. (2006). Potential distribution and relative abundance of swede midge, *Contarinia nasturtii*, an invasive pest in Canada. *Entomologia Experimentalis et Applicata*, 120(3), 221–228.

Ovaskainen, O., Hottola, J. & Siitonen, J. (2010). Modeling species co-occurrence by multivariate logistic regression generates new hypotheses on fungal interactions. *Ecology*, 91(9), 2514–2521.

Pearce, J. & Ferrier, S. (2000). Evaluating the predictive performance of habitat models developed using logistic regression. *Ecological Modelling*, 133(3), 225–245.

Pearson, G. P., Thuiller, W., Araujo, M. B., et al. (2006). Model-based uncertainty in species range prediction. *Journal of Biogeography*, 33(10), 1704–1711.

Pearson, R. G. (2007). *Species' distribution modeling for conservation educators and practitioners*. New York: American Museum of Natural History. Available from http://ncep. amnh.org.

Peterson, A. T. (2003). Predicting the geography of species' invasions via ecological niche modeling. *The Quarterly Review of Biology*, 78(4), 419–433.

Peterson, A. T. (2006). Uses and requirements of ecological niche models and related distributional models. *Biodiversity Informatics*, 3, 59–72.

Peterson, A. T. & Nakazawa, Y. (2008). Environmental data sets matter in ecological niche modelling: An example with *Solenopsis invicta* and *Solenopsis richteri*. *Global Ecology and Biogeography*, 17(1), 135–144.

Peterson, A. T., Soberón, J., Pearson, R. G., et al. (2011). *Ecological niches and geographic distributions*. Princeton, NJ: Princeton University Press.

Phillips, S. J., Anderson, R. P. & Schapire, R. E. (2006). Maximum entropy modeling of species geographic distributions. *Ecological Modelling*, 190(3–4), 231–259.

Phillips, S. J., Dudík, M., Elith, J., et al. (2009). Sample selection bias and presence-only distribution models: Implications for background and pseudo-absence data. *Ecological Applications*, 19(1), 181–197.

Phillips, S. J. & Elith, J. (2011). Logistic methods for resource selection functions and presence-only species distribution models. In *Proceedings of the Twenty-Fifth AAAI Conference on Artificial Intelligence* (pp. 1384–1389). San Francisco, CA: AAAI Press.

Pollock, L. J., Tingley, R., Morris, W. K., et al. (2014). Understanding co-occurrence by modelling species simultaneously with a Joint Species Distribution Model (JSDM). *Methods in Ecology and Evolution*, 5(5), 397–406.

Porter, W. P., Sabo, J. L., Tracy, C. R., Reichman, O. J. & Ramankutty, N. (2002). Physiology on a landscape scale: Plant-animal interactions. *Integrative and Comparative Biology*, 42(3), 431–453.

Potts, J. M. & Elith, J. (2006). Comparing species abundance models. *Ecological Modelling*, 199(2), 153–163.

Pulliam, H. R. (2000). On the relationship between niche and distribution. *Ecology Letters*, 3(4), 349–361.

Randin, C. F., Dirnböck, T., Dullinger, S., et al. (2006). Are niche-based species distribution models transferable in space? *Journal of Biogeography*, 33(10), 1689–1703.

Rangel, T. F. L. V. B., Diniz-Filho, J. A. F. & Bini, L. M. (2006). Towards an integrated computational tool for spatial analysis in macroecology and biogeography. *Global Ecology and Biogeography*, 15(4), 321–327.

Ray, N. & Burgman, M. A. (2006). Subjective uncertainties in habitat suitability maps. *Ecological Modelling*, 195(3–4), 172–186.

Reddy, S. & Dávalos, L. M. (2003). Geographical sampling bias and its implications for conservation priorities in Africa. *Journal of Biogeography*, 30(11), 1719–1727.

Renner, I. W., Elith, J., Baddeley, A., et al. (2015). Point process models for presence-only analysis. *Methods in Ecology and Evolution*, 6(4), 366–379.

Reusser, D. A. & Lee II, H. (2008). Predictions for an invaded world: A strategy to predict the distribution of native and non-indigenous species at multiple scales. *ICES Journal of Marine Science*, 65(5), 742–745.

Richardson, D. M. & Thuiller, W. (2007). Home away from home – objective mapping of high-risk source areas for plant introductions. *Diversity and Distributions*, 13(3), 299–312.

Robertson, M. P., Cumming, G. S. & Erasmus, B. F. N. (2010). Getting the most out of atlas data. *Diversity and Distributions*, 16(3), 363–375.

Rocchini, D., McGlinn, D., Ricotta, C., Neteler, M. & Wohlgemuth, T. (2011). Landscape complexity and spatial scale influence the relationship between remotely sensed spectral diversity and survey-based plant species richness. *Journal of Vegetation Science*, 22(4), 688–698.

Rodda, G. H., Jarnevich, C. S. & Reed, R. N. (2009). What parts of the US mainland are climatically suitable for invasive alien pythons spreading from Everglades National Park? *Biological Invasions*, 11(2), 241–252.

Rodda, G. H., Jarnevich, C. S. & Reed, R. N. (2011). Challenges in identifying sites climatically matched to the native ranges of animal invaders. *PloS ONE*, 6(2), e14670.

Rödder, D. & Lötters, S. (2010). Explanative power of variables used in species distribution modelling: An issue of general model transferability or niche shift in the invasive greenhouse frog *(Eleutherodactylus planirostris)*. *Naturwissenschaften*, 97(9), 781–796.

Rouget, M. & Richardson, D. M. (2003). Inferring process from pattern in plant invasions: A semimechanistic model incorporating propagule pressure and environmental factors. *American Naturalist*, 162(6), 713–724.

Roura-Pascual, N., Brotons, L., Peterson, A. T. & Thuiller, W. (2009). Consensual predictions of potential distributional areas for invasive species: A case study of Argentine ants in the Iberian Peninsula. *Biological Invasions*, 11(4), 1017–1031.

Rout, T. M., Moore, J. L. & McCarthy, M. A. (2014). Prevent, search or destroy? A partially observable model for invasive species management. *Journal of Applied Ecology*, 51(3), 804–813.

Rykiel, E. J., Jr. (1996). Testing ecological models: The meaning of validation. *Ecological Modelling*, 90(3), 229–244.

Schröder, B. (2008). Challenges of species distribution modeling belowground. *Journal of Plant Nutrition and Soil Science*, 171(3), 325–337.

Schulman, L., Toivonen, T. & Ruokolainen, K. (2007). Analysing botanical collecting effort in Amazonia and correcting for it in species range estimation. *Journal of Biogeography*, 34(8), 1388–1399.

Soberón, J. & Nakamura, M. (2009). Niches and distributional areas: Concepts, methods, and assumptions. *Proceedings of the National Academy of Sciences of the USA*, 106(Suppl. 2), 19644–19650.

Steiner, F. M., Schlick-Steiner, B. C., VanDerWal, J., et al. (2008). Combined modelling of distribution and niche in invasion biology: A case study of two invasive *Tetramorium* ant species. *Diversity and Distributions*, 14(3), 538–545.

Stohlgren, T. J., Ma, P., Kumar, S., et al. (2010). Ensemble habitat mapping of invasive plant species. *Risk Analysis*, 30(2), 224–235.

Sutherst, R. W. (2003). Prediction of species geographical ranges. *Journal of Biogeography*, 30(6), 805–816.

Sutherst, R. W. & Maywald, G. F. (1985). A computerised system for matching climates in ecology. *Agriculture, Ecosystems and Environment*, 13(3–4), 281–299.

Sutherst, R. W., Maywald, G. F. & Kriticos, D. J. (2007). *Climex version 3: User's guide*. South Yarra, Australia: Hearne Scientific Software.

Taylor, S. & Kumar, L. (2012). Sensitivity analysis of CLIMEX parameters in modelling potential distribution of *Lantana camara* L. *PloS ONE*, 7(7), e40969.

Thomas, C. D. & Ohlemüller, R. (2010). Climate change and species' distributions: an alien future? In C. Perrings, H. Mooney & M. Williamson (eds.), *Bioinvasions and globalization: Ecology, economics, management and policy* (pp. 19–29). Oxford: Oxford University Press.

Thuiller, W. (2003). BIOMOD – Optimizing predictions of species distributions and projecting potential future shifts under global change. *Global Change Biology*, 9(10), 1353–1362.

Thuiller, W., Albert, C., Araújo, M. B., et al. (2008). Predicting global change impacts on plant species' distributions: Future challenges. *Perspectives in Plant Ecology, Evolution and Systematics*, 9(3–4), 137–152.

Thuiller, W., Richardson, D. M., Pysek, P., et al. (2005). Niche-based modelling as a tool for predicting the risk of alien plant invasions at a global scale. *Global Change Biology*, 11(12), 2234–2250.

Tyberghein, L., Verbruggen, H., Pauly, K., et al. (2012). Bio-ORACLE: A global environmental dataset for marine species distribution modeling. *Global Ecology and Biogeography*, 21(2), 272–281.

Václavík, T. & Meentemeyer, R. K. (2009). Invasive species distribution modeling (iSDM): Are absence data and dispersal constraints needed to predict actual distributions? *Ecological Modelling*, 220(23), 3248–3258.

van Klinken, R. D., Lawson, B. E. & Zalucki, M. P. (2009). Predicting invasions in Australia by a Neotropical shrub under climate change: The challenge of novel climates and parameter estimation. *Global Ecology and Biogeography*, 18(6), 688–700.

Van Niel, K. P. & Austin, M. P. (2007). Predictive vegetation modeling for conservation: Impact of error propagation from digital elevation data. *Ecological Applications*, 17(1), 266–280.

Venette, R. C., Kriticos, D. J., Magarey, R. D., et al. (2010). Pest risk maps for invasive alien species: A roadmap for improvement. *BioScience*, 60(5), 349–362.

Ward, G., Hastie, T., Barry, S. C., Elith, J. & Leathwick, J. R. (2009). Presence-only data and the EM algorithm. *Biometrics*, 65(2), 554–563.

Warton, D. I., Renner, I. W. & Ramp, D. (2013). Model-based control of observer bias for the analysis of presence-only data in ecology. *PloS ONE*, 8(11), e79168.

Warton, D. I. & Shepherd, L. C. (2010). Poisson point process models solve the 'pseudo-absence problem' for presence-only data in ecology. *The Annals of Applied Statistics*, 4(3), 1383–1402.

Williams, J. W., Jackson, S. T. & Kutzbac, J. E. (2007). Projected distributions of novel and disappearing climates by 2100 AD. *Proceedings of the National Academy of Sciences of the USA*, 104(14), 5738–5742.

Williams, N. S. G., Hahs, A. K. & Morgan, J. W. (2008). A dispersal-constrained habitat suitability model for predicting invasion of alpine vegetation. *Ecological Applications*, 18(2), 347–359.

Wintle, B. A., McCarthy, M. A., Parris, K. M. & Burgman, M. A. (2004). Precision and bias of methods for estimating point survey detection probabilities. *Ecological Applications*, 14(3), 703–712.

Wolmarans, R., Robertson, M. P. & Van Rensburg, B. J. (2010). Predicting invasive alien plant distributions: How geographical bias in occurrence records influences model performance. *Journal of Biogeography*, 37(9), 1797–1810.

Woodbury, P. B. & Weinstein, D. A. (2008). Availability of spatial data. In *Forest Encyclopedia Network*. Available from www.forestencyclopedia.net/p/p3233

Wu, S.-H., Rejmanek, M., Grotkopp, E. & DiTomaso, J. M. (2005). Herbarium records, actual distribution, and critical attributes of invasive plants: genus *Crotalaria* in Taiwan. *Taxon*, 54(1), 133–138.

Yemshanov, D., Koch, F. H., Ben-Haim, Y. & Smith, W. D. (2010). Robustness of risk maps and survey networks to knowledge gaps about a new invasive pest. *Risk Analysis*, 30(2), 261–276.

Ysebaert, T., Meire, P., Herman, P. M. J. & Verbeek, H. (2002). Macrobenthic species response surfaces along estuarine gradients: Prediction by logistic regression. *Marine Ecology Progress Series*, 225, 79–95.

Zimmermann, N., Edwards, T., Moisen, G., Frescino, T. & Blackard, J. (2007). Remote sensing-based predictors improve distribution models of rare, early successional and broadleaf tree species in Utah. *Journal of Applied Ecology*, 44(5), 1057–1067.

Zimmermann, N. E., Yoccoz, N. G., Edwards, T. C., et al. (2009). Climatic extremes improve predictions of spatial patterns of tree species. *Proceedings of the National Academy of Sciences of the USA*, 106(Suppl. 2), 19723–19728.

Zurell, D., Elith, J. & Schröder, B. (2012). Predicting to new environments: Tools for visualizing model behaviour and impacts on mapped distributions. *Diversity and Distributions*, 18(6), 628–634.

6 Mapping Risks and Impacts of Invasive Alien Species with Dynamic Simulation Models

Denys Yemshanov, Frank H. Koch, John W. Coulston and William D. Smith

6.1 Introduction

Invasive alien species have been acknowledged as a serious ecological and economic concern worldwide. Significant global impacts of invasive alien species on the agricultural, forestry and public health sectors (Colautti et al., 2006; Dawson, 2002; Westbrooks, 1998) underline the need for reliable assessments of the risks posed by organisms that have been, or are likely to be, introduced into new environments outside their native ranges. The pertinent risks include the likelihood of successful establishment of the invading organism as well as the likelihood and magnitude of economic or ecological impacts (e.g. damage or mortality of a commercially important host resource). Dynamic simulation models are attractive techniques, not only to develop reliable estimates of these risks but also to quantify uncertainty around the risk estimates.

Invasions may affect large and diverse geographical areas. Assessing the potential risks in a geographical domain is always desired and helps when investigating regional variation in the predicted invasion outcomes. For plant protection organisations and land management agencies, mapping pest risks aids in developing surveillance and control strategies (e.g. early warning survey networks), appropriate phytosanitary regulations and effective counter-measures. Unlike road or physiographic maps, pest risk maps are models that show predictive rather than observed data, and thus have associated errors or uncertainty. These predictive maps have proven to be effective aids in raising awareness and helping to address public concerns regarding regulation and control of new invaders.

Ideally, a pest risk map, and its underlying model, should simultaneously address both the likelihood and the impact of invasion by the pest species (Venette et al., 2010). In practice, these two aspects have typically been examined distinctly, sometimes with an ad hoc combination of outputs as a last step (FHTET, 2010; Magarey et al., 2011). Most pest risk maps and models have focused narrowly on particular stages of the invasion process, such as pathways or mechanisms of introduction (Koch et al., 2011), or the distribution of environmentally suitable areas where a species is likely to persist if introduced (Andersen et al., 2004a; FHTET, 2010; Venette et al., 2010; see Chapter 5). Regardless of whether a risk map has limited scope, its risk estimates may be influenced by the nature of the mapped information or by specific factors associated with the pest of interest (e.g. the area being infested, the rate of spread of the invader, the amount and susceptibility of the local host resource or the time the invading population has occupied a given area). Furthermore, because an invader can usually become established only at a minimum population size, there must be a minimum level of impact on the pest's host resource for any risk estimate to be meaningful.

As these points suggest, for a risk map to provide adequate decision support, the underlying model of invasion risk should represent all key aspects of invasion (including the time horizon of interest) in an explicit or implicit manner. A simulation-based approach offers an opportunity to dynamically combine the various aspects and stages of a pest's invasion into an integrated, temporally explicit risk framework. Stochastic models also offer the capacity to generate numerous plausible outcomes of an invasion through independent randomised simulations; in turn, these model outputs, collected over multiple model realisations, can be used to generate distributions of potential invasion outcomes and estimate the variation of invasion risks over large geographical areas. Geographically explicit simulation models can generate risk estimates at large spatial scales, but with spatial accuracy sufficient to demarcate particular hotspots of high risk, thereby providing important management information in a broad geographical context.

6.2 Dynamic Simulation Risk Models

6.2.1 Basic Concept

In general, an invasion model portrays the trajectory of an outbreak through its fundamental stages (i.e. entry, establishment, spread and impact) as a sequential simulation process. The process starts with one or more introduction events as a result of trade or other human activities (Williamson, 1996). Once established in a new locale, the invading organism spreads through the landscape, causing host mortality and subsequent ecological damage that may trigger socio-economic impacts. These processes occur under diverse environmental conditions that variably influence the behaviour of the pest of interest (e.g. host density, connectivity and level of susceptibility or degree of climatic suitability for the pest) and generate a chain of events that determine the expansion of the invasion in time and geographical space (Figure 6.1). The results may be depicted as a map of the invasion risks for a given forecast period. Overall, a simulation-based approach offers better opportunity to estimate the long-term cumulative risks of multiple introductions. This is because all relevant components of invasion (such as spread, survival and establishment of the invader) are integrated in these models and feedback that occurs in time and space as a result of multiple introductions or interactions between existing and newly established pest populations can be taken into account (Rafoss, 2003).

The computational and structural complexity of the selected invasion model is guided by the nature and amount of available information about the pest. In its

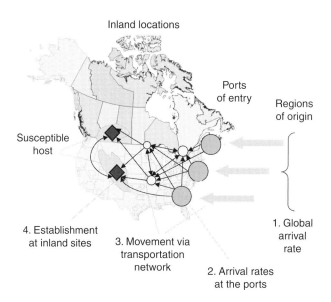

Figure 6.1.   A schematic representation of the basic elements of an invasion process.

simplest form, the model is usually fitted to experts' beliefs regarding the pest's behaviour in its new environment (which may be informed by evidence from other parts of the world, despite the differences between these environments). The model structure becomes more sophisticated when knowledge about the organism is more comprehensive (e.g. the emerald ash borer, *Agrilus planipennis* Fairmaire, model in BenDor et al., 2006). For relatively simple models of invasion, key invasion stages can be depicted in a generalised fashion with a functional calculus where the model dependencies are described using a set of continuous functions that often have analytical solutions (see example in Sharov & Liebhold, 1998). More complex processes of spread and population growth based on empirical and geographically distributed data are commonly modelled using a discrete event approach (but see Gibson & Austin 1996; see also Fuentes & Kuperman, 1999; Yemshanov et al., 2009b).

In this chapter, we provide a brief overview of basic modelling components and approaches that may be used to depict critical steps of an invasion and estimate the risk and impact of new infestations.

6.2.2   Entry

The majority of non-indigenous species have been introduced to North America via transport of imported goods (Costello et al., 2007; Levine & D'Antonio, 2003). This method of entry has become increasingly important as the volume of global trade has risen rapidly. For decades, inspections at ports of entry have routinely detected unwanted organisms, not just in cargoes but – particularly with respect to wood-boring insect pests – in their packing materials as well (Brockerhoff et al., 2006; Haack, 2006).

For many invading organisms, risk assessment starts from estimating their entry potential. Entry potential is described by a set of probabilities, across individual locations of interest, which quantify the likelihood that the invader will be introduced with imported goods and commodities. This step can be seen as two linked analyses: identification of likely pathways for the invading organism to travel from the region(s) where it is already established (Andersen et al., 2004b) and subsequent estimation of the particular entry potential at individual locations within the geographical area of interest, which may include inland locations beyond initial ports of entry.

The first analysis involves evaluation of the worldwide distribution of the species of concern to identify possible regions of origin (Magarey et al., 2009). It also includes assessment of likely import pathways (i.e. the commodities and cargo types with which the pest has been associated historically). This can be accomplished by examining pest interception records from ports of entry as well as the status of commercial activities (e.g. timber production) with which the species is associated in the identified origin regions (Baker et al., 2005; Magarey et al., 2007; Piel et al., 2008). Data on recent levels of international trade at broad scales offer an initial way to quantify a pest's entry potential based on origin and pathway information. For example, Figure 6.2 shows the probabilities of introduction for an invasive wood wasp, *Sirex noctilio* Fabricius, at North American marine ports of entry. Given the broad geographical distribution of *S. noctilio*, Koch et al. (2009) and Yemshanov et al. (2009b) concluded that these likelihoods (i.e. the pest's entry potential) could be reasonably estimated as a function of the total value of commodities (Costello & McAusland, 2003; Levine & D'Antonio, 2003; Yamamura & Katsumata, 1999; Yamamura et al., 2001) received at each port from regions where *S. noctilio* is known to exist and has a significant economic impact. Such analyses may be refined by looking only at the values or volumes of commodities specifically associated with the species of interest, rather than total import values or volumes (e.g. Koch et al., 2011).

The increasing proportion of containerised shipments that do not have to be opened at a port of entry, but instead are opened at their final destination, together with the elaborate transportation networks found in North America and elsewhere, highlight the need to consider the domestic (i.e. intercity) flow of pest-associated commodities via major transportation corridors (Black, 1972; De Jong et al., 2004; LeSage & Kelley Pace, 2008; LeSage & Polsek, 2006; O'Sullivan & Ralston, 1974; Porojan, 2001). Hence, the second phase of analysis focuses on the subsequent movement of imported goods after they have entered at the ports. To represent the entry potential at final destination locations (such as urban areas), the entry potential at each port, which is based on the volumes of pest-associated cargo that the port has historically received, is apportioned to the inland locations to which it is linked by domestic trade routes (Figure 6.3).

Unfortunately, historical data relevant for calculating entry potential are often incomplete and inconsistent; for example, data for both domestic and international commodity flows are usually provided at broad scales (i.e. the data are summarised

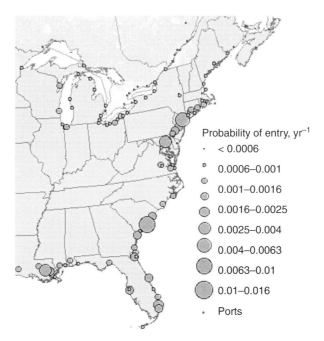

Figure 6.2.   An example of *Sirex noctilio* entry potential at major marine ports in eastern North America from the world regions where the pest is known to exist.
[Reproduced with permission from Yemshanov, D., Koch, F. H., McKenney, D. W., Downing, M. C. and Sapio, F. (2009b). Mapping invasive species risks with stochastic models: A cross-border United States–Canada application for Sirex noctilio Fabricius. Risk Analysis, 29(6), 868–884. See source for further details.]

at a regional level) and lack sufficient fine-scale geographical details to permit allocation of flows to specific geographical locations (e.g. urban centres) that might be of interest with respect to invasive pests (Baker et al., 2005). One potential solution is to predict the entry potential at two levels: a global (i.e. broad-scale) likelihood of entry for the entire region of interest and a geographically distributed set of local entry probabilities that apportion the region-wide entry potential into location-specific estimates for the individual ports of entry and other destination locations of interest (Herborg et al., 2007; Koch et al., 2011; Yemshanov et al., 2009b). This approach allows one to combine separate data assumptions for global and local estimates and test a wide range of local entry hypotheses independently of the global entry potential. For example, inland sites (such as distribution centres and urban areas) can be incorporated into the apportionment of entry potential among individual locations without changing the global entry potential. This approach also offers the opportunity for linkage with more advanced transportation network and commodity flow models (similar to de Vos et al., 2004 and Yemshanov et al., 2012a) to quantify the long-distance movement of invasive organisms via transportation corridors.

Notably, entry potential is a dynamic variable that changes with time. Several studies have modelled entry potential as a function of changing climate (Magarey

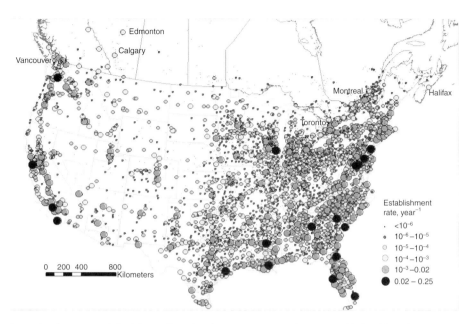

Figure 6.3.   Introduction potential of forest invasive insects at ports of entry and inland locations across Canada and the United States from all world regions (2000–2010 estimate). [Reproduced with permission from Koch, F. H., Yemshanov, D., Colunga-Garcia, M., Magarey, R.D. and Smith, W. D. (2011). Potential establishment of alien-invasive forest insect species in the United States: Where and how many? Biological Invasions, 13(4) 969–985 and Yemshanov, D., Koch, F., Ducey, M. and Koehler, K. (2012). Trade-associated pathways of alien forest insect entries in Canada. Biological Invasions, 14(4), 797–812. See sources for further details.]

et al. 2007), specific weather phenomena (such as El Niño), socio-political and economic events such as the recent global financial crisis (Koch et al., 2011) or the impact of new trade rules (Costello et al., 2007). Representing entry as a dynamic variable in a stochastic model is likely to be more realistic than point-based techniques (Jarvis & Baker, 2001) because it provides a more reliable depiction of multiple reintroductions over time (Rafoss, 2003; see also Koch et al., 2009; Yemshanov et al., 2009b).

6.2.3   Spread

The spread of invading organisms is one of the most intensively studied aspects of ecological invasions (Nathan, 2005; Neubert & Caswell, 2000; Okubo & Levin, 2002; Royama, 1992). There are two broad modelling approaches for forecasting the spread of non-indigenous species (Hastings, 1996). The first approach employs theory-based analytical spread models such as reaction-diffusion, travelling wave or stratified diffusion models (Kot et al., 1996; Sharov & Liebhold, 1998; Shigesada et al., 1995), essentially fitting one of these analytical models to historical rates of spread based on observational data (Holmes, 1993; Kovacs et al.,

2010; Pitt et al., 2009; Tobin et al., 2007). These analytical models are relatively simple and have been well studied (e.g. Royama, 1992), but they often lack feedbacks to ecological and economic drivers that shape a species' particular pattern of invasion. Analytical models have been long criticised for their poor capacity to predict long-distance dispersal and their tendency to underestimate true rates of spread (Waage et al., 2005).

The second modelling approach incorporates various empirical data about the ecology and behaviour of the invading organism and makes use of more complex mechanistic algorithms that do not have analytical solutions. This approach can accommodate various environmental feedbacks (BenDor et al., 2006; Sharov & Colbert, 1996), but the parameter-fitting procedures are often less transparent and rely more on expert knowledge about an invader (or on data collected in other, usually foreign, regions where the invader is known to exist) than analytical models. Although these complex mechanistic models may be considered more realistic than analytical models with their incorporation of species' life cycles and environmental preferences (Sharov & Colbert, 1996), they can be difficult to validate. It can also be challenging to determine the sources of any identified errors (which could, for example, arise due to a failure to recognise important interactions that result in missing or incorrectly specified model parameters). In general, spread models include at least three key components in various implementations: population growth, spatial spread (i.e. dispersal) and establishment of an invasive organism at newly colonised locations (BenDor et al., 2006; Nathan, 2005; Neubert & Caswell, 2000).

6.2.4   Population Growth and Dispersal

In conceptual terms, dispersal models link the positions of newly emerging individuals to the positions of their parents (van den Bosch et al., 1992). This can be depicted as a dispersal kernel $K(x, y, t)$ that denotes the probability, at time t, that an offspring from an individual born at location x will start life at location y. More practically, kernel K specifies how emerging adults spread to other locations, and can usually be defined as a probability density function (Neubert & Caswell, 2000) for location y to which an individual at location x disperses.

The shape of the dispersal kernel K greatly affects the rate of spread (Kot et al., 1996), but choosing the kernel's shape and fitting it to actual spread rates calculated from field surveys can be problematic. For example, the Gaussian probability density function produces diffusion-like spread with constant velocity (Kot et al., 1996). However, a Gaussian kernel does not capture well the long-distance spread events that have been observed in many historical invasions (Chapman et al., 2007). While rare events of long-distance dispersal have been widely recognised as key contributors to rates of spread (Clark et al., 1998; Nathan, 2003), they are notoriously difficult to calibrate to field observations (Higgins & Richardson, 1999; Shigesada & Kawasaki, 1997). A special group of fat-tailed probability density functions provides an increased probability of long-distance dispersal events and may be better able to simulate the accelerating rates of spread seen in many invasions (Chapman et al., 2007; Clark et al., 1998; Kot et al., 1996). Alternatively, long-distance dispersal can be portrayed with a two-staged stratified diffusion model (Shigesada et al., 1995) that adds a distance-dependent probability of creating new population nuclei (or colonies) at distances beyond the main front of an organism's spread. Another approach simulates long-distance spread as a spreading and coalescing colony, with the probability of creating new population nuclei calculated as a function of the geographical distance from already established infestations (Sharov & Liebhold, 1998).

The analytical approaches described in the preceding text depend on simplifying assumptions and may not resolve the issue of severe uncertainties when it comes to predicting long-distance spread of invasion (Melbourne & Hastings, 2009). Another issue is that long-distance dispersal of invaders is often a result of human activities, and cannot be well explained by biological, kernel-based models alone. One approach to predicting human-mediated long-distance dispersal is to use gravity models (Bossenbroek et al., 2001). Gravity models predict the degree of interactions between invaded and non-invaded locations, weighted by the geographical distance between them, in a manner similar to a gravity law (Bossenbroek et al., 2001; Muirhead & MacIsaac, 2005). These models assume that the migration of invading organisms is guided by the attractiveness of potential destinations, which is often based on statistical hypotheses about economic activities, infrastructure and transportation networks (Muirhead et al., 2006).

The accuracy of predicting human-mediated, long-distance spread of invasive organisms can be further improved via explicit modelling of flows of freight, commodity types or vehicles that could harbour the organisms. Instead of relying on theoretical dispersal or gravity models, the approach makes use of network models built upon empirical data about these flows to estimate the likelihood of movement of an invader via directional pathways in the network. For instance, it is possible to estimate the flows of pest-specific commodities through a transportation network linking cities and other populated areas (de Vos et al., 2004; Koch et al., 2011; Yemshanov et al., 2012a).

6.2.5 Establishment

This phase describes the process of the pest's growth and reproductive activities in a newly colonised location. An invading organism requires certain resources and conditions to establish a persistent population in this new environment; most obviously, the likelihood of survival depends on the presence of appropriate hosts and suitable ranges of a number of constraining environmental factors. Several studies have demonstrated the effect of host resource distribution on species' spread rates (Durrett & Levin, 1994; Shigesada & Kawasaki, 1997; Weinberger, 2002), population growth (Jules et al., 2002) and severity of impact of new invaders (Condeso &

Meentemeyer, 2007). For invaders of forested ecosystems, any major tree species that can serve as hosts are typically of primary interest. National forest inventories (e.g. Gillis, 2001; Woudenberg et al., 2010) usually represent the most reliable source of tree species geographical distribution data. When detailed inventory data are unavailable, various interpolation techniques that link species information from field observations with satellite imagery (Lowe et al., 2005; McRoberts et al., 2005; Yemshanov et al., 2009a) can be used.

At broad geographical scales, the potential distributions of invasive organisms are often limited by climatic conditions that fundamentally affect fecundity, mortality, development time and other aspects of population ecology (Magarey et al., 2007). Typically, modelling of a non-indigenous organism's bioclimatic range, or environmental niche, within an area of interest requires information on the historical or present distributions of the pest in other regions with known climatic profiles. The reference climatic data used in these analyses are widely available at global (Hijmans et al., 2005) and continental scales (Hamlet & Lettenmaier, 2005; Magarey et al., 2007; McKenney et al., 2007).

Maps of the potential climatic distribution ranges of invasive alien species have become commonplace in pest risk assessments (Elith & Leathwick, 2009; Venette et al., 2010), and various statistical prediction methods have been introduced, especially in recent decades (Elith et al., 2006; Worner & Gevrey, 2006; see Chapter 5). Final predictions of climatic ranges are often affected by the choice of analytical techniques, number of known species observations, and the way information about the presence and absence of a species is translated in the model (Phillips & Elith, 2010). As a result, assumptions about the pest's underlying distribution records and the choice of the climatic variables can lead to a delineation of different distribution ranges (Elith & Graham, 2009) and overestimation (or underestimation) of the potential establishment range of a species of interest.

6.2.6   Integrated Modelling Approach as a Risk Modelling Tool

Integrating the invasion model in a geographical setting facilitates incorporation of the spatial variation of known biophysical and economic drivers in the final invasion risk map. For example, entry and spread are spatial processes per se and fit naturally into a geographical framework. Host data provide spatially heterogeneous input, affecting establishment and survival of an invasive pest that can serve as a probabilistic constraint. Integrated models also better estimate the cumulative impacts of invasion that may occur at different locations over time. This becomes especially valuable for assessing complex situations, including the combination of existing infestations scattered across large and diverse regions with anticipated new introductions of a pest (Pitt et al., 2009; Rafoss, 2003; Yemshanov et al., 2009b). These models may also be used to reveal the importance of key aspects of invasion (e.g. entry potential, population growth or presence of host) via sensitivity analyses of their relative influence on invasion outcomes (Koch et al., 2009; Neubert & Caswell, 2000; Watkinson et al., 2000).

6.3   Case Study Application: Sirex Wood Wasp

A simulation-based approach to estimate risk of ecological invasions can be illustrated with the following example of a risk model for *Sirex noctilio* Fabricius, an invasive wood wasp that was first detected in North America in 2005 (Yemshanov et al., 2009a). *S. noctilio* is considered a threat to pine (*Pinus* spp.) forests throughout the eastern United States and Canada (Borchert et al., 2007; Corley et al., 2007; Haugen et al., 2006).

The invasion model provides a generalised depiction of *S. noctilio* spread and impact on pine host resources across eastern North America over a 30-year period. The simulations started from a map of known *S. noctilio* infestations (De Groot et al., 2006), followed by anticipated additional introductions of the pest in subsequent years at eastern North American marine ports (Yemshanov et al., 2009b). The pest's potential for future entry was modelled as a function of the value of imported commodities (Costello & McAusland, 2003; Levine & D'Antonio, 2003) and incorporated the impact of new international phytosanitary standards for all wood packaging and raw wood materials (FAO-IPPC, 2006), which were implemented by the United States and Canada in 2006. For each port, a local probability of entry was estimated from the volumes of received shipments of commodities capable of harbouring *S. noctilio* (FHTET, 2007a); for known infestations, the probability of *S. noctilio* introduction was set to 1 (Figure 6.2).

The successful entries and already established infestations were then used to simulate spread of the pest through North America using a coalescing colony model (Sharov & Liebhold, 1998; Yemshanov et al., 2009a, 2009b). The choice of a relatively simple model was dictated by limited knowledge about the pest's behaviour in North America, because the bulk of information about its ecology is based on studies in pine plantation forests in the Southern Hemisphere (Carnegie et al., 2006; Haugen 2006; Haugen & Hoebeke, 2005; Hurley et al., 2007). The model estimated population spread as dependent on the probability of colonisation in the nearest adjacent map location as well as the distance from the nearest known infested location, constrained by the maximum distance at which new locations may be successfully invaded by biological means. In successfully invaded locations, the maximum annual *S. noctilio* population size – and thus the total damage to the host resource – was constrained by a population carrying capacity (Yemshanov et al., 2009a).

The establishment of *S. noctilio* populations depended on the availability and susceptibility of hosts (i.e. various pine species). The susceptibility value sets the establishment probability for new colonies, and was modelled in this case as a species-specific function of pine stand age; higher susceptibility values generally translate to a higher chance of pest survival and more severe host damage. The model also required tracking the geographical distribution of pine forests and their growth over time. Maps of pine composition and age were derived from the National Forest Inventory for Canada (Gillis, 2001) and the USDA Forest Service Forest Inventory and Analysis database (Reams et al., 2005; USDA FS, 2007).

The growth of the pine resource and the amount of host surviving after *S. noctilio* infestation were modelled using tree species growth rate curves, defined separately for the United States (Dixon, 2002) and Canada (Yemshanov et al., 2009a).

In summary, three linked simulation events occurred at each time step: (1) generation of *S. noctilio* introduction events at the ports of entry, performed stochastically based on the local entry probability values; (2) stochastic spread from locations where the pest was already established or had been introduced recently; and (3) establishment of the pest at new locales with abundant susceptible hosts. This model structure is common in geographically explicit modelling of ecological invasions (see Pitt et al., 2009 for an example of a spread model for the Argentine ant, *Linepithema humile* Mayr). We assumed annual time steps, in keeping with the estimated *S. noctilio* development cycle in North America (see Borchert et al., 2007; Haugen & Hoebeke, 2005). The results depict a progressive expansion of the pest's invaded range over time. The final output is a single realisation of anticipated establishments of *S. noctilio* populations over a specified forecast period. In this modelling framework, multiple model realisations can be used to generate distributions of the plausible outcomes of an invasion that, in turn, can be used to calculate a probabilistic estimate of risk. For *S. noctilio*, the invasion risk was calculated for each geographical location (map cell) in the study region as the probability of the pest establishing a viable population at that location within the 30-year time horizon:

$$P_j = \frac{\sum_{d=1}^{D_{\text{reps}}} \tau_{j,d}}{D_{\text{reps}}} \ \forall \ \tau_{j,d} = [0\,|\,1], \tag{6.1}$$

where $\tau_{j,d}$ is the presence–absence of an infestation at location j at the end of the forecast horizon for a single model realisation d, and D_{reps} is the total number of randomised model replications. Notably, this stochastic implementation also offers the opportunity to calculate basic measures of the uncertainty associated with the model; for example the standard deviation of the probabilistic risk estimate calculated in Eq. 6.1 (Koch et al., 2009; Yemshanov et al., 2009b; Figure 6.4). Furthermore, the discrete nature of the stochastic realisations also provides a setting for various model manipulation scenarios (e.g. systematic increases in the variability of key parameter values; see Koch et al., 2009) through which it may be possible to discriminate sources of uncertainty in the risk estimates, such as natural variability or data input errors (Elith et al., 2002; Regan et al., 2002).

6.3.1   Incorporating Uncertainties in Risk Mapping

Given the extensive use of risk maps in managing biological invasions, it is surprising that very few studies have attempted to address some of the uncertainties in the risk mapping process and thus improve map utility for decision makers and other stakeholders. While widely acknowledged as a problem, quantifying uncertainties

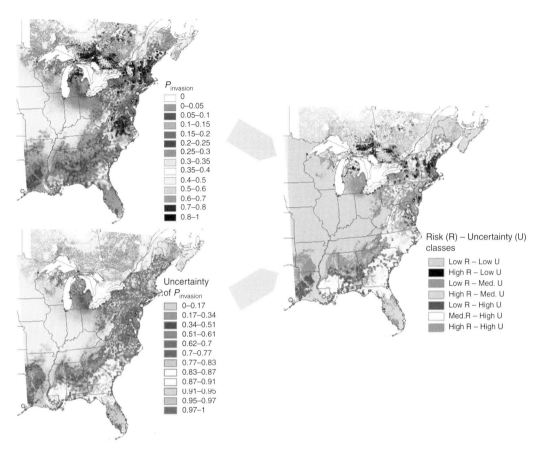

Figure 6.4. Combining maps of invasion risk and uncertainty in a single data product (a *Sirex noctilio* example).
[Reproduced with permission from Yemshanov, D., Koch, F. H., McKenney, D. W., Downing, M. C. and Sapio, F. (2009). Mapping invasive species risks with stochastic models: A cross-border United States–Canada application for Sirex noctilio Fabricius. Risk Analysis, 29(6), 868–884. See source for further details.]

of risk estimates for geographically and temporally specific analyses is challenging. As a result, uncertainties are often omitted from risk modelling outputs, and in turn, the output risk predictions are presented as effectively certain to end users (FHTET, 2007b; Meentemeyer et al., 2004; Woodbury, 2003). In truth, proper consideration of the uncertainties associated with a set of risk estimates is likely to change the meaning and implications of those estimates for decision makers (e.g. see recent climate change forecasts in Morgan & Dowlatabadi, 1996 and Reichert & Borsuk, 2005; see Chapter 12). Thus, incorporation of uncertainties in a risk map would greatly enhance its value as a decision support product.

As a starting point, a simple combination of broad risk and uncertainty categories in a single map can serve as a practical guide for decision makers (Figure 6.4). However, this can be used only for relatively simple scenarios with few ordinal combinations of risk-uncertainty classes (such as high–low classes; see Yemshanov et al., 2009b). For more complex scenarios, simple classifications may overlook subtle variations and potential trade-offs between these two important outputs and make the results difficult to interpret overall.

Other techniques that have been proposed to characterise or quantify uncertainties include sensitivity analysis (Henderson-Sellers & Henderson-Sellers, 1996; Morgan & Henrion, 1990; Swartzman & Kaluzny, 1987; Walley, 1991), ensemble prediction systems (Demerit et al., 2007; Worner & Gevrey, 2006) and multi-criteria valuation techniques (Keeney & Raiffa, 1976; Stewart, 1992; von Winterfeldt & Edwards, 1986). More advanced approaches for incorporating uncertainties in risk assessments take into account decision makers' preferences about risk and use techniques that were originally developed for asset valuation under uncertainty in corporate finance (Arrow, 1971; Levy & Markowitz, 1979; Markowitz, 1952; Sharpe, 1964). These techniques help delineate particular types of uncertainties in a risk model, such as parametric uncertainty, model structure uncertainty or model output uncertainty (Refsgaard et al., 2007; Regan et al., 2002; Walker et al., 2003). These techniques also provide a more concise depiction of the impact of uncertainty on decision making (i.e. to what degree it distorts the risk value; Götze et al., 2008).

To illustrate this concept in more detail, one possible approach is based on the well-known mean-variance rule that suggests if two choices have the same risk values but the second has a higher variance in its risk value (i.e. greater uncertainty), then the first choice should be preferred (Markowitz, 1952). In the pest risk mapping context, the basic idea is to rank map locations by their expected mean risk values, $\bar{E}$, and the variance of those risk estimates, σ^2, which represents a simple measure of uncertainty. Gerber and Pafumi (1998) proposed a certainty equivalent that adds the risk premium caused by uncertainties to the mean impact estimate. The certainty equivalent is calculated using

$$\mathrm{CE} = -\bar{E} - 0.5\alpha\sigma^2, \tag{6.2}$$

where $\bar{E}$ is the expected impact of an action or event (e.g. invasion of a location by a pest; the minus sign assumes that the impact is negative), α is the degree of a decision maker's risk aversion and σ^2 is the variance of the impact values. Thus, all elements of a risk map can be ranked in terms of the certainty equivalent.

A more advanced approach for combining risk and uncertainty is to depict all potential map locations in dimensions of expected invasion risk and its variance (or another uncertainty measure). Essentially, this portrays all map locations as a point cloud in dimensions of $\bar{E}$ and σ^2 (Figure 6.5). The points in the outermost boundary of the cloud depict the worst combinations of risk and uncertainty, i.e. a mean–variance two-attribute frontier, and are ranked as the locations of highest concern (Yemshanov et al., 2013). These points are temporarily removed from the analysis and a second frontier is determined from the rest of the cloud; this is assigned the next highest rank and then temporarily removed. The process is repeated until every point in the cloud has been assigned an integrated risk rank. The ranked points are then referenced back to the original geographical locations

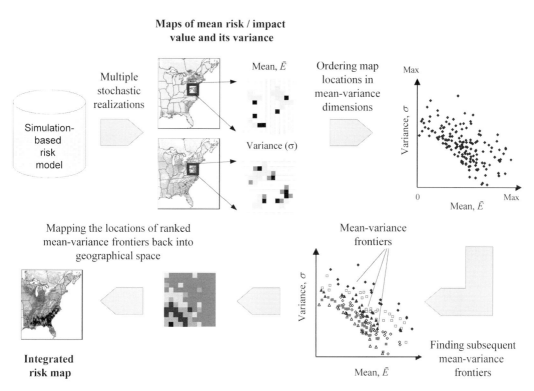

Figure 6.5.   Estimating risk as a mean–variance frontier.
[Reproduced with permission from Yemshanov, D., Koch, F.H., Ben-Haim, Y. et al. (2013). A new multicriteria risk mapping approach based on a multiattribute frontier concept. Risk Analysis, 33(9), 1694–1709.]

and plotted as a single risk map, which shows the locations' ordinal risk rankings, each representing a subsequent mean–variance frontier (Figure 6.5).

Another promising approach for incorporating uncertainties in risk modelling and mapping employs the stochastic dominance concept (Levy, 1992, 1998). As mentioned in Section 6.1, simulation-based risk models can generate a distribution of potential outcomes of an invasion for any given location of interest. Compared with a mean-variance approach, stochastic dominance considers the entire probability distribution of the potential outcomes when comparing risk between one location and another. The stochastic dominance concept has been widely used in portfolio valuation and asset pricing to differentiate efficient and inefficient sets of financial investments (Hadar & Russell, 1969). Stochastic dominance can be evaluated at different levels (Levy, 1998) that are largely related to the anticipated risk preferences of the decision makers who will be using the risk model output. First-degree stochastic dominance simply supposes that a decision maker prefers more benefit rather than less benefit. Thus, when comparing the cumulative distributions of invasion outcomes x at two different risk map locations, f and g, represented by their cumulative distributions F and G, respectively, location f dominates alternative location g by first-degree stochastic dominance if

$$G(x) - F(x) \geq 0 \text{ for all realisations of } x$$
$$\text{and} \tag{6.3}$$
$$G(x) - F(x) > 0 \text{ for at least one } x.$$

Second-degree stochastic dominance adds the assumption that the decision maker is risk averse. Higher-order stochastic dominance criteria have also been developed (e.g. third-degree stochastic dominance; Whitmore, 1970). For example, third-degree stochastic dominance adds the assumption of a preference for positive skewness of the probability distributions of the risk estimates, therefore supposing that a decision maker is decreasingly risk averse (in absolute terms) as the value-at-risk increases.

Notably, the stochastic dominance approach is not restricted to any particular distribution type and can be applied to rank all map locations through pairwise comparisons in terms of their integrated risk. Caulfield (1988) compared the stochastic dominance and mean-variance approaches for forestry applications and concluded that the stochastic dominance concept is more useful as a screening technique for making decisions under risk. However, Hildebrandt and Knoke (2011) concluded that second-degree stochastic dominance should be seen only as a method to separate high-risk alternatives, while a precise ranking among these alternatives should be carried out with other approaches. Overall, the stochastic dominance concept offers a reliable way to incorporate the uncertainty in a model-based assessment into the final risk values, and can be adapted for a partial delineation of high-risk and low-risk areas (Yemshanov et al., 2012b).

6.3.2   Technical Aspects

Although there are many advantages to the model-based risk mapping approach, there are of course potential drawbacks. Gathering the volume of information needed to model the entire invasion process can be demanding, and may be beyond the capacity and time constraints of many pest surveillance and research programs. Validation and calibration of integrated models also represents a special challenge; finding independent validation data for newly detected invaders is extremely difficult because the invasion process is often in a relatively early stage of expansion. Furthermore, these models are often focused on assessing the potential long-term outcomes as opposed to time-step-specific risks. Nevertheless, one possible approach is to model the potential spread of a long-established invasive species and then test model predictions against actual spread data obtained from historical occurrence records for that species (see Higgins et al., 2001). This method can be used only for species with a detailed observation record in the region of interest and has limited application for recently detected invasions.

Computing time represents another notable technical hurdle for wide implementation of simulation-based risk assessments. Stochastic implementation of a geographically explicit model generally means that risk and impact values have to be estimated for a large number of map units (cells or polygons) over multiple randomised realisations. The spatial extent of a risk map could exceed 10 to 20 million map units for continent-wide assessments, and 10^3 to 10^5 independent stochastic model replications are often required to get a representative distribution of invasion outcomes. This places high demand on available computing capacity, and for the sake of practicality, may limit the geographical extent (or spatial resolution) of the final risk maps. Recent advances in parallel computing will certainly help resolve this issue, and hopefully will encourage the use of dynamic simulation models to analyse risk and subsequently inform the development of pest management and regulatory policies.

References

Andersen, M. C., Adams, H., Hope, B. & Powell, M. (2004a). Risk assessment for invasive species. *Risk Analysis*, 24(4), 787–793.

Andersen, M. C., Adams, H., Hope, B. & Powell, M. (2004b). Risk analysis for invasive species: General framework and research needs. *Risk Analysis*, 24(4), 893–900.

Arrow, K. J. (1971). *Essays in the theory of risk bearing*. Chicago: Markham Publishing.

Baker, R., Cannon, R., Bartlett, P. & Barker, I. (2005). Novel strategies for assessing and managing the risks posed by invasive alien species to global crop production and biodiversity. *Annals of Applied Biology*, 146(2), 177–191.

BenDor, T. K., Metcalf, S. S., Fontenot, L. E., Sangunett, B. & Hannon, B. (2006). Modelling the spread of the emerald ash borer. *Ecological Modelling*, 197(1–2), 221–236.

Black, W. R. (1972). Interregional commodity flows: Some experiments with the gravity model. *Journal of Regional Science*, 12(1), 107–118.

Borchert, D., Fowler, G. & Jackson, L. (2007). Organism pest risk analysis: Risks to the conterminous United States associated with the woodwasp, *Sirex noctilio* Fabricius, and the symbiotic fungus, *Amylostereum areolatum* (Fries: Fries) Boidin. Raleigh, NC: USDA-APHIS-PPQ-CPHST-PERAL.

Bossenbroek, J. M., Kraft, C. E. & Nekola, J. C. (2001). Prediction of long-distance dispersal using gravity models: Zebra mussel invasion of inland lakes. *Ecological Applications*, 11(6), 1778–1788.

Brockerhoff, E. G., Bain J., Kimberley M. & Knížek, M. (2006). Interception frequency of exotic bark and ambrosia beetles (Coleoptera: Scolytinae) and relationship with establishment in New Zealand and worldwide. *Canadian Journal of Forest Research*, 36, 289–298.

Carnegie, A. J., Matsuki, M., Haugen, D. A., et al. (2006). Predicting the potential distribution of *Sirex noctilio* (Hymenoptera: Siricidae), a significant exotic pest of *Pinus* plantations. *Annals of Forest Science*, 63(2), 119–128.

Caulfield, J. P. (1988). A stochastic efficiency approach for determining the economic rotation of a forest stand. *Forest Science*, 34(2), 441–457.

Chapman, D. S., Dytham, C. & Oxford, G. S. (2007). Modelling population redistribution in a leaf beetle: An evaluation of alternative dispersal functions. *Journal of Animal Ecology*, 76(1), 36–44.

Clark, J. S., Fastie, C., Hurtt, G., et al. (1998). Reid's paradox of rapid plant migration: Dispersal theory and interpretation of paleoecological records. *BioScience*, 48(1), 13–24.

Colautti, R. I., Bailey, S. A., van Overdijk, C. D. A., Amundsen, K. & MacIsaac, H. J. (2006). Characterised and projected costs of nonindigenous species in Canada. *Biological Invasions*, 8(1), 45–59.

Condeso, T. E. & Meentemeyer, R.K. (2007). Effects of landscape heterogeneity on the emerging forest disease sudden oak death. *Journal of Ecology*, 95(2), 364–375.

Corley, J. C., Villacide, J. M. & Bruzzone, O. A. (2007). Spatial dynamics of a *Sirex noctilio* woodwasp population within a pine plantation in Patagonia, Argentina. *Entomologia Experimentalis et Applicata*, 125(3), 231–236.

Costello, C. & McAusland, C. (2003). Protectionism, trade, and measures of damage from exotic species introductions. *American Journal of Agricultural Economics*, 85(4), 964–975.

Costello, C., Springborn, M., McAusland, C. & Solow, A. (2007). Unintended biological invasions: Does risk vary by trading partner? *Journal of Environmental Economics and Management*, 54(3), 262–276.

Dawson, M. (2002). Plant quarantine: A tool for preventing the introduction and spread of alien species harmful to plants. In R. Claudi, P. Nantel & E. Muckle-Jeffs (eds.), *Alien invaders in Canada's waters, wetlands and Forests* (pp. 243–51). . Ottawa, Canada: Canadian Forest Service.

de Groot, P., Nystrom, K. & Scarr, T. (2006). Discovery of *Sirex noctilio* (Hymenoptera: Siricidae) in Ontario, Canada. *Great Lakes Entomologist*, 39(1–2), 49–53.

de Jong, G., Gunn, H. F. & Walker, W. (2004). National and international freight transportation models: An overview and ideas for further developments. *Transport Reviews*, 24(1), 103–124.

de Vos, C. J., Saatkamp, H. W., Nielen, M. & Huirne, R. B. (2004). Scenario tree modeling to analyze the probability of classical swine fever virus introduction into Member States of the European Union. *Risk Analysis*, 24(1), 237–253.

Demeritt, D., Cloke, H., Pappenberger, F., et al. (2007). Ensemble predictions and perceptions of risks, uncertainty, and error in flood forecasting. *Environmental Hazards*, 7(2), 115–127.

Dixon G. E. (2002). *Essential FVS: A user's guide to the forest vegetation simulator. Internal Report*. Fort Collins, CO: USDA Forest Service, Forest Management Service Center. Available from www.fs.fed.us/fmsc/ftp/fvs/docs/gtr/EssentialFVS.pdf

Durrett, R. & Levin, S. (1994). The importance of being discrete (and spatial). *Theoretical Population Biology*, 46(3), 363–394.

Elith, J., Burgman, M. A. & Regan, H. M. (2002). Mapping epistemic uncertainties and vague concepts in predictions of species distribution. *Ecological Modelling*, 157(2), 313–329.

Elith, J. & Graham, C. G. (2009). Do they? How do they? WHY do they differ? On finding reasons for differing performance of species distributions models. *Ecography*, 32(1), 66–77.

Elith, J. & Leathwick, J. (2009). Species distribution models: Ecological explanation and prediction across space and time. *Annual Review of Ecology, Evolution and Systematics*, 40(1), 677–697.

Elith, J., Graham, C. H., Anderson, R. P., et al. (2006). Novel methods improve prediction of species' distributions from occurrence data. *Ecography*, 29, 129–151.

Elith, J., Kearney, M. & Phillips, S. (2010). The art of modelling range-shifting species. *Methods in Ecology and Evolution*, 1(4), 330–342.

FAO-IPPC. (2006). Guidelines for regulating wood packaging material in international trade. ISPM No.15. In *International standards for phytosanitary measures* (pp. 174–183). Rome,

Italy: Food and Agriculture Organisation of the United Nations–Intergovernmental Panel on Climate Change.

FHTET (US Department of Agriculture, Forest Health Technology Enterprise Team). (2007a). *Commodities likely associated with Sirex noctilio*. Available from www.fs.fed.us/foresthealth/technology/pdfs/assoc_commodities_sirex.pdf

FHTET (US Department of Agriculture, Forest Health Technology Enterprise Team). (2007b). *Invasive pest risk maps: Sirex woodwasp – Sirex noctilio*. Available from www .fs.fed.us/foresthealth/technology/invasives_sirexnoctilio_riskmaps.shtml

FHTET (US Department of Agriculture, Forest Health Technology Enterprise Team). (2010). *Invasive pest risk maps: Oak splendor beetle* – Agrilus biguttatus (*Fabricus*). Available from fs.fed.us/foresthealth/technology/invasives_agrilusbiguttatus_riskmaps.shtml

Fuentes, M. A. & Kuperman, M. N. (1999). Cellular automata and epidemiological models with spatial dependence. *Physica A*, 267(3–4), 471–486.

Gerber, H. U. & Pafumi, G. (1998). Utility functions: From risk theory to finance. *North American Actuarial Journal*, 2(3), 74–100.

Gibson, G. J. & Austin, E. J. (1996). Fitting and testing spatio-temporal stochastic models with application in plant epidemiology. *Plant Pathology*, 45(2), 172–184.

Gillis, M. D. (2001). Canada's national forest inventory, responding to current information needs. *Environmental Monitoring and Assessment*, 67(1–2), 121–129.

Götze, U., Northcott, D. & Schuster, P. (2008). *Investment appraisal: Methods and models*. Berlin, Germany: Springer-Verlag.

Haack, R. A. (2006). Exotic bark- and wood-boring Coleoptera in the United States: Recent establishments and interceptions. *Canadian Journal of Forest Research*, 36(2), 269–288.

Hadar, J. & Russell, W. R. (1969). Rules for ordering uncertain prospects. *American Economic Review,* 59(1), 25–34.

Hamlet, A. F. & Lettenmaier, D. P. (2005). Production of temporally consistent gridded precipitation and temperature fields for the continental United States. *Journal of Hydrometeorology*, 6(3), 330–336.

Hastings, A. (1996). Models of spatial spread: Is the theory complete? *Ecology*, 77(6), 1675–1679.

Haugen, D. A. (2006). *Sirex noctilio*, Exotic Forest Pest Information System for North America. North American Forest Commission, Available from http://spfnic.fs.fed.us/exfor/data/pestreports.cfm?pestidval=33&langdisplay=english

Haugen, D. A. & Hoebeke, E. R. (2005). *Pest Alert: Sirex woodwasp – Sirex noctilio F. (Hymenoptera: Siricidae)*. USDA Forest Service NA-PR-07-05. Available from http://na.fs.fed.us/spfo/pubs/pest_al/sirex_woodwasp/sirex_woodwasp.htm

Henderson-Sellers, B. & Henderson-Sellers, A. (1996). Sensitivity evaluation of environmental models using fractional factorial experimentation. *Ecological Modelling*, 86(2–3), 291–295.

Herborg, L.-M., Jerde, C. L., Lodge, D. M., Ruiz, G. M. & MacIsaac, H. J. (2007). Predicting invasion risk using measures of introduction effort and environmental niche models. *Ecological Applications*, 17(3), 663–674.

Higgins, S. I., & Richardson, D. M. (1999). Predicting plant migration rates in a changing world: The role of long-distance dispersal. *American Naturalist*, 153(5), 464–475.

Higgins, S. I., Richardson, D. M. & Cowling, R. M. (2001). Validation of a spatial simulation model of a spreading alien plant population. *Journal of Applied Ecology* 38(3), 571–584.

Hijmans, R. J., Cameron, S. E., Parra, J. L., Jones, P. G. & Jarvis, A. (2005). Very high resolution interpolated climate surfaces for global land areas. *International Journal of Climatology*, 25(15), 1965–1978.

Hildebrandt, P. & Knoke, T. (2011). Investment decisions under uncertainty – A methodological review on forest science studies. *Forest Policy and Economics*, 13(1), 1–15.

Holmes, E. E. (1993). Are diffusion models too simple? A comparison with telegraph models of invasion. *American Naturalist*, 142(5), 779–795.

Hurley, B. P., Slippers, B. & Wingfield, M. J. (2007). A comparison of the control results for the alien invasive woodwasp, *Sirex noctilio*, in the southern hemisphere. *Agricultural and Forest Entomology*, 9(3), 159–171.

Jarvis, C. H. & Baker, R. H. A. (2001). Risk assessment for non-indigenous pests: I. Mapping the outputs of phenology models to assess the likelihood of establishment. *Diversity and Distributions*, 7(5), 223–236.

Jules, E. S., Kauffman, M. J., Ritts, W. D. & Carroll, A. L. (2002). Spread of an invasive pathogen over a variable landscape: A nonnative root rot on Port Orford cedar. *Ecology*, 83(11), 3167–3181.

Kaplan, S. & Garrick, B. J. (1981). On the quantitative definition of risk. *Risk Analysis*, 1(1), 11–27.

Keeney, R. L. & Raiffa, H. (1976). *Decisions with multiple objectives*. New York: John Wiley & Sons.

Koch, F. H., Yemshanov, D., Colunga-Garcia, M., Magarey, R.D. & Smith, W. D. (2011). Potential establishment of alien-invasive forest insect species in the United States: Where and how many? *Biological Invasions*, 13(4) 969–985.

Koch, F. H., Yemshanov, D., McKenney, D. W. & Smith, W. D. (2009). Evaluating critical uncertainty thresholds in a spatial model of forest pest invasion risk. *Risk Analysis*, 29(9), 1227–1241.

Kot, M., Lewis, M. A., & van den Driessche, P. (1996). Dispersal data and the spread of invading organisms. *Ecology*, 77(7), 2027–2042.

Kovacs, K. F., Haight, R. G., McCullough, D. G., et al. (2010). Cost of potential emerald ash borer damage in U.S. communities, 2009–2019. *Ecological Economics*, 69(3), 569–578.

LeSage, J. P. & Kelley Pace, R. (2008). Spatial econometric modeling of origin-destination flows. *Journal of Regional Science*, 48(5), 941–967.

LeSage, J. P. & Polasek, W. (2006). *Incorporating transportation network structure in spatial econometric models of commodity flows*. Economics Series 188. Vienna, Austria: Institute for Advanced Studies.

Levine, J. M. & D'Antonio, C.M. (2003). Forecasting biological invasions with increasing international trade. *Conservation Biology*, 17(1), 322–326.

Levy, H. (1992). Stochastic dominance and expected utility: Survey and analysis. *Management Science*, 38(4), 555–593.

Levy, H. (1998). *Stochastic dominance: Investment decision making under uncertainty*. Boston: Kluwer Academic.

Levy, H. & Markowitz, H. M. (1979). Approximating expected utility by a function of mean and variance. *American Economic Review*, 69(3), 308–317.

Lowe, T., Cieszewski, C. J., Zasada, M. & Zawadzki, J. (2005). Distributing FIA information onto segmented Landsat Thematic Mapper images stratified with industrial ground data. In R. E. McRoberts, G. A. Reams, P. C. Van Deusen, W. H. McWilliams & C. J. Cieszewski (eds.), *Proceedings of the Fourth Annual Forest Inventory and Analysis Symposium* (pp. 111–116). St. Paul, MN: US Department of Agriculture, Forest Service, North Central Research Station.

Magarey, R. D., Borchert, D. M., Engle, J. S., et al. (2011). Risk maps for targeting exotic plant pest detection programs in the United States. *EPPO Bulletin*, 41(1), 1–11.

Magarey, R. D., Borchert, D. M., Fowler, G. L., et al. (2007). NAPPFAST: An internet system for the weather-based mapping of plant pathogens. *Plant Disease*, 91(4), 336–345.

Magarey, R. D., Colunga-Garcia, M. & Fieselmann, D. A. (2009). Plant biosecurity in the United States: Roles, responsibilities, and information needs. *Bioscience*, 59(10), 875–884.

Markowitz, H. (1952). Portfolio selection. *The Journal of Finance*, 7(1), 77–91.

McKenney, D., Papadopol, P., Lawrence, K., Campbell, K. & Hutchinson. M. (2007). *Customized spatial climate models for Canada*. Canadian Forest Service. Technical Note No. 108.

McRoberts, R. E., Holden, G. R., Nelson, M. D., Liknes, G. C. & Gormanson, D. D. (2005). Using satellite imagery as ancillary data for increasing the precision of estimates for the Forest Inventory and Analysis program of the USDA Forest Service. *Canadian Journal of Forest Research*, 35(12), 2968–2980.

Meentemeyer, R., Rizzo, D., Mark, W. & Lotz, E. (2004). Mapping the risk of establishment and spread of sudden oak death in California. *Forest Ecology and Management*, 200(1–3), 195–214.

Melbourne B. A. & Hastings, A. (2009). Highly variable spread rates in replicated biological invasions: Fundamental limits to predictability. *Science*, 325(5947), 1536–1539.

Morgan, M. G. & Dowlatabadi, H. (1996). Learning from integrated assessment of climate change. *Climatic Change*, 34(3–4), 337–368.

Morgan, M. G. & Henrion, M. (1990). *Uncertainty: A guide to dealing with uncertainty in quantitative risk and policy analysis*. Cambridge: Cambridge University Press.

Muirhead, J. R., Leung, B., van Overdijk, C., et al. (2006). Modelling local and long-distance dispersal of invasive emerald ash borer *Agrilus planipennis* (Coleoptera) in North America. *Diversity and Distributions*, 12(1), 71–79.

Muirhead, J. R. & MacIsaac, H. J. (2005). Development of inland lakes as hubs in an invasion network. *Journal of Applied Ecology*, 42(1), 80–90.

Nathan, R. (2003). Seeking the secrets of dispersal. *Trends in Ecology and Evolution*, 18(6), 275–276.

Nathan, R. (2005). Long-distance dispersal research: Building a network of yellow brick roads. *Diversity and Distributions*, 11(2), 125–130.

Neubert, M. G., & Caswell, H. (2000). Demography and dispersal: Calculation and sensitivity analysis of invasion speed for structured populations. *Ecology*, 81(6), 1613–1628.

Okubo, A. & Levin, S.A. (2002). *Diffusion and ecological problems: Modern perspectives*. New York: Springer Science+Business Media.

O'Sullivan, P. & Ralston, B. (1974). Forecasting intercity commodity transport in the U.S.A. *Regional Studies*, 8(2), 191–195.

Phillips, S. J. & Elith, J. (2010). POC-plots: Calibrating species distribution models using presence-only data. *Ecology*, 91(8), 2476–2484.

Piel, F., Gilbert, M., De Cannière C. & Grégoire, J.-C. (2008). Coniferous round wood imports from Russia and Baltic countries to Belgium: A pathway analysis for assessing risks of exotic pest introductions. *Diversity and Distributions*, 14(2), 318–328.

Pitt, J. P. W., Worner, S. P. & Suarez, A. V. (2009). Predicting Argentine ant spread over the heterogeneous landscape using a spatially explicit stochastic model. *Ecological Applications*, 19(5), 1176–1186.

Porojan, A. (2001). Trade flows and spatial effects: The gravity model revisited. *Open Economies Review*, 12(3), 265–280.

Rafoss, T. (2003). Spatial stochastic simulation offers potential as a quantitative method for pest risk analysis. *Risk Analysis*, 23(4), 651–661.

Reams, G. A., Smith, W. D., Hansen, M. H., et al. (2005). The Forest Inventory and Analysis sampling frame. In W. A. Bechtold & P. L. Patterson (pp. 11–26). *The enhanced forest inventory and analysis program – National sampling design and estimation Procedures.* Asheville, NC: USDA Forest Service, Southern Research Station.

Refsgaard, J. C., van der Sluijs, J. P., Højberg, A. L. & Vanrolleghem, P. A. (2007). Uncertainty in the environmental modelling process – A framework and guidance. *Environmental Modelling and Software*, 22(11), 1543–1556.

Regan, H. M., Colyvan, M. & Burgman, M. A. (2002). A taxonomy and treatment of uncertainty for ecology and conservation biology. *Ecological Applications*, 12(2), 618–628.

Reichert, P. & Borsuk, M. E. (2005). Does high forecast uncertainty preclude effective decision support? *Environmental Modelling and Software*, 20(8), 991–1001.

Royama, T. (1992). *Analytical population dynamics.* London: Chapman and Hall.

Sharov, A. A. & Colbert, J. J. (1996). A model for testing hypotheses of gypsy moth *Lymantria dispar* L., population dynamics. *Ecological Modelling*, 84(1–3), 31–51.

Sharov, A. A. & Liebhold, A. M. (1998). Model of slowing the spread of gypsy moth (Lepidoptera: Lymantriidae) with a barrier zone. *Ecological Applications*, 8(4), 1170–1179.

Sharpe, W. F. (1964). Capital asset prices: a theory of market equilibrium under conditions of risk. *Journal of Finance*, 14(3), 425–442.

Shigesada, N. & Kawasaki, K. (1997). *Biological invasions: Theory and practice.* Oxford: Oxford University Press.

Shigesada, N., Kawasaki, K. & Takeda, Y. (1995). Modeling stratified diffusion in biological invasions. *American Naturalist*, 146(2), 229–251.

Stewart, T. J. (1992). A critical survey on the status of multiple criteria decision making theory and practice. *Omega*, 20(5–6), 569–586.

Swartzman, G. L. & Kaluzny, S. P. (1987). *Ecological simulation primer*. New York: Macmillan USA.

Tobin, P. C., Liebhold, A. M. & Roberts, E. A. (2007). Comparison of methods for estimating the spread of a non-indigenous species. *Journal of Biogeography*, 34(2), 305–312.

USDA FS (USDA Forest Service). (2007). *Forest inventory and analysis database: Database description and users guide version 3.0.* USDA Forest Service, Forest Inventory and Analysis Program. Available from www.fia.fs.fed.us/tools-data/docs/pdfs/FIADB_user%20guide%203-0_P3_6_01_07.pdf

van den Bosch, F., Hengeveld, R. & Metz, J. A. J. (1992). Analysing the velocity of animal range expansion. *Journal of Biogeography,* 19(2), 135–150.

Venette, R. C., Kriticos, D. J., Magarey, R., et al. (2010). Pest risk maps for invasive alien species: A roadmap for improvement. *BioScience*, 60, 349–362.

von Winterfeldt, D. & Edwards, W. (1986). *Decision analysis and behavioral research.* London: Cambridge University Press.

Waage, J. K., Fraser, R.W., Mumford, J. D., Cook, D. C. & Wilby, A. (2005). *A new agenda for biosecurity.* A Report for the Department for Food, Environment and Rural Affairs. London: Faculty of Life Sciences, Imperial College London.

Walker, W. E., Harramoës, P., Rotmans, J., van der Sluijs, J. P., van Asselt, M. B. A., Janssen, P. & Krayer von Krauss, M. P. (2003). Defining uncertainty: A conceptual basis for uncertainty management in model-based decision support. *Integrated Assessment*, 4(1), 5–17.

Walley, P. (1991). *Statistical reasoning with imprecise probabilities*. London: Chapman and Hall.

Watkinson, A. R., Freckleton, R. P. & Dowling, P. M. (2000). Weed invasions of Australian farming systems: From ecology to economics. In C. Perrings, M. Williamson, & S. Dalmazzone *The economics of biological invasions* (pp. 94–114). Cheltenham, UK: Edward Elgar.

Weinberger, H. F. (2002). On spreading speeds and travelling waves for growth and migration models in a periodic habitat. *Journal of Mathematical Biology*, 45(6), 511–548.

Westbrooks, R. (1998). *Invasive plants, changing the landscape of America: Fact book*. Washington, DC: Federal Interagency Committee for the Management of Noxious and Exotic Weeds.

Whitmore, G. A. (1970). Third degree stochastic dominance. *American Economic Review*, 60(3), 457–459.

Williamson, M. (1996). *Biological invasions*. London: Chapman and Hall.

Woodbury, P. B. (2003). Dos and don'ts of spatially explicit ecological risk assessments. *Environmental Toxicology and Chemistry,* 22(5), 977–982.

Worner, S. P. & Gevrey, M. (2006). Modelling global insect pest species assemblages to determine risk of invasion. *Journal of Applied Ecology*, 43(5), 858–867.

Woudenberg, S. W., Conkling, B. L., O'Connell, B. M., et al. (2010). *The Forest Inventory and Analysis Database: Database description and Users Manual Version 4.0 for Phase 2*. General Technical Report RMRS-GTR-245. Fort Collins, CO: United States Department of Agriculture, Forest Service, Rocky Mountain Research Station.

Yamamura, K. & Katsumata, H. (1999). Estimation of the probability of insect pest introduction through imported commodities. *Researches on Population Ecology*, 41(3), 275–282.

Yamamura, K., Katsumata, H. & Watanabe, T. (2001). Estimating invasion probabilities: A case study of fire blight disease and the importation of apple fruits. *Biological Invasions*, 3(4), 373–378.

Yemshanov, D., Koch, F.H., Ben-Haim, Y., et al. (2013). A new multicriteria risk mapping approach based on a multiattribute frontier concept. *Risk Analysis*, 33(9), 1694–1709.

Yemshanov, D., Koch, F., Ducey, M. & Koehler, K. (2012a). Trade-associated pathways of alien forest insect entries in Canada. *Biological Invasions*, 14(4), 797–812.

Yemshanov, D., Koch, F.H., Lyons, B., et al. (2012b). A dominance-based approach to map risks of ecological invasions in the presence of severe uncertainty. *Diversity and Distributions*, 18(1), 33–46.

Yemshanov, D., Koch, F. H., McKenney, D. W., Downing, M. C. & Sapio, F. (2009b). Mapping invasive species risks with stochastic models: A cross-border United States–Canada application for *Sirex noctilio* Fabricius. *Risk Analysis*, 29(6), 868–884.

Yemshanov, D., McKenney, D. W., de Groot, P., et al. (2009a). A bioeconomic approach to assess the impact of a nonnative invasive insect on timber supply and harvests: A case study with *Sirex noctilio* in eastern Canada. *Canadian Journal of Forest Research*, 39(1), 154–168.

7 Models for Understanding Disease Dynamics

Michael P. Ward, M. Graeme Garner, Joanne M. Potts and Brendan D. Cowled

7.1 Introduction

Disease systems consist of interactions between pathogens or pests (for simplicity, referred to here as diseases), their hosts and the environment. Disease systems are also influenced by, and have an influence on, other biotic and abiotic elements such as human behaviour and commercial considerations. As a simplified representation of a complex system, a model can increase appreciation and understanding of that system (Thrusfield, 2007). Models enable us to understand the effect of external influences on outputs, such as the consequences of management actions on disease dispersal in a landscape, and to communicate ideas about the behaviour of the system (Keeling, 2005; Taylor, 2003).

Models have a long history of use in human and animal health. For example, Ross developed a mathematical model of malaria transmission that was published in 1908 and later refined by MacDonald and colleagues in the 1950s (Smith et al., 2012). Models have been used to understand the disease dynamics and management of endemic diseases and to assess the impact and control options for emergency and transboundary diseases. In the past two decades, the latter application has become increasingly important as government agencies invest in preparedness and planning.

Recently, simulation models have been applied within a decision-support framework (Chadès et al., 2011) because this approach allows disease to be considered in a broader context of physical, economic, technological, management and political constraints. Some recent examples of simulation models to investigate emergency and transboundary disease spread within the animal health sector include AusSpread for foot-and-mouth disease (FMD) (Garner & Beckett, 2005; Ward et al., 2009), equine influenza (Garner et al., 2011) and classical swine fever (CSF) (Cowled et al., 2012a); the North American Animal Disease Spread Model for FMD, Aujezsky's disease and avian influenza (Reeves et al., 2011); InterSpread and InterSpread Plus for FMD (Morris et al., 2001; Owen et al., 2011) and CSF (Boklund et al., 2009; Jalvingh et al., 1999); and the Davis Animal Disease Spread Model for FMD (Bates et al., 2003; Carpenter et al., 2011) and CSF (Durr et al., 2013; Pineda-Krch et al., 2010).

Although there are many examples of the use of disease models in human health and in animal health, there are few examples of the application of disease models in plant health (Jeger et al., 2007). The use of modelling for plant health has been slower than for animal health, perhaps because of the slower progression of many plant diseases, the generally longer delays between disease incursions and detection, the greater variety of plant hosts and their diseases, and the lack of animal welfare concerns that can drive development of appropriate disease response strategies in animal health (e.g. the negative public response to large-scale culling of animals during the FMD outbreak in Britain in 2001).

The animal health sector benefits from sometimes having extensive data from censuses and systems for tracking livestock movements (Garner & Beckett, 2005). Plant disease incursions might be considered more challenging because there can be a long lag between incursion and detection (in some cases years, meaning that the estimation of when the incursion first occurred is highly uncertain); there is a greater variety of plant hosts and their diseases; and the distributions and habitats of many plant hosts and their diseases are highly uncertain.

Fox et al. (2009) investigated surveillance protocols for Chilean needle grass (*Nassella neesiana*) by integrating a spatially explicit simulation model (including plant demography and dispersal vectors) within a geographical information system. Plant weed invasion is conceptually similar to an incursion of an animal disease, and analytical and individual-based models may be useful for guiding actions for weed management and eradication (e.g. Travis et al., 2011). These types of plant disease (including weed) spread models typically generate complex unique solutions rather than general frameworks or rules for managing a range of plant diseases in different environments. Potts et al. (2013) developed a spatially explicit stochastic state-transition model of citrus canker (*Xanthomonas citri*) and tested the adequacy of various searching strategies for detecting infected host populations. Their citrus canker model includes disease spread between susceptible populations through different mechanisms such as wind dispersal and the movement of diseased plant material. The model also includes uncertainty in host species distribution and detectability of diseased hosts.

Dispersal of animal and plant diseases is a complex process in which susceptible populations may be exposed to a pathogen via numerous pathways. Models should accommodate the frequency of dispersal between an infected and non-infected population (Gertzen et al., 2011) and the cumulative effect of multiple dispersals. Importantly, infection is a chance process affected by many factors such as environmental conditions and the presence and susceptibility of the host species.

To model both plant and animal diseases successfully, the model structure should be realistic and have appropriate parameters. Here, we define success as the development of a robust and reliable tool that is considered fit for purpose (Garner & Hamilton, 2011) and is appropriate to assist with disease management or policy formulation. The usefulness of models for disease management and policy formulation declines with increasing uncertainty about the underlying structure of the model and its parameters. Model formulation requires data collection, but this is usually hampered by cost and time restrictions (because managers often need model outputs to inform their decision-making quickly).

In this chapter, we describe the principles, approaches and applications of disease spread models. We briefly discuss different modelling approaches, outline stages in model development, describe some important considerations in designing a model and provide guidelines for the critical evaluation of models. We demonstrate the application of disease spread models by presenting three case studies – examples of livestock, wildlife and plant disease spread models.

7.1.1   Principles of Building Disease Spread Models

Generic steps in model building are to determine the system and objectives of the modelling study; collect information and data on the study population and the disease; develop and validate a conceptual model; formulate, verify and validate the model; conduct sensitivity analysis; and interpret outputs and communicate results (Garner & Hamilton, 2011).

7.1.2   Approaches to Modelling Disease Spread

Disease spread models can vary from simple deterministic mathematical models through to complex spatially explicit stochastic simulations and decision support systems. The approach used should depend on the purpose of the study, how well transmission and spread of the disease are understood, the amount and quality of data available and the experience of the modelling team. Disease spread models can be categorised depending on their treatment of variability, chance and uncertainty (deterministic or stochastic), time (continuous or discrete intervals), space (non-spatial or spatial) and the structure of the population (homogeneous or heterogeneous mixing).

How disease transmission is represented is central to disease spread models. Disease transmission could be represented by a simple spread rate parameter that allows the outbreak to grow. This can be readily estimated from field data, but does not attempt to explain how new infections occur and limits opportunities to investigate control strategies. At the other end of the spectrum, a model may explicitly represent discrete transmission pathways. Although realistic values for the parameters included in these models can be difficult to obtain, these models offer greater opportunities to understand disease spread and evaluate mitigations. How the population at risk is represented is the second central characteristic of disease spread models. These two themes – disease transmission and population – are key elements in all disease spread models.

The most appropriate type of model to use will depend on the issues being studied and the objectives of the study. For example, simple deterministic models can be useful for understanding basic transmission dynamics, but they are of limited use as a predictive tool because every epidemic is unique and unlikely to follow an average pattern (Green & Medley, 2002). Stochastic models are more complicated to construct, but are particularly useful for assessing risks and can be used to investigate the likelihood of different outcomes (Taylor, 2003). Spatial models can be used to study the importance of geographical factors in the spread of disease and test spatially targeted control strategies.

Disease models in animal health have had a strong mathematical foundation (Hurd & Kaneene, 1993), relying on mass-action or chain-binomial approaches to represent movements of individuals between different disease states. These approaches generally involve simple population structures with homogeneous mixing of the population and simplified transmission parameters to represent the spread of disease. New approaches include detailed spatial simulation models that consider location, geographical and population heterogeneity (Dubé et al., 2007a; Garner & Beckett, 2005; Harvey et al., 2007), network modelling using contact network structures to explicitly capture complex patterns of interaction that underlie disease transmission (Bansal et al., 2007; Dubé et al., 2009; Hamede et al., 2012) and large agent-based models in which a system is modelled as a collection of autonomous entities that individually make decisions according to a set of rules and allow for the behaviour of entities to evolve over time (Macal & North, 2007; Perez & Dragicevic, 2009).

7.1.3   Application and Use of Models

Models can be used to study disease processes (Perez et al., 2002; Smith & Grenfell, 1990), generate hypotheses about factors involved in the persistence of endemic diseases in populations to direct further studies (Chapagain et al., 2008), provide advice on risks associated with exotic diseases and emerging disease threats (Baylis et al., 2001; Le Menach et al., 2005), assess the economic impact of diseases and evaluate control strategies at various scales (Bates et al., 2003; Cacho et al., 2006, 2010, 2011; Garner & Lack, 1995; Groenendaal et al., 2003; Hagerman et al., 2012; Pasman et al., 1994; Schoenbaum & Disney, 2003; Yoon et al., 2006), assess the effectiveness of surveillance and control programmes (Hopp et al., 2003; Leslie et al., 2012; Parnell et al., 2010; Potts et al., 2012; Rovira et al., 2007; van Asseldonk et al., 2005) and provide inputs and scenarios for training activities (Harvey et al., 2007; Jeger et al., 2007; Mangano et al., 2011). Modelling can be particularly useful in situations in which it is impractical, unethical or impossible to conduct experimental or field studies (Garner & Beckett, 2005) and to conduct retrospective analysis of epidemics to investigate different control strategies (Mangen et al., 2001).

To be useful in policy development, models should be fit for purpose and appropriately verified and validated (Garner & Hamilton, 2011). This involves ensuring that the model is an adequate representation of the system under study and that its outputs are sufficiently accurate and precise for the intended purpose. Sections 7.2 to 7.4 present examples of how disease models are being used to support planning and management of livestock, wildlife and plant disease threats.

7.2   FMD Preparedness in Livestock Systems

Introduced animal diseases have the potential to cause significant impacts on animal health, public health, the economy and the environment. The greatest economic threat to Australia by an animal disease is FMD. A recent study estimated the present value of total direct economic losses over 10 years for a large multistate outbreak at $A52 billion (Buetre et al., 2013). In response to the threat, Australia invests considerable resources in FMD prevention and planning, including surveillance, early warning systems, comprehensive emergency plans (AUSVETPLAN; available from www.animalhealthaustralia.com.au/our-publications/ausvetplan-manuals-and-documents/) and training and awareness programmes. A thorough understanding of the likely behaviour of FMD under Australian conditions is a necessary component of effective preparation and response planning. Australia has not had an outbreak of FMD since the late nineteenth century. Thus, disease spread modelling is an important tool to investigate the potential spread of disease and the effectiveness of eradication strategies under different outbreak scenarios.

To support FMD preparedness, the Australian Government Department of Agriculture has developed a disease simulation model called AusSpread (Beckett & Garner, 2007; Garner & Beckett, 2005; Roche et al., 2014b). AusSpread is a stochastic spatial simulation model of the spread and control of FMD in livestock populations. The model uses the farm as the unit of interest and simulates disease spread in daily steps while allowing for interactions between farms with different animal species and different production types, and incorporating the role that these interactions might play in the epidemiology of an outbreak of FMD.

7.2.1   Description

Unlike many other spatial simulation models, AusSpread operates within a geographical information system environment (MapBasic/MapInfo®). This offers significant advantages to the user, including ready access to specialised geographical information system functions and statements, the ability to incorporate additional spatial datasets that may be important in spread and control of disease and high-quality visual outputs (see Figure 7.1). It incorporates the attributes and spatial locations of individual farms, sale yards, weather stations, local government areas and other features of the regional environment. The user can define a custom farm type or choose from seven default farm types: specialist beef, dairy, sheep, pig, mixed beef–sheep, smallholders and feedlots. The model allows for the spread of disease through the following five pathways:

1. Direct farm-to-farm contact spread through movements of animals
2. Local spread of FMD to farms close (<3 km) to an infected farm where the actual source of the infection is not known and more than one possible conveyor can be identified (Gibbens et al., 2001)
3. Indirect farm-to-farm contact spread through movements of contaminated products, equipment and other fomites, including people and vehicles that could carry FMD from one farm to another
4. Wind-borne longer distance aerosol spread
5. Spread through sale yards and markets

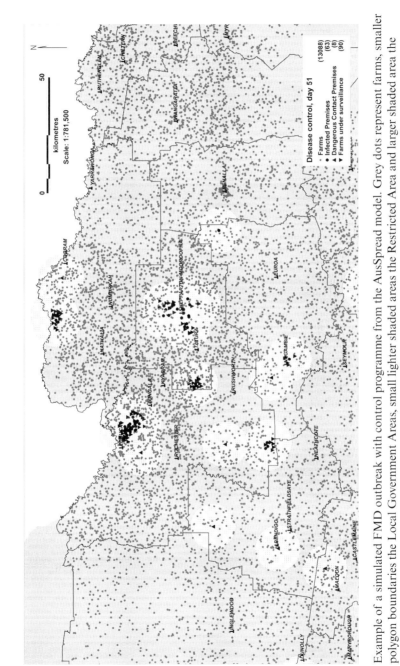

Figure 7.1. Example of a simulated FMD outbreak with control programme from the AusSpread model. Grey dots represent farms, smaller polygon boundaries the Local Government Areas, small lighter shaded areas the Restricted Area and larger shaded area the Control Area.

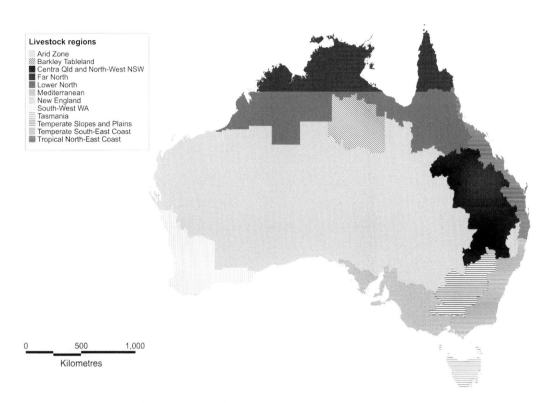

Livestock regions
- Arid Zone
- Barkley Tableland
- Centra Qld and North-West NSW
- Far North
- Lower North
- Mediterranean
- New England
- South-West WA
- Tasmania
- Temperate Slopes and Plains
- Temperate South-East Coast
- Tropical North-East Coast

0   500   1,000
Kilometres

Figure 7.2.   Australian livestock production regions.

Control Measures

AusSpread is configured to support the range of mitigations described in Australia's AUSVETPLAN manual for FMD (Animal Health Australia, 2014). Users can select mitigations including quarantine and movement restrictions; stamping out (destruction of infected and suspected infected animals); surveillance; and tracing, culling and vaccination. The efficacy, efficiency and eventual success of a control operation will depend on the availability of resources. In AusSpread, the user can specify the availability of teams to undertake surveillance, culling and vaccination, and the effectiveness of activities such as surveillance and vaccination. If available resources are insufficient to accommodate all of the operational activities scheduled for a given day, a backlog accumulates.

Livestock Information and Model Parameters

AusSpread has been designed to operate at a regional scale, where a region is part of Australia delimited by natural or geopolitical boundaries and characterised by reasonably homogeneous animal production industries and systems. Using the beef cattle industry, Australia has been divided Australia into 12 livestock production regions taking into account environmental, production and marketing factors (Roche et al., 2014b) (Figure 7.2). To simulate a large multifocal outbreak involving several regions, separate versions of the model can be set up and movements from one region to another can be used to initiate new foci of disease.

AusSpread is built around a dataset that contains information about each farm in the study population. This includes the number and type of each animal species present, the production type or types, as well as information about the farm's spatial location. Values for disease parameters in the model are based on the published literature, analyses of livestock industry information, databases (including the National Livestock Identification System; see www.animalhealthaustralia.com .au/programs/biosecurity/national-livestock-identification-system/) and expert opinion.

Verification and Validation

Verification is the process that ensures that the logic, formulae and computer code of the model correctly reproduce the logical framework conceived by the model's designer (Taylor, 2003). Validation ensures that the assumptions underlying the model are correct and that the model's representation of the study system is reasonable for the intended purpose. Verification, validation and sensitivity analysis of the AusSpread model is discussed in Garner and Beckett (2005). AusSpread has also been part of comparative studies, in which models from Australia, the Netherlands, New Zealand, North America and the United Kingdom have been compared in a series of scenarios of increasing complexity (Dubé et al., 2007b; Roche et al., 2014a; Sanson et al., 2011).

7.2.2 Applications

Vaccination in an FMD Response

Vaccination to control an outbreak of FMD in a previously FMD-free country is increasingly being recognised as a potentially important component of the response. For major livestock exporting countries such as Australia, the implications of vaccination, particularly the management of vaccinated animals, requires careful consideration because of current international guidelines on regaining FMD-free status after an outbreak (OIE, 2012). AusSpread has been used to explore the cost-effectiveness of vaccination (Abdalla et al., 2005). Three control strategies involving stamping out with or without emergency vaccination were compared in an intensive livestock-producing region of Australia. The study found that vaccination may be a cost-effective option when disease spreads rapidly and if available resources are insufficient to maintain effective stamping out. The study also reinforced the importance of early detection as a key factor influencing the probability of containment.

The AusSpread model has also been used to study FMD control in an integrated livestock production system in Texas (Ward et al., 2009). This study found that vaccination did not offer significant advantages over culling strategies under the assumptions of the study, either because it increased the time to eradicate the disease or because it increased the average number of herds depopulated.

Several countries including Australia, New Zealand, Canada, the United States, the United Kingdom and the Netherlands are undertaking a comprehensive collaborative modelling study aimed at addressing operational issues related to the use of vaccination for FMD (Roche et al., 2014a). Under the Great Britain outbreak scenario studied, all models demonstrated reduction in predicted epidemic size and duration with vaccination compared to non-vaccination baseline control strategy. For all models there were advantages in vaccinating cattle-only rather than all species, using 3-km vaccination rings immediately around infected premises and starting vaccination earlier in the control programme. This study showed that certain vaccination strategies are robust even to substantial differences in model configurations. AusSpread has also been used in Australia to model FMD outbreak scenarios to examine control options and resource implications of managing a large FMD outbreak and to conduct socioeconomic impact studies (Buetre et al., 2013; Garner et al., 2014; Roche et al. 2014b).

Welfare

Interest in animal welfare is growing among stakeholders, including governments, veterinarians, livestock industries and the broader community. A study was designed to investigate the possible extent of animal welfare problems arising from moderate and severe outbreaks of FMD in pig farms in two intensive livestock production regions (East et al., 2014). Three welfare management strategies were evaluated: the full culling of all grower and finisher pigs on farms with welfare problems, partial culling of finisher pigs only and permits for controlled movement of finisher pigs to slaughter.

Results suggested that in moderate outbreaks, resources were adequate to maintain an effective stamping-out strategy. Welfare management strategies did not significantly increase the duration or extent of these outbreaks, and welfare problems were adequately addressed under all three welfare management strategies. The partial culling strategies were more effective than the full culling strategy because fewer animals needed to be removed. In the more severe outbreaks, resources were insufficient to control disease under a stamping-out policy. In these situations, the duration and extent of the outbreaks quickly built up. Welfare problems could not be addressed with full or partial culling because of lack of resources. Welfare is particularly important in the pig industry, where the numbers of pigs on infected premises quickly increase as pregnant sows continue to farrow, quickly leading to issues of overcrowding. Maintaining adequate feed supplies is another problem. In the face of resource constraints, sending pigs direct to slaughter proved to be the most effective option for managing welfare issues. These results, which would be inaccessible by any other means, illustrate the kinds of questions that can be explored by complex models for which data and understanding are relatively complete.

Surveillance and Early Detection

The importance of early detection in the subsequent size of an outbreak of an emergency animal disease (EAD) is well recognised (Abdalla et al., 2005; Carpenter et al., 2011; Ward et al., 2009). Animal health authorities in Australia commissioned a study to identify and describe the relative likelihood of the introduction, establishment and spread of significant diseases, including FMD, across Australia and to assess the consequences of delayed detection (Hester & Garner, 2012).

Disease modelling was used to evaluate the potential spread of FMD that could occur between introduction and time to detection in each of the 12 Australian livestock production regions. The study confirmed that there is considerable heterogeneity in the likely size of outbreaks between regions and highlighted the importance of taking regional and seasonal factors into account when assessing disease risks (East et al., 2016). Work has also been undertaken to assess the effectiveness of the general surveillance system for detecting an incursion of FMD (Martin et al., 2015) and to test different approaches to improving early detection (Garner et al., 2016).

The findings have provided valuable information to assist preparedness planning in terms of surveillance, management and the resource implications for responding to outbreaks of FMD in different parts of Australia.

7.3 Wildlife Disease: CSF and Feral Pigs

7.3.1 Background

Infectious disease in wildlife can have ecological, biodiversity and societal impacts (Jones et al., 2008; Li et al., 2005; McCallum et al., 2009; Normile, 2008). However, management responses required for mitigation are frequently limited by poor understanding of disease epidemiology in wildlife (Cowled et al., 2012b). Disease modelling is one approach for providing new insights into wildlife disease epidemiology.

Wild pigs (*Sus scrofa*) are of international significance because they are found on every continent except Antarctica (Oliver & Leus, 2008) and are variously considered a damaging invasive (feral pigs), a valued endemic (wild boar) or a highly sought after game species. In Australia, domestic pigs became feral following their introduction at European settlement. They are now found across 38% of the continent (Choquenot et al., 1996) and have been estimated to number as many as 13.5 million (Hone, 1990). The distribution of populations continues to expand through mechanisms such as illegal translocations by hunters (Spencer & Hampton, 2005).

Feral pigs have been infected by a range of important pathogens including CSF (Laddomada, 2000). CSF is an important transboundary disease of both domestic and feral pigs (OIE, 2011) and has caused outbreaks costing billions of dollars (Meuwissen et al., 1999). CSF has a wide geographical distribution and is found throughout much of the world (including South-East Asia) but not Australia (although it occurs close to Australia in Indonesia). This case study focuses on modelling the epidemiology and control of highly virulent CSF in northern Australian feral pig populations that was initiated to enhance emergency disease preparedness (Cowled et al., 2012a).

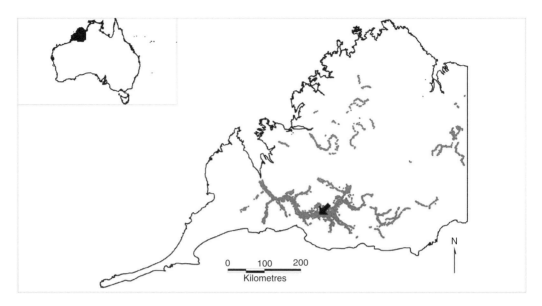

Figure 7.3.   Feral pig distribution in the Kimberley region. The dots represent simulated pig herds within known feral pig distributions. The arrow indicates the introduction site for all simulations. The insert shows the location of the Kimberley region in north-west Australia.
[Reprinted with permission from Cowled, B. D., Garner, M. G., Negus, K. & Ward, M. P. (2012). Controlling disease outbreaks in wildlife using limited culling: Modelling classical swine fever incursions in wild pigs in Australia. *Veterinary Research*, 43, 3.]

7.3.2   Modelling Approach

The approach was similar to that described in Section 7.2. The model was extensively respecified to account for the important unique features of feral pig ecology and epidemiology (Cowled & Garner, 2008). Two models were developed: a within-herd model and a between-herd model. The within-herd model simulated the spread of infection within herds and allowed estimation of important epidemiological probability distributions (e.g. infectious and immune periods). Outputs of the within-herd model were then used as input parameters for the between-herd model.

The between-herd model simulated the spread of infection within a feral pig population in the Kimberley region of north-western Australia (see Figure 7.3). The Kimberley region is remote and sparsely settled; it has an extensive beef cattle pastoral industry and feral pigs are widely dispersed across the region. The between-herd model simulated pig herds across the landscape using published information on population densities, group sizes (e.g. Twigg et al., 2005) and known feral pig distributions (Cowled et al., 2009). The model captured much of the known ecology and behaviour of feral pigs. For example, feral pigs were aggregated into herds and adult males were allowed to exist as lone individuals. Pigs were given a seasonal home range and the majority were assigned high fidelity to that home range (e.g. Caley, 1997). Most pigs moved within a small part of their seasonal home range

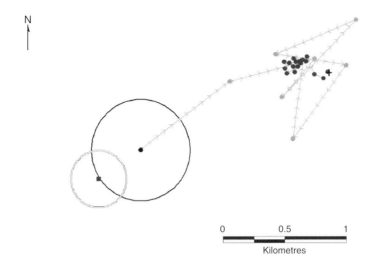

Figure 7.4.   Representation of a typical disease transmission event and subsequent daily movements of the newly infected herd in the process model (Cowled et al., 2012a). An infected herd (red square) and susceptible herd (blue circle) have overlapping daily home ranges (red and blue circles, respectively). CSF transmission may occur according to an arbitrary probability. Following infection, the incubating herd continues to move normally for several days (yellow dots) before becoming clinically affected (red dots) with shortened daily movements and eventually having all herd members killed (black cross). This infected herd does not contact another herd and CSF is not transmitted to another herd.
[Reprinted with permission from Cowled, B. D., Garner, M. G., Negus, K. & Ward, M. P. (2012). Controlling disease outbreaks in wildlife using limited culling: Modelling classical swine fever incursions in wild pigs in Australia. *Veterinary Research*, 43, 3.]

each day, but some pigs were able to leave their home range and move to adjacent pig home ranges if the distance was biologically plausible. Given the sociability of feral pigs, home ranges overlapped. Pig distributions were structured along large watercourses, reflecting the pigs' requirements for riverine habitat for thermoregulation and water (Choquenot & Ruscoe, 2003; Cowled et al., 2006).

The model used daily steps and was spatially explicit. Disease transmission was possible if the daily home range of an infected pig herd (or individual) overlapped with an adjacent uninfected herd on a particular day (see Figure 7.4). If daily home ranges overlapped, transmission was modelled by sampling an appropriate probability distribution. Following the introduction of an infection, the epidemic could progress as long as transmission between adjacent pig groups and individuals occurred before a herd had either been extirpated by infection or recovered from such an infection.

Surveillance and control steps following detection of an outbreak were also implemented in the model by assuming that disease was detected six weeks after introduction and that surveillance occurred to delineate infection. Control using aerial culling or aerial vaccination was then modelled to reflect attempts to contain and eradicate the outbreak.

7.3.3   Major Findings

The model showed that epidemics could persist for many years in the Kimberley, and would generally progress in gradual epidemic waves along river systems where appropriate densities of feral pigs existed in a continuous population. Importantly, the modelling revealed that the epidemic would fade out when the epidemic wave reached an area of low or discontinuous feral pig density, although this would generally take several years.

The surveillance and control modules indicated that under the assumptions of realistic resources, detection at six weeks and no artificial movements of feral pigs, disease could be contained and eradicated within weeks. This occurred by first delineating an infected feral pig population and then by implementing control zones where a proportion of feral pigs was culled or vaccinated at the periphery of the outbreak. The outbreak could then fade out within a contained area as the number of susceptible herds declined over time. Several combinations of the width of the control zone and the proportion of pigs culled were successful at eradicating infection, but as a rule-of-thumb, if 60% to 80% of populations were culled within 20 km to 30 km of an outbreak, containment and eradication were very likely to be achieved. Vaccination was also successful, but was less effective than aerial culling.

Sensitivity analysis was conducted to ascertain the relative importance of the different assumptions. The assumed density of feral pigs, the linear distance a herd can move in a day, the virulence of the strain of CSF, and the transmission probability between adjacent herds can all have a substantial influence on the model outputs. Density is especially important because following good rainfall, when feral pig populations are likely to be larger and denser, the likelihood that CSF could establish is higher. Conversely, in dry years or if the estimate of feral pig density was too high, infection may not establish. The influence of transmission probabilities suggests that further information is required to enhance modelling outcomes.

7.4   Plant Disease: Citrus Canker as an Example

Citrus canker (*Xanthomonas citri* (Hasse) Vauterin) is a plant-pathogenic bacterium that causes lesions on leaves, shoots, branches and fruit of several susceptible species within the Rutaceae family (Goto, 1992; Gottwald et al., 2002). In Australia, the detection of citrus canker triggers immediate quarantine restrictions and disrupts the movement of fresh fruit (Dempsey et al., 2002). The last outbreak of citrus canker in Australia was in Emerald, Queensland, in July 2004 (Gambley et al., 2009). During the four and a half years it took to eradicate the citrus canker outbreak, approximately 495,000 commercially grown citrus trees planted on 1,100 hectares, 4,235 citrus trees planted on 1,238 residential properties, and 175,000 native *Citrus glauca* trees in bushland were destroyed in the 3,150-km^2 pest quarantine region around Emerald (Senate Rural and Regional Affairs and Transport Legislation Committee, 2006). The eradication campaign was completed in 2009 at an estimated cost of A\$17.6 million (Gambley et al., 2009), excluding the cost to the industry (Alam & Rolfe, 2006).

During an incursion of citrus canker, the main aim of the biosecurity response is to achieve disease-free status as quickly as possible. One of the critical initial response activities involves tracing known movements to and from an infected property. During an incursion response, managers allocate surveillance resources to follow-up these movements in order of priority. Ranking priorities is difficult in plant health and is typically subjective because for many plant diseases, there is a lag between initial infection and detection that causes uncertainty in estimating the day of initial infection. In addition, host species or their distributions are not known with certainty and dispersal mechanisms may be unknown. Although subjective judgment can be reliable in contexts in which repetition and feedback are substantial, most incursions of plant disease are essentially novel. The novelty and complexity make decision makers especially susceptible to contextual and cognitive frailties, rendering judgments potentially unreliable (Perry et al., 2001; Slovic, 1999; Wilkinson et al., 2011). This creates a need for simple rules-of-thumb that result in robust and effective strategies for searching during responses to incursions.

This case study outlines a simulation-based spatially explicit stochastic state-transition model, in which several dispersal mechanisms (e.g. wind or human-assisted movement of diseased plant material) can spread a disease from infected to susceptible host populations. In this model, not all host populations in the landscape must be known. Susceptible populations of suitable host species can exist, receive the disease and spread the disease until these host populations are discovered via surveillance. This is different to many models of disease spread in animals that typically assume all host populations are known (e.g. Garner et al., 2011). Patterns of disease dispersal emerge by running many iterations of the simulation model over a range of scenarios.

7.4.1   Model Description

A Network of Nodes

The simulation model is based on a network of nodes that represent areas of interest that may contain potential host species or suitable habitats that are spatially clustered (e.g. an orchard) or act as a pathway for disease dispersal (e.g. a fruit-packing shed). Each node comprises a unique spatial location within the network and is defined by several features including node type, area, the number of

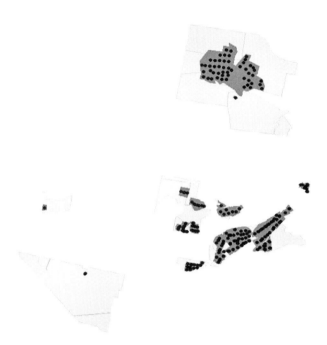

Figure 7.5.   Map of a hypothetical citrus-growing region (based on Emerald, Queensland), with areas containing host species represented as a network of nodes. Each node (solid black dot) is defined by a spatial location and area, and contains a number of citrus plants with a mean tree age. Commercial citrus growing areas are shaded dark grey and properties that contain commercial citrus areas are shaded light grey.
[Reprinted with permission from Potts, J. M., Cox, M. J., Barkley, P., et al. (2013). Model-based search strategies for plant diseases: A case-study using citrus canker (*Xanthomonas citri*). *Diversity and Distributions*, 19(5–6), 590–602.]

susceptible host plants and the mean age of host plants. The geographical layout of our case study is shown in Figure 7.5 and includes three node types: *block*, comprising commercially grown citrus trees that are assumed to be exposed to the same management practices such as pruning, harvesting and pest-spraying; *backyard*, in which individual trees are grown in backyard settings where management practices such as pest-spraying may be more haphazard; and *commercial nursery*, where host plant material is propagated for planting in commercial citrus blocks. For each iteration of the simulation study, a node was randomly chosen to be the first infected property.

Incubation, Infectiousness, Citrus Canker Dispersal, and Susceptibility

Once the first node in the network becomes infected, citrus canker has an incubation period of two weeks before the node becomes contagious and dispersal mechanisms can transport bacteria to other uninfected nodes in the network. The number of host trees, their mean age and tree canopy area determine infectiousness, which represents the level of citrus canker bacteria each node can produce and disperse to other nodes (i.e. nodes with many infected trees have greater capability to produce

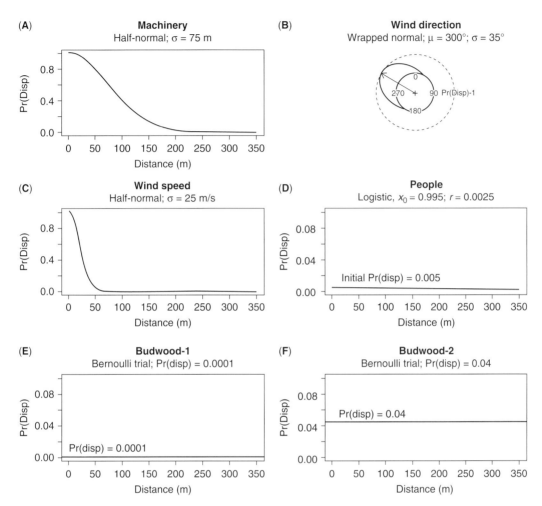

Figure 7.6. Five examples of dispersal functions, with probability of dispersal, Pr(Disp), on the *y*-axis. Wind direction and wind speed-based dispersal are varied at each time step based on weather data. The budwood pathway (panels **E** and **F**) have node-type dependent parameters with Budwood-1 parameterised with Pr(disp) = 0.0001 for citrus block to citrus block and citrus block to commercial nursery pathways. Budwood-2 was parameterised with Pr(disp) = 0.04 for commercial nursery to all other node types. Note the varying *y*-axis scales: panels **A** and **C** have Pr(disp) range 0 to1, while panels **D** to **F** have Pr(disp) range 0 to 0.1.
[Reprinted with permission from Potts, J. M., Cox, M. J., Barkley, P., et al. (2013). Model-based search strategies for plant diseases: A case-study using citrus canker (*Xanthomonas citri*). *Diversity and Distributions*, 19(5–6), 590–602.]

more bacteria than nodes with fewer infected trees). When a contagious node is sufficiently infectious, a dispersal mechanism may transmit citrus canker bacteria from the contagious node to an uninfected node. In our simulations, the dispersal mechanisms included wind and rain as well as the movement of contaminated farm machinery, people (e.g. bacteria on clothing) and plant material (e.g. budwood, Figure 7.6). Dispersal mechanisms are directional, and a dispersal event of moving plant material from a citrus block to a commercial nursery had a lower probability (Figure 7.6E) than the opposite dispersal event of moving plant material from a commercial nursery to a citrus block (Figure 7.6F).

Importantly, although citrus canker bacteria might be successfully dispersed from a contagious node to an uninfected node, the uninfected node must be susceptible to infection before citrus canker can become established. That is, there must be suitable habitats or host plants at the uninfected node, host plants must be in a growth stage that is susceptible to infection and environmental conditions must be conducive. Susceptibility of the uninfected node was governed by temperature in a given time step and mean tree age at the node (Dalla Pria et al., 2006).

Detectability

Detectability relates to two processes. Initially, a new disease in a region is unlikely to be detected because people are unlikely to be actively searching for it, and the disease's signs, if they are observed, may go undiagnosed. This initial detectability is modelled as being proportional to an infected node's infectiousness (i.e. as a node becomes more infectious, detectability of the disease increases).

After initial disease discovery, detectability increases as awareness is increased, and surveillance officers and property owners begin to search actively for the disease on host species. We model this detectability for the ith node as a function of the duration of infection at the ith node (i.e. the time between when the ith node first became infected and when it was inspected for disease presence) and the infectiousness of the ith node, given the minimum period required for visual signs of infection to appear. The appearance of visual signs of infection is highly variable and can occur from as early as 7 to 10 days post-infection (Gottwald et al., 1989; Graham et al., 2004) to as long as 60 days or more postinfection under adverse environmental conditions (Dalla Pria et al., 2006; Gottwald & Graham, 1992). The detectability parameter was varied in the simulation scenarios.

7.4.2   Simulation Scenarios

We simulated two scenarios for the dispersal and establishment of citrus canker – Emerald and Mildura, a location with a more temperate climate (Figure 7.7) – that were based on hypothetical rearrangements of a real incursion (Emerald, Queensland; Figure 7.5) but modified to reflect a wider range of initial conditions and environments. Weather data were taken from the Australian Bureau of Meteorology between July 2009 and July 2010. Weather conditions interact with node infectiousness and susceptibility. For example, citrus canker bacteria cannot survive above in temperatures greater than 42°C (Dalla Pria et al., 2006) and because of extremely hot temperatures in Mildura after week 50 (panel 2, Figure 7.7), the infectiousness, probability of dispersal and probability of detection (panels 3, 4 and 6 in Figure 7.7, respectively) declined significantly for the Mildura simulation scenario. Each simulation was run for two years (104 weekly time steps) and repeated 1,000 times. For each simulation, the time step at which a dispersal event occurred,

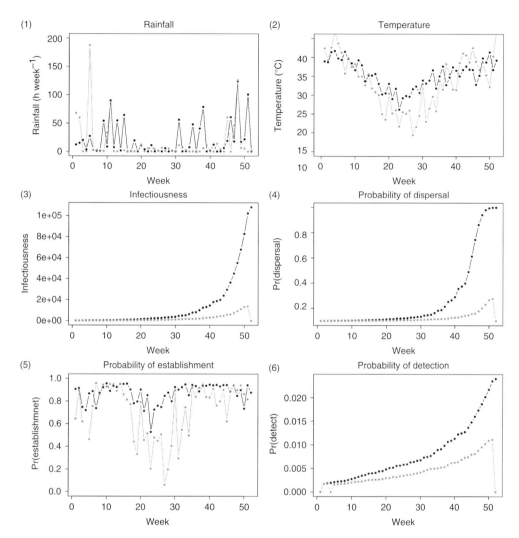

Figure 7.7.   Weekly rainfall duration (panel 1) and temperature (panel 2) as related to infectiousness (panel 3), probability of dispersal (panel 4), probability of establishment (panel 5) and probability of detection (panel 6). The *x*-axis shows weeks from 1 July 2009. Data are from the Australian Bureau of Meteorology for Emerald, Queensland (black line) and Mildura, Victoria (grey line). Given these input parameters, infectiousness (panel 3) is calculated for a node containing 1,000 two-year-old trees. Dispersal probability is dependent on infectiousness and duration of infection. Establishment probability is based on citrus variety, mean tree age and temperature. The drop in infectiousness, probability of dispersal and detection for the Mildura scenario (grey line) occurred because of extreme weather events (temperatures exceeding 42°C) that kill all citrus canker bacteria.

[Reprinted with permission from Potts, J. M., Cox, M. J., Barkley, P., et al. (2013). Model-based search strategies for plant diseases: A case-study using citrus canker (*Xanthomonas citri*). *Diversity and Distributions*, 19(5–6), 590–602.]

the node the pest came from, the node(s) it infected and the dispersal mechanism, were recorded.

7.4.3   Using Model Outputs to Develop Searching Strategies for Citrus Canker Eradication

We tested the efficacy (number of infected nodes detected and the number of nodes visited) of the three search strategies. The three search strategies we investigated were:

1. **Adaptive radius:** A circular search area was established around the first detected node (not necessarily the node that was the first infected). The radius of this circle was proportional to the number of months, t_1, since the node was first infected such that $r = t_1 d$, where d is an arbitrary distance. This type of search makes no assumptions about search direction (forward or backward tracing). In the citrus canker example, we varied d from 50 m to 1,000 m in intervals of 50 m. We used a truncated normal distribution in which input the values of the distribution parameters were derived using expert opinion.
2. **Closest n nodes:** A given number of n nodes closest to the node where the disease was first detected were searched with internode distance calculated as the Euclidian distance from node edge to node edge. This type of search makes no assumptions about search direction. In the citrus canker example, we varied the number of closest n nodes from 1 to 100 in steps of 1.
3. **Adaptive search of probability space:** This search strategy is also centred on the node where a disease outbreak is initially detected. Using knowledge of dispersal and establishment probabilities, a matrix of all possible dispersal and establishment probabilities was calculated from each node to every other node in the network.

In simulations of both hypothetical scenarios, either no spread occurred from the point of initial infection (Emerald, 3.1%; Mildura, 42.7%) or the disease spread but remained undetected during surveillance (Emerald, 0.1%; Mildura, 18.5%). The detected proportion was typically greater in Emerald, where weather conditions were more conducive to citrus canker spread, than in Mildura, where fewer nodes became infected. Regardless of which simulation parameters were used and regardless of the probability of the detectability of citrus canker if present (set at 1.0, 0.7 and 0.3), the adaptive radius search method outperformed the other search methods (see Figure 7.8) in terms of detecting the most number of infected nodes in the network. However, this method also used more survey effort, consistently searching a greater proportion of nodes on the network than the other two strategies.

The adaptive radius rule set is similar to the approach in Gottwald et al. (2001) that stipulates a 580-m removal zone around every infected host species for 30 days following initial infection. Importantly, none of the search strategies we investigated (including the adaptive radius strategy) consistently found all infected nodes

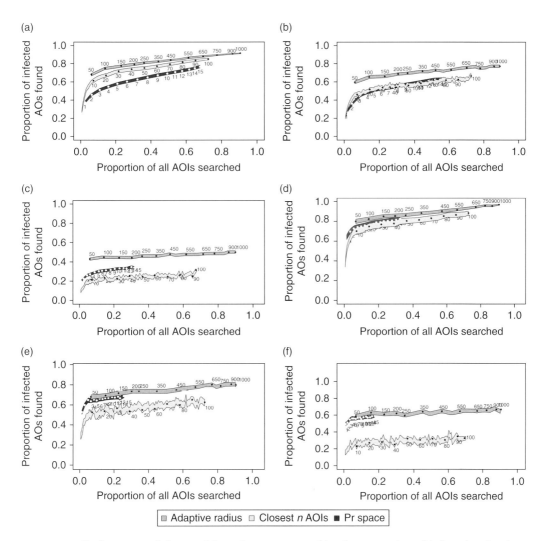

Figure 7.8.   Performance of the searching rule sets measured by the proportion of infected nodes that were detected (*y*-axis) compared with all nodes that were searched (*x*-axis). The top and bottom rows use Emerald and Mildura weather conditions, respectively. The left, middle and right columns had detection probabilities of 1.0 (perfect detection), 0.7 and 0.3, respectively. The proportion of infected areas of interest found using the adaptive radius method (shaded dark grey) was calculated using a radius of between 50 m and 250 m (at 50-m intervals) and between 250 m and 1,000 m (at 100-m intervals). The closest *n* areas of interest (shaded light grey) searched between the closest 10 and 100 nodes (in intervals of 10 nodes). The Pr space method (shaded black) searched between 1 and 15 nodes with the highest probability of transmitting the disease (calculated using the transmission matrix, Figure 7.6). If the disease was detected at any of the searched nodes, the next set of nodes was selected until no disease was detected.

[Reprinted with permission from Potts, J. M., Cox, M. J., Barkley, P., et al. (2013). Model-based search strategies for plant diseases: A case-study using citrus canker (*Xanthomonas citri*). *Diversity and Distributions*, 19(5–6), 590–602.]

without searching all susceptible nodes in the region. However, the model would allow estimation of the probability of detecting 95% of the infected nodes and thus the effectiveness and reliability of different search strategies for different phases of surveillance (e.g. delimiting versus proof of pest eradication).

The model was developed with flexibility in mind to allow users to investigate the behaviour of different strategies for searching and ranking the priority of traces of citrus canker in other regions and for other plant pests and diseases. Potts et al. (2012) and Potts et al. (2013) fully describe the model. Potential model extensions include exploring the implementation of control measures (e.g. destroying all host plants within a node) and calculating the cost of implementing control measures.

7.5   Conclusions

In an emergency disease situation, policy decisions regarding control often have to be made in the face of uncertainty and with imperfect understanding of how interactions between the agent, environment and host affect transmission and development of disease. Disease models offer a means to provide assistance for decision-makers by combining available information from field and experimental studies with the opinion of experts to gain insight into the dynamics of infection and disease control.

As computing power has increased, more user-friendly software has become available, and with the greater availability of disease and population data (including spatially referenced data), the scope and complexity of disease models have increased. Developments in geographical information systems, remote sensing, data analysis methods, network theory and complex systems science are leading to a new generation of models.

Disease systems are inherently variable and predictions based on disease spread models may not be sufficiently accurate and precise for use in the day-to-day management of the response. The use of disease models to direct decision making during fast-moving epidemics remains controversial (Garner et al., 2007) because realistic parameter values that reflect the local situation are likely to be incomplete. Indeed, the use of models as decision support tools in the 2001 FMD disease epidemic in the United Kingdom has attracted much criticism in both the scientific literature and popular media (Kitching et al., 2006; Mansley et al., 2011; Nerlich, 2007).

Adding complexity to a model may not necessarily improve the quality of outputs (Green & Medley, 2002). Modelling invariably involves trade-offs in terms of complexity versus availability of data and in model specification (i.e. a model that is highly specified for a particular population time or location may not be applicable to other populations, times or places). Models are just one tool for providing technical advice and should not be considered in isolation from other sources of information.

7.5.1 Future Directions

By definition, disease spread models are an abstraction of the real-life process of disease transmission. Models attempt to capture the key mechanisms that determine how diseases spread from one area or group of animals or plants to another. In the processing of simplifying a model to make it tractable, we can inadvertently fail to include characteristics that make the model useful for decision making and policy development to plan for and respond to disease threats. Disease spread models are likely to continue to become more sophisticated by using the increasingly available computer resources and data. However, there will continue to be a trade-off between what can be achieved technically and what is needed to support decision making and policy development.

In the future, there will likely be an increasing reliance on the outputs of disease spread models to guide decisions on preparedness and response strategies, and to justify the policies that are developed. To determine if models are fit for purpose, the following questions can be asked:

• What scale of resolution is needed? Is it (for example) the individual farm or an entire region?
• How important is the dimension of time? Do we need to understand how a disease spreads at a daily resolution, or monthly?
• What data are the model built on and are these appropriate?
• How was expert opinion incorporated into the model? Were these opinions obtained in a systematic and transparent manner?
• Is the model flexible enough to allow a range of management and control strategies to be tested?
• Does the model require specialist software and a super-computer for it to be run?
• Does the model incorporate real-life issues (e.g. transportation networks and non-homogeneous mixing) to generate realistic outputs?

One of the major benefits of developing disease spread models is that they can be readily adapted to explore different scenarios to inform disease management policy (Garner & Beckett, 2005; Pech et al., 1992, 1995). However, despite this potential utility, disease spread models have not been routinely used to comprehensively explore practical and realistic mitigation strategies under a variety of disease and spread incursion scenarios. To date, disease spread models have had limited impact on animal and plant health policy development. One possible reason is a lack of communication between disease modellers and decision makers – the stakeholders in any disease modelling programme. More effort needs to be spent on developing close working relationships between disease modellers and stakeholders. The latter need to clearly express their objectives in terms of how they would use model outputs and what critical questions need to be answered. The former must strive to explain both the modelling process and the interpretation of model outputs to inform policy and influence decision making.

References

Abdalla, A., Beare, S., Cao, L., Garner, G. & Heaney, A. (2005). *Foot and mouth disease: evaluating alternatives for controlling a possible outbreak in Australia*, ABARE eReport 05.6. Canberra: Australian Bureau of Agricultural and Resource Economics.

Alam, K. & Rolfe, J. (2006). Economics of plant disease outbreaks. *Agenda*, 13(2), 133–146.

Animal Health Australia. (2014). *Disease strategy: foot-and-mouth disease (version 3.4), Australian Veterinary Emergency Plan (AUSVETPLAN)*, edition 3. Canberra: Primary Industries Ministerial Council.

Bansal, S., Grenfell, B. T. & Meyers L. A. (2007). When individual behaviour matters: Homogeneous and network models in epidemiology. *Journal of the Royal Society Interface*, 4(6), 879−891.

Bates, T. W., Thurmond, M. C. & Carpenter, T. E. (2003). Results of epidemic simulation modeling to evaluate strategies to control an outbreak of foot-and-mouth disease. *American Journal of Veterinary Research*, 64(2), 205−210.

Baylis, M., Mellor, P. S., Wittmann, E. J. & Rogers, D. J. (2001). Prediction of areas around the Mediterranean at risk of bluetongue by modelling the distribution of its vector by satellite imaging. *Veterinary Record,* 149(21), 639−643.

Beckett, S. & Garner, M. G. (2007). Simulating disease spread within a geographic information system environment. *Veterinaria Italiana*, 43(3), 595−604.

Boklund, A., Toft N., Alban L. & Uttenthal, A. (2009). Comparing the epidemiological and economic effects of control strategies against classical swine fever in Denmark. *Preventive Veterinary Medicine*, 90(3–4), 180−193.

Buetre, B., Wicks, S., Kruger, H., et al. (2013). *Potential socioeconomic impacts of an outbreak of foot-and-mouth disease in Australia*. ABARES Research Report, Canberra, September. CC BY 3.0. Research report 13.11.

Cacho, O. J. & Hester, S. M. (2011). Deriving efficient frontiers for effort allocation in the management of invasive species. *Australian Journal of Agricultural and Resource Economics*, 55(1), 72−89.

Cacho, O. J., Spring, D., Hester, S. & Mac Nally, R. (2010). Allocating surveillance effort in the management of invasive species: A spatially-explicit model. *Environmental Modelling & Software*, 25(4), 444−454.

Cacho, O. J., Spring, D., Pheloung, P. & Hester, S. (2006). Evaluating the feasibility of eradicating an invasion. *Biological Invasions*, 8(4), 903−917.

Caley, P. (1997). Movements, activity patterns and habitat use of feral pigs (*Sus scrofa*) in a tropical habitat. *Wildlife Research*, 24(1), 77−87.

Carpenter, T. E., O'Brien, J. M., Hagerman, A. D. & McCarl, B. A. (2011). Epidemic and economic impacts of delayed detection of foot-and-mouth disease: A case study of a simulated outbreak in California. *Journal of Veterinary Diagnostic Investigation*, 23(1), 26−33.

Chadès, I., Martin, T. G., Nicol, S., et al. (2011). General rules for managing and surveying networks of pests, diseases and endangered species. *Proceedings of the National Academy of Sciences of the USA*, 108(20), 8323–8328.

Chapagain, P. P., Van Kessel, J. S., Karns, J. S., et al. (2008). A mathematical model of the dynamics of *Salmonella cerro* infection in a US dairy herd. *Epidemiology and Infection*, 136(2), 236−272.

Choquenot, D., McIlroy, J. & Korn, T. (1996). *Managing vertebrate pests: Feral pigs*. Canberra: Bureau of Resource Sciences, Australian Government Publishing Service.

Choquenot, D. & Ruscoe, W. A. (2003). Landscape complementation and food limitation of large herbivores: Habitat-related constraints on the foraging efficiency of wild pigs. *Journal of Animal Ecology*, 72(1), 14−26.

Cowled, B. & Garner, G. (2008). A review of geospatial and ecological factors affecting disease spread in wild pigs: Considerations for models of foot-and-mouth disease spread. *Preventive Veterinary Medicine*, 87(3–4), 197−212.

Cowled, B. D., Garner, M. G., Negus, K. & Ward, M. P. (2012a). Controlling disease outbreaks in wildlife using limited culling: Modelling classical swine fever incursions in wild pigs in Australia. *Veterinary Research*, 43(1), 3.

Cowled, B. D., Giannini, F., Beckett, S. D., et al. (2009). Feral pigs: Predicting future distributions. *Wildlife Research*, 36(3), 242−251.

Cowled, B. D., Lapidge, S. J., Hampton, J. O. & Spence, P. B. S. (2006). Measuring the demographic and genetic effects of pest control in a highly persecuted feral pig population. *Journal of Wildlife Management*, 70(6), 1690−1697.

Cowled, B. D., Ward, M. P., Laffan, S. W., et al. (2012b). Integrating survey and molecular approaches to better understand wildlife disease ecology. *PLoS ONE*, 7(10), e46310.

Dalla Pria, M., Christiano, R. C. S., Furtado, E. L., Amorim, L. & Bergamin Filho, A. (2006). Effect of temperature and leaf wetness duration on infection of sweet oranges by Asiatic citrus canker. *Plant Pathology*, 55(5), 657−663.

Dempsey, S., Evans, G. & Szandala, E. (2002). *A target list of high risk pathogens of citrus*. Canberra: Department of Agriculture, Fisheries and Forestry.

Dubé, C., Garner, G., Stevenson, M., et al. (2007a). The use of epidemiological models for the management of animal diseases. Paper presented to *75th General Session of the International Committee of the World Organization for Animal Health* (*OIE*), Paris, 20−25 May 2007.

Dubé, C., Ribble, C., Kelton, D. & McNab, B. (2009). Comparing network analysis measures to determine potential epidemic size of highly contagious exotic diseases in fragmented monthly networks of dairy cattle movements in Ontario, Canada. *Transboundary and Emerging Diseases*, 55(9–10), 382−392.

Dubé, C., Stevenson, M. A., Garner, M. G., et al. (2007b). A comparison of predictions made by three simulation models of foot-and-mouth disease. *New Zealand Veterinary Journal*, 55(6), 280−288.

Dürr, S., zu Dohna, H., Di Labio, E., Carpenter, T. E. & Doherr, M. G. (2013). Evaluation of control and surveillance strategies for classical swine fever using a simulation model. *Preventive Veterinary Medicine*, 108(1), 73−84.

East, I. J., Martin, P. A. J., Langstaff, I., et al. (2016). Assessing the delay to detection and the size of the outbreak at the time of detection of incursions of foot and mouth disease in Australia. *Preventive Veterinary Medicine*, 123, 1–11.

East, I. J., Roche, S. E., Wicks, R. M., de Witte, K. & Garner, M. G. (2014). Options for managing animal welfare on intensive pig farms confined by movement restrictions during an outbreak of foot and mouth disease. *Preventive Veterinary Medicine*, 117(3–4), 533–541.

Fox, J. C., Buckley, Y. M., Panetta, F. D., Bourgoin, J. & Pullar, D. (2009). Surveillance protocols for management of invasive plants: Modelling Chilean needle grass (*Nassella neesiana*) in Australia. *Diversity and Distributions*, 15(4), 577−589.

Gambley, C. F., Miles, A. K., Ramsden, M., et al. (2009). The distribution and spread of citrus canker in Emerald, Australia. *Australasian Plant Pathology*, 38(6), 547−557.

Garner, M. G. & Beckett, S. D. (2005). Modelling the spread of foot-and-mouth disease in Australia. *Australian Veterinary Journal*, 83(12), 30−38.

Garner, M. G., Bombarderi, N., Cozens, M., et al. (2014). Estimating resource requirements to staff a response to a medium to large outbreak of foot and mouth disease in Australia. *Transboundary and Emerging Diseases.* doi: 10.1111/tbed.12239

Garner, M. G., Cowled, B., East, I. J., Moloney, B. J. & Yung, N. Y. (2011). Evaluating the effectiveness of early vaccination in the control and eradication of equine influenza – A modelling approach. *Preventive Veterinary Medicine*, 99(1), 15−27.

Garner, M. G., Dubé, C., Stevenson, M. A., et al. (2007). Evaluating alternative approaches to managing animal disease outbreaks – the role of modelling in policy formulation. *Veterinaria Italiana*, 43(2), 285−298.

Garner, M. G., East, I. J., Kompas, T., et al. (2016). Comparison of alternatives to passive surveillance to detect foot and mouth disease incursions in Victoria, Australia. *Preventive Veterinary Medicine*, 128, 78–86.

Garner, M. G. & Hamilton, S. A. (2011). Principles of epidemiological modelling. *OIE Scientific and Technical Review*, 30(2), 407−416.

Garner, M. G. & Lack, M. B. (1995). An evaluation of alternate control strategies for foot- and mouth disease in Australia: A regional approach. *Preventive Veterinary Medicine*, 23(1–2), 9−32.

Gertzen, E. L., Leung, B. & Yan, D. (2011). Propagule pressure, Allee effects and the probability of establishment of an invasive species (*Bythotrephes longimanus*). *Ecosphere*, 2(3), art30.

Gibbens, J. C., Wilesmith, J. W., Sharpe, C. E., et al. (2001). Descriptive epidemiology of the 2001 foot-and-mouth disease epidemic in Great Britain: The first four months. *Veterinary Record*, 149(24), 729–743.

Goto, M. (1992). Citrus canker. In J. Kumar, H. S. Chaube, U. S. Singh & A. N. Mukhopadhyay (eds.), *Plant diseases of international importance* (pp. 250–269). Englewood Cliffs, NJ: Prentice Hall.

Gottwald, T. R. & Graham, J. H. (1992). A device for precise and nondisruptive stomatal inoculation of leaf tissue with bacterial pathogens. *Phytopathology*, 82(9), 930–935.

Gottwald, T. R., Graham, J. H. & Schubert, T. S. (2002). Citrus canker: The pathogen and its impact. *Plant Health Progress.* doi:10.1094/PHP-2002-0812-01-RV

Gottwald, T. R., Sun, X., Riley, T. D., et al. (2001). Geo-referenced, spatiotemporal analysis of the urban citrus canker epidemic in Florida. *Phytopathology*, 92(4), 361−377.

Gottwald, T. R., Timmer, L. W. & McGuire, R. G. (1989). Analysis of disease progress of citrus canker in nurseries in Argentina. *Phytopathology*, 79(11), 1276−1283.

Graham, J. H., Gottwald, T. R., Cubero, J. & Achor, D. (2004). *Xanthomonas axonopus* pv. *citri*: Factors affecting successful eradication of citrus canker. *Molecular Plant Pathology*, 5(1), 1–15.

Green, L. E. & Medley, G. F. (2002). Mathematical modelling of the foot and mouth disease epidemic of 2001: Strengths and weaknesses. *Research in Veterinary Science*, 73(3), 201−205.

Groenendaal, H., Nielen, M. & Hesselink, J. W. (2003). Development of the Dutch Johne's disease control program supported by a simulation model. *Preventive Veterinary Medicine*, 60(1), 69−90.

Hagerman, A. D., McCarl, B. A., Carpenter, T. E., Ward, M. P. & O'Brien, J. (2012). Emergency vaccination to control foot-and-foot disease: Consequences of its inclusion as a US policy option. *Applied Economic Perspectives and Policy*, 34(1), 119–146.

Hamede, R., Bashford, J., Jones, M. & McCallum, H. (2012). Simulating devil facial tumour disease outbreaks across empirically derived contact networks. *Journal of Applied Ecology*, 49, 447–456.

Harvey, N., Reeves A. P., Schoenbaum, M. A., et al. (2007). The North American Animal Disease Spread Model: A simulation model to assist decision making in evaluating animal disease incursions. *Preventive Veterinary Medicine*, 82(3–4), 176–197.

Hester, S. & Garner, M. G. (2012). *Post-border surveillance techniques: Review, synthesis and deployment*. Final Report: ACERA Project No. 1004. Available from www.acera.unimelb.edu.au/materials/core.html

Hone, J. (1990). How many feral pigs in Australia. *Australian Wildlife Research*, 17(6), 571–572.

Hopp, P., Webb, C. R. & Jarp, J. (2003). Monte Carlo simulation of surveillance strategies for scrapie in Norwegian sheep. *Preventive Veterinary Medicine*, 61(2), 103–125.

Hurd, H. S. & Kaneene, J. B. (1993). The application of simulation models and systems analysis in epidemiology: A review. *Preventive Veterinary Medicine*, 15(2–3), 81–99.

Jalvingh, A. W., Nielen, M., Maurice H., et al. (1999). Spatial and stochastic simulation to evaluate the impact of events and control measures on the 1997–1998 classical swine fever epidemic in the Netherlands. I. Description of simulation model. *Preventive Veterinary Medicine*, 42(3–4), 271–295.

Jeger, M. J., Pautasso, M., Holdenrieder, O. & Shaw, M.W. (2007). Modelling disease spread and control in networks: Implications for plant sciences. *New Phytologist*, 174(2), 279–297.

Jones, K. E., Patel, N. G., Levy, M. A., et al. (2008). Global trends in emerging infectious diseases. *Nature*, 451, 990–993.

Keeling, M. J. (2005). Models of foot-and mouth disease. *Proceedings of the Royal Society B: Biological Sciences*, 272(1569), 1195–1202.

Kitching, R. P., Thrusfield M. V. & Taylor N. M. (2006). Use and abuse of mathematical models: An illustration from the 2001 foot and mouth disease epidemic in the United Kingdom. *OIE Scientific and Technical Review*, 25(1), 293–311.

Laddomada, A. (2000). Incidence and control of CSF in wild boar in Europe. *Veterinary Microbiology*, 73(2–3), 121–130.

Le Menach, A., Legrand, J., Grais, R. F., et al. (2005). Modeling spatial and temporal transmission of foot-and-mouth disease in France: Identification of high risk areas. *Veterinary Research*, 36(5–6), 699–712.

Leslie, E., Cowled, B., Garner, M. G. & Ward, M. P. (2012). Effective surveillance strategies following a potential classical swine fever incursion in a remote feral pig population in north-western Australia. *Transboundary and Emerging Diseases*, 61(5), 432–442.

Li, W., Shi, Z., Yu, M., et al. (2005). Bats are natural reservoirs of SARS-like coronaviruses. *Science*, 310(5748), 676–679.

Macal, C. M. & North, M. J. (2007). Agent-based modeling and simulation: Desktop ABMS. In S. G. Henderson, B. Biller, M.-H. Hsieh, J. Shortle, J. D. Tew & R. Barton (eds.), *Proceedings of the 2007 Winter Simulation Conference*, Washington, DC (pp. 95–106).

Mangano, P., Hardie, D., Speijers, J., et al. (2011). The capacity of groups within the community to carry out plant pest surveillance detection. *The Open Entomology Journal*, 5, 15–23.

Mangen, M. J., Jalvingh, A. W., Nielen, M., et al. (2001). Spatial and stochastic simulation to compare two emergency-vaccination strategies with a marker vaccine in the 1997/1998 Dutch classical swine fever epidemic. *Preventive Veterinary Medicine*, 48(3), 177−200.

Mansley, L. M., Donaldson, A. I., Thrusfield, M. V. & Honhold, N. (2011). *Destructive tension: Mathematics versus experience – the progress and control of the 2001 foot-and-mouth disease epidemic in Great Britain. OIE Scientific and Technical Review,* 30(2), 483−498.

Martin, P. A. J., Langstaff, I., Iglesias, R. M., et al. (2015). Assessing the efficacy of general surveillance for detection of incursions of livestock diseases in Australia. *Preventive Veterinary Medicine,* 121, 215–230.

Matthews, K. (2011). *A review of Australia's preparedness for the threat of foot-and-mouth disease.* Canberra: Australian Government Department of Agriculture, Fisheries and Forestry.

McCallum, H., Jones, M., Hawkins, C., et al. (2009). Transmission dynamics of Tasmanian devil facial tumor disease may lead to disease-induced extinction. *Ecology,* 90(12), 3379−3392.

Meuwissen, M. P., Horst, S. H., Huirne, R. B. & Dijkhuizen, A. A. (1999). A model to estimate the financial consequences of classical swine fever outbreaks: Principles and outcomes. *Preventive Veterinary Medicine*, 42(3–4), 249−270.

Morris, R. S., Wilesmith, J. W., Stern, M. W., Sanson, R. L. & Stevenson, M. A. (2001). Predictive spatial modelling of alternative control strategies for the foot-and-mouth disease epidemic in Great Britain, 2001. *Veterinary Record*, 149(5), 137−144.

Nerlich, B. (2007). Media, metaphors and modelling: how the UK newspapers reported the epidemiological modelling controversy during the 2001 foot and mouth outbreak. *Science, Technology and Human Values*, 32(4), 432−457.

Normile, D. (2008). Driven to extinction. *Science*, 319(5870), 1606−1609.

OIE. (2011). *Classical swine fever, general disease information sheets.* Paris: World Organisation for Animal Health.

OIE. (2012). Foot and mouth disease. In *Terrestrial animal health code*, Vol. 2. Available from www.oie.int/en/international-standard-setting/terrestrial-code

Oliver, W. & Leus, K. (2008). *Sus scrofa*. In IUCN Red List of Threatened Species, version 2010.4. Available from www.iucnredlist.org/details/41775/0

Owen, K., Stevenson, M. A. & Sanson, R. L. (2011). A sensitivity analysis of the New Zealand standard model of foot and mouth disease. *OIE Scientific and Technical Review*, 30(2), 513−526.

Parnell, S., Gottwald, T. R., Gilligan, C. A., Cunniffe, N. J. & van den Bosch, F. (2010). The effect of landscape pattern on the optimal eradication zone of an invading epidemic. *Phytopathology*, 100(7), 638−644.

Pasman, E. J., Dijkhuizen, A. A. & Wentink, G. H. (1994). A state-transition model to simulate the economics of bovine virus diarrhoea control. *Preventive Veterinary Medicine*, 20, 269−277.

Pech, R. P., McIlroy J. C. & Clough, M. F. (1995). Models for predicting the dynamics and control of contact-spread diseases in feral pigs (*Sus scrofa*) in Australia. *Ibex: Journal of Mountain Ecology*, 3, 95−97.

Pech, R. P., McIlroy, J. C., Clough, M. F. & Green, D. G. (1992). A microcomputer model for predicting the spread and control of foot and mouth disease in feral pigs. In J. E. Boorrecco & R. E. Marsh (eds.), *Proceedings of the 15th Vertebrate Pest Conference*, University of California, Davis (pp. 360−364).

Perez, A. M., Ward, M. P., Charmandarian, A. & Ritacco, V (2002). Simulation model of within-herd transmission of bovine tuberculosis in Argentine dairy herds. *Preventive Veterinary Medicine*, 54(4), 361–372.

Perez, L. & Dragicevic, S. (2009). An agent-based approach for modeling dynamics of contagious disease spread. *International Journal of Health Geographics*, 8, 50–67.

Perry, B., McDermott, J. & Randolph, T. (2001). Can epidemiology and economics make a meaningful contribution to national animal-disease control? *Preventive Veterinary Medicine*, 48(4), 231–260.

Pineda-Krch, M., O'Brien, J. M., Thunes, C. & Carpenter, T. E. (2010). Potential impact of introduction of foot-and-mouth disease from wild pigs into commercial livestock premises in California. *American Journal of Veterinary Research*, 71(1), 82–88.

Potts, J. M., Cox, M. J., Barkley, P., et al. (2013). Model-based search strategies for plant diseases: A case-study using citrus canker (*Xanthomonas citri*). *Diversity and Distributions*, 19(5–6), 590–602.

Potts, J. M., Cox, M. J. & Burgman, M. A. (2012). Model-based search strategies for plant diseases: A case-study using citrus canker (*Xanthomonas citri*). The University of Melbourne submitted to the Department of Agriculture, Fisheries and Forestry.

Reeves, A., Salman, M. D. & Hill, A. E. (2011). Approaches for evaluating veterinary epidemiological models: Verification, validation and limitations. *OIE Scientific and Technical Review*, 30(2), 499–512.

Roche, S. E., Garner, M. G., Sanson, R. L., et al. (2014a). Evaluating vaccination strategies to control foot-and-mouth disease: A model comparison study. *Epidemiology and Infection*, 143(6), 1256–1275.

Roche, S. E., Garner, M. G., Wicks, R. M., et al. (2014b). How do resources influence control measures during a simulated outbreak of foot and mouth disease in Australia? *Preventive Veterinary Medicine*, 113, 436–446.

Rovira, A., Reicks, D. & Muñoz-Zanzi, C. (2007). Evaluation of surveillance protocols for detecting porcine reproductive and respiratory syndrome virus infection in boar studs by simulation modeling. *Journal of Veterinary Diagnosis Investigation*, 19(5), 492–501.

Sanson, R. L., Harvey, N., Garner, M. G., et al. (2011). Foot and mouth disease model verification and 'relative validation' through a formal model comparison. *OIE Scientific and Technical Review*, 30(2), 527–540.

Schoenbaum, M. A. & Disney T. W. (2003). Modeling alternative mitigation strategies for a hypothetical outbreak of foot-and-mouth disease in the United States. *Preventive Veterinary Medicine*, 58(1–2), 25–52.

Senate Rural and Regional Affairs and Transport Legislation Committee. (2006). *The Administration by the Department of Agriculture, Fisheries and Forestry of the Citrus Canker Outbreak*, June 2006. Canberra: Senate Rural and Regional Affairs and Transport Legislation Committee.

Slovic, P. (1999). Trust, emotion, sex, politics, and science: surveying the risk-assessment battlefield. *Risk Analysis*, 19(4), 689–701.

Smith, D. L., Battle, K. E., Hay, S. I., et al. (2012). Ross, Macdonald, and a theory for the dynamics and control of mosquito-transmitted pathogens. *PLoS Pathogens*, 8(4), e1002588.

Smith, G. & Grenfell, B. T. (1990). Population biology of pseudorabies in swine. *American Journal of Veterinary Research*, 51(1), 148–155.

Spencer, P. B. S. & Hampton, J. O. (2005). Illegal translocation and genetic structure of feral pigs in Western Australia. *Journal of Wildlife Management*, 69(1), 377–384.

Taylor, N. (2003). *Review of the use of models in informing disease control policy development and adjustment*, A report for DEFRA. Reading, UK: Veterinary Epidemiology and Economics Research Unit (VEERU).

Thrusfield, M. (2007). *Veterinary epidemiology*, 3rd ed. Oxford: Blackwell Science.

Travis, J. M. J., Harris, C. M., Park, K. J. & Bullock, J. M. (2011). Improving prediction and management of range expansions by combining analytical and individual-based modelling approaches. *Methods in Ecology and Evolution*, 2(5), 477−488.

Twigg, L. E., Lowe, T., Martin, G. & Everett, M. (2005). Feral pigs in north-western Australia: Basic biology, bait consumption, and the efficacy of 1080 baits. *Wildlife Research*, 32(4), 281−296.

van Asseldonk, M. A. P. M., van Roermund H. J. W., Fischer E. A. J., de Jong M. C. M. & Huirne R. M. B. (2005). Stochastic efficiency analysis of bovine tuberculosis-surveillance programs in the Netherlands. *Preventive Veterinary Medicine*, 69(1–2), 39−52.

Ward, M. P., Laffan, S. W. & Highfield, L. D. (2009). Modelling spread of foot-and-mouth disease in wild white-tailed deer and feral pig populations using a geographic-automata model and animal distributions. *Preventive Veterinary Medicine*, 91(1), 55−63.

Wilkinson, K., Grant, W. P., Green, L. E., et al. (2011). Infectious diseases of animals and plants: An interdisciplinary approach. *Philosophical Transactions of the Royal Society B: Biological Sciences*, 366(1573), 1933−1942.

Yoon, H., Wee, S.-H., Stevenson, M. A., et al. (2006). Simulation analyses to evaluate alternative control strategies for the 2002 foot-and-mouth disease outbreak in the Republic of Korea. *Preventive Veterinary Medicine*, 74(2–3), 212−225.

8 Bayesian Networks for Import Risk Assessment

Ann E. Nicholson and Kevin B. Korb

8.1 Introduction

Bayesian networks are an increasingly popular paradigm for reasoning under uncertainty. A Bayesian network (Korb & Nicholson, 2011; Pearl, 1988) is a directed, acyclic graph whose nodes represent the random variables in the problem. A set of directed links connect pairs of vertices, representing the direct dependencies (which are often causal connections) between the variables. The set of nodes pointing to a node X are called its parents and are denoted $pa(X)$. The relationship between variables is quantified by conditional probability tables (CPTs) associated with each node, namely $P(X|pa(X))$. Together, the conditional probability tables compactly represent the full joint distribution. Users can set the values of any combination of nodes in the network that they have observed. This evidence, e, propagates through the network, producing a new posterior probability distribution $P(X|e)$ for each variable in the network. There are a number of efficient exact and approximate inference algorithms for performing this probabilistic updating, providing a powerful combination of predictive, diagnostic and explanatory reasoning. In the biosecurity context, the typical use is predictive; given the scenario of a proposed importation of a product that may be a pathway for a particular pest, a Bayesian network can be used to incorporate evidence about the pest and its biological features, assessments made by analysts about the likelihood of live pests on the product at each stage in the pathway and so on.

Bayesian networks can be extended with two other types of nodes – decision nodes and utility nodes – to form a so-called Bayesian decision network.[1] Decision nodes represent controllable actions that have an effect on the system, while utility nodes are used to assign a value to combinations of outcomes (e.g. costs and benefits). A Bayesian decision network can then be used to automatically compute the so-called expected utility of alternative decisions, supporting rational decision making based on decision theory (Russell & Norvig, 2010). When considering biosecurity risk assessment, a Bayesian decision network not only can provide predictions of the probability of entry, establishment and spread, but these probabilities

---

[1] Decision networks are also known, sometimes confusingly, as influence diagrams (Howard & Matheson, 1981).

can also be combined with estimates of the costs of these outcomes and the cost of mitigation measures, to compute the expected utility of both the unmitigated and mitigated risk.

Over the past 10 years, Bayesian networks have been widely used in ecological modelling [see Section 5.2.3 in Korb and Nicholson (2011) for a survey], with a number of modelling guidelines published (e.g. Borsuk et al., 2004; Renken & Mumby, 2009; Varis & Kuikka, 1999), while Uusitalo (2007) has reviewed their features and use in modelling environmental applications. Bayesian networks have been developed for local pest detection and eradication for sheep lice (Horton et al., 2009), red imported fire ant (Burgman et al., 2010; Dambacher et al., 2008), dengue fever (Murphy et al., 2010) and non-native trout (Peterson et al., 2008). Hood (2009) has developed a Bayesian network for an import risk assessment of the importation of giant African snail into Australia. There have also been a number of assessments of Bayesian networks as biosecurity tools (e.g. Baker & Stuckey, 2009; Hood et al., 2009; Hosack et al, 2008; Walshe & Burgman, 2010; Wintle & Nicholson, 2014). Bayesian networks have also been used in PRATIQUE, a European Union project to enhance pest risk analysis techniques (Baker et al., 2009). For example, Holt et al. (2012) have used the GeNIe[2] Bayesian network software to compute and visualise combinations of uncertain risk assessments, while Mengersen et al. (2012) have described an approach using control point–Bayesian networks, where the Bayesian networks are generated in a standard template from a spreadsheet of questions and expert assessments of uncertainty. Kuhnert and Hayes (2009) have shown how Bayesian networks can be used to quantify and improve the qualitative risk assessment developed by the European and Mediterranean Plant Protection Organization; in this chapter, our focus is very similar, except we model the Australian process.

One advantage of Bayesian networks in these applications is that the graphical structure provides visualisation of the relationships between variables, such as cause and effect, and can be easily modified to incorporate new factors and new understandings of the relationships. Bayesian networks can be constructed using information from a range of sources such as empirical data, the research literature, the opinion of experts and output from other models. Both the relationships between variables and the outcomes are expressed probabilistically, so uncertainly is embedded and explicit.

8.2   Biosecurity Case Study: An Insect on Fruit

We develop our Bayesian network framework for the pest risk assessment for a hypothetical insect on fruit; this case study was developed and used in Burgman

---

[2] GeNIe is made available in a compiled form that is free of charge from the Decision Systems Laboratory, University of Pittsburgh (http://genie.sis.pitt.edu).

Unrestricted Risk

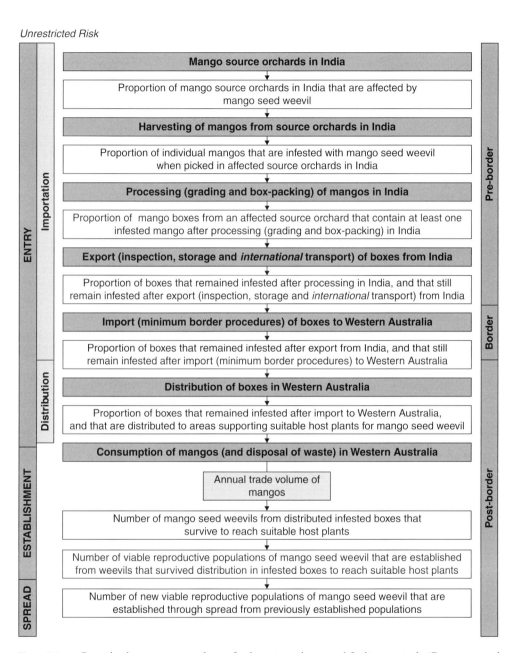

Figure 8.1.   Steps in the exposure pathway for insects on imported fruit case study (Burgman et al., 2011, Figure 2.2).

et al. (2011). Figure 8.1 shows the exposure pathway for the insect, which is represented as an exposure tree; this structure was used as a template for the Bayesian network construction. There are seven basic steps in the pathway, beginning with the source orchards in the exporting country, through to consumption of the fruit

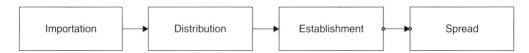

Figure 8.2   Steps in Biosecurity Australia's model (Burgman et al., 2011, Figure 2.1).

and waste disposal (in the specific area of Western Australia chosen for this case study). At each step, there is a description of the quantity representing the risk from the pest that must be assessed at each point. This progresses from the proportion of source orchards, to the proportion of individual fruit, to the proportion of fruit boxes and to the number of pests and viable populations.

The terms *affected* and *infested* in Figure 8.1, and in this chapter, refer to the presence of at least one pest. The proportion of boxes that remain infested is the net effect of pest survivorship and cross-contamination, which in our case study, we assume to be zero. We assume that, if infested fruits are found during inspection, the affected boxes are disposed of and the remaining boxes are inspected further, but the entire shipment is not cancelled and the pathway is not changed. Each of the steps in Figure 8.1 represent bundled detailed steps covering the multiple steps and factors considered in import risk assessments. After the first step, each of the steps is conditional on the previous step.

The steps in the exposure pathway can be grouped in different ways, as can be seen from the different divisions of the vertical bars (to the left and right) in Figure 8.1. To comply with the World Trade Organization framework, the methodology documented by Biosecurity Australia (2008) provided four estimates, one each for importation, distribution, establishment and spread (Figure 8.2), basically combining the first five steps in Figure 8.1 into a judgement of the likelihood of importation. That judgement is typically based on a subjective consideration of a range of factors (Burgman et al., 2011), including

- Distribution and incidence of the pest in the source area
- Occurrence of the pest in a life stage that would be associated with the commodity
- Volume and frequency of movement of the commodity along each pathway
- Seasonal timing of imports
- Pest management, cultural and commercial procedures at the place of origin
- Speed of transport and conditions of storage compared with the duration of the life cycle of the pest
- Vulnerability of the life-stages of the pest during transport or storage
- Incidence of the pest likely to be associated with a consignment
- Commercial procedures (e.g. refrigeration) during transport and storage in the country of origin and during transport to Australia.

We note that importation and distribution are often together referred to as entry (as shown on the left of Figure 8.1).

Table 8.1. Probability intervals employed by Biosecurity Australia (2008)

Likelihood	Descriptive definition	Indicative probability range
High	The event would be very likely to occur.	$0.7 < p \leq 1.0$
Moderate	The event would occur with an even probability.	$0.3 < p \leq 0.7$
Low	The event would be unlikely to occur.	$0.05 < p \leq 0.3$
Very low	The event would be very unlikely to occur.	$10^{-3} < p \leq 0.05$
Extremely low	The event would be extremely unlikely to occur.	$10^{-6} < p \leq 10^{-3}$
Negligible	The event would almost certainly not occur.	$0 < p \leq 10^{-6}$

Reprinted with permission from Biosecurity Australia (2008). *Final import risk analysis report for fresh mango fruit from India.* Technical report. Canberra, Australia: Biosecurity Australia. Available from www.agriculture.gov.au/SiteCollectionDocuments/ba/plant/ungroupeddocs/Final_IRA_-_Mangoes_from_India.pdf

	High	Moderate	Low	Very low	Extremely low	Negligible
High	High	Moderate	Low	Very low	Extremely low	Negligible
Moderate		Low	Low	Very low	Extremely low	Negligible
Low			Very low	Very low	Extremely low	Negligible
Very low				Extremely low	Extremely low	Negligible
Extremely low					Negligible	Negligible
Negligible						Negligible

Figure 8.3.   Matrix showing rules for how the qualitative likelihoods are combined in the methodology reported in Biosecurity Australia (2008, Table 2.1).
[Reprinted with permission from Biosecurity Australia (2008). Final import risk analysis report for fresh mango fruit from India. Technical report. Canberra, Australia: Biosecurity Australia. Available from www.agriculture.gov.au/SiteCollectionDocuments/ba/plant/ungroupeddocs/Final_IRA_-_Mangoes_from_India.pdf]

8.3   Business as Usual

First we show how a Bayesian network can be constructed from an exposure pathways tree that represents Biosecurity Australia's 2008 qualitative assessment method.

8.3.1   Biosecurity Australia's Qualitative Likelihoods

In many of its import risk assessments, Biosecurity Australia defined a set of intervals associated with words that reflect likelihoods of importation, distribution, establishment and spread (Table 8.1). These intervals were intended only to be indicative guides to the meanings of the words. These qualitative likelihoods are combined with a set of rules, distilled into a matrix in Figure 8.3.

Next, we show how this assessment process can be modelled in a Bayesian network using the same qualitative measures of risk (e.g. negligible, extremely low, very low, low, moderate and high) and when combining the risks for each stage in the same way (based on the matrix shown in Figure 8.3).

8.3.2   A Simple Deterministic Bayesian Network

This process can be modelled by a simple Bayesian network with deterministic relationships (Figure 8.4a). In this network, each of the main steps of the pathway becomes a node in the network: Importation, Distribution, Establishment and Spread. These are so-called *root nodes* in the Bayesian network because they have no parents (i.e. there are no incoming arcs). They are the input or evidence nodes, for which values will be supplied by the import risk assessor. The assessments for these main steps in the pathway are combined pairwise in sequence, represented in this Bayesian network by so-called intermediate nodes, namely Entry (combining Importation and Distribution), and EntryAndEstablishment.[3] The result of the final combination is a leaf node, a node with no children (i.e. there are no outgoing arcs), giving the overall likelihood of entry, establishment and spread. Because this is the output node of interest, in Bayesian network terminology, it is also called a target or query node.

Following the 2008 documented practice, the possible values for each node are {High, Moderate, Low, VeryLow, ExtremelyLow, Negligible}, representing a qualitative likelihood. The entries in the deterministic conditional probability tables (CPTs; see Figure 8.4b) were taken from the matrix in Figure 8.3 that shows how to combine qualitative likelihoods.

The model in Figure 8.4a has uniform priors for the root nodes because, at this point, we have not incorporated any information about a particular situation. Priors for the root nodes for an individual case study should be obtained from experts. The overall assessments across these scenarios are uneven because of the threshold effect of the rules (e.g. a combination of VeryLow with any of High, Moderate or Low gives VeryLow). As shown, the probability mass is concentrated around the 'Negligible' end of the scale and is a by-product of the matrix rules.

Other than the uncertainty in the categorisation of risk, the documented method doesn't use any distribution over that risk. We can represent this in a Bayesian network by viewing the category low, for example, as a state (setting aside for the moment that it is indicative of a range of probabilities). Recall that a Bayesian network can be used for predictive risk assessment by adding evidence about what is now. Here, we add evidence as a fixed setting for each of Importation, Distribution, Establishment and Spread. The Bayesian network software then propagates this evidence through the rest of the network, which in this case gives us a new posterior

---

[3] This combination of steps isn't given a name in the pathway model, and is instead reflected by the node's name.

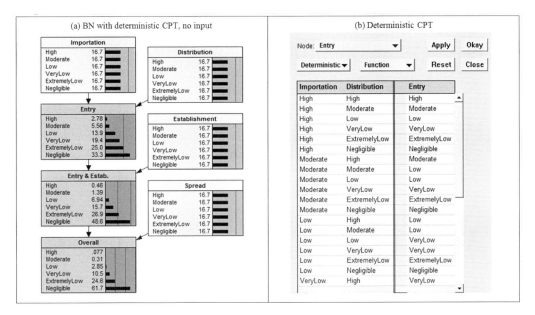

Figure 8.4. (a) Bayesian network representing Biosecurity Australia qualitative risk assessment for the case study with deterministic conditional probability tables for combining qualitative likelihoods. [Reprinted with permission from Wintle, B. C. & Nicholson, A. E. (2014). Exploring risk judgments in a trade dispute using Bayesian networks. Risk Analysis, 34(6), Figure 1.] No input likelihoods added, deterministic nodes indicated by the darker shade. (b) Deterministic conditional probability table (incomplete) for Entry node.
[These and all subsequent figures are screenshots from the Netica® Bayesian network software (Norsys, 2012).]

probability distribution for the other nodes, including the main node of interest, the Overall node, representing the summarised overall risk assessment. Figures 8.5 to 8.8a show four such scenarios where all the risk inputs are considered certain and are entered as a fixed 100% in the Bayesian network. Case 1 in Figure 8.5 shows a combination of Low, VeryLow and ExtremelyLow resulting in Negligible overall risk. Case 2 in Figure 8.6 shows how a combination of High and Moderate results in Moderate overall risk. Case 3 in Figure 8.7 and Case 4 in Figure 8.8a are examples of how different combinations of risk can result in the same overall risk (VeryLow in this example).

8.4 Incorporating Uncertainty

There are two types of uncertainty in the documented process: uncertainty in the risk assessments for each of the stages and uncertainty in how the risks are combined. In this section we describe how these can be represented in the Bayesian network.

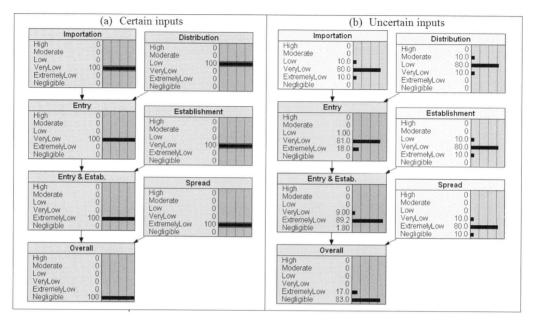

Figure 8.5.   Case 1: Low input risks (Bayesian network with deterministic conditional probability table) resulting in a negligible overall risk, comparing **(a)** certain and **(b)** uncertain inputs.

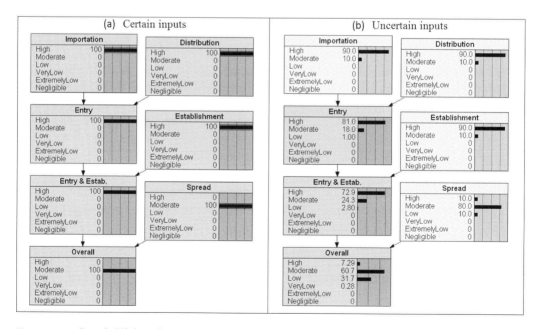

Figure 8.6.   Case 2: High and moderate input risks (Bayesian network with deterministic conditional probability table) resulting in a moderate overall risk, comparing **(a)** certain and **(b)** uncertain inputs.

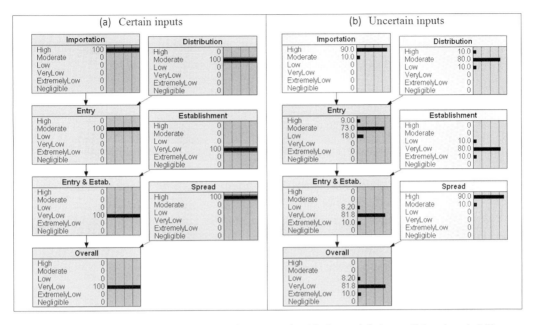

Figure 8.7.   Case 3: Mixed input risks (Bayesian network with deterministic conditional probability table) resulting in a very low overall risk, comparing **(a)** certain and **(b)** uncertain inputs.

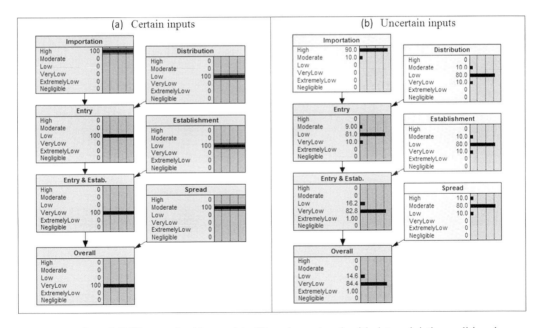

Figure 8.8.   Case 4: Different mixed input risks (Bayesian network with deterministic conditional probability table) resulting in a very low overall risk, comparing **(a)** certain and **(b)** uncertain inputs.

8.4.1   Representing Uncertainty about Input Likelihoods

The input likelihoods for the Importation, Distribution, Establishment and Spread can be entered as uncertain in the Bayesian network in two ways:

1. By setting a prior distribution for each node (this possible because each node is a root node)
2. By adding so-called likelihood (uncertain) evidence

Examples comparing certain and uncertain inputs are shown in Figures 8.5 to 8.8. In each case, uncertainty in the inputs results in a distribution over the Overall likelihood, although the highest probability falls in the same category. In this example, we continue to think about input likelihoods as states. Uncertainties in the inputs represent uncertainty in beliefs that a particular input is in a given state.

8.4.2   Adding Uncertainty to the Combinations of Likelihoods

We can also represent the uncertainty in the way the likelihoods are combined. Each qualitative likelihood reflects an indicative probability range, as shown in Table 8.1. The deterministic combination of qualitative likelihoods is very coarse and is inaccurate, particularly when the probability range is large. For example, the deterministic table says that *High* × *Low* → *Low*. However, multiplying the lower range values of 0.7 and 0.05 gives 0.035, which is in the VeryLow range. This means that the deterministic Bayesian network, which gives *P(Entry = Low | Importation = High, Distribution = Low)* = 1, is only approximating the distribution that would result if the actual ranges were used (see Section 5 of Burgman et al., 2011).

It is straightforward to represent the uncertainty arising from combining discretised probability range in the Bayesian network by making the nodes represent continuous variables, each ranging from 0 to 100. In the Bayesian network software Netica® (Norsys, 2012), we discretise the nodes using exactly the labels and indicative ranges from Table 8.1. The arithmetic combination of likelihoods is calculated using an equation, for example, *P(Entry | Importation, Distribution)* = *Importation* × *Entry* / 100 (see Figure 8.9a). This equation is used to generate a conditional probability table for the node (using a stochastic sampling method; see Figure 8.9b).

Figure 8.10 shows the resultant Bayesian network with uniform priors for the root nodes; for comparison, see Figure 8.4a for the corresponding qualitative Bayesian network. Note that there is a slight change in the Netica visualisation for discretised continuous nodes. Rather than simply display discrete categories, there is an additional section at the bottom of each node showing the mean and the standard deviation of the current calculated posterior distribution.

We can see that with no informative inputs, the resultant distribution for the Overall likelihood for the continuous model is not very different, as expected given that the qualitative combination matrix was calibrated with the indicative probability ranges. Figures 8.11 and 8.12 show the result of entering the certain input

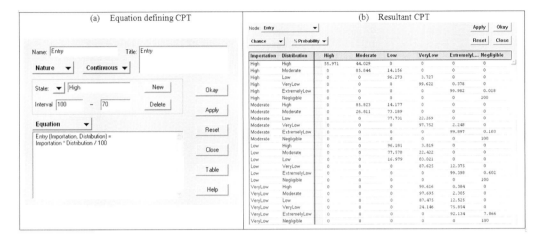

Figure 8.9. Netica screenshots for the entry node, showing **(a)** the specification of the continuous range for high, and the equation for combining the likelihoods of the parent nodes, importation and distribution; and **(b)** the resultant conditional probability table (incomplete), from stochastic sampling.

risks into the new Bayesian network. The distributions for the Overall risk for Cases 1, 3 and 4 are similar to the previous Bayesian network. However, Case 2 (High and Moderate inputs) provides an example of how the Overall assessment can change when explicitly modelling the indicative probability ranges; here the highest probability outcome is $P(Overall = Low \mid Case\ 2\ Inputs) = 0.551$, whereas the documented qualitative method gives a Moderate Overall combined likelihood (Figure 8.6a).

8.5 Improving the Bayesian Network Structure

There are limitations with the documented process as modelled by the Bayesian networks in Figures 8.4 to 8.12. Here we analyse these limitations and show how changes to the structure of the Bayesian network can overcome them.

8.5.1 Representing Dependencies between Likelihoods at Different Stages

The Bayesian network modelling discussed in Section 8.4 combines the risks for the different stages in a way that assumes they are independent. For example, in the Bayesian network in Figure 8.10, Importation and Distribution are independent parents of Entry:

$$P(Entry) = P(Importation) \times P(Distribution).$$

However, this is not how the likelihood of Distribution is assessed by the analyst; the qualitative assessment is the likelihood of Distribution if the pest has been

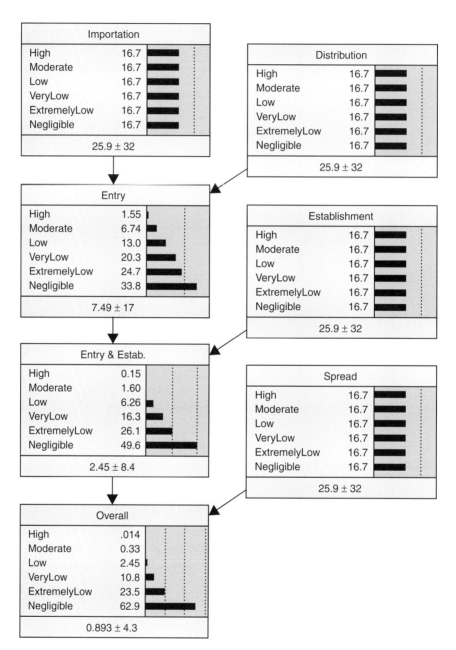

Figure 8.10.   Bayesian network where the nodes represent a continuous variable, discretised according to the indicative ranges from Table 8.1, with the combination of likelihoods done using an equation (used by Netica to generate the conditional probability tables; see Figure 8.9).

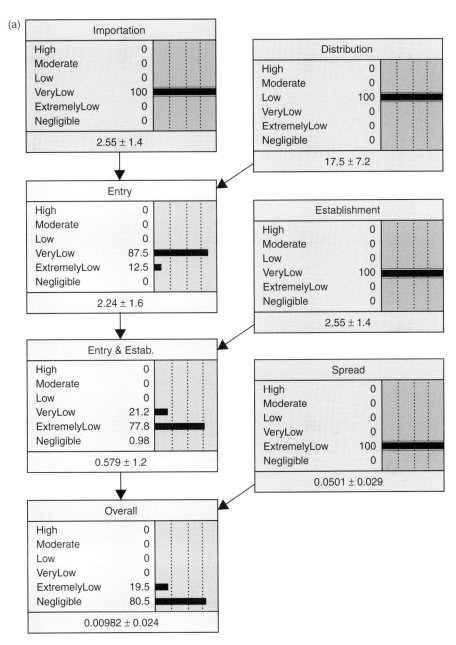

Figure 8.11. Input risk for Case 1 and Case 2 (compare with Figures 8.5 and 8.6) for the discretised continuous Bayesian network, with conditional probability table defined by equation (see Figure 8.9).

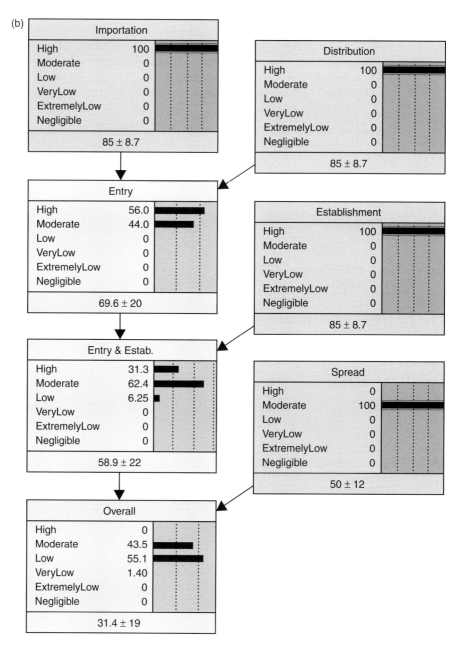

Figure 8.11 *(continued)*

imported. So the qualitative method is actually providing a conditional likelihood that we haven't captured in the Bayesian network models given earlier. The definition of Entry is then

$$P(Entry) = P(Distribution \mid Importation) \times P(Importation).$$

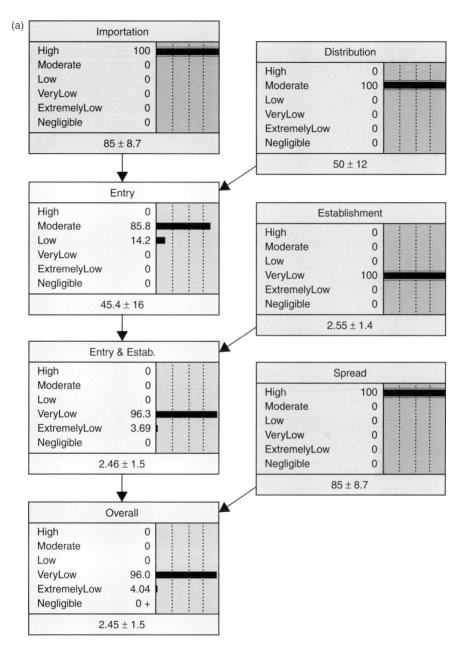

Figure 8.12. Input risk for Case 3 and Case 4 (compare with Figures 8.7 and 8.8) for the discretised continuous Bayesian network, with conditional probability table defined by equation (see Figure 8.9).

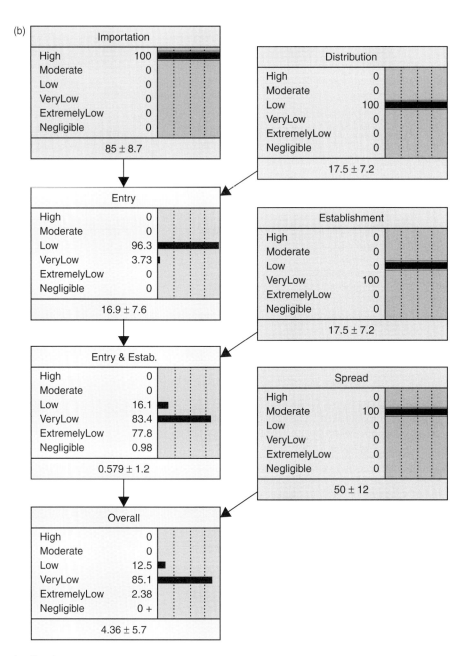

Figure 8.12   (*continued*)

8.5.2   Representing Pest Volume

The second problem is that the preceding Bayesian network modelling is doing a kind of meta-reasoning, producing probability distributions over likelihoods that represent indicative probability ranges. Given pest likelihood at one stage, the Bayesian network produces a distribution over the likelihood of infestation at the next stage. This improperly conflates aspects of volume (such as amount of fruit in a container and how prevalent the pest is on the fruit) with probability. These problems can be overcome by making the modelling changes shown in the example Bayesian network in Figure 8.13.

First, Entry is modelled explicitly as being conditional on Importation given Distribution. So instead of three nodes (one each for Importation, Entry and Distribution), there are now only two.

Second, we have changed the states of the nodes to explicitly represent the volume (number) of the pest for the Importation, Entry and Establishment nodes, while Spread models area. In Figure 8.13 these are discrete nodes in the Bayesian network with the names of the states representing (unspecified) qualitative levels; the pest volume states are {High, Medium, Low and Negligible} while the spread states are {Large, Medium, Small and Negligible}. In practice, for any specific import risk assessment, the number of states can be modified to reflect the number of levels that are expected to make a difference to risk. Also, the nodes should be turned into continuous nodes in the Bayesian network software, with each state specified by an interval (in the same way that we explicitly represented the intervals for the qualitative likelihoods given earlier). With the new state space, the risk level is then the posterior distribution computed by the Bayesian network reasoning algorithm for each volume, or the area.

8.5.3   Modelling Consequences

In Figure 8.13, the consequences are modelled as simple three-valued nodes {High, Low, Negligible}, with the cost of each consequence modelled by an associated utility node (represented by hexagons). The utility functions were obtained through methods such as described in Section 11 of Burgman et al., (2011). The Netica software requires that the utility function be represented by a utility table, with a single real number associated with each combination of parent node values; Figure 8.14 shows an example utility table for the Domestic Trade Cost node. The utility scale is arbitrary, but it is important that the same scale be used for all utility functions that represent the costs of actions, outcomes and benefits (although there are no benefits represented in the Bayesian network presented here). Here, we have chosen to represent the costs as negative, and although our qualitative utility nodes are similar to Biosecurity Australia's levels from A to G, the way we have included them in the decision network does not mirror Biosecurity Australia's documented matrix method for combining qualitative consequences (Biosecurity Australia, 2008).

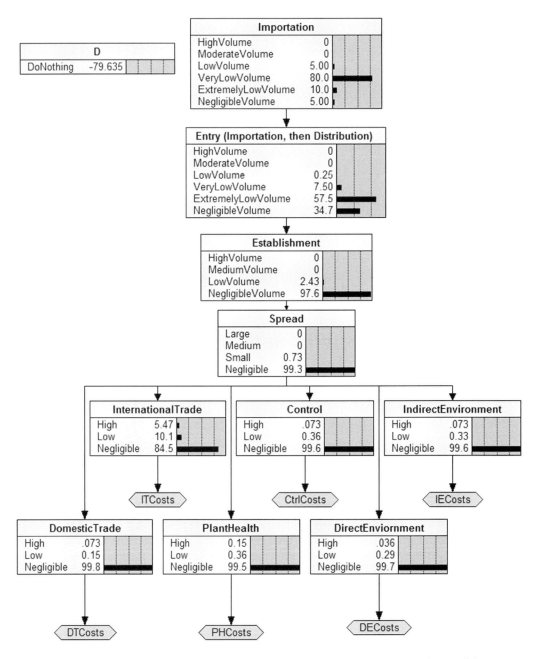

Figure 8.13. Alternative Bayesian network structure that includes correct dependencies; explicit representation of pest volume and spread area; and representation of consequences, costs and the Do Nothing action of unrestricted risk. The scenario starts with a distribution over a predominantly very low volume importation assessment.

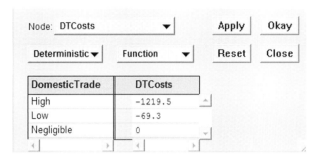

Figure 8.14.   Example utility table, representing the utility function for the cost associated with the consequences of the impact of entry, establishment and spread on domestic trade.

8.5.4   Modelling Risk at Each Stage

Thus far, we have modelled only the basic stages used previously in the Biosecurity Australia qualitative risk assessment process. However, an advantage of Bayesian networks is that they can explicitly model the other information and factors being incorporated into the risk assessment. We do this by incorporating additional nodes that feed into the "Stage" nodes. For example, in Figure 8.15 the importation assessment may depend on a large range of factors such as prevalence in the place of origin, inspection procedures at the export location and the ability of the pest to survive transportation. The layout of the process reflects the sequence of stages and the model includes the possibility of detection (say through inspection at source) and whether or not the pest survives transportation.

8.5.5   Modelling Risk Mitigation Actions in Bayesian Decision Networks

It is also possible to add nodes to the Bayesian network to represent the causal factors influencing the unmitigated risk, as shown in Figure 8.16. All the posterior probabilities (shown by the bars) are uniform, because no parameters (CPTs) have been entered for this Bayesian network. In this example, the LocalEnvironment node allows us to model the difference between the establishment of the pest, given that it has entered, depending on whether the local environment is benign or hostile. The second causal factor, RegionalFruitTransport, has an impact on the spread of the pest.

   In import risk assessment, if the unmitigated risk is high enough to warrant further modelling, typically the next stage is to look at risk mitigation actions and their associated costs. This is another straightforward extension of the unmitigated Bayesian network. In Figure 8.16, the possible actions modelled (as decision nodes) are the level of inspection on entry {High, Low, None} and whether or not to apply pesticides on entry or on local farms. Each action has an associated cost, which is modelled in the table for the utility nodes (*InspCost*, *PCost1* and *PCost2*). This results in a Bayesian decision network.

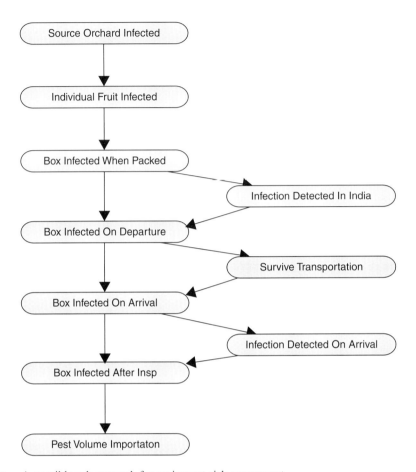

Figure 8.15.   A possible sub-network for an import risk assessment.

8.6   Knowledge Engineering Bayesian Networks

The development of useful robust methodologies for constructing and using Bayesian networks – which we call the knowledge engineering process – is a well-established and active area of research (e.g. Boneh, 2010; Laskey & Mahoney, 2000; Pollino et al., 2007). However, there are certain principles that should be followed if Bayesian networks become a standard technique in the biosecurity risk assessment process.

The basic modelling steps are to select the nodes, determine the structure, elicit the probabilities and evaluate the outcome. The knowledge engineering process should be iterative and incremental (e.g. Boneh, 2010; Korb & Nicholson, 2011). This was done informally for this case study. Thus, during the development of the models presented above, there were a number of instances of revisiting past modelling choices following improved understanding of the problem domain. For example, during the elicitation of parameters from our expert, the values for the

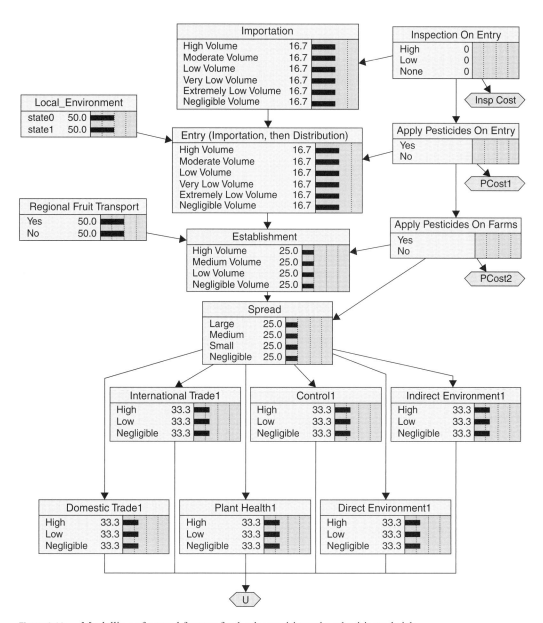

Figure 8.16. Modelling of causal factors for both unmitigated and mitigated risk.

consequence nodes (DomesticTrade etc.) were changed from {Yes, No} to {High, Low, Negligible}.

The focus of this case study is the development of the Bayesian network structure: the nodes, their states and the relationships between them. The issue of how best to parameterise a Bayesian network is a research area in its own right (e.g. Druzdzel & van der Gaag, 2000). For the Bayesian networks presented in this case study, some parameters in the conditional probability table were obtained during an elicitation workshop that produced probability intervals (we simply used the best-guess point probabilities in the conditional probability tables). Other parameters were obtained by elicitation of single point estimates from a single expert. Where we compared direct elicitation with an elicitation tool based on verbal cues, there were no significant differences in the time for elicitation or the parameters elicited. Our focus was simply to obtain plausible parameters for illustrative purposes. In practice, probabilities should be elicited from multiple experts, and there is a large body of research on how this can be done and how their estimates can be combined. For example, rather than using a single point estimate, better results can be obtained using a three-point (or even four-point) method (Martin et al., 2012; Speiers-Bridge et al., 2010) with multiple experts.

An important part of the knowledge engineering process is evaluating the Bayesian network at each stage. Once the network is parameterised, sensitivity analysis is an important tool for understanding the uncertainty embedded in the Bayesian network. While elicited distributions for parameters are not used by Bayesian networks, distributions can (and should, when available) be used to support analysis of sensitivity to parameters. For example, if a normal distribution were supplied by the elicitation process, the mean would be used in the conditional probability tables. However, values at, say, two standard deviations above and below the mean could be checked to see whether the resulting distributions under observations remain sensible and whether any indicated decisions or utility values have made dramatic shifts. Unfortunately, some of the better methods for analysis of sensitivity to parameters (e.g. Coupé et al., 2000) are not available in Bayesian network software such as Netica. Another form of sensitivity analysis that is available in Netica and is commonly used with Bayesian networks is the sensitivity to findings, which is the use of mutual information to rank the relative influence of nodes in a Bayesian network on a node of interest. For example, in the Bayesian network shown in Figure 8.16, sensitivity to findings can be used to indicate which of the factors Local_Evironment or Regional Fruit Transport has the most impact on the probability of Spread.[4]

In the Bayesian network research literature, many methods have been proposed for validating a Bayesian network (whether constructed through expert elicitation, from data, or a combination of both) against data (Korb & Nicholson, 2011). Unfortunately, when doing import risk assessments, there is often little data available with which to validate the network. Certainly, case studies from other countries for the same or similar products and pests can be used for "what-if" scenarios (entering evidence), to see if the Bayesian network's risk assessment matches what happened in practice. But the value of this is limited when the physical and environmental factors in the importing country differ from the case study data.

---

[4] However, care needs to be taken when using such measures not to read too much into such rankings, because the way the mutual information is computed means that nodes further away in the graph tend to have less influence anyway.

We have illustrated how sub-networks could be used in the biosecurity context; a full evaluation of their use is beyond the scope of this chapter. Templates of sub-networks with the range of factors for each stage could be developed. Then, when a Bayesian network is to be developed for a new risk assessment, relevant factors would be selected and parameterised for the specific situation. We note that the Netica software used for our prototype Bayesian networks does not provide direct support for the use of sub-networks. As a result, risk assessment Bayesian networks may quickly become large, unwieldy and difficult for the risk analyst to build and validate. Other Bayesian network software (e.g. GeNIe[5]) does provides support for the templates and sub-networks needed for the flexible development of case-specific Bayesian networks. We note that Mengersen et al. (2012), with their use of control point Bayesian networks, also advocate more structured, rather than ad hoc, use of Bayesian networks.

The routine deployment of knowledge engineering for import risk assessments would require investment in skill development. Naïve users of these tools often make several predictable mistakes that may compromise the legitimacy of the analyses. Appropriate skills may be developed in people with no quantitative background in a few days of dedicated training, given follow-up support and review.

Although development of skills may be an initial hurdle, the approach holds the potential to capture current experienced thinking in a more formal framework that can accommodate expert judgements and whatever data may become available. Over time, sub-networks developed for specific pests, diseases and commodities will form a library of templates that will inform and improve the efficiency of future efforts.

8.7 Conclusions

A recurring constraint on the application of Bayesian networks is the reticence of many to nominate precise quantities for their uncertainties and values. People are much more comfortable with qualitative assessments. Rain today is unlikely, not 10.5% likely; gastroenteritis is unpleasant, not pleasant to a degree of −53 utiles. But these qualms are not relevant in the end. As we show at the beginning of this chapter, whatever can be done in reasoning about uncertainty with qualitative tools, such as the import risk assessment model examined here, can be mimicked using Bayesian networks. But Bayesian networks can also do more than that. When precise quantities are available – whether because the relevant expertise or the relevant data are available – Bayesian networks can use them, allowing us to better understand and predict the systems we are working with. For example, meaningful sensitivity analysis, such as determining tipping points when changed probabilities or values require changing our interventions, can only be done with quantitative tools; qualitative representations are simply too crude for them. Bayesian network

---

[5] http://www.bayesfusion.com

are at least as good, and sometimes better, than qualitative tools. We hope the biosecurity community will take full advantage of this productive, and still emerging, technology.

References

Baker, J. & Stuckey, M. (2009). *Prioritising the impact of exotic pest threats using Bayes Net and MCDA methods*. Melbourne, Australia: Australian Centre of Excellence for Risk Analysis, The University of Melbourne. Available from www.acera.unimelb.edu.au/materials/endorsed/0707_Final_Report.pdf

Baker, R. H. A., Battisti, A., Bremmer, J., et al. (2009). PRATIQUE: A research project to enhance pest risk analysis techniques in the European Union. *EPPO Bulletin*, 39(1), 87–93.

Biosecurity Australia (2008). *Final import risk analysis report for fresh mango fruit from India*. Technical report. Canberra, Australia: Biosecurity Australia. Available from www.agriculture.gov.au/SiteCollectionDocuments/ba/plant/ungroupeddocs/Final_IRA_-_Mangoes_from_India.pdf

Biosecurity New Zealand (2006). Risk analysis procedures, version 1. April 2006.

Boneh, T. (2010). Ontology and Bayesian decision networks for supporting the meteorological forecasting process. Ph.D. thesis, Monash University, 455 pp.

Borsuk, M. E, Stow, C. A. & Reckhow, K. H. (2004). A Bayesian network of eutrophication models for synthesis, prediction and uncertainty analysis. *Ecological Modelling*, 173(2–3), 219–239.

Burgman, M., Colyvan, M., Christian, R., et al. (2011). *Demonstrating risk analysis capabilities*. ACERA Project 0901. Melbourne, Australia: Australian Centre of Excellence for Risk Analysis, The University of Melbourne. Available from http://cebra.unimelb.edu.au/__data/assets/pdf_file/0008/1290491/0901_final-report.pdf

Burgman, M. A., Wintle, B. A., Thompson, C. A., et al. (2010). Reconciling uncertain costs and benefits in Bayes nets for invasive species management. *Risk Analysis*, 30(2), 277–284.

Coupé, V. M. H., van der Gaag, L. C. & Habbema, J. D. F. (2000). Sensitivity analysis: An aid for belief-network quantification. *Knowledge Engineering Review*, 15(3), 1–18.

Dambacher, J. M., Shenton, W., Hayes, K. R., Hart, B. T. & Barry, S. (2008). *Qualitative modelling and Bayesian network analysis for risk-based biosecurity decision making in complex systems*. Melbourne, Australia: Australian Centre of Excellence for Risk Analysis, The University of Melbourne. Available from www.acera.unimelb.edu.au/materials/endorsed/0601.pdf

Druzdel, M. J. & Van Der Gaag, L. C. (2000). Building probabilistic networks: "Where do the numbers come from?" *IEEE Transactions on Knowledge and Data Engineering*, 12(4), 481–486.

Holt, J., Leach, A. W., Knight, J. D., et al. (2012). Tools for visualizing and integrating pest risk assessment ratings and uncertainties. *EPPO Bulletin*, 42(1), 35–41.

Hood, G. (2009). *Risk of introduction to Australia of giant African snail via shipping containers*. Canberra, Australia: Bureau of Rural Sciences.

Hood, G. M., Barry, S. C. & Martin, P. A. J. (2009). Alternative methods for computing the sensitivity of complex surveillance systems. *Risk Analysis*, 29(12), 1686–1698.

Horton, B. J., Evans, D. L., James, P. J. & Campbell, N. J. (2009). Development of a model based on Bayesian networks to estimate the probability of sheep lice presence at shearing. *Animal Production Science*, 49(1), 48–55.

Hosack, G. R., Hayes, K. R. & Dambacher, J. M. (2008). Assessing model structure uncertainty through an analysis of system feedback and Bayesian networks. *Ecological Applications*, 18(4), 1070–1082.

Howard, R. & Matheson, J. (1981). Influence diagrams. In R. Howard and J. Matheson (eds.), *Readings in Decision Analysis* (pp. 763–771). Menlo Park, CA: Strategic Decisions Group.

Korb, K. B. & Nicholson, A. E. (2011). *Bayesian artificial intelligence*, 2nd ed. Boca Raton, FL: CRC/Chapman Hall.

Kuhnert, P. M. & Hayes, K. R. (2009). How believable is your BBN? In *18th World IMACS/MODSIM Congress*, Cairns, Australia.

Laskey, K. B. & Mahoney, S. M. (2000). Network engineering for agile belief network models. *IEEE Transactions on Knowledge and Data Engineering*, 12(4), 487–498.

Martin, T. G., Burgman, M. A., Fidler, F., et al. (2012). Eliciting expert knowledge in conservation science. *Conservation Biology*, 26, 29–38.

Mengersen, K., Quinlan, M. M., Whittle, P. J. L., et al. (2012). Beyond compliance: Project on an integrated systems approach for pest risk management in South East Asia. *EPPO Bulletin*, 42(1), 109–116.

Murphy, B., Jansen, C., Murray, J. & De Barro, P. (2010). *Risk analysis on the Australian release of Aedes aegypti (L.) (Diptera: Culicidae) containing Wolbachia*. Indooroopilly, Australia: CSIRO Entomology.

Norsys (2012). *Netica*. Vancouver, Canada: Norsys Software Corp. Available from www.norsys.com/

Pearl, J. (1988). *Probabilistic reasoning in intelligent systems: Networks of plausible inference*. San Mateo, CA: Morgan Kaufmann.

Peterson, D. P., Rieman, B. E., Dunham, J. B., Fausch, K. D. & Young, M. K. (2008). Analysis of trade-offs between threats of invasion by nonnative brook trout (*Salvelinus fontinalis*) and intentional isolation for native westslope cutthroat trout (*Oncorhynchus clarkii lewisi*). *Canadian Journal of Fisheries and Aquatic Sciences*, 65(4), 557–573.

Renken, H. & Mumby, P. J. (2009). Modelling the dynamics of coral reef macroalgae using a Bayesian belief network approach. *Ecological Modelling*, 220(9–10), 1305–1314.

Russell, S. J. & Norvig, P. (2010). *Artificial intelligence: A modern approach*, 3rd ed. Upper Saddle River, NJ: Prentice Hall.

Speirs-Bridge, A., Fidler, F., McBride, M., Flander, L., Cumming, G., & Burgman, M. (2010). Reducing overconfidence in the interval judgments of experts. *Risk Analysis*, 30, 512–523.

Uusitalo, L. (2007). Advantages and challenges of Bayesian networks in environmental modelling. *Ecological Modelling*, 203(3–4), 312–318.

Varis, O. & Kuikka, S. (1999). Learning Bayesian decision analysis by doing: Lessons from environmental and natural resources management. *Ecological Modelling*, 119(2–3), 177–195.

Walshe, T. & Burgman, M. (2010). A framework for assessing and managing risks posed by emerging diseases. *Risk Analysis*, 30(2), 236–249.

Wintle, B. C. & Nicholson, A. E. (2014). Exploring risk judgments in a trade dispute using Bayesian networks. *Risk Analysis*, 34(6), 1095–1111.

9 Getting the Message Right: Tools for Improving Biosecurity Risk Communication

Jane Gilmour, Ruth Beilin, Tamara Sysak and Marta Hernández-Jover

9.1   Introduction

Communicating effectively about biosecurity risk is a key responsibility for managers. Tools used in other fields of risk communication and risk management can provide useful knowledge and inform the way managers communicate.

An area of increasing concern to agencies charged with the responsibility of assuring Australia's protection against unwanted diseases and pests is the growing number of peri-urban landholders. The transformation of land use around urban areas has been extensively documented. Buxton et al. (2006) report widespread agreement that the peri-urban area is expanding significantly in its geographic extent. The phenomenon is occurring not only in Australia, but also in the United States, Canada and Europe (Buxton et al., 2006). Daniels (1986) points to the proliferation of hobby farms in exurban areas on the fringes of American cities.

These peri-urban landholders are assumed to lack the knowledge and experience of established farmers, and they are therefore expected to be less likely to follow approved practices. They are also believed to be less likely to access the communication channels traditionally used by the responsible agencies to disseminate information. While conventionally such biosecurity messages are targeted as political rather than technical issues focused on specific crops (Higgins & Dibden, 2011), the peri-urban elicits a more general concern from government. In the eyes of these agencies, peri-urban landholders represent an unknown and potentially significant biosecurity risk factor.

Initial Australian studies on peri-urban landholders added to the conviction that these newcomers increased biosecurity risk. These studies identified the challenge of communicating with peri-urban landholders due to the fact that little is known about their numbers, behaviours, attitudes, knowledge of biosecurity and land use practices (Maller et al., 2007). These studies confirmed that the primary focus of these landholders was on lifestyle, amenity and environmental factors, not on primary production (Aslin et al., 2004). The assumption was that people not engaged in primary production would not have the appropriate information to manage biosecurity risks effectively. Therefore, there was little to appease the concerns of government agencies, even though the actual levels of biosecurity knowledge within this group were unknown.

A trial biosecurity risk communication was proposed by the relevant government agency for the Yass Valley region in New South Wales, Australia (see Gilmour et al., 2011). This region is adjacent to the nation's capital, Canberra, and has experienced significant demographic change in recent years. Larger landholdings have been subdivided into smaller lots. More people live in the region and work in the capital city, and there is increased land use diversity including small-scale production (e.g. vineyards and alpaca farms) and other ventures that are driven predominantly by lifestyle decisions.

Government agencies have a tendency to rely heavily on scientific advice when communicating risk. They are likely to take a top-down approach and work from what is effectively an information deficit model, where they assume that the provision of information alone will address the problem. Government agencies are generally reluctant to acknowledge scientific uncertainty and they rarely seek to engage local people in scoping problems and identifying solutions. Subsequent to this field work, research by Linkov et al. (2009) indicates the ongoing importance of bringing together agency decision-makers and stakeholder risk perceptions and behaviour for more effective risk management. Gaillard and Mercer (2013) reinforce the need for integrative processes that engage with the science; and Lazrus et al. (2016) affirm the localised constructions of risk that will inform risk communication. These three tenets – sourcing local understanding, acknowledging uncertainty and building local meanings to better inform risk communication – are central to empowering risk management approaches.

We had previously developed an approach to risk management that was based on stakeholder analysis and mapping – that is, an approach informed by the above ideas. We proposed that this, together with mental models analysis, was a means of capturing current knowledge, behaviours, values and beliefs, as well as information about communication and other networks. This would provide a useful framework for the development of a strategic approach to biosecurity risk communication for the peri-urban community in question. We therefore undertook a 12-month study to find out who the stakeholders in the issue were, what their networks of communication and influence were with respect to biosecurity, and the extent of their current knowledge and practice around biosecurity. (See Gilmour et al., 2009 for the report of this study.) The tools we used for these purposes were stakeholder identification, analysis and mapping, and mental models analysis.

The tenets referenced in the preceding text are built on a number of principles that informed our approach. First, building effective relations with stakeholders and incorporating their knowledge improves decision making and contributes to stakeholder acceptance of policy decisions (McDaniels et al., 1999; Wynne, 1996). Second, we believed that a consultative process would ensure that local knowledge and values would be taken into account and would contribute to the development of solutions; and that these solutions would necessarily need to encompass multiple layers of biosecurity governance (Higgins et al., 2016). Finally, we explored the assumption that involving people in the process of thinking about biosecurity risk would contribute to more effective risk governance outcomes in the longer term. In a similar vein, Bocking (2004) proposes that 'dealing with risk is best viewed as a collective process, in which all interested parties participate in negotiating the definition of a problem, learning more about it and coming up with solutions' (p. 160).

9.2   Being Sure about Who the Target Audience Is

Our target group was landholders in an area adjacent to Canberra, but we needed to be clear about how we were defining these peri-urban landholders. Peri-urban landholders are often defined by the size of their landholding. In Australia, these have been proposed as either 1–2 to 100 hectares (Guise & Narducci, 2005; Hollier et al., 2004) or 1 to 200 hectares (Maller et al., 2007). Other studies have defined members of the peri-urban population according to their lifestyle, values or sources of income, and have given them various titles including lifestylers, hobby farmers and tree changers. Another Australian study defines the peri-urban area in terms of population density, proportion of employment in non-rural industries and proportion of new residents (Houston, 2005).

For the purposes of our study, we adopted a broad definition of peri-urban as 'the transitional zone between rural and urban Australia' (Maller et al., 2007, p. 4) and intended to confine our study to landholdings up to a certain size. We were dissuaded from this approach at our first stakeholder consultation meeting. Those present questioned whether there was any difference between smaller landholders and larger commercial producers in terms of knowledge and practices in relation to biosecurity. They argued there was a mix of expertise and knowledge across both groups. It was agreed that the project would not be limited by landholding size, and that all landholding sizes would be investigated within the area of the Yass Valley local government area. Based on our consultations, the project study area was amended to encompass the whole of the Yass Valley local government area and the full spectrum of landholding sizes (Yass Valley council, 2008).

9.3   Methods and Tools

Our methods included stakeholder identification, analysis and mapping, and mental model analysis. These were informed by two stakeholder consultation meetings, in-depth interviews with 33 stakeholders and a survey that was distributed to a stratified sample of 930 landholders

9.3.1   Step 1. Stakeholder Identification Analysis

Knowing who the stakeholders are in an issue and what the relationships among them are can provide valuable information for the development of an effective communication strategy. There may be some organisations or agencies that are more trusted than others. There are inevitably some that have better networks

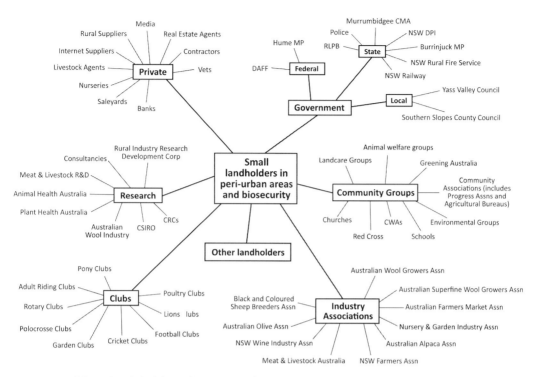

Figure 9.1.   Map of stakeholders relevant to peri-urban landholders and biosecurity risk in the Yass LGA.

than others. As we found in this study, there are some organisations or individual agents that are unexpectedly important to the issue but had been previously disregarded. We used two different forms of stakeholder mapping to depict the information we gathered through our processes of stakeholder identification, analysis of data from stakeholder interviews and surveys and ongoing stakeholder consultation.

Tool 1: Stakeholder Identification Map

The first step in our research study was to draw up a list of all the possible agencies or individuals that could affect or be affected by biosecurity risk outcomes within the Yass Valley local government area. Within the extensive literature on stakeholders, this is the widely accepted definition of stakeholder. (See Gilmour and Beilin, 2007, for a detailed review of this literature and its application to risk issues.)

By establishing some broad categories of stakeholder (e.g. government agencies, community groups, research agencies, industry groups and professional associations), we were able to start building our list of stakeholders. We consulted local websites and talked to local people to ensure that the list included all relevant people and organisations. The resulting stakeholder map (see Figure 9.1) was then used as a prompt for people in subsequent interviews. As the research progressed, there were further additions and deletions from the map.

Tool 2: Stakeholder Interest/Influence Map

Our next step was to identify agencies that were trusted by the landholders and therefore more likely to be able to influence outcomes. We also sought to understand the relative interest of different agencies in biosecurity risk management in the area. This mapping process is particularly useful with respect to risk communication issues because it provides insights into organisations and individuals that, even though they may not have high levels of interest in biosecurity risk issues, are widely trusted within the community and therefore could be usefully co-opted as participants in the development and implementation of a risk communication strategy.

At our first stakeholder consultation meeting, we invited those present to reflect on these two questions. After some discussion, they decided that the answers to these questions would be different depending on whether we were talking about weed risk or animal disease risk. We therefore determined that we would need to develop two maps showing the relative interest and influence of the key stakeholders: one for weeds and one for animal diseases. We started to build these maps with the stakeholders at that first meeting and then used the data from interviews and surveys to complete them.

We defined interest from the point of view of the agency, that is, the extent to which biosecurity risk fell within its remit. Influence was defined from the point of view of the landowners and was based on the trust that landowners had in the agency, the agency's perceived effectiveness and the regularity of landowner contacts with it (Figure 9.2).

The final consultation meeting with stakeholders was an opportunity to triangulate the grids. These discussions highlighted the complexity and the multi-faceted nature of interactions within communities. The position of the key national agencies responsible for biosecurity risk management was firmly endorsed. Local people did not see these agencies as having a role at the local level and therefore these agencies were not seen to have any capacity to influence outcomes locally. The capacity of the national agencies to influence would always be through other agencies. There was general agreement about the role of the key local government agencies, the Department of Primary Industry and the Rural Lands Protection Board. The latter, however, was about to evolve into a different organisation and there was some concern about its ongoing capacity to service the region. The discussion also confirmed the role of pony clubs and adult riding clubs in an area with a high percentage of horse ownership. Their role in the recent equine influenza outbreak had been significant and they enjoyed high levels of trust and extensive networks within the community. Rural suppliers were also confirmed as trusted agents within the community. Although the New South Wales Farmers' Association was acknowledged as having a significant level of interest in minimising animal disease risk, it was seen as having limited influence because its support in the area has declined over the years, largely as a result of its role in the outbreak of ovine Johne's disease some years earlier.

As organisations change, or in response to their interactions with the community, their position on this map will also change. Stakeholder maps need to be reviewed

Influence/interest map: animal diseases
(Yass Local Government Area)

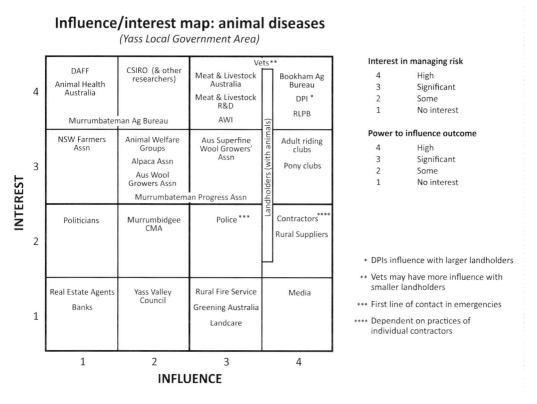

Figure 9.2.   Stakeholder influence/interest grid.

on a regular basis if they are to continue to provide useful information for risk managers and communicators. Importantly, stakeholder beliefs as part of cognitive mapping processes may frequently give rise to actions. Making this as transparent as possible for managers can elucidate and inform planning processes (Wood et al., 2012) embedding stakeholder and manager needs.

9.3.2   Step 2. Mental Models Analysis

Mental models are useful for eliciting people's intuitive knowledge or understanding of a specific risk (Brummette, 2013; Fischhoff et al., 2002; Morgan et al., 2002). Mental models have been defined as 'the mechanisms whereby humans are able to generate descriptions of system purpose and form, explanations of system functioning and observed states, and predictions of future system states' (Rouse & Morris 1986, p. 351). If these mental models do not encompass the potential seriousness of a risk or a complete understanding of exposure pathways, they can lead to erroneous conclusions, even in situations where people are otherwise well-informed about an issue (Morgan et al., 2002).

It has been suggested that mental models analysis starts from a knowledge deficit framework where an expert mental model is presented against which lay knowledge is measured. Usually, the development of a mental model representation of a process will start from an expert or influence diagram based on the knowledge of experts. Other knowledge is added to this as it emerges and mental models can also incorporate values and beliefs to create a comprehensive picture of the complexity of people's perceptions of the salient features of a particular issue. In this way, mental models can assist in integrating the fact that stakeholders may have different values and concerns about risks from the experts, as well as differences in their technical understanding of a risk (Shepherd, 2008).

Mental models can also address some of the issues around language and terminology. The importance of using lay language in risk communication is well established (Abel et al., 1998; Daly & Wade, 2013; Finucane & Holup, 2006). Mental models analysis can help identify where there is the potential for miscommunication and misunderstanding due to the language or terminology being used. An example of this, as we found, is the use of the word biosecurity; the continuing recognition that multiple interpretations of the terminology are likely to exist and that this may give rise to inherent tensions (Beilin & Bohnet, 2015) is a critical step in the definition of stakeholders and their inclusion. Clearly defining stakeholders can increase the possibility of engagement but does not guarantee the quality of such engagement in terms of effective responses (Marzano et al., 2015). Therefore, we emphasise again that the more transparent the mental models are, checked with stakeholders and end-users, the better the likelihood of mutual understanding among participants and decision-making agencies.

Tool 3: Expert models or pathways diagrams

We created two separate pathways diagrams: one for weeds and one for animal diseases. Through discussions with specialists and people working with these issues in the Yass Valley, we developed an understanding of the types of biosecurity and land management issues present in the area as well as potential biosecurity risks. We asked people to list the top five endemic and exotic animal diseases and weeds that exist or pose a potential threat to the area and then reviewed the literature on those to develop the initial diagrams. In building these diagrams, we used the widely accepted conceptual risk pathway framework of prevention, point of entry detection, establishment, spread, intervention or management (Maller et al., 2007).

The resulting diagrams were reviewed by two experts, one specialising in veterinary pathology and the other specialising in plant physiology and ecology. The outcome for animal disease is shown in Figure 9.3.

These diagrams were then presented to a workshop of specialists in risk analysis and modifications were made to reflect feedback from these professionals. A number of the factors affecting establishment, such as detectability of the disease, weather conditions and the disease incubation period, were not controllable. We needed to understand people's mental models around the controllable factors. We therefore decided to focus the diagrams on entry, spread and management variables. We also included attitude and awareness variables that were based on the literature because we expected these would influence people's management actions. This iterative

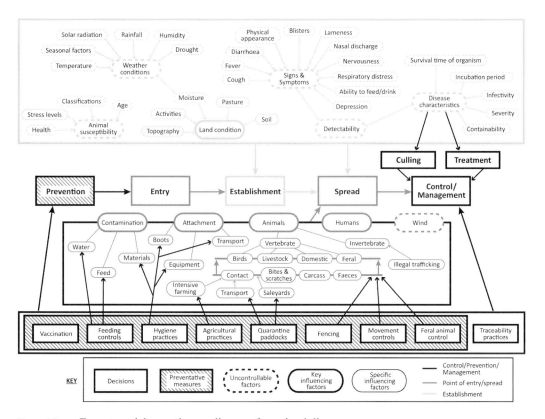

Figure 9.3.   Expert model or pathways diagram for animal diseases.

process was important because it meant that we were able to focus our subsequent data collection on the key variables that would be relevant to biosecurity risk communication and management.

Tool 4: Semi-structured Interviews to Elicit Information about Local Knowledge, Behaviours, Beliefs and Attitudes

These diagrams formed the basis for developing interview questions on biosecurity knowledge, awareness and practices. We also included some demographic questions to assist with comparing our data with other peri-urban studies (see Guise & Narducci, 2005; Hollier et al., 2004). Importantly, the survey included questions relating to sources of information and networks to help us understand the levels of influence of different agencies within the community.

Thirty-three semi-structured ethnographic interviews were conducted by one researcher who was locally based for the period of this field work. The interviewees were selected from five different landholding sizes: 0–2 hectares, 2–40 hectares, 40–100 hectares, 100–500 hectares and more than 500 hectares. These were determined after consultation with key stakeholders in the Yass Valley and after referring to a map of holding areas by hectares provided by local government. Interviews were also held with a selection of people representing key stakeholder

Table 9.1. Survey distribution and return rate

	Yass Valley local government area (1 hectare and over)	Surveys sent	Surveys returned	Surveys returned as % of surveys sent
0–2 hectares	519	190	18	9
2–40 hectares	1465	204	36	18
40–100 hectares	661	196	28	14
100–500 hectares	553	191	38	20
Over 500 hectares	150	150	23	15
Overall	**3,350**	**930**	**144**	**15**

groups. Interviewees were identified through a number of processes including website searches, snowball sampling, cold sampling, attendance at events and an article placed in the local council newsletter.

The semi-structured interviews averaged about one hour and were held at participants' properties, offices or local meeting places. The interviews focused on eliciting respondents' insights into, and awareness of, biosecurity, and also established their practices, sources of information and communication networks. Immediately following the interviews, the researcher recorded her own commentary and impressions of the interview. All interviews were recorded and transcribed soon after, as were the researcher's comments.

The locally based researcher also visited relevant businesses including local shops, nurseries, real estate agents, equipment hire companies, newsagencies and an information service centre to gain further insight into the area. Observations from these visits were also recorded and transcribed by the researcher.

The responses were then analysed against the expert model. Key points from the interview data were abstracted and added to the diagrams to represent the full extent of the known and expected pathways associated with the particular risks.

Tool 5: Survey

The survey instrument was based on the semi-structured interviews and influence diagrams. The objective was to understand how well concepts are understood, whether there are misconceptions, and if so, whether they are widely shared. Ten pilot surveys were sent to landholders and key stakeholders in the region asking for feedback about completion time, ease of reading and comprehension. Six of these were returned completed and with comments, prompting some further amendments to the survey instrument. The final survey instrument included 33 questions covering demographic data, activity on property, biosecurity knowledge and networks, travel patterns, and communication. The survey took 20 to 30 minutes to complete and the majority of the questions were closed questions. Surveys were sent to a stratified sample of 930 people across the landholding size groups (Table 9.1). The sample size per group was determined on the basis of statistical advice to allow for comparability of responses between landholding sizes. A follow-up card was sent four weeks later to the same people and a reminder announcement was made on Yass community radio. The overall return rate was 15%.

Tool 6: Data Analysis

All survey data were entered and analysed using the statistical package SPSS version 17.0. Not all respondents completed the whole survey, choosing to skip some questions. Chi-square tests, using the conventionally accepted 0.05 as the significance level, were applied to a number of the comparisons to identify any significant statistical relationships between responses and landholding size.

9.3.3 Step 3. Identifying the Key Data from the Interviews and Survey Relevant to People's Attitudes to, Knowledge of and Behaviour with Respect to Biosecurity

Identifying What People Know about Biosecurity

We were able to determine that many landholders were not clear about the meaning of biosecurity, which reflects the findings of previous researchers (Hollier et al., 2006). Only 22% said they were familiar with the term; 62% said they were somewhat familiar and 16% indicated they were not familiar. Nonetheless, respondents generally had a comprehensive understanding of the factors contributing to the spread of pests and diseases, indicating that they had practical knowledge, but they did not necessarily see how this related to a broader understanding of biosecurity. All the pathways identified as important by the experts were acknowledged as having either some or significant impact by 60% or more of respondents. Other people's practices, lack of information, people not seeing disease and weed spread as a risk, and people's failure to recognise diseases or weeds were all widely recognised as contributing factors. There were, however, some factors that had much lower recognition, with between 20% and 40% of people saying that they did not see water, movement of people, movement of equipment and machinery and ineffective quarantine practices as having any impact.

Across the different landholding sizes there was very little difference in people's understandings of the factors contributing to the spread of weed and animal disease (Figure 9.4).

There were some gaps in knowledge. Respondents had greater knowledge of weeds and weed pathways than of animal diseases. More than half of the respondents (58%) were able to name five or more weeds, with only 8% leaving the question blank. In contrast, only 13% of respondents were able to list five or more animal diseases that they thought were or could become significant in the area, and 34% left the question blank or indicated they did not know. Those on larger landholdings had better knowledge of animal diseases than those on smaller landholdings.

Identifying People's Biosecurity Practices

A number of comments from interviews suggested that, even if people are aware of the factors contributing to spread of pests and diseases, it cannot necessarily be

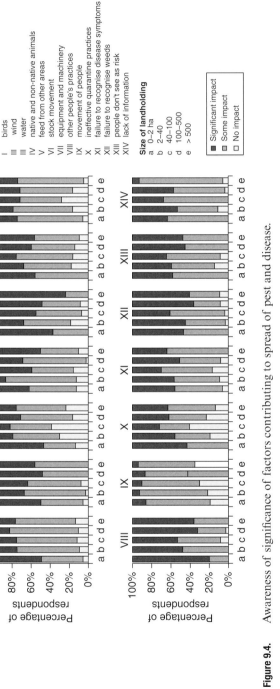

Figure 9.4. Awareness of significance of factors contributing to spread of pest and disease.

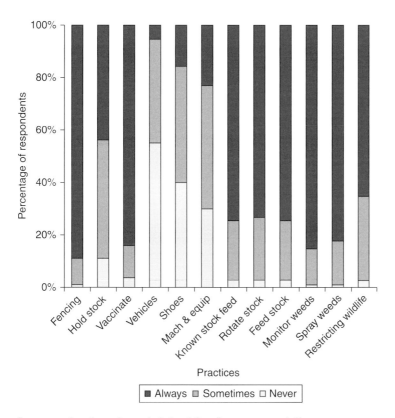

Figure 9.5. Steps people take to keep their land free from pests and diseases.

assumed that they will act on this knowledge. This is not an uncommon finding, as indicted by the study of Sayers et al. (2014) of dairy farm veterinarians and advisors. In our research, one interviewee commented that he had a couple of clients who had been running farms for 50 years but refused to drench (the use of an oral dose of medicine, particularly for sheep against worms). Another commented that complacency leads to people not complying with required procedures. Nonetheless, with the exception of hygiene practices (washing shoes, vehicles and equipment), people responded that they regularly undertook the appropriate behaviours to minimise the spread of weeds and animal diseases, including maintaining their fences, holding new stock in separate paddocks, vaccinating stock and monitoring for and spraying weeds (see Figure 9.5).

Despite overall low level of knowledge of animal diseases, the majority (82%) of respondents said they would ask a specialist if they noticed unusual symptoms in one of their animals.

Providing Insights into Landholder Attitudes and Motivations
By asking about people's reasons for managing weeds on their property, we were able to use this as a proxy for their motivations. The most common responses were

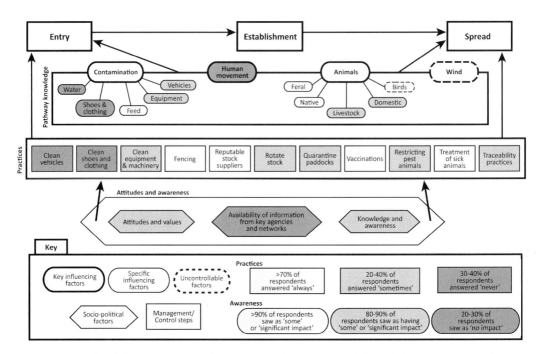

Figure 9.6. Animal diseases pathway diagram indicating landholder's knowledge, awareness and practice.

good land management (89%), pasture protection (61%) and responsibility to neighbours (35%).

9.3.4 Step 5. Applying the Findings to the Mental Model Diagrams

The findings from the interviews and survey were then correlated with the mental model diagrams, to identify areas where awareness and practice suggested there was reason for concern. Figure 9.6 represents the combined data from the interviews and surveys relating to people's knowledge, actions and general awareness of the biosecurity risk posed by animal diseases. It shows that there is generally poor awareness of animal diseases and that there is reason for concern about people's attitudes to the risk of animal disease. It also shows the lack of knowledge around some specific pathways and the fact that precautionary practices are not followed rigorously.

A similar diagram with respect to weeds indicated a lack of knowledge around certain pathways and failure to implement the associated management practices. Overall awareness and understanding of weed risk was, however, much higher.

The diagrams were presented at the final stakeholder meeting as a form of triangulation to clarify findings, identify any responses that seemed improbable, reinforce positive practices and encourage local engagement. Initially, the models required some decoding before participants felt confident to engage with the information they contained. However, after working through the models in detail, participants found them to be a useful way of representing the data.

9.4 Implications for a Communication Strategy

9.4.1 Getting the Message Right

Biosecurity is not a term with which people feel comfortable. We suggest that using the word biosecurity in any form of communication will be ineffective without some discussion of its meaning. Overall, landholders in this region had good knowledge of the possible pathways for the incursion and spread of weeds and animal diseases, and based on this knowledge, good management practices are widely followed. Policymakers and communications experts need to note that this is not a high priority area for any form of top-down generic biosecurity risk message, and any communication needs to relate to specific practices or specific risks. There was no need for a message that was directed specifically towards smaller landholders. With few exceptions, the data did not indicate any major differences in awareness, knowledge or practice between large and smaller landholders.

The lack of knowledge about animal diseases could represent a threat in the region. However, another finding from the survey – that the majority of landholders would seek expert advice if they noticed any unusual symptoms in an animal – suggests that the threat of animal disease is not seen as an active management issue for landholders. If a disease occurs then it becomes a priority, but not otherwise. Landholding size did make a difference in terms of knowledge of animal diseases, with fewer than 20% of people on smaller landholdings (0–40 hectares) able to name three or more animal diseases compared with 65% of people on landholdings of more than 500 hectares. We noted that the traditional channels for communication about animal diseases are directed primarily to commercial farmers. This suggests that, with respect to animal diseases, communication needs to be directed through a diverse set of channels to reach the non-commercial scale landholders.

The lack of awareness of the significance of the risks posed by individual pathways – specifically the movement of people, vehicles and equipment and hence the importance of hygiene practices – may indicate the need for specific attention, particularly in circumstances of a disease outbreak. Other studies have found that people's mental models of natural phenomena are better developed where the physical processes are more immediately comprehensible. Lazrus et al. (2016) noted the diversity of understanding among the 26 mental model interviews about flash flooding in Colorado. Wagner (2007) found that people had more comprehensive mental models of flash floods than of landslides. This research revealed that people were less aware of the risks posed by water and people movement. Alternatively, people may simply have made a heuristic assessment that these pathways were in fact of much less significance than others.

If responsible agencies want to address the risks posed by these pathways, they need to address the beliefs, rather than the behaviours that stem from the beliefs. Fischhoff et al. (2003) found that people who hold strongly to erroneous beliefs are not likely to seek advice before making a decision, with the result that neither the belief nor the practice is challenged. If you don't think the risk posed by people movement is high, you will be unlikely to clean your footwear and clothing. The communication therefore needs to be directed at changing people's knowledge about pathways for them to be motivated to change their practice.

9.4.2   Appealing to People's Motivations and Values

Communication needs to appeal to people's values and motivations; and Liu and Cook (2016) note the importance of establishing how best to represent diverse values through formal and structured decision analysis of the issues. Pannell et al. (2006) found that landholders' adoption of practices depends on their expectation that it will allow them to better achieve their goals. This study found that landholders are motivated by considerations of good land management, pasture protection and good neighbourliness (with respect to weed management). Landholders were also motivated by economic considerations because it is cheaper to deal with weeds before they get out of control. Where information assists people to achieve their goals, they are more likely to implement recommended practices. Biosecurity risk communication therefore needs to make the connection between biosecurity risk and good farm management, stock health (particularly for those on smaller landholdings) and good neighbourliness, and address concerns about cost and cost-saving. While standardising public practices can improve risk communication, messages must still be local and particular enough to be useful for all, including disadvantaged populations (Dickmann et al., 2016), whether this disadvantage is due to socio-economic, distance, isolation or other causes. Biosecurity risk communication needs to present a whole of landscape solution to the issue rather than focusing solely on the actions of individual landholders. Finally, any biosecurity risk message needs to address real risks and tangible outcomes, not some potential risk that people cannot see as important in the day-to-day heuristic triage they conduct with respect to what they can do and what they do not have time (or money) to do.

9.4.3   Working Locally

Importantly, any risk communication strategy needs to be developed in consultation with local stakeholders and involve the different networks operating within the region to ensure that it reaches all landholders. There is a diversity of formal and informal networks, some of which have already been involved in different ways. As we have seen, the Pony Club, for example, played an important role in communicating to local people at the time of the equine influenza outbreak. Other local organisations are actively involved in natural resource management communication with varying focus on biosecurity risk issues. Other organisations, such as rural suppliers, contractors, garden clubs and nurseries, are not involved in natural resource management communication. A comprehensive biosecurity risk communication strategy should look at how it can involve organisations and agencies that enjoy the confidence and trust of the local community and are, as set out in the interest/influence grid, seen by the local stakeholders as having the capacity to influence the issue.

9.5 Conclusion

This chapter describes an investigation that started from the premise of an assumed biosecurity risk communication need. A series of tools were developed using local and expert knowledge. These elicited what landholders know, believe and do with respect to biosecurity, who they trust within the community and which organisations they see as being able to influence the outcome. A continuing process of stakeholder consultation was built into the study and all findings were verified with a stakeholder consultative group.

The mental models analysis proved to be an effective way of capturing people's knowledge, attitudes and practices with respect to biosecurity risk. It allowed us to highlight areas where there are gaps in knowledge; areas where there are differences between people on different landholding sizes, indicating the need for different communication strategies; and areas where changing attitudes and beliefs may be critical to changing behaviour. The mental models diagrams proved to be effective tools for communicating and engaging with stakeholders on these issues. To the responsible agencies, they provided some level of comfort that, although there were some specific gaps in knowledge and practice, overall understanding of risk pathways was good and there was fairly widespread compliance with good risk management practice.

The investigation revealed that the initial assumption that smaller-scale peri-urban landholders posed a greater biosecurity risk than traditional larger-scale commercial landowners was unfounded. It also demonstrated a framework for any future risk communication that incorporates expert opinion, draws on local knowledge, addresses landholder motivations and values and involves multiple local networks.

Risk communication needs to be undertaken within an interdisciplinary framework that takes into consideration scientific knowledge, cultural perceptions and norms, together with stakeholder (or lay) knowledge, beliefs and preferences. Information about what people already know and understand, what their attitudes and values are with regard to a potential risk, whether there are people within the community whose opinions and actions they trust above others and whether there are issues that are of major concern to them that may or may not affect their response to a risk situation are all critical to the development of an effective stakeholder communication process.

The tools we have described allowed us to generate detailed information about the Yass Valley with respect to biosecurity risk. These tools could easily be used by this or any other local community, with the help of a facilitator, to address ongoing biosecurity risk management issues while recognising the need for, and the dynamic nature of, adaptive management processes.

Box 9.1 Stakeholder Interest and Influence Mapping to Inform Risk Communication for Improved Biosecurity among Small-scale Pig Producers in Australia

This box presents the finding of a separate study that applied the methodologies of stakeholder mapping to another biosecurity risk communication issue in Australia. Recent studies among small-scale pig producers in Australia suggest that this sector could pose a biosecurity risk to the commercial livestock industry due, for example, to being less informed about potential risks for disease introduction and spread and less engaged with industry and government agencies (Hernández-Jover et al., 2012a; Schembri et al., 2006). Producers' active engagement and participation within the pig industry could be enhanced with better extension and communication networks among producers and industry and government stakeholders. However, a better understanding of these producers' biosecurity practices, current networks, relationships with stakeholders and what the influences and interests of both producers and stakeholders are, is essential for improving communication effectiveness and subsequently the management of the potential biosecurity risks.

On-farm biosecurity and health practices of pig producers in Australia have been previously investigated (Hernández-Jover et al., 2012b; Schembri, 2009; Schembri et al., 2014, 2015) and a summary of the main findings of these studies is presented in Table 1. As suggested by these studies, on-farm biosecurity practices and disease knowledge and reporting behaviour, especially among small-scale pig producers, could be improved. Some of the barriers to disease reporting identified by Schembri (2009) included the economic impact of the disease, over-reaction from the media and government agencies, the fear of negative consequences and the previous negative experiences with authorities.

Evaluation of the Interest and Influence of Stakeholders

Two influence/interest maps were created to investigate industry and government stakeholders' perceptions of their influence and interest on on-farm management practices, and disease reporting attitudes. On-farm management encompasses a range of producers' practices related to biosecurity, including general husbandry, health management, feeding practices and biosecurity measures such as isolation of new animals and footwear and clothing precautions. Producer reporting refers to the mandatory requirement for all notifiable diseases to be reported to the relevant authority.

Box 9.1, Table 1. A review of on-farm practices related to biosecurity of small and large-scale pig producers in Australia reported in previous studies

Small-scale pig producers (<100 sows) (Schembri et al, 2014, 2015; Hernández-Jover et al., 2012a)		Large-scale pig producers (>100 sows) (Hernández-Jover et al., 2012b)	
Practice	Producers applying the practice, *n* (%)	*Practice*	Producers applying the practice, *n* (%)
On-farm biosecurity practices		*On-farm biosecurity practices*	
Footwear precautions in piggery	49 (50.5)	I provide visitors with overalls and/or boots.	89 (84.0)
Overalls provided for visitors/staff	12 (12.4)	I do not let any visitor inspect my pigs.	39 (36.8)
Visitors allowed in piggery	68 (70.1)	I have a controlled entry preventing visitors contacting my pigs.	85 (84.9)
Pig isolation practices		I keep records of visitors to my pig farm.	80 (75.5)
Nothing	38 (39.2)	I display quarantine sings for visitors at my farm entry.	80 (80.2)
>30 days and >100 m isolation	3 (3.1)	I allow my staff to contact pigs other than my own.	9 (8.5)
		I record movements of pigs on and off my farm.	93 (87.7)
Herd health management		*Herd health management*	
Keeping health records	49 (50.5)	I inspect my herd regularly for unusual signs of disease.	96 (90.6)
Exotic Animal Disease training	5 (5.2)	I regularly consult my vet or pig health specialist.	95 (89.6)
Contact a veterinarian in the last 12 months	16 (16.5)		
Disease knowledge		*Disease knowledge and reporting*	
Foot-and-mouth disease	95 (97.9)	I train workers in emergency disease recognition.	68 (64.2)
Erysipelas	77 (79.4)		
Ringworm	67 (69.1)		

(*continued*)

Box 9.1, Table 1 continued

Small-scale pig producers (<100 sows) (Schembri et al, 2014, 2015; Hernández-Jover et al., 2012a)		Large-scale pig producers (>100 sows) (Hernández-Jover et al., 2012b)	
Practice	Producers applying the practice, *n* (%)	*Practice*	Producers applying the practice, *n* (%)
Disease reporting			
Would you report foot-and-mouth disease?	93 (95.9)		
Seek veterinary advice if unusual signs of disease	83 (85.6)		
Feeding practices			
Home table scraps	14 (14.4)		
Retail waste food (café, shops)	5 (5.2)		

Adapted with permission from Hernández-Jover, M., Gilmour, J., Schembri, N. et al. (2012a). Use of stakeholder analysis to develop risk communication and extension strategies for improved biosecurity among small-scale pig producers. *Preventive Veterinary Medicine*, 104(3–4), 258–270; Hernández-Jover, M., Taylor, M., Holyoake, P. & Dhand, N. (2012b). Pig producers' perceptions of the influenza pandemic H1N1/09 outbreak and its effect on their biosecurity practices in Australia. *Preventive Veterinary Medicine*, 106(3–4), 284–294; Schembri, N. (2009). *Biosecurity practices of producers trading pigs at saleyards*. PhD thesis. Farm Animal and Veterinary Public Health, University of Sydney, Camden, Australia; and Schembri, N., Hernandez-Jover, M., Toribio, J.-A. L. M. L. & Holyoake, P. K. (2013). Demographic and production practices of pig producers trading at saleyards in eastern Australia. *Australian Veterinary Journal*, 91(12), 507–516.

Small-scale Pig Producers' Perceptions of Influence of Stakeholders

In addition, the influence that stakeholders had on producers' practices, as perceived by producers, was estimated from information on communication networks and trusted sources of information on small-scale pig producers gathered during previous studies (Schembri, 2009). This information included perceived influence on their on-farm management and disease reporting practices.

Key Findings

Figure A shows the industry and government stakeholders' self-rating interest/influence ranking for (a) on-farm management practices and (b) disease reporting. Figure B represents the influence of stakeholders as perceived by small-scale pig producers.

The self-ranking interest/influence of stakeholders on on-farm management practices and disease reporting suggests that veterinarians, the Australian Quarantine Inspection Service, the State Food Authority and other producers

On-farm practices

Interest	Influence 1	Influence 2	Influence 3	Influence 4
4		Animal Health Australia Australian Pork Limited Researchers		Veterinarians AQIS
		— DPI Victoria —— LHPA —		
3	DAFF	DPI NSW DAFF	Food authority	Other producers
2	PIRSA	Abattoirs DEEDI	Saleyards/ livestock agents	
1				

Disease reporting

Interest	Influence 1	Influence 2	Influence 3	Influence 4
4	Animal Health Australia DAFWA	DAFF DEEDI LHPA PIRSA Researchers	Other producers	Veterinarians
	— DPI Victoria —			
3		DPI NSW	Food authority AQIS saleyards	
2	Australian Pork Limited	Abattoirs		
1				

Box 9.1, Figure A Influence/interest map representing the self-ranking influence and interest of stakeholders on (a) producer on-farm practices and (b) disease reporting behaviour of small-scale pig producers (< 100 sows) in Australia. Influence level is categorised as: 1, no influence; 2, some influence; 3, significant influence; and 4, high influence. Interest level is categorised as: 1, no interest; 2, some interest; 3, significant interest; and 4, high interest. (Adapted from Hernández-Jover et al., 2012a).
Abbreviations: AQIS, Australian Quarantine Inspection Service; DAFF, Department of Agriculture, Fisheries and Forestry; DEEDI, Department of Employment, Economic Development and Innovation Queensland; DPI NSW, Department of Primary Industries New South Wales; DPI Victoria, Department of Primary Industries Victoria; LHPA, Livestock Health and Pest Authorities; PIRSA, Primary Industries and Resources South Australia

On-farm practices

Influence	
4	Veterinarians Other producers Family
3	Livestock agents Rural suppliers Abattoirs Buyers
2	State Department of Primary Industries Australian Pork Limited
1	Animal Health Australia Department of Agriculture, Fisheries and Forestry

Box 9.1, Figure B Influence of stakeholders on on-farm practices, as perceived by Australian small-scale pig producers (<100 sows). Influence level is categorised as: 1, no influence; 2, some influence; 3, significant influence; and 4, high influence. (Adapted from Hernández-Jover et al., 2012a).

consider themselves as having high interest and influence on these producers' practices. In addition, saleyards and livestock agents, although having limited interest, believe they have significant influence on producers' practices. Industry organisations, such as Australian Pork Limited and Animal Health Australia, and government agencies have significant interest in these producers' practices but their self-perceived influence is limited.

When looking at the influence of stakeholders as perceived by producers, we can see that industry organisations and government agencies are seen to have limited or no influence on their practices, while other producers, family members and veterinarians are considered highly influential.

Although coarse agreement between the self-ranked influence of stakeholders and that perceived by producers was observed, this study has identified anomalous situations where stakeholders with high interest in achieving a particular outcome have limited to no influence on producers' practices. To improve biosecurity among small-scale pig producers using an extension approach, government and industry agencies need to work with producers and with stakeholders who have the capacity to influence them. Understanding the extension needs of this sector and building alliances with trusted stakeholders is crucial for the effectiveness of any extension program aimed at improving producers' practices. Successful biosecurity risk management will depend on shared responsibility among all the stakeholders.

References

Abel, N., Ross, H. & Walker, P. (1998). Mental models in rangeland research, communication and management. *Rangeland Journal,* 20(1), 77–91.

Aslin, H., Kelson, S., Smith, J. & Lesslie, R. (2004). *Peri-urban landholders and biosecurity issues – A scoping study*. Canberra, Australia: Bureau of Rural Sciences, Commonwealth of Australia.

Beilin, R. & Bohnet, I. C. (2015). Culture-production-place and nature: the landscapes of somewhere. *Sustainability Science,* 10(2): 195–205.

Bocking, S. (2004). *Nature's experts: Science, politics and the environment*. New Brunswick, NJ: Rutgers University Press.

Brummette, J. (2013). *Mental models approach to risk communication*. Thousand Oaks, CA: SAGE.

Buxton, M., Tieman, G., Bekessy, S., et al. (2006). *Change and continuity in peri-urban Australia – State of the peri-urban regions: Review of the literature*. Melbourne, Australia: RMIT University.

Daly, D. & Wade, S. (2013). Message mapping for CCUS outreach: Testing communications through focus group discussion. In T. Dixon & K. Yamaji (eds.), *Ghgt-11*, 37, 7346–7352.

Daniels, T. L. (1986). Hobby farming in America: Rural development or threat to commercial agriculture? *Journal of Rural Studies*, 2(1), 31–40.

Dickmann, P., Abraham, T., Sarkar, S., et al. (2016). Risk communication as a core public health competence in infectious disease management: Development of the ECDC training curriculum and programme. *Eurosurveillance*, 21(14), 24–28.

Finucane, M. & Holup, J. L. (2006). Risk as value: Combining affect and analysis in risk judgments. *Journal of Risk Research*, 9(2), 141–164.

Fischhoff, B., Bostrom, A. & Jacobs Quadrel, M. (2002). Risk perception and communication. In R. Detels, J. McEwan, R. Reaglehole & H. Tanaka (eds.), *Oxford textbook of public health*, 4th ed., (pp. 1105–1123). London: Oxford University Press.

Fischhoff, B., Gonzalez, R. M., Small, D. A. & Lerner, J. S. (2003). Evaluating the success of terror risk communications. *Biosecurity and Bioterrorism: Biodefense Strategy, Practice, and Science*, 1(4), 255–258.

Gaillard, J. C. & Mercer, J. (2013). From knowledge to action: Bridging gaps in disaster risk reduction. *Progress in Human Geography*, 37(1), 93–114.

Gilmour, J. & Beilin, R. (2007). *Stakeholder mapping for effective risk communication*. Melbourne, Australia: Australian Centre of Excellence for Risk Analysis. Available from www.acera.unimelb.edu.au/materials/core.html

Gilmour, J., Beilin, R. & Sysak, T. (2009). *Using stakeholder mapping and analysis with a mental models approach for biosecurity risk communication with peri-urban communities*. Melbourne, Australia: Australian Centre of Excellence for Risk Analysis. Available from www.acera.unimelb.edu.au/materials/core.html

Gilmour, J., Beilin, R. & Sysak, T. (2011). Biosecurity risk and peri-urban landholders – using a stakeholder consultative approach to build a risk communication strategy. *Journal of Risk Research*, 14(3), 281–295.

Guise, N. & Narducci, M. (2005). Small landholder extension delivery in practice: Western Australian approach. Paper presented at *Rural Lifestyle and Landscape Change: Emerging Challenges for Extension: a National Forum*. Barton, Australia: Rural Industries Research and Development Corporation.

Hernández-Jover, M., Gilmour, J., Schembri, N., et al. (2012a). Use of stakeholder analysis to develop risk communication and extension strategies for improved biosecurity among small-scale pig producers. *Preventive Veterinary Medicine*, 104(3–4), 258–270.

Hernández-Jover, M., Taylor, M., Holyoake, P. & Dhand, N. (2012b). Pig producers' perceptions of the influenza pandemic H1N1/09 outbreak and its effect on their biosecurity practices in Australia. *Preventive Veterinary Medicine*, 106(3–4), 284–294.

Higgins, V., Bryant, M., Hernández-Jover, M., et al. (2016). Harmonising devolved responsibility for biosecurity governance: The challenge of competing institutional logics. *Environment and Planning A*, 48(6), 1133–1151.

Higgins, V. & Dibden, J. (2011). Biosecurity, trade liberalisation, and the (anti)politics of risk analysis: The Australia-New Zealand apples Dispute. *Environment and Planning A*, 43(2), 393–409.

Hollier, C., Francis, J. & Reid, M. (2004). Rural-peri-urban interface and extension. Paper presented at the *National Extension Policy Forum*, Sydney.

Hollier, C., Reid, M. & Reed, D. (2006). *Small lifestyle farms and biosecurity*. Rutherglen, Australia: Department of Primary Industries. Available from www.dpi.vic.gov.au/__data/assets/pdf_file/0004/24493/Small-Farms-Biosecurity.pdf

Houston, P. (2005). Re-valuing the fringe: Some findings on the value of agricultural production in Australia's peri-urban regions. *Geographic Research*, 43(2), 209–223.

Lazrus, H., Morss, R., Demuth, J. L., et al. (2016). Know what to do if you encounter a flash flood: Mental models analysis for improving flash flood risk communication and public decision making. *Risk Analysis,* 36(2), 411–427.

Linkov, I., Wood, M., Bridges, T., et al. (2009). Cognitive barriers in floods risk perception and management: A mental modeling framework and illustrative example. In *2009 IEEE International Conference on Systems, Man and Cybernetics* (pp. 3940–3945). San Antonio, Texas, United States.

Liu, S. & Cook, D. (2016). Eradicate, contain, or live with it? Collaborating with stakeholders to evaluate responses to invasive species. *Food Security,* 8(1), 49–59.

Maller, C., Kancans, R. & Carr, A. (2007). *Biosecurity and small landholders in peri-urban Australia.* Canberra, Australia: Bureau of Rural Sciences, Department of Agriculture, Fisheries and Forestry.

Marzano, M., et al. (2015). Part of the solution? Stakeholder awareness, information and engagement in tree health issues. *Biological Invasions* 17(7), 1961–1977.

McDaniels, T. L., Gregory, R. S. & Fields, D. (1999). Democratizing risk management: Successful public involvement in local water management decisions. *Risk Analysis*, 19(3), 497–510.

Morgan, M. G., Fischoff, B., Bostrom, A. & Atman, C. J. (2002). *Risk communication: A mental models approach.* Cambridge: Cambridge University Press.

Pannell, D. J., Marshall, G. R., Barr, N., et al. (2006). Understanding and promoting adoption of conservation practices by rural landholders. *Australian Journal of Experimental Agriculture*, 46(2), 1407–1424.

Rouse, W. & Morris, N. (1986). On looking into the black box: Prospects and limits in the search for mental models. *Psychological Bulletin*, 100(3), 349–363.

Sayers, R. G., Good, M. & Sayers, G. P. (2014). A survey of biosecurity-related practices, opinions and communications across dairy farm veterinarians and advisors. *Veterinary Journal,* 200(2), 261–269.

Schembri, N. (2009). *Biosecurity practices of producers trading pigs at saleyards.* PhD thesis. Farm Animal and Veterinary Public Health, University of Sydney, Camden, Australia.

Schembri, N., Hart, K., Petersen, R. & Whittington, R. (2006). Assessment of the management practices facilitating the establishment and spread of exotic diseases of pigs in the Sydney region. *Australian Veterinary Journal*, 84(10), 341–348.

Schembri N., Hernández-Jover M., Toribio J.-A. L. M. L. & Holyoake P. K. (2014). Demographic and production practices of pig producers trading at saleyards in Eastern Australia. *Australian Veterinary Journal*, 91 (12), 507–516.

Schembri, N., Hernandez-Jover, M., Toribio, J. A., & Holyoake, P. K. (2015). On-farm characteristics and biosecurity protocols for small-scale swine producers in eastern Australia. *Preventive Veterinary Medicine*, 118(1), 104–116.

Shepherd, R. (2008). Involving the public and stakeholders in the evaluation of food risks. *Trends in Food Science and Technology*, 19(5), 234–239.

Wagner, K. (2007). Mental models of flash floods and landslides. *Risk Analysis*, 27(3), 671–682.

Wood, M. D., Bostrom, A., Bridges T., et al. (2012). Cognitive mapping tools: Review and risk management needs. *Risk Analysis,* 32(8), 1333–1348.

Wynne, B. (1996). May the sheep safely graze? A reflexive view of the expert–lay knowledge divide. In S. Lash, B. Szerniski & B. Wynne (eds.), *Risk, environment and modernity: Towards a new ecology* (pp. 44–83). London: SAGE.

Yass Valley Council. (2008). *Yass valley LGA.* Available from www.yass.nsw.gov.au/files/9191/File/3_YassValleyLGA.pdf

10 Cost–Benefit Analysis for Biosecurity Decisions

Tom Kompas, Tuong Nhu Che, Pham Van Ha and Hoang Long Chu

10.1 Introduction

Economists normally praise the benefits of international and regional trade. But trade it is not an unqualified good. Rapid increases in trade and tourism throughout the world have increased the likelihood of the incursion, establishment and spread of exotic diseases and pests. These can do great harm and can be devastating to local industry, the environment and the health of animals, plants and humans. Foot-and-mouth disease (FMD), severe acute respiratory syndrome (SARS), bovine spongiform encephalopathy disease and avian influenza are recent headline concerns, but there are hundreds of other key pests and diseases that can cause substantial damages. Traditional approaches to prevent these threats have focused on pre-border, border and post-border quarantine measures; local surveillance programmes; and eradication and containment campaigns when a pest or disease has already been detected in the environment. In many cases, these biosecurity measures are undertaken by local, state and national governments. In other cases, private industry and volunteer groups provide effective measures against invasive threats.

All of this activity generates at least a few essential economic questions. In particular, how much should be spent, or what costs for biosecurity should be incurred, to protect the environment as well as animal, plant and human health? How should resources be allocated across the large number of threats? Who of industry, taxpayers, government or consumers should pay for this activity? How should expenditure be allocated across biosecurity measures? How much should be spent at the border? How much for local surveillance to ensure the early detection of an invasive threat? Should an invasive threat be eradicated or contained, or should it simply be ignored and potentially treated at a later date or not treated at all?

Most of the work on biosecurity by economists has, by far, focused on relatively standard cost–benefit analyses (CBA) of eradication and containment campaigns. With the identification of an invasive threat, an economist is often asked to evaluate the relative costs and benefits of a control measure and to form an assessment of the cost-effectiveness of various actions. When ratios of benefits to costs are greater than one, action is usually undertaken, subject to budget constraints or available resources.

Not until recently has more elaborate work been done on CBA for optimal border quarantine and surveillance measures, and much less has been done on allocating scarce resources across different biosecurity measures and invasive threats. Along with highlighting some problems and establishing basic principles for the use of CBA in biosecurity measures, the purpose of this chapter is to describe recent extensions to standard CBA approaches to the economics of biosecurity and provide a better understanding of how economics can assist in answering some of the essential questions surrounding biosecurity measures.

The main sections of this chapter focus on the principles for CBA in biosecurity as well as economically justifiable approaches to containment, eradication, optimal surveillance and border quarantine measures. Practical case studies are included to provide a set of simple examples of how economists approach CBA for biosecurity. Although these case studies deal with specific diseases, the concepts are equally applicable to any pest or pathogen.

10.2   Problems and Principles for CBA in Biosecurity Measures

Biosecurity is defined as measures to reduce the risk of disease incursion and spread of an invasive species, one that affects the environment or the well-being of humans, plants or animals. Consequently, CBA in biosecurity focuses on the costs and benefits of implementing these measures. In other words, a CBA exercise will compare the cost of one or a combination of these measures with the avoided losses that would have occurred if the biosecurity measures were not implemented. Costs and benefits, all properly discounted, are simply compared to determine whether it is economically rational to take a control action.

The application of CBA in biosecurity faces several key challenges. First, the benefits of biosecurity measures often cannot be easily measured or measured directly. As a result, simulation methods and choice experiments must often be used. These are complicated procedures and are not easy to implement (but see Chapter 11). Second, biosecurity measures applied in one sector can influence other sectors of an economy, so that total costs and total benefits are rarely (if ever) comprehensively evaluated. For example, the loss caused by an animal disease outbreak can be much greater than simply multiplying the average value of an infected animal by the quantity infected because the disease outbreak also has an impact on other sectors of the economy (e.g. food suppliers, domestic consumers, exporters and so on). Some authors, such as Gohin and Rault (2013), Keogh-Brown et al. (2009), Smith et al. (2011) and Wittwer et al. (2005), address this issue with computable general equilibrium models, but most of the usual CBA work is done in a simple sector-specific partial equilibrium framework.

The third challenge is the difficulty in measuring the benefits of biosecurity measures relating to a human disease or the environment. For human diseases, some authors use the concept of quality-adjusted life years (e.g. Prieto & Sacristan, 2003), but the monetary value of a quality-adjusted life year is still under intense debate (Nord et al., 1999). Regarding the environment, it is usually difficult (if not impossible) to obtain an exact monetary measure for the environmental services saved by a biosecurity measure, simply because there is no market price for them. Choice experiment techniques have been used to provide statistical estimates of these values (e.g. Choi et al., 2010 or Wang et al., 2007), but the high cost of this kind of research along with its inherent econometric difficulties are still key obstacles.

There are 10 basic or general principles for implementing a CBA exercise in biosecurity. These are important and not always followed. First, the measure of benefits should be calculated from all known avoided losses from the biosecurity measure. Avoided losses, depending on context, may include losses to plant, animal and human health; damage to the environment; losses from trade bans that often accompany a disease or pest incursion; and spillover effects to other industries and areas.

Second, the measure of benefits must be conditional on both an area and density spread model for the disease or pest and the specific biosecurity actions taken (and their likely effects). A proper CBA for containment or eradication measures avoided losses *marginally* at each point in time and relative to the time-dependent effects of the biosecurity measure, and not as the simple difference between the disease-free state and the total potential avoided damages assuming maximum saturation of the pest or disease in the environment. Avoided damages and the costs of the campaign have to be evaluated and discounted at each relevant point in time. The further forward in time the avoided losses and costs, the more heavily discounted and smaller they are in terms of present value.

Third, the measure of cost should include the full range of specific containment or eradication actions (e.g. sprays, vaccinations, screening, inspections, blood tests, public awareness campaigns and so on). Fourth, because prices and costs used to measure avoided losses and the cost of a biosecurity action may vary over time (e.g. an outbreak of an animal disease can affect the price of meat and the resulting value of the animal over time) and by region, these values must also be measured as time dependent. Fifth, where dollar amounts of costs and benefits cannot be measured by market values, non-market valuations should be used wherever possible. Examples of these are contingent value estimates, hedonic pricing and choice modelling exercises.

Sixth, because streams of costs and benefits vary over time and potentially occur at different points in time, all dollar amounts must be discounted to the present. Because a dollar today is worth more tomorrow if it is invested and given a bank rate of return, a dollar tomorrow is worth less today given the same rate of return. Seventh, the discount rate is typically the inflation-adjusted real rate of return, the Treasury bill rate or bank rate (i.e. the common or non-risk adjusted real rate of return). For environmental assets it is not uncommon to use lower or time-contingent discount rates, or rates that decline through time (see Pearce et al., 2006). Eighth, the time horizon for discounting is normally contingent on the full period of time over which damages occur or on a point in time where the present value of future benefits or costs is zero.

Ninth, the present value of all benefits and costs should reflect likely outcomes based on given or estimated probability distributions for key parameter values.

Calculations should account for the variance in the spread rate along with the variance in the estimated values of costs, prices and measured avoided losses. The resulting CBA should report a range of potential values and a probability distribution for costs and benefits. Finally, sensitivity analysis of parameter values should be reported to determine their relative importance. In some cases, the analysis will be especially sensitive to the discount rate, the probability of entry and spread and various cost and price assumptions on the potential damages and costs of the campaign.

10.3   Eradication and Containment

10.3.1   Control Strategies and Associated Economic Components

Once a disease or a pest is confirmed to be present in an area, there are two basic economic strategies for dealing with it: eradication and doing nothing. A combination of these two options is containment (Cacho et al., 2008), which is to eradicate a sub-area and keep the disease inside the remaining area, which is often referred to as a containment zone. Because the benefit of doing something is the avoided losses that would have occurred from a potential disease spread, spread rates are always a key variable in a CBA exercise of a control measure. A rule-of-thumb is that if the spread rate is larger than the discount (or interest) rate, then the net benefit of eradication is almost always positive (Harris et al., 2001).

The cost of an eradication programme normally includes (1) the cost of actual removal (or slaughter in the case of animals), which may have to be repeated due to re-incursions, and (2) the cost of monitoring activities to make sure eradication objectives are met. For example, Schoenbaum and Disney (2003) at the time of their study calculate the cost of slaughtering cattle with FMD in the United States is roughly US$17 per animal plus US$5,000 to US$7,000 per farm for post-slaughter cleaning. In addition, the cost for a testing and monitoring visit is between US$200 and US$500 per farm. Hinrichs et al. (2006) estimate that the costs per bird for culling poultry with H5N1 are US$0.25 in Vietnam and US$1 in Nigeria. For animal diseases, the eradication cost is often calculated by multiplying the affected number by a constant unit cost and adding this to an expenditure for culling-related activities.

For plants and small pests, calculating eradication costs is often more complicated and available estimates are often very broad. It is generally agreed that the cost of eradicating invasive plants or pests increases exponentially with infestation size, and after some point becomes practically unaffordable (Adamson et al., 2000; Hester et al., 2004). However, rough estimates for the unit cost of a successful eradication do not always exhibit this trend (see Cunningham et al., 2003; Rejmánek and Pitcairn, 2002; Woldendorp and Bomford, 2004), but these estimates may be biased because they generally exclude eradication feasibility issues. Taking into account this eradication feasibility, Panetta et al. (2011b) estimate that among the 41 Class-I invasive plants under the Queensland Land Protection Act 2002, only one cannot be practically eradicated, 12 could be eradicated at a cost of more than A$1 million, and 28 could be eradicated for less than A$1 million.

One feature of the eradication cost for invasive plants is that it often includes cost components over a long period of time because eradicating an invasive plant often takes more than 10 years (Panetta & Lawes, 2007). For example, Panetta et al. (2011a), using a stochastic dynamic model, estimate that to eradicate branched broomrape in South Australia would take, on average, 73 years at a net benefit of A$68 million. For other weeds (Cunningham et al., 2003; Woldendorp & Bomford, 2004), the time horizon may not be so long, but a significant component of the total eradication cost should be devoted to monitoring activities over a fairly lengthy period of time (see Chapter 16).

10.3.2 When Eradication or Containment Is Cost-Effective

Kompas et al. (2013) derive a condition that determines when eradication is more cost effective than doing nothing: $d + c \times r \geq c \times \rho$, where d, r, c and ρ are respectively the annual damage caused by the disease, the annual spread rate of the disease, the eradication cost and the discount rate. The left-hand side of this expression presents the avoided loss if eradication is delayed for one year, which includes the damage d caused in that year plus the cost of eradicating the new infection $c \times r$. The right-hand side is the opportunity cost of immediate eradication which is the interest paid on the upfront eradication cost $c \times \rho$. When considering this condition in an area containing heterogeneous locations where the damage, eradication cost and spread rate can vary spatially, it often turns out that parcels that satisfy the condition belong to eradication zones and the rest belong to containment zones.

The condition not only determines the cost-effectiveness of eradication measures, but also has an important implication for the cost-effectiveness of surveillance measures. Surveillance measures are desirable only when one needs to detect a disease so that eradication can take place early. If the eradication measures are not cost effective, then it is not worth paying for early detection. When the benefit of eradication is larger than the cost, the size of this gap will determine the attractiveness of early detection.

10.4 Local Surveillance Measures

10.4.1 Fundamental Factors in a CBA for Surveillance

Surveillance is the search for unknown incursions. It can be implemented either when there are unknown incursions or when known incursions are confirmed but their locations are unknown. The cost of surveillance is the money spent to implement the search, and the benefit of surveillance is the value of early detection in terms of avoided losses that would have resulted otherwise. Thus, surveillance has a

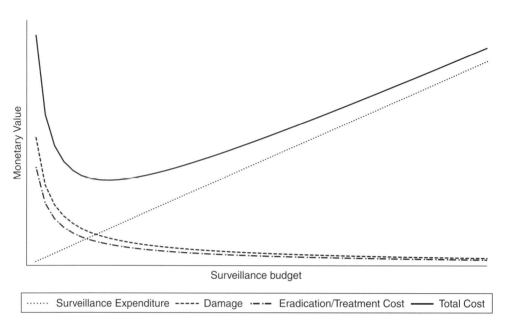

Figure 10.1.   Fundamental factors in a CBA exercise for surveillance.

benefit only when the control actions, such as eradication or containment, are cost effective.

The comparison between the costs and benefits of a surveillance programme depend on how early a search can detect an unknown incursion if it is present. An ambitious surveillance programme can detect a disease very early, but it may be too expensive; an inexpensive programme may not provide satisfactory detectability or detect early enough. Quantitatively, the relationship between surveillance effort and detectability plays a key role in determining the cost-effectiveness of surveillance measures.

Figure 10.1 illustrates the basic idea in a CBA exercise when surveillance, to some degree, is desirable. From left to right, in return for an increase in surveillance expenditure, the damage caused by a disease and the eradication/treatment costs diminish thanks to early detection. It follows that total costs will be minimised when a $1 increase in surveillance expenditure is compensated by a $1 reduction in the damage and eradication costs. If too much is spent on surveillance (the points to the right of the minimum point on the bold line for total cost), the cost is too high because of the high cost of the surveillance programme itself; if too little is spent (the points to the left of the minimum point), detection is not early enough and the damages that result are too high. In practice, quantifying the three cost components in Figure 10.1 often requires models that can connect economic, technical and biological variables. Chapter 14 provides an overview of how these three elements inform optimal resource allocation. In the text that follows we describe and illustrate coherent integration of economic, technical and biological variables in more detail.

10.4.2   A Model of Optimal Surveillance Design

An optimal surveillance model normally has three main components: (1) a bio-logical component to describe the growth and density of infected herds (in the case of animals), (2) a surveillance expenditure function that maps the cost of surveil-lance to the spread of the disease and the point of detection and (3) a measure of production losses before detection occurs, disease management costs and trade and other losses that result during the disease management period (either in terms of disease containment or the time it takes for eradication). The resulting model will evaluate the sum of the three components for each surveillance design and choose the one that minimises the total cost.

Growth and Density Growth of Infected Livestock
As an example, take the unit of measurement as a herd, subject to a disease incur-sion where the growth in the number of infected herds is assumed to follow a Verhulst–Pearl logistic function, so that

$$dN(t) = gN(t)\left(1 - \frac{N(t)}{N_{max}}\right)dt + \sigma_n N(t)dW_n + N_0 dQ_i - N_e dQ_e, \tag{10.1}$$

where $N(t)$ is the number of infected herds at time t, g is the intrinsic or biological growth rate, N_{max} is the maximum number of infected herds relative to the environ-mental carrying capacity, W_n is a Brownian process that captures the natural uncer-tainty in the infected population and Q_i and Q_d are Poisson processes that capture the disease incursion and detection.

   The arrival rate λ_d for disease detection depends on the number of infected herds and the target number (subject to determination of the best surveillance level) of infected herds X in the following way:

$$\lambda_d = \theta \frac{N(t)/X}{N(t)/X + \delta}, \tag{10.2}$$

where θ and δ are positive coefficients. The functional form ensures that the rate of detection will be maximised when the number of infected herds reaches the target value X, and be zero when $N(t) = 0$.

   In a similar fashion, density growth is given by

$$dD(t) = zD(t)\left(1 - \frac{D(t)}{D_{max}}\right)dt + \sigma_d D(t)dW_d + D_0 dQ_i - D_e dQ_e, \tag{10.3}$$

where z is the density growth rate, $D(t)$ is the ratio of the number of infected herds to total herds and D_{max} is the maximum density rate.

Surveillance Expenditure Function
Following Kompas et al. (2004), a surveillance expenditure function maps sur-veillance expenditure to a point of early detection of a disease incursion and is expressed in terms of the number of potentially infected animals in the population.

Larger surveillance expenditure (e.g. blood and viral tests, screening or physical examination) generally result in points of earlier detection and a smaller number of potentially infected livestock. Define R_m as the number of infected animals occurring at the natural detection point, or where the disease incursion is self-evident or recognised by farmers or the public without any surveillance expenditure. In addition, let E_m be the amount of surveillance expenditure that will ensure the earliest possible detection, or where the number of infected animals is near zero (depending on the efficacy of border quarantine measures) or the incursion is detected before the spread of the disease. This amount of expenditure can be finite, but it may also be infinite. The surveillance expenditure function is given by

$$E(X, \eta) = \frac{E_m(R_m - X)}{R_m(\eta X + 1)},\qquad(10.4)$$

where X is the target number of infected animals that potentially enter a population and $\eta \geq 0$ is a surveillance effectiveness parameter. The higher the value of η, the lower the expenditure on surveillance for a given number of infected livestock, or the more convex the expenditure function. When $\eta = 0$, the expenditure function is linear. When $\eta > 0$, the marginal benefit of surveillance decreases with a decrease in the target value X.

Production, Disease Management, Trade and Tourist Losses

The potential production cost before detection depends on both the length of time over which the disease has developed and the time to eradication. Assume that production loss at time t depends both on the number and the density of herds and is given by

$$C_p(t) = c_p N(t)D(t),\qquad(10.5)$$

where c_p is the average production loss per herd. For simplicity, it is assumed that any reduction in infected herds (through containment or eradication) implies that both density and infected herd numbers are reduced proportionately.

A disease can immediately generate disease management costs. One possibility is that all infected herds are destroyed and costs for disinfection and cleaning activities must be incurred. Vaccination costs may also be imposed for all herds entering the affected area for a period of time after a successful eradication campaign. Assuming that all costs are proportional to the target number of potentially infected herds X gives

$$C_{me} = c_{me}X \qquad C_{mv} = c_{mv}\phi X,\qquad(10.6)$$

where C_{me} is the eradication cost and C_{mv} is the vaccination cost, with average cost parameters c_{me} and c_{mv}.

Another possible cost component of an outbreak is a trade ban for importing related products into a disease-free area. This is often the most significant cost component. In addition, the tourism industry also suffers losses due to travel restrictions and quarantine provisions. In general, the larger the number of infected herds, the longer the disease management period. Let the length of time for disease management (T_m) be given by

$$T_m = \alpha_0 + \beta X, \tag{10.7}$$

where α_0 is the minimum time for disease management and is a given parameter. Thus, trade and tourism losses (C_{tt}) are

$$C_{tt} = \left(\alpha_1 Y_{tr} + \alpha_2 Y_{tou}\right) T_m, \tag{10.8}$$

where Y_{tr} and Y_{tou} are the gross value of livestock trade and relevant tourism respectively, and α_1 and α_2 are parameters.

Objective Function

The problem of identifying the optimal surveillance scheme is to choose the one that minimises the present value of all three cost components. Mathematically, the problem is to minimise the total cost

$$
\begin{aligned}
C(N(0),D(0)) = \min_{X} E \Bigg\{ &\int_0^\infty \left[\frac{E_m(R_m - X)}{R_m(\eta X + 1)} + c_p N(t)D(t) \right] e^{-\rho t} dt \\
&+ \int_0^\infty \left[(c_m + c_{mc}\phi)X + (\alpha_1 Y_{tr} + \alpha_2 Y_{tou})T_m \right] e^{-\rho t} dQ_e \Bigg\}
\end{aligned}
\tag{10.9}
$$

subject to motion Eqs. 10.1 and 10.3, where the control variable is the target number of potentially infected herds X, and E is the usual expectations operator. The functional representation after invoking Ito lemma is[1]

$$
\begin{aligned}
\rho C(N,D) = \max_{X} \Bigg\{ &\frac{E_m(R_m - X)}{R_m(\eta X + 1)} + c_p N \times D + \lambda_d (c_{me} + c_{mc}\phi)X \\
&+ \lambda_d (\alpha_1 Y_{tr} + \alpha_2 Y_{tou})T_m + \lambda_i \left[C(N + N_0, D + D_0, X) - C(N,D) \right] \\
&+ \lambda_d \left[C(N_e, D_e) - C(N,D) \right] \\
&+ C_{ng}N\left(1 - \frac{N}{N_{max}}\right) + C_d z D\left(1 - \frac{D}{D_{max}}\right) + 0.5C_{nn}\sigma_n^2 N^2 + 0.5C_{dd}\sigma_d^2 D^2 \Bigg\}.
\end{aligned}
\tag{10.10}
$$

Equation 10.10 has no analytical solution and must be solved using numerical techniques for each value of the parameter values that determine the surveillance expenditure. The solution algorithm will choose the value that minimises the total cost function $C(.)$. In Section 10.4.3, we provide a case study as a basic example that calibrates the model to FMD in the United States at an aggregate level and subject to a time period when data are publicly available.

---

[1] Here, we assume that Brownian processes are uncorrelated and drop the time subscript t for simplicity.

10.4.3   Calibration to FMD in the United States

Baseline Scenario: Parameters and Optimal Surveillance Expenditure

Key incursion and biological parameters are drawn from the GAO (2002) and Bates et al. (2001, 2003a, 2003b). The probability of an FMD incursion is the most difficult parameter to determine. The probability of an incursion is thought to be increasing over time with increases in international trade and the growing prevalence of the disease in various parts of the world, but its precise measure for the United States is unclear. With current quarantine restrictions in place, a possibility of an outbreak once every 30 years is commonly assumed. Subject to sensitivity analysis, the annual probability of an incursion λ_i is thus approximately 0.03.

The transmission or growth rate of FMD is more easily known, with studies drawn from the recent United Kingdom experience (GAO, 2002) and Uruguay (Chowell et al., 2005). The value g is taken as 0.45% per week and density growth z is 0.2% per week. According to United States Department of Agriculture estimates (GAO, 2002), the potential number of initial infected herds N_0 is 15 and the maximum number of infected herds N_{max} is 81,000. The initial density D_0 is taken as 5% of a given herd, the maximum density D_{max} is 75% and the eradication zone is typically (in practice) set at a radius nine times the radius of the original area in which infected livestock were found. To determine the detection rate, values of $\theta = 52 \times 1.1$ and $\delta = 0.1$ are assumed.

The parameter values for the surveillance expenditure function are based on Bates et al. (2003a, 2003b). At this time, surveillance expenditure for FMD in the United States was roughly US$8.29 million. This is based on foreign animal disease operating expenses of US$24 million and associated capital (laboratories and equipment) of more than US$140 million. The cost of surveillance for FMD, given the 834 foreign animal disease investigations for a number of different diseases, is thought to be about 25% of the total operating budget and roughly 35% of the value of all labs and equipment. A 5% interest rate is used to account for capital costs. Detecting FMD in the first week of an outbreak is estimated to require at least 2,000 individual foreign animal disease inspections for FMD alone, compared with 200 in 2005. The natural detection point R_m is calculated to be 4,000 herds and E_m is 10 times current expenditure, or US$82.9 million. The value of the surveillance effectiveness parameter is approximated by $\eta = 0.0021$.

Herd size varies across different livestock, as does the cost of production losses associated with an FMD outbreak. In this simulation, it is assumed that the cost of the disease in terms of production loss occurs only at the farm level (e.g. directly affecting milk and meat production) and not to the indirect farm sector (e.g. transportation, retail and supporting industries). It is also assumed that only the beef, dairy, sheep and pig industries are potentially subjected to FMD. The production losses are drawn from a United States Department of Agriculture study (USDA, 2005) with a value of $c_p = 0.224$ and are comparable to average production losses in the 2001 United Kingdom outbreak (GAO, 2002).

Average indemnity cost is estimated to be roughly US$224,000 per herd. This value is estimated from the average market value of livestock (Bates et al., 2003a), average herd sizes and the proportional share of dairy, beef, pig and sheep farms in susceptible areas (USDA 2005). The market value per head for dairy heifer, heifer calves, sheep and pigs is US$1,200, US$602, US$231 and US$120 respectively (Bates et al., 2003a). The average cost of cleaning and disinfection is US$18,062 per herd and average vaccination costs are US$2,960 per herd (Bates et al., 2003a). The vaccination zone is taken as eight times the size of the radius of the initial infestation, as simulated in the study of a hypothetical outbreak of FMD in California (Bates et al., 2001). Thus, ϕ is 8, and the calculated average disease management costs, c_{mv} and c_{mv}, are 0.018 and 0.00296 respectively.

The value of α_0 is 24 weeks, the usual minimum time requirement for FMD-free status assuming that the disease can be detected and eradicated in the first week of incursion. For time periods longer than this, $\beta = 0.008$, based on the United Kingdom experience (DEFRA, 2002). Losses from trade bans and falls in tourism depend on the length of time needed for disease management. The average weekly gross value of exported livestock is US$5.7 million (USDA, 2005) and the average weekly value of all tourist activities is estimated to be US$0.7 billion (USCB, 2005). Clearly, only a small fall in tourist revenue should be expected from an FMD outbreak. The values of α_1 and α_2 are specified to be 0.1 and 0.005, roughly the same proportions as in the recent United Kingdom experience (DAFRD, 2002; GAO, 2002).

Using the baseline parameter values, the minimum mean-value cost function obtained by varying the number of potentially infected herds X is given in Figure 10.2. All growth and density rates and potential damages are translated into yearly measures. The approximated optimal value of X is 405 herds at a potential disease incursion cost of US$4,309 million or roughly US$4.3 billion. Using Eq. 10.4, optimal surveillance expenditures for an FMD incursion amount to roughly US$40.3 million per year. Annual surveillance expenditures for this time period are approximately US$8.29 million, far below optimal values. Current expenditures, assuming that current policy was consistently applied with Eq. 10.3 operating, act as if the target was 2,000 potentially infected herds rather than 405. There is a common and characteristic flatness near the optimal point, but current surveillance measures are far outside this point.

Sensitivity Analysis

Sensitivity across key parameter values varies considerably. For example, a change in the growth rate of disease transmission is relatively insensitive; a 16-fold increase in the growth rate results in only a 0.01% change in total incursion costs and a negligible variation in the target value of X. A change in the density growth rate has even less effect, with virtually no change in the target number of infected herds over a wide range of parameter values (tables indicating all results for changes in growth and density rates across a range of parameter values are available from the authors on request). The reason for these outcomes is straightforward. Although a higher

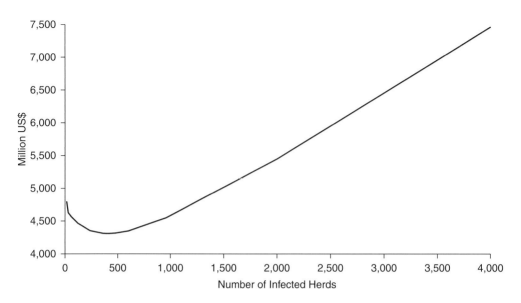

Figure 10.2.   Surveillance for FMD: Baseline scenario.

growth rate for disease transmission causes more damage, it is also more likely to be detected earlier and, therefore, controlled and eradicated. In terms of density growth, higher density growth rates do create more production losses initially, but an outbreak of FMD immediately creates an eradication zone in which all animals are destroyed regardless of their density growth.

In terms of the sensitivity results, differences in the probability of an FMD incursion do matter. Table 10.1 shows that the total costs of a disease incursion (million US$) with different probabilities (p) of a disease incursion and the optimal target number of infected herds (X). The benchmark case is $p = 0.03$ and $X = 405$. An increase in the probability of an incursion to 0.036 results in the optimal target for X falling to 330; a fall in the probability of an incursion to 0.024 increases X to 510. It is important to note that, even at a very low incursion rate and target of optimal surveillance, expenditures are still US$28.8 million dollars, or nearly three and a half times more than the surveillance expenditures in the United States at the time of writing. In Table 10.2, an increase in average production losses clearly decreases the optimal target X. The benchmark case is $c_p = 0.22$. If c_p increases to 0.31, X decreases to 385, with an annual surveillance expenditure of roughly US$41.4 million. Table 10.3 shows limited sensitivity between the size of the eradication zone and the optimal target number of infected herds X. The benchmark is 8. The larger the eradication zone, the larger the resulting damages in production and disease management costs, and thus the smaller the target number of infected herds.

Finally, a change in the natural detection point results in large changes in optimal results. This implies that education and extension services, designed to generate early detection on farms independently of formal surveillance activities, matter a great deal. For example, values of R_m of 3,000, 2,000 and 1,000 herds (from the

Table 10.1. Total costs of a FMD incursion in US$ million with different probabilities (p) of disease incursion and the optimal target number of infected herds (X)*

P	X										
	265	270	325	330	335	405	495	510	515	665	670
0.018	3,002.88	2,998.32	2,954.73	2,951.31	2,947.98	2,909.37	2,877.98	2,874.39	2,873.29	**2,858.45**	2,858.48
0.024	3,671.45	3,668.02	3,636.86	3,634.58	3,632.37	3,609.57	3,598.46	**3,598.25**	3,598.27	3,617.14	3,618.29
0.030	4,339.60	4,337.29	4,318.51	4,317.34	4,316.27	**4,309.18**	4,318.24	4,321.39	4,322.53	4,374.91	4,377.17
0.036	5,007.32	5,006.14	4,999.66	**4,999.62**	4,999.66	5,008.20	5,037.33	5,043.81	5,046.06	5,131.76	5,135.13
0.042	5,674.63	**5,674.56**	5,680.33	5,681.40	5,682.55	5,706.65	5,755.72	5,765.52	5,768.88	5,887.69	5,892.16

* Bold indicates baseline in all cases relative to sensitivity results.

Table 10.2. Total costs of a FMD incursion in US$ million with variations in average production losses (c_p) and the optimal target number of infected herds (X)*

C_p	X										
	380	385	390	395	400	405	410	415	425	430	435
0.134	4,289.78	4,289.19	4,288.67	4,288.22	4,287.84	4,287.52	4,287.27	4,287.08	4,286.89	**4,286.88**	4,286.93
0.179	4,299.94	4,299.48	4,299.1	4,298.79	4,298.54	4,298.35	4,298.23	**4,298.17**	4,298.24	4,298.37	4,298.55
0.224	4,310.1	4,309.78	4,309.53	4,309.35	4,309.23	**4,309.18**	4,309.19	4,309.27	4,309.6	4,309.86	4,310.18
0.269	4,320.26	4,320.07	4,319.96	**4,319.91**	4,319.92	4,320.01	4,320.15	4,320.36	4,320.96	4,321.35	4,321.81
0.314	4,330.42	**4,330.37**	4,330.38	4,330.47	4,330.62	4,330.83	4,331.11	4,331.45	4,332.32	4,332.85	4,333.43

* Bold indicates baseline in all cases relative to sensitivity results.

Table 10.3. Total costs of a FMD incursion in US$ million with variations in the size of the eradication zone (ϕ) and the optimal target number of infected herds (X)*

Φ	X					
	395	400	405	410	415	420
4.8	4,307.82	4,307.68	4,307.61	**4,307.60**	4,307.65	4,307.77
6.4	4,308.93	4,308.81	**4,308.75**	4,308.76	4,308.82	4,308.95
8	4,310.05	4,309.94	**4,309.90**	4,309.91	4,310.00	4,310.14
9.6	4,311.17	4,311.07	**4,311.04**	4,311.07	4,311.17	4,311.33
11.2	4,312.28	4,312.2	**4,312.18**	4,312.23	4,312.34	4,312.51

* Bold indicates baseline in all cases relative to sensitivity results.

benchmark case of 4,000) lowers optimal surveillance expenditure to US$37.9, US$32.7 and US$18.15 million respectively. At a value of R_m of 630 herds, optimal surveillance expenditure is zero.

10.5 Border Quarantine

10.5.1 The Costs and Benefits of Border Quarantine

Quarantine measures at the border are designed to reduce or eliminate the probability of an incursion. As usual, there are costs and benefits from this activity. The benefits are avoided losses from a disease entry. In terms of costs, apart from administrative and border quarantine service expenditure, losses in consumer welfare caused by restricted trade flow are usually seen to be the most significant cost of a quarantine measure (Mumford, 2002). In a few cases, some authors claim that the cost of restricting trade flow may be so significant that bans should be lifted until a more clearly quantified risk of incursion is confirmed. An extreme example of this is a partial equilibrium analysis of the Australian banana market by Anderson and James (1998), who show that the benefit of free trade is, on average, enough to compensate, even if the whole domestic banana industry is wiped out by an imported disease. This is, somewhat, supported by another analysis by Leroux and MacLaren (2011), who show that the net cost of restricting the flow of goods is, on average, positive but reduced by uncertainties and the relative irreversibility of bans once they are in place. In these works, cost is generally more than the avoided losses or benefits of stopping an incursion, so it is not cost effective to have a quarantine programme.

Other studies provide more clear evidence for quarantine activity. For example, Cook et al. (2011) show that the price difference between imported apples and the autarkic price is insufficient to outweigh the increase in expected damages resulting from an increased fire blight risk. Soliman et al. (2013) calculate that the economic impact of the invasion of the plant pathogenic bacterium in Europe is, on average,

€114 million per year more than the benefit of a completely non-quarantined flow of trade. Another estimate from Breukers et al. (2008) shows that reducing monitoring frequency in brown rot quarantine increases the costs to €12.5 million per year in the Dutch potato production chain, 60% of which are export losses. According to these authors, the benefit far exceeds the cost and establishing a quarantine programme clearly improves economic welfare.

The key idea of a CBA exercise for border quarantine is to minimise the sum of the direct costs of a potential disease incursion, the cost of the quarantine programme itself and the resulting welfare losses from quarantine restrictions. This is achieved through a variation in the potential number of, say, infected livestock that enter a region or a country. Clearly, the larger the expenditure on a quarantine activity, the larger the welfare losses and cost of the quarantine programme. However, the more severe the quarantine activity, the smaller the risk of a disease incursion and the direct costs of the disease to the affected industry. In principle, there will be cases in which the disease is so devastating that the direct cost of an incursion will require vast expenditure on quarantine services and large welfare losses to guarantee that the risk of a disease entry is virtually zero. On the other hand, for some diseases, reducing the risk of a disease incursion to zero may imply that the cost of the quarantine measures and the resulting welfare losses more than surpass the (present value) of the direct cost of the disease to the local industry. Finding the correct value of the likelihood of disease entry, and with it the associated expenditure level and optimal quarantine activity, requires minimising all of the (properly discounted) potential and actual costs associated with managing imported livestock.

10.5.2   An Optimal Quarantine Model

Assume that the disease incursion happens with an arrival rate that depends on the quarantine expenditure $\lambda(q) = q$, where q is the risk of infected rams entering per month under the current quarantine scheme. The initial number of sick animals crossing the border at any disease or incursion outbreak is assumed to be some value x_0. The number of infected animals then increases according to a quadratic growth function

$$dx(q) = gx(x_m - x)dt + d\aleph(q), \tag{10.11}$$

where $\aleph$ is a Poisson random variable with arrival rate q, which represents the outbreak incursion, and the rate of the production loss is $C(q) = c \times x(q)$, where c is the production and management cost coefficient.

The next relevant component in the cost is the quarantine expenditure. Following Kompas and Che (2009), the quarantine expenditure can be defined as a decreasing function of the number of entering infected animals (say rams used for breeding in a sheep import scheme):

$$E(q) = \frac{E_m(q_m - q)}{q_m(\eta q + 1)}, \tag{10.12}$$

where q is the risk of infected rams entering under the current quarantine scheme and q_m is the risk of infected rams entering under no quarantine.

Finally, quarantine activities can restrict trade, much like tariffs. To approximate welfare losses from restricting imports with a quarantine activity, assume linear supply and demand schedules for livestock. The welfare loss from quarantine activity can then be calculated by

$$L(q) = \alpha E(q)M - \frac{\alpha^2 E(q)^2 M}{2(p^0 - p^*)},\qquad (10.13)$$

where M, p^* are the import and price without quarantine and p^0 is the domestic price.

The total cost of the quarantine programme is the present value of a cost flow consisting of the three components, or

$$C(x_0) = \min_q E \int_0^\infty \left\{ \frac{E_m(q_m - q)}{q_m(\eta q + 1)} + cx + \alpha \frac{E_m(q_m - q)}{q_m(\eta q + 1)} M \left(1 - \frac{\alpha E_m(q_m - q)}{2q_m(p^0 - p^*)(\eta q + 1)} \right) \right\} dt$$

or in functional-equation representation

$$\rho C(x) = \min_q \left\{ \frac{E_m(q_m - q)}{q_m(\eta q + 1)} + cx \right.$$

$$+ \alpha \frac{E_m(q_m - q)}{q_m(\eta q + 1)} M \left[1 - \frac{\alpha E_m(q_m - q)}{2q_m(p^0 - p^*)(\eta q + 1)} \right]$$

$$\left. + C_x gx(x_m - x) + q[C(x + 1) - C(x)] \right\} \qquad (10.14)$$

10.5.3 Calibration to Ovine Johne's Disease Quarantine Measures in Western Australia

Equation 10.14 is a partial differential equation that must be solved using numerical techniques (e.g. finite difference or projection methods). Specifying the optimal arrival rate (q) generally requires that the equation be solved with a grid of possible values and then picking the one that minimises the total cost of the quarantine programme.

Figure 10.3 calibrates the model to calculate the optimal budget for an ovine Johne's disease quarantine scheme in Western Australia. Following Kompas and Che (2009), the baseline parameter values are (all parameters are on monthly basis unless otherwise indicated): $g = 2.7110^{-9}$ (reaches maximum after 80 years), $q_m = 18.5$, $x_m = 6.7610^6$, $\sigma = .05$, $E_m = \$500,000$, $\eta = 3.13$, $c_p = \$14$ per year, $\alpha = 0.001875$, $M = 550$, $p^0 - p^* = \$1,000$ and $\rho = 0.05$ per year. Figure 10.3 shows a typical trade-off between production cost and quarantine related expenses. A very strict quarantine programme may minimise production losses, but it also induces substantial quarantine costs and trade impacts. A less restrictive quarantine scheme, allowing for a higher probability of a disease incursion, is less expensive but production losses

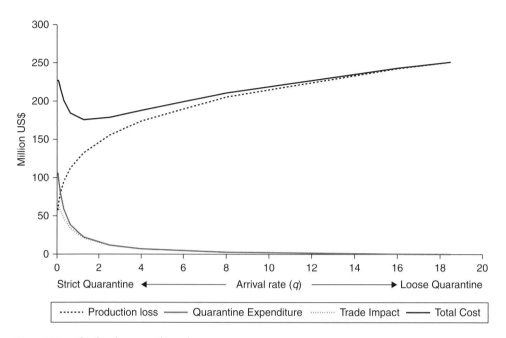

Figure 10.3.   Optimal quarantine scheme.

are also significantly higher. On balance, the optimal quarantine budget is one that minimises the sum of all cost components. Nevertheless, depending on the curvature of the production loss, quarantine expenditure and trade impact functions, the total cost may rise when we depart from an extreme zero-incursion quarantine regime (see Table 10.4). This happens when production cost rises very quickly as we start to relax our quarantine measure and outweighs the reduction in quarantine expenses. As we depart further from a zero-incursion quarantine regime, the quarantine expenditure will decrease at a faster rate and, at some point, the trade-off argument will apply. This complicated feature forces us to check the whole range of possible quarantine measure values, not just to find a local minimum point.

Sensitivity tests again give a sense of the importance of parameter values. Table 10.4 shows how sensitive the optimum quarantine measure is to a change in the growth rate of the disease. As expected, the extreme trade-off between quarantine expenditure and disease management costs exists only when the growth rate is low. A higher growth rate for disease transmission clearly indicates that more should be spent on quarantine measures.

The magnitude of the maximum quarantine cost raises the value of the zero target arrival rate. At some point, it reduces the optimum quarantine expenditure from its maximum point. Table 10.5 shows that as the value of the maximum quarantine measure increases, less should be spent on quarantine. On the other hand, the management cost parameter (c_p) is very important in determining the optimum quarantine measure. Table 10.6 shows that the increase in the cost parameter means a stricter quarantine measure throughout.

Table 10.4. Sensitivity with respect to the intrinsic growth rate (A$ million)*

G	Target incursion probability										
	0	0.04	0.08	0.16	0.32	0.64	1.28	2.5	4	8	18.5
6.30E-10	185.74	177.26	166.33	147.76	121.82	93.92	72.07	61.23	**59.88**	66.21	85.54
1.70E-10	185.74	194.54	187.35	173.16	152.39	130.55	115.68	**112.42**	116.89	132.49	164.02
7.10E-10	185.74	223.81	221.3	212.22	197.18	181.69	**173.68**	177.4	186.9	210.08	250.77
2.50E-10	**185.74**	262.25	264.54	260.45	250.79	241.03	238.93	248.34	261.76	290.52	337.49
7.90E-10	**185.74**	306.43	313.21	313.6	308.6	303.68	306.38	320.17	336.48	369.15	420.15

* Bold indicates baseline in all cases relative to sensitivity results.

Table 10.5. Sensitivity with respect to the maximum quarantine cost (A$ million)*

E_m	Target incursion probability										
	0	0.04	0.08	0.16	0.32	0.64	1.28	2.5	4	8	18.5
0.3	**125.37**	167.57	168.36	165.25	159.45	155.19	157.6	168.72	181.76	208.21	250.9
0.4	**157.88**	197.48	196.27	189.72	178.86	168.68	165.72	173.08	184.34	209.15	250.83
0.5	185.74	223.81	221.3	212.22	197.18	181.69	**173.68**	177.4	186.9	210.08	250.77
0.6	208.97	246.56	243.44	232.75	214.42	194.25	**181.5**	181.67	189.45	211.01	250.7
0.7	227.55	265.71	262.71	251.3	230.57	206.34	189.16	**185.91**	191.99	211.94	250.64

* Bold indicates baseline in all cases relative to sensitivity results.

Table 10.6. Sensitivity with respect to the production cost (A$ million)*

c_p ($/month)	Target incursion probability										
	0	0.04	0.08	0.16	0.32	0.64	1.28	2.5	4	8	18.5
0.7	185.74	201.29	194.36	180.23	159.3	136.9	120.76	**115.24**	117.33	127.92	150.33
0.93	185.74	212.55	207.83	196.23	178.24	159.3	147.22	**146.32**	152.12	169	200.55
0.17	185.74	223.81	221.3	212.22	197.18	181.69	**173.68**	177.4	186.9	210.08	250.77
0.4	**185.74**	235.07	234.76	228.22	216.12	204.09	200.15	208.48	221.69	251.16	300.99
0.63	**185.74**	246.33	248.23	244.21	235.06	226.48	226.61	239.55	256.48	292.24	351.21

* Bold indicates baseline in all cases relative to sensitivity results.

10.6   Closing Remarks

CBA is an important exercise for evaluating the economic efficiency of biosecurity measures. However, the costs and benefits of each measure, whether it be border quarantine, post-incursion control or local surveillance, are rarely trivial to esti-mate. We often need to develop complicated bioeconomic models to calculate the cost and benefit components adequately. These approaches will normally require integrating substantial biological and economic information. Standard cost–benefit analysis will simply not do.

Along with some basic problems and principles of CBA applied to biosecurity measures, in this chapter we have illustrated some relatively new optimal bioeconomic modelling approaches to containment, eradication, surveillance and border quarantine measures. These are the approaches that economists would normally use now, or at least should use, with their emphasis on optimal expenditure, discounting and time contingent measures of all relevant costs and benefits. These approaches are especially useful to decision makers who are allocated fixed or limited budgets to obtain biosecurity outcomes.

The models illustrated here are still relatively simple. More complicated versions should endeavour to include more sophisticated biological models and spatial dimensions. This can still be done for the economist, in otherwise comparable bioeconomic models, although such models are computationally much more difficult to handle. In many cases, optimal results will not be obtainable. It will depend on the algorithm employed and computing capacity.

Nevertheless, the goal for the economist in all cases will be the same: to find expenditure values that minimise the cost of any biosecurity measure, including the cost of the quarantine, eradication or surveillance programme itself. This general principle is illustrated in all approaches given in the preceding text, and should be a guide for all economic modelling, however complicated.

10.7   Acknowledgements

The computations in this chapter were performed with the help of Portable, Extensible Toolkit for Scientific Computation (PETSc) at Argonne National Laboratory (Balay et al., 1997, 2013a, 2013b). We would like to thank the people at Argonne National Laboratory for making PETSc available for researchers all over the world.

References

Adamson, D., Bilston, L. & Lynch, K. (2000). The potential economic benefits of the Siam weed (*Chromolaena odorata*) eradication program. Working paper. Queensland, Australia: Department of Natural Resources and Mines.

Anderson, K. & James, S. (1998). On the need for more economic assessment of quarantine policies. *Australian Journal of Agricultural and Resource Economics*, 42(4), 425–444.

Balay, S., Brown, J., Buschelman, K., et al. (2013a). *PETSc users manual*. Technical Report ANL-95/11, Revision 3.4. Argonne, IL: Argonne National Laboratory.

Balay, S., Brown, J., Buschelman, K., et al. (2013b). *PETSc: Portable extensible toolkit for scientific computation*. Available from www.mcs.anl.gov/petsc

Balay, S., Gropp, W. D., McInnes, L. C. & Smith, B. F. (1997). Efficient management of parallelism in object oriented numerical software libraries. In E. Arge, A. M.

Bruaset & H. P. Langtangen (eds.), *Modern software tools in scientific computing* (pp. 163–202).Basel: Birkhäuser.

Bates, T. W., Carpenter, T. E. & Thurmond, M. C. (2001). Direct and indirect contact rates among beef dairy, goat, sheep, and swine herds in three California counties, with reference to control of potential foot-and-mouth disease transmission. *American Journal of Veterinary Research*, 62(9), 1477.

Bates, T. W., Carpenter, T. E. & Thurmond, M. C. (2003a). Benefit-cost analysis of vaccination and preemptive slaughter as a means or eradicating foot-and-mouth disease. *American Journal of Veterinary Research*, 64(7), 805–812.

Bates, T. W., Thurmond, M. C., Hietala, S. K., et al. (2003b). Surveillance for detection of foot-and-mouth disease. *Journal of the American Veterinary Association*, 223(5), 609–614.

Breukers, A., Mourits, M., van den Werf, W. & Lansink, A. O. (2008). Costs and benefits of controlling quarantine diseases: A bio-economic modeling approach. *Agricultural Economics*, 38(2), 137–149.

Cacho, O. J., Wise, R. M., Hester, S. M. & Sinden, J. A. (2008). Bioeconomic modelling for control of weeds in natural environments. *Ecological Economics*, 65(3), 559–568.

Choi, A. S., Ritchie, B. W., Papandrea, F. & Bennett, J. (2010). Economic valuation of cultural heritage sites: A choice modeling approach. *Tourism Management*, 31(2), 213–220.

Chowell, G., Rivas, A. L., Hengartner, N. W., Hyman, J. M. & Castillo-Chavez, C. (2005). *The role of spatial mixing in the spread of foot-and-mouth disease.* http://math.lanl.gov/~gchowell/publications

Cook, D. C., Carrasco, L. R., Paini, D. R. & Fraser, R. W. (2011). Estimating the social welfare effects of New Zealand apple imports. *Australian Journal of Agricultural and Resource Economics*, 55(4), 599–620.

Cunningham, D. C., Woldendorp, G., Burgess, M. B. & Barry, S. C. (2003). Prioritising sleeper weeds for eradication: Selection of species based on potential impacts on agriculture and feasibility of eradication. Working Paper. Canberra, Australia: Bureau of Rural Sciences.

DEFRA (Department for Environment, Food and Rural Affairs). (2002). Origin of the UK foot-and-mouth disease epidemic in 2001, June. Unpublished Report.

GAO (United States General Accounting Office) (2002). Foot and mouth disease: To protect U.S. livestock: USDA must remain vigilant and resolve outstanding issues. Report to the Honorable Tom Daschle, U.S. Senate. July 2003.

Gohin, A. & Rault, A. (2013). Assessing the economic costs of a foot and mouth disease outbreak on Brittany: A dynamic computable general equilibrium analysis. *Food Policy*, 39, 97–107.

Harris, S., Brown, J. & Timmins, S. (2001). *Weed surveillance: How often to search? Science for Conservation* 175. Wellington, New Zealand: Department of Conservation.

Hester, S. M., Odom, D. I. S., Cacho, O. J. & Sinden, J. A. (2004). Eradication of exotic weeds in Australia: Comparing effort and expenditure. Working paper. Armidale, Australia: University of New England.

Hinrichs, J., Sims, L. & McLeod, A. (2006). Some direct costs of control for avian influenza. In *Proceedings of the 11th International Society for Veterinary Epidemiology and Economics*, Cairns, Australia.

Keogh-Brown, M. R., Smith, R. D., Edmunds, J. W. & Beutels, P. (2009). The macroeconomics impacts of pandemic influenza: Estimates from models of the United Kingdom, France, Belgium and the Netherlands. *European Journal of Health Economics*, 11(6), 543–554.

Kompas, T. & Che, T. N. (2009). *A practical border quarantine measure for imported livestock*. Canberra, Australia: Australian Centre for Biosecurity and Environmental Economics, Australian National University.

Kompas, T., Che, T. N., Cao, L. Y. & Klijn, N. (2004). *Optimal surveillance measures against an imported pest or disease: An application to Papua fruit fly in Australia*. Canberra, Australia: Australian Bureau of Agricultural and Resource Economics, Commonwealth of Australia.

Kompas, T., Chu, L., Che, T. N., Nguyen, H. & White, K. (2013). *Optimal surveillance measures against exotic weeds: An application to hawkweed in Australia*. Canberra, Australia: Australian Centre for Biosecurity and Environmental Economics, Australian National University.

Leroux, A. & MacLaren, D. (2011). The optimal time to remove quarantine bans under uncertainty: The case of Australian bananas. *Economic Record*, 87(276), 140–152.

Mumford, J. D. (2002). Economic issues related to quarantine in international trade. *European Review of Agricultural Economics*, 29(3), 329–348.

Nord, E., Pinto, J. L., Richardson, J., Menzel, P. & Ubel, P. (1999). Incorporating societal concerns for fairness in numerical valuations of health programmes. *Health Economics*, 8(1), 25–39.

Panetta, F. D., Cacho, O. J., Hester, S. M. & Sims-Chilton, N. M. (2011a). Estimating the duration and cost of weed eradication programmes. In C. R. Veitch, M. N. Clout & D. R. Towns (eds.), *Island invasives: Eradication and management: Proceedings of the International Conference on Island Invasives* (pp. 472–476). Gland, Switzerland: IUCN, and Auckland, New Zealand: Centre for Biodiversity and Biosecurity.

Panetta, F. D., Csurhes, S. M., Markula, A. & Hannan-Jones, M. A. (2011b). Predicting the cost of eradication for 41 Class 1 declared weeds in Queensland. *Plant Protection Quarterly*, 26(2), 42–46.

Panetta, F. D. & Lawes, R. (2007). Evaluation of the Australian branched broomrape (*Orobanche ramosa*) eradication program. *Weed Science*, 55(6), 644–651.

Pearce, D., Atkinson, G. and Mourato, S. (2006) *Cost-benefit analysis and the environment: recent developments*. Organisation for Economic Co-operation and Development, Paris, France. ISBN 9264010041

Prieto, L. & Sacristán, J. A. (2003). Problems and solutions in calculating quality-adjusted life years (QALYs). *Health and Quality of Life Outcomes*, 1, 80.

Rejmánek, M. & Pitcairn, M. J. (2002). When is eradication of exotic pest plants a realistic goal? In C. R. Veitch & M. N. Clout (eds.), *Turning the tide: The eradication of invasive species* (pp. 249–253). Gland, Switzerland and Cambridge, UK: IUCN SSC Invasive Species Specialist Group.

Schoenbaum, M. A. & Disney, W. T. (2003). Modeling alternative mitigation strategies for a hypothetical outbreak of foot-and-mouth disease in the United States. *Preventive Veterinary Medicine*, 58(1–2), 25–52.

Smith, R. D., Keogh-Brown, M. R. & Barnett, T. (2011). Estimating the economic impact of pandemic influenza: An application of the computable general equilibrium model to the UK. *Social Science and Medicine*, 73(2), 235–244.

Soliman. T, Mourits. M. C. M., Oude-Lansink A. G. J. M. & van der Werf, W. (2013). Economic justification for quarantine status – the case study of 'Candidatus Liberibacter solanacearum' in the European Union. *Plant Pathology*, 62(5), 1106–1113.

USCB (US Census Bureau). (2005). Tourist statistics. Available from www.tia.org/research-pubs/economic_research_impact_tourism.html.

USDA (United States Department of Agriculture). (2005). National Agricultural Statistics Service. Available from www.usda.gov/nass/

Wang, X., Bennett, J., Xie, C., Zhang, Z. & Liang, D. (2007). Estimating non-market environmental benefits of the Conversion of Cropland to Forest and Grassland Program: A choice modeling approach. *Ecological Economics*, 63(1), 114–125.

Wittwer, G., McKirdy, S. & Wilson, R. (2005). Regional economic impacts of a plant disease incursion using a general equilibrium approach. *Australian Journal of Agricultural and Resource Economics*, 49(1), 75–89.

Woldendorp, G. & Bomford, M. (2004). *Weed eradication: Strategies, timeframes and costs.* Canberra, Australia: Bureau of Rural Sciences.

11 Valuing Protection against Invasive Species Using Contingent Valuation

John Rolfe and Jill Windle

11.1 Introduction

Invasive species create particular challenges for policymakers who need to identify and evaluate appropriate management responses (Born et al., 2005; Perrings et al., 2000). Although some deliberately introduced species contribute significantly to agricultural production and other purposes, many invasive weed and animal pests have the potential to generate substantial costs through impacts on agricultural production, biodiversity, ecosystem services, infrastructure and communities (Lovell et al., 2006; Pimentel et al., 2005). For example, Pimentel et al. (2005) estimated that invasive species in the United States cost more than US$138 billion per year in damages and control, while McLeod (2004) reported that the impact of invasive animals in Australia generates costs of more than A$700 million per year.

In economic terms, efforts to control invasive species should be assessed by comparing the potential costs of the control against the benefits that may be generated, such as through the application of cost–benefit analysis (Born et al., 2005; Burnett et al., 2008). Control efforts can be categorised into three broad groups: prevention efforts (such as quarantine protocols) are aimed at preventing establishment, eradication measures can be applied at any time after establishment and control measures are aimed at restricting spread at some point after establishment (Born et al., 2005). The justification for each of these measures, and the distribution of effort between measures, should be based on an assessment of the net benefits arising from the different options (Burnett et al., 2008).

There are several factors that complicate the application of a simple cost–benefit framework (Born et al., 2005). First, biological invasions occur over space and time, and many benefits of control relate to the avoidance of future impacts and reducing the risks that impacts might occur. Second, there is a great deal of uncertainty about the current and potential impacts of biological invasions, making it difficult to assess impacts precisely (Burnett et al., 2008). This is complicated by the dynamic, non-linear growth patterns of most biological pests and the difficulties of predicting spread and impact over time (Olson, 2006; Perrings et al., 2000). Third, many of the benefits of control are difficult to value, especially those involving reduced impacts on human health and the protection of environmental assets and ecological processes (Born et al., 2005; Lovell et al., 2006). Fourth, there are a large number of different invasive species, and both the costs and benefits of control often involve cooperation and complementarities. Fifth, invasive species usually involve multidimensional and partial impacts (sometimes offsetting; Pimentel et al., 2005), requiring net marginal impacts to be considered (Born et al., 2005). Sixth, impacts and the costs and benefits of control vary over locations, so it is not appropriate to assume uniform values across diverse locations (Olson, 2006).

Born et al. (2005) identify a number of deficiencies with the current pool of economic studies of invasive species. Key research gaps include a lack of systematic valuation studies that assess non-use values, particularly those relevant to environmental impacts; a focus on ex post evaluation instead of ex ante studies; a focus on control measures instead of distinguishing among prevention, control and eradication options; and deficiencies arising from uncertainty rarely being considered as an explanatory factor.

The focus of this chapter is on valuing the benefits of controlling invasive pest species using a non-market valuation technique. The study was conducted with households in Brisbane, Australia to identify awareness of invasive species and values to avoid future outbreaks. Brisbane has had major outbreaks and subsequent control efforts for red imported fire ants, and one goal of the survey was to identify awareness of issues associated with fire ants and the attempts to eradicate the outbreaks. The chapter is structured as follows. In Section 11.2, the underlying economic framework is described together with a review of previous studies in this field. An overview of the contingent valuation method (CVM) is provided in Section 11.3, followed by a description of the case study and application of the experiment in Section 11.4. Study results are described in Section 11.5, and discussion and conclusions are presented in Section 11.6.

11.2   Outlining the Economic Framework

Many public policy frameworks dealing with invasive species involve at least an implicit consideration of the benefits and costs of different control efforts or policy changes. An extended cost–benefit analysis formalises this process and is one of the key approaches that can be used in an economic evaluation of control options for invasive species (Born et al., 2005). The advantages of a cost–benefit study are that it attempts to be inclusive in terms of measuring all the outcomes of a proposed action, explicitly values the different impacts and outcomes and provides a framework in which very different outcomes may be assessed against each other. The methodical approach of cost–benefit analysis helps in the evaluation of issues and can guard against rent-seeking behaviour by special-interest groups.

A key stage in the analysis of environmental values is to categorise the types of benefits that might be associated with controlling or avoiding pest invasions (Born et al., 2005; Figure 11.1):

• *Direct use values* are benefits that directly accrue to individuals, and can be either extractive or non-extractive. Extractive use values include harvesting of natural

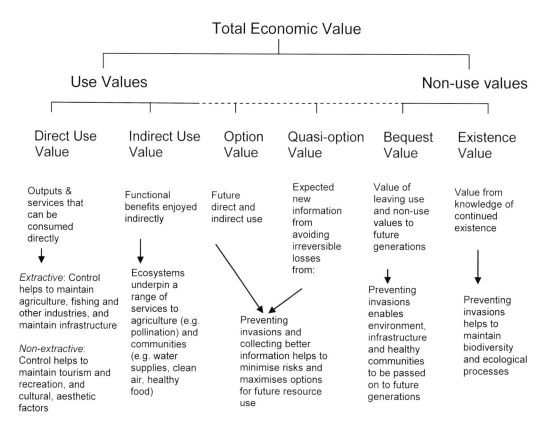

Figure 11.1.   Total economic value and attributes of values for controlling invasive species. [Adapted from Born, W., Rauschmayer, F. and Brauer, I. (2005). Economic evaluation of biological invasions – a survey. Ecological Economics, 55, 321–336.]

resources such as fishing and agriculture. Non-extractive values involve tourism, research and education.

- *Indirect use values* are gained indirectly from the natural resource, usually through support and protection of other economic activities. Examples include support to agriculture, fisheries, water quality, community lifestyles and indigenous culture.

- *Non-use values* to society arise indirectly, either through potential future uses or through the knowledge of the presence of the resource. These can be divided into option values, quasi-option values, existence values and bequest values. Option values are for use in the future, existence values are for knowledge of their presence and bequest values arise from wanting to preserve the public good for future generations. Non-use values can be derived without any actual current human use of the resource.

In many cases, it is difficult to estimate each component of value separately. Under the Total economic value approach, values arising from controlling an invasive species are either estimated jointly in a single valuation exercise or values from separate estimation exercises are summed to give a total value estimate of the asset of interest.

Most efforts to value the benefits of controlling invasive species have focused on the extractive direct-use values, such as those associated with agriculture losses or treatment costs (Lovell et al., 2006; Olson, 2006; Pimentel et al., 2005). Some studies have involved the use of the travel cost method to estimate non-extractive use values for recreation that are affected by invasive species (Lovell et al., 2006). Although direct and indirect use values are important for some types of invasive species, they rarely represent the total economic value, and may not be very significant for other invasive species. Other studies (e.g. Sinden & Griffith, 2007) have focused on estimation of the costs of control and mitigation strategies as a weak proxy for the value that society assigns to avoiding invasive species. Estimation of values through replacement costs or defensive expenditures is unlikely to represent underlying community preferences for control, particularly where large non-use values are involved (Shogren et al., 2006).

A more comprehensive approach to valuing benefits of controlling invasive species requires the assessment of both non-use and use values. Non-use values can be assessed through the application of stated preference techniques such as the CVM or choice modelling experiments. Applications involve people being presented with hypothetical scenarios about different options for resource management and the associated costs. Analysis of the preferred choices reveals how people would make trade-offs between different environmental outcomes and the monetary cost, allowing predictions of value to be made.

There has been limited application of stated preference techniques to issues involving invasive species (Born et al., 2005; Lovell et al., 2006), although the number of studies has increased in recent years. Turpie et al. (2003) use the CVM to estimate loss of existence values from invasive species in the Cape Floristic Region in South Africa. Numes and Van Den Burgh (2004) report the use of a joint travel cost study (to estimate recreation benefits) and a CVM (to estimate non-use benefits) associated with the removal of harmful algal-bloom species along the coast of the Netherlands. Other studies have used choice modelling experiments to estimate the benefits from controlling algal blooms in Lake Tenkiller, Oklahoma (Roberts et al., 2008); the Black Sea Coast of Bulgaria (Taylor & Longo, 2010); and in a region of the South Island in New Zealand (Beville et al., 2012). Both Horsch and Lewis (2009) and Zhang and Boyle (2010) have use hedonic pricing model property values over time to estimate the impact of a common aquatic invasive species (milfoil) on lakefront property values in Wisconsin and Vermont respectively. Champ et al. (2005) apply the CVM to assess the benefits of a weed control program in the United States, while Carlsson and Kataria (2008) use choice modelling experiments to assess the benefits from weed-control programs in both Sweden and the United States. Other studies transfer benefit estimates from recreation, property, health or environmental valuation studies to infer the benefits of controlling an invasive pest species (Lovell et al., 2006).

11.3   The Contingent Valuation Method

The application of the CVM involves people being asked to indicate their preferred trade-off between changes in the quantity of an environmental good and an opportunity cost, usually money. Respondents are asked, through a survey mechanism, for their willingness to pay (WTP) for a specific change in the provision of an environmental good. In the open-ended format, respondents are asked to nominate their preferred trade-off, while the dichotomous choice format involves respondents being asked to indicate 'yes' or 'no' to whether they would support a nominated trade-off. The technique has been in use since the early 1960s, when direct interviews and bidding games were used to value the benefits of outdoors recreation (Mitchell & Carson, 1989). Since then, the technique has been widely used to help quantify, in monetary terms, social preferences for a variety of environmental and other outcomes (Carson, 1997).

The random utility model is the behavioural basis of the dichotomous choice CVM (Hanemann, 1984; Hanemann & Kanninen, 1996), and it provides a base for a mechanical assessment of preferences that may be used to describe how an individual or group of people might be likely to choose between different items. In choosing whether to answer 'yes' or 'no' to a dichotomous choice CVM survey, it is assumed, on the basis of utility maximisation, that individuals choose options that offer more utility. For a situation where a survey respondent is offered an increase in an environmental good (from q^0 to q^1) at a specified trade-off ($\$a$), the probability of a 'yes' response is given by the probability that the new situation has more utility for the individual than the old, as follows:

$$\Pr(\text{response is yes}) = \Pr\{v(p, q^1, y - a, s) + \varepsilon \geq v(p, q^0, y, s) + \varepsilon\}, \qquad (11.1)$$

where v represents the indirect utility function for the individual, p the price of market goods, q the non-market good of interest, y the individual's income, a the cost of the trade-off, s other factors and influences and ε the unexplained component of each choice (Bockstael et al., 1989).

This outcome can also be expressed in terms of compensating surplus (c), which is the individual's WTP for a change from q^0 to q^1 that holds the initial level of utility constant. Under this formulation, compensating surplus is the amount that satisfies the relationship

$$v(p, q^1, y - c, s) + \varepsilon \geq v(p, q^0, y, s) + \varepsilon. \qquad (11.2)$$

Compensating surplus represents the individual's maximum WTP for the change in the quantity of the environmental amenity. It follows that when the nominated bid a in a CVM survey is less than the maximum WTP c, individuals will answer 'yes', and vice versa. The random utility model implies that this compensating surplus measure has some random element (Hanemann & Kanninen, 1996). While individuals presumably know what their WTP for a change is, it appears to the outside observer to have some random components. Thus, although responses to a particular bid value will indicate, through some statistical estimation process, what the likely WTP amount would be, the stochastic nature of the responses means that the estimated WTP will lie within specific confidence intervals.

There are a range of different models that can be used to generate estimates of compensation surplus (Hanemann & Kanninen, 1996). If the cumulative distribution frequency for the WTP amounts is specified as a standard logistic distribution, the choices can be estimated with a logit model. Welfare measures are calculated from the resulting models by estimating either the mean or the median of the estimated WTP function. For example, the mean WTP can be calculated from the logit model as

$$\text{Mean WTP} = (1/\beta_1)\ln(1 + e^{\beta_0}) \qquad (11.3)$$

where β_1 is the slope of the function plotted against price and β_0 is the intercept value (Loomis & Ekstrand, 1997).

11.4 The Case Study and Design of the Survey

Queensland is a decentralised Australian state with a large land mass and substantial variety in land types and biodiversity. Its tropical and sub-tropical position means that it is susceptible to a variety of pests and diseases that might generate risks to human and animal health, agricultural crops, and to the natural environment. There are particular risks of entry for some pests and diseases at the Torres Strait in the north, and major industries, such as the horticulture and livestock sectors, rely on effective biosecurity controls to keep diseases out of the country.

In recent years, there have been a number of well-publicised outbreaks of exotic diseases and pests that have entered Queensland. Some of the outbreaks have centred on the agricultural sector. In the north, there were outbreaks of Papaya fruit fly in 1995 and Black Sigatoka (in bananas) in 2001, with active control measures successful in eradicating the pests. In central Queensland, citrus canker was discovered in orchards at Emerald in 2004; it was eradicated by 2009 after every citrus tree in the district was removed. Sugarcane smut was detected in the cane industry in 2006, but inability to eradicate the disease meant that cane growers have had to plant different varieties of cane that are resistant to the disease.

Red imported fire ants were accidentally introduced to Australia, with infestations found in the port areas and south-western suburbs of Brisbane in February 2001. Follow-up surveillance identified scattered infestations in more than 300 km² of the area (Scanlon & Vanderwoude, 2006). Modelling suggested that the pest could invade half of Australia within 35 years if it was not controlled (Kompas & Che, 2001; Scanlon & Vanderwoude, 2006). The Queensland government led a vigorous eradication policy funded by the Australian and state governments to identify and control outbreaks; this included regular inspections and control efforts,

---

Foreign diseases and pests that have entered Queensland in the past 10 years include:
- Equine Influenza (horse flu) – major outbreak in 2008

- Papaya fruitfly – first detected in 1995; eradicated in 1998

- Sugarcane smut – first detected in 2006; outbreak not fully eradicated

- Red imported fire ants – first detected in 2001; outbreak not fully eradicated

- Citrus canker – first detected 2004; eradicated in 2009

- Black Sigatoka (banana disease) – first detected 2001; now eradicated

Increasing quarantine inspections and surveillance could reduce the rate of new disease and pest imports to about half the current rate. If it cost an additional $260 per household per year, would you be willing to participate? This would be $260 **each year** for the next **10 years** to avoid approximately three serious foreign pests and diseases entering into Queensland.

Please answer this question bearing in mind how much you are able to pay (after taking into account all your other commitments) (please tick one)

☐ Yes   ☐ No   ☐ Not sure

Figure 11.2.   The contingent valuation question.

such as restrictions over the movement of soil and garden waste in areas at risk. Equine influenza, also known as horse flu, was introduced to southern Queensland in August 2007 after the virus spread from Japanese race horses at a quarantine station in Sydney. The outbreak led to a shutdown of horse movements across large areas of eastern Australia, with substantial disruption to racing and other equestrian events. The controls over horse movements and other activities were quickly successful in limiting further spread of the disease, and all controls were lifted by February 2008.

Brisbane is the capital city of Queensland. In the survey of Brisbane residents, a key goal was to identify values for avoiding future outbreaks of exotic diseases and pests. Part of the survey focused on red imported fire ants, and provided background information on the pest, its discovery in Brisbane and subsequent efforts to control it. This helped to frame the valuation exercises. Specific questions about potential control mechanisms for the red imported fire ant were designed to test whether residents would support mandatory control measures, the use of preventative baiting and the use of chemicals in baiting and controls. For the contingent valuation experiment, respondents were provided with summary information about major pest and diseases outbreaks in Queensland in the previous 10 years. They were then asked about their WTP to reduce the rate of future outbreaks. Six different price trade-offs, ranging from $50 to $1,000 (Australian dollars (AUD)) were used as bid values. The information provided and the trade-off question is shown in Figure 11.2.

Table 11.1. Respondent socio-demographic characteristics

	Sample population	ABS population
Mean age (within the range sampled)	43	43
Proportion of females	52%	51%
Proportion of households with children	38%	
Education:		
Post-school qualification	59%	56%
Tertiary education	42%	24%
Mean household income (AUD)	$62,665	$66,112

The survey design was tested and refined during 2009 with four focus groups of Brisbane residents (each with eight to ten participants). The final survey instrument included the following five key sections:

- Background information to define the issues and refer respondents to further information if required
- Collection of data about knowledge, attitudes and experience with red imported fire ants
- A choice modelling experiment (not reported in this chapter)
- A contingent valuation survey about reducing future outbreaks
- Collection of data about respondent characteristics.

The survey was conducted online with a private organisation employed to host the survey and to provide access to an internet panel of Brisbane residents. Three hundred and twenty-nine respondents were surveyed from the Brisbane metropolitan area, with similar proportions answering each of the three versions. Fifty-six per cent of the respondents were living within a Fire Ant Restricted Area[1] and 44% were living outside the restricted area. The survey responses were collected during a three-week period in August 2009.

There were some small differences between the study sample and the census data for Brisbane. The average age of respondents, as well as the gender proportion, was similar to that of the general population (based on 2006 census data from the Australian Bureau of Statistics; Table 11.1). The average household income was slightly lower than that from the general population. The education of the respondent group was slightly higher than that of the general Brisbane population, with 3% more having post-school qualifications and many more having tertiary education.

The majority of respondents were long-term residents of Brisbane, with close to 60% living in the area for 15 years or more. Two-thirds of the respondents intended to stay in the city for at least the next 10 years, with more than half intending to

---

[1] As defined by the Queensland Government dated 15 May 2009.

stay the rest of their lives. Most respondents lived in houses, with more than 50% owning their homes. Nearly 90% of respondents had access to a yard or garden, with 70% of them using the space often or very often.

11.5   Study Results

It is important in CVM studies that respondents are familiar with or understand the issue of interest and the trade-offs being presented, and that the way the trade-offs are framed does not generate hypothetical bias or protests. The evidence from many of the contextual questions in the survey were that respondents were familiar with red imported fire ants and the risks of infestation, and viewed ongoing efforts to control the pest as realistic.

The large majority of respondents (95%) indicated that they were concerned about pest and weed species in their city. When asked to name three major pest or weed species, more than half (53%) were able to name three different species. Of those that named pest species, fire ants were mentioned by 60% and cane toads were mentioned by 58%. Other pest species that respondents named were: ants (species other than fire ants) (9%), lantana (16%), termites or white ants (8%), hares or rabbits (7%) and rats or mice (6%).

A majority of respondents (88%) were aware of the outbreaks of red imported fire ants in Brisbane, with only 5.5% of respondents not aware of the pest at all. Two-thirds of respondents (66%) were concerned about the impact of fire ants on themselves and the wider community. Fire ants can impact the community in many ways, and respondents were asked to rate common impacts on a Likert scale ranging from 1 for 'not concerned' to 5 for 'very concerned'. The summary of responses in Figure 11.3 demonstrates that most concerns are on personal impacts around loss of recreational use of their backyards and risks of painful stings. Respondents were least concerned with damage to buildings and the impacts to golf and sporting fields.

Respondents were asked how they viewed the effectiveness of control measures for red imported fire ants over the next five years. Only 4% were confident there would be full eradication, while most (53.2%) thought the chance of a full eradication was somewhere between 10% and 66%. When asked about types of control measures (Figure 11.4) the preferred approach toward eradication (88% support) was for the government to undertake mandatory inspections in areas at risk. Many (59%) preferred targeted baiting in infested areas rather than preventative baiting in areas at risk of infestation (41%); the use of chemical baiting was preferred (71%) over non-chemical options (29%).

The responses to the CVM trade-offs are shown in Figure 11.5, and demonstrate that the willingness to support measures that would reduce the rate of future outbreaks falls as the bid level rises. The responses are confounded by a large percentage (44%) of 'not sure' responses. When these are coded as 'no' responses, support

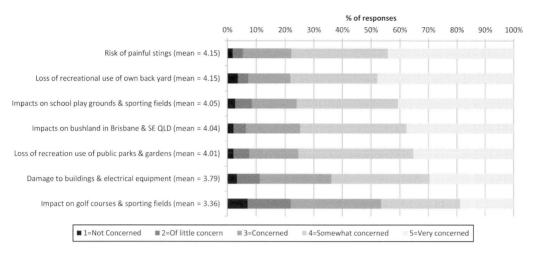

Figure 11.3.   Respondent concerns regarding the impact of fire ants on themselves and their community.

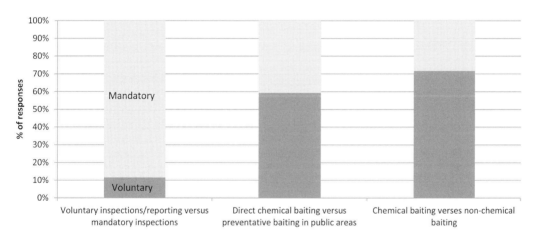

Figure 11.4.   Preferences of respondents between different control options.

for the payment level falls from 45.8% at the $50 bid level to 15.5% at the $1,000 bid level. However, if the 'not sure' responses are removed from the data set, then support levels range from 71% down to 25% over the same bid levels.

Logit models were developed to explain the influences on participants' responses to the contingent valuation question. Two main models were developed; one where the 'unsure' responses were treated as 'no' responses (model 1) and the second where the 'unsure' responses were not included in the analysis (model 2). Details of the variables used in the logit models are presented in Table 11.2 and model results are presented in Table 11.3.

Both models are statistically significant with chi-square values higher than the test statistic. The socio-demographic characteristics of respondents were not strong

Table 11.2. Model variables

Variable	Description
Constant	Accounting for the unexplained influences in the model
Contingent cost	Cost levels presented to respondents: $50, $100, $200, $400, $750 and $1,000 (AUD)
Gender	Female = 1; Male = 0
Age	Respondent's age in years
Number of children	Number of children in the household
Education	Coded from 1 = primary to 5 = tertiary degree or higher
Income	Five categories; the mid-point of each category was used for analysis with 50% added to the highest category.
Living in a RIFA area	1 = living in a RIFA restricted area; 0 = not living in a RIFA restricted area

RIFA, red imported fire ant.

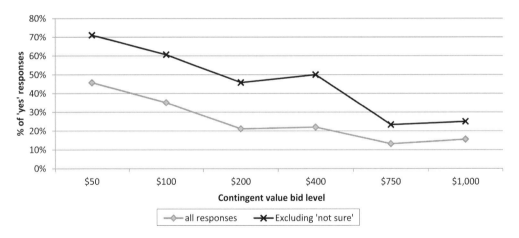

Figure 11.5. Percent support for reducing future outbreaks by CVM bid level.

influencing factors, and only gender was significant in model 1, with females being less likely to say 'yes' to one of the payment levels. Age was weakly significant (at the 10% level) in model 2. Removing the 'unsure' responses resulted in a stronger model fit (with higher McFadden pseudo R^2 value).

The results of these analyses demonstrate that the average respondent has substantial values to reduce the rate of future invasions, with annual WTP (in Australian dollars) estimated at $306 per household when all responses were considered, and $535 when the 'not sure' responses were excluded. The CVM experiment was to reduce the rate of serious outbreaks by three outbreaks over 10 years, and the value to avoid a single outbreak was approximately $102 per household per year. Values were not dependent on whether or not respondents lived in an area infested with red imported fire ants, suggesting that the results may be transferable across the population.

Table 11.3. Logit models with responses to the contingent valuation question

	Model 1 (all data)		Model 2 (excluding 'Not sure')	
	Coefficient	*SE*	*Coefficient*	*SE*
Constant	−0.470	0.882	−0.239	1.091
Contingent cost	−0.002***	0.000	−0.002***	0.000
Gender	−0.779***	0.273	−0.523	0.337
Age	0.009	0.009	0.019*	0.011
Number of children	0.018	0.099	0.010	0.107
Education	0.114	0.128	0.164	0.159
Income	3.2E-06	3.1E-06	2.9E-06	3.6E-06
Living in RIFA area	0.269	0.269	0.183	0.329
Model statistics				
Number of observations	329		183	
Log-likelihood	−172.915		−111.022	
AIC	1.101		1.301	
McFadden R^2	0.080		0.122	
Chi square (dof)	30.107 (7)		30.723 (7)	
Mean WTP[a]	$306		$535	
95% confidence interval	$202–$623		$373–$947	

*** Significant at the 1% level; * significant at the 10% level; AIC, Akaike information criterion; RIFA, red imported fire ant; SE, standard error; WTP, willingness to pay.
[a] calculated from a model with contingent valuation and constant only.

11.6 Conclusions

The research reported in this chapter has focused on the potential for stated preference techniques such as the CVM to assess values for preventing or addressing outbreaks of invasive species. Benefit estimates are required to perform more systematic analysis of intervention strategies in frameworks such as cost–benefit analysis. There is a current paucity of studies that estimate benefits involving non-use values, such as those affecting communities and the environment. Given the range of invasive species that have major non-commercial impacts, a demonstration that stated preference techniques can address these information gaps is important.

The study shows that respondents in Brisbane have significant values to reduce the rate of future outbreaks of exotic pests and diseases in Queensland, with the value to avoid a major incursion estimated at $102 per household per year over a 10-year period.

The total present value of these 10-year payments for the Brisbane population [based on a population of 2 million, an average household size of 2.7 (2011 Population Census], and a 5% discount rate) was estimated at $602.7 million (ranging from $379.8 million to $1,236.9 million) to avoid a major outbreak from an exotic pest or disease. If a 10% discount rate was applied, the total present value was estimated at $479.6 million (ranging from $316.6 million to $984.2 million) to avoid a major outbreak from an exotic pest or disease.

The high value estimates are likely to be underpinned by values that Brisbane residents have for maintaining their health, lifestyles and environment. This information will help policy makers to evaluate different management options and engage in the political economy of generating support and providing information back to communities. The estimated values suggest that many, if not most, quarantine and other protection policies are likely to generate net benefits to society and support efforts to avoid major biosecurity incursions.

Two key caveats about the size of the benefit estimates should be noted. First, the survey was conducted at a time when major pest and disease incursions were prominent in the media, and risks of other outbreaks, such as avian bird flu, were well publicised. It is possible that concerns over these issues have led to high WTP values that may not be maintained over time. Second, the methodology used has not allowed values to be differentiated according to the risks and issues involved in a pest and disease outbreak, with the result that the value estimated may be only applicable to major biosecurity incursions. Further research to provide more detailed estimates of values is recommended.

11.7   Acknowledgements

This study has been funded through the Commonwealth Environmental Research Fund for the Environmental Economics Research Hub. The contributions of Tom Kompas and Jeff Bennett in the design of the experiments, and of Gail Tucker in the analysis of results, are gratefully acknowledged.

References

Beville, S. T., Kerr, G. N. & Hughey, K. F. D. (2012). Valuing impacts of the invasive alga *Didymosphenia geminata* on recreational angling. *Ecological Economics*, 82, 1–10.

Bockstael, N. E., McConnell, K. E. & Strand, I. E. (1989). A random utility model for sport fishing: Some preliminary results for Florida. *Marine Resource Economics*, 6(3), 245–260.

Born, W., Rauschmayer, F. & Brauer, I. (2005). Economic evaluation of biological invasions – a survey. *Ecological Economics*, 55(3), 321–336.

Burnett, K. M., D'Evelyn, S., Kaiser, B. A., Namtamanasikarn, P. & Roumasset, J. A. (2008). Beyond the lamppost: Optimal prevention and control of the brown tree snake in Hawaii. *Ecological Economics*, 67(1), 66–74.

Carlsson, F. & Kataria, M. (2008). Assessing management options for weed control with demanders and non-demanders in a choice experiment. *Land Economics*, 84(3), 517–528.

Carson, R. T. (1997). Contingent valuation: Theoretical advances and empirical tests since the NOAA Panel. *American Journal of Agricultural Economics*, 79(5), 1501–1507.

Champ, P. A., Alberini, A. & Correas, I. (2005). Using contingent valuation to value a noxious weeds control program: The effects of including an unsure response category. *Ecological Economics*, 55(1), 47–60.

Hanemann, W. M. (1984). Welfare evaluations in contingent valuation experiments with discrete responses. *American Journal of Agricultural Economics*, 66(3), 332–341.

Hanemann, M. & Kanninen, B. (1996). The statistical analysis of discrete-response CV data. Working Paper No. 798. Berkeley, CA: Department of Agricultural and Resource Economics, Division of Agriculture and Natural Resources, University of California at Berkeley.

Horsch, E. J. & Lewis, D. J. (2009). The effects of aquatic invasive species on property values: Evidence from a quasi-experiment. *Land Economics*, 85(3), 391–409.

Kompas, T. & Che, N. (2001). *An economic assessment of the potential costs of red imported fire ants in Australia*. Canberra, Australia: Report for the Department of Primary Industries, Queensland.

Loomis, J. B. & Ekstrand, E. (1997). Economic benefits of critical habitat for the Mexican spotted owl: A scope test using a multiple-bounded contingent valuation survey. *Journal of Agricultural and Resource Economics*, 22(2), 356–366.

Lovell, S. J., Stone, S. F. & Fernandez, L. (2006). The economic impacts of aquatic invasive species: A review of the literature. *Agricultural and Resource Economics Review*, 35, 195–208.

McLeod, R. (2004). *Counting the cost: Impact of invasive animals in Australia, 2004*. Canberra, Australia: Pest Animal Control Cooperative Research Centre.

Mitchell, R. C. & Carson, R. T. (1989). *Using surveys to value public goods: The contingent valuation method*. Washington, DC: Resources for the Future.

Nunes, P. A. L. D. & van den Bergh, J. C. J. M. (2004). Can people value protection against invasive marine species? Evidence from a Joint TC–CV survey in the Netherlands. *Environmental and Resource Economics*, 28(4), 517–532.

Olson, L. (2006). The economics of terrestrial invasive species: A review of the literature. *Agricultural and Resource Economics Review*, 35(1), 178–194.

Perrings, C., Williamson, M. & Dalmazzone, S. (eds.) (2000). *The economics of biological invasions*. Cheltenham, UK: Edward Elgar.

Pimentel, D., Zuniga, R. & Morrison, D. (2005). Update on the environmental and economic costs associated with alien-invasive species in the United States. *Ecological Economics*, 52(3), 273–288.

Roberts, D.C., Boyer, T.A. and Lusk, J.C. (2008). Preferences for environmental quality under uncertainty. Ecological Economics, 66 (4), 584–593.

Scanlan, J. C. & Vanderwoude, C. (2006). Modelling the potential spread of *Solenopsis invicta* Buren (Hymenoptera: Formicidae) (red imported fire ant) in Australia. *Australian Journal of Entomology*, 45(1), 1–9.

Shogren, J. F., Finnoff, D., McIntosh, C. & Settle, C. (2006). Integration-valuation nexus in invasive species policy. *Agricultural and Resource Economics Review*, 35(1), 11–20.

Sinden, J. A. & Griffith, G. (2007). Combining economic and ecological arguments to value environmental gains from control of 35 weeds in Australia. *Ecological Economics*, 61(2–3), 396–403.

Taylor, T. & Longo, A. (2010). Valuing algal bloom in the Black Sea coast of Bulgaria: A choice experiment approach. *Journal of Environmental Management*, 91(10), 1963–1971.

Turpie, J. K., Heydenrych, B. J. & Lamberth, S. J. (2003). Economic value of terrestrial and marine biodiversity in the Cape Floristic Region: Implications for defining effective and socially optimal conservation strategies. *Biological Conservation*, 112(1–2), 233–251.

Zhang, C. & Boyle, K. J. (2010). The effect of an aquatic invasive species (Eurasian watermilfoil) on lakefront property values. *Ecological Economics*, 70(2), 394–404.

12   Management of Invasive Species: Info-Gap Perspectives

Yakov Ben-Haim

12.1   Introduction

Invasive species create difficult challenges for environmental managers. Invasive species may disrupt existing processes and behave in new and unpredictable ways, and thus reduce the relevance of ecological experience and established scientific understanding in managing them.

Scientific models are extremely useful for evaluating and selecting strategies for managing invasive species (see, e.g. Potts et al., 2013). However, because the real ecological system may differ in unknown ways from the system represented in the model, managers should use such models cautiously. In particular, model-based predictions of optimal outcomes may be very unrealistic when there is a mismatch between the mathematical model and the ecological system. This means that evaluating a strategy in terms of its model-based predicted outcome, and choosing a strategy whose predicted outcome is best, may be unrealistic. A management strategy asserting that 'This is the best model we have' (which is probably true), 'so we should use this model to identify and strive for the best possible outcome', is wishful thinking. The best possible outcome is unknown because the model errs in unknown ways. We simply cannot reliably identify a strategy whose outcome will be better than all other strategies.

Gigerenzer and Selton (2001) take a very different approach, by attempting to achieve adequate – rather than optimal – outcomes. This approach employs the concept of *satisficing* introduced by Simon (1955, 1956) and motivated by the limited information and information-processing ability of the decision maker, which Simon referred to as *bounded rationality*. To satisfice has come to mean 'To decide on and pursue a course of action that will satisfy the minimum requirements necessary to achieve a particular goal' (*Oxford English Dictionary*, online version, 1989). Satisficing makes very good sense in situations of severe uncertainty such as managing many invasive species. When one's understanding may be very deficient, it is bad policy to exploit that understanding too extensively. Satisficing strategies seek solutions that deliver minimally acceptable outcomes, even when the true ecological system turns out to be very different from the model system.

The goal of this chapter is to provide a conceptual framework for selecting management strategies that satisfice, rather than optimise, the outcome. We show how the decision maker can choose a strategy to achieve maximal confidence of adequate outcome. We will see when outcome optimisation is the strategy of choice, and when it is not. Our work is based on info-gap decision theory (Ben-Haim, 2006).

We discuss a few examples of the management of invasive species. The aim is not to advocate specific models, or to develop real-life policy recommendations. Rather, the goal is to illustrate the info-gap decision methodology so the reader can understand how an info-gap robustness analysis is used in the selection of a management strategy, and what insights it provides. No attempt is made to explain the mathematical details of how the info-gap analysis is actually performed, which is described extensively elsewhere (Ben-Haim, 2006; Burgman, 2005; http://info-gap.com; Regan et al., 2005).

We will consider three examples of progressive complexity. In Section 12.2 the manager must allocate a limited budget between culling the invasive species and studying the ecology of the system. The purpose of this example – which is static, simplistic and stylised – is to introduce the central ideas of info-gap uncertainty and robustness. In Section 12.3 we consider a dynamic model and illustrate the ways in which the info-gap robustness analysis supports the choice of a time-varying culling effort. We extend this example in Section 12.4 to include both uncertainty in the parameters of the ecological model as well as conflicting expert opinion on the structure of the model itself. Our examples employ versions of the Lotka–Volterra model of population dynamics, providing an opportunity to study the implications of model uncertainty for the selection of management strategies.

12.2   Culling and Learning: An Allocation Problem

12.2.1   Problem Statement

Consider a feral cat population preying on an indigenous bird species. Our aim is to keep the bird population viable. We can exert effort to control the cat population, but we are unable to eradicate all cats; it is simply too hard to find them all. Furthermore, our understanding of the population dynamics is limited. How many cats should we cull in order to confidently maintain a healthy bird population? Should we allocate some of our management budget to study the population dynamics so that we can choose a more effective and reliable culling strategy? Initially we will consider a simplified static example.

Assume that we have access to a team of analysts who have built a Lotka–Volterra model for the two-species interaction between cats and birds (Krebs, 1978; Pielou, 1969; Royama, 1992). Regarding birds, the model states that the bird population would grow exponentially if they were not predated by cats. Regarding cats, the model states that the cat population would decay exponentially if they were not able to consume birds.

This model predicts two possible stable states for the bird–cat interaction. Either both species become extinct, or both species stabilise at population sizes that depend on the properties of the dynamic interactions. The equilibrium size of the bird population, B_{eq}, as it interacts with the cat population, is

$$B_{eq} = \frac{\gamma_1}{\gamma_2}. \qquad (12.1)$$

The equilibrium size of the bird population is the ratio of the rate at which the cat population would decline in the absence of birds, γ_1, to the rate at which the cat population grows as a result of each bird–cat encounter, γ_2. (An analogous expression describes the equilibrium size of the cat population but it needn't concern us here.)

We can influence the size of the equilibrium bird population by management actions such as investing effort in culling cats or investing resources in studying the population dynamics so that culling efforts can be more effectively deployed. Our management goal is to keep the equilibrium bird population viable. We would like to stabilise with at least 200 individuals, which is the minimal acceptable equilibrium population size for birds, denoted B_{min}. If the equilibrium bird population is no less than B_{min}, then the management activity has succeeded. We would like to know if it is feasible to equilibrate at no less than 200 birds, and what management strategy is needed to reliably achieve this.

12.2.2   Uncertainty and Robustness

Our analysts should be able to help answer these questions. However, their quantitative model is uncertain. Our analysts are using an adaptation of the best available model developed in similar situations, but the specifics of our situation are unique. This particular invasive species (the cat) has not been studied before in this habitat with this particular prey (the bird). In addition, we suspect that the habitat is changing, perhaps due to urbanisation, or climate change, or other factors.

Our analysts are fully aware of the limitations of their model. They therefore recognise that, in order to use the models for selecting a management strategy, it is essential to evaluate robustness-to-uncertainty, as we will demonstrate. By *strategy* they mean the fraction of a fixed budget that is allocated to the culling of cats, while the remaining budget is devoted to studying the ecosystem and improving the population dynamics model. By the *robustness* of a strategy they mean how good the strategy will be, even if the model is wrong. The concept of robustness can be expressed more precisely in two different – but complementary – ways.

One way to understand the idea of the robustness of a strategy is as an answer to the following question: if we want to achieve an acceptable outcome (yielding a bird population no less than B_{min}), then how large an error in the estimated species-interaction model can we tolerate? Robustness is a measure of our immunity to model error while achieving a specified required outcome. The strategy is robust if acceptable bird population size is maintained even at large modelling error.

If the robustness of a particular strategy is large, then an acceptable outcome will be achieved even if the best model we can think of is very wrong. That is, large robustness means that the bird population at equilibrium will not fall below the specified minimal value even if the real interaction dynamics are greatly different from the mathematical model. On the other hand, small robustness of a strategy means that the outcome requirements are confidently achieved only if the habitat dynamics are quite close to our analysts' model. We will tend to prefer a strategy that is more robust over a strategy that is less robust.

The other way to understand the robustness of a strategy is as an answer to the following question: how small could the bird population be if our model contains errors up to a specified magnitude? This turns things around. Rather than specifying the minimal acceptable population size, we specify the magnitude of error of the model and ask: how much could the bird population fall, given this strategy, if our model errs by this amount? The strategy is robust if bird loss is small even with large modelling error.

Whichever of the two interpretations of robustness that we use, the robust preference between strategies will be the same.

The robustness can also be used to evaluate the feasibility of different choices of the minimal acceptable population size, B_{min}. For a given strategy, we can ask: what value of B_{min} has large (or small) robustness? Values of B_{min} that, for a given strategy, have large robustness are more feasible (with that strategy) than values of B_{min} that have low robustness. We illustrate these ideas with some graphs.

12.2.3   Interpreting Robustness Curves

Our analysts display the robustness of a specified strategy in terms of its *robustness curve*, as shown in Figure 12.1. The vertical axis is the minimal acceptable population size, while the horizontal axis is the robustness. This curve is for a specific strategy: an allocation between culling cats and studying the ecosystem.

The interpretation of the scale on the robustness axis depends on how the uncertainty is modelled. Our analysts have estimated the values of the coefficients in the equation for the equilibrium size of the bird population, γ_1 and γ_2 in Eq. 12.1, and they have estimated the errors of these estimated coefficients (e.g. standard errors, or spread of expert opinion, etc.) Uncertainty may be expressed as an unknown fractional error of each coefficient with respect to its estimated error. Robustness is the greatest fractional error of the estimated parameters of the model up to which all models yield acceptable outcome. Thus, for instance, a robustness of 0.5 means that any magnitude of error in all coefficients of the model, up to 50% error, does not jeopardise the corresponding minimum bird-population size requirement, which is 600 birds for this value of robustness, as we see in Figure 12.1. Similarly, a robustness of 1.4 means that γ_1 and γ_2 can each err by as much as 140% (each coefficient with respect to its estimated error) if the minimal requirement is for 176 birds.

Three features of all robustness curves appear in Figure 12.1: trade-off, cost of robustness and zeroing.

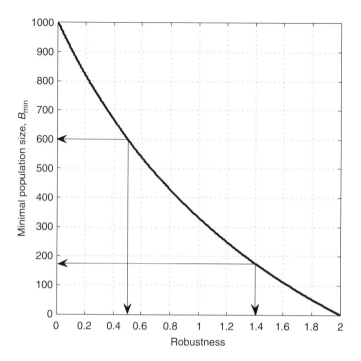

Figure 12.1.   Robustness vs. minimal bird population size, B_{min}, for strategy S_1.

The negative slope of the robustness curve in Figure 12.1 represents the *trade-off* between robustness and performance: better performance (larger minimal population size) is obtained in exchange for lower (worse) robustness to uncertainty. The negative slope in Figure 12.1 quantifies the ordinary intuition that higher aspirations (for large values of B_{min}) entail greater vulnerability (lower robustness) than lower aspirations. The negative slope enables us to evaluate how much immunity against model-error must be foregone in exchange for an increase in our performance requirement. For instance, we see from Figure 12.1 that requiring an equilibrium population size of birds no less than 800 has a robustness of 0.22: the bird population will not fall below 800 provided no model coefficient errs by more than 22%. Allowing the equilibrium size to be as small as 400 birds entails a robustness of 0.86.

The trade-off property is manifested in the slope of the robustness curve which can be understood as a *cost of robustness*. A shallow slope means that a unit decrease in the minimal population size entails a large increase in robustness. A steep slope means that a unit decrease in population size results in only a small gain in robustness. For instance, we see in Figure 12.1 that decreasing B_{min} from 300 to 100 birds results in an increase in robustness of about 0.5. In contrast, a decrease from 1,000 to 800 results in an increase in robustness of only 0.2. The cost of robustness is lower at the lower right than at the upper left of the curve in Figure 12.1. Shallow slope means low cost of robustness, while steep slope means that robustness is very costly in units of decreased performance.

The trade-off property has a further important implication for strategy selection. Recall that a robustness curve is evaluated for a specific management strategy; Figure 12.1 is for a strategy labelled S_1. Using this strategy, the analysts tell us that the estimated model predicts an equilibrium population of 1,000 birds. As we see in Figure 12.1, this is precisely the value of B_{min} at which the robustness equals zero. This illustrates a property of all robustness curves: the robustness of a strategy is zero when attempting to achieve the outcome which is *predicted* for that strategy. Best-model predictions have zero robustness. This is called the *zeroing* property.

This means that we should not evaluate a strategy in terms of the predicted outcome of that strategy, because this prediction is an unreliable indication of how the strategy will fare. Rather, we should evaluate a strategy by its full robustness curve. Using the concept of trade-off between robustness and performance, we can evaluate the robustness of poorer-than-predicted outcomes; these are the only outcomes which have positive robustness against modelling error.

A further implication has to do with outcome optimisation. A common approach to selecting a management strategy is to seek the best outcome that can be achieved, based on our best model (why settle for less?). The problem with this approach is that best-model predictions have no robustness against uncertainty, so outcome optimisation can be wishful thinking as we will see.

Each strategy has its own robustness curve that reflects the trade-off and zeroing properties of that strategy. Why are some curves steep and some curves shallow? What does this indicate about the corresponding strategies? A strategy has large predicted equilibrium bird population (hence the robustness becomes zero at a large value of B_{min}) if that strategy effectively exploits the properties of the system as represented by the estimated model of the population dynamics. A strategy will have low cost of robustness (and hence a shallow robustness curve) if that strategy is insensitive to the gap between the estimated and the correct model. These two properties of a strategy – predicted outcome and robustness against error in the predictive model – together determine the slope and intercept of the robustness curve.

The method for selecting a management strategy that is indicated by these considerations is called *robust-satisficing*. Identify an outcome that you can accept, and seek a management strategy that maintains at least an acceptable outcome over the widest possible range of deviation of reality from your model. That is, satisfice (rather than optimise) the outcome and robustify against modelling error. This is illustrated in Figure 12.2.

12.2.4   Selecting between Management Strategies

Figure 12.2 shows robustness curves for two management strategies, e.g. different allocations between culling cats and studying the population dynamics. Strategy S_1 entails more culling of cats and less modelling effort than strategy S_2. The best-model prediction for S_1 is that the equilibrium bird population will have 1000 individuals while S_2 predicts only 500. On the other hand, because S_2 is based on a more

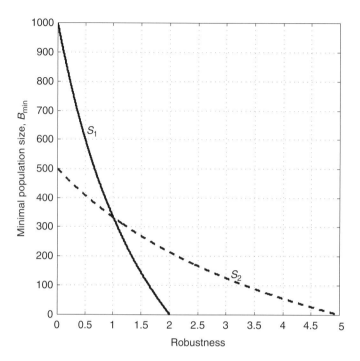

Figure 12.2.   Robustness vs. minimal bird population size, $B_{\min}$, for strategies S_1 and S_2.

thorough study of the bird–cat interaction, the cost of robustness is lower with S_2 than with S_1. That is, the robustness curve for S_2 is shallower than for S_1.

Consider strategy S_1. The predicted equilibrium size of the bird population, based on S_1, is 1,000 individuals. However, the robustness to uncertainty in this value is zero, so we cannot rely on stabilising at 1,000 birds if we implement strategy S_1. Only smaller populations have positive robustness against modelling error. We are aiming to maintain at least 200 individuals, and we see from the solid curve in Figure 12.2 that the robustness for this requirement is 1.3; the coefficients of the Lotka–Volterra model can all err up to 130% without jeopardising the requirement that the final population not fall below 200 individuals.

Now consider strategy S_2, whose robustness curve is the dashed line in Figure 12.2. The predicted outcome of S_2 is only 500 birds (because we are culling fewer cats than with S_1). Nominally – based on the best-model predictions – we would prefer S_1 over S_2 (because 1,000 birds is better than 500). However, because predicted outcomes have zero robustness, this is not a good basis for comparing these strategies. Rather, we see that the robustness for achieving a population no smaller than 200 birds is 2.1 with strategy S_2 (as opposed to 1.3 with S_1). Using S_2 (with its larger share of ecosystem research), the model coefficients can all vary up to 210% without allowing the equilibrium bird population to fall below 200. Strategy S_2 is more robust to uncertainty than strategy S_1; the robust preference – given the requirement for at least 200 birds – is for S_2 rather than S_1. What has happened is a reversal

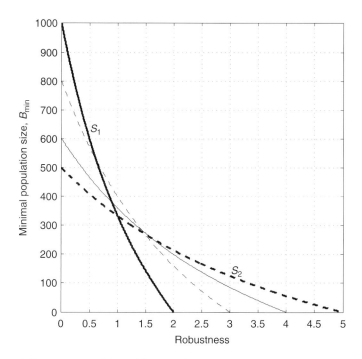

Figure 12.3. Robustness vs. minimal bird population size, B_{min}, for strategies S_1, S_2 and 2 others.

of preference between these strategies, resulting from the fact that their robustness curves cross one another.

Let's summarise the robust-satisficing approach to strategy selection. Strategy S_1 is nominally preferred over S_2: the best-model prediction is better with S_1 than with S_2. However, best-model predictions have zero robustness. Furthermore, the robustness curves of these two strategies cross one another at a value of B_{min} denoted B_x. If an outcome below the crossing point is acceptable (B_{min} less than B_x) then S_2 is more robust and hence preferable over S_1. S_1 is preferred if we need a population larger than B_x.

There are many management strategies that are intermediate between S_1 and S_2, all with the same total budget. The robustness curves of two such intermediates are shown as thin curves in Figure 12.3, together with the curves for S_1 and S_2. The four strategies all show the trade-off and zeroing properties, as well as extensive curve crossing. Most notably, however, we see that – to a good approximation – the robustness curves for S_1 and S_2 enclose the intermediate strategies. This means that either S_1 or S_2 is more robust than the other strategies which thus need not be considered.

12.3 Variable Culling Effort

We now extend the example of Section 12.2 to include variation of the culling effort over time. Our aim, as before, is to maintain a healthy bird population threatened by an invasive cat. We have a fixed budget that determines the total culling effort that can be exerted over a specified duration. However, when the cat population is small, a large effort is needed to remove additional cats, while culling from a large population requires less effort. The question is how to allocate culling effort over time in order to reliably maintain a viable bird population in light of uncertainty in the population dynamics.

12.3.1   Formulation

The analysts estimate that the amount of effort, E_t, required to remove n_t cats (at any time step t) depends on the current size of the cat population, C_t, as:

$$E_t = \frac{\varepsilon}{C_t - n_t} - \frac{\varepsilon}{C_t} \tag{12.2}$$

where ε is a constant. Removing no cats ($n_t = 0$) requires no effort, but as n_t approaches the size of the cat population (i.e. as we attempt to remove all but the last few cats) the required effort increases without bound. This equation can be inverted to express the number of cats culled as a function of the effort and the size of the cat population. We denote this as $n_t(E_t, C_t)$. (Strictly speaking, this is the greatest integer less than the value of n_t which satisfies Eq. 12.2.) This is a *feedback* strategy because the size of the cat population feeds back to influence the culling action.

The discrete-time Lotka–Volterra equations that the analysts use are:

$$B_{t+1} = (1 + \gamma_3) B_t - \gamma_4 B_t C_t \tag{12.3}$$

$$C_{t+1} = (1 - \gamma_1) C_t + \gamma_2 B_t C_t - n_t(E_t, C_t) \tag{12.4}$$

The coefficients γ_1 and γ_2 are the same as in Eq. 12.1. γ_3 is the fractional growth rate of birds in the absence of predation, and γ_4 is the death rate of birds per bird–cat encounter. Equation 12.4 contains the cat-culling term, $n_t(E_t, C_t)$, that depends on the size of the cat population and on the culling effort that is allocated for the current step.

Our management goal is to maintain the size of the bird population above a specified minimum value, $B_{\min}$, throughout the planning period T. That is, we require that $B_t \geq B_{\min}$ for each time step t from $t = 1$ to $t = T$. Our budget determines the total culling effort that can be exerted, E, and our task is to allocate this effort over time subject to the budget constraint, $E = \sum_{t=1}^{T} E_t$.

We will consider three different strategies for allocating the culling effort. The effort, E_t, can be constant over time, or it can increase linearly from zero to maximal effort at time T, or it can decrease linearly to zero effort at time T. While there are other time varying strategies, these three will suffice to illustrate the decision methodology. We will also consider the impact of different total budget sizes, E.

The robustness of a strategy can be understood exactly as in Section 12.2, where we discussed two equivalent definitions. The robustness of a specified strategy

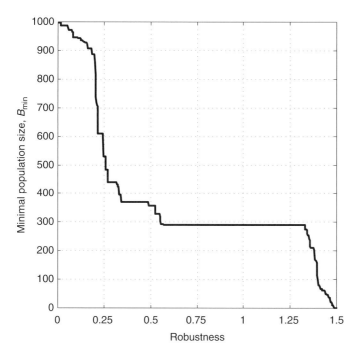

Figure 12.4. Robustness vs. minimal bird population size, B_{min}, for constant culling effort.

(allocation of effort over time) is the greatest uncertainty in the parameters of the model that can be tolerated while also maintaining the bird population above the minimal requirement, B_{min}, throughout the management duration. Equivalently, the robustness of a strategy can be understood as the smallest size that the bird population could attain, given a specified level of error in the model. In this latter definition, robust strategies ensure large bird populations even with large model errors.

12.3.2 Results

Figure 12.4 shows a robustness curve for constant culling effort over a duration in which both the bird and the cat populations display more or less periodic fluctuations. The number of cats that are culled varies up and down over time as the size of the cat population changes, in accord with Eq. 12.2, even though the total effort expended on both culling and learning, E_t, is constant.

We see the same three generic features of the robustness curves that were observed in Section 12.2. First, robustness trades off against performance: requiring that the bird population not fall below a large minimal size entails low robustness against modelling error. Second, the robustness can be significantly increased without substantially reducing the population minimum only if the slope is shallow. Third, the robustness equals zero at the population size that is predicted by the estimated model for this strategy.

The striking difference between the robustness curve in Figure 12.4 and those in Section 12.2 is that here the robustness is jagged and piece-wise flat. The step-like shape in Figure 12.4 results from the discrete culling process in which small numbers of cats are culled, typically between 0 and 10 per time step. Thus for instance the long plateau in the robustness curve at a value of B_{min} about 300 results from both the culling, and the extremes of the fluctuating bird population, staying the same for the corresponding wide range of different models.

This long plateau is quite significant because it shifts the lower right part of the robustness curve to substantially larger robustness values. For instance, we see from Figure 12.4 that the robustness is 1.38 if our goal is to maintain at least 200 birds throughout the management period. This means that fractional errors in all of the model parameters of 138% (each with respect to its own estimated error) do not jeopardise this requirement. In contrast, the robustness is only 0.55 if we require a B_{min} of 300 birds.

Figure 12.5 shows robustness curves for three different culling strategies, all with the same total effort. The curve with constant culling effort is reproduced from Figure 12.4. The dashed curve that crosses the constant-culling curve has linearly increasing effort starting with zero effort in the first time step. The robustness curve in the lower left corner has linearly decreasing culling effort reaching zero effort in the last time step. The numbers of cats that are culled in each step are different in each case, and fluctuate as the cat population fluctuates due to the feedback from population size to actual culling.

The first thing to conclude from Figure 12.5 is that the decreasing-effort strategy is vastly more vulnerable to error in the model than either the constant-effort or the increasing-effort strategies. From among these three options (at the total budget considered) one would never choose the decreasing effort strategy.

The choice between constant and increasing effort is more subtle, because their robustness curves cross one another, which raises the possibility of preference-reversal between them, as discussed in Section 12.2. Nominally, these strategies are almost the same: their predicted minimal population sizes are nearly identical. In contrast, their robustness curves are substantially different over part of the range of B_{min}. For instance, for a minimal acceptable bird population size of 500, the robustness of the constant-culling strategy is 0.26 while the robustness of the linearly increasing strategy is 0.58, more than twice as robust. On the other hand, at B_{min} of 200 the preferences are reversed though the robustness advantage of the constant-effort strategy is not as dramatic.

Figure 12.6 shows robustness curves for constant-effort culling strategies at three different total budgets of culling effort. The overall trend is clear and unsurprising: more total effort is usually more robust. A total budget of $E = 2.0$ is strictly more robust than a total budget of $E = 1.5$, though the robustness advantage of the greater effort is not constant over the range of B_{min} values. A budget of $E = 2.0$ is more robust than $E = 1.0$ over most, but not all, of the B_{min} values.

Figure 12.7 shows a close-up of Figure 12.6 in the high-performance low-robustness corner of the graph. Here we see extensive curve-crossing, with the

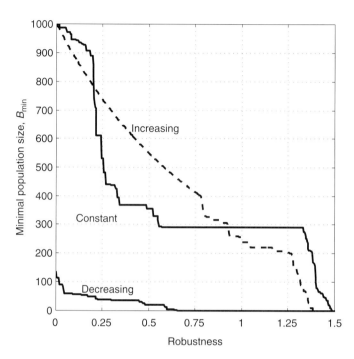

Figure 12.5. Robustness vs. minimal bird population size, B_{min}, for three different culling effort strategies.

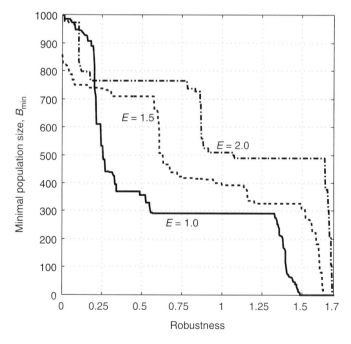

Figure 12.6. Robustness vs. minimal bird population size, B_{min}, for constant culling effort at three different total budgets.

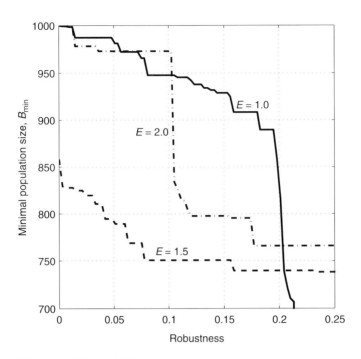

Figure 12.7.   Close-up of Figure 12.6.

associated potential for reversal of preferences among these management options. In particular, for B_{min} between 800 and 900 birds, the *lower* effort has *twice* the robustness of the higher effort, when comparing $E = 1.0$ against $E = 2.0$. If a very large bird population is required – and recognising that the associated robustness is relatively low – then one might prefer the lower total effort (from among these constant-effort strategies).

This somewhat counterintuitive conclusion is a result of the non-linear population dynamics and the feedback between population size and actual culling. Culling too many cats can lead to a rise in the bird population, which can then cause a sharp rise in the number of cats, which in turn may drive the bird population below the acceptable level. We can't predict this at all precisely because the model is uncertain, but the robustness analysis reveals this mechanism and steers us away from being too trigger happy.

These examples illustrate how the choice of a dynamic state-feedback culling strategy is supported by analysis of robustness to modelling uncertainty. These models capture uncertainties in the model parameters. Other uncertainty models would be required to explore other sources of uncertainty; for instance, we explore uncertainty in model structure in the text that follows. The most important thing to emerge in this initial analysis is the qualitative understanding this provides of the impact of uncertainty on the managers' objectives. Such explicit consideration of uncertainty provides important insight into the strategies that may determine population viability.

12.4   Conflicting Experts

Experts often disagree with one another. For instance, the Intergovernmental Panel on Climate Change presents suites of science-based models predicting different global climate futures (IPCC-AR4, 2007). Likewise, macroeconomic processes can be modelled in many conceptually distinct but credible ways. Nonetheless, the axiomatic, conceptual and predictive disparity among these models is substantial (Snowdon et al., 1994).

Ecological models and experts are no exception. Expert opinions on matters of fact – how large a population can this habitat sustain, how low a rainfall can this species tolerate, and so on – can vary greatly. Experts' opinions depend on how the questions are formulated, how the elicitation interview is structured, and many other factors. Experts tend to be overconfident in assessing statistical confidence intervals, which can be ameliorated only by careful design of the elicitation procedure (Speirs-Bridge et al., 2010). Opinions can differ on the conceptual foundations and mathematical structure of predictive models for ecological processes. Several distinct paradigms are in use for describing spatial and temporal population dynamics, including the Lotka–Volterra model, time series modelling (Turchin & Taylor, 1992), meta-population modelling (Hanski, 1999) and others. Even within the class of Lotka–Volterra models, specific realizations vary widely.

In this section we study the choice of a time-varying culling strategy when our team of analysts is divided in two groups, each supporting a different model of the population dynamics. Both models are uncertain, their predictions are different, and we must choose a culling strategy before the scientists are able to work out their differences. We have no reason to believe, or to disbelieve, one model more than the other. We are not able to bet on either model. Both models cannot be true, and in fact both are uncertain so both are likely to be false. And yet each model is founded on sound evidence and supported by credible scientific opinion. It is not due to negligence or incompetence that the scientists disagree among themselves. The specific ecological situation that must be managed is unique in important ways. We may believe that the scientists, given time and resources, would work out their differences. But we must choose a management strategy for the current situation now. In this section we illustrate an info-gap robustness approach to strategy selection in this predicament.

12.4.1   Two Models

The two models used by our team of analysts are both finite-difference Lotka–Volterra models, but their structures are different and some of each model's parameters are fractionally uncertain as described in Section 12.2.3.

The **first model** is specified in Eqs. 12.3 and 12.4 with the culling quantity determined by Eq. 12.2 in terms of the culling effort. That is, the culling strategy determines the culling effort at each time step, and the actual number of cats that are removed with this effort depends on the size of the cat population.

The **second model** is also a finite difference Lotka–Volterra model with a different structure (this model is motivated by Krebs, 1978, p. 242):

$$B_{t+1} = \left(1 - \frac{B_t}{\varsigma_2}\right)\varsigma_3 B_t - \varsigma_4 B_t C_t \tag{12.5}$$

$$C_{t+1} = \varsigma_1 B_t C_t - n_t\left(E_t, C_t\right) \tag{12.6}$$

The coefficients, ς_i, are all positive. ς_2 is the carrying capacity of birds in the habitat in the absence of predation by cats. ς_3 is the fractional growth rate of birds in the absence of predation and far below the carrying capacity. ς_4 is the death rate of birds per bird-cat encounter. ς_1 is the growth rate of cats per bird-cat encounter. $n_t\left(E_t, C_t\right)$ is determined by Eq. 12.2.

The dramatic predictive difference between the two models is illustrated in Figures 12.8 and 12.9. These figures show bird and cat population sizes versus time for each of the two models, given a constant culling effort. The first model shows fairly stable and nearly harmonic oscillation of the populations, while the second model shows rapid and highly damped convergence to an equilibrium in which cats have been eradicated. The same total budget for culling effort is available in both cases, but the second model actually expends far less effort because the cats are eradicated fairly early. Thus the policy implications of these models are quite different, and we will see that their robustnesses to uncertainty are different as well.

Our management goal, as in Section 12.3, is to maintain the size of the bird population above a specified minimum value, $B_{\min}$, for times $t = 1$ through $t = T$. We must choose the culling effort at each step, E_t, subject to the budget constraint, $E = \sum_{t=1}^{T} E_t$. The question is: how to choose a culling strategy? The answer is based on the idea of robustness.

12.4.2   Robustness

We define the robustness for each model just as we did in Section 12.3. Indeed, model 1 here is the same as the model used in that section so the robustness is the same as well. We denote the robustness functions for these two models as $\hat{h}_1\left(B_{\min}\right)$ and $\hat{h}_2\left(B_{\min}\right)$. In each case, we can understand the robustness in either of the senses introduced in Section 12.2. If we specify a lowest acceptable bird population size, $B_{\min}$, then the robustness is the greatest fractional error of the model parameters at which the bird population will not fall below $B_{\min}$. Equivalently, if we postulate the magnitude of fractional error, then the robustness function determines the lowest size that the bird population can reach. The robustness function depends on the culling strategy. More robustness is better than less robustness, so the robustness function generates preferences on culling strategies.

Figure 12.10 shows robustness functions for the two models with constant culling effort. The difference in the dynamic predictions of these models, which was illustrated in Figures 12.8 and 12.9, is transformed here into dramatic difference

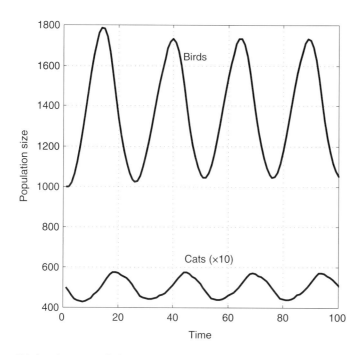

Figure 12.8.   Bird and cat populations predicted with model 1; constant culling effort.

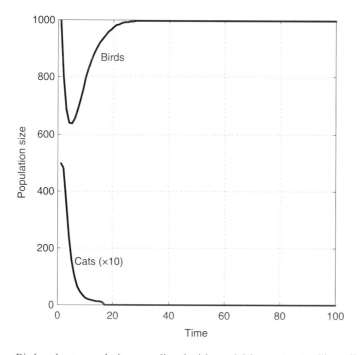

Figure 12.9.   Bird and cat populations predicted with model 2; constant culling effort.

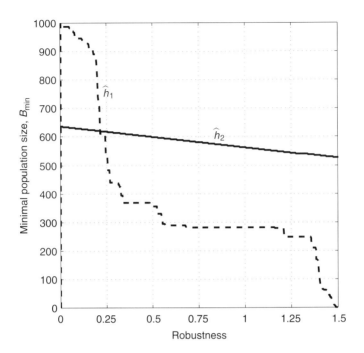

Figure 12.10. Robustness versus minimal bird population size, B_{min}, with constant culling effort, for two conflicting models.

in robustness. Model 1, which predicts persistence of both populations and hence persistent removal of small numbers of cats, shows the step-like robustness curve that we encountered in Section 12.3. Model 2 predicts smooth and rapid extinction and its robustness curve is smooth as well.

Model 2 is more robust than model 1 for acceptable bird-population sizes below 600. For instance, requiring no less than $B_{min} = 200$ birds, we are vastly more robust if we can rely on model 2 rather than model 1 ($\hat{h}_2 (200)$ is off scale far to the right). But we are not in a position to favour model 2 over model 1. And furthermore, if we need a larger bird population, say $B_{min} = 800$, then model 1 is more robust than model 2.

How should we choose among culling strategies? The approach is to extend the info-gap model of uncertainty beyond the fractional errors of the parameters and to include the structural uncertainty as well (as reflected in having two models rather than one). For any minimal acceptable population size, B_{min}, the robustness is the greatest fractional error in the parameters of either model, so that the corresponding model satisfies the population requirement. We don't know the actual fractional errors of the parameters of either model, and we don't know which of these models we really should pay attention to. Consequently, we attend to both models and evaluate a culling strategy according to whichever model is more vulnerable at the specified minimal population size. The robustness of a culling strategy is the robustness of the more vulnerable of the two models. We state this formally as

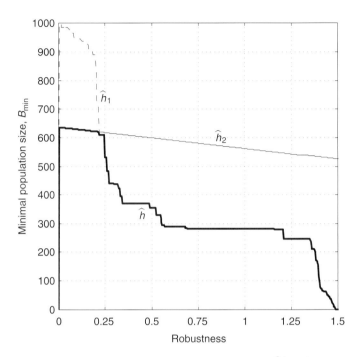

Figure 12.11. Same as Figure 12.10, indicating overall robustness, $\hat{h}(B_{\min})$.

$$\hat{h}(B_{\min}) = \min\{\hat{h}_1(B_{\min}), \ \hat{h}_2(B_{\min})\} \tag{12.7}$$

The thick curve in Figure 12.11 is the overall robustness, $\hat{h}(B_{\min})$, evaluated from the two model robustnesses displayed as thin curves. The constant-effort culling strategy is evaluated as the worst of the two alternatives. We don't know which model is in fact more accurate, so we evaluate the strategy in terms of whichever model is more vulnerable to error because we are unwilling to favour either model over the other.

12.4.3   Strategy Selection

Having established what we mean by robustness to conflicting uncertain models, we are now ready to evaluate alternative culling strategies.

Figure 12.12 shows the overall robustnesses for the three different culling strategies described in Section 12.3.1. The culling effort can be either constant over time, linearly increasing, or linearly decreasing. The total budget of effort is fixed.

Figure 12.12 is a truncated version of Figure 12.5. We can understand this truncation by considering Figure 12.11 in which the robustness curve for model 1 is truncated by the robustness curve for model 2. Much of the discussion of strategy selection in Figure 12.5 applies here as well. The decreasing culling effort would not be chosen because it is dominated by the other two strategies. The robustness curves for constant and linearly increasing effort cross one another so the preference

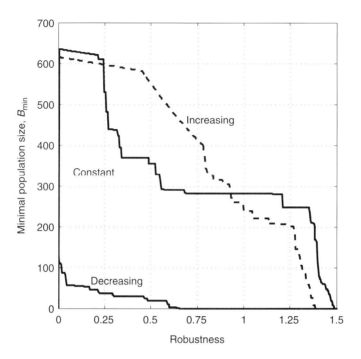

Figure 12.12. Robustness vs. minimal bird population size, B_{min}, for three different culling effort strategies.

between them depends on our performance requirement as discussed in Section 12.3.2.

The policy impact of having two conflicting models is demonstrated in Figure 12.12. At high performance ($B_{min} > 600$) the robustness is determined by model 2 for which the constant culling strategy is more robust. At lower performance ($B_{min} < 600$) the robustness is determined by model 1 for which either constant or increasing culling is more robust, depending on B_{min}.

Figure 12.13 shows robustness curves for three different total budgets of culling effort, all with constant effort over time. This is a truncated version of Figure 12.6. The presence of two conflicting models has eliminated all curve crossing and established an unambiguous preference ordering: more culling effort is preferred over less in this specific case, unlike the situation in Figure 12.6.

12.5   Conclusion

Science-based models are useful, even when applied to systems that deviate in unknown ways from those for which the models were developed. However, it is then necessary to deal with the info-gap between model and reality. Management strategies cannot be evaluated only by their model-based predicted outcomes, because these predictions have no robustness against error in the model. We discussed three

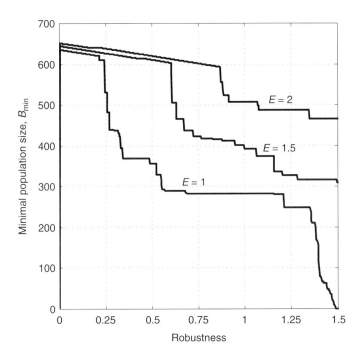

Figure 12.13. Robustness vs. minimal bird population size, $B_{\min}$, for constant culling effort at three different total budgets.

examples in which an info-gap robustness analysis is used to select a management strategy in attempting to reliably achieve an acceptable outcome.

These examples can be extended in many directions (relevant examples can be found in Ben-Haim, 2006). We could explore the robustness of the predator population, and the management implications of considering both predator and prey robustness. Our analysis can be applied to systems with three or more species. We could study how monetary allocations are translated into models of population dynamics. This would introduce additional uncertainties that must be modelled and managed. One might wish to consider uncertainty about the size of the smallest viable prey population. We have represented uncertainty in the population dynamics with non-probabilistic info-gap models of uncertainty. In some situations we have probabilistic information that, although valuable, may itself be uncertain. One may like to consider adaptive extensions: use part of the budget for exploratory management, improve the dynamic model from what is learned, and then invest the remaining budget. These and other extensions can be explored using info-gap techniques.

12.6   Acknowledgements

This chapter was written in part while the author was the Alan Richards Fellow in Grey College, Durham University, Durham, UK The author expresses his gratitude for the support of the College. The author also gratefully acknowledges the support of the UK Royal Academy of Engineering.

References

Ben-Haim, Y. (2006). *Info-gap decision theory: Decisions under severe uncertainty*, 2nd ed. London: Academic Press.

Burgman, M. (2005). *Risks and decisions for conservation and environmental management.* Cambridge: Cambridge University Press.

Gigerenzer, G. & Selton, R., ed. (2001). *Bounded rationality: The adaptive toolbox.* Boston: MIT Press.

Hanski, I. (1999). *Metapopulation ecology*. Oxford: Oxford University Press.

IPCC-AR4 (2007). Global climate projections. In S. Solomon, D. Qin, M. Manning, Z. Chen, M. Marquis, K. B. Averyt, M. Tignor, & H. L. Miller (eds.), *Climate change 2007: The physical science basis. Contribution of Working Group I to the Fourth Assessment Report of the Intergovernmental Panel on Climate Change*. Cambridge: Cambridge University Press. Available from www.ipcc.ch.

Krebs, C. J. (1978). *Ecology: The experimental analysis of distribution and abundance*. New York: Harper & Row.

Oxford English Dictionary (1989). 2nd ed. Oxford: Oxford University Press.

Pielou, E. C. (1969). *An introduction to mathematical ecology*. New York: John Wiley & Sons.

Potts, J. M., Cox, M. J., Barkley, P., et al. (2013). Model-based search strategies for plant diseases: A case-study using citrus canker (*Xanthomonas citri*). *Diversity and Distributions*, 19(5–6), 590–602.

Regan, H. M., Ben-Haim, Y., Langford, B., et al. (2005). Robust decision making under severe uncertainty for conservation management. *Ecological Applications*, 15(4), 1471–1477.

Royama, T. (1992). *Analytical population dynamics*. London: Chapman & Hall.

Simon, H. A. (1955). A behavioral model of rational choice. *Quarterly Journal of Economics*, 69(1), 99–118.

Simon, H. A. (1956). Rational choice and the structure of the environment. *Psychological Review*, 63(2), 129–138.

Snowdon, B., Vane, H. & Wynarczyk, P. (1994). *A modern guide to macroeconomics: An introduction to competing schools of thought*. Cheltenham, UK: Edward Elgar.

Speirs-Bridge, A., Fidler, F., McBride, M., et al. (2010). Reducing overconfidence in the interval judgments of experts. *Risk Analysis*, 30(3), 512–523.

Turchin, P. & Taylor, A. D. (1992). Complex dynamics in ecological time series. *Ecology*, 73(1), 289–305.

13 Decisions with Relative Robustness

Colin J. Thompson

13.1 Introduction

Allocation of resources among alternative strategies or options is a common and important problem in many areas of environmental management, including biodiversity, species conservation and threats from invasive species. A general theoretical framework for analysing this problem was presented by McCarthy et al. (2010), who stressed that management should indicate overall objectives in terms of the benefits (and costs) derived from allocation of resources to available management options. The problem then reduces to optimising objectives. Several applications of this approach can be found in McCarthy et al. (2010) and similar problems were addressed in Wintle et al. (2010).

The benefits derived from individual management options for a given allocation of resources will typically be subject to severe uncertainty. This issue was discussed recently by Thompson et al. (2012) in the context of surveillance for threatened and invasive species. The purpose of this chapter is to present a simple example of resource allocation under severe uncertainty to illustrate how different methods in decision theory (French, 1986) and robust optimisation (Kouvelis & Yu, 1997) can provide different robust-optimal solutions, depending on the method and choice of management objectives.

13.2 Model Objective Functions

The general theory of McCarthy et al. (2010) considers the problem of allocating a fraction x_i of a total budget to n management options with expected benefits p_i (x_i) for options $i=1,2,\ldots,n$. They assume that the management objective is to maximise the overall expected benefit, that is, the sum of p_i (x_i), subject to the budget constraint where the sum of the fractions x_i is unity. In the case of two management options, the objective function can be written as

$$V(x;\lambda) = p_1(x) + p_2(1-x) \quad 0 \le x \le 1, \tag{13.1}$$

where the fraction x of the budget is allocated to option 1, $1-x$ is allocated to option 2 and λ denotes some parameter set that characterises the functional form of p_1 and p_2. McCarthy et al. (2010) considered exponential, hyperbolic and linear

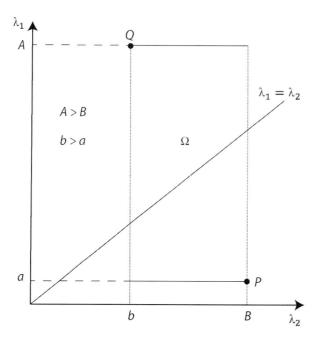

Figure 13.1.   Region of uncertainty Ω for model parameters λ_1 and λ_2.

functional forms, while Thompson et al. (2012) explored functions inversely proportional to their respective allocation. Wintle et al. (2010), on the other hand, considered more general situations involving products of functions of x and $(1-x)$.

Here, for illustrative purposes, we consider the linear model

$$V(x,\lambda) = x\lambda_1 + (1-x)\lambda_2 \qquad 0 \le x \le 1, \tag{13.2}$$

which can be thought of as a simple portfolio model of two assets with the expected returns λ_1 and λ_2. Given this formulation, one would clearly like to choose x to maximise the overall benefit $V(x, »)$ in Eq. 13.1. For the portfolio example in Eq. 13.2,

$$V_M(\lambda) = \begin{matrix} \max \\ 0 \le x \le 1 \end{matrix} V(x,\lambda) = \{ \begin{matrix} \lambda_1 \text{ when } \lambda_1 > \lambda_2 \ (x=1) \\ \lambda_2 \text{ when } \lambda_1 < \lambda_2 \ (x=0) \end{matrix} \tag{13.3}$$

which is an all $(x=1)$ or nothing $(x=0)$ solution assuming that one actually knows λ_1 and λ_2. In reality, of course, λ_1 and λ_2 are unknown and are possibly subject to severe uncertainty.

13.3   Classical Maximin Solutions

We assume that $\lambda = (\lambda_2, \lambda_1)$ is unknown and lies in some possibly large rectangular region of uncertainty Ω as shown in Figure 13.1.

In classical decision theory (French, 1986), there are several methods to determine an appropriate asset allocation x, depending on the management objective function. For example, the Wald maximin rule chooses x to maximise the worst case (scenario) outcome. For the objective function (Eq. 13.2), the worst case (for $\lambda \in \Omega$) occurs at the lower left-hand vertex of Ω, where $\lambda_1 = a$ and $\lambda_2 = b$. From the preceding discussion and assuming $b > a$, the Wald solution is $x_W = 0$, which is a very conservative solution.

An alternative objective function is the Savage regret rule (French, 1986)

$$S(x,\lambda) = V_M(\lambda) - V(x,\lambda), \tag{13.4}$$

which measures the deviation of $V(x,\lambda)$ from its true unknown maximum $V_M(\lambda)$ (Eq. 13.3). Savage's regret rule then chooses $x = x_s$ to minimise the maximum regret (Eq. 13.4) taken over $\lambda \in \Omega$, which is easily seen to occur at either vertex P or vertex Q. The value of $x = x_s$ is precisely where the maximum regret functions at P and Q are equal, viz after a little algebra,

$$x_s = (A - b)/(A - b + B - a), \tag{13.5}$$

which is clearly a much less conservative solution than Wald's all-or-nothing solution ($x_W = 0$ when $b > a$).

From a management perspective, a better objective function (as a measure of overall performance) may be the dimensionless ratio

$$R(x,\lambda) = V(x,\lambda)/V_M(\lambda), \tag{13.6}$$

which measures the performance $V(x,\lambda)$ relative to its true unknown maximum $V_M(\lambda)$ in Eq. 13.3.

The Wald maximin rule applied to Eq. 13.6 shows that the (worst case) minimum of $R(x,\lambda)$ with respect to $\lambda \in \Omega$ again occurs at either vertex P or vertex Q, with a maximum at the point at which they are equal, giving the solution

$$x_R = (1 - b/A)/(1 - a/B + 1 - b/A), \tag{13.7}$$

which differs from both the Wald and Savage solutions.

13.4   Acacia Rust: A Hypothetical Case Study

Rust fungi pose serious threats to horticulture, crops and indigenous flora. To illustrate the use of the approaches outlined in the preceding text, we use a hypothetical case study for a hypothetical disease. We suppose there are very little data and considerable uncertainty, which is the case in many real situations, especially those involving new and emerging pests and diseases. We further suppose that there are many possible pathways for entry of the hypothetical rust, including air cans and tourists returning from Kenya (especially those who have been on safari).

In our hypothetical example, we assume that detection of rust spores is proportional to both the approach rates along pathways and the number of inspections carried out on each pathway. The linear model above (Eq. 13.2) is a measure of the overall detection rate along the two pathways. In this context, the parameters λ_1 and λ_2 in Eq. 13.2 are the approach rates along the two pathways, x is the proportion of inspections targeting tourists and $(1 - x)$ is the proportion of inspections targeting air cans. The objective is to maximise the overall detection rate defined by Eq. 13.2. The problem, of course, is that the approach rates λ_1 and λ_2 are unknown and subject to possibly severe uncertainty.

For our hypothetical case study, we consider the uncertainty region Ω in Figure 13.1 and choose (in some appropriate units) $A = 6$, $a = 1$, $B = 3$ and $b = 2$. From the solutions described in the previous section, we then use Eqs. 13.2, 13.3, 13.5 and 13.7 to obtain

$$x_W = 0, \quad x_s = \frac{2}{3}, \quad x_R = \frac{1}{2}. \tag{13.8}$$

This result shows that different methods in classical decision theory can lead to different values for decision variables (which is not unusual).

We note that in the present hypothetical example, the choices $A = 6$ and $B = 3$ reflect a belief that returning tourists may be twice as likely to import rust spores (on clothing, shoes etc.) than air cans. The Savage regret value of $x_s = \frac{2}{3}$ then seems (intuitively) to be a reasonable solution (compared with $x_W = 0$ and $x_R = \frac{1}{2}$).

We further note that if one sets $a = b = 0$ in this example (allowing for the possibility of zero approach rates), one obtains the same solutions for x_s and x_R in Eq. 13.8 (from Eqs. 13.5 and 13.7), but with x_W indeterminant. In fact, it will be seen from Eq. 13.7 that when $a = b = 0$, $x_R = \frac{1}{2}$ for any choice of A and B. This generalises, in an obvious way, to equal numbers of inspections across any number of pathways (which could, in some circumstances, be seen as quite reasonable). The generalisation of the Savage solution (Eq. 13.5), however, is not as obvious.

13.5   Robust Optimal Solutions

Rather than optimising some objective function, Simon (1959) argued that under conditions of uncertainty, one should aim to satisfy some minimally acceptable performance requirements. For example, one could require that $V(x; \lambda)$ in Eq. 13.2 be within some fraction ε of its true unknown maximum $V_M(\lambda)$ in Eq. 13.3. For the regret function (Eq. 13.4) and the ratio (Eq. 13.6), this requirement is equivalent to

$$R(x; \lambda) \geq 1 - \varepsilon. \tag{13.9}$$

In the important field of robust optimisation (Kouvelis & Yu, 1997), we note that Eq. 13.9 is similar to the so-called relative robustness framework, and the requirement $S(x; \lambda) \leq \varepsilon$ for the Savage regret rule (Eq. 13.4) is similarly related to the so-called robust deviation approach.

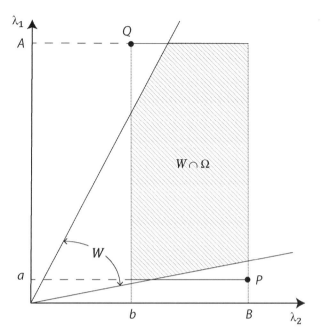

Figure 13.2. Performance requirement of Eq. 13.9 requires $\lambda = (\lambda_2, \lambda_1)$ to lie in the shaded region $W \cap \Omega$.

From Eq. 13.6 it is easily seen that Eq. 13.9 requires $\lambda = (\lambda_2, \lambda_1)$ to lie in both Ω and the wedge W bounded by two straight lines i.e. in the shaded region $W \cap \Omega$ shown in Figure 13.2. From Eqs. 13.3 and 13.6, the slopes of the upper and lower boundary lines defining W are, respectively, $x/(x-\varepsilon)$ and $(1-\varepsilon/(1-x))$, assuming $\varepsilon < x < 1-\varepsilon$ and showing that for small $\varepsilon > 0$, one or both of these lines pass through Ω. It follows that for small ε, one must sacrifice some level of uncertainty to satisfy Eq. 13.9.

To quantify this loss of uncertainty, we follow the pioneers of robust optimisation, Gupta and Rosenhead (1968; see also Rosenhead et al., 1972) and define (as in Thompson et al., 2012) the $G - R$ robustness $g_{R(x)}$ to be the area of $W \cap \Omega$ divided by the area of Ω. The $(G - R)$ robust optimal solution then occurs at $x = x_{GR}$, where $g_{R(x)}$ is a maximum (corresponding to a minimal loss in the uncertainty region Ω).

Clearly, for large enough $\varepsilon \geq \varepsilon^*$, W encloses Ω corresponding to a maximum $g_{R(x)}$ of unity. The borderline case, when

$$\varepsilon = \varepsilon^* = \left(1 - \frac{a}{B}\right)\left(1 - \frac{b}{A}\right) \Big/ \left[1 - \frac{a}{B} + 1 - \frac{b}{A}\right] \tag{13.10}$$

corresponds to the bounding lines of W passing through the vertices P and Q shown in Figure 13.2. For $\varepsilon \geq \varepsilon^*$ it is then not difficult to show that x_{GR} where $g_{R(x)}$ takes its maximum is precisely the Wald value x_R for the objective function $R(x, \lambda)$ in Eq. 13.6.

When $\varepsilon < \varepsilon^*$, it is possible to derive explicit expressions for $g_{R(x)}$ and x_{GR} and to generalise the above results when management has more than two choices for allocation of resources. For example, when $n = 2$, $A > B$ and $b > a$,

$$x_{GR} = 1 - \varepsilon \Big/ \left(1 - \frac{b}{A}\right), \qquad (13.11)$$

with $g_{R(x)}$ in general a non-decreasing function of ε. As a numerical example with $A = 6$, $a = 1$, $B = 3$ and $b = 2$ (cf. Eq. 13.8), we have $\varepsilon^* = 1/3$ (from Eq. 13.10), $x_R = \frac{1}{2}$ and $g_{R(x_R)} = 1$. For a higher performance aspiration of $\varepsilon = 0.2$ one has

$x_{GR} = 0.7$ (from Eq. 13.11) and $g_{R(x_{GR})} = 0.73$ showing a 27% loss in robustness to uncertainty to achieve the higher level of performance.

13.6   Info-gap Robustness

Unlike the robust optimisation approach outlined in the previous section, info-gap theory (Ben-Haim, 2006) begins with best-guess estimates for the uncertainty variables (e.g. for the $n = 2$ portfolio model, $\lambda = \tilde{\lambda} = \left(\tilde{\lambda}_2, \tilde{\lambda}_1\right)$) and considers a nested set of uncertainty regions $U(\alpha)$ that expand as the horizon of uncertainty α increases and contract to the best guess $\tilde{\lambda}$ when $\alpha = 0$. This is shown schematically in Figure 13.3, which also shows a dotted rectangle to indicate the original region of uncertainty Ω and the wedge regions W determined by Eq. 13.9 (as in Figure 13.2).

To satisfy the performance requirement in Eq. 13.9 for all $\lambda \in U(\alpha)$, it is clear that $U(\alpha)$ (shown in Figure 13.3 as the sequence of rectangles expanding outwards from $\tilde{\lambda}$) must be enclosed by the wedge $U(\alpha) \subset W$. The largest value $\tilde{\alpha}$ of α, for which $U(\alpha) \subset W$, is called the info-gap robustness corresponding to at least one vertex of $U(\alpha)$ touching a boundary line of W. Further maximisation of $\tilde{\alpha} = \tilde{\alpha}(x)$ with respect to x then gives the robust-optimal info-gap solution x_{IG}. We will not present any details or examples here except to note that, in general, one would expect the region $U(\tilde{\alpha})$ to be smaller than $W \cap \Omega$, particularly for $\varepsilon < \varepsilon^*$, and that x_{IG} will depend on $\tilde{\lambda}$, providing different solutions to those derived in previous sections. Further discussion on the info-gap approach can be found in Chapter 12.

References

Ben-Haim, Y. (2006). *Info-gap decision theory: Decisions under severe uncertainty*, 2nd ed. Oxford: Academic Press.

French, S. (1986). *Decision theory: An introduction to the mathematics of rationality*. Chichester, UK: Ellis Horwood.

Gupta, S. K. & Rosenhead, J. (1968). Robustness in sequential investment decisions. *Management Science*, 15(2), B18–B29.

Kouvelis, P. & Yu, G. (1997). *Robust discrete optimization and its applications*. Dordrecht, Netherlands: Kluwer Academic Publishers.

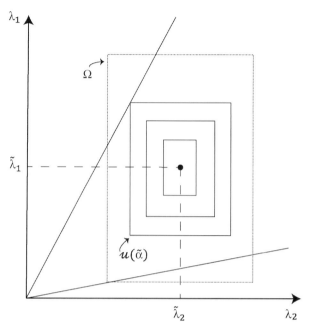

Figure 13.3. Expanding info-gap regions of uncertainty around the best-guess estimate $\tilde{\lambda} = \left(\tilde{\lambda}_2, \tilde{\lambda}_1 \right)$.

McCarthy, M. A., Thompson, C. J., Hauser, C., et al. (2010). Resource allocation for efficient environmental management. *Ecology Letters*, 13(10), 1280–1289.

Rosenhead J., Elton, M. & Gupta, S. K. (1972). Robustness and optimality as criteria for strategic decisions. *Operations Research Quarterly*, 23(4), 413–431.

Simon, H. A. (1959). Theories of decision-making in economics and behavioral science. *American Economic Review*, 49(3), 253–283.

Thompson, C. J., Cannon, R. M. & Burgman, M. A. (2012). Surveillance for threatened and invasive species when uncertainty is severe. *Diversity and Distributions*, 18(4), 410–416.

Wintle, B. A., Runge, M. C. & Bekessy, S. A. (2010). Allocating monitoring effort in the face of unknown unknowns. *Ecology Letters*, 13(11), 1325–1337.

14 Optimising Resource Allocation

Cindy E. Hauser and Tracy M. Rout

14.1 Introduction

Compared with the scale of impacts caused by invasive species worldwide, resources available for managing them are limited (Pimentel et al., 2005). It is, therefore, important for managers to allocate these resources to the greatest effect. However, in systems that are logistically and ecologically complex, it is difficult to determine intuitively how to achieve the best outcome.

These issues are not unique to invasive species management, and techniques have been developed to solve resource allocation problems in fields such as stock portfolio management, project and production management and marketing and natural resource management (Sethi & Thompson, 2006). Decision making can be improved by posing and solving problems in a logical and structured way. At a basic level, this involves specifying three things (Howard, 2007):

1. *What we want* – the management objective(s) describing preferences about the outcome of the decision
2. *What we can do* – the alternative options we must choose from
3. *What we know* – a description of the system, including the likely outcomes of each alternative.

In this chapter, we address situations in which the objective can be expressed in a single currency such as monetary value. We outline several scenarios in which the alternative options are the different ways that resources – in the form of money, time or effort – can be allocated to manage an invasive species. There are some common resource allocation questions for invasive species management: Which species should we manage? How should we manage them? And where should we manage them? We discuss structured approaches and efficient strategies for resource allocation in each case.

14.2 Which? Allocating Resources across Species

There is often a long list of candidate invasive species that managers could be searching for, containing, controlling or eradicating. A common question is, therefore, on which taxa should we be focusing our effort? Some species may be known to occur, while others may not be known to occur and are at some risk of being introduced. To make the most of limited resources, it is essential to have a transparent and repeatable procedure for prioritising species.

In developing a list of candidate species for management action, we must assess the current or potential impact of each species on the local environment. If considering pre-border quarantine or surveillance, we must also assess the likelihood of each species entering, establishing and spreading (see Chapter 8). In addition, we need some understanding of how these values will change if a species is managed. A natural objective for this resource allocation problem is to minimise the total impacts caused by all species.

However, given that a species' entry, establishment, spread, impact and response to management are likely to be uncertain, the precise form of the objective should also reflect the manager's tolerance of risk. A risk-neutral manager focuses on the impacts that are most likely or can be expected on average. A risk-averse manager places more emphasis on avoiding undesirable outcomes, while a risk-prone manager focuses on opportunities for unusually beneficial outcomes. A range of objective functions and solution techniques are available in each case, and we discuss these further in Section 14.6.

Joseph et al. (2009) developed a heuristic scheme for prioritising species conservation projects that takes a risk-neutral approach. They rank projects using the score

$$E_i = W_i \times B_i \times \frac{S_i}{C_i}, \tag{14.1}$$

where W_i is a weighting incorporating social, political or biological values for species i; B_i is the benefit of investing in a project conserving species i; S_i is the probability that the project is successful; and C_i is the cost of investing in the project. These parameters could be redefined in a biosecurity context with W_i being the impact of an unmanaged species i infestation; B_i the expected proportional reduction in impact brought about by detection and response; S_i the probability that infestation management is successful; and C_i the cost of infestation management.

The highest scoring projects are selected for investment until the budget is exhausted, and these projects yield the highest expected return per unit invested. This ranking approach approximates an optimisation of expected total impact, subject to an investment budget, and is known as the *greedy algorithm* (Martello & Toth, 1990). It should provide optimal or near-optimal solutions when the cost of individual projects tends to be much smaller than the total budget.

In the study of Joseph et al. (2009), conservation projects are of a predefined size; each comes at a known cost and is expected to yield a single corresponding outcome. McCarthy et al. (2010) explored a set of resource allocation problems in which investment in a given option (i.e. species) can be varied continuously with corresponding variation in outcomes. The more a manager invests in managing species i, the less impact species i is expected to have on the local environment.

When the relationship between species impact and management investment is linear or displays diminishing returns, the solution can easily be represented

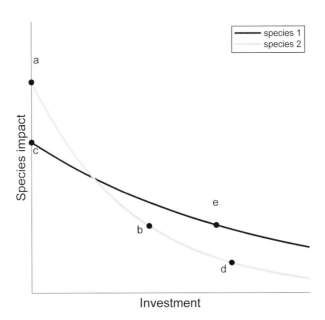

Figure 14.1.   Graphical representation of optimal investment in management of species to minimise overall impacts. Each curve represents the relationship between investment and ultimate impact for a different species. Species 2 is prioritised for investment because of its steep slope at point *a*. If the total budget exceeds the investment at point *b*, then it is optimal to invest in both species 1 and 2 because the slope at point *c* is equal to the slope at point *b*. The budget should be exhausted such that positions on each investment curve have the same slope (e.g. points *d* and *e*).

graphically (see Figure 14.1). The rate at which impacts are reduced per unit of investment (the gradient or steepness of the slope) determines the cost-effectiveness of an option. The optimal strategy is, therefore, to 'invest in the options for which the marginal benefits [impact reduction per unit investment] are large, and invest to a level in each such that the marginal benefits are equal' (McCarthy et al., 2010, p. 1281). In Figure 14.1, the relationship between investment and consequent species impact is plotted for hypothetical species 1 and 2. Investment in species 2 is initially more cost effective because impact reduction per unit investment (the slope of the graph) is largest at point *a*. When investment exceeds point *b*, returns on investment have diminished so that investment in species 1 and species 2 is equally cost effective: the slope of the graph at point *b* equals the slope of the graph at point *c*. When the investment budget is exhausted, the optimal allocation invests to a level in each species so that cost-effectiveness is equal (e.g. points *d* and *e*, where the curves have the same slope).

While this graphical approach may be useful for a small set of candidate species, algorithms are required to optimise investment across many species. McCarthy et al. (2010) provide explicit solutions to this problem when the relationship between expected impact and investment is linear, exponential or hyperbolic. A spreadsheet is available to solve the exponential case (Hauser, 2009). McCarthy et al. (2010)

found that when the impact–investment relationship is uncertain, resources should be invested across a broader range of options (i.e. species), thus avoiding reliance on the few investments that are currently thought to be highly cost effective.

The prioritisation methods proposed by Joseph et al. (2009) and McCarthy et al. (2010) measure the impact W_i of invasive species in a single currency. However, species may have an impact on a range of values relating to the environment, economic revenue or public health. Methods exist for weighing various impact types and aggregating values into a single currency, such as cost–benefit analysis and multi-criteria decision-analysis. Multi-criteria decision-analysis is increasingly being used for prioritisation in a biosecurity context because it offers scope to elicit preferences from a range of stakeholders (e.g. Benke et al., 2011; Cook & Proctor, 2007; Hurley et al., 2009). Criteria must be scaled carefully to ensure that the process is well calibrated and subsequent species rankings are robust (Steele et al., 2009).

14.3 How? Allocating Resources across Management Actions

When an invasive species has been identified as warranting management, there are usually a range of potential management actions. These actions could be different control methods, for example, burning, herbicide application or mechanical removal. Alternatively, they could be actions that target different stages of invasion, for example, choosing to invest in quarantine versus surveillance or containment versus eradication.

If the set of candidate management actions are independent, that is, the benefit of implementing an action does not depend on the amount invested in other actions, then this allocation problem can be solved using the methods described in the Section 14.2. The methods of Joseph et al. (2009) and McCarthy et al. (2010) can be easily adapted to this problem by taking the index i to refer to candidate management actions rather than candidate taxa.

Dependencies between management actions become particularly important when allocating across the biosecurity continuum, that is, between pre- and post-border management of a species. For example, the earlier an invasion is detected, the more successful control and eradication efforts can be. The amount invested in surveillance to detect an invasion can, therefore, affect the subsequent amount of control effort needed. There has been considerable research into these types of questions, with models exploring the trade-offs between quarantine and control (Burnett et al., 2006, 2008; Finnoff et al., 2007; Finnoff & Tschirhart, 2005; Leung et al., 2002; Olson & Roy, 2005), surveillance and control (Bogich et al., 2008; Epanchin-Niell & Hastings, 2010; Mehta et al., 2007), quarantine and surveillance (Moore et al., 2010) and between all three actions (Polasky, 2010; Rout et al., 2011, 2014).

Moore et al. (2010) used a simple model of island invasion to find the optimal allocation of resources for quarantine and surveillance, and were able to identify some general rules of thumb for management. They describe the invasive species as being absent, localised or widespread on the island (Figure 14.2). If localised,

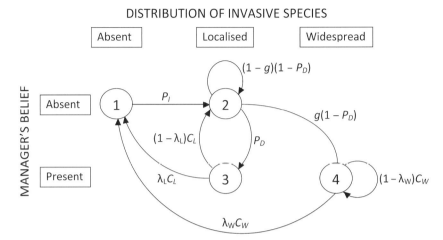

Figure 14.2.   A diagram describing the island invasion model, adapted from Moore et al. (2010). Given the possible combinations of species distribution and the manager's belief about the species, the species can be (1) absent, (2) localised and undetected, (3) localised and detected or (4) widespread and detected. The probability of incursion P_I is a function of the amount invested in quarantine, while the probability of detection P_D is a function of the amount invested in surveillance. If not detected when localised, the species has probability g of becoming widespread. Localised and widespread invasions are successfully eradicated with probabilities λ_L and λ_W respectively, and their combined costs of eradication and impact are C_L and C_W respectively.
[Reprinted with permission from Moore, J., Rout, T. M., Hauser, C. E., Moro, D., Jones, M., Wilcox, C. & Possingham, H. P. (2010). Protecting islands from pest invasion: optimal allocation of biosecurity resources between quarantine and surveillance. Biological Conservation, 143(5), 1068–1078.]

the invasive species can be detected only by investing in surveillance. If widespread, the invasive species is certain to be detected, even without surveillance. There are benefits to detecting the species early; if it is detected while localised, it has only a small impact and costs a small amount to eradicate, while if it becomes widespread, it has a much larger impact and costs much more to eradicate. The probability of quarantine and surveillance being successful increases as investment in each action increases, albeit with diminishing returns. While Moore et al. (2010) illustrated their model with a case study of black rat invasion on an island, this general model could be applied equally well to animal or plant invasion of any isolated site.

Moore et al. (2010) take a risk-neutral approach, minimising the total expected cost of keeping the island invasion free. This expected cost includes investment in management as well as the ecological, economic and social costs of the impact of an invasive species. When aiming to minimise the total cost, it will never be optimal to invest more in preventative management than the cost of the worst possible outcome. The expected cost of the species entering and becoming widespread (its impact and cost of eradication) provides an upper limit on the total amount to invest in quarantine and surveillance.

The effectiveness of quarantine and surveillance, that is, the rate at which their probability of success increases as investment is increased, affects the optimal amount to invest in each. Moore et al. (2010) found that if quarantine is more effective than surveillance, it is best to invest only in quarantine. However, if surveillance is more effective, it can be best to invest in both quarantine and surveillance simultaneously. Surveillance is useful only if there is a benefit to catching the invasion early, so the amount to invest in surveillance also depends on the ratio of the impact of localised invasions to the impact of widespread invasions. Even the outcome of an optimal decision is likely to be expensive unless quarantine is cost effective.

14.4   Where? Allocating Resources across Space

When post-border management of an invasive species has been prioritised, resources must typically be deployed in a heterogeneous environment. The species is more likely to be introduced and become established at some locations rather than others. The species may be more visible or amenable to control in some circumstances over others. The species may have an impact on some features of the landscape more severely than others. How should resources be allocated to account for such variation?

Hauser and McCarthy (2009) determined how to allocate staff time to surveys for a weed. They divide a heterogeneous landscape into equal-sized cells that can be treated as homogeneous units. For each cell, they require a measure of the following:

1. *The probability that the weed is present*, based on its likely introduction, spread and establishment
2. *The benefit of successfully detecting the weed*, based on the cost of weed control and the value of the cell
3. *The detectability of the weed*, based on local conditions for survey.

They assumed that the probability of successfully detecting the weed in a cell, when it is present, depends on both local conditions and the time spent searching (Garrard et al., 2008; Moore et al., 2011). Believing the vegetation type to be the key influence on detection, they developed contrasting detection functions for shrubby and low grassy cells (Figure 14.3).

Hauser and McCarthy (2009) adopted a risk-neutral approach, focusing on the expected (mean) impact in cells containing undetected weeds. They examined the survey design problem from two different perspectives:

1. Allocating survey effort to optimally trade its cost against the expected (mean) impacts caused by undetected invaders
2. Allocating a survey budget to minimise the expected (mean) impacts caused by undetected invaders.

In both cases, they found that the importance of including each cell in the survey could be rated using the same score,

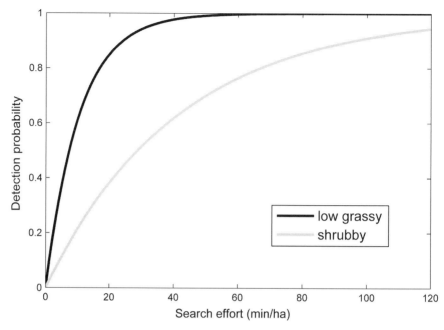

Figure 14.3.   Detection functions proposed by Hauser and McCarthy (2009) for ground searches of
flowering orange hawkweed plants in south-eastern Australia. The probability of detecting
the weed, when it is present, depends on the surrounding vegetation (low grassy or
shrubby) and time spent searching.
[Reprinted with permission from Hauser, C. E. & McCarthy, M. A. (2009). Streamlining
'search and destroy': Cost-effective surveillance for invasive species management. Ecology
Letters, 12(7), 683–692.]

$$\text{cell score} = \frac{\text{probability of}}{\text{weed occurrence}} \times \frac{\text{benefit of weed}}{\text{detection}} \times \frac{\text{local weed}}{\text{detectability}}, \quad (14.2)$$

with the highest-scoring cells offering the greatest potential for reducing weed
impact from survey. These cells are likely to contain the weed; offer large benefits
from detecting and treating any weeds present; and provide conditions under which
any weeds can be detected easily, relative to other cells.

The optimal survey duration at each cell is a more complicated function of the
input variables (see equations 2, 5–7 in Hauser & McCarthy, 2009). The more likely
it is that the weed is present, the longer the optimal search time (Figure 14.4a).
Likewise, higher benefits associated with weed detection and treatment yield longer
optimal search times (Figure 14.4b). However, these relationships are non-linear,
and only a small additional search time is justified at the highest levels of these
parameters. The effect of weed detectability on optimal search time is more complex still (Figure 14.4c). Cells in which it is extremely difficult to find the weed
should not be surveyed at all. Cells in which it is somewhat difficult to find the
weed require long search times to determine the species' presence or absence with

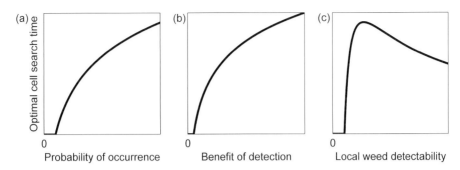

Figure 14.4.   Optimal search time for a cell as a function of **(a)** the probability that the cell contains the weed, **(b)** the benefits obtained by detecting and treating the weed and **(c)** the detectability of the weed under local conditions.

confidence. Cells in which it is easy to find the weed require only short searches to achieve equivalent confidence.

The optimal allocation of surveillance resources can be calculated using a spreadsheet with one row per cell (Hauser, 2009). Data can be imported and exported from a spreadsheet, allowing for useful visualisations such as maps (Figure 14.5). High-priority areas for surveillance can be identified clearly in space and related back to the input data. Williams et al. (2008) predicted the likelihood of orange hawkweed occurrence across south-eastern Australia's Alpine National Park as a function of likely seed dispersal from the known source and habitat suitability for hawkweed establishment (Figure 14.5a). Hauser and McCarthy (2009) identified the broad vegetation type in each cell from the data of Williams et al. (2008) (Figure 14.5b) and associated these with detection functions (Figure 14.3). The search time that optimally trades survey costs against expected impacts from detection failures is influenced by both of these inputs (Figure 14.5c). Effort is most concentrated in regions with a high likelihood of seed arrival and establishment; within these regions, shrubby locations require longer searches to accumulate sufficient confidence that hawkweed is absent, rather than present and undetected.

Hauser and McCarthy's (2009) study effectively treated each cell in the landscape independently. They ignored the variable costs of travelling between cells during the survey (later addressed by Moore and McCarthy, 2016), and intended that the spatial correlations between cells and the dynamics of management be captured using the input data. Many other studies have taken a more strategic approach to invasive species management by explicitly modelling population and management dynamics; a range of these are summarised in Section 2.2.

14.5   Combining Allocation Questions

While many management problems can be related to one of the three questions outlined in Sections 14.2 to 14.4, there are situations when it is necessary or

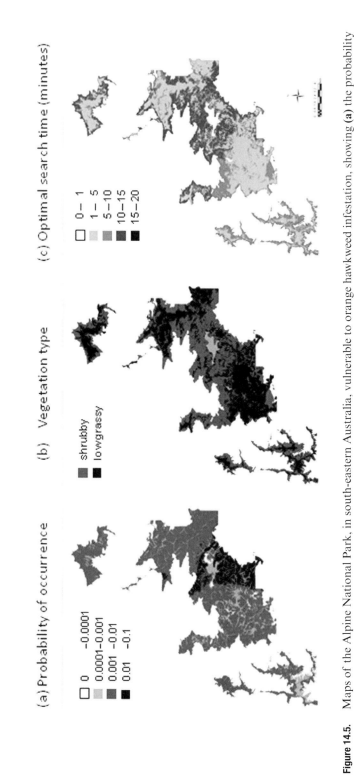

(a) Probability of occurrence   (b)   Vegetation type   (c) Optimal search time (minutes)

Probability of occurrence legend:
- 0 – 0.0001
- 0.0001–0.001
- 0.001 –0.01
- 0.01 –0.1

Vegetation type legend:
- shrubby
- lowgrassy

Optimal search time legend:
- 0 – 1
- 1 – 5
- 5 – 10
- 10 – 15
- 15 – 20

Figure 14.5.   Maps of the Alpine National Park, in south-eastern Australia, vulnerable to orange hawkweed infestation, showing **(a)** the probability of occurrence, as predicted by Williams et al. (2008), **(b)** vegetation type (affecting detectability as in Figure 14.3) and **(c)** search time (in minutes) that optimally trades survey cost against expected impact, when a detection failure is expected to incur 100-fold costs beyond successful detection and treatment.

[Reprinted with permission from Hauser, C. E. & McCarthy, M. A. (2009). Streamlining 'search and destroy': cost-effective surveillance for invasive species management. Ecology Letters, 12(7), 683–692.]

advantageous to consider more than one question simultaneously. For instance, the question of which species to manage can be inextricably linked to the question of where to manage them. Evans et al. (2011) considered both these questions for invasive rabbits and foxes in Australia, and found that incorporating spatial dependencies in the impact of these species increased the cost-effectiveness of management. The interactions between rabbits and foxes and the native species they threaten mean that, in some areas, the benefit of managing both species simultaneously is much greater than the summed benefits of managing them separately. There can also be spatial dependencies in the costs of management, and managing multiple species in a single area can be cheaper than the sum of managing each species separately (Evans et al., 2011).

While these interdependencies may be important for some management problems, expanding the scope of a problem comes at a price: the more complex a problem becomes, the more difficult it is to solve and to understand and communicate the results. Decision problems must, therefore, be framed in a parsimonious way, incorporating only the elements that are really influential within the system and important to the decision maker.

14.6   Uncertainties and Risk Tolerance

Resource allocation occurs in the face of uncertainty and natural variation. The allocation examples discussed in this chapter have focused on risk-neutral strategies, which produce the best outcomes when we average over all plausible scenarios. Managers may instead have a risk-prone (emphasis on positive outcomes) or risk-averse (emphasis on negative outcomes) attitude towards uncertainty; for invasive species management risk-neutral and risk-averse objectives are generally most relevant.

Early literature on optimal portfolio investment (Markovitz, 1952; Roy, 1952) recognised that decision makers are likely to be interested in both positive average outcomes and reliable outcomes across the range of uncertainty (i.e. low variation in outcomes). Among the set of efficient allocations, there is typically a trade-off between positive average outcomes and high reliability. A manager's level of risk tolerance could be placed at any point along this trade-off curve, from risk-neutral (maximising average outcomes with no concern for variation) to entirely risk-averse (minimising variation in possible outcomes with no concern for positive outcomes).

To derive an optimal solution to a resource allocation problem, the decision maker's relative preferences for positive outcomes and reliability must be articulated in some sense. Because the risk-neutral approach takes an average across all possible scenarios, a set of probabilities or belief weightings need to be ascribed to the full range of plausible scenarios. Not all approaches require weightings. For example, a worst-case analysis identifies the worst possible outcome under each candidate allocation and selects the allocation with the best outcome. This is an extremely risk-averse approach, where the solution is derived from the single worst outcome for each scenario.

Another risk-averse approach is the use of a regret function (see Chapter 13 for more detail). A regret function shows the losses incurred from selection of a candidate allocation instead of the optimal allocation when the true underlying scenario is known (i.e. in the case without uncertainty). Decision makers can view those losses across all plausible scenarios and select an allocation that yields tolerable losses across all scenarios. This selection can be made by weighting and averaging scenarios or by focusing on the greatest loss scenario for each candidate allocation; these same methods can be applied to the outcomes themselves in the risk-neutral and worst-case approaches already discussed.

There are also a range of methods that impose thresholds on acceptable and unacceptable outcomes. The *safety first* approach was introduced early in the development of investment portfolio theory (Roy, 1952), and has since been applied to the management of veterinary diseases (Prattley et al., 2007). The safety first approach requires that a target outcome be set, and identifies an allocation of resources that maximises the probability that the target will be met. Info-gap theory (see Chapter 12) identifies the resource allocation that meets a target outcome under the broadest range of plausible scenarios, without weighting the relative likelihood of each scenario.

Although minimising impact is a common objective for most invasive species management, there are an infinite number of ways that preferences can be expressed, particularly with regard to the trade-off between expected impact and plausible variation around the mean expectation. It is important that the objective function selected reflects the preferences of the stakeholders involved with, or affected by, the resource allocation decision.

14.7   Conclusion

Deciding how to best allocate limited resources is a pervasive problem in the management of invasive species. Fortunately, tools exist for answering resource allocation questions. Risk-neutral approaches are the most common among invasive species studies, including those we have covered in detail in this chapter. Other risk-averse approaches have been introduced to the invasive species literature more recently, and the solution techniques discussed here can be adapted for this purpose by altering the objective. Chapters 12 and 13 discuss risk-averse methods for decision making under uncertainty. The optimal resource allocation is driven by the stated objective, and it is, therefore, most important that the objective function reflects the preferences and risk tolerance of the stakeholders involved with, or affected by, the resource allocation decision.

When optimal solutions to resource allocation problems are sought, quantitative optimisation techniques are required. Some of the solution approaches discussed here [e.g. the project prioritisation protocol of Joseph et al. (2009) and the efficient environmental management of McCarthy et al. (2010)] are highly adaptable to a range of problems. Others (e.g. the quarantine and surveillance allocation of Moore et al. (2010) and fox and rabbit management of Evans et al. (2011)] are tailored to more specific problem structures. The original articles offer more detailed accounts of the optimisation techniques used, and many other resource allocation problems for invasive species have been solved and published in the academic literature. More general literature on optimisation methods for scientists and engineers (e.g. Bhatti, 2000; Sarker & Newton, 2008; Sethi & Thompson, 2006) may assist in posing and solving unique problems of resource allocation management.

14.8   Acknowledgements

The authors thank Mark Burgman, John Kean, Terry Walshe and Susie Hester for helpful comments and contributions. CEH was supported by an Australian Research Council Linkage Grant (LP100100441), and TMR was supported by an Australian Research Council Discovery Grant (DP110101499).

References

Benke, K. K., Steel, J. L., & Weiss, J. E. (2011). Risk assessment models for invasive species: Uncertainty in rankings from multi-criteria analysis. *Biological Invasions*, 13(1), 239–253.

Bhatti, M. A. (2000). *Practical optimization methods: With mathematica applications*. New York: Springer-Verlag.

Bogich, T. L., Liebhold, A. M. & Shea, K. (2008). To sample or eradicate? A cost minimization model for monitoring and managing an invasive species. *Journal of Applied Ecology*, 45(4), 1134–1142.

Burnett, K. M., D'Evelyn, S., Kaiser, B. A., Nantamanasikarn, P. & Roumasset, J. A. (2008). Beyond the lampost: Optimal prevention and control of the brown tree snake in Hawaii. *Ecological Economics*, 67(1), 66–74.

Burnett, K. M., Kaiser, B. A., Pitafi, B. A. & Roumasset, J. A. (2006). Prevention, eradication, and containment of invasive species: Illustrations from Hawaii. *Agricultural and Resource Economics Review*, 35(1), 63–77.

Cook, D. & Proctor, W. (2007). Assessing the threat of exotic plant pests. *Ecological Economics*, 63(2–3), 594–604.

Epanchin-Niell, R. S. & Hastings, A. (2010). Controlling established invaders: Integrating economics and spread dynamics to determine optimal management. *Ecology Letters*, 13(4), 528–541.

Evans, M. C., Possingham, H. P. & Wilson, K. A. (2011). What to do in the face of multiple threats? Incorporating dependencies within a return on investment framework for conservation. *Diversity and Distributions*, 17(3), 437–450.

Finnoff, D., Shogren, J. F., Leung, B. & Lodge, D. (2007). Take a risk: Preferring prevention over control of biological invaders. *Ecological Economics*, 62(2), 216–333.

Finnoff, D. & Tschirhart, J. (2005). Identifying, preventing and controlling invasive plant species using their physiological traits. *Ecological Economics*, 52(3), 397–416.

Garrard, G. E., Bekessy, S. A., McCarthy, M. A. & Wintle, B. A. (2008). When have we looked hard enough? A novel method for setting minimum survey protocols for flora surveys. *Austral Ecology*, 33(8), 986–998.

Hauser, C. (2009). Where and how much? A spreadsheet that allocates surveillance effort for a weed. *Plant Protection Quarterly*, 24(3), 94–97.

Hauser, C. E. & McCarthy, M. A. (2009). Streamlining 'search and destroy': Cost-effective surveillance for invasive species management. *Ecology Letters*, 12(7), 683–692.

Howard, R. A. (2007). The foundations of decision analysis revisited. In W. Edwards, R. F. Miles Jr. & D. Von Winterdfeldt (eds.), *Advances in decision analysis: From foundations to applications* pp. 32–56. Cambridge: Cambridge University Press.

Hurley, M., Lowell, K., Cook, D., et al. (2009). How model outputs can be used to improve decision-making: Using bio-economic model outputs in deliberative multi-criteria evaluation to prioritize invasive pest species. In R. S. Anderssen, R. D. Braddock & L. T. Newham (eds.), *Proceedings of the 18th World IMACS Congress and MODSIM09 International Congress on Modelling and Simulation* (pp. 2894–2900).Modelling and Simulation Society of Australia and New Zealand and International Association for Mathematics and Computers in Simulation.

Joseph, L. N., Maloney, R. F. & Possingham, H. P. (2009). Optimal allocation of resources among threatened species: A project prioritization protocol. *Conservation Biology*, 23(2), 328–338.

Leung, B., Lodge, D., Finnoff, D., et al. (2002). An ounce of prevention or a pound of cure: Bioeconomic risk analysis of invasive species. *Proceedings of the Royal Society of London B: Biological Sciences*, 269(1508), 2407–2413.

Markovitz, H. (1952). Portfolio selection. *Journal of Finance*, 7(1), 77–91.

Martello, S. & Toth, P. (1990). *Knapsack problems: Algorithms and computer implementations*. Chichester: John Wiley & Sons.

McCarthy, M. A., Thompson, C. J., Hauser, C., et al. (2010). Resource allocation for efficient environmental management. *Ecology Letters*, 13(10), 1280–1289.

Mehta, S. V., Haight, R. G., Homans, F. R., Polasky, S. & Venette, R. C. (2007). Optimal detection and control strategies for invasive species management. *Ecological Economics*, 61(2–3), 237–245.

Moore, A. L. & McCarthy, M. A. (2016). Optimizing ecological survey effort over space and time. *Methods in Ecology and Evolution*, 7(8), 891–899.

Moore, J. L., Hauser, C. E., Bear, J. L., Williams, N. S. G. & McCarthy, M. A. (2011). Estimating detection-effort curves for plants using search experiments. *Ecological Applications*, 21(2), 601–607.

Moore, J., Rout, T. M., Hauser, C. E., et al. (2010). Protecting islands from pest invasion: Optimal allocation of biosecurity resources between quarantine and surveillance. *Biological Conservation*, 143(5), 1068–1078.

Olson, L. J. & Roy, S. (2005). On prevention and control of an uncertain biological invasion. *Review of Agricultural Economics*, 27(3), 491–497.

Pimentel, D., Zuniga, R. & Morrison, D. (2005). Update on the environmental and economic costs associated with alien-invasive species in the United States. *Ecological Economics*, 52(3), 273–288.

Polasky, S. (2010). A model of prevention, detection and control for invasive species. In C. Perrings, H. A. Mooney & M. Williamson (eds.), *Bioinvasions and globalisation: Ecology, economics, management, and policy* (pp. 100–109). New York: Oxford University Press.

Prattley, D. J., Morris, R. S., Stevenson, M. A. & Thornton, R. (2007). Application of portfolio theory to risk-based allocation of surveillance resources in animal populations. *Preventive Veterinary Medicine*, 81(1–3), 56–69.

Rout, T. M., Moore, J. L. & McCarthy, M. A. (2014). Prevent, search or destroy? A partially observable model for invasive species management. *Journal of Applied Ecology*, 51(3), 804–813.

Rout, T. M., Moore, J. L., Possingham, H. P. & McCarthy, M. A. (2011). Allocating biosecurity resources between preventing, detecting, and eradicating island invasions. *Ecological Economics*, 71, 54–62.

Roy, A. D. (1952). Safety first and the holding of assets. *Econometrica*, 20(3), 431–449.

Sarker, R. A. & Newton, C. S. (2008). *Optimization modelling: A practical approach.* Boca Raton, FL: CRC Press.

Sethi, S. P. & Thompson, G. L. (2006). *Optimal control theory: Applications to management science and economics*, 2nd ed. New York: Springer Science+Business Media.

Steele, K., Carmel, Y., Cross, J. & Wilcox, C. (2009). Uses and misuses of multi-criteria decision analysis (MCDA) in environmental decision-making. *Risk Analysis*, 29(1), 26–33.

Williams, N. S. G., Hahs, A. K. & Morgan, J. W. (2008). A dispersal-constrained habitat suitability model for predicting invasion of alpine vegetation. *Ecological Applications*, 18(2), 347–359.

15 Value of Information Analysis as a Decision Support Tool for Biosecurity

Michael C. Runge, Tracy M. Rout, Daniel A. Spring and Terry Walshe

15.1   Introduction

Invasive species managers often make decisions in the face of considerable uncertainty (Parma et al., 1998). For example, they may be uncertain about the spatial extent of an invasion, the efficacy of treatment options or the various life-history characteristics of species.

In some cases, managers have the option of reducing uncertainty by investing in monitoring or experimentation. However, this often means diverting resources away from control actions, or delaying actions until the results of research are known. It is therefore important for managers to assess the benefits and costs of collecting this additional information. Some uncertainties, although scientifically interesting to resolve, may not actually affect decision making. Managers must determine whether investing in collecting additional information will lead to a better management outcome, and if so, how much better?

These questions can be answered using a method known as value of information (VOI) analysis (Raiffa & Schlaifer, 1961). VOI analysis was developed within the theory of information economics and has been applied to decision problems in diverse fields such as medicine (Groot Koerkamp et al., 2008; Singh et al., 2008), epidemiology and health risk management (Shea et al., 2014; Yokota & Thompson, 2004a, 2004b) and resource exploration (Eidsvik et al., 2008). In the domain of invasive species, Wiles (2004) emphasises the relevance of decision science and VOI analysis to weed management. D'Evelyn et al. (2008) identify circumstances in which information on population size obtained via catch-per-unit effort in a species control program can contribute substantially to reducing total costs. Sahlin et al. (2011) apply VOI analyses to evaluate the benefit of improving the accuracy of a trait-based screening model of species invasiveness. Ward and Kompas (2010) provide an illustrative analysis of the value of resolving uncertainty in the magnitude of damages caused by fire ants in Australia arising from the transfer of estimated impacts in the United States. Applications in environmental management beyond invasive species are emerging (Maxwell et al., 2015; Moore & Runge, 2012; Runge et al., 2011; Williams et al., 2012), suggesting that the tool may be underutilised.

VOI analysis has been recommended particularly as a decision support tool for complex problems with high stakes and large uncertainties (Yokota & Thompson, 2004b). To be more specific, VOI analysis is useful in situations in which

- A decision must be made, for example, choosing between candidate management actions.
- There is uncertainty in elements of this decision.
- Information can be collected to resolve all or part of this uncertainty.
- There is debate about whether the benefits of resolving uncertainty outweigh the direct and opportunity costs of gathering the information.

VOI analysis assesses the benefit of collecting this information while considering the context of the decision to be made.

Assume a manager must choose between several possible management actions, and this choice is affected by an uncertain variable. The simplest type of VOI calculation is the expected value of perfect information (EVPI; Howard, 1966). This calculates the expected improvement in the outcome of the decision if all uncertainty could be resolved. The equation for the EVPI is

$$\text{EVPI} = \int_{s \in S} [\max_{a \in A} u(a,s)] f(s) \, ds - \max_{a \in A} [\int_{s \in S} u(a,s) f(s) \, ds], \qquad (15.1)$$

where $f(s)$ is the probability of the uncertain variable taking value s, and $u(a, s)$ is the utility of taking action a when the uncertain variable has value s.

The first half of this equation calculates the expected utility with perfect information, assuming that if the decision maker knew the value s of the uncertain variable, he or she would choose the action with the highest utility for that particular value. This utility is then multiplied by the probability that the true value is s, and summed for all possible values of s. The second half of the equation describes the scenario under uncertainty, assuming the decision maker will take the action with the highest expected utility across all possible values of the uncertain variable. In this way, the equation finds the difference in expected utility between the best decision given perfect information and the best decision under uncertainty. That is, the calculation answers the question, 'what is the difference in the expected outcome of the decision under certainty and uncertainty?' If the utilities are measured in dollars, then the output of this calculation is the absolute maximum that should be spent on research or monitoring to improve knowledge about this uncertain variable.

Biosecurity is the applied management field that deals with the effect of invasive organisms on a nation, state or community's economic livelihood, health, recreation or well-being. Agencies responsible for biosecurity sometimes distinguish among pre-border activities (preventing the arrival of an invasive species by taking action before it reaches the border), border activities (detection and treatment at the moment of arrival, e.g., at ports of entry) and post-border activities (management of invasive species after its arrival and possible establishment). In this chapter we demonstrate how VOI analysis could be used for practical decision making in biosecurity, focusing on the common post-border decision problem of choosing whether to eradicate or contain an invasion. Throughout this chapter, we use the value of perfect information to find the maximum amount to invest in reducing uncertainty. We show how the analysis can be tailored to a specific management problem, illustrated with a case study of red imported fire ants in south-east Queensland.

15.2   Prototype for a Post-border Biosecurity Decision

Here we develop a prototype VOI analysis for deciding whether to eradicate or contain an existing infestation. We consider the decision a one-off, irrevocable allocation of resources to either eradication or containment. The expected costs and benefits of either action are a function of the extent of the infestation. From analysis of these costs and benefits we can determine a threshold extent, above which it is optimal to contain, and below which it is optimal to eradicate. Uncertainty in the extent of the infestation induces uncertainty about the optimal decision. In the circumstances we consider, we have the option to learn the extent of infestation precisely before committing our resources. We calculate the expected improvement in management from obtaining that information, allowing us to determine whether it is worth the cost to acquire it.

15.2.1   The Decision Model

Let x be the extent of a circular infestation in hectares (square hectometres, hm²). If we choose the contain action, we will incur an expense that is proportional to the perimeter of infestation, and we will seek to contain the infestation at that extent for the indefinite future. The cost would be spread over the time frame of interest. This might be a fixed time horizon, or might be viewed as the net present value of annual payments made over an infinite time horizon; either way, the cost is finite. Thus, the cost of containment (Figure 15.1a) is

$$\text{Cost}(C) = c_1 \cdot 2\sqrt{\pi x}, \tag{15.2}$$

where c_1 is the long-term cost of containment per hectometre (hm, 100 m) of perimeter.

If we choose the eradicate action, we incur a large, immediate expense that is proportional to the areal extent of infestation. If the eradication succeeds, the infestation is removed and there are no further costs. If the eradication fails, then the containment cost is incurred and we assume, for the sake of simplicity, that the infestation remains at the original extent in perpetuity. The probability of failure is an increasing function of the extent of infestation, taking a sigmoid shape (Figure 15.1b),

$$p(\text{failure}) = \frac{1}{1 + e^{-m(x-a)}}, \tag{15.3}$$

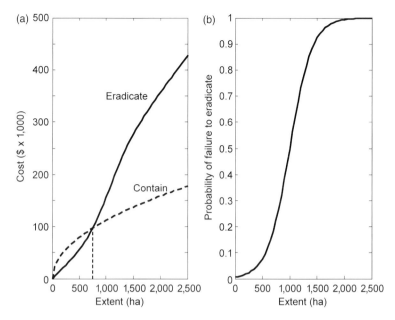

Figure 15.1. Costs of management actions as a function of extent of infestation. **(a)** Costs of eradication and containment, where the cost of containment (c_1) is \$1,000 per 100 m of perimeter and the cost of eradication (c_2) is \$100 per hectare. The total costs of containment and eradication are equal when the extent of infestation is 753 ha. **(b)** Probability of failure to eradicate as a function of extent of infestation, where the half-effectiveness area (a) is 1,000 ha and the efficiency slope (m) is 0.005. Note: All costs are given in Australian dollars.

where a is the half-effectiveness area (at which the probability of failure is 50%), and m measures how steep the failure curve is near the inflection point. Then, the expected cost of eradication (Figure 15.1a) is

$$\text{Cost}(E) = c_2 x + \frac{2c_1 \sqrt{\pi x}}{1 + e^{-m(x-a)}}, \tag{15.4}$$

where c_2 is the cost of eradication per hectare, and the second term is the cost of containment times the probability of failure to eradicate.

In addition to the costs of management, we need to consider the losses associated with the long-term presence of the infestation (due to loss of production, social amenity, etc.). It is reasonable that these losses are proportional to the extent of infestation. If the contain action is taken, the long-term extent of infestation is the current extent of infestation, x. If the eradication action is taken, the long-term extent of infestation is 0 if eradication succeeds, and x if eradication fails. Therefore, the expected loss, as a function of the initial extent of infestation, is

$$\text{Loss} = \begin{cases} c_3 x & \text{if containment} \\ \dfrac{c_3 x}{1 + e^{-m(x-a)}} & \text{if eradication} \end{cases}, \tag{15.5}$$

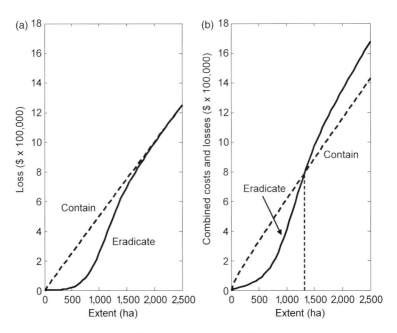

Figure 15.2. Production and amenity losses **(a)** combined with management costs **(b)** as a function of initial extent of infestation, for two management actions. The production and amenity loss rate (c_3) is \$500 per hectare. The decision threshold occurs at 1,321 ha; if the extent of infestation is less than this, the best course of action is eradication; otherwise, the best course of action is long-term containment. At this level of infestation, the cost of eradication is \$239,000 and the cost of containment is \$129,000, but eradication is expected to reduce the production and amenity losses more than containment. All costs are given in Australian dollars.

where c_3 is the net present value of the long-term loss per hectare of infestation (Figure 15.2a).

The combined losses and costs, T, can be found by summing Eqs. 15.2, 15.4 and 15.5,

$$T = \begin{cases} 2c_1\sqrt{\pi x} + c_3 x & \text{if containment} \\ c_2 x + \dfrac{2c_1\sqrt{\pi x} + c_3 x}{1+e^{-m(x-a)}} & \text{if eradication} \end{cases} \tag{15.6}$$

The objective to minimise the combined losses and costs gives rise to a threshold extent of infestation, x^*, below which it is optimal to attempt eradication, and above which it is optimal to commit to long-term containment (Figure 15.2b):

$$x^* : 2c_1\sqrt{\pi x^*} + c_3 x^* = c_2 x^* + \dfrac{2c_1\sqrt{\pi x^*} + c_3 x^*}{1+e^{-m(x^*-a)}}. \tag{15.7}$$

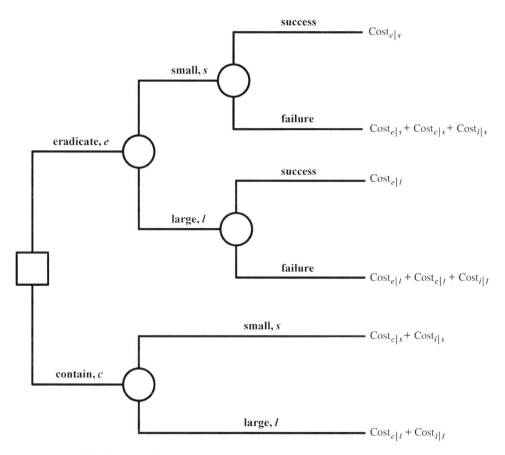

Figure 15.3.   A decision tree illustrating the choice between eradication e and containment c for the scenario with binary uncertainty in the extent of the infestation (small s, or large l). The costs of eradication, containment, and impact i are greater for large infestations, as given by Eqs. 15.2, 15.4 and 15.5. The probability that eradication will fail is also greater for large infestations, as given by Eq. 15.3. The tree assumes that if eradication fails, management reverts to containment.

15.2.2   Binary Uncertainty

Now, suppose that we are uncertain about the extent of infestation, x. This uncertainty about the state of the system may induce uncertainty about which action to take. Further, let us suppose that we could undertake a survey that would allow us to reduce this uncertainty before we had to make the decision (and suppose that the survey could be conducted fast enough so there were no consequences associated with delaying action, other than the cost of the survey). How much would this survey be worth to us?

First, by way of a simple illustration of the value of perfect information, imagine that our uncertainty is binary, that is, the extent is either 750 ha (small) or 1,750 ha (large; Figure 15.3).

Table 15.1. Expected value of perfect information with binary uncertainty in the extent of infestation

	Small extent (750 ha)	Large extent (1,750 ha)	Weighted average
	Belief = 0.4	Belief = 0.6	
Action: Contain	$472,080	$1,023,300	$802,810
Action: Eradicate	$180,130	$1,174,800	$776,920
Best	$180,130	$1,023,300	$686,030
EVPI			$ 90,890

The entries are the combined costs and losses associated with each action and the extent of the infestation. The parameters for the cost and loss functions are those given in Figures 15.1 to 15.3. The value of information is expressed in Australian dollars.

A standard analysis of the expected VOI (Eq. 15.2) using the parameters given in Figures 15.1 to 15.3, gives the total costs and losses shown in Table 15.1.

With a prior belief of 0.4 that the extent is small, the best action to take in the face of uncertainty is to eradicate, because the expected total loss is $776,900 versus $802,800 (losses are given in Australian dollars). If we could resolve that uncertainty ahead of time, we would eradicate if the extent is small (expected loss = AU$180,100), and contain if the extent is large (expected loss = AU$1.023 million). Averaging over the prior beliefs that we would discover those states of nature, the expected total loss, provided we can resolve uncertainty first, is $686,000. Thus, by reducing uncertainty, we decrease our expected loss by $90,890. So the expected value of perfect information is $90,890, and we should be willing to pay up to that amount for the survey that would let us know the extent of the infestation.

15.2.3   Continuous Uncertainty

Next, consider a more realistic situation, and suppose instead that our uncertainty about the extent of infestation is continuous and can be expressed by a probability distribution, $f(x)$, defined for $0 \leq x < \infty$. For example, our prior belief that the extent is x might be described by a lognormal distribution with mean μ and standard deviation σ:

$$f(x) = \frac{1}{x\sqrt{2\pi\sigma^2}} e^{\frac{-(\ln x - \mu)^2}{2\sigma^2}} = \frac{1}{\sigma x} \phi\left(\frac{\ln x - \mu}{\sigma}\right), \tag{15.8}$$

where $\phi(z)$ is the standard normal probability density function.

The expected cost (EC) of taking the contain action is found by integrating the total loss (Eq. 15.6) over the range of possible extents, weighted by our prior belief in the extent, that is,

$$\text{EC("contain")} = \int_x T(x\,|\,\text{"contain"})f(x)\,dx$$
$$= \int_0^\infty \left(2c_1\sqrt{\pi x} + c_3 x\right)f(x)\,dx. \tag{15.9}$$

The expected cost of taking the eradicate action is found in a similar manner:

$$\text{EC("eradicate")} = \int_x T(x\,|\,\text{"eradicate"})f(x)\,dx$$
$$= \int_0^\infty \left(c_2 x + \frac{2c_1\sqrt{\pi x} + c_3 x}{1 + e^{-m(x-a)}}\right)f(x)\,dx. \tag{15.10}$$

The best action in the face of uncertainty is the minimum of Eqs. 15.9 and 15.10, that is, the action that minimises the expected total loss. The expected total loss in the face of uncertainty, EC_u, is

$$\text{EC}_u = \min\left[\int_x T(x\,|\,\text{"eradicate"})f(x)\,dx, \int_x T(x\,|\,\text{"contain"})f(x)\,dx\right]. \tag{15.11}$$

If we can resolve uncertainty about the extent first, before making the decision, then we would take the eradicate action if we find out that x is less than x^*, and the contain action if we find out that x is greater than x^*. Thus, prior to collecting that information, the expected cost of the decision under certainty, EC_c, is

$$\text{EC}_c = \int_0^{x^*} T(x;\text{"eradicate"})f(x)\,dx + \int_{x^*}^\infty (x;\text{"contain"})f(x)\,dx$$
$$= \int_0^{x^*} \left(c_2 x + \frac{2c_1\sqrt{\pi x} + c_3 x}{1 + e^{-m(x-a)}}\right)f(x)\,dx + \int_{x^*}^\infty \left(2c_1\sqrt{\pi x} + c_3 x\right)f(x)\,dx \tag{15.12}$$

and the expected VOI is the difference between the expected cost under uncertainty and the expected cost under certainty:

$$\text{EVPI} = \text{EC}_u - \text{EC}_c. \tag{15.13}$$

Consider the set of parameters given above, for which $x^* = 1{,}321$ ha. Suppose that our belief about the extent of infestation can be characterised as a lognormal distribution with $\mu = \ln(1{,}000)$ and $\sigma = 0.3$ (Figure 15.4). The probability that the extent of infestation is less than the decision threshold is 0.823 (Figure 15.4). In the face of uncertainty, the expected total loss of taking the contain action is $636,154, and the expected total loss of taking the eradication action is $481,526. The best course of action is eradication, reflecting the weight of evidence that the extent is lower than the decision threshold. But there is a 17.7% risk of making the wrong decision. If the extent of infestation can be determined before the decision is made, the expected total loss is $465,663. Thus, the expected VOI is $15,863, which is the maximum we should spend reducing uncertainty in the extent of the invasion.

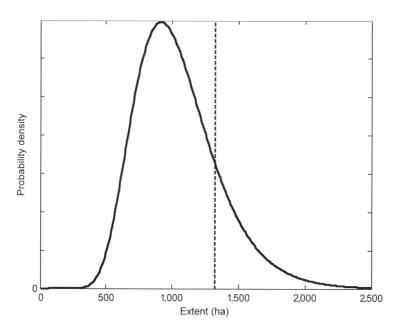

Figure 15.4.   Uncertainty in the extent of infestation, expressed as a lognormal distribution with mean $\mu = \ln(1,000)$ and standard deviation $\sigma = 0.3$. The probability that the extent is less than the threshold (x^*) is 0.823.

15.3   Tailoring the Analysis to a Specific Management Problem

We now illustrate how our prototype VOI analysis can be applied to a specific management situation, using an example of red imported fire ant management in southeast Queensland. Red imported fire ants (*Solenopsis invicta*, hereafter fire ants) were first detected in Brisbane in early 2001 (Moloney & Vanderwoude, 2002). Since that time they have been the subject of a major eradication campaign (Moloney & Vanderwoude, 2002). One of the world's 100 worst invaders (Lowe et al., 2000), fire ants damage agricultural crops, injure livestock and affect human health and ecosystems (Moloney & Vanderwoude, 2002). Fire ants are a significant pest in the United States, with estimated costs of control, medical treatment and damage to property greater than US$6 billion annually (Lard et al., 2006).

In the early stages of the Brisbane eradication campaign, fire ants were present at high density within a relatively small area. While eradication efforts successfully reduced population density, occasional long-distance dispersal has led to a very large area (hundreds of thousands of hectares) being occupied at a low density (Keith & Spring, 2015). Reflecting these changed circumstances, the focus of management has shifted from intensive surveillance and treatment of a small area to methods better suited to eradication over a larger area.

This new approach has been informed by quantitative models of fire ant spread under alternative surveillance and control strategies (Keith & Spring, 2013; Schmidt et al., 2010; Spring et al., 2010). One of the main findings of modelling research is that if eradication is to be a viable option, new methods will be required to search larger areas at lower cost. Remote sensing technology, which uses an infra-red camera from a helicopter, was identified as a candidate method and recommended for further evaluation. Modelling work indicates there is a threshold level of sensitivity of remote sensing, below which eradication is unlikely to be feasible.

Other cost-effective strategies for containment and eradication are also being considered. One potential strategy is extensive application over general areas of infestation of broadcast pesticide baits (baiting), which are so-named because the poison is designed to be palatable to fire ants, which take the baits to their nests. Managers are currently conducting trials to further evaluate the efficacy of baiting and thereby determine its cost-effectiveness as a containment or eradication method.

To show how VOI analysis can answer practical management questions, we calculate the value of learning about two uncertain variables: the sensitivity of remote sensing and the efficacy of baiting. VOI analysis can tell us how much effort should be expended on research and evaluation of these methods, or if it may be more cost-effective to simply implement these methods despite uncertainty. As in our prototype analysis, we also consider uncertainty about the current spatial extent of the invasion.

15.3.1 Fire Ant Treatment Methods

Several different actions are employed to detect and kill fire ant nests (Table 15.2). Two kill methods are used: baiting, in which bait is broadcast over a large area, and nest injection, in which poison is applied directly into detected fire ant nests. Baits contain an attractant and poison, so they are taken back to undetected nests by fire ant workers (Moloney & Vanderwoude, 2002). Baits can be distributed on foot, from all-terrain vehicles or from the air (Moloney & Vanderwoude, 2002). Experience in North America indicates that baiting is between 80% and 95% effective (Barr et al., 2005), although its efficacy for fire ants in Queensland is uncertain. Given this uncertainty, we use a modal value of 80% and consider the effect of uncertainty (Table 15.2). Nest injection is fully effective in killing fire ant nests (Table 15.2) but can be applied only after a nest is detected.

The most effective detection method is surveying with odour detection dogs, which have close to a 100% nest detection rate given optimal search routines that account for the distance from which a dog can detect a nest (Wylie et al., 2016). This surveillance method is also the most expensive (Table 15.3) because two handlers must accompany the dog and relatively few hectares can be searched per day. Visual surveillance, in which trained field staff form an evenly spaced line and move forward uniformly to scan an area for fire ant nests, has an 80% nest detection rate (National Red Imported Fire Ant Eradication Program, pers. comm.). Visual surveillance is both less effective and more expensive than canine surveillance (Table 15.3).

Remote sensing involves capturing images of a landscape with an infra-red camera from a helicopter and analysing the images to map the location of fire ant nests

Table 15.2. Efficacy of fire ant nest detection and kill methods

Kill method	Estimated efficacy $\lambda = p$(killing nest)
Nest injection	1
Baiting	Currently uncertain, best estimate is 0.8 (Barr et al., 2005)
Detection method	Estimated sensitivity $\delta = p$(detecting nest | present)
Canine surveys	0.99 (Wylie et al., 2016)
Visual surveys	0.8 (NRIFAEP, pers. comm.)
Remote sensing	Currently unknown

Table 15.3. Costs of fire ant nest detection and kill methods

Parameter	Cost per ha	Source
Cost of tracking with dogs + nest injection (/ ha)	$184	D. Spring, pers. comm.
Cost of visual surveys + nest injection (/ ha)	$276	D. Spring, pers. comm.
Cost of remote sensing + nest injection (/ ha)	$108	D. Spring, pers. comm.
Cost of baiting (/ ha)	$195	Three different baiting methods are used, depending on land type. Costs range from $147 to 240/ha, average $195 (NRIFAEP, pers. comm.)

All costs are given in Australian dollars.

(Vogt, 2004). Testing in North America has found this method to be capable of detecting up to 79% of fire ant nests within an area, with a false-positive rate of only 4% in the habitats in which the detection algorithm was tuned (Vogt & Wallet, 2008). The false-positive rate was much higher (17.5%) when the method was applied to a habitat with different features than the one it was tuned to, suggesting site-specific or habitat-specific tuning is needed. The technology is currently being developed for application in south-east Queensland, and its efficacy in this setting is currently unknown (Table 15.2). Because large areas can be covered quickly and easily with remote sensing, it is expected to be substantially cheaper per hectare than ground-based surveillance methods when a large area needs to be searched (Table 15.3).

15.3.2   The Decision Model

We frame the decision in the same way as in the previous section, that is, broadly as a choice between eradication and containment of fire ants. Let x be the extent of the fire ant infestation in hectares, which for simplicity we assume to be roughly

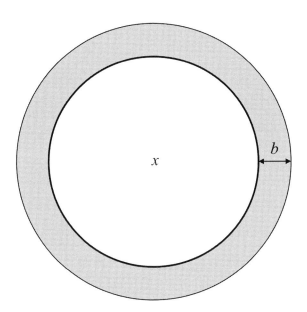

Figure 15.5. Diagram showing the infestation area x (outlined in bold), and the area in which containment actions are applied (shaded in grey) defined by buffer width b.

circular. If eradication is chosen, a one-off treatment will be applied across the entire extent x, which may or may not be successful in eradicating fire ants. If containment is chosen, treatment will be applied annually to a ring of width b (measured in hm) around the outside of the infestation (Figure 15.5), which we assume will successfully contain the infestation to area x.

The annual cost of containment is then $c_1\left(2\sqrt{\pi x b} + \pi b^2\right)$, where c_1 is the annual per hectare cost of the treatment applied. Containment will be applied every year from now ($t = 0$) indefinitely into the future ($t = \infty$). Using standard exponential discounting, the net present cost of containment is therefore

$$\text{Cost}(C) = \sum_{t=0}^{\infty} \frac{c_1\left(\sqrt{\pi x b} + \pi b^2\right)}{(1+j)^t} = c_1\left(2\sqrt{\pi x b} + \pi b^2\right)\left(\frac{1+j}{j}\right), \qquad (15.14)$$

where j is the annual discount rate. Throughout this section we use a discount rate of $j = 0.05$. Eradication is a one-off management expenditure, but if eradication fails we assume containment must then be enacted. The cost of eradication is therefore

$$\text{Cost}(E) = c_2 x + (1 - p(\text{success}))\text{Cost}(C), \qquad (15.15)$$

where c_2 is the one-time per hectare cost of eradication and $p(\text{success})$ is the probability that eradication will be successful.

The probabilities that eradication will be successful and that containment will eliminate all nests within the treatment buffer depend on the combination of detection and kill actions used as part of the eradication or containment strategy. A strategy may comprise a number of dog surveys, visual surveys, remote sensing surveys and rounds of baiting. Assuming these actions are independent, the probability an individual nest will survive treatment is

$$p(\text{survive}) = (1 - \delta_{\text{dogs}})^{n_{\text{dogs}}} (1 - \delta_{\text{visual}})^{n_{\text{visual}}} (1 - \delta_{\text{remote}})^{n_{\text{remote}}} (1 - \lambda_{\text{bait}})^{n_{\text{bait}}}, \quad (15.16)$$

where δ_y is the sensitivity of detection method y, n_y is the number of surveys with method y, λ_{bait} is the probability the nest will be killed with bait and n_{bait} is the number of rounds of bait applied.

We assume the nests have a density γ across the extent, which means the total number of nests is given by γx. The probability that all nests within the treatment area will be killed is then

$$p(\text{success}) = (1 - p(\text{survive}))^{\gamma z}, \quad (15.17)$$

where z is the treatment area, which is

$$z = \begin{cases} 2b\sqrt{\pi x} + \pi b^2 & \text{if containment} \\ x & \text{if eradication} \end{cases}. \quad (15.18)$$

Throughout this analysis we assume a fire ant density in the treated area of $\gamma = 1$ nest per hectare (Antony, 2009).

Along with the cost of managing fire ants, there will be losses incurred as a result of the fire ant presence. We assume this impact is proportional to the area occupied. If containment is chosen, the long-term extent of the infestation will remain at the current extent x. If eradication is chosen, the long-term extent of the infestation will be zero if eradication is successful and x if eradication fails. The expected loss caused by the long-term presence of fire ants is therefore given by

$$\text{Loss} = \begin{cases} \displaystyle\sum_{t=0}^{\infty} \frac{c_i x}{(1+j)^t} = \frac{c_i x(1+j)}{j} & \text{if containment} \\[4mm] (1 - p(\text{success})) \displaystyle\sum_{t=0}^{\infty} \frac{c_i x}{(1+j)^t} = (1 - p(\text{success})) \frac{c_i x(1+j)}{j} & \text{if eradication} \end{cases}$$

$$(15.19)$$

where c_i is the per hectare annual cost of impact and j is the annual discount rate. For simplicity, we assume that the impact losses and costs of management are discounted at the same exponential rate.

A recent cost–benefit analysis estimated the potential loss due to the long-term presence of fire ants in south-east Queensland to be as much as AU$43 billion (Antony et al., 2009). We simplified the method applied in that analysis to derive an annual cost of fire ant impact of AU$1,031.48 per hectare. As in Antony et al. (2009), this includes the costs of ongoing private treatment of fire ant infested areas, the health care costs associated with fire ant stings, and the impact of fire ants on ecosystem services.

The combined total cost and loss of each action, T, can thus be found by summing Eqs. 15.14, 15.15 and 15.19:

$$T = \begin{cases} \dfrac{\left(c_1\left(2b\sqrt{\pi x} + \pi b^2\right) + c_i x\right)(1+j)}{j} & \text{if containment} \\[3em] c_2 x + \left(1 - p\left(\text{success}\right)\right)\dfrac{\left(c_1\left(2b\sqrt{\pi x} + \pi b^2\right) + c_i x\right)(1+j)}{j} & \text{if eradication} \end{cases}.$$

(15.20)

If all model parameters are certain, the most cost-effective management strategy is the one with the lowest total cost, as given by Eq. 15.20 above.

15.3.3 Uncertainty in the Extent of the Infestation

We now investigate the VOI for one uncertain parameter at a time, starting with the extent of the infestation, which is estimated to be hundreds of thousands of hectares (Keith & Spring, 2015); we'll assume approximately 200,000 ha for the purposes of this analysis. To confine our uncertainty to a single variable, we consider only management strategies involving detection and kill methods with a known efficacy.

We compare two management strategies:

- A containment strategy applied to a buffer ($b = 10$ hm) around the perimeter of the infestation, involving two canine surveys and two visual surveys per year and injection of detected nests with poison
- An eradication strategy applied over the entire extent of the infestation, involving two canine surveys and one visual survey, and injection of detected nests with poison.

These strategies were chosen to provide an interesting conceptual model and are not based on current practice. For the containment strategy, the intensive combination of canine and visual surveys is necessary to give a high probability of eliminating all nests within the containment buffer (Figure 15.6), consistent with the model assumption that containment is successful in maintaining the infestation at its current extent.

Given the cost estimates in Table 15.3, the containment strategy will cost $920 per hectare per year ($19,320 per hectare, net present value of all annual treatments over time), while the eradication strategy will cost $644 per hectare over a larger area (unless stated otherwise, all costs are given in Australian dollars). The total cost of each strategy includes the cost of management as well as the costs of fire ant impact (Eq. 15.20). The most cost-effective strategy depends on the extent of the infestation (Figure 15.7). Eradication is optimal for an infestation size of up to 179,449 ha, while containment is optimal if the infestation is any larger (Figure 15.7). At an extent of $x = 200,000$ ha, the expected treatment cost for eradication

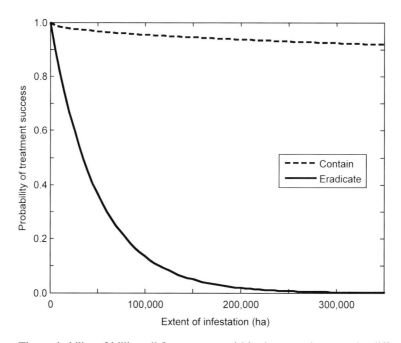

Figure 15.6.   The probability of killing all fire ant nests within the treated area under different management strategies, and for different infestation extents. The treatment area is either the containment buffer (containment) or the entire extent (eradication). The probabilities are calculated with Eq. 15.17, using the parameter estimates in Table 15.2.

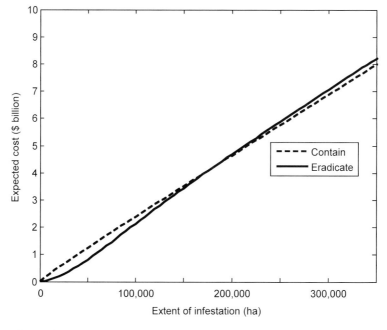

Figure 15.7.   The total expected cost of different management strategies for different extents of the fire ant infestation, calculated with Eq. 15.20.

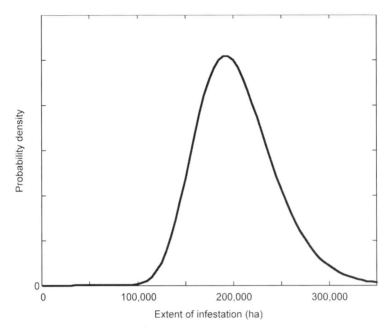

Figure 15.8. The lognormal probability distribution (Eq. 15.21) expressing uncertainty in the extent of the RIFA infestation. The mean μ = ln(200 000), and the standard deviation σ = 0.2.

is $435 million, but the probability of success is only 1.8%, so the expected amenity cost is $4.253 billion and the total expected cost is $4.688 billion. By comparison, the long-term treatment cost for containment is $312 million, the amenity cost is $4.332 billion and the total cost is $4.645 billion. With this extent of infestation, eradication is more expensive than containment and is unlikely to succeed, making containment more advantageous.

But what if the extent of infestation is not known with certainty? Given that the extent of the infestation affects which strategy is the most cost effective, the decision maker may be concerned that uncertainty in extent could influence the decision. To calculate the value of resolving uncertainty about the extent, we first describe this uncertainty with a lognormal distribution:

$$ f(x) = \frac{1}{x\sqrt{2\pi\sigma^2}} e^{\frac{-(\ln x - \mu)^2}{2\sigma^2}}. \tag{15.21}$$

We use a mean μ = ln(200,000) and standard deviation σ = 0.2 to describe uncertainty about the extent (Figure 15.8).

The expected cost of each management strategy can be found by integrating the total cost (Eq. 15.20) across the range of possible extents, weighted by our prior belief that each is the true extent (Eq. 15.21):

$$ EC(\text{containment}) = \int_0^{x_{max}} T(x\,|\,\text{containment}) f(x) dx $$
$$ EC(\text{eradication}) = \int_0^{x_{max}} T(x\,|\,\text{eradication}) f(x) dx. \tag{15.22}$$

To be consistent with Antony et al. (2009), the largest possible extent we consider is x_{max} = 2.7 million ha.

The best strategy in the face of uncertainty is the strategy that minimises the total expected cost given the prior distribution for the uncertain variable. That is, if Figure 15.8 represents our belief about the likelihood of different infestation sizes, we should choose the strategy with the lowest expected cost across these possible extents. Taking this best strategy, the expected cost under uncertainty is

$$EC_u = \min[EC(\text{containment}), EC(\text{eradication})], \qquad (15.23)$$

where the expected costs are given by Eq. 15.22. The best strategy under uncertainty is containment, with an expected cost of approximately AU$4.734 billion.

If we could find out what the true extent was before making our decision, we would choose the strategy with the lowest expected cost for that particular extent. That means we would choose eradication if we knew the extent was less than x^* = 179,449 ha, and we would choose containment if we knew the extent was more than 179,449 ha. Prior to collecting information about the extent, the expected cost of the decision is

$$EC_c = \int_0^{x^*} T(x\,|\,\text{eradication})f(x)dx + \int_{x^*}^{x_{max}} T(x\,|\,\text{containment})f(x)dx, \qquad (15.24)$$

which is equal to AU$4.717 billion.

The expected value of perfect information about the extent is the difference between the expected cost under uncertainty and the expected cost under certainty:

$$EVPI(x) = EC_u - EC_c, \qquad (15.25)$$

which in this case is only AU$15.2 million. Although perfect information about the extent of the infestation is not likely to be possible, this puts an upper limit on the amount that should be spent acquiring information about the extent.

Why is information about the extent worth relatively little, when our analysis shows the choice of strategy depends on the extent? According to our prior belief distribution (Figure 15.8), it is likely (70.6%) that the infestation is large enough for containment to be the most cost-effective strategy, but there is still a substantial chance (29.4%) that eradication is the best strategy. But, for extents near 200,000 ha, the total costs of the two actions do not differ greatly (Figure 15.8); thus the cost of choosing the wrong strategy is not large.

15.3.4   Uncertainty in the Sensitivity of Remote Sensing

We now explore the value of learning about the sensitivity of remote sensing, another uncertain parameter in this model. To do this, we compare three possible management strategies. In addition to the containment and eradication strategies considered previously, we add a new eradication strategy with two canine surveys and two remote sensing surveys, where detected nests are injected with poison.

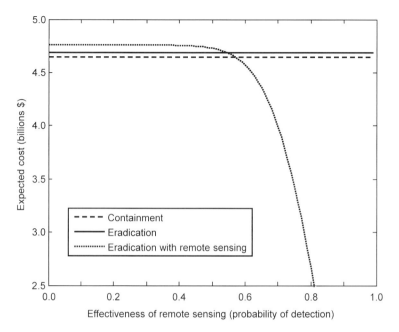

Figure 15.9. The total expected cost of different management strategies for different values of the effectiveness of remote sensing, calculated with Eq. 15.20.

Given the cost estimates in Table 15.3, this new strategy will cost AU$584 per hectare (compared with AU$920 per hectare per year for containment and AU$644 per hectare for the eradication strategy without remote sensing). Again, these three management strategies are chosen for illustrative purposes and do not reflect current or intended future practice.

The total expected cost calculations show that the cost-effectiveness of including remote sensing in an eradication strategy depends on its effectiveness (Figure 15.9). The eradication strategy with remote sensing is optimal if the probability of detecting a nest with remote sensing is greater than 0.571. Otherwise, the original eradication strategy is more cost effective. Note that these calculations are for an infestation extent of $x = 200,000$ ha.

Previous analyses of remote sensing found that eradication using this technology is feasible at much lower levels of sensitivity than 0.571 (Spring et al., 2010). Although feasibility and cost-effectiveness are not equivalent measures, differences in the fire ant models may have led to differences in the results of these analyses. In particular, this analysis has several simplifying assumptions, for example, that fire ant nests are uniformly distributed across the infestation extent.

To calculate the expected VOI, we start by describing our uncertainty in the sensitivity of remote sensing, using a beta distribution:

$$f(\delta_{remote}) = \frac{\delta_{remote}^{\alpha-1}(1-\delta_{remote})^{\beta-1}}{B(\alpha,\beta)}, \qquad (15.26)$$

where α and β are shape parameters, and $B(\alpha, \beta)$ is the beta function:

$$B(\alpha, \beta) = \int_0^1 u^{\alpha-1}(1-u)^{\beta-1}\, du. \tag{15.27}$$

The beta distribution is defined on the interval [0,1] and is thus a suitable and commonly used distribution for describing probabilities. To reflect the ongoing development of remote sensing technology and the subsequent high level of uncertainty involved, we use a prior distribution with shape parameters $\alpha = 1$ and $\beta = 1$, equivalent to a uniform distribution over the interval [0,1].

Again, the expected cost of each management strategy can be found by integrating the total cost (Eq. 15.20) across the range of the uncertain variable, weighted by our prior belief that each value is the true value (Eq. 15.26):

$$EC(\text{containment}) = \int_0^1 T(\delta_{\text{remote}} \mid \text{containment}) f(\delta_{\text{remote}})\, d\delta_{\text{remote}} = T(\text{containment})$$

$$EC(\text{eradication}) = \int_0^1 T(\delta_{\text{remote}} \mid \text{eradication}) f(\delta_{\text{remote}})\, d\delta_{\text{remote}} = T(\text{eradication})$$

$$EC(\text{eradication with RS}) = \int_0^1 T(\delta_{\text{remote}} \mid \text{eradication with RS}) f(\delta_{\text{remote}})\, d\delta_{\text{remote}}. \tag{15.28}$$

The best strategy in the face of uncertainty is the strategy that minimises the total expected cost, given the prior probability distribution:

$$EC_u = \min\left[EC(\text{containment}), EC(\text{eradication}), EC(\text{eradication with RS})\right]. \tag{15.29}$$

In this case, the best strategy under uncertainty is the eradication with remote sensing strategy, with an expected cost of AU\$3.841 billion.

Under certainty, we would choose eradication with remote sensing if the effectiveness of remote sensing is greater than $\delta_{\text{remote}}^* = 0.571$, and we would choose the containment strategy if the effectiveness is less than 0.571. The expected cost of the decision under certainty is

$$EC_c = \int_0^{\delta_{\text{remote}}^*} T(\delta_{\text{remote}} \mid \text{eradication}) f(\delta_{\text{remote}})\, d\delta_{\text{remote}}$$

$$+ \int_{\delta_{\text{remote}}^*}^1 T(\delta_{\text{remote}} \mid \text{eradication with RS}) f(\delta_{\text{remote}})\, d\delta_{\text{remote}}$$

$$= p\left(\delta_{\text{remote}} < \delta_{\text{remote}}^*\right) T(\text{eradication})$$

$$+ \int_{\delta_{\text{remote}}^*}^1 T(\delta_{\text{remote}} \mid \text{eradication with RS}) f(\delta_{\text{remote}})\, d\delta_{\text{remote}} \tag{15.30}$$

which equals AU\$3.780 billion.

The expected value of perfect information is the difference between the expected cost under uncertainty and the expected cost under certainty:

$$EVPI(\delta_{\text{remote}}) = EC_u - EC_c, \tag{15.31}$$

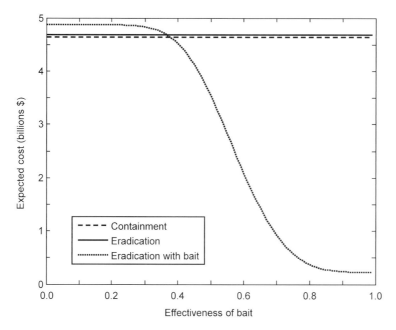

Figure 15.10. The total expected cost of different management strategies for different values of the efficacy of baiting, calculated with Eq. 15.20.

which is AU$60.6 million. The value of perfect information is substantial in this case because we assume so little is known about the sensitivity of remote sensing, and this ignorance is likely to affect the outcome of the decision, especially given the large difference in the expected cost of the strategies when the effectiveness of remote sensing is high (Figure 15.9).

15.3.5 Uncertainty in Bait Efficacy

The third uncertain parameter in this model is the efficacy of baiting undetected fire ant nests. To calculate the value of learning about this parameter, we again compare the original containment and eradication strategies with a new eradication strategy, this time involving two canine surveys (where found nests are injected with poison) and four rounds of baiting. This new eradication strategy will cost AU$1,148 per hectare compared with AU$920 per hectare per year for containment and AU$644 per hectare for the original eradication strategy. Again, these three management strategies are chosen purely for illustrative purposes.

The baiting strategy is the most cost-effective strategy if the efficacy of baiting is 0.377 or greater (Figure 15.10). For values below this, the containment strategy is optimal. This outcome is consistent with the findings of previous modelling that aggressive containment using extensive baiting can be an effective eradication strategy when combined with high-sensitivity visual surveillance (Spring et al., 2010). Note again that these calculations are for an infestation extent of $x = 200,000$ ha.

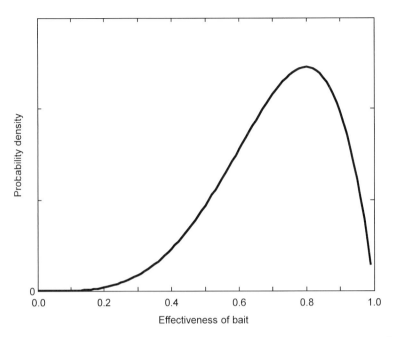

Figure 15.11. The beta probability distribution (Eq. 15.32) expressing uncertainty in the efficacy of baiting (parameters $\alpha = 5$ and $\beta = 2$).

We use a beta distribution to describe uncertainty in the effectiveness of baiting:

$$f(\lambda_{\text{bait}}) = \frac{\lambda_{\text{bait}}^{\alpha-1}(1-\lambda_{\text{bait}})^{\beta-1}}{B(\alpha,\beta)}. \qquad (15.32)$$

Our intuition about the efficacy of baiting is stronger than that of remote sensing, but still contains substantial uncertainty. We use shape parameters $\alpha = 5$ and $\beta = 2$ to give an asymmetric distribution with a mode $((\alpha - 1)/(\alpha + \beta - 2))$ of 0.8 (Figure 15.11), which is the current best estimate of bait efficacy.

The expected cost of each management strategy is found by integrating the total cost (Eq. 15.20) across the range of the uncertain variable, weighted by our prior belief that each value is the true value (Eq. 15.32):

$$EC(\text{containment}) = \int_0^1 T(\lambda_{\text{bait}} \mid \text{containment}) f(\lambda_{\text{bait}}) d\lambda_{\text{bait}} = T(\text{containment})$$

$$EC(\text{eradication}) = \int_0^1 T(\lambda_{\text{bait}} \mid \text{eradication}) f(\lambda_{\text{bait}}) d\lambda_{\text{bait}} = T(\text{eradication})$$

$$EC(\text{baiting}) = \int_0^1 T(\lambda_{\text{bait}} \mid \text{baiting}) f(\lambda_{\text{bait}}) d\lambda_{\text{bait}}.$$

$$(15.33)$$

Again, the best strategy in the face of uncertainty is the one that minimises the total expected loss given the prior probability distribution, which makes the expected cost under uncertainty

$$EC_u = \min\left[EC(\text{containment}), EC(\text{eradication}), EC(\text{baiting})\right]. \qquad (15.34)$$

The best strategy under uncertainty is eradication with baiting, which has an expected cost of AU\$1.313 billion.

If we could fully reduce uncertainty, we would choose the containment strategy if the bait efficacy is less than $\lambda_{\text{bait}}^* = 0.377$, and we would choose eradication with baiting if the bait efficacy is 0.377 or greater. The expected cost of the decision under certainty is

$$\text{EC}_c = \int_0^{\lambda_{\text{bait}}^*} T(\lambda_{\text{bait}} \mid \text{eradication}) f(\lambda_{\text{bait}}) d\lambda_{\text{bait}}$$
$$+ \int_{\lambda_{\text{bait}}^*}^1 T(\lambda_{\text{bait}} \mid \text{baiting}) f(\lambda_{\text{bait}}) d\lambda_{\text{bait}}$$

$$= p\left(\lambda_{\text{bait}} < \lambda_{\text{bait}}^*\right) T(\text{eradication}) + \int_{\lambda_{\text{bait}}^*}^1 T(\lambda_{\text{bait}} \mid \text{baiting}) f(\lambda_{\text{bait}}) d\lambda_{\text{bait}}, \quad (15.35)$$

which equals AU\$1.309 billion.

The expected value of perfect information is the difference between the expected cost under uncertainty and the expected cost under certainty:

$$\text{EVPI}(\lambda_{\text{bait}}) = \text{EC}_u - \text{EC}_c, \quad (15.36)$$

which is AU\$4.52 million. The value of perfect information is quite small in this case because, although we are uncertain about the effectiveness of baiting, our prior belief is very high (96.9%) that it is at least 0.377. Thus, although we are uncertain about the parameter, we are not uncertain about what action to take.

15.4 Discussion and Future Directions

This chapter provides an introduction to VOI analysis, in particular the expected value of perfect information, and describes how this analysis can be useful for biosecurity decision making. VOI analysis enables managers to identify which uncertainties affect the outcome of management decisions, thus allowing the managers to prioritise investment in research and monitoring. An EVPI calculation requires

- Clearly defined alternative actions
- A description of uncertainty, whether as discrete probabilities or a continuous probability distribution
- Predictions of how alternative actions perform under different possible values of the uncertain variable.

The output of this calculation, the expected value of perfect information, is the amount by which resolving all uncertainty is expected to improve the decision outcome. This provides managers with an upper limit on the amount that should be spent on research or monitoring to reduce their uncertainty.

Although our models capture the basic elements of the eradicate-or-contain decision problem, further work is needed to increase the realism of the models. First, reducing uncertainty through research or monitoring takes time and delays decisions, which might allow further spread of the invader during the delay. This opportunity cost could be substantial, but could be accounted for in the decision analysis if estimates of the rate of spread were available. Second, we have not accounted for the consequences if containment fails. Third, we have treated containment as a fixed long-term strategy, but there might be dynamics that increase or decrease its efficacy over time. Fourth, we have not considered long-distance dispersal (naturally occurring or human mediated) of the invader past the containment ring. Fifth, we have not considered constraints on the availability of various treatments (e.g., whether there are enough trained dogs to search the area of interest). In short, there are many other aspects of this general problem that might need to be treated in more detail in specific settings, but the insights from this prototype still provide guidance.

While our fire ant case study demonstrates the flexibility of VOI analysis, we note that it is primarily a conceptual model and embodies strong simplifying assumptions about fire ant biology. Those simplifying assumptions may have a substantial effect on the choice of management strategy and on decisions regarding research and monitoring to reduce uncertainty. For the particular case of fire ants in Queensland, a number of important details have been, or are being, built into predictive models, including the specific spatial arrangement of known infestations, the probability of opportunistic detection by individual members of the public, the effect of incentive programs for detection and the timing of action relative to the spread of ants. One of the findings of this predictive modelling (Keith & Spring 2013) is that areas known or likely to be infested by fire ants occupy a small proportion of the delimited area. Management strategies being considered that address this spatial pattern of infestation include searching only part of the delimited area, rather than the entire area as implied in our formulation. Another feature of some of the management strategies currently being considered is to conduct surveillance both near the estimated invasion boundary and in selected areas of higher infestation likelihood within the delimited area. These strategies blur the sharp distinction made in our formulation between containment and eradication strategies because elements of both strategies are likely to be applied in practice, regardless of whether the objective is containment or eradication. Despite the need for such elaborations for practical application, our model still provides a basis for the development of a decision support tool.

In this chapter we have focused on the EVPI, which gives an upper bound on the value of any reduction in uncertainty. Other types of VOI calculations can deal with more nuanced measures of information value. For example, when a decision involves multiple sources of uncertainty simultaneously, the expected value of partial information can be used to assess the relative importance of resolving the uncertainty from each source and is the best way of performing a sensitivity analysis in a decision context (Runge et al., 2011). The expected value of partial information calculates the difference in expected utility between the best decision with perfect information about a variable x (but with uncertainty in other variables y), and the best decision given uncertainty in both x and y. In Section 15.3 we performed three separate EVPI calculations for three uncertain variables, each considering different candidate management options. By simultaneously incorporating the uncertainty around multiple variables, the expected value of partial information gives a measure of the relative importance of resolving uncertainty in each variable, and would enable simultaneous consideration of all possible management options.

Obtaining perfect information is impossible for many systems; thus the decision maker must instead rely on imperfect sample information that reduces but does not eliminate uncertainty. The expected value of sample information, another form of VOI analysis, takes the imperfect acquisition of information into account and can be used to evaluate what level of investment in research or monitoring is warranted (Runge et al., 2011).

In some applied environmental contexts, VOI methods are difficult to use, because they require two important prerequisites: the framing of the problem as a decision (with articulation of objectives and development of alternatives) and a reasonable basis for estimating the outcomes of alternative interventions across the range of uncertain states. But the recognition of the utility of VOI analyses can motivate the prerequisite steps, which may be even more important than the subsequent analysis. The full framing of environmental problems as *decisions* opens up access to the rich array of tools from decision analysis (Gregory et al., 2012). Many biosecurity problems, by virtue of their economic impact and the public attention brought to them, are considerably well developed: they have often been framed as economic decisions; baseline information exists; and funding for surveillance, research and intervention is available. Thus, the prerequisites for VOI analysis are met, and the agencies with responsibility will often have the technical expertise to conduct them. The VOI framework brings the same rigour to the question of reducing uncertainty as has already been brought to the analysis of the potential damage, and it does so from the standpoint of the decision-making agencies with responsibility to take action.

A VOI analysis, in contrast to a traditional sensitivity analysis, changes the focus of attention from the influence of uncertainty on the predictions to the influence of uncertainty on the decisions recommended. Although this seems like a subtle change in wording, it can represent a profound change in direction and can help agencies avoid spending scarce resources on surveillance, monitoring or research that will not help them make a materially better decision.

In summary, although VOI analysis is an established and extensively used decision support tool, it is not currently widely applied within the field of biosecuity management. This chapter provides a first step in increasing the use of VOI analysis for biosecurity decision support, demonstrating its potential utility and outlining several directions for future research and application.

References

Antony, G., Scanlan, J., Francis, A., Kloessing, K. & Nguyen, Y. (2009). *Revised benefits and costs of eradicating the red imported fire ant*. Brisbane, Australia: Queensland Department of Primary Industries and Fisheries.

Barr, C. L., Davis, T., Flanders, K., et al. (2005). *Broadcast baits for fire ant control.* Texas Imported Fire Ant Research & Management Project.

D'Evelyn, S. T., Tarui, N., Burnett, K. & Roumasset, J. A. (2008). Learning-by-catching: Uncertain invasive-species populations and the value of information. *Journal of Environmental Management,* 89(4), 284–292.

Eidsvik, J., Bhattacharjya, D. & Mukerji, T. (2008). Value of information of seismic amplitude and CSEM resistivity. *Geophysics,* 73(4), R59–R69.

Gregory, R., Failing, L., Harstone, M., et al. (2012). *Structured decision making: A practical guide for environmental management choices.* West Sussex, UK: Wiley-Blackwell.

Groot Koerkamp, B., Nikken, J. J., Oei, E. H., et al. (2008). Value of information analysis used to determine the necessity of additional research: MR imaging in acute knee trauma as an example. *Radiology,* 246(2), 420–425.

Howard, R. A. (1966). Information value theory. *IEEE Transactions on Systems Science and Cybernetics,* 2(1), 22–26.

Keith, J. M. & Spring, D. (2013). Agent-based Bayesian approach to monitoring the progress of invasive species eradication programs. *Proceedings of the National Academy of Sciences of the USA,* 110(33), 13428–13433.

Keith, J. M. & Spring, D. (2015). *Has the Brisbane fire ant infestation been delimited?* Unpublished report to Queensland Department of Agriculture and Fisheries.

Lard, C. F., Schmidt, J., Morris, B., et al. (2006). *An economic impact of imported fire ants in the United States of America.* Project Report. College Station, TX: Texas A&M University.

Lowe, S., Browne, M., Boudjelas, S., & De Poorter, M. (2000). 100 of the world's worst invasive alien species: a selection from the global invasive species database. *Aliens* 12(pull-out), 1–12.

Maxwell, S. L., Rhodes, J. R., Runge, M. C., et al. (2015). How much is new information worth? Evaluating the financial benefit of resolving management uncertainty. *Journal of Applied Ecology,* 52(1), 12–20.

Moloney, S. & Vanderwoude, C., (2002). Red imported fire ants: A threat to eastern Australia's wildlife? *Ecological Management and Restoration,* 3(3), 167–175.

Moore, J. L. & Runge, M. C. (2012). Combining structured decision making and value-of-information analyses to identify robust management strategies. *Conservation Biology,* 26(5), 810–820.

Parma, A. M., Amarasekare, P., Mangel, M., et al. (1998). What can adaptive management do for our fish, forests, food and biodiversity? *Integrative Biology: Issues, News and Reviews,* 1(1), 16–26.

Raiffa, H. & Schlaifer, R. O. (1961). *Applied statistical decision theory.* Cambridge, MA: Division of Research, Graduate School of Business Administration, Harvard University.

Runge, M. C., Converse, S. J. & Lyons, J. E. (2011). Which uncertainty? Using expert elicitation and expected value of information to design an adaptive program. *Biological Conservation,* 144(4), 1214–1223.

Sahlin, U., Rydén, T., Nyberg, C. D. & Smith, H. G. (2011). A benefit analysis of screening for invasive species – base-rate uncertainty and the value of information. *Methods in Ecology and Evolution,* 2, 500–508.

Schmidt, D., Spring, D., Mac Nally, R., et al. (2010). Finding needles (or ants) in haystacks: Predicting locations of invasive organisms to inform eradication and containment. *Ecological Applications,* 20(5), 1217–1227.

Shea, K., Tildesley, M. J., Runge, M. C., Fonnesbeck, C. J. & Ferrari, M. J. (2014). Adaptive management and the value of information: Learning via intervention in epidemiology. *PLoS Biology*, 12(10), e1001970.

Singh, S., Nosyk, B., Sun, H., et al. (2008). Value of information of a clinical prediction rule: Informing the efficient use of healthcare and health research resources. *International Journal of Technology Assessment in Health Care*, 24(1), 112–119.

Spring, D., Cacho, O. & Jennings, C. (2010). *The use of spread models to inform eradication programs: Application to red imported fire ant*. Australian Centre for Biosecurity and Environmental Economics Discussion Paper. Available from www.acbee.anu.edu.au/pdf/publications/2010/IDEC10-03.pdf

Vogt, J. T. (2004). Quantifying imported fire ant (Hymenoptera: Formicidae) mounds with airborne digital imagery. *Environmental Entomology*, 33(4), 1045–1051.

Vogt, J. T. & Wallet, B. (2008). Feasibility of using template-based and object-based automated detection methods for quantifying black and hybrid imported fire ant (*Solenopsis invicta* and *S. invicta* × *richteri*) mounds in aerial digital imagery. *The Rangeland Journal*, 30(3), 291–295.

Ward, M. & Kompas, T. (2010). *The value of information in biosecurity risk-benefit assessment: An application to red imported fire ants*. Environmental Economics Research Hub Research Reports. Canberra, Australia: Australian National University.

Wiles, L. J. (2004). Economics of weed management: principles and practices. *Weed Technology*, 18, 1403–1407.

Williams, B. K., Eaton, M. J. & Breininger, D. R., (2012). Adaptive resource management and the value of information. *Ecological Modelling*, 222(18), 3429–3436.

Wylie, R., Jennings, C., McNaught, M. K., Oakey, J. & Harris, E. J. (2016). Eradication of two incursions of the red imported fire ant in Queensland, Australia. *Ecological Management & Restoration*, 17(1), 22–32.

Yokota, F. & Thompson, K. M. (2004a). Value of information analysis in environmental health risk management decisions: Past, present, and future. *Risk Analysis*, 24(3), 635–650.

Yokota, F. & Thompson, K. M. (2004b). Value of information literature analysis: A review of applications in health risk management. *Medical Decision Making*, 24(3), 287–298.

16 Declaring Eradication of an Invasive Species

Tracy M. Rout

16.1 Introduction

Imperfect detection methods mean that it is difficult to tell whether a species is absent from a site or remains undetected. For this reason, the decision to conclude an eradication program and declare a species successfully eradicated is fraught with uncertainty (Morrison et al., 2007). There are two errors that can be made (Regan et al., 2006). First, if the species is declared eradicated when it is still present, its population could grow undetected, causing large economic and environmental damages. There are costs associated with reinitiating the eradication campaign and reducing the species' population to a low level. Second, monitoring cannot continue indefinitely, and continuing to survey when a species has already been eradicated uses resources that could be better deployed elsewhere. This chapter reviews statistical models that can be used to quantify the certainty that a species has been successfully eradicated from a site. It then describes how to analyse logically the decision to declare eradication, considering the risks and consequences of getting it wrong.

16.2 Quantifying Certainty of Species Absence

A range of statistical models have been used in the literature to quantify certainty of species absence. Choosing the most suitable model for a particular species depends primarily on the amount and type of data that are available. This can range from a basic time series of sightings or detections, to detailed information on the number of individuals removed during an eradication campaign and the management effort employed over time. This section summarises different statistical methods from the literature, using hypothetical case studies to illustrate how they can be applied.

16.2.1 Sighting Data

It is possible to quantify certainty of species absence when the only information available is a series of sightings over time (e.g. Table 16.1). In these cases, we can apply simple statistical methods that test whether the recent lack of sighting is exceptional, given the previous frequency with which the species was sighted (or otherwise detected). Such methods are known as *sighting record methods* (Boakes

Table 16.1. Hypothetical survey data for bottleweed, an imaginary weed species

Date of survey	Detected?
9 Sep 2001	Yes
5 Sep 2002	Yes
8 Sep 2003	No
11 Sep 2004	Yes
4 Sep 2005	No
6 Sep 2006	No
12 Sep 2007	Yes
8 Sep 2008	No
2 Feb 2009	No
6 Sep 2010	No

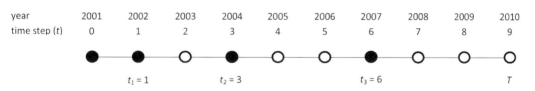

year	2001	2002	2003	2004	2005	2006	2007	2008	2009	2010
time step (t)	0	1	2	3	4	5	6	7	8	9

$t_1 = 1$ $t_2 = 3$ $t_3 = 6$ T

Figure 16.1. A schematic representation of the sighting record for the imaginary bottleweed. Closed circles represent surveys when bottleweed was detected, while open circles represent surveys when it was not detected. Surveys occurred annually, beginning in 2001 ($t = 0$) and ending in 2010 ($t = T$). After the beginning of the surveys, there were three sightings, with the most recent in the sixth time step ($t_3 = 6$).

et al., 2015). Although these methods were originally developed to test for the extinction of rare or cryptic species of conservation interest (Solow, 1993a), they can also be applied to assessing the success of eradication campaigns. Although referred to as testing *extinction*, this is synonymous with the eradication or extirpation of a species from the site where it was previously seen.

The record of sightings is described as occurring over a defined time interval, from 0 to T. For bottleweed (Table 16.1), the first sighting in 2001 defines the start of this interval ($t = 0$), which then goes for nine years ($T = 9$) (Figure 16.1). During this time there were n sightings, with the most recent at time t_n. Because the first sighting defines the start of the record, it is not included in the total number of sightings, so for bottleweed, $n = 3$ and $t_n = 6$ (Figure 16.1). This way of classifying the sighting data is common to all sighting record methods.

Sightings are assumed to represent a realisation of a Poisson process, which is a stochastic process in which events (in this case, sightings) occur continuously and independently. Other events that can be modelled as a Poisson process include the arrival of telephone calls to a switchboard and the radioactive decay of atoms. Within a Poisson process, events occur at a certain rate; for species sightings, this rate is driven by both species abundance and the amount of effort that went into observation. To make inferences about the exceptionality of a recent lack of sightings, it is necessary to make some assumptions about this sighting rate parameter. The simplest assumption is that the sighting rate is constant before eradication (known as a homogeneous Poisson process), and then after eradication the sighting rate drops to zero. We can then test whether successful eradication is likely to have occurred before the end of the sighting period, which is usually the present time.

Taking a hypothesis-testing approach, the p-value for the null hypothesis that the species remains present at the site is (Solow, 1993a)

$$p = \left(\frac{t_n}{T}\right)^n. \tag{16.1}$$

This p-value is the probability of obtaining the observed data (or more extreme data) if the null hypothesis were true. Hence, a low p-value gives support to the alternative hypothesis that the species has been successfully eradicated. For our example of bottleweed, the p-value is $(6/9)^3 = 0.3$, lending little support to the hypothesis that eradication has been successful. Traditionally, a null hypothesis is rejected if the p-value is less than 0.05, an arbitrary threshold of certainty that may not reflect the consequences of being wrong, as discussed in detail in Section 16.3.

This constant sighting rate model has been modified in several ways, with authors developing hypothesis tests that accommodate multiple sightings in a single time step (Burgman et al., 1995), account for differences in observational effort (McCarthy, 1998) and remove the influence of the length of observation period (McInerny et al., 2006).

This model can also be applied in a Bayesian framework (Solow, 1993a). Instead of calculating a p-value for the null hypothesis that a species is still present, the Bayesian version directly calculates the probability the species is present as

$$p(\text{presence}) = \frac{1}{\left(1 + \dfrac{1-\pi}{\pi B}\right)}, \tag{16.2}$$

where B is the Bayes factor

$$B = \frac{n-1}{\left(\dfrac{T}{t_n}\right)^{n-1} - 1},$$

and π is the prior probability of presence, that is, the probability that the species is present independent of its observed sighting record.

This prior probability can be estimated by obtaining values from one or more experts (McCarthy, 2007) or by modelling the success rate of eradication programs for similar species (Rout et al., 2009a). For example, Campbell and Donlan (2005) summarised the success and failure of goat (*Capra hircus*) eradications on islands and found that 120 out of 130 documented eradications were successful. From this,

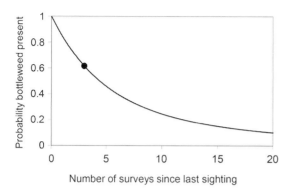

Figure 16.2. The probability that bottleweed is present despite being undetected for a number of surveys, calculated with the Bayesian constant sighting rate model (Eq. 16.2), with $\pi = 0.5$. There have been three surveys since bottleweed was last sighted (marked with circle), making the probability it remains present 0.6.

we can estimate a prior probability of eradication failure (and thus a prior probability that goats remain following an eradication attempt) of 0.08. In some cases, the probability of eradication failure can be predicted as a function of site or species characteristics. For example, Campbell and Donlan (2005) found that the failure rate on larger islands was higher than on smaller islands. McCarthy and Masters (2005) illustrated this approach by predicting annual survival rates of bird species from regression models of published data. Informative prior information has been found to increase the precision of estimates without systematically reducing accuracy (Morris et al., 2015). The ability to incorporate prior information is a major advantage of Bayesian methods (McCarthy, 2007). However, if no prior information is available, an uninformative prior probability of 0.5 can be used, and the posterior probability of presence will be driven solely by the observed sighting data.

Another advantage of this Bayesian method is that the output – the probability of presence – is much easier to use and interpret than a p-value. Indeed, in the literature, the p-value for the null hypothesis that the species is present is often interpreted incorrectly as the probability that the species is present. It is important to note that these are not the same quantity, and calculating them with the same data will give different results. Take the example of the imaginary bottleweed. After the three most recent surveys failed to detect bottleweed, the probability it is still present (with $\pi = 0.5$) is 0.62, whereas the p-value for the null hypothesis that it is present is 0.30.

It can also be useful to examine how the probability of presence will decrease as future surveys fail to detect the species (Figure 16.2). Because of bottleweed's short sighting record (and in particular its small n), the probability that it is present decreases quite slowly as the number of surveys since the last detection increases. After 20 surveys without detection, the probability that bottleweed is present is 0.10.

The methods described so far have modelled the sighting record as an homogeneous Poisson process, assuming that the rate of sightings is constant prior to eradication. The sighting record can also be modelled as a non-homogeneous Poisson process, where the pre-eradication sighting rate changes with time, for example, declining exponentially at an unknown rate (Solow, 1993b). Boakes et al. (2015) summarise and illustrate the current range of sighting record methods, including constant and declining sighting rate methods, as well as a number of non-parametric tests that make no assumptions about the distribution of the pre-eradication sighting rate. More recent methods can also take into account uncertainty in the veracity of individual sighting records (Boakes et al., 2015).

As with any statistical method, users should be aware of the underlying assumptions of these models and the implications of those assumptions (see Boakes et al. (2015) for a summary of the assumptions underlying each method). Assuming a constant sighting rate implies (in the simplest case) that both species abundance and observational effort are constant over time. This makes the model suitable for species with a low but stable population, where individuals that are detected and removed are replaced through reproduction. We might reasonably expect that, during an eradication campaign, the abundance of the species would decrease as the campaign progresses, making a decreasing sighting rate model more appropriate.

As mentioned, these sighting record methods were developed for rare species with incidental observations over time, rather than for species that were systematically and repeatedly surveyed. Sighting record methods can be applied in their original form to bottleweed because the surveys occurred at regular time intervals, in this case years, which can be used as the base unit for the sighting record. If surveys occur at irregular time intervals, then observational effort is not continuous through time, and this violates an assumption of the Poisson process model.

In these cases, the Poisson model can still be applied by using the number of surveys as the base unit for the sighting record (Rout et al., 2009a). This means interpreting T as the total number of surveys for the species, n as the number of surveys in which the species was detected and t_n as the survey number when the most recent observation was made. This means that the sighting rate is modelled across surveys rather than over time. This distinction is subtle when considering a constant sighting rate, but becomes important when using non-constant models. For example, modelling a decreasing sighting rate means that either abundance or observational effort is decreasing with every survey performed, even when individuals are not detected. This may be a realistic assumption for abundance if herbicide is applied or poison baits are dropped across the target site whenever surveys are conducted. Note that, although the timing of surveys becomes irrelevant when using surveys as the base unit of the sighting record, surveys must occur far enough apart in time to be considered independent observations.

16.2.2   Data on Persistence and Detectability

If the species has been surveyed at regular intervals and there is some information about its life history, then the model of Regan et al. (2006) may be suitable for

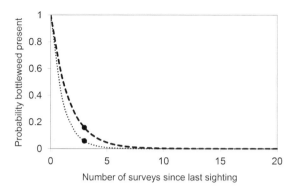

Figure 16.3. The probability that bottleweed is present despite being undetected for a number of surveys calculated with the persistence and detectability model (Eq. 16.3), with $s = 0.9$, and two different values for q: 0.4 (dotted line), and 0.57 (dashed line). The current probability that bottleweed is present, after three surveys without detection, is between 0.06 and 0.16 (marked with circles).

calculating the probability of presence. Under this model, the probability that a species is still present following d surveys without being detected is

$$p(\text{presence}) = \left(s(1-q)\right)^d , \qquad\qquad (16.3)$$

where s is the probability that the species persists in the time interval between surveys and q is the probability a survey will detect the species if it is present. The probability of persistence can be estimated with life history data such as seed bank longevity (Regan et al., 2006). The probability of detection can be estimated from survey data or more rigorously as a function of local conditions such as the surrounding vegetation type and the amount of time spent searching (see Chapter 14; Garrard et al., 2008; Moore et al., 2011).

Imagine we obtain information about the seed bank longevity of bottleweed that allows us to estimate its annual probability of persistence as $r = 0.9$. We can use the sighting data in Table 16.1 to estimate the probability that bottleweed will be detected in a survey if it is present. Bottleweed was detected in four surveys and was present for at least seven surveys (up until the last sighting) and perhaps up to ten surveys (up until the last survey). The probability of detecting bottleweed if it is present is, therefore, somewhere between 0.4 (four out of ten) and 0.57 (four out of seven). Using the model of Regan et al. (2006), the probability that bottleweed is currently present after three surveys without detection is between 0.06 and 0.16 (Figure 16.3).

16.2.3   Data from a Single Survey

The two previous models are suitable for species with multiple surveys or observations over time. For some species, it may be more appropriate to calculate the probability that the species is present in an area after a single extensive survey has failed to detect it. Scott et al. (2008) addressed this problem for several birds of conservation interest by developing a Bayesian model based on the proportion of the species' range that has been effectively surveyed. They assume that there is a well-defined range or target area for the species, that individuals are uniformly distributed over this area and that they are detected independently. The probability that a species remains present despite being undetected by the survey is

$$p(\text{presence})=1-e^{-m\left(1-\frac{E}{A}\right)}, \tag{16.4}$$

where m is the mean of a Poisson distribution describing the prior belief about population size, E is the effective survey area and A is the species' range area. In their appendix, Scott et al. (2008) provide an alternative calculation in which the prior belief in species abundance is described with a geometric distribution.

To show how this method can be applied, let us consider another hypothetical eradication campaign, this time of feral cats (*Felis catus*) on an island. Following an extensive baiting program, managers described their belief about the number of cats remaining on the island with a Poisson probability distribution with a mean and variance of $\lambda = 2$ (Figure 16.4). Note that a prior probability distribution could also be constructed more rigorously using data on the number of individuals removed, if available; see Section 16.2.4.

Under the distribution the managers described, the most likely number of cats remaining is either one or two (both are equally likely with a probability of 0.27). The probability that fewer than five cats remain is 0.95, while the probability that no cats remain is 0.14 (Figure 16.4).

A spotlighting survey was then conducted, comprising 20 line transects, each 200 m long. This survey failed to detect cats. The effective area of this spotlighting survey can be calculated as (Scott et al., 2008)

$$E=2Lw, \tag{16.5}$$

where L is the total transect length and w is the effective detection distance. A previous test on the island found that the eye-shine of a cat could be detected by spotlight from up to 40 m away, giving an effective survey area of $E = 2 \times 4,000$ m $\times$ 40 m $= 0.32$ km^2.

The entire island area of 42 km^2 is considered as potential cat habitat ($A = 42$ km^2). Using Eq. 16.4 to combine the managers' prior belief with the spotlighting data, we can calculate the probability of cat presence on the island as

$$p(\text{presence})=1-e^{-2\left(1-\frac{0.32}{42}\right)}=0.86. \tag{16.6}$$

This detection model assumes that all individuals could potentially be detected if the survey effort were high enough. For invasive plants with undetectable seed banks, this model can be used to assess the likelihood that adults and seedlings are present, but cannot make inferences about the complete eradication of the species. This model is unlikely to be suitable for gregarious animal species because of

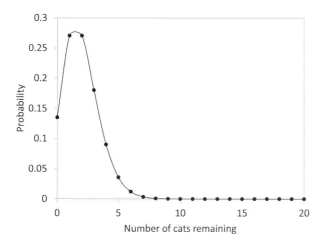

Figure 16.4. The prior probability distribution for the number of cats remaining on a hypothetical island following a baiting program – a Poisson distribution with a mean of 2.

the assumption that individuals are uniformly distributed over the target area. For example, the tendency for feral pigs to congregate means that their detection is not independent, and this is well known and often exploited by eradication managers.

16.2.4 Removal Data

If data are available on the number and timing of individuals removed throughout an eradication campaign, this can be used to model the population and calculate the probability that individuals remain at the conclusion of the eradication campaign. Solow et al. (2008) analysed trapping data from the unsuccessful eradication of Asian shrews (*Suncus murinus*) from a Mauritian island. Their Bayesian model assumed the population was closed and non-reproducing during the eradication campaign, and the population size – both before and after the campaign – was unknown. They used the record of individual trapping times to make inferences about the population size at the conclusion of the campaign, when successful eradication was mistakenly declared.

Solow et al. (2008) began by describing a prior probability distribution for the number of shrews remaining that was estimated independently of the observed trapping data. As with the single survey model (see Section 16.2.3), they used a Poisson probability distribution to describe this prior belief (e.g. Figure 16.4). They modelled the trapping data as a realisation of a non-homogeneous Poisson process, and the assumptions discussed in Section 16.2.1 apply, namely that trappings are stochastic and occur continuously and independently of one another. They then used Monte Carlo simulation to generate the posterior probability distribution for the number of shrews remaining. Using this approach, they found that the probability that the eradication was successful (i.e. that zero shrews remained at the conclusion of the eradication campaign) was only 0.27. They argue that this analysis could have prevented the mistake of declaring eradication prematurely (because presumably managers would have required a higher certainty of absence than 0.27).

The assumption of a closed population makes this model suitable for species in which the eradication is conducted outside the breeding season (as for the case study of shrews) or occurs on a short time scale compared with the generation time of the species. This assumption may make this model unsuitable for plant species in which there is ongoing germination from the undetectable seed bank.

16.2.5   Removal and Effort Data

When there are data on the amount of management effort employed during an eradication campaign as well as the number of individuals removed (or sighted) over time, this information can be used to assess the likelihood of eradication success and the effectiveness of different management methods. Ramsey et al. (2009), Ramsey et al. (2011) and Rout et al. (2014) apply catch–effort models to the island eradications of feral pigs, cats and foxes respectively.

These three studies model the relationship between effort and detection rate for different types of search and removal activities, for example, trapping, hunting with dogs, surveillance with cameras, and searching for scats. In these Bayesian models, prior estimates are required to calculate the probability of eradication success and the sensitivity of each search and removal method. Although Ramsey et al. (2009) and Ramsey et al. (2011) both assume that the pest population is closed and non-reproducing during the eradication campaign, it is possible to accommodate violations of this assumption using catch–effort models using data on reproduction (or germination), mortality and immigration or emigration rates (Seber, 1982). For example, Rout et al. (2014) used data from an independent study of an unharvested fox population as an estimate of the natural population growth rate. These models also assume that, given a particular sampling period and method, all individuals have an equal probability of detection.

The advantage of these catch–effort models is that they can incorporate data from different management methods by including a combination of removal data from trapping or hunting, and observation data from search-only methods such as camera surveillance. Catch–effort models can also incorporate variations in the amount of management effort employed over time.

16.3   Deciding to Declare Eradication

Section 16.2 described methods for quantifying the certainty that a species has been successfully eradicated, using either a null hypothesis test or a direct estimation of the probability that the species remains present. The absence of a species can never really be proven, although confidence in absence increases as more searches fail to find the species (e.g. Figures 16.2 and 16.3). How certain do we need to be to stop searching and declare eradication?

One option is for managers to set a threshold level of certainty that will trigger the decision to declare eradication. For example, in the eradication of pigs from Santa Cruz Island, managers and consulting scientists agreed that eradication be declared when they could be 95% sure that no pigs remained (Ramsey et al., 2009). However, setting an arbitrary threshold does not take into account the relative consequences of making a mistake. If there are huge negative consequences to declaring eradication prematurely, it would be sensible to set the threshold level of certainty very high. Conversely, if surveying is very expensive and the consequences of falsely declaring eradication are insubstantial, it would be best to set a much lower threshold.

These risks and consequences can be considered explicitly using decision theory. Regan et al. (2006) posed and solved this problem by using economic cost to quantify the consequences of error. They calculated the net expected cost of declaring eradication after d surveys without detection as

$$\mathrm{NEC}(d) = (d-1)C_s + p(\text{presence} \mid d)C_e, \tag{16.7}$$

where C_s is the cost of one survey, C_e is the expected cost of declaring eradication prematurely and $p(\text{presence}|d)$ is the probability that the species is present when it has not been detected for d surveys. Regan et al. (2006) then found the point at which this expected cost is minimised as the optimal point at which to declare eradication.

Regan et al. (2006) interpreted the cost of declaring eradication prematurely as the expected cost if the species were to escape from the eradication site and cause damage. This was calculated using

$$C_e = P_{\text{escape}} \times P_{\text{damage}} \times C_{\text{damage}}, \tag{16.8}$$

where P_{escape} is the probability that the species will escape, P_{damage} is the probability that it will cause damage and C_{damage} is the cost of that damage. This cost could be an economic cost, such as a loss in agricultural production, or it could be an environmental loss that has been monetised using economic valuation methods (Spangenberg & Settele, 2010). Alternatively, the cost of declaring eradication prematurely could be the cost of having to re-start the eradication program and repeat the treatments applied (Ramsey et al., 2009; Rout et al., 2014).

For example, consider again the imaginary bottleweed. A single survey for bottleweed costs A$1,000. If falsely declared eradicated, bottleweed has a 0.4 probability of escaping its previous area of infestation, and there is a 0.5 chance it will cause A$1 million worth of agricultural damage. The expected cost of escape is, therefore, $Ce = 0.4 \times 0.5 \times 1,000,000 = A\$200,000$. The probability that bottleweed remains present after several surveys without detection was calculated previously using the Bayesian sighting record method (Eq. 16.2 and Figure 16.2). This probability can be used within Eq. 16.7 to calculate the net expected cost of declaring bottleweed eradicated (Figure 16.5).

Declaring eradication after only a few surveys without detection has a very high net expected cost that is driven by the expected cost of falsely declaring eradication.

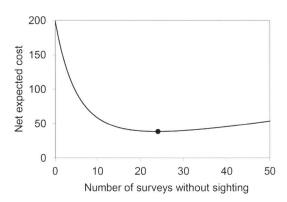

Figure 16.5.   The net expected cost of declaring eradication of bottleweed after different numbers of surveys without detection. The net expected cost is shown as a ratio compared to the cost of one survey. The probability bottleweed remains present is calculated using the Bayesian sighting record method (Eq. 16.2; see Figure 16.2). It is optimal to declare bottleweed eradicated after 24 surveys without detection (black dot).

For bottleweed, this expected cost is 200 times the cost of a single survey. The net expected cost of declaring eradication increases again after many surveys without detection as the cost of conducting surveys accumulates. For bottleweed, it is optimal to declare eradication after 24 surveys without detection, when the expected cost is lowest.

Within Eq. 16.7, the probability that the species is present when it has not been detected for d surveys can be calculated using any of the Bayesian methods described Section 16.2. There are several examples of this in the literature: Regan et al. (2006) apply the persistence and detectability model (Eq. 16.3) to find the optimal time to declare eradication of a weed species; Rout et al. (2009a) apply sighting data models, including the constant (equation 16.2) and declining sighting rate models, to the same weed species as Regan et al. (2006), Ramsey et al. (2009), Ramsey et al. (2011) and Rout et al. (2014) apply catch–effort models to find the optimal time to declare eradication of feral pigs, cats and foxes. Hypothesis testing calculations (e.g. Eq. 16.1) cannot be used within this framework, although Field et al. (2004) describe how to optimise the error thresholds of a hypothesis test to account for the consequences of making the wrong management decision.

The framework of Regan et al. (2006) is risk neutral, focusing on the best estimates of parameters and the mean expected outcomes. A risk-averse decision maker would focus instead on the worst plausible values of uncertain parameters and avoid the worst outcomes, while a risk-tolerant (or risk-prone) decision maker would focus on the best plausible values and outcomes.

Rout et al. (2009b) apply an info-gap uncertainty analysis to the framework of Regan et al. (2006) for declaring eradication. They take a risk-averse approach, seeking decisions that have an acceptable net expected cost while being most robust to uncertainty in the probability of presence. In info-gap analysis, uncertainty is propagated around a nominal, or best-guess, estimate, and the best decision (i.e. the number of surveys without detection after which eradication should be declared) is known as the robust-optimal decision (see Chapter 12). Rout et al. (2009b) used the model of Regan et al. (2006) (Eq. 16.3) as the nominal model for how the probability of presence declines with the number of surveys without detection. They derive a general result for any convex nominal model of the probability of presence: the robust-optimal solution will always be greater than the optimal solution using that nominal model. In other words, if managers are uncertain about their model of the probability of presence, they should survey for longer than the solution that minimises the net expected cost (Eq. 16.7).

Another parameter in this framework that is likely to be uncertain is the cost of declaring eradication prematurely (C_e). As discussed in Section 16.3, this cost can be interpreted in different ways, for example, as a potential cost of impact of the invasive species or as the cost of restarting the eradication campaign. When there is no clear best method for estimation, it could be advantageous to combine costs or use the limits of multiple estimates as a plausible interval for this cost. Ramsey et al. (2009) point out that many potential indirect costs of falsely declaring eradication, such as political costs or opportunity costs, are likely to be both substantial and essentially unknowable. Underestimating C_e by ignoring these costs could lead to underestimating the amount of search effort needed before eradication can be declared. If this is a concern, it could be prudent to take a risk-averse approach, such as relative regret or info-gap analysis (see Chapters 12 and 13).

16.4 Conclusion

The decision to declare eradication can be difficult, with large risks and large uncertainties. Formulating a formal decision problem has several advantages. By explicitly considering the different risks involved, managers can provide a formal justification for their decisions. This could be helpful in many ways, particularly because a bad outcome does not imply a bad decision. For example, a species can be rediscovered even when the probability of it being present is extremely small. A formal analysis could also be helpful in securing resources for additional surveys. This being said, decision tools need not dictate precisely which action should be taken. Rather, they can be used as decision support to help managers understand and communicate the implications of their decisions, and to form a basis for further discussion and compromise between managers and stakeholders.

16.5 Acknowledgements

Thanks to Terry Walshe and Joslin Moore for helpful feedback on earlier drafts. This work was supported by an ARC Discovery Grant (DP110101499).

References

Boakes, E. H., Rout, T. M. & Collen, B. (2015). Inferring species extinction: the use of sighting records. *Methods in Ecology and Evolution*, 6, 678–687.

Burgman, M. A., Grimson, R. C. & Ferson, S. (1995). Inferring threat from scientific collections. *Conservation Biology*, 9(4), 923–928.

Campbell, K. & Donlan, C. J. (2005). Feral goat eradications on islands. *Conservation Biology*, 19(5), 1362–1374.

Field, S. A., Tyre, A. J., Jonzen, N., Rhodes, J. R. & Possingham, H. P. (2004). Minimizing the cost of environmental management decisions by optimizing statistical thresholds. *Ecology Letters*, 7(8), 669–675.

Garrard, G. E., Bekessy, S. A., McCarthy, M. A. & Wintle, B. A. (2008). When have we looked hard enough? A novel method for setting minimum survey protocols for flora surveys. *Austral Ecology*, 33(8), 986–998.

McCarthy, M. A. (1998). Identifying declining and threatened species with museum data. *Biological Conservation*, 83(1), 9–17.

McCarthy, M. A. (2007). *Bayesian methods for ecology*. Cambridge: Cambridge University Press.

McCarthy, M. A. & Masters, P. (2005). Profiting from prior information in Bayesian analyses of ecological data. *Journal of Applied Ecology*, 42(6), 1012–1019.

McInerny, G. J., Roberts, D. L., Davy, A. J. & Cribb, P. J. (2006). Significance of sighting rate in inferring extinction and threat. *Conservation Biology*, 20(2), 562–567.

Moore, J. L., Hauser, C. E., Bear, J. L., Williams, N. S. G. & McCarthy, M. A. (2011). Estimating detection-effort curves for plants using search experiments. *Ecological Applications*, 21(2), 601–607.

Morris, W. K., Vesk, P. A., McCarthy, M. A., Bunyavejchewin, S. & Baker, P. J. (2015). The neglected tool in the Bayesian ecologist's shed: a case study testing informative priors' effect on model accuracy. *Ecology and Evolution*, 5, 102–108.

Morrison, S. A., Macdonald, N., Walker, K., Lozier, L. & Shaw, M. R. (2007). Facing the dilemma at eradication's end: Uncertainty of absence and the Lazarus effect. *Frontiers in Ecology and the Environment*, 5(5), 271–276.

Ramsey, D. S. L., Parkes, J. & Morrison, S. A. (2009). Quantifying eradication success: The removal of feral pigs from Santa Cruz Island, California. *Conservation Biology*, 23(2), 449–459.

Ramsey, D. S. L., Parkes, J. P., Will, D., Hanson, C. C. & Campbell, K. J. (2011). Quantifying the success of feral cat eradication, San Nicolas Island, California. *New Zealand Journal of Ecology*, 35(2), 163–173.

Regan, T. J., McCarthy, M. A., Baxter, P. W. J., Panetta, F. D. & Possingham, H. P. (2006). Optimal eradication: When to stop looking for an invasive plant. *Ecology Letters*, 9(7), 759–766.

Rout, T. M., Kirkwood, R., Sutherland, D.R., Murphy, S., & McCarthy, M.A. (2014). When to declare successful eradication of an invasive predator? *Animal Conservation*, 17(2), 125–132.

Rout, T. M., Salomon, Y. & McCarthy, M. A. (2009a). Using sighting records to declare eradication of an invasive species. *Journal of Applied Ecology*, 46(1), 110–117.

Rout, T. M., Thompson, C. J. & McCarthy, M. A. (2009b). Robust decisions for declaring eradication of invasive species. *Journal of Applied Ecology*, 46(4), 782–786.

Scott, J. M., Ramsey, F. L., Lammertink, M., et al. (2008). When is an 'extinct' species really extinct? Gauging the search efforts for Hawaiian forest birds and the Ivory-Billed Woodpecker. *Avian Conservation and Ecology*, 3(2), 3.

Seber, G. A. F. (1982). *The estimation of animal abundance*. London: Charles Griffin.

Solow, A. R. (1993a). Inferring extinction from sighting data. *Ecology*, 74(3), 962–964.

Solow, A. R. (1993b). Inferring extinction in a declining population. *Journal of Mathematical Biology*, 32(1), 79–82.

Solow, A. R., Seymour, A., Beet, A. & Harris, S. (2008). The untamed shrew: On the termination of an eradication programme for an introduced species. *Journal of Applied Ecology*, 45(2), 424–427.

Spangenberg, J. H. & Settele, J. (2010). Precisely incorrect? Monetising the value of ecosystem services. *Ecological Complexity*, 7(3), 327–337.

17 Surveillance for Detection of Pests and Diseases: How Sure Can We Be of Their Absence?

Tony Martin

17.1 Introduction

17.1.1 Context: Trade in Animals, Plants and Their Products

The Agreement on Sanitary and PhytoSanitary measures of the World Trade Organisation requires member countries to follow international standards when establishing measures to protect the life and health of their humans, animals and plants in international trade. These standards are set by the World Organisation for Animal Health, the International Plant Protection Convention and the Codex Alimentarius Commission. Measures taken by a country to protect its livestock, agriculture and natural environment from the potential introduction of pests and diseases as a result of international trade in animals, plants and their products should be the minimum (least trade-restrictive) necessary to provide a level of protection consistent with the country's appropriate level of protection. Where there is no applicable international standard, or where a country wishes to impose measures different from those specified in the international standards, the measures imposed must be supported by a science-based import risk analysis.

International standards and import risk analysis both necessarily recognise that for a pest or a disease, its presence in, or absence from, the exporting country, zone, compartment or area is critical in determining the risks associated with importations from that area, and thus in determining appropriate protection measures. Similarly, the appropriate protection measures to be applied by the importing country depend on its own pest or disease status. Surveillance for detection of the pest or disease is the means by which its presence can be determined (by detecting it) and also the means by which evidence for its absence can accumulate (by not detecting it). Although in the absence of the pest or disease, surveillance may be planned to provide a reassuring level of confidence in its absence, the level of confidence must be documented and quantified if trading partners are to be convinced.

17.1.2 Evidence for Absence

If we are going to be sure that a pest or disease is not present, we have to be sure that we would detect it if it were present. Detection of pests and diseases in an area or in a population is achieved by surveillance, which includes all processes by which the pests and diseases might be detected. A surveillance system for an exotic pest or disease typically comprises several different surveillance system components (SSCs), any one of which might detect its presence. The commonest SSC is the general diagnostic, or passive, reporting system; others might include sentinel herds, flocks or farms, a random cross-sectional survey of a population, or routine testing of products intended for export.

Without a perfect test applied simultaneously to the entire population, we can never *prove* freedom from any pest or disease. The best we can do is to demonstrate a high level of confidence, or certainty, concerning its absence. Supporting evidence for the absence of a pest or disease is provided by all functioning SSCs when they do not detect it. The more likely the SSCs would be to find the pest or disease if it were present, the greater the supporting evidence they provide.

Rephrasing this in the language of surveillance, a surveillance system for a pest or disease has a *sensitivity*, which is the probability that it will detect the pest or disease that is present in the population at some specified level (the *design prevalence*). The higher the sensitivity (i.e. the more likely it is that the surveillance system will detect the disease), the greater our confidence that the pest or disease is truly absent if the surveillance system has not found it. This chapter explores how we can quantify the sensitivities of all types of SSCs, and accumulate evidence for freedom to derive a quantitative estimate of the resulting level of confidence that a pest or disease is not present in a population. These methods are applicable to invasive species (vertebrates, invertebrates and plants) and to diseases of plants and animals, in both terrestrial and aquatic environments, and will be illustrated using a series of examples.

17.1.3 Terminology and Assumptions

Authorities in a member country of the World Trade Organization is interested in knowing whether or not it is free from pests and diseases that may affect trade, and to this end they conduct surveillance aimed at detecting the presence of a pest or disease of interest. In using the results of this surveillance as evidence for freedom from the pest or disease, we must assume that the pest or disease has not been found, and all surveillance outcomes are negative (see Results and Outcomes in this section below). If the pest or disease has been found, then it is present and the country is not free of it. The following terminology is used throughout this chapter. Key terms are emphasised in italics.

Pests and Diseases
This chapter presents a method that may be applied to any unwanted organisms, most of which are normally covered by one or other of the terms *pest* and *disease*. Reference to *pests and diseases* in the text is clearly intended to be comprehensive; reference to one or the other does not imply that the method under discussion is applicable only to that one, but is simply using the appropriate term for the example presented. *Pest* is a term usually used to imply a free-living species that is unwanted

because of its adverse impacts on the environment or agriculture. A *disease* is the unwanted manifestation in a host species of infection or infestation with a parasitic organism. This organism is often microscopic (e.g. bacteria, viruses and fungi), and although it is the organism that is actually unwanted, it is its manifestation (the *disease*) to which we often refer.

Infection and Infestation

Pests are generally said to *infest*, and diseases to *infect* their hosts. The two terms are taken to have the same meaning in this chapter.

Units, Groups and Populations
General Description

Within a country (or other jurisdiction), surveillance is conducted in or on a *population*. A population is made up of some number of population *elements*, and the smallest collection of elements that is assessed or *processed* by the surveillance forms a surveillance *unit*. The units that are processed (tested) form a subset or *sample* (≤100%) of the *population under surveillance*. This sample may be representative of the population under surveillance (i.e. randomly selected) or it may be biased (i.e. non-representative). The population under surveillance consists of all units with a non-zero probability of being processed. Results from the surveillance might be extrapolated to a wider *reference population*, which may or may not be equivalent to the whole population of the country. So, if:

- the sample of units processed is 100% of the population under surveillance;
- the population under surveillance is the same as the reference population; and
- the reference population includes all the population elements in the country

then the surveillance is effectively a census of the population.

There are many possibilities and options in this description of the hierarchy of population elements, and this is inevitable when defining terms to cover a comprehensive range of scenarios and surveillance programmes. Surveillance units are often, but certainly not always, considered to form clusters or *groups* of units based on shared attributes, such as

- How they are managed
- Who owns them
- Their categorisation by administrative bodies
- Their spatial location
- Their exposure to factors affecting their probability of being infected
- Their exposure to factors affecting the probability of infection being detected.

Application to Pests

A *pest* infests a plot of land, an area of forest, a district, a river system, a field or some other spatial entity. When we conduct surveillance for this pest (to detect the pest if it is present) we carry out inspections, or in some other way test for the presence of the pest, on individual plots of land, areas of forest, districts, river systems, fields or other entities. These are then the *surveillance units*. So we might inspect an orchard for the presence of a fruit fly, or we might inspect ponds for the presence of an aquatic weed, or suburban gardens for the presence of an ant species. The surveillance unit in these examples is the orchard, the pond and the suburban garden, respectively. When considering the presence of pests or wildlife species in an environment, the elements that constitute the assessable population are generally at the small end of a continuous spatial scale. The method presented here deals with discrete *units* of population; hence the need to define, somewhat arbitrarily, recognisable and assessable collections of elements as forming surveillance units. The population under surveillance in these examples is the population of fruit trees, the population of ponds and the population of suburban gardens that might be tested in the surveillance programme.

When analysing the surveillance results, useful groupings of surveillance units might be areas (e.g. towns or districts), shared ownership (e.g. farms) or vegetation types (e.g. dense scrub). The reference population of units is the wider population of units that we believe to be represented by the units under surveillance. In the examples presented, the reference populations might be all fruit farms in the country for fruit fly, all waterways in the country for the aquatic weed, or the whole country for ants.

Application to Diseases

A *disease* infects an animal or a plant, and in this scenario individual animals or individual plants are the elements of the population. Surveillance to detect the disease may deal with individual animals or plants (e.g. in the diagnostic laboratory), in which case the individual population elements are the surveillance units. Alternatively, a surveillance activity may perform its test on a collection of animals (e.g. a herd, a shed or a farm) or a collection of plants (e.g. a crop, an orchard or a farm), and in this case the herd, shed or farm is the surveillance unit. The population under surveillance might be, for example, all beef cattle in the country or all chipping potatoes, and the reference populations might be all cattle in the country and all potatoes grown in the country.

If the individual cow is the surveillance unit, surveillance results will often accumulate or be summarised at the herd level. An individual herd is then a group of units, and herds in general form a *grouping level* for summarising surveillance results. It is possible further to summarise results at the regional (or other) level, and in this case regions form another grouping level. Alternatively, the herd of cows may be the surveillance unit. In the terminology defined here, the herd is not a group of units because it is simply a single unit. Results can still be aggregated at the regional level, and in this case a region would be a group of units.

The level at which the surveillance observations are made defines the surveillance unit, and with animal diseases this is most commonly the individual animal of the host species. For plant diseases, an area of land where the plant grows is more commonly the surveillance unit, or a unit may even be a quantity of seed (e.g. Hammond, 2010).

Surveillance Systems and Components

Typically a *surveillance system* for detection of a pest or disease has multiple contributing SSCs, each of which comprises a separate surveillance activity. Each such activity consists of applying a test for the presence of the pest to a unit of the population. This unit has then been processed in the SSC.

Sensitivity and Specificity

The efficacy of a surveillance activity or system for detection of a pest or disease is assessed from its *sensitivity*. This term may be used for a test applied to an individual surveillance unit (i.e. the test sensitivity), a testing procedure applied to a group of units such as a herd of cattle (i.e. the herd sensitivity) or the whole surveillance system applied to the population (i.e. the sensitivity of the surveillance system). Sensitivity in this context is the probability that the test, group test or surveillance system will give a positive outcome when the pest or disease is present in the surveillance unit, group of units or population. This use of the word sensitivity is analogous to the *diagnostic sensitivity* of a diagnostic laboratory test – the probability that the test will give a positive result when it is applied to a specimen from an infected individual (or other entity). This is different from the *analytic sensitivity*, which is a measure of the minimum quantity of the assayed substance that a test can detect.

The *specificity* of a test on a surveillance unit, or a group test or a population test (an SSC or the whole surveillance system), is the probability that the test will give a negative result when the unit/group/population is *not* infected.

Results and Outcomes

An SSC for detection of a pest or disease applies at least one test to each unit processed. Each test has a dichotomous *result*: positive or negative. For example, the inspectors saw ants at a site (positive) or they did not (negative); the laboratory test for the presence of antibodies in a blood specimen gave a positive result or it did not. Tests for which the results are expressed other than dichotomously need to be considered here to have given a negative result or a non-negative (positive) result.

An SSC applied to a unit gives a dichotomous *outcome*: positive or negative. Positive implies truly infected and detected. Negative outcomes may be obtained either when the unit is uninfected or when it is infected and undetected (i.e. truly uninfected or a false negative).

Box 17.1 Enzootic Bovine Leukosis

Authorities in country A consider its dairy cattle population to be free from the viral infection enzootic bovine leukosis (EBL). EBL infection can cause a range of disease syndromes in infected animals, particularly lymphatic system tumours, which are seen most commonly in mature animals. The virus is commonly transmitted from infected adults (cows and bulls) to their progeny and may also be transmitted by any process that transmits blood lymphocytes from one animal to another (e.g. biting flies feeding on multiple animals; or shared injection needles). Once infected, an animal remains infected (and infectious) for life and also develops an immune response to the infection. The disease may be detected clinically (by recognising the tumours or other clinical signs of disease) or at the abattoir during post-mortem inspection, and infection may also be detected by tests for antibodies in the blood or milk. Viruses may be detected in a range of tissues from infected animals.

The country exports dairy heifers, which are individually tested before export, using a blood test for antibodies to EBL. There is also routine six-monthly testing of all dairy herds supplying milk to processing plants, using a test for antibodies to EBL that is applied to a sample of bulk tank milk. Other SSCs for EBL detection in this country are the general (passive) surveillance component in which clinical disease is diagnosed, and both ante-mortem and post-mortem inspection at the abattoir, where tumours can be detected.

17.1.4   Perfect Specificity

Consider the country in the example in Box 17.1. Suppose that it exports dairy products and dairy heifers, and suppose that importing countries require that both dairy products and heifers should be free from EBL. Heifers may be individually blood-tested prior to export, and the importers are satisfied with this because the test, an enzyme-linked immunosorbent assay (ELISA) for antibodies or immune proteins in the blood, has a sensitivity of greater than 99.9% (i.e. fewer than one in a thousand infected heifers will incorrectly pass the test by giving a false-negative ELISA result). Since the population from which they are drawn is believed to be free of infection, this provides an extremely high level of confidence that a heifer that tests negative will be uninfected. (Even if, contrary to our belief, infection is present in the population, we can still be at least 99.9% confident that a heifer that tests negative will be uninfected.)

But what if a heifer gives a positive ELISA result? Is she genuinely infected, or is this a false-positive test result? The importing country will refuse to accept her (and possibly all other heifers from country A) unless this is resolved and the heifer is proven to be uninfected. For this purpose, the exporter must follow up with a definitive test (detection of virus antigen in the heifer's blood), which will provide the required certainty. Although the antigen detection test may be less sensitive than the ELISA, in theory (i.e. barring laboratory mix-ups) it cannot give false positive results; it has perfect specificity. It is a kind of backstop, ensuring perfect specificity for the testing procedure applied to each heifer. Such perfect specificity is necessary for all testing procedures used to demonstrate freedom from a pest or disease because positive test results are unacceptable when the population is supposedly free from the pest or disease. Unless a positive test result can be demonstrated to be a false positive by use of a follow-up test with perfect specificity, it will be taken to indicate the potential presence of the pest or disease.

This follow-up testing forms an integral part of the SSC, and any associated reduction in the sensitivity of the SSC must be incorporated into calculations of the SSC's sensitivity. In practice, when dealing with a disease that is believed to be absent from the population, the programme of testing used to follow up a positive test on a unit often involves testing all neighbouring or otherwise associated units. This theoretically enhances the overall sensitivity of the SSC by testing further high-risk units, and in such situations it is often reasonable to assume that follow-up testing has a sensitivity of 100%.

Returning to the export of dairy products, the importing country requires that these are also EBL-free, which means that the herd or herds from which they came must be shown to be free from EBL. For a herd to be free from EBL, *all* the cows in the herd must be uninfected. If the products are derived from the milk of a single herd, evidence for freedom of the herd from EBL might be derived from a single test applied to a well-mixed sample of bulk tank[1] milk (again, an ELISA for antibodies). The sensitivity of this single test applied to the whole herd will depend on the herd size (the number of cows contributing milk to the bulk tank).[2] The test's specificity, as with the blood test on the heifer, may be less than perfect, but arrangements for follow-up testing in the event of a positive ELISA result will ensure that the whole testing procedure has 100% specificity. In this case, because the test is applied to the whole milking herd and the dairy cow population is believed to be free of EBL, follow-up will probably include individual testing of all cows that contributed to the bulk milk, using the ELISA for antibodies. Follow-up testing of any cows giving positive ELISA results would ensure that the overall herd-level specificity of the procedure would effectively be 100%, while the herd-level sensitivity would be considerably enhanced (for detection of a single infected cow, to 99.9%).

Suppose now that instead of using the bulk milk ELISA, the herd was tested by taking a specimen of blood from each of the 100 cows in the herd. Although 100 ELISAs were run, the end result for the herd is a single herd test with a negative outcome (i.e. all 100 blood ELISAs gave negative results). The sensitivity of this herd test is the probability of getting one or more positive results if the herd were infected. What about its specificity? Again, agreed testing arrangements need to include follow-up testing to resolve any positive blood ELISA results into true positives (an infected herd) and negatives, resulting in a herd test with perfect specificity.

---

[1] The bulk tank is where milk from all milking cows in the herd is mixed, awaiting collection by the dairy company.

[2] The ELISA has a certain *analytic sensitivity* (the minimum number of molecules of antibody that must be present in the test well for the assay to give a positive result). Since an infected herd is one in which there is at least one infected animal, the ELISA applied to the bulk tank milk must be able to detect antibodies from a single infected cow. The *diagnostic sensitivity* of this test is then the probability that it will give a positive result when milk from a single infected cow is mixed with milk from all the other (uninfected) cows in the milking herd. The concentration of antibodies in the bulk milk, and thus the capacity of the test to detect them, will therefore depend on the number of cows in the milking herd, decreasing with increasing numbers of cows.

In the context of exotic[3] pests and diseases, all surveillance processes and all testing procedures must include any necessary follow-up testing to resolve positive test results into true positive outcomes and negative outcomes. The surveillance process or testing procedure may then be said to have perfect specificity. We will assume henceforth that all surveillance processes providing evidence for freedom from pests or diseases have perfect specificity.

17.1.5 The Surveillance System as a Diagnostic Test Applied to the Population

In the preceding section we saw that the herd test for EBL might be a single bulk milk ELISA (with appropriate follow-up) or the summary outcome of 100 individual cow blood tests. In the same way, a surveillance component may be seen as a single test for the presence or absence of disease that is applied to a whole population.

Continuing with the example in Box 17.1, suppose the dairy products to be exported are derived from milk drawn from many herds in the population. In this case, the importing country needs evidence that the entire dairy population of the exporting country is free from EBL. To support this claim, a test is applied to the reference population of dairy herds. This test, which might be carried out every six months, consists of testing each dairy herd in the country using the bulk milk ELISA. This population-level test has a certain sensitivity (the probability that a positive test outcome will be obtained when the population of dairy herds is infected), and like all population-level tests in disease-free contexts (see Section 17.1.4) it will have perfect specificity. The sensitivity of the population-level test may be calculated from the sensitivities of the individual herd bulk milk tests and the proportion of herds that would be infected were the population infected (the design prevalence; see Section 17.1.7). Like any diagnostic test applied to an individual unit of the population, the performance of the test applied to the group (herd), or in this case to the whole population, may be described in practice using various test attributes, of which sensitivity, specificity and *negative predictive value* (NPV) are of use to us here.

17.1.6 Confidence in Freedom, and Some Notation

The NPV of a diagnostic test applied to an individual is the probability that the individual is truly uninfected given that the test gave a negative result. In notation used throughout this chapter, this is $Pr(D-|T-)$. For the herd test for EBL, the same principle applies, as it does also for the SSC (a test applied to the population). In the latter case, the NPV is the probability that the population is truly uninfected (free of EBL; D–) given that the six-monthly testing of all herds had a negative outcome; $Pr(D-|S-)$, where S– indicates a negative surveillance outcome. Note that, in the case of group (herd) tests or population-level tests (SSCs), it is necessary to qualify the definition of the NPV by including the design prevalence, which is effectively

---

[3] Exotic: not present in the population.

the (hypothetical) level of infection in the herd or population that constitutes the cut-off between infected and uninfected.

The NPV is equivalent to the level of confidence we have concerning the pest-free or disease-free status of the population, given currently available surveillance findings. The term *confidence in freedom* is often used to convey this concept. The word *confidence* is also used in other contexts to mean different things (e.g. in hypothesis testing, for $1 - \text{Pr(type I error)}$, or when evaluating an SSC, the sensitivity of the SSC is referred to as the confidence of detecting the pest or disease). It is thus important to use the word with care, and in this chapter we use it only to denote confidence in freedom, or the probability that the population is free from the pest or disease at the design prevalence.

NPV is predicated on a negative test outcome and clearly the same is true for any statement about confidence in freedom from the pest or disease. If any positive surveillance outcomes are obtained, the unit, group or population cannot be considered free of the pest or disease, whatever the design prevalence may be.

17.1.7   Design Prevalence

The sensitivity of any SSC or surveillance system is the probability that it will detect the pest or disease if it is present. Clearly, it cannot be detected if it is absent. To estimate sensitivity, we therefore need to assume that the pest or disease is (hypothetically) present. For an SSC applied to a population this means we must specify the amount or frequency of the pest or disease that marks the artificial boundary between its presence and its absence. This boundary is necessarily artificial, and is used simply as the standard at which SSC sensitivity is estimated.

Some might like to specify the presence of a single 'element' of the pest or disease agent (e.g. a virus, a bacterium, an insect egg, a bird, or a fungal spore) as marking its presence in the population. In most circumstances, the probability that this single element will be detected will be extremely low, whatever the nature of the SSC. However, given a reasonably sensitive test, we are highly likely to detect the pest or disease when it is present in most population units, but the value of being able to do so is questionable because the principles of surveillance suggest that the information generated (in this case, the presence of the pest or disease) should be acted upon, and in most situations early detection will be important. It is therefore sensible to select an amount of pest or disease that defines its presence in the population that is

- Reasonably detectable
- Low enough not to cause unacceptable impacts on human health, the environment or other values
- Low enough that action could be taken to eliminate or control the pest or disease if it were detected
- Acceptable to trading partners (or others with an interest in the outcome) as a level defining presence or absence.

The level selected is known as the *design prevalence* (denoted by P^*) and is generally expressed as the proportion of population units in which the pest or disease is present. The design prevalence is the minimum amount of the pest or disease that will be present if it is present at all. In the case of rapidly spreading disease, this may well be a substantial proportion of units (say 25%), but with a slowly spreading pest or disease it will probably be a smaller proportion.

Often, and particularly within small groups, the within-group design prevalence may be specified as one infested/infected unit in the group because the group cannot be infested/infected if no individual units are infested/infected. The herd of dairy cows tested for EBL (see the example in Box 17.1) is considered infected with EBL if one or more cows is infected, and the within-herd design prevalence is therefore the inverse of the number of cows in the herd. Another example is that of surveillance for bovine tuberculosis in farmed deer (see More et al., 2009).

For the SSC testing herds using the bulk milk ELISA, the design prevalence will probably be expressed as a proportion of dairy herds that are infected with EBL, for example 0.002, which is the design prevalence prescribed by the World Organisation for Animal Health (2012) for EBL. As another example, serological surveillance of poultry for notifiable avian influenza in the European Union is designed and assessed using two levels of design prevalence: an among-flock design prevalence [the (hypothetical) proportion of all poultry flocks that is infected] of 0.05, and a within-flock design prevalence (the proportion of birds that is infected within an infected flock) of 0.3 (European Commission, 2007).

In quantifying the probability of having achieved eradication of tuberculosis-infected possums from an area, Anderson et al. (2013) superimposed a grid over the area, and the surveillance unit was one grid cell. The design prevalence in their analysis was then the proportion (0.0004) of grid cells containing infected possums if the area were infected.

Design prevalence, is an integral part of all quantitative estimates concerning probability of detection or confidence in freedom. Thus, the sensitivity of an SSC is its sensitivity at a specified design prevalence. When this sensitivity is then used to estimate confidence in freedom, the estimate is the confidence in the population being free of the pest or disease at the design prevalence. Thus confidence in disease freedom must be conditioned on an underlying design prevalence.

17.1.8   Clustering of Infection

In animal diseases, and sometimes in other applications, infectious disease clusters. Typically, there is clustering at the level of the management group, and for domestic livestock this is very often the farm. Once introduced to a farm, a disease can spread among animals that are kept in close contact. The disease may not spread so readily to animals on other farms if there is little contact between them. Even in an area containing many neighbouring farms with the same species of livestock, some farms will be infected and others will stay uninfected. This is due to varying degrees of contact between pairs of farms, in particular movement of animals between farms, as experienced in the foot and mouth disease epidemic in the United Kingdom in 2001 (Ortiz-Pelaez et al., 2006).

Where clustering is likely to occur, the probability that an individual animal (or other surveillance unit) is infected is not the same across all population units; an animal in an infected herd has a different probability of being infected from an animal in an uninfected herd. When estimating SSC sensitivity in these circumstances, it is necessary to specify two design prevalences, one at the farm level (P_H^*) and one at the animal level (P_U^*). In the EBL example in Box 17.1, if the individual cow is the surveillance unit, there is a need for an among-cow, within-herd, design prevalence, and in estimating population-level SSC sensitivity there is also a need for an among-herd design prevalence (the proportion of herds in the population that are infected). P_U^* is the design prevalence *within an infected herd*. The prevalence in an uninfected group (herd) is zero.

It is possible to specify numerous design prevalences, each applying to a grouping level in the population. In practice, one or two are generally used. Note that the overall proportion of the population which is notionally infected is the product of the design prevalences, $P_H^* \times P_U^*$.

Box 17.2 Red Imported Fire Ants

Red imported fire ants (RIFAs; *Solenopsis invicta*) are difficult to live with and difficult to control. Under suitable conditions, RIFAs form extensive super colonies that have multiple queens, that spread rapidly. They are omnivorous opportunistic feeders that prey on invertebrates, vertebrates and plants. RIFAs destroy seeds, harvest honeydew from specialised invertebrates and scavenge. Their foraging can affect whole ecosystems by reducing plant populations and through competition with native herbivores and insects for food. RIFAs have a fiery sting that is unusual in that blisters and pustules develop at the sites of the stings, which are generally numerous[4].

RIFAs are assumed not to be present in country X, which receives many shipments of imported goods, including many that could harbour soil and possibly RIFAs. If RIFAs are to be eradicated, early detection is essential and an active surveillance programme is conducted around all ports and associated high-risk sites such as import depots. This programme consists of periodic visits to all high-risk sites by a team of trained inspectors who examine the sites for evidence of RIFAs and take samples of any suspicious-looking ants for identification by entomologists.

Other components of the surveillance programme include reporting of unusual or unwanted ants by the public and reports from medical practitioners of cases of blisters and pustules following ant bites.

---

[4] See Wikipedia (2013) and Collins and Scheffrahn (2001) for more information on the biology of RIFAs.

17.2   Surveillance Systems, Components and Their Applicability

In this chapter, a *surveillance system* for a pest or disease refers to all of the surveillance activities that might detect the pest or disease in question. The surveillance system comprises one or more surveillance system components and applies to a particular reference population.

17.2.1   Reference Population

The *reference population* is the population of surveillance units to which the surveillance system is applied, for which surveillance data are available for each of the SSCs and about which inference will be made based on any analysis of the surveillance findings (see Section 17.1.3).

17.2.2   Defining Infection or Infestation

When conducting surveillance for detection of a pest or disease that is believed to be absent, a positive surveillance outcome must involve definitive identification of the pest or disease. Many SSCs may, however, aim primarily to detect something different; this is particularly true in animal health, where an immunological response to infection is often used as a proxy for actual infection. In the example in Box 17.1, the export heifers are tested for antibodies to the EBL virus. This is a valid proxy for detecting EBL virus because infected animals develop antibodies to the virus and also remain infected for life. However, many viral infections are transient (e.g. influenza and foot-and-mouth disease) and detection of antibodies merely implies a past infection. In fact, in many viral infections, by the time an animal has developed a measurable level of antibodies, it will no longer be infected. In both plants and animals, a disease syndrome may be pathognomonic for a single causative agent and an SSC may focus on detection of this syndrome.

Clearly, these complications serve to emphasise that care should be taken in defining what constitutes a positive surveillance outcome, and as discussed in Section 17.1.4, all SSCs should include any necessary follow-up testing needed for resolving positive results from the initial screening test into true positives and negatives.

17.2.3   Random and Non-random Surveillance Components

SSCs may provide data on a representative sample of the reference population, as in the case of a structured, random, cross-sectional survey; or they may provide information that is either deliberately or accidentally non-representative of the population. Factors that affect the probability that a pest or disease will be detected in the population (i.e. that surveillance will have a *positive outcome*) are those that affect the probability of infection or infestation as well as factors that affect the probability of detection of infected units. So to be truly representative of the population (i.e. unbiased), a sample of units must be representative of the distribution of these factors in the population, or at least be stratified by levels of the key factors affecting probability of infection and probability of detection.

SSCs often process units opportunistically, without regard to representativeness or to relevant factors affecting the probability of a positive outcome. An example of this is the SSC described in Box 17.1 in which heifers intended for export are tested for EBL antibodies. The heifers are not representative of the dairy population of the country: among other things they are all female, they are from a few specific farms, they are all between 12 and 30 months old and none of them has had a calf or lactated.

Many surveillance components are deliberately designed to process units that are more likely to give positive outcomes; if you really want to find a pest or disease, look where you are most likely to find it if it is present. This is *risk-based surveillance*, and a good example is the strategy of inspecting high-risk sites for red imported fire ants (RIFAs) described in Box 17.2. Negative findings in this SSC provide greater reassurance of the absence of RIFAs than if the inspections were conducted at a random sample of sites across the country.

Whether deliberately or accidentally acquired, data from biased samples of population units generate valuable information. If the units are high risk (i.e. they have an above-average chance of being infested or infected), negative outcomes give us more confidence in the population being free from disease than do negative outcomes from units with only an average chance of being infested or infected. Similarly, for low risk units, negative surveillance outcomes are less convincing (with regard to the population being free of the pest or disease) than those from units at average risk.

Similar reasoning applies to the probability that an infected unit will be detected. Negative results from infected units with a high chance of being detected provide better evidence for freedom than negative results from those with an average or low chance of being detected. In the case of EBL in the example in Box 17.1, infected animals generally develop clinical signs (tumours) later in life, if at all. Noting that no young animals (e.g. the heifers being exported) have clinical disease is not at all convincing, and the same observation for cows more than over 10 years old would carry much more weight.

The differential surveillance benefits gained from units with different probabilities of infection or detection, or both, are readily quantified in estimating the sensitivity of an SSC, provided the necessary information on the relevant factors affecting these probabilities is available to the analyst, for each unit processed, and (in summary form) for the whole of the reference population. The sensitivity of the overall surveillance system can readily be estimated by combining the sensitivities of random and non-random SSCs.

> **Box 17.3** Newcastle Disease in Poultry
>
> Country C has commercial poultry industries involving chickens, ducks and turkeys. In addition, around 30% of people keep backyard poultry. The country is believed to be free of Newcastle disease, a viral infection that, in its virulent form, causes very high mortality in poultry. The virus may be transmitted from bird to bird and via faeces and environmental contamination. Wild birds may spread the virus and non-virulent strains of the virus can mutate to virulence. From all perspectives, authorities in country C are keen to maintain its disease-free status and want to detect infection as early as possible should it occur. To this end a surveillance programme is planned, and the efficacy and value of the general diagnostic (passive surveillance) system is being estimated because it is thought likely that this should be the cornerstone of surveillance to detect a disease with obvious clinical signs. Active, targeted surveillance can then be designed to supplement the general diagnostic system as necessary.

17.2.4 Coverage of the Reference Population

Some SSCs process every population unit, and thus have comprehensive coverage of the population. Passive general surveillance forms an important component of many surveillance systems for exotic pests and diseases. This is the process whereby people who manage domestic animals or plants, or who live in the region under surveillance, report or seek diagnostic or other assistance with pest occurrences or clinical signs of disease. Each population unit has a chance of being infected and a chance of being detected. It is important to be clear whether an SSC has comprehensive or partial coverage of the population. In the EBL example (Box 17.1), milking cows, dry cows, bulls, calves, steers and heifers that are not exported have no chance of giving positive surveillance outcomes in the SSC that tests export heifers for EBL, so this SSC does not have comprehensive coverage of the population of dairy cattle. It is important to be aware that where some units are systematically excluded from an SSC, it will sometimes not be possible to include those units in the reference population. In the example in Box 17.2, if high risk site inspections are conducted in only one of several regions in the country, the results of this SSC may well not be applicable to the other regions.

17.3 Principles of Analysis

17.3.1 Confidence in Freedom

As discussed in Section 17.1.6, our level of confidence in a population's pest-free or disease-free status (taking into account current surveillance evidence) is given by the NPV of the surveillance system when we consider the surveillance system to be a diagnostic test applied to the population.

The NPV for a diagnostic test applied to an individual unit may be given by an application of Bayes' theorem:

$$NPV = \Pr(D-|T-) = \frac{\Pr(T-|D-) \times \Pr(D-)}{\Pr(T-|D-) \times \Pr(D-) + \Pr(T-|D+) \times \Pr(D+)}, \quad (17.1)$$

This theorem states that the probability of the unit being uninfected, given a negative test result, is equal to the probability of getting a negative test result from an uninfected unit divided by the total probability of all possible ways of getting a negative test result.

This can be transcribed into the notation of sensitivity (Se = test sensitivity) and specificity (Sp = test specificity):

$$NPV = \Pr(D-|T-) = \frac{Sp \times (1-p)}{Sp \times (1-p) + (1-Se) \times p}, \quad (17.2)$$

where p is our pre-test estimate of the probability that the unit was infected. This *prior probability* that the unit was infected is commonly estimated by the prevalence of infection in the population, or in the case of an exotic disease, by the design prevalence, P^*. The NPV is then our revised, or *posterior*, estimate of the probability that the unit is *not* infected, given a negative result to the test.

When we apply the same formulae to the surveillance system (system sensitivity = SSe, system specificity = SSp, and prior probability of infection = $PriorPInf$), we get

$$NPV = \Pr(D-|S-) = \frac{SSp \times (1-PriorPInf)}{SSp \times (1-PriorPInf) + (1-SSe) \times PriorPInf}. \quad (17.3)$$

Now unlike the diagnostic test applied to the individual unit, our surveillance system has perfect specificity (see Section 17.1.4), so this reduces to

$$NPV = \Pr(D-|S-) = \frac{1 - PriorPInf}{1 - SSe \times PriorPInf}. \quad (17.4)$$

It is apparent from this equation that the two quantities required for estimating the probability that the population is free from disease (at the design prevalence) given a negative surveillance system outcome, are

1. An estimate of the prior (pre-surveillance) probability that the population was infected (at the design prevalence)
2. An estimate of the sensitivity of the surveillance system (at the design prevalence).

The prior probability of the population being infected ($PriorPInf$) might be estimated in various ways:

- *Expert opinion.* An estimate based on one or more person's expert knowledge of the pest or disease, its global distribution, its potential for establishment in the region concerned, the probability of it having been introduced, the capacity of the country's surveillance system to detect it if present, past surveillance findings and any other relevant considerations.

- *Agreement by interested parties.* A figure that is acceptable to key stakeholders in the process.
- *A conservative or 'uninformed' estimate* (one not allowing any bias towards the disease being either present or absent). This implies that prior to the surveillance which has recently been conducted there was no information on which to base an estimate, and we had no idea whether the country was infected (at the design prevalence) or not. Such an estimate might be 0.5.
- *Past surveillance findings.* The estimate of *PriorPInf* for this year can be derived from the last year's posterior estimate of confidence in freedom (i.e. last year's NPV). This can be repeated sequentially over multiple periods (see Section 17.9).

The sensitivity of the surveillance system at the design prevalence is the only measure of the efficacy of our surveillance that is needed for estimating confidence in freedom. *SSe* is a measure of how hard we have looked for the pest or disease. If we have put a great deal of effort into finding the pest or disease or looked in all the most likely places, or both, then we can be confident that it is not present. On the other hand, if we didn't see the pest or disease simply because we didn't look very hard, or because we looked in the least likely places, we won't be very confident that it is absent. The rest of this chapter focuses on estimating *SSe* and the sensitivity of the contributing SSCs.

17.3.2 Group Sensitivity

This section describes calculation of sensitivity for a group, cluster or aggregation of similar units such as herd-level sensitivity in the EBL example (Box 17.1) when this is assessed from results of individual animal blood tests. Where there is no intermediate grouping of units, this approach applies equally to calculation of SSC sensitivity such as the RIFA SSCs described in Box 17.2 or the bulk milk testing SSC for EBL (Box 17.1).

The sensitivity of any diagnostic test is the probability that it will give a positive result when applied to an infected individual. This assumes a dichotomous test outcome. The same assumption is made when considering tests applied to groups of individuals. A single test applied to the group (e.g. the bulk milk ELISA for EBL antibodies in the dairy herd) has easily defined positive and negative results. The sensitivity of the test varies with the optical density value used as the cut-off between positive and negative in the laboratory, and with the dilution of milk from infected cows in the bulk tank. When the group test consists of a series of individual tests applied to a sample of the units comprising the group, a negative outcome for the group test occurs when all the individual tests have negative results. A positive group test outcome is when at least one of the individual tests has a positive result.

For an individual surveillance unit in an infected group to give a positive outcome, it must be both infected and detected. If the sensitivity of the diagnostic test(s) applied to the unit is SeU and the probability that it is infected is P_U^*, then the probability that it will give a positive outcome is

$$\Pr(U+) = \Pr(D+) \times \Pr(T+|D+) = P_U^* \times SeU. \tag{17.5}$$

This follows from the probability of a positive test result being conditional on the disease status of the unit; SeU is actually $\Pr(T+|D+)$, where D+ denotes an infected unit. Furthermore, because an SSC has perfect specificity, we can ignore the possibility that uninfected units generate positive test results; these will not be demonstrated to be true positives in the follow-up testing.

If we assume that the group is homogeneous with regard to probabilities of infection and detection, and in a group-testing procedure we process n units in this infected group, then if n is small relative to the group size N ($n < 0.1N$), it is reasonable to assume that each unit has the same probability of giving a positive outcome. For each of them, $\Pr(U+) = P_U^* \times SeU$, and $\Pr(U-) = 1 - P_U^* \times SeU$. For the group test, the probability that one or more of the n tested units gives a positive test result is the complement of the probability that all n give negative results:

$$\text{Group test sensitivity} = SeH = 1 - \left(1 - P_U^* \times SeU\right)^n \tag{17.6}$$

or one minus the product of all processed units' probabilities of having a negative outcome. The assumptions made here, if valid, allow use of a binomial probability formula (Cameron & Baldock, 1998).

Non-homogeneous Groups

Where subgroupings of units can be identified as having different probabilities of being infected or detected, group sensitivity can be calculated separately for each subgroup using Eq. 17.6. Each subgroup to which Eq. 17.6 is applied should be homogeneous with regard to probability of infection and probability of detection.

If group-level sensitivity is to be calculated for non-homogeneous groups whose constituent units are independent of each other (i.e. their probabilities of infection or detection are not dependent on the infection or detection status of other units in the group), the probability that one or more members of the group will give a positive outcome is

$$\text{Group test sensitivity} = SeH = 1 - \prod_{j=1}^{n}\left(1 - EPIU_j \times SeU_j\right) \tag{17.7}$$

where $EPIU_j$ is the effective probability of infection for the jth unit among the n units processed (see Section 17.5), and SeU_j is the sensitivity of the detection process applied to it.

In the EBL example (Box 17.1), suppose a sample of h out of a total of H dairy herds in the country is tested for EBL using an ELISA on individual cow blood samples, with a varying number of animals tested in each of the h herds. For each herd tested, the sensitivity of the herd test is

$$SeH_i = 1-\left(1- P_U^* \times SeU\right)^{n_i},\qquad(17.8)$$

where the subscript i denotes the individual herd and n_i is the number of animals tested in the ith herd.

Hypergeometric Probability Formula; Small Groups

In many surveillance activities, however, the number of units processed may well be more than 10% of the group (or population) size. In these cases, a hypergeometric probability formula should be used instead of the binomial, and a simple formula for SeH approximating the hypergeometric probability is

$$SeH = 1-\left(1-\frac{n}{N}\times AveSeU\right)^{N\times P_U^*},\qquad(17.9)$$

where $AveSeU$ is the average unit sensitivity for those processed in the group (Cameron & Baldock, 1998; MacDiarmid, 1988). In this formula, $N \times P_U^*$ is the number of infected units in the group. In general, it is appropriate to round this quantity to a whole number, since a fraction of a unit makes little sense – each unit is either infected or not infected. When estimating surveillance sensitivity and confidence in freedom, rounding *down* is generally a good idea, since it will lead to more conservative sensitivity estimates.

If the probability that units are infected also varies among the units processed in this group (see Section 17.5), the same hypergeometric probability formula can be used with the average probability of infection ($AveEPIU$) for the units processed:

$$SeH = 1-\left(1-\frac{n}{N}\times AveSeU\right)^{N\times AveEPIU}.\qquad(17.10)$$

Exact Probability Formula; All Units Tested

Where *all* the units in the group are processed ($n = N$), an *exact* probability formula should be used. In this case, given the design prevalence, we *know* how many infected units have been processed if the group is infected: $N \times P_U^*$. The probability that one or more of them will give a positive outcome is one minus the probability that they will all give negative outcomes. Because we have perfect specificity, the uninfected units cannot give positive outcomes. The probability that an infected unit will give a positive outcome is SeU (or $AveSeU$ if SeU varies among units) and the group level sensitivity is

$$SeH = 1-\left(1- AveSeU\right)^{N\times P_U^*},\qquad(17.11)$$

which is a straightforward derivation from Eq. 17.9.

In the EBL example, where a within-herd design prevalence is the inverse of the herd size (i.e. one animal infected), this simplifies further to

$$SeH = 1 - (1 - SeU)^1 = SeU. \tag{17.12}$$

17.3.3   Among-Group Sensitivity

Having calculated the sensitivity for each group of units processed, the same logic and principles apply to calculating the sensitivity of the SSC in which units are organised in groups for the analysis: the among-group sensitivity. In the EBL example, where herd sensitivity was calculated based on the individual animals on which blood tests were performed, the next step is to calculate the SSC sensitivity based on the individual herds that have been tested. This two-stage process deals appropriately with the clustering of infection within herds. In theory, this can be repeated at multiple levels (where there are multiple grouping levels, each with a design prevalence specified). In most cases, two levels are sufficient (e.g. Christensen et al., 2011; Hadorn & Stärk, 2008; Martin, 2008; Frössling et al., 2009).

In among-group estimation of SSC sensitivity (*CSe*) we can use binomial, hypergeometric or exact probability formulae as dictated by circumstances (see Table 17.1).

17.4   Visualising Surveillance Processes Using Scenario Trees

A scenario tree is a logical branching structure that depicts how a surveillance unit *processed in an SSC* gives a positive outcome in the SSC. A scenario tree can summarise the structure of an SSC to show how the SSC relates to the reference population and the entire population of the country, what is done in the SSC, what is done to individual units and any groups to which they belong, and how the SSC can give a positive outcome. The scenario tree can be useful for some calculations, and is valuable in showing exactly what information is needed to estimate the sensitivity of the SSC.

The scenario tree representing an SSC should include all the factors affecting the probability that a unit is infected, and all factors affecting the probability that it will be detected. In estimation of the sensitivity of the SSC, its principal uses are to

- Define the structure of the SSC
- Represent the SSC visually
- Identify inputs required for estimation of SSC sensitivity
- Calculate average sensitivity for a processed unit – useful where unit-specific data are not available on factors affecting probabilities of infection or detection.

In the context of modelling surveillance components, a scenario tree is a model of all possible ways that a surveillance unit can give a positive outcome in the SSC. The starting point is the reference population being infected or infested with the

Table 17.1. Formulae for calculation of among-group or SSC sensitivity in different circumstances

Circumstances	Formula		Within-group equivalent
Where all groups processed have equal probabilities of infection and detection AND are independent of each other $(h < 0.1H)$	$CSe = 1 - \left(1 - P_H^* \times SeH\right)^h$	(17.13)	Eq. 17.6
Where groups have differing probabilities of infection, differing sensitivities, AND are independent of each other $(h < 0.1H)$	$CSe = 1 - \prod_{i=1}^{H}\left(1 - EPIH_i \times SeH_i\right)$	(17.14)	Eq. 17.7
Where groups have equal or varying sensitivities, equal probabilities of infection, AND $h > 0.1H$	$CSe = 1 - \left(1 - \dfrac{h}{H} \times AveSeH\right)^{H \times P_H^*}$	(17.15)	Eq. 17.9
Where groups have varying sensitivities, differing probabilities of infection, AND $h > 0.1H$	$CSe = 1 - \left(1 - \dfrac{h}{H} \times AveSeH\right)^{H \times AveEPIH}$	(17.16)	Eq. 17.10
Where all groups in the population have been processed	$CSe = 1 - \left(1 - AveSeH\right)^{H \times P_H^*}$	(17.17)	Eq. 17.11
Where all groups in the population have been processed, and the design prevalence is based on one group being infected $(P_H^* = 1/H)$	$CSe = AveSeH$	(17.18)	Eq. 17.12

Key to new notation used in this table

Variable	Meaning
$AveSeH$	Average group sensitivity for the groups processed in the SSC
$EPIH$	Effective Probability of Infection for a group (see Section 17.5)
$AveEPIH$	Average EPIH for all groups processed in the SSC

disease or pest at the design prevalence. A branching structure breaks this population down into its component subpopulations and units, separating these into infected and uninfected, and then detected and undetected subsets. This process is illustrated in Figures 17.1a, 17.1b, 17.2 and 17.3. The scenario tree consists of a series of nodes, each of which marks a branching point and represents a factor affecting the probability that a surveillance unit will give a positive outcome. The perfect specificity of SSCs for exotic pests and diseases allows considerable simplification of model structure. Uninfected units cannot yield positive surveillance outcomes and redundant limbs can therefore be truncated.

Figure 17.1a shows a scenario tree representing a model of the bulk milk testing SSC of the example in Box 17.1, while Figure 17.1b shows a tree for the testing of individual animals prior to export. In Figure 17.2, a scenario tree is shown for the example in Box 17.2 in which high-risk sites are inspected for RIFAs. Figure 17.3 illustrates a scenario tree for the general surveillance component of Newcastle disease surveillance described in Box 17.3. These diagrams illustrate the three main node types used in scenario tree models of surveillance components. These are (using the nodes in Figure 17.2 as illustrations)

- Infection nodes (e.g. SITE STATUS) dividing units or groups into those that are *infected* and those that are *uninfected*
- Detection nodes (e.g. RIFAs DETECTED) dividing infected units into those that are *detected* and those that are *not detected*
- Category nodes (e.g. PATHWAY, HABITAT and DETECTION DIFFICULTY) dividing the population or group into subpopulations or subgroups, or categorising an individual unit, according to the factor specified by the node.

Category nodes are generally of three kinds:

- Risk category nodes, or risk nodes, which divide the population into subpopulations with different risks of being infected or infested. In Figure 17.2, the PATHWAY risk node divides the country into five different categories of sites with different probabilities of RIFAs being introduced. In this case these are artificial categories representing five qualitative levels of probability of introduction from *very low* (1) to *very high* (5). The HABITAT risk node further divides the population of sites into five categories representing different levels of habitat suitability for RIFA establishment from *very low* (1) to *very high* (5). In Figure 17.3, the MANAGEMENT node divides each of the turkey, chicken and duck populations into *Backyard* and *Commercial* flocks because *Backyard* flocks are thought to be at greater risk of infection than *Commercial* flocks.
- Grouping category nodes, or grouping nodes, which divide the population into subpopulations based on administrative categories. They do not per se have different probabilities of infection or detection, but represent subpopulations within which the data for the SSC are grouped, or by which the results need to be reported (e.g. REGION in Figures 17.1a and 17.1b and SPECIES in Figure 17.3).
- Detection category nodes, which divide the population into subgroups with different probabilities of being detected. The node DETECTION DIFFICULTY in Figure 17.2 splits inspection sites into five different categories based on their vegetation cover and topography. Again, these are contrived categories for which detection difficulty is estimated qualitatively from very difficult (1) to very easy (5).

All factors affecting probability of infection or probability of detection need to be included in any model of the SSC, since the goal is to calculate its sensitivity.

Each branch of each node has a probability (infection and detection nodes) or proportion (category nodes) associated with it. At any node, all possible outcomes are specified by its branches so that branch probabilities or proportions sum to 1

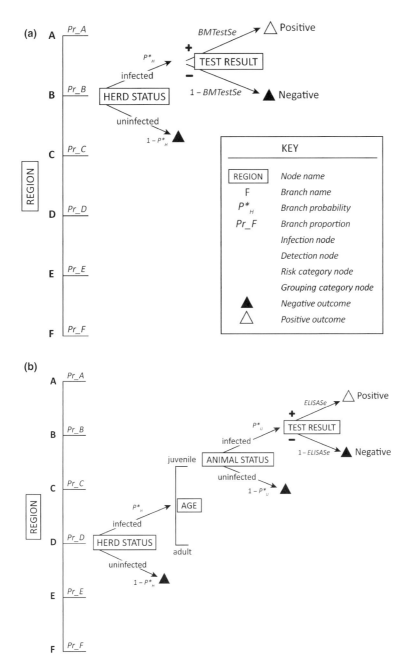

Figure 17.1. (a) Scenario tree for the *Bulk Tank Testing* SSC described in Box 17.1. All six regions have identical limb structure, but for clarity only region B is completed. (b) Scenario tree representing the SSC comprising individual animal blood testing prior to export, as described in Box 17.1. Only one limb is shown, but all truncated limbs have the same structure. Refer to part (a) for a key to the symbols and notation.

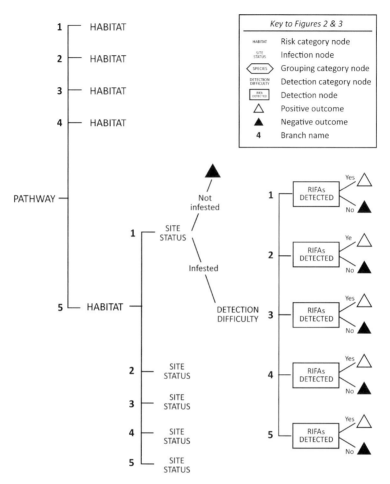

Figure 17.2. Scenario tree for the SSC *Inspection of high-risk sites* as described in Box 17.2. The complete structure is shown for only one instance of PATHWAY and HABITAT; they all have the same structure.

at each node in the tree. Each branch probability or proportion is conditional on all preceding nodes in its limb of the tree. In the expanded limb of the Newcastle disease general surveillance SSC shown in Figure 17.3, the probability associated with the *Yes* branch of the CLINICAL SIGNS node is the probability of clinical signs occurring in an infected flock of commercial turkeys in country C. Branch probabilities or proportions associated with a particular node will vary among occurrences of that node in the tree. This model is of those *units that are processed in the SSC*, and the category node branch proportions required for SSC sensitivity calculations are proportions of units actually processed.[5] This structure allows for

---

[5] As will be seen in the section on differential risk, proportions of the reference population must also be specified for branches of risk nodes. These proportions and the associated estimates of relative risk must be specified for all branches of a risk node; hence the inclusion of PATHWAY categories 1, 2, 3 and 4 in Figure 17.3.

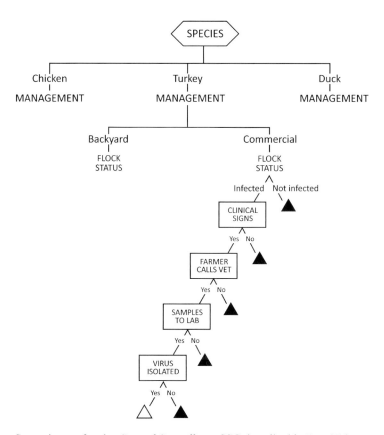

Figure 17.3. Scenario tree for the *General Surveillance* SSC described in Box 17.3.

easy visualisation of all the probabilities and proportions that must be estimated to estimate SSC sensitivity.

17.4.1 Alternative Representations of SSCs for Computation of Sensitivity

Hood et al. (2009) presented two alternative formats for visualisation of SSCs and computation of component sensitivity. Matrix algebra may be used for calculation of average sensitivity (see Section 17.5), and Bayesian belief networks may be used to visualise the surveillance process and compute the component sensitivity. Readers should refer to the paper by Hood et al. for further information; here we stick to the straightforward logic of the scenario tree formulation.

17.4.2 Calculating Average Sensitivity

The structure of the scenario tree allows calculation of the sensitivity for the average surveillance unit or group. The scenario tree is a model of all possible ways in which a randomly selected, processed unit can give a positive outcome in the SSC. The probability that this randomly selected unit will give a positive outcome given that the population is infected at the design prevalence(s) is then the sum of the limb probabilities for all limbs with positive outcomes. This is of use where hypergeometric or exact probability formulae are to be used in calculating CSe, or where relevant attributes (e.g. SPECIES and MANAGEMENT in Figure 17.3) of individual processed units are not known. In these situations, an *average* probability is required, either because of the computational requirements of the formula approximating the hypergeometric probability (Eqs. 17.9, 17.10, 17.11, 17.12, 17.15, 17.16, 17.17 and 17.18) or because in the absence of unit-specific data on relevant factors, the best we can do is to use an average figure for all units processed. However, we hope we have data for all or most of the units processed.

The average probability of a positive outcome can be calculated at any level of the tree; common examples are as follows. Averages for *processed* units (as opposed to all units in the reference population) are calculated using the relevant proportions of units processed (notated $PrSSC\_xxx$) where these data are available, rather than population proportions.

a. Average probability that a processed unit will have a positive outcome given that the population is infected at the design prevalence(s).

In the tree in Figure 17.3, this is obtained for the illustrated limb with a positive outcome by multiplying together all branch proportions and probabilities on the limb:

Pr(U+ for *Commercial Turkey* flocks) $=PrSSC\_Turkey \times PrSSC\_Commercial|Turkey \times EPI\_Commercial|Turkey \times$Pr(Clinical signs|*Infected Commercial Turkey* flock) $\times$Pr(Farmer calls vet|Clinical signs in *Infected Commercial Turkey* flock) $\times$Pr(Samples to lab|Vet called; Clinical signs; *Infected Commercial Turkey* flock) $\times$Pr(Virus isolated|Samples; Vet; Clinical signs; *Infected Commercial Turkey* flock)   (17.19)

where $PrSSC\_Turkey$ is the proportion of flocks processed that are *Turkey* flocks; $PrSSC\_Commercial|Turkey$ is the proportion of *Turkey* flocks processed that are *Commercial*, and $EPI\_ Commercial|Turkey$ is the effective probability of infection for *Commercial Turkey* flocks (see Section 17.5). Positive-outcome limb probabilities are calculated similarly for *Backyard Turkey* flocks, *Commercial Chicken* flocks, and so on. Then the average probability of a unit (flock) having a positive outcome is the sum of all these positive outcome limb probabilities.

Note that in this example, the SSC has comprehensive coverage of the population, so the proportions processed are the same as the population proportions.

b. The average sensitivity for a unit within an infected group is the average probability that an infected processed unit will have a positive outcome given that the group is infected.

In the tree in Figure 17.2, the average site sensitivity might be needed if the DETECTION DIFFICULTY of some individual sites has not been recorded. It may be calculated as

$$AveSiteSe_{p,h} = \sum_{d=1}^{5}\left(PrSSC_{d,p,h} \times \mathrm{Pr}(\mathrm{RIFA\ detected})_{d,p,h}\right), \qquad (17.20)$$

where $AveSiteSe_{p,h}$ is the average site sensitivity for processed sites of PATHWAY category p and HABITAT category h, $PrSSC_{d,p,h}$ is the proportion of units processed that are DETECTION DIFFICULTY d in PATHWAY category p and HABITAT category h, and $\mathrm{Pr}(\mathrm{RIFA\ detected})_{d,p,h}$ is the sensitivity of the inspection for a site of DETECTION DIFFICULTY d in PATHWAY category p and HABITAT category h. Then the inspected sites in HABITAT h and PATHWAY p for which no detection difficulty was recorded can be allocated a site sensitivity of $AveSiteSe_{p,h}$. (For sites with a complete inspection record, the site sensitivity is simply $\mathrm{Pr}(\mathrm{RIFA\ detected})_{d,p,h}$.)

17.5 Differential Risk of Infection

Although the population is deemed to be infected at the design prevalence (for the purposes of estimation of SSC sensitivity) this does not mean that infection is necessarily uniformly distributed across the population. Surveillance units exposed to risk factors for infection are more likely to be infected than those that are not, and infection may cluster in groups. The latter scenario (clustering) is effectively accommodated by specifying separate among-cluster and within-cluster design prevalences, and the use of two-stage (or multistage) calculation of SSC sensitivity as laid out in Sections 17.3.2 and 17.3.3. The former scenario (differential risk arising from differential exposure to risk factors) is the subject of this section.

Where an SSC processes units based on convenience or any other non-random selection process, the processed units cannot be assumed to be representative of the reference population. Within the population, there may be subpopulations of units with different probabilities of being infected, given that the population is infected at the design prevalence. In the RIFA site inspection SSC (Box 17.2; Figure 17.2) the presence of RIFAs depends on the ants having been introduced to the site and the suitability of the habitat at the site. It is more likely that RIFAs will be present at a site to which imported goods are taken regularly than at a randomly selected site, to which it is unlikely that imported goods would ever be taken directly from the port. Site inspections are therefore aimed at the high risk sites. There is greater surveillance benefit from inspecting high risk sites and surveillance benefit is measured in terms of SSC sensitivity.

Differential risk is most readily quantified using the concept of *relative risk* (RR), which is the risk (or probability[6]) of infection in one group relative to the risk of infection in another. The reference, or lowest, risk group is generally assigned a RR of 1. A higher risk group might have a RR of 5, implying that units in this group are five times as likely to be infected as those in the reference group. In the Newcastle

---

[6] Here and throughout this chapter, *risk* refers to likelihood (probability) only.

disease general surveillance SSC (Box 17.3; Figure 17.3), we might estimate that *Backyard* flocks are five times as likely to be infected as *Commercial* flocks, given that the population is infected at the design prevalence P^*.

Without any information on differential risk associated with MANAGEMENT, P^* is the best estimate of the probability that a flock is infected. By specifying RRs for the sub-populations *Backyard* and *Commercial*, we are effectively assigning different infection probabilities to flocks in these two risk groups. When estimating SSC sensitivity and confidence in freedom, we do so for the specified design prevalence P^*, so it is important that the average prevalence across the population should be P^*. The *effective probabilities of infection* (EPIs) that result from application of the RRs in our calculations must therefore average P^* over the reference population. This is achieved by applying *adjusted relative risks* (ARs) such that the ARs retain the relativity of the RRs and they average 1 over the reference population. Then

$$EPI \_ Backyard = AR \_ Backyard \times P^* \qquad (17.21)$$

such that

$$\frac{AR \_ Backyard}{AR \_ Commercial} = \frac{RR \_ Backyard}{RR \_ Commercial} \qquad (17.22)$$

and

$$(AR\_Backyard \times PrP\_Backyard) + (AR\_Commercial \times PrP\_Commercial) = 1, \qquad (17.23)$$

where *PrP_Backyard* and *PrP_Commercial* are the proportions of flocks *in the reference population* that are *Backyard* and *Commercial* respectively; in the expanded limb of Figure 17.3 this will be the proportion of *Turkey* flocks in the reference population that are *Backyard*. Simplifying and generalising the two conditions above

$$AR_k = \frac{RR_k}{\sum_{k=1}^{K}(RR_k \times PrP_k)}, \qquad (17.24)$$

where AR_k, RR_k and PrP_k are the AR, RR and population proportion for risk group k of K risk groups.

In calculating group and among-group sensitivities, the calculated EPI is then used as the probability that a unit (or group) is infected. In so doing, EPIs are applied to all the units processed in the SSC, and where the proportions of units processed are different from the population proportions used in equation 17.24, the calculated sensitivity will be different from that obtained when the units are proportionally representative of the reference population. Sensitivity will be higher if a relatively high proportion of high risk units is processed and lower if a relatively high proportion of low risk units is processed.

Clearly, it is not reasonable to specify relative risks that are inconsistent with the design prevalence and population proportions. Analysts should be careful not to apply logically impossible RRs to P^*, or the EPI may exceed one.[7]

17.5.1   Multiple Risk Factors

Where there are multiple risk factors for infection, represented by multiple sequential risk nodes in a scenario tree model, effective probabilities of infection can be estimated by calculating ARs for each contributing category of each applicable risk factor, and then combining them multiplicatively with the design prevalence.

For example, in Figure 17.2 the PATHWAY and HABITAT risk nodes both apply to the probability of infestation for an inspection site. RRs are specified for each branch of the PATHWAY node relative to the lowest risk branch and also for each branch of the HABITAT node relative to its lowest risk branch. ARs are calculated (separately) for both of these nodes, using the appropriate population proportions. For the expanded limb of the scenario tree shown in Figure 17.2, the EPI for a site in PATHWAY category 5 (P5) and HABITAT category 1(H1) is then

$$EPI\_P5\_H1 = AR\_P5 \times AR\_P5\_H1 \times P^*, \qquad (17.25)$$

where AR_P5 is the AR for sites in P5 (relative to other PATHWAY categories), and AR_P5_H1 is the AR for sites in H1 (relative to the other HABITAT categories) within Pathway category 5.

This may be followed for more than two risk nodes. In all cases, it is important that the appropriate population proportions should be used to adjust the RRs. Where only a single risk factor is present, this is generally straightforward, although the issues raised in this section should still be considered. Where there are multiple risk nodes, or one risk node and one or more grouping category node, the following considerations apply.

Using the terminology of scenario trees, the population proportion applicable to a branch of a category node is conditional (dependent) on all preceding node branches in the limb on which the node occurs. In the expanded limb shown in Figure 17.2, the proportion of inspection sites in HABITAT category 1 is the proportion of P5 sites that are H1. The same is true for the relative risk; RR_H1 may, theoretically, vary among branches of the PATHWAY node.

ARs calculated in this way will be specific to the PATHWAY category for which they are calculated, and this is appropriate when the HABITAT category is not independent of the PATHWAY category. However, if HABITAT is independent of PATHWAY, ARs should be calculated using overall population proportions (i.e. independent of the

---

[7] For example, if the within-group design prevalence is high (as is often appropriate for highly contagious diseases – say 30%) and the proportion of high risk units in the group is low, the maximum possible relative risk is the reciprocal of the design prevalence (3.33 in this case), so estimates of the RR should be constrained accordingly.

PATHWAY category; the same values for each occurrence of the HABITAT node). This is true whether PATHWAY is a risk node or simply a grouping category node.

In general, where a risk factor is independent of higher level category nodes, population proportions used for adjusting the RRs at the risk node should be summed across all branches of those higher nodes. Where a risk factor is not independent of a higher level risk or grouping node, its RRs should be adjusted based on population proportions within the branches of the higher level node(s). Where multiple risk nodes are independent of each other, they may be combined into a single multibranch risk node with branch proportions calculated assuming independence of the individual contributing risk factors (i.e. by multiplication), and these branch proportions should be used to adjust the RRs of each branch (which are also calculated multiplicatively).

17.6 Differential Detection Probability

In estimating the sensitivity of an SSC that gives a series of negative outcomes when surveillance units are processed, we need to know the probability that each of those units would give a positive outcome if infected. This is the SeU_j of Eq. 17.7. This may be constant among units, for example the sensitivity of the blood ELISA on an individual infected heifer in the EBL example (Box 17.1), or it may vary among units. In the RIFA example in Box 17.2, as illustrated in Figure 17.2, inspection sites are categorised according to their level of DETECTION DIFFICULTY. For each of the five categories of site, there is a different probability of detecting RIFAs if they are present (SeU), and within a category, all sites have the same SeU.

It is also possible that each site has a unique value for SeU. Continuing with the RIFA example, the probability of detecting RIFAs (when a nest is present) at a site may be calculated as a function of several variables:

- Detection difficulty (1, 2, 3, 4 or 5) – a measure of the density and type of vegetation and the topography of the site
- Area of the site
- Number of inspectors and experience or skill of inspectors
- Time spent inspecting.

Similarly, in the bulk milk testing SSC described in Box 17.1, the sensitivity of the test applied to the bulk tank milk varies with the number of cows contributing milk to the tank and the amount of milk they each contribute, since an infected herd contains at least one infected cow(s), and the milk from the infected cow or cows is diluted by the milk from the rest of the herd.

In these cases, if unit-specific data are not available for calculation of SeU, an average SeU will have to be used. Although this may give a mean group sensitivity estimate close to that obtained by calculating unit-specific $SeUs$, variability associated with diverse unit properties will not have been incorporated and the group sensitivity estimate will be inaccurate if its individual units are not typical of the population.

17.7 Combining SSCs

Sensitivities of individual SSCs comprising the surveillance system for the pest or disease in question may be combined into a surveillance system sensitivity (*SSe*) as follows:

$$SSe = 1 - \prod_{l=1}^{L}(1 - CSe_l) \qquad (17.26)$$

This is valid if the *L* contributing SSCs are independent of each other, with no processing of the same units (or the same groups) in multiple SSCs.

17.7.1 Overlap and Non-independence of SSCs

Within a surveillance system for detection of a particular pest or disease, SSCs may not be independent of each other if some units or groups of units have been processed in both. Even where there is no clustering of the pest or disease in groups of units, if some of the same units have been processed in both SSCs using tests that are related (i.e. tests for the same manifestation of infection), they cannot be considered independent, and Eq. 17.26 cannot be used without first making some adjustments for this lack of independence as follows.

Where overlap has occurred, the sensitivity of the detection process in the second SSC must be adjusted for the fact that a negative result has already been obtained in the first SSC. In the example in Box 17.1, suppose that a dairy herd that exports heifers has two sets of evidence for its freedom from EBL: blood tests done on the heifers prior to export (SSC1) and a herd test consisting of the same blood test applied to all non-milking animals in the herd (SSC2). If both SSCs are contributing *current* information, for example the testing was all carried out in the same surveillance period (see Section 17.9)], then any heifer tested twice can have only one test counted because the second test simply duplicates the first. Animals exported before the herd test was carried out can be added to the herd test results because they had only one test. If different laboratory tests were used for the SSCs for animals that were tested twice, the sensitivity used for the second test should be its sensitivity when it is applied to animals that have already given a negative result in the first test. Once the adjusted sensitivity of the second SSC has been calculated (i.e. accounting for the overlap and non-independence of the diagnostic tests), Eq. 17.26 may be used.

The same principles apply when considering non-independence of SSCs with one or more grouping levels. Continuing with the EBL example in Box 17.1, SSC1 and SSC2 are supplemented at the national level by bulk milk testing for antibodies to EBL (SSC3). Combination of the sensitivities of SSC1 and SSC2 was dealt with by combining them at the herd level and incorporating appropriate adjustments for overlap in duplication of testing. Each processed herd then has a herd-level sensitivity, SeH_12_i, based on SSC1 and SSC2. SSC3 provides only herd-level information.

Within the herd, it can be considered independent of SSC1 and SSC2 because it processes only milking cows, which have not been blood tested. At the national level, however, SSC3 is not independent of SSC1 and SSC2, because it provides additional information about the same herds.

One way of looking at this is that after getting negative results for a herd in SSC1 and SSC2, we already have some evidence that the herd is free from EBL, and the additional evidence provided by a negative outcome in SSC3 will not raise our confidence in its free status by as much as it would if we had no information from SSC1 or SSC2. In this case

$$SeH\_123_i = 1-(1-SeH\_1_i)\times(1-SeH\_2_i)\times(1-SeH\_3_i), \qquad (17.27)$$

which is a within-herd application of Eq. 17.26. This assumes that the non-independence of test results within the herd has been accounted for in the calculation of SeH_1_i, SeH_2_i and SeH_3_i (see also Cannon, 2002). This is the simplest way to deal with the overlap in herd coverage of SSCs. The sensitivity of the surveillance system, SSe, is then calculated using one of Eqs. 17.14 to 17.18, as appropriate (see Table 17.1).

17.8   Comparison of SSCs

If the efficacies of different SSCs, or combinations of SSCs, in a surveillance system are to be compared using their calculated sensitivities ($CSes$), it is important that the same risk node structure and design prevalence(s) are used in each. Comparison may then be made directly between the component sensitivities. Alternatively, the CSe of an SSC may be compared to the CSe that would be obtained if the same SSC were used with random or representative sampling of surveillance units from the reference population. This type of comparison illustrates the sensitivity benefits or costs of any non-random or risk-based sampling used in the SSC.

17.9   Use of Historical Surveillance Information

Past surveillance findings can be used as the basis for quantitative estimation of the prior probability that the population is infected at the design prevalence, thereby:

- Quantifying what we naturally do in our heads when making a subjective qualitative estimate
- Deriving the otherwise elusive prior probability of population freedom that is necessary for estimating the posterior (post-surveillance) probability that the population is free from the pest or disease
- Using otherwise-redundant historical surveillance findings in an appropriate way.

Here we explore how this is done. Suppose we have been conducting surveillance for an exotic pest or disease for two years and have not detected it. If our surveillance period is one year (as might be appropriate for the examples in Boxes 17.1 and 17.2) we can divide the accumulated surveillance findings into two one-year data sets. In so doing, we assume that sequential observations on the same unit or same group of units are independent of each other when they occur in different periods. (When there is a constant threat of introduction and a surveillance period that defines the required frequency of reassessment of pest or disease status, this seems appropriate.)

For each of these two periods, we can calculate the surveillance system sensitivity, SSe_{tp}, where tp represents the year. Before conducting the surveillance we had no evidence one way or the other as to whether the disease was present, so we calculate our confidence in freedom from the disease (at the design prevalence) after the first year's surveillance ($tp = 1$) using a value of 0.5 for $PriorPInf_1$ (see Section 17.3.1) in Eq. 17.4:

$$PostPFree_1 = \frac{1 - PriorPInf_1}{1 - PriorPInf_1 \times SSe_1}.$$ (17.28)

We now have a post-surveillance estimate of the probability that the population was infected at the end of year 1:

$$PostPInf_1 = 1 - PostPFree_1.$$ (17.29)

SSe_1 is bound to be greater than zero, so $PostPInf_1$ will be less than $PriorPInf_1$. As evidence for freedom accumulates, the probability that infection is present decreases.

17.9.1 Probability of Introduction

The only reasons why the probability of the disease being present might change between the end of year one and the end of year two are that the disease might be introduced during the year or the disease might be eradicated during the year.

There can be no ongoing eradication programme because the disease is believed to be absent, and it is reasonable to assume that spontaneous eradication does not occur. A new introduction of the disease is therefore the only means by which disease status of the population might be changed. All reference to disease status in this context necessarily includes *at the design prevalence*, so here we are saying that the only way the probability that the population is infected at the design prevalence can change from one year to the next (without inclusion of any new evidence for presence or absence) is through the possibility of the introduction of disease at the design prevalence. The concept of introduction at the design prevalence includes an increase in the prevalence of pre-existing disease to cross the design prevalence threshold. If we assume that the probability of introduction of the disease is reasonably constant from one period to the next, and that the likely rate of spread of the disease following introduction does not vary from one period to the next, then the probability of the prevalence becoming $>P^*$ during a period is equal to the probability of introduction during a period.[8] Using this convenient proxy for the probability of disease being introduced at the design prevalence, during period 2 the probability that the population is infected at the design prevalence increases due to the constant threat of introduction. So when we come to estimate a level of confidence in population freedom following the second period's surveillance evidence, our prior probability of the population being infected is derived as

$$\mathrm{Pr}\,iorPInf_2 = PostPInf_1 + PIntro_2 - (PostPInf_1 \times PIntro_2) \qquad (17.30)$$

because it is possible that infection was present at $>P^*$ at the end of period 1, and that it was also introduced during period 2. ($PIntro_{tp}$ is the probability of infection being introduced (at P^*) during time tp.)

This prior probability then feeds into period 2's Bayesian revision of the probability that the population is infected at the design prevalence. Applying Eq. 17.4,

$$PostPFree_2 = \frac{1 - PriorPInfl_2}{1 - PriorPInfl_2 \times SSe_2}. \qquad (17.31)$$

This same process can be followed through sequential periods with negative surveillance outcomes, steadily increasing or decreasing our confidence in freedom, depending on the balance between $PIntro$ and SSe[9] (see Figure 17.4). The equilibrium level of confidence obtainable ($PFreeEquil$; see Watkins et al., 2009) may be calculated for constant $PIntro_{tp}$ and constant SSe_{tp}:

$$PFreeEquil = \frac{1 - PIntro_{tp}/SSe_{tp}}{1 - PIntro_{tp}}. \qquad (17.32)$$

$PIntro_{tp}$ is generally estimated as part of an import risk analysis. For the process described here, quantitative estimates are required.

17.10   Dealing with Uncertainty

It is inevitable that most of the quantities needed for quantitative evaluation of surveillance for detection of pests and diseases will not be known for certain. Either estimates need to be made from available data or, in the absence of relevant data, from expert opinion. These estimates may be represented in the calculations by their most likely values, but generally it will be preferable to incorporate the uncertainty associated with the estimates into the calculations using stochastic modelling software. A comprehensive discussion of this process is given by Vose (2008).

---

[8] If these assumptions are not valid, alternative methods for estimating the probability of infection being introduced at the design prevalence, for each period, will need to be used. See, for example, Martin (2008).

[9] Confidence in freedom will decrease in period tp if the probability that disease will be introduced during that period outweighs the evidence for freedom derived from the surveillance evidence accumulated over the same period. Specifically, if $PIntro_{tp}$ is less than the product of SSe_{tp} and $PriorPInf_{tp}$, $PostPFree_{tp}$ will increase, and it will decrease if $PIntro_{tp} > (SSe_{tp} \times PriorPInf_{tp})$.

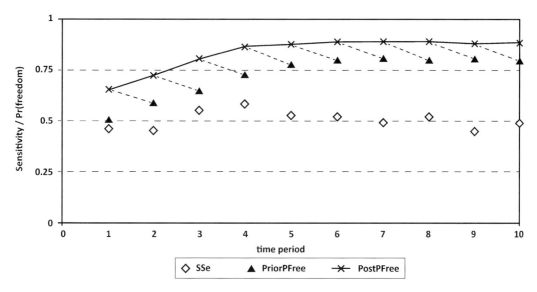

Figure 17.4. Probability of population freedom from infection (at the design prevalence), given ongoing negative surveillance findings (over 10 surveillance periods) from a system delivering a sensitivity in the range 0.4 to 0.6 and constant probability of introduction of infection of 0.1 per period.
[After Martin, P. A. J., Cameron, A. R. & Greiner, M. (2007). Demonstrating freedom from disease using multiple complex data sources 1: A new methodology based on scenario trees. *Preventive Veterinary Medicine*, 79(2–4), 71–97, with permission.]

17.11   Summary

This chapter presents methods for quantifying the sensitivity of a surveillance system for detection of a pest or disease believed to be absent from a country or region. The sensitivity of the surveillance system may then be used to provide quantitative estimates of confidence in the pest-free or disease-free status of the country or region, and this level of confidence may be revised following further surveillance conducted in sequential periods. This approach provides an objective quantitative basis for otherwise subjective qualitative assessments of confidence in freedom. Both random (representative) and non-random (biased or risk-based) sampling strategies in components of the surveillance system are equally amenable to this quantitative evaluation.

A significant component of most surveillance programmes for exotic pests and diseases is the general (passive) surveillance component. The value of this component can be quantified and incorporated into quantitative estimates of confidence in freedom of the population or country from the pest or disease.

The approach described in this chapter may be applied to any evaluation of the efficacy of surveillance for detection of pests or diseases. It is typically used for assessing the efficacy of surveillance in support of claims to disease or pest freedom.

Design and evaluation of surveillance for notifiable avian influenza in Canada (Christensen et al., 2011) and Europe (Alba et al., 2010; Welby et al., 2010) has been based on this approach, as has evaluation of surveillance for bovine tuberculosis in Europe (More et al., 2009), Australia (Sergeant et al., 2010), Sweden (Wahlström et al., 2010), Denmark (Carlo-Artavia et al., 2013) and New Zealand (Anderson et al., 2013). Other animal disease applications include brucellosis in the United Kingdom (Hesterberg et al., 2009), Switzerland and Bosnia (Hadorn et al., 2008); porcine reproductive and respiratory syndrome in Sweden (Frössling et al., 2009); classical swine fever (hog cholera) in Denmark (Martin et al., 2007b); bovine Johne's disease in Sweden (Frössling et al., 2009) and Australia (Martin, 2008), and *Trichinella* in Denmark (Alban et al., 2008).

Applications to plant pests and diseases are less common, although surveillance in this field is equally amenable to quantitative evaluation and risk-based design (Hammond, 2010). Surveillance for unwanted vertebrate pest species may also be evaluated in this way, and Anderson et al. (2013) have used this approach to quantification of confidence in freedom for assessment of possum eradication in control of bovine tuberculosis in New Zealand.

Watkins et al. (2009) assessed acute flaccid paralysis surveillance for human poliomyelitis in Australia, but instances of freedom from disease in human medicine are rare outside global eradication campaigns.

Quantification of the value of surveillance for pest and disease detection, in particular the valuation of differential risk, opens the door for wider use of risk-based (and therefore potentially more cost-effective) surveillance in support of freedom claims in international trade. It also makes possible the adoption of output-based standards for surveillance (More et al., 2009), freeing surveillance planners and funders from prescriptive input-based requirements. Whittle et al. (2013) describe a quantitative, probabilistic approach for designing a cost-effective, risk-based, multiple-pest, output-driven surveillance system, when tackling conservation of the ecology of a small island in the face of new industrial activity.

Accumulation of surveillance evidence gathered over time into a current quantitative estimate of confidence in freedom implies less reliance on annual testing for maintenance of an acceptable level of confidence. This has the potential to reduce costs and free resources for a broader surveillance programme.

17.12   Further Reading

Food and Agriculture Organization of the United Nations. (2014). *Risk-based disease surveillance – a manual for veterinarians on the design and analysis of surveillance for demonstration of freedom from disease*. FAO Animal Production and Health Manual No. 17. Rome, Italy. Available from www.fao.org/publications/card/en/c/1440fee4-be47-4d38-8571-4dad3f3036d6/

Willeberg, P., Paisley, L. G. & Lind, P. (2011). Epidemiological models to support animal disease surveillance activities. *Scientific and Technical Review of the OIE*, 30(2), 603–614.

References

Alba, A., Casal, J., Napp, S. & Martin, P. A. (2010). Assessment of different surveillance systems for avian influenza in commercial poultry in Catalonia (north-eastern Spain). *Preventive Veterinary Medicine*, 97(2), 107–118.

Alban, L., Boes, J., Kreiner, H., et al. (2008). Towards a risk-based surveillance for *Trichinella* spp. in Danish pig production. *Preventive Veterinary Medicine*, 87, 340–357.

Anderson, D. P., Ramsey, D. S. L., Nugent, G., et al. (2013). A novel approach to assess the probability of disease eradication from a wild-animal reservoir host. *Epidemiology and Infection*, 141(7), 1509–1521.

Carlo-Artavia, F. F., Alban, L. & Nielsen, L. R. (2013). Evaluation of surveillance for documentation of freedom from bovine tuberculosis. *Agriculture*, 3, 310–326.

Collins, L. & Scheffrahn, R. H. (2001). *Red imported fire ant*. University of Florida. Available from http://entomology.ifas.ufl.edu/creatures/urban/ants/red_imported_fire_ant.htm

Cameron, A. R. & Baldock, F. C. (1998). A new probability formula for surveys to substantiate freedom from disease. *Preventive Veterinary Medicine*, 34(1), 1–17.

Cannon, R. M. (2002). Demonstrating disease freedom – combining confidence levels. *Preventive Veterinary Medicine*, 52(3–4), 227–249.

Christensen, J., Stryhn, H., Vallières, A. & El Allaki, F. (2011). A scenario tree model for the Canadian notifiable avian influenza surveillance system and its application to estimation of probability of freedom and sample size determination. *Preventive Veterinary Medicine*, 99(2–4), 161–175.

European Commission. (2007). Commission decision on the implementation of surveillance programmes for avian influenza in poultry and wild birds to be carried out in the member states, and amending decision 2004/450/EC (2007/268/EC). *Official Journal of the European Union*, L115, 3–17.

Frössling, J., Ågren, E. C. C., Eliasson-Selling, L. & Lewerin, S. S. (2009). Probability of freedom from disease after the first detection and eradication of PRRS in Sweden: Scenario-tree modelling of the surveillance system. *Preventive Veterinary Medicine*, 91(2–4), 137–145.

Frössling, J., Ågren, E. C. C., Wahlström, H., Lindberg, A. & Sternberg Lewerin, S. (2009). Evaluation of the surveillance system for MAP infection in Swedish cattle. In *Procedings of the 10th International Colloquium on Paratuberculosis*. Available from www.paratuberculosis.info/images/stories/pdfs/443.pdf

Hesterberg, U. W., Cook, A. J., Stack, J. A. & Martin, P. A. J. (2009). Evaluation of the sensitivity of the British brucellosis surveillance system using stochastic scenario tree modelling. Paper presented at the *12th International Symposium on Veterinary Epidemiology and Economics (ISVEE XII)*, Durban, South Africa, 9–14 August 2009.

Hadorn, D. C., Haracic, S. S. & Stärk, K. D. C. (2008). Comparative assessment of passive surveillance in disease-free and endemic situation: example of *Brucella melitensis* surveillance in Switzerland and in Bosnia and Herzegovina. *BMC Veterinary Research*, 4, 52.

Hadorn, D. C. & Stärk, K. D. C. (2008). Evaluation and optimization of surveillance systems for rare and emerging infectious diseases. *Veterinary Research*, 39(6), 57.

Hammond, N. E. B. (2010). *Evaluation of emergency plant pathogen surveillance and surveillance methods for demonstrating pest freedom in Western Australia*. PhD thesis, Murdoch University, Perth, Australia.

Hood, G. M., Barry, S. C. & Martin, P. A. J. (2009). Alternative methods of computing the sensitivity of complex surveillance systems. *Risk Analysis*, 29(12), 1686–1698.

MacDiarmid, S. C. (1988). Future options for brucellosis surveillance in New Zealand beef herds. *New Zealand Veterinary Journal*, 36(1), 39–42.

Martin, P. A. J. (2008). Current value of historical and ongoing surveillance for disease freedom: Surveillance for bovine Johne's disease in Western Australia. *Preventive Veterinary Medicine*, 84(3–4), 291–309.

Martin, P. A. J., Cameron, A. R., Barfod, K., Sergeant, E. S. G. & Greiner M. (2007b). Demonstrating freedom from disease using multiple complex data sources 2: case study – classical swine fever in Denmark. *Preventive Veterinary Medicine*, 79(2–4), 98–115.

Martin, P. A. J., Cameron, A. R. & Greiner, M. (2007a). Demonstrating freedom from disease using multiple complex data sources 1: a new methodology based on scenario trees. *Preventive Veterinary Medicine*, 79(2–4), 71–97.

More, S. J., Cameron, A. R., Greiner, M., et al. (2009). Defining output-based standards to achieve and maintain tuberculosis freedom in farmed deer, with reference to member states of the European Union. *Preventive Veterinary Medicine*, 90(3–4), 254–267.

Ortiz-Pelaez, A., Pfeiffer, D. U., Soares-Magalhães, R. J. & Guitian, F. J. (2006). Use of social network analysis to characterize the pattern of animal movements in the initial phases of the 2001 foot and mouth disease (FMD) epidemic in the UK. *Preventive Veterinary Medicine*, 76(1–2), 40–55.

Sergeant, E., Happold, J., Hutchison, J. & Langstaff, I. (2010). Evaluation of Australian surveillance for freedom from bovine tuberculosis. Project AL.121R Report prepared for the Australian Biosecurity CRC for Emerging Infectious Disease. Available from www1.abcrc.org.au/uploads/5c94f8f6-7dc1-4f74-a9e4-86479f7786f8/docs/Report_surveillance_freedom_from_bovine_tb.pdf

Vose, D. (2008). *Risk analysis: a quantitative guide*, 3rd ed. Chichester, UK: John Wiley & Sons.

Wahlström, H., Frössling, J., Lewerin, S. S., Ljung, A., Maria Cedersmyg M. & Cameron, A. (2010). Demonstrating freedom from *Mycobacterium bovis* infection in Swedish farmed deer using non-survey data sources. *Preventive Veterinary Medicine*, 94(1–2), 108–118.

Watkins, R. E., Martin, P. A. J., Kelly, H., Madin, B. & Watson, C. (2009). An evaluation of the sensitivity of acute flaccid paralysis surveillance for poliovirus infection in Australia. *BMC Infectious Diseases*, 9, 162.

Welby, S., van den Berg, T., Marché, S., Houdart, P. & Hooyberghs, J. (2010). Redesigning the serological surveillance program for notifiable avian influenza in Belgian professional poultry holdings. *Avian Diseases*, 54(Suppl 1), 597–605.

Whittle, P. J. L., Stoklosa, R., Barrett, S., Jarrad, F., Majer, J., Martin, P. & Mengersen, K. (2013). A method for designing complex biosecurity surveillance systems: detecting non-indigenous species of invertebrates on Barrow Island. *Diversity and Distributions*, 19(5–6), 629–639.

Wikipedia (2013). Red imported fire ant. Available from http://en.wikipedia.org/wiki/Red_imported_fire_ant

World Organisation for Animal Health (2012). Enzootic bovine leukosis. *Terrestrial Animal Health Code*. Available from www.oie.int/index.php?id=169&L=0&htmfile=chapitre_1.11.9.htm

18 Some Questions to Ask Yourself

Rob Cannon

18.1 Introduction

Words with almost the same meaning have become entrenched in the different disciplines that deal with biosecurity. Using either *pest* or *disease* by itself in a general context inevitably results in a suggestion that the other be added. We use *infected* for diseases and *infested* for pests. *Prevalence*, *density* and *infestation rate* are other examples of words with similar usage. There are even more options for describing the proportion of times a procedure will do what it is meant to do: sensitivity and specificity (serological tests), efficacy (treatments), effectiveness (inspection) and confidence (statistics). The action being done will depend on context, for example, testing, surveying or inspecting. When reading this chapter, please translate these types of words into a context you are familiar with.

18.2 How Much Surveillance Is Required to Demonstrate Freedom?

'Why do we want to demonstrate freedom?' is probably the first question to ask ourselves. It might be to facilitate trade, it might be to allay public concern, or it might be because we have been told to do so. Whatever the reason, the answer to that question will be taken as known. This section discusses some of the key questions you need to ask yourself about the broad design of such a surveillance programme.

18.2.1 Can Surveillance Demonstrate Freedom?

Sometimes we can use the biology of the pest to *prove* freedom of an area when no pests are found by a survey. The number of pests in a region will vary over time, but will generally increase. As discussed later, despite this variation and uncertainty, we may still be able to agree on a minimum pest density (*MinDen*) that would be present *at the time of the survey* if the area being surveyed were infested. From our knowledge of the pest's biology, we can say

1. If the pest is present, its density will be greater than *MinDen*.

We would design our survey so that it is large enough to be able to say

2. A survey that finds no pests implies that the pest density is less than *MinDen*.

If we find no pests in the survey, we can conclude from statement (2) that the density is less than *MinDen,* and then from statement (1), we can say that the pest cannot be present. Of course, statement (2) should really be qualified by the phrase 'with a certain degree of confidence'. Our confidence that the pest is not present when we have a negative survey is equal to the probability that the pest would have been detected if its density were *MinDen*.

This argument can't be used in every situation; sometimes we cannot, or do not want to, specify a minimum density. If we have no statement (1) to fall back on, we must specify a design prevalence and base our survey size on it. We can then simply say that, if the pest had been present at a density greater than or equal to the design prevalence, we would have detected it with the required confidence.

18.2.2 Can the Pest Still Get in?

The standard (and completely correct) criticism about using surveys to demonstrate freedom is that the pest might have only recently entered the region and its density would not have increased to a level that could be reliably detected by the survey. To demonstrate that a region is free from a pest, we must be able to demonstrate that strong measures are (and were) being taken to reduce the chance of infestation or reinfestation. This might be achieved by inspection at the border of everything entering the region, by a host-free zone around the region or by appropriate surveillance of a buffer zone around the region.

18.2.3 What Is the Minimum Pest Density?

When designing a survey, we use the minimum pest density expected in an infested area to determine the survey size that will achieve the desired confidence of detecting the pest. For some pests, infestation rates in similar regions overseas might provide useful information. In other cases, we may decide to model the increase in pest density over time because we may be doing surveys over a number of years. Ideally, the modelling would also include information that would help us determine the sensitivity of the inspection methods by modelling not just (say) the proportion of trees infested in an orchard but also the proportion of an infested tree that is affected. The modelling would begin with a small pest population that had just been introduced or had survived eradication. The starting day would be the date quarantine measures were imposed, the date of a possible incursion or the date the last control treatments were applied after an eradication campaign. A simple answer to the minimum density question is not possible. While the pest's biology is of prime importance, other factors such as weather, availability of hosts and methods of transmission might need to be considered. Chapters 5, 6 and 7 have more to say on this topic.

18.2.4   What Level of Confidence Do We Need?

Before tackling this question, let's remind ourselves what we mean by *confidence* in a statistical sense: it's the probability that the conclusion drawn from our data is correct.

Although we wouldn't need the concept of confidence limits in this chapter, given how often they are calculated, it seems worthwhile mentioning them. When we analyse data to determine a numerical characteristic (or parameter) of a population, for example the proportion of passengers who have failed to declare prohibited goods, we typically want two things: a point estimate (our best bet) and, to cover ourselves, an interval estimate (also called confidence limits) that gives a range of values for the parameter for which the observed results are not too unlikely. Because we can devise any number of algorithms for calculating interval estimates, we need a way to measure how well they perform. One way to do this is to ask: 'What is the probability that the calculated interval would include the value of the parameter?' This question is often expressed as: 'What is the probability that the parameter is within the confidence intervals?' Superficially, these two formulations of the question are the same. However, the emphasis has changed; the second suggests (wrongly) that it is the parameter that can vary – it is the end points of the interval that vary depending on the observations.

The probability that the calculated interval will include the value of the parameter is called the confidence level. In some cases (typically with continuous data), the confidence level is the same for all values of the parameter. For other cases (typically with discrete data), the confidence level depends on the actual value of the parameter, and we can say things such as 'the method gives at least 95% confidence' or 'the probability our interval covers the true value averages out at 95% but is sometimes slightly better and sometimes slightly worse'. Box 18.1 shows this for binomial limits. We can view our algorithms as black boxes with numbers such as 95% or 99% stamped on the side. Which black box should we use?

For surveys to demonstrate freedom, the confidence provided by the survey is the probability that the survey would detect the disease or pest if it were present (and strictly speaking, we should add 'at the specified disease level'). The overall level of confidence that we want a survey to achieve will depend on a number of factors. Comparing the cost of sampling with the likely cost if we wrongly conclude the area is free of disease may be one consideration in setting the confidence level, especially if the survey is for home consumption. Sometimes we do not have to ask this question: the confidence required of the survey will be specified by some (international) agreement or by the people requiring the survey. If we are relying solely on a survey to demonstrate freedom, a very high level of confidence would be required at the overall level – maybe 99% or higher. We may not want to use the same level of confidence for every region; we might want a greater confidence that we would detect the pest in regions that have been at a greater risk of an incursion. Such a high level of confidence might not be required if the survey is just one

Box 18.1 Confidence Limits

This example shows how the level of confidence achieved by an interval estimate may not be the same for all possible values of the parameter. Three ways of determining 95% confidence limits for the prevalence p of a binomial distribution when we find x positive items in a sample of size n can be expressed in terms of the percentage points of the beta distribution (Betainv) as

(Normal): $x/n \pm 1.96 \sqrt{[x/n\,(1 - x/n)\,/n]}$
(Clopper–Pearson): Betainv(0.025, x, $n - x + 1$) to Betainv(0.975, $x + 1$, $n - x$);
     Lower limit 0 if $x = 0$; upper limit 1 if $x = n$
(Jeffreys): Betainv(0.025, $x + 0.5$, $n - x + 0.5$) to Betainv(0.975, $x + 0.5$, $n - x + 0.5$)

Figure 18.B1 graphs the probability that the true value of the parameter would be included in the calculated confidence limits for $n = 50$. The shape is similar for other values of n. The graphs are a mirror image for values of p greater than 0.5.

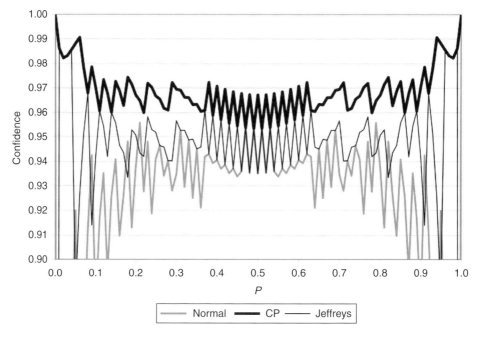

Figure 18.B1. Interval estimation: how the confidence depends on the parameter value. The figure shows the confidence obtained by three different methods to calculate interval estimates based on a sample of 50 observations from a binomial distribution.

The Clopper–Pearson confidence limits always provide greater than 95% confidence. The Jefferys confidence limits provide about 95% confidence on average, sometimes more, sometimes less. For small or large values of p, all three methods behave poorly: the Clopper–Pearson give more confidence than required, and the other two methods give considerably less confidence for some values of p. The Normal approximation is generally less than 95% and averages about 90%.

component of a set of evidence of freedom; instead, we would be happy with the survey providing, say, 95% confidence of detecting the pest if it were present.

Unfortunately, survey design often revolves around just two questions: 'How much money do I have?' and 'How much does a sample cost?' Dividing one by the other gives the size of the survey. If this is the case, the important question to ask becomes 'What level of confidence would this give me?' This would probably be followed by a request for more funds.

18.2.5   What Do We Do about False Negatives?

Unfortunately, our conclusion when examining a specimen (or doing a test) won't be correct every time. An error occurs when we classify an infested plant as not infested – a false negative. When demonstrating freedom, false negatives are more of an annoyance than a problem. We can compensate (and take more samples) by incorporating the test sensitivity into the calculations used to determine the required survey size.

In contrast, when inspecting consignments at the border, false negatives are a problem because there is no second chance – once the consignment has been cleared, that's it. Sometimes the problem can be resolved by using a better method of inspection. However, this might not be a practical or optimal solution if the better inspection costs more or, as a more likely restraint, takes longer. This question arises later when we ask how to optimise the effort expended on a test.

18.2.6   What Do We Do about False Alarms?

The opposite error, a false positive, incorrectly concludes the pest is present when it isn't. This is a much greater problem in a survey aiming to show freedom. These false positives or false alarms might occur only occasionally for serological tests or might be quite frequent when lay people are reporting sightings of the pest. Further, when a specimen is in such a poor state that a definitive identification cannot be made, an uncertain result can be just as bad as a positive result in some situations. We have to ask ourselves what we will do about false alarms and document the answers, preferably before starting the survey.

We want our survey method to be specific so that we will have a positive result only if the specimen is actually the pest. The specificity of a test is the proportion of pest-free samples that return a negative test. The false-positive rate (one minus the specificity) is possibly a better and more familiar term in some contexts. The importance of false positives depends on why we are doing the test.

For border control purposes, unless too frequent, false positives are of no great concern (except to the owners of the inspected items) and are a cost to be borne. Indeed, in many applications a two-stage procedure provides an ideal compromise between cost and accuracy. The first stage is a quick and cheap screening procedure that must have a very high sensitivity and an adequate specificity. Any items bought to our attention by the screening procedure undergo the second stage of inspection, a generally slower and more expensive definitive procedure that has extremely high specificity. For example, passenger bags can be X-rayed, with any suspicious bags inspected fully. As another example, we might look at a number of plants in a glasshouse and submit only leaves with symptoms for further tests.

At the start of a pest or disease eradication campaign, false positives may be considered as just an unfortunate extra cost. But as the campaign continues, false positives become a greater problem because they hide the fact that eradication may have been achieved. At the final stage of an eradication campaign, or when we are doing surveys to confirm freedom, false positives become a huge problem.

One approach to false positives can be described as test, retest and test again. As an integral part of designing a survey to demonstrate freedom, we must specify what will be done if positive or suspicious results are detected. Typically, a further (and more expensive) sequence of tests on the same specimen, or extra surveillance of the area in question would be required, so that for all practical purposes, the protocol gives 100% specificity (i.e. no false positives). Including more testing in the protocol to increase the overall specificity will decrease the overall sensitivity, and the calculation of the survey size required must reflect that.

What happens if this approach is not possible and false positives can still occur? The statistical problem posed by the survey changes completely: a single positive is no longer proof that the pest is present. We then need to design our survey so that we can distinguish between the number of false positives found if the region is free of pests and the number of false and true positives found if the region is infested. This inevitably means that we need to specify a tolerance limit for the number of positive samples found before the survey is considered positive. It cannot be stressed too much that this tolerance limit must be increased if the number of samples taken is increased. In determining the survey protocol – the survey size and the tolerance – we need to specify two error levels: our confidence (or the sensitivity) that the survey would conclude pests were present if they were present at the design prevalence and the specificity of the survey (or one minus the probability we would conclude the pest was present when it wasn't).

The problem becomes more complicated if we are dealing with animals in herds (or trees in orchards) because we have to set two tolerance values: one for the number of animals testing positive in a herd and one for the number of apparently positive herds in the area. We also need to set the number of animals per herd and the number of herds to be tested. Our choice of tolerance value will determine the herd-level sensitivity and specificity. We then need to define a tolerance for the number of positive herds that would be consistent with the area being free of the disease. Box 18.2 provides an example. For a given number of animals being tested,

Box 18.2 Tolerance Level versus Survey Confidence

This example illustrates how the tolerance values and accuracy from our survey are related. Suppose that if the area were infected, at least 5% of the herds would be infected, each with at least 20% of their animals infected. The available test has sensitivity of 95% and a specificity of 90%. Our problem is to differentiate between an apparent prevalence of 10% in a non-infected herd and 27% in an infected herd. Because the survey has no international implications, we decide that it would be adequate to be 95% certain that we detect an infected area and 95% certain that we don't claim a non-infected area is infected. Just for this example, it is convenient if 50 animals are randomly sampled from each of 200 randomly chosen large herds.

Table 18.B2 shows how our choice of tolerance values affects the accuracy of the survey. At the herd level, one obvious point from the first half of the table is that as the tolerance is increased the sensitivity (probability of concluding an infected herd is positive) decreases while the specificity increases.

Table 18.B2 The effect of tolerance value on the accuracy of a survey for the text's example

We will say that …	Tolerance / sensitivity (%) / specificity (%)						
A herd is positive if more than … positive animals	10	11	12	13	14	15	16
Probability infected herd classed as positive	82.99	73.29	61.63	49.01	36.69	25.75	16.89
Probability non-infected herd classed as negative	99.06	99.68	99.90	99.97	99.99	100.00	100.00
An area is infected if more than … positive herds	4	3	2	1	0	0	0
Probability infected area classed as infected	97.49	95.88	95.45	95.98	97.57	92.53	81.68
Probability non-infected area classed as non-infected	95.90	99.58	99.89	99.84	98.53	99.65	99.92

The second half of the table looks at the overall accuracy of the survey. The first five pairs of tolerance values each define a survey that meets our requirements, but clearly some are better than others. However, as the last two columns show, it is possible to increase specificity at the herd level so much that it is not possible to achieve the desired overall sensitivity for the survey.

It is interesting to compare this result with an opportunistic survey that could reasonably be assumed to look at randomly chosen animals from the area. We need to be able to differentiate between an apparent prevalence of 10% and 10.85%. The tolerance (expressed as the proportion of positives in the sample) would be a point about midway between these two values. For convenience, we shall use the point that gives the same sensitivity and specificity for the survey. For the same number (10,000) of animals as the herd survey, we would achieve 91.8% sensitivity and specificity. To increase this to 95% we would need about 13,800 samples, and to achieve 98.0%, a level comparable to the farm survey, we would need about 22,000 samples.

a strategy that has a tolerance of zero for the number of herds classified as infected will usually provide the preferred survey.

18.2.7   Have We Set an Impossible Task?

This question can arise when the survey is based on a very small design prevalence and a non-perfect test. The number of samples required will be very large, and may be the same regardless of the population size. For a small population we may need to use a design prevalence that is inversely proportional to the population size to limit the amount of survey effort.

As an example, consider the requirements of the World Organisation for Animal Health (OIE) for country freedom from bovine spongiform encephalitis.[1] The animal surveillance requirement is based on detecting a ten-in-a-million prevalence and requires the equivalent of 300,000 randomly selected animals being tested over a number of years. The prevalence of bovine spongiform encephalitis in animals showing neurological signs will be higher than in the general population and the 300,000 tests can be reduced by targeting symptomatic animals. Nonetheless, the number of animals to be sampled still poses an impossible target for a country with only a small cattle population. Further, a prevalence of ten-in-a-million is totally unrealistic if there are only 25,000 animals in the country. To resolve this problem, the design prevalence for small populations (of less than a million in OIE's code) was expressed as an absolute number – 10 infected animals in the population. The design prevalence would therefore be larger for smaller populations of animals. This has the effect of putting a limit on the proportion of the population that must be tested so that the same proportional effort is required regardless of the number of animals in the country.

This example reminds us that we must be pragmatic. It also reminds us of a very important question we should answer before our survey gets underway: 'Who has to be convinced?'

18.2.8   Who Do We Have to Convince?

After we have determined the parameters needed to calculate the survey size (such as the test sensitivity and design prevalence), it is worthwhile circulating these values to the people or organisations that have to be convinced by our assertion of freedom. It is best if all parties agree that the survey design will be adequate to detect the pest. It's not a bad idea to ask yourself if you, deep down, would accept your arguments if somebody else were proposing them.

---

[1] http://www.oie.int/international-standard-setting/terrestrial-code/access-online/

18.3   What Is the Best Surveillance Method?

There are often several ways that we can look for pests. As an example, suppose that
we are looking for exotic mussels in a port. We could look at keels when boats are
in dry dock. We could create artificial pontoons on which the mussels might grow.
A diver could inspect underwater surfaces such as pier pylons. We could trawl for
plankton using either gene probes or visual identification. We could simply rely
on members of the public noticing strange mussels on flotsam. How do we choose
which method to use?

In addition, we will often have information from several sources, all of which
indicate that the pest is not present. Surveys might have been done each year, with
the value of each successive year's survey increasing because the density of the pest,
and hence the likelihood that it would have been detected, would have increased.
Alternatively, we may have several sources of information: formal surveys, opportunistic observations and passive monitoring

Humans like to classify, and there is more than an adequate opportunity to classify sources of information. For example, some surveys such as walking a transect
through scrub can be considered to be continuous, while others such as inspecting
individual boxes can be considered discrete. For others, the distinction between
continuous and discrete information may not be clear cut.

The words *active* and *passive* are often used to describe information gathering: the former implies that we have organised information gathering while the latter implies that we are waiting for information to trickle in or that we will use the
lack of adverse reports as confirmatory evidence. *Opportunistic* information gathering is when we take advantage of an unrelated event to obtain information for our
purposes. Sometimes this differentiation of surveillance types is beneficial, sometimes it is not; whatever the case, we would like a way to combine the confidence
obtained from different sources.

18.3.1   When and Where Should We Look?

'Look in the most likely places at the time when they would be most prolific' is
a quick answer to the when and where question. This gives the greatest chance
of detecting the pest. It might be prudent to look in other places as well in case
our underlying assumptions are wrong. If it is you who made the claim that there
are no pests present, you would need to provide acceptable justification for your
choice for your survey design. On the other hand, if someone else has claimed
that there are no pests present, it is acceptable to target your inspection on areas
where you expect the pest to congregate at times when you expect the pests to be
most obvious. When you are looking for several pests, some care is required when
designing targeted surveys based on one pest's behaviour. In contrast, when the
task is to estimate pest density, a targeted survey is usually not appropriate unless

the relationship between the average density and the density in the targeted areas is well known.

18.3.2   What Is the Most Economical Test?

Each surveillance method will have a different cost per sampling unit. Each method will also have a different chance of detecting pests and this chance might vary according to the time of the year and the location. Roughly speaking, the number of tests required to achieve a desired level of confidence is inversely proportional to the sensitivity – the lower the sensitivity, the greater the number of samples required. Dividing the sensitivity by the cost of the method provides a convenient way to measure the efficiency of the method.

Sometimes it is straightforward to determine the most economic test method; sometimes more complicated mathematics is required. As an example, increasing the number of trees inspected in an orchard increases the likelihood of detecting a pest in the orchard. This in turn decreases the number of orchards we need to inspect to demonstrate freedom. However, depending on the ratio of the incremental cost of inspecting another tree in an orchard to the incremental cost of inspecting another orchard, there will be an optimal number of trees to inspect in an orchard. This example is discussed in Box 18.3.

Logically we would choose the most cost-efficient method. But there may be other reasons why we would prefer to use other methods. There may be insufficient opportunities to use the most efficient method or laboratory capacity might be the limiting factor. We would like to protect ourselves from our assumptions being slightly incorrect. For example, although it might be cheapest to concentrate our inspection effort to a small part of the region, to provide some protection from our assumption of homogeneity being wrong, we might choose a wider-based but more expensive method. The benefit of good public relations might mean that low-cost, low-sensitivity passive surveillance is worthwhile even though the added cost of false alarms must be accounted for.

18.3.3   What Is the Confidence Obtained from a Survey?

The probability (γ) that a survey will detect the presence of the target species depends on the density (ρ) of the pest, the effectiveness of the inspection (ϕ), the area of a sample unit (a), the number of sampling units (n), the spatial and temporal distribution of the target species, and the design of the survey. Occasionally, slightly different terms are required. For example, in a line transect, the area of the survey might correspond to an effective sweep reach (or some similar term) that takes into account how inspection effectiveness decreases with distance to the left and right of the transect path.

Box 18.3 How Many Consignments and How Many Oranges?

This example shows how our sampling design changes according to what we hope to do. Suppose our survey inspects consignments of oranges for disease. An exporter might want to use these inspections to demonstrate that his suppliers are disease-free. An importer simply wants to find as many diseased consignments as possible.

Both the importer and the exporter have agreed that if there were a problem, the proportion of diseased consignments would be at least q, and that the proportion of diseased oranges in a diseased consignment would be at least p. For this example, assume that it costs on average $\$f$ to open a consignment for inspection and an extra $\$c$ per orange inspected. They agree that the method will detect disease with probability T_{se} and that n oranges will be inspected from each of m consignments. This example could also be couched in different terms, for example, herds and animals, or orchards and trees. We have $\$F$ to spend on this survey. How should we determine m and n?

We pretend that n and m can be fractional and convert the solution to integers. Our fixed budget determines the relationship between m and n. Because inspecting n oranges in a consignment costs $\$(f + cn)$, the number of consignments we can afford to inspect is

$$m = F / (f + cn). \tag{18.B3.1}$$

We shall assume the binomial distribution is adequate to determine the probability that at least one of the n inspected oranges or m inspected consignments is found to be infected. Hence the confidence C_{se} that a diseased consignment would be detected and the confidence S_{se} that the survey would detect disease are

$$C_{se} = 1 - (1 - pT_{se})^n \text{ and } S_{se} = 1 - (1 - qC_{se})^m = 1 - (1 - qC_{se})^{(F/(f + cn))}. \tag{18.B3.2}$$

To demonstrate freedom, the exporter would usually want to determine n and m to give the most economic survey in terms of survey confidence divided by survey cost. Because the survey cost is fixed, this is the same as finding the survey with the greater overall confidence S_{se}. From Eq. 18.B3.2, calculus gives the following equation that can be solved iteratively for n:

$$\frac{c}{f + cn} = \frac{\ln(1 - pT_{se})}{\ln(1 - q(1 - (1 - pT_{se})^n))} \times \frac{q(1 - pT_{se})^n}{1 - q(1 - (1 - pT_{se})^n)}. \tag{18.B3.3}$$

In contrast, the importer wants to maximise the number of diseased consignments found, namely mqC_{se}, which is equal to $qFC_{se} / (f + cn)$. This criterion is equivalent to finding the most economic consignment-level survey in terms of consignment sensitivity divided by cost of testing a consignment. Calculus shows the best value for n is obtained when

$$\frac{c}{f + cn} = -\ln(1 - pT_{se})\frac{(1 - pT_{se})^n}{1 - (1 - pT_{se})^n}. \tag{18.B3.4}$$

For small q, both criteria give almost the same value for n. However, for larger values of q, the difference is greater. This reflects the fact that we need to find only one diseased consignment to disprove freedom.

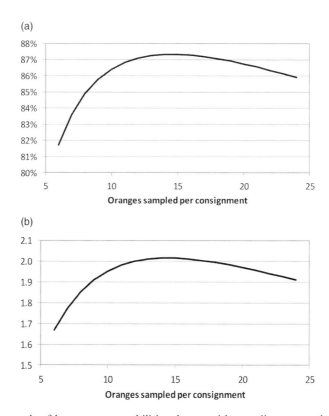

Figure 18.B3. An example of how survey capabilities change with sampling rate under a fixed budget.

For completeness, suppose we want to maximise the expected number of dis-
eased oranges ($m\ q\ n\ p\ T_{se}$) found. This can be rewritten as $q\ p\ T_{se}\ F\ n\ /\ (f + c\ n)$,
which has a maximum when n is infinite. With this criterion we would look at just one
consignment and at as many oranges as the budget allowed – not a strategy one would
recommend!

As a numeric example, suppose that $p = 5\%$ of consignments from a diseased supplier
have diseased fruit at a level of $q = 20\%$ if the consignment is diseased. The inspection process has a sensitivity $T_{se} = 95\%$ and costs \$20 per consignment and \$0.25 per
fruit. We don't want to spend more than \$1,000. Figure 18.B3 shows the relationship
between the number of oranges inspected in each consignment and the average number
of diseased consignments found and the probability that we would detect a diseased supplier. The maximum for the two curves occur at $n = 14.42$ and 14.54 respectively. Each
corresponds to sampling a fraction more than 42 consignments. In practice we might use
$m = 42$ and $n = 15$. It should be noted that spending \$1,000 will at best give us 87.26\%
confidence of detecting a diseased supplier. We would need to spend \$1,450 by inspecting
an extra 19 consignments to raise this to 95\% confidence.

In a continuous survey, if the probability of detecting each target individual in the sampling unit is the same, and if the individuals are independently distributed at a constant density, then the number of target individuals detected in a sampling unit can be treated as a Poisson random variable with a mean (E) that is proportional to the area sampled and the likelihood that pests are found:

$$E = \rho \times a \times \phi. \tag{18.1}$$

The mean E is sometimes called the encounter function or rate. The level of confidence obtained by inspecting n sampling units is simply one minus the probability that no target species are detected:

$$\gamma = 1 - \exp(-n \times E). \tag{18.2}$$

Taking logarithms of Eq. 18.2 gives a relationship that we shall make extensive use of later, and from which we can easily calculate the survey size required to give the desired confidence:

$$n \times E = -\ln(1 - \gamma). \tag{18.3}$$

In a discrete survey, if there is the same probability (E) of detecting the target species at each possible survey site, the number of sites at which the target species is detected by the survey can be treated as a binomial random variable. Again, the confidence obtained by inspecting n sampling units is simply one minus the probability that no target species are detected:

$$\gamma = 1 - (1 - E)^n \cong 1 - \exp(-n \times E). \tag{18.4}$$

Equation 18.4 includes the Poisson approximation to the binomial distribution. There are some points to be made. If this approximation is used to calculate the sample size, the number calculated will be slightly higher than needed, by a factor of $-\ln(1 - E) / E$. The approximation is adequate when the pest density is likely to be low if pests are indeed present. More importantly, the approximation shows that Eq. 18.4 can be replaced by Eq. 18.2, with the probability E being equivalent to the encounter function – the same equation can often be used for both discrete and continuous surveys.

Encounter functions usually can be determined for most survey methods and Eq. 18.2 forms the basis of the next section when we look at how to combine the confidence obtained from a number of surveys.

Before doing that, there is one important final point. We have assumed that the distribution of pests is random. However, often pests will be found in clusters. If so, we must focus on clusters rather than individuals and, if these clusters occur randomly, we can use the methods being discussed to determine the survey size.

18.3.4   Combining the Information from a Number of Sources

The scenario trees and pathways analysis discussed in Chapters 16 and 17 provide one approach to determine the confidence obtained when combining information from a number of sources. The remainder of this section uses the Poisson approximation in Eq. 18.4 as a quick way to combine information from a number of surveys.

The sum of a number of Poisson distributions is a Poisson distribution with a mean equal to the sum of the means, which, in terms of the encounter functions of our different sources, is $\Sigma n_i E_i$. When designing a survey program that uses information from k independent sources, any combination of n_i source units where

$$n_1 E_1 + n_2 E_2 + \cdots + n_k E_k = -\ln(1 - \gamma) \tag{18.5}$$

will have the same confidence of detecting the pest. It is a convenient approach, even though it does overestimate the total number of source units that would be required.

As a simple illustration of the use of Eq. 18.5, if an identical survey is done in an environment with twice the expected density, the encounter function would be twice as large, and consequently the survey would require only half as many samples to have the same probability of detecting the target species. Another example of Eq. 18.5 has been implicitly used in Section 18.2.4. If the pest density (and hence the encounter function) is proportional to the population size, then the survey size required will also be proportional to the population size.

Equation 18.5 justifies the comment made in Section 18.3.2 about using sensitivity divided by cost as a way to compare tests. Suppose we want to choose between a quicker inspection method with 80% effectiveness and a slower method giving 95% effectiveness. Using the quicker but less effective method requires about 19% more samples (0.95/0.80) to achieve the same level of accuracy. However, providing its cost was less than 0.80/0.95 (about 84%) of the slower, it would be more economical to use it.

Another example of the use of Eq. 18.5 would be to measure the amount of passive and opportunistic information obtained during the year and then determine the size of the formal survey required to top up the surveillance to reach the desired level of confidence.

18.3.5   Inspecting the Same Sample Unit Twice

Some care is needed in determining the encounter function for methods that inspect the same unit twice, and indeed this applies to any statistical analyses of the data. As an example, consider the inspection of a plant or animal in two successive years for a disease for which the symptoms are slow to show. The encounter function for the second year would correspond to the change in the likelihood that the disease was discernible. Similarly, when two tests are performed on the same specimen, the encounter function is equal to the sum of the two encounter functions minus the probability that both tests would detect the problem.

18.4 How Should We Allocate Surveillance Resources between Regions?

So far we have concentrated on finding the most economical way of performing surveillance in a homogeneous region. From now on, we shall assume that has been resolved and we can concentrate on how we should allocate our resources between different regions, not just for demonstrating freedom from a pest or disease but for other biosecurity reasons.

An example seems the easiest way to introduce this section. Suppose we have an ongoing monitoring program for exotic mosquitoes at international airports. Doing the same monitoring at each airport is an obvious approach; it is operationally simple and is often adequate. But each airport is different; the risks depend on the proportion of planes coming from mosquito-ridden countries, busier airports have a greater chance of an incursion, an incursion may have greater consequences in more populous cities and dry or cooler climates might be less suitable for mosquito breeding. We could ask if we can increase the benefit of the monitoring program by taking into account these differences.

The most important thing is to ask is: 'What do we want to achieve?' to which we must add 'on our limited budget'. We will discuss several options after giving a general method to solve to the problem.

18.4.1 The Best Allocation of Resources on a Limited Budget

We want to divide our total resources (F) between k regions to give the greatest overall benefit, the definition of which we shall leave until later. For the time being, we know that a benefit $B_j(f_j)$ is obtained from using f_j resources in region j. It will usually be more convenient to treat f_j as a continuous variable, even though it may not be possible in practice. We'll give the formal solution first and then an informal explanation.

Our aim to maximise the total benefits subject to our restricted budget can be expressed as

$$\text{maximise } \Sigma \, B_j(f_j) \text{ subject to the restriction } \Sigma f_j = F. \tag{18.6}$$

The solution can be found using calculus in terms of the derivatives $B_j'(f_j)$ and a constant whose value is determined (often iteratively) from the resource limit F as

$$B_1'(f_1) = \cdots = B_k'(f_k) = \text{a constant.} \tag{18.7}$$

We can derive this solution informally as follows. The derivative $B_j'(f_j)$ simply measures the incremental benefit obtained from slightly changing the amount of resources used. If we had allocated our resources so that the incremental benefit in region i was greater than in region j, we could obtain a greater overall benefit by moving resources from region j to region i. We can keep on shuffling our resources like this until we obtain a combination of resources that has the same incremental benefit for each region. This is the optimal solution and is simply Eq. 18.7.

Occasionally, the optimal solution is negative for some regions, especially when there are only a few resources available. We would not allocate any resources to these regions (other than under the proviso mentioned in Chapter 1 that we must do some monitoring in each region to know what is happening in each region). If the optimal amount of resources is greater than what is available in the region, we would use all that we could. In either case, we would recalculate the optimal values for the other regions based on the resources remaining.

18.4.2   The Optimum Is a Guide, Not the Master

Although we can determine an optimal solution, we will usually be more than satisfied with a close to optimal solution because of practicality or other intangible benefits. At a trivial level, the continuous precise optimal values will need to be converted to integers. The chance that procedures will not be followed correctly increases with their complexity. It may be that we might prefer to use a standard set of rates for operational ease, for example rounding numbers up to a multiple of 10. Some sampling rate calculations might be based on an estimate of future throughput and the actual numbers tested in a year will be different from those used in the calculations. We will assume that the amount of resources available is flexible enough to accommodate some uncertainty, although the resources being used should be monitored during the year and the optimal solution re-evaluated if necessary.

Occasionally the optimum allocates no resources to some categories. However, when border control is primarily done to find and rectify non-compliance, we also need to monitor the non-compliance rate in case it has changed (either intentionally or non-intentionally) and should re-allocate resources to do so. Inspecting none of particular types of items would not be prudent. Similarly, when surveying for disease, there may be reasons why it is unacceptable to survey only some regions, and hence a slightly less than optimal solution might be essential. One approach could be to allocate a certain amount of resources as general monitoring and use the remainder for targeted inspection or surveillance. Chapter 1 relates to a slightly different problem: setting the resources for each pathway so that it is unlikely that the undetected items of concern (the leakage) will exceed a specified level.

The analysis might also need to consider the uncertainty in the estimated probabilities that underpin the optimal solution. Because of this, a more robust solution based on fewer assumptions may be preferred (Chapter 13 and Box 18.4). Regardless, it would be useful to compare the result of other allocation strategies with the optimum; this may indicate that there is little difference or suggest an acceptable compromise. In short, treat the calculated optimal solution as a guide rather than a fixed rule that must be obeyed.

18.4.3 Maximise the Number of Pests Found

In this, and the next few sections, we consider different ways to define *best* and *benefit*. Maximising the number of pests found is not an appropriate objective for a survey to demonstrate freedom. It is wasteful because we only need to find one pest to dismiss the claim of freedom. It is, however, a very good objective for border control when we are trying to ensure that no pests enter or re-enter a region. We would like to inspect all incoming goods, but with a limited budget, we might only have sufficient resources to inspect (say) 60% of incoming goods. As a result, we would expect to only find about 60% of incoming pests. How can we do better?

By examining data from previous inspections we can often divide the incoming goods into a number of streams (or pathways) that have different proportions of non-compliant items, a process that is often called profiling. It is important that an item can easily be assigned to a stream by inspectors. It is easy to show that we will find the most non-compliant items for a given amount of resources if we only inspect the streams with the higher proportions of non-conforming items (often called the approach rate). The number of inspections allowed under the budget and the expected number of items that would arrive in each stream will determine which streams will be fully inspected and which will have no inspection at all. But, and this is a very big but, if we don't inspect any goods in some streams, we will have no way of knowing if the risk has changed and hence we have no way to determine when to change our inspection strategy. Consequently, we need to allocate some of our resources to monitoring the lower risk streams. Chapter 1 discusses this in more detail.

Occasionally, it is possible to adjust the effectiveness of inspection by changing the number of items in a consignment that are inspected. If we can determine effectiveness as a function of inspection effort, we can mathematically determine an appropriate inspection rate for each stream that will maximise the amount found. The second part of Box 18.3 gives an example. In situations in which the theoretical optimal sampling rate is not sufficient to monitor changes in the approach rate in some streams, a less than optimal scheme will be necessary.

18.4.4 Minimise the Time Pests Remain Undetected

Minimising the time that pests remain undetected is another aim that is not directly pertinent to proving pest freedom, although it is relevant to finding an economical way of demonstrating that pests have not arrived. It is a more appropriate aim when we are monitoring such as surveillance at sea ports or airport for arriving pests, auditing the compliance of fumigators, or checking for incursions into a buffer zone around a pest-free production area. We need to ask ourselves about how the cost of a delay in detection is related to how long it takes to detect the problem. The risk from an arriving pest will often be proportional to the time undetected. Sometimes we might consider that the risk is proportional to the square of the time undetected because the increasing pest population would be more likely to escape the surveillance area. Other formulations for the risk posed could take into account, for example, there being two or more pest incursions before the trap is emptied.

A limit on the number of insect traps that can be processed each year means that we may have to decide between the number of sites for traps and the time between collecting the traps. If we change traps frequently, we detect pests quickly and can treat the buffer area (we hope) before the pests have escaped into the wider area. We will, of course, use our resources more quickly and not be able to cover as many sites. Increasing the time between inspecting the traps will increase the number of sites we can cover but will also increase the likelihood that the pests escape the area around the trap before the incursion is detected. Box 18.4 gives an example.

18.4.5   Maximise the Probability of Detecting the Pest

Maximising the probability of detecting the pest is a good objective for a survey to demonstrate pest freedom. It is usually straightforward to write down the probability that the survey would fail to detect the pest although solving the resultant equations might be harder. Box 18.3 gives an example. However, if we are allocating resources between regions, there is one important point to consider: we need to specify the (relative) probabilities that each region might have become infested and, if so, the prevalence within each region. These probabilities would take into account other information that we must collect, such as the amount of arriving trade and density of hosts in the region. If we assume that all regions have become infested, the probability of detecting the pest is maximised by taking all of our samples from the region with the highest expected prevalence, not a good strategy.

18.4.6   Maximise the Benefit of the Survey

Maximising the number of regions in which pests are detected – as distinct from maximising the number of pests detected – is a good objective when we want to demonstrate freedom. This criterion has a solution that is approximately the same as maximising the probability of detecting a pest. It leads to slightly simpler calculations, but more importantly, it can be modified to apply weights to the regions according to other criteria such as the likelihood and cost of an incursion. Chapter 14 discusses this approach in greater detail.

18.4.7   Minimise the Consequences of a Wrong Allocation

So far, the tacit assumption has been that the various probabilities and costs are known reasonably precisely. Sometimes, we only know the relative values of the parameter. For example, the best we can say is that the risk will be proportional to

---

Box 18.4 Insect Trapping

Insect traps are often placed at entry points (like ports) to detect the arrival of pests. 'Detect them as quickly as possible' would seem to be a good way to decide how many traps should be placed at each port and how often they should be checked when we have a fixed budget. Although this example ignores many things that would need to be considered in practice such as seasonal variation, biological limitations and the effect of multiple traps, it provides a simple way to illustrate some of the points in this chapter.

Suppose that occasionally colonies of pests arrive at ports. The rate of arrival, λ_i per year, at port i would depend on factors such as the throughput of the port and origin of the vessels. The average delay until a pest is caught in one of the traps around the port is μ_i. Traps are regularly inspected n_i times per year, adding an extra $1/(2n_i)$ to the average time to detection. The effort of visiting a port is the dominant component of the cost and about the same for each port. Our budget sets a limit $N = \Sigma n_i$ for the number of visits. We want to allocate our resources to minimise the average delay until the pest is detected.

The average time, T, expressed in terms of colony-days, that pest colonies are undetected over a year, is

$$T = \sum \lambda_i \left(\mu_i + \frac{1}{2n_i} \right). \tag{18.B4.1}$$

Minimising this subject to the limit on the number of visits shows that the relative effort at each port should be proportional to the square root of the arrival rate:

$$T_{min} = \sum \lambda_i \mu_i + \frac{L^2}{2N} \quad \text{when } n_j = N\sqrt{\lambda_j}/L \text{ and } L = \sum \sqrt{\lambda_i}. \tag{18.B4.2}$$

As a numerical example, suppose we have budgeted to visit each of three ports every four weeks (which gives $N = 39.13$). Experiments have shown that the average time until an insect enters the trap is $\mu = 0.03$ years, which is just under 11 days. The arrival rates λ_i are 0.75, 0.50 and 0.25, respectively, giving an average of 1.5 arrivals per year. During the year, we would be waiting 16.44 days for the insects to enter the trap and 21.00 days it to be emptied, 37.44 days in total. Using Eq. 18.B4.2 to minimise the average delay gives $n_1 = 16.35 = 39.13 \times \sqrt{0.75}/(\sqrt{.75} + \sqrt{.50} + \sqrt{0.25})$, $n_2 = 13.35$ and $n_3 = 9.44$. This corresponds to visiting the ports every 22.34, 27.36 and 38.70 days respectively and reduces the average delay by about a day, to 36.49 days. For a practical schedule, these values might be rounded so visits were done every 3, 4 and 6 weeks ($n_i = 17.39$, 13.04 and 8.70). This gives an average delay of 36.56 days.

Suppose, however, that the arrival rates are not known precisely and that the λ_i above are the mid-points of the ranges (0.5–1.0, 0.25–0.75 and 0.1–0.4) reflecting our uncertainty for λ_i. Section 18.4.7 discusses why our approach must change when there is a considerable degree of uncertainty about the values of the parameters. While we still want to minimise the average delay until discovery, we need to assess each allocation choice by comparing the delay resulting from the choice with the best we could achieve. Our regret could be expressed in absolute or relative terms as either

Table 18.B4. Examples of how regret changes for different allocations of resources
Over a year, 39 visits need to be allocated among three sites. The table gives the regret (T/T_{min}) over making the wrong allocation for the extreme values of the parameters (λ_i) and the numbers of visits per site (n_i).

T/T_{min}		λ_1	0.50	0.50	0.50	0.50	1.00	1.00	1.00	1.00
		λ_2	0.25	0.25	0.75	0.75	0.25	0.25	0.75	0.75
		λ_3	0.10	0.40	0.10	0.40	0.10	0.40	0.10	0.40
n_1	n_2	n_3								
14.00	15.40	9.74	1.0265	1.0422	1.0202	1.0054	**1.0825**	1.0583	1.0375	1.0059
15.00	14.78	9.35	1.0149	1.0421	1.0206	1.0114	**1.0604**	1.0472	1.0275	1.0023
16.48	**13.33**	**9.32**	1.0047	**1.0355**	**1.0355**	1.0233	**1.0355**	1.0285	1.0257	1.0011
17.00	13.03	9.10	1.0026	1.0391	**1.0391**	1.0296	1.0284	1.0268	1.0244	1.0028
18.00	12.46	8.68	1.0007	1.0481	**1.0481**	1.0438	1.0173	1.0257	1.0240	1.0081
17.39	13.04	8.70	1.0010	**1.0478**	1.0379	1.0355	1.0234	1.0300	1.0206	1.0051
16.35	13.35	9.44	1.0056	1.0336	1.0357	1.0217	**1.0375**	1.0283	1.0269	1.0008
13.04	13.04	13.04	1.0532	1.0108	1.0713	1.0098	**1.1161**	1.0478	1.0865	1.0184

$$T-T_{min} = \sum \frac{\lambda_i}{2n_i} - \frac{L^2}{2N} \quad \text{or} \quad \frac{T}{T_{min}} = \frac{\sum \lambda_i \mu + \sum \frac{\lambda_i}{2n_i}}{\sum \lambda_i \mu + \frac{L^2}{2N}} \qquad (18.B4.3)$$

This example uses the minimax algorithm with T/T_{min} as the regret function to allocate the resources. For each set of n_i, the maximum regret over the parameter values will occur at one (or more) of the eight vertices of the cube defined by the ranges of λ_i. Although an analytic solution can be found for this example, a systematic search can be used: choose a value for n_1, find the value of n_2 that gives the smallest maximum regret, readjust n_1 and repeat. The first five rows of Table 18.B4 shows the regret for five of the many steps in this process with the maximum in bold The shaded sixth row shows the consequences of rounding the optimum to a practical survey schedule.

Using the bolded optimum values for n_i leads, at worst, to a 3.55% larger average period pests remain undetected compared to what could be achieved if we knew the values of λ_i. These values correspond to visiting every 22.2, 27.4 and 39.2 days respectively. As before, we might round these values to visits being made every 3, 4 and 6 weeks, respectively. The shaded row shows that we would be at most 4.78% worse off if we did.

The second bottom row of the table uses the values 16.35, 13.35 and 9.44 for n_i that we calculated earlier using the mid-points of the ranges for λ_i. It shows that this is not much different from the optimum, giving at worst an increased delay of 3.75%. The final row has our resources being evenly deployed between the ports: the maximum increase in waiting time would be 11.61%, showing that there is a benefit in adjusting our resource allocation according to risk.

the number of vessels arriving. This may not be a problem because often the optimum resource allocation depends only on the relative values of the parameters. But what should we do if we only have a limited knowledge – say just a range – for the possible values of the parameters?

While we must still decide on a particular objective (such as maximising the chance of detecting a pest), our approach to allocating resources must change to minimising our *regret* about making a non-optimal choice. For any set of parameter values, our regret compares what we will achieve if we use a particular set of resources with what we would achieve if we used the optimum resources for those parameter values. Our comparison could either be the difference or the ratio of these two.

If our uncertainty about the parameter values could be expressed as a probability distribution, we would consider the regret averaged over the parameter range and choose the allocation that minimised this. Otherwise a method such as the minimax algorithm could be used so that for each allocation choice we would determine the maximum regret over the possible parameter values and then use the allocation that gives the smallest maximum. Box 18.4 gives an example. Allocation of resources under uncertain knowledge is discussed further in Chapter 13.

18.5 Summary

One should view the theoretical solution as a guide. Actions can be summed up as

- Define the problem.
- Obtain estimates of the parameters.
- Determine a preliminary solution.
- Confirm that the parameter values are acceptable to all concerned.
- Re-analyse the problem if necessary.
- Convert the precision of the theoretical answer into a practical solution.
- Check that the benefits haven't strayed too far from the optimum benefits.
- Finally, promise yourself that next time you will seek statistical advice beforehand.

Index